Jonathan Guinness is the elder son of the late Diana Mosley, by her first marriage to Bryan Guinness, now Lord Moyne. He has worked in journalism and banking and has been a Conservative candidate as well as chairman of the Monday Club.

Catherine Guinness worked in New York in the 1970s as a journalist and editor on Andy Warhol's *Interview* magazine and *Viva* magazine. She has five children and divides her time between Southport and London. She is a keen gardener, oenophilist and fisherman. Her husband Robert Hesketh died in 2004.

# The House of Mitford

## JONATHAN GUINNESS
### WITH CATHERINE GUINNESS

PHOENIX

A PHOENIX PAPERBACK

First published in Great Britain in 1984
by Hutchinson and Co. (Publishers) Ltd
This paperback edition published in 2004
by Phoenix,
an imprint of Orion Books Ltd,
Orion House, 5 Upper St Martin's Lane,
London WC2H 9EA

An Hachette UK company

7 9 10 8 6

A CIP catalogue record for this book
is available from the British Library.

ISBN 978-0-7538-1803-9

Typeset at the Spartan Press Ltd,
Lymington, Hants

Printed in Great Britain by
Clays Ltd, St Ives pic

The Orion Publishing Group's policy is to use papers
that are natural, renewable and recyclable products and
made from wood grown in sustainable forests. The logging
and manufacturing processes are expected to conform to
the environmental regulations of the country of origin.

www.orionbooks.co.uk

# Contents

CONTENTS

# Preface to the New Edition

When this book was first published in 1984 – twenty years ago – the reviewer for the *Sunday Express* wondered: 'Who cares now, anyway?' Quite a few, seems to be the answer. One can see the reviewer's point; the sisters were already ageing by then, their main activities belonged to the past, and times had changed. Yet interest in the family had not waned, and it still continues. In response, the Mitford Industry has proceeded unabated: see the bibliography. Both of us have been continually asked for copies of this book during the time that it was out of print and hard to obtain. Why is this?

For one thing, four of the Mitfords have been writers, namely Nancy, Diana, Decca and Debo. All have books in print, implying that people still read them. For another, members of the family knew some of the key figures of early twentieth-century politics, and witnessed important events such as the Spanish Civil War, the *Anschluss* of Austria with Germany, the build-up to the Second World War. But the family's uniqueness, the reason why attention returns to them again and again, is that their stark variations in opinion mirrored the great world conflicts of their time.

It is true that the family is scarcely of any historical *importance* at all; it is hard to think of anything that would have turned out very differently had none of them existed. What the Mitfords do possess is historical *interest*. The interplay of nations, ideologies, economic doctrines, statesmen and armies; these are what constitute history. Yet when they are all that is described they are unlikely to satisfy any but the driest academic; one can compare the result to a film in black and white. History while it is proceeding is seen by contemporaries in colour, and future generations reading about a period in the past thirst for the colour to be reinserted. The educated public has always liked biographies, letters and diaries, just because they do this. The French Revolution is vividly described by historians such as Michelet or de Tocqueville or Furet. Chateaubriand, who personally knew so many of the protagonists, is also an interesting read. But the old documents unearthed by G. Lenotre, concerning players of the second rank or lower, and published in six volumes, are so particularly riveting because they show how it actually was for a variety of fairly ordinary people. That is what the general reader wants, a sense of what it was like to be alive and aware at the time. To be aware, whether at the time or later, means to be partisan. The Mitfords were partisan, all right.

For the rest, we stand by our earlier Introduction. This has always been a decent and sensitive family. They have also been sparklingly funny; but with the jokes came an intensity of passion in love and politics. Some find this disturbing. A reviewer of the first edition of Diana's memoirs, *A Life of Contrasts*, felt that he had come across ground glass in a *bombe surprise*.

We still believe that the Mitfords' grandfathers explain much about the seven, and are interesting in themselves. We have not re-written our text very much; our work still belongs essentially to the early 1980s. However, we now know much more about Susannah Bowles, the mother of the Mitfords' maternal grandfather. This has entailed revising Chapter 10 and adding to it. Again, we feel there is no longer any reason to omit the fact that Sir Oswald Mosley, in the 1930s, was living a double life between Diana and Lady Alexandra Metcalfe, sister of his first wife. The fact that Diana was aware of this and put up with it seems in retrospect almost incredible. She was, of course, unusually dedicated politically; but even more unusual, it seems to us, is the rock-solid confidence it shows that she was first in Mosley's affections. This continued throughout their life together. She could be angry about his flings with others; she never seems to have been in the least worried. Few people, we think, possess such granite self-confidence. Diana's MI5 file, released in November 2003, tells us a certain amount that is new, notably revealing that she was already under observation as early as 1934 in connection with her visits to Italy. It also shows that Nancy not only denounced Diana as a national danger in June 1940, before her imprisonment under Regulation 18b, but that in November of the same year she urged that Diana should be kept inside and that Pam, among others, should be kept under observation. Nancy also denounced two other people. We are so convinced that they were totally innocent that we are withholding their names. To do the authorities justice, they paid no attention.

We are also adding a chapter to bring the story up to date.

Jonathan Guinness and
Catherine Guinness, 2004

# Introduction

David Freeman-Mitford, second Lord Redesdale, had seven children by his wife Sydney, née Bowles. They were christened:
Nancy, Pamela, Thomas, Diana, Unity, Jessica and Deborah.
This book is about them, their parents and their grandfathers.
Nicknames for these people have been numerous; the following
list gives some of them. We have put in italics the names we
actually decided to use in the book.

Algernon Bertram Mitford, Lord Redesdale (1837–1916), was
always known as *Bertie*, pronounced Barty.

*Thomas* Gibson Bowles (1841–1921), in his maturity, seems
usually to have been known as Gibson, but the newspapers and
cartoonists called him Tommy. His children always called him
Tap. We thought it best, after some hesitation, to use his first
name in full.

*David* Bertram Ogilvy Mitford, Lord Redesdale (1878–1958),
was usually called by his first name. His brothers and sisters
sometimes called him The Old Ape; his children called him Farve
and also Forgy, Forgery, T P O M (The Poor Old Male), The
Old Chap, Chaplayn (*sic*).

*Sydney* Bowles (1880–1963), later Lady Redesdale, was called
by her first name. Her children called her Muv and also Aunt Syd,
TPOF (The Poor Old Female), (The) Fem.

*Nancy* (1904–73) when small was Koko to her parents, sometimes Blob-Nose to her father. Pam, Tom and Diana called her
Naunce-(ling); Decca called her Susan; Debo and others called
her Natch and Debo's children, Aunt Natch. Later Debo called her
The Old French Lady or the French Lady Writer. Catherine
christened her Octopus Untruth.

Pamela (1907–94) was shortened to *Pam*, but the others also very commonly call her (The) Woman, or sometimes Wooms or Woomling.

Thomas (1909–45) was almost always called *Tom* or Tud.

*Diana* (1910–2003) was Dina(h) to David and Dana to Sydney. Nancy called her Bodley because of her big head. Pam called her Nard(y), as did Tom and Unity. To Decca she was Cord(uroy), to Debo and her children she was Honks or Aunt Honks.

*Unity* Valkyrie (1914–48) when small was known to her parents as Baby, then Boby, then Bobo, which became the name most commonly used by family and friends. She was Aunt Bobo to Jonathan and Desmond. We could have used Bobo throughout this book, but it was not quite universal; Hitler called her Unity. Decca called her (The) Boud; some others took over the name including Nancy who spelled it Bowd. This developed into Birdie, often used by Diana and Debo. For a time, in the 1930s, Unity was known as William.

Jessica Lucy (1917–96) became *Decca*. Sydney called her Little D, Nancy called her Susan, to Unity she was (The) Boud and to Debo Henderson.

Deborah Vivian (born 1920) is shortened to *Debo*. Sydney called her Stubby, and for a time in her teens she was known as Swyne. Afterwards Nancy took to calling her Miss, or Nine, or The Nine-year-old, this being supposed to refer to her mental age. Decca called her Henderson.

When they were young, someone described the seven as always being in shrieks or floods: shrieks of laughter, that is, or floods of tears. Nancy, the eldest, initiated a good deal of both, since she made jokes and inflicted teases; it was also she who first put a version of their life into print in her novels, notably *The Pursuit of Love*. But Nancy's literary success began only in 1945, and some years before that date three of her sisters had already become well known in ways only dimly indicated in her books. Diana became a supporter of the Fascist leader Sir Oswald Mosley, marrying him in Berlin in 1936 with a wedding reception at the house of Dr Josef Goebbels. Unity, in the first instance through Diana, went to Germany and made friends with Hitler, of whom she then became a notorious supporter; she shot herself on the outbreak of war in 1939, but survived as a brain-damaged invalid till 1948. Decca, in sharp contrast, became a Communist sympathizer; she eloped in

1937 with a cousin of the same tendency who had fought in the Spanish Civil War. She is now an eminent left-wing journalist and author.

There is, then, more to the Mitfords than can be found in Nancy's novels, and it has not failed to find its way into print. Jessica published her two volumes of autobiography, *Hons and Rebels* and *A Fine Old Conflict*. Diana followed more recently with *A Life of Contrasts*. Unity's life was the subject of a study by David Pryce-Jones; Sir Harold Acton wrote a 'memoir' on Nancy, on whom a full-scale life was written by Selina Hastings. On television, there have been a programme of reminiscences about Nancy, a series based on two of her novels, and a dramatized version of Unity's life, based largely on Pryce-Jones's book. There has even been a musical play, *The Mitford Girls*. This the survivors of the seven, four well-preserved ladies in their sixties and seventies, watched – not all on the same occasion, to be sure – in a state of mild bemusement. The management issued each of them with a badge proclaiming: 'I really am a Mitford Girl.'

All this may mean that a word of explanation will be expected for writing what will, no doubt, be described as 'yet another' book about the Mitfords, although it is in fact the first to try to tell the story in full and as it was. For the material that has appeared so far has mostly been either fictional or political. Nancy's novels are fiction, and light fiction at that. To have had what the Germans call an *Auseinandersetzung* (roughly, 'set-to') with the serious side of her sisters' beliefs and activities would have ruined her work. In fact the very word, long, solemn and Germanic, would have excited her wildest mockery and her deadliest, most private fears; so her view of her family avoids any such thing. On the other hand, there are the writings of and about Nancy's politically active sisters. Neither Decca nor Diana, and least of all David Pryce-Jones, are people to shun an *Auseinandersetzung*. To be sure, Decca and Diana can manage to engage in one without being too heavy-handed, but it does not alter their main purpose in writing. That aim is, as Marx claimed for his own work, not to interpret the world but to change it. Their writings, that is to say, are in great part designed to prove points and to grind axes.

The image of the family in Nancy's novels is a half-truth, designed to suit her caricaturist's talent and her humorist's purpose. But something like it also suits the quite different aim of Decca, to whose left-wing Pilgrim's Progress her family represents, as it were, the City of Destruction; the original home for which one may feel a private regret, but of which one is obliged to disapprove. Diana does something to correct and amplify the image, but her main purpose is to counter the general political disapproval of herself and her husband. David Pryce-Jones writes of Unity, and therefore of her family, from a point of view too hostile to permit much insight.

So the story has at best appeared fitfully and partially and usually in relation to some particular person. But is there, properly speaking, a story at all? This is a fair question. The fact that a family contains a number of well-known people does not in itself mean that there is anything particular binding them all together. The whole may, but it also quite easily may not, be more than the sum of its parts. We believe that in the case of the Mitfords it is; that there is a story that is worth treating as a thing in itself.

To see this, it is helpful to start two generations before the seven. For the Mitfords did not spring, as Nancy's novels imply, unexpectedly and in their full variety from one backwoods peer and his vague wife. David Redesdale was in real life the son of a minor celebrity, and Sydney the daughter of another; and there are numerous ways in which the characters of Bertie Mitford and Thomas Bowles can be seen reappearing in their descendants. It was the times in which they lived which were different. Mitford and Bowles were young under Queen Victoria and ageing under Edward VII. During their adult life it was possible, simply because it was customary, for an educated and sensitive Englishman to be by and large content with things as they were and unquestioning in his patriotism and national pride. This does not exclude social conscience, which in Bowles's case, at least, was strong, though of a type now unfashionable; but it means that necessary improvement was seen as being possible within society as it existed. By their grandchildren's time this unquestioning acceptance had begun to disappear. A slow change was coming over opinion. One might suggest that the war had discredited patriotism and the slump had made people question the structure of society; but perhaps to link the change to particular events, even such great ones, is a little too glib. In any case the change occurred, one of those mysterious transformations in mood and climate that can overtake a society. It was starting when the seven Mitfords were growing up, in the 1920s. Diana's favourite authors in late adolescence, she tells us, were Lytton Strachey, Bertrand Russell, Aldous Huxley and J. B. S. Haldane. 'I loved them for their wit and irreverence *and their rejection of accepted standards.*' (Our italics.) The significance here is the wish to question standards just because they are accepted. We see this as an invariable characteristic of intelligent youth, but it was not always so. Diana's grandfathers would not, at the equivalent age, have seen their favourite writers in these terms. Nor, of course, did most people of the Mitfords' age and class, or even all the Mitfords themselves. But a great deal of the interest in the Mitford story lies in comparing the seven to their grandfathers, to see two intelligent men exercising their talents in an age of security, and then consider their rather similar descendants when things were breaking up.

We are, therefore, beginning this book by looking at Bertie Mitford and Thomas Bowles: Bertie with his sense of history and class, and with the scholarly talents and the acute curiosity that enabled him to write his *Tales of Old Japan*, and Thomas, proprietor of *Vanity Fair*, with his inquiring mind, his egoism, his insistence on thinking everything through for himself and his addiction to teasing. Teasing was a habit among the Mitfords, starting when they were children but continuing all their lives. Some people attribute it to the rough and tumble of the large family. Not all large families develop it to this degree, but the Mitfords were descended from Thomas Bowles, and Bertie Mitford married into that great family of teases, the Stanleys.

One work did go some way towards telling the story as it should be told, though this was, in a sense, by mistake. Julian Jebb's television film on Nancy, featuring all her surviving sisters as well as some film of Nancy herself, was a skilful piece of work. The programme was supposed to be designed round its subject, and its angle was essentially hers. However, the political dispute between Diana and Decca erupted during its preparation. First Decca, then in reaction Diana, insisted that certain material must be included if they were not to withhold cooperation. This material, on both sides, had little to do with Nancy herself, but its inclusion meant that more of the general story was told than the producer really wanted. The subjects took charge, as in Pirandello's *Six Characters in Search of an Author*.

For the Mitfords can be formidable, surprising as this might be to anyone who has only seen *The Mitford Girls* and therefore thinks of them as social butterflies. This view is a caricature of a caricature; remotely related to certain passages in Nancy's and Decca's works, it does not survive a close reading even of *The Pursuit of Love*, let alone of *Hons and Rebels*. But the view predates the musical. It possibly originated in the division of labour in Fleet Street which has given us, among other special kinds of journalism, the gossip column. Not only within, but also outside, gossip columns themselves, people classified as suitable gossip column material receive coverage that is, in a special combination, both breathless and patronizing.

It is, in fact, just about the opposite of the truth. A social butterfly lives for parties, pleasure and 'kicks'. No one can say this of any of the Mitfords. They have been remarkably stable in their personal lives and sober in their habits; more so, of course, as they have grown older. There is a variant of the social butterfly view, according to which Unity was a Hitler 'groupie', like those who were later to scream for Mick Jagger. Some reviewers of Pryce-Jones's book took this line, as did Lesley-Anne Down who played the part of Unity in John Mortimer's television play. It does not stand up to examination.

The social butterfly view does help to escape the discomfort inherent in the Mitfords' serious side; it enables writers of the pedestrian sort to dismiss and to pontificate. Nancy's concentration on the shrieks and floods is another evasion, if a more elegant one. Those who do regard the Mitfords as serious do not always like them much. Some people find it particularly hard to swallow their self-assured front, their aversion to the public confessional. This is evident in both grandfathers, especially Thomas Bowles. It is also associated with their class, the landed gentry. Literary and social fashion among the talking classes, anyway of the rising generation, is now hostile to this class; so anti-Mitford sentiment is given an extra bite, especially as no Mitford, even Decca, is in the least ashamed of her origins. As to Nancy, she positively flaunted these origins, making millions of people self-conscious about their speech through the controversy about U and Non-U. Perhaps it was partly in revenge for this massive national tease that the talking classes later decreed that the landed gentry would become unacceptable except in certain defined roles, such as that of 'twit' in the style of Wodehouse's Bertie Wooster. This prevents appreciation of a basic wisdom in the Mitfords that can be a real help in coping with life. They have all, underneath the shrieks and floods and the compulsive articulateness, a deep reticence and a deep kindness. It is connected with their technique of making everything, not necessarily into a joke, but into a story. This originated with Nancy, but the others have practised it with equal skill. Phrase-making also helps. Compare the typical Mitford phrase 'shrieks and floods' with the more normal 'joys and sorrows'. The very expression 'shrieks and floods' conveys a feeling that the shrieks take precedence, that there is something really rather funny about floods, much as we may suffer when we are actually in them. In 'joys and sorrows' we feel rather that there is something a little gloomy about the joys. Those who describe the Mitfords as affected or callous miss the point of this. It is not just frivolity; it is also a way of making life tolerable. Jonathan once watched, with Nancy, the film *The Best Years of Their Lives*, which tells the story of four American servicemen being demobilized after the war. One of them is Homer, a sailor, who has lost both his hands, each of which is replaced by a pair of hooks. Adjustment is difficult, but his fiancée stands by him and finally they marry. There is a moment of poignant embarrassment when during the ceremony Homer fumbles with the ring and drops it. Emerging from the cinema, Nancy commented: 'Of course, if Homer had been in our family, we'd have got him all right in two ticks; as soon as we saw him, we'd have said "Oh, Homer, you *are* clever with your hooks, *do* show how they work"; and nobody would have minded at the wedding.'

# The Grandfathers

The story of the seven Mitfords begins in the 1890s with the acquaintanceship, and rather short-lived political collaboration, of two remarkable men: Algernon Bertram Mitford and Thomas Gibson Bowles. Mitford was later created Lord Redesdale. It was because the Bowles family used to come and stay with the Mitfords at Batsford in Gloucestershire that Mitford's son David and Bowles's daughter Sydney met as children, ultimately to marry and become 'Farve' and 'Muv' to our main subjects.

The two men came to know each other well when both were elected to Parliament as new Conservative members at the General Election of 1892 although, since they dined out in similar circles in London, they could easily have met before. Each certainly knew of the other by reputation, for both were well known. Mitford was born in 1837. He was always known as Bertie, pronounced 'Barty' by his contemporaries from the old usage of pronouncing Bertram as 'Bartram'. He had passed his early life in the Diplomatic Service, and had later spent twelve years at the Office of Works, where he helped restore the Tower of London and remodel Hyde Park. The Dell, the small landscaped area at the downstream end of the Serpentine, is his creation. In 1886 he inherited Batsford from a cousin, together with large estates in Gloucestershire and Oxfordshire; so he resigned from the Office of Works and moved there with his growing family to devote himself to his new local responsibilities. He became Member of Parliament for Stratford. But his claim to fame was a book he had published in 1873 called *Tales of Old Japan*. This is a medley of reminiscences, descriptions, legends and fairy stories, told with skill and charm. It gives a vivid impression of Japanese politics, culture and folklore as Bertie had found them when he was with the British diplomatic mission there from 1866 to 1868. The book was an instant success, and has proved an enduring one; it ran to many impressions on publication and has rarely been out of print ever since, our copy being a paperback printed in Tokyo in 1978. Robert Louis Stevenson and Dante Gabriel Rossetti were among its distinguished admirers; extracts occur in anthologies as diverse as Andrew Lang's Fairy Books and at least one modern collection of horror stories, where the extract in question, the blood-drenched 'Story of the Forty-seven Ronins', is by no means out of place. Bertie's eye-witness description of a ceremonial hara-kiri is possibly the best-known passage in the book. The Japanese themselves sometimes quote Bertie with respect, as for example Inazo Nitobe in his short treatise on the chivalric ethic of Bushido.

The publication date was exactly right for the *Tales*, for they came out not long after the opening of Japan to the West, when there was an intense curiosity about Japan and very little knowledge of it. But this was not the only reason for the book's success; it is a considerable achievement in itself. Bertie was, like so many of the best Victorian travellers, both scholarly and adventurous. His older friend, Sir Richard Burton, comes to mind. Formed, as all educated people then were, in the severe but fruitful discipline of the classics, Bertie was also an uncannily brilliant natural linguist who quickly became fluent in spoken Japanese, having already, during a spell in China, learnt the Chinese ideographic writing that serves also as vehicle for the classical literature of Japan. But what makes the book live is his love of the country. Japan was made for Bertie, and he for it. He reacted to Japanese ways with fascination, with amusement, sometimes with frank incomprehension, but always with respect and never with that condescension which can mar Victorian writing about alien cultures. The gruesome side of Japan is rather dwelt on than glossed over, but it is presented in its cultural context; the strangeness is given full force, but never permitted to hinder the reader from seeing the Japanese as people basically like himself. There is an elegiac note. Well aware that the old Japan he describes is doomed to pass away, Bertie often draws a parallel between the Japanese feudalism that he witnessed, and the feudalism of the European Middle Ages whose passing, at least with his emotions, he regretted. To him, the writing of the *Tales* and the restoration of the Tower of London were both ways of preserving for posterity the memory of heroic times.

The nature of Bertie's affection for Japan is thrown into relief by the fact that he quite evidently felt differently during his time in China. He wrote a book about his Chinese experiences, *An Attaché in Peking*, which, though full of interest and liveliness, entirely lacks the resonance of respect that makes the *Tales of Old Japan* a classic. It was the Japanese samurai that impressed the author, with their customs of blood feud and ritual suicide for the sake of honour, not the smooth class of landowning scholars who provided China with its mandarin administrators. Bertie warmed to a fighting feudalism. Old family traditions needed for him to be validated by martial qualities; and he explicitly compared the samurai with the class to which he himself belonged, the English gentry with roots in the chivalry of old. Bertie's explicit pride in these origins was much more accepted in his time than it is today; but even making this allowance, one must concede that he was rather a snob. Nevertheless, his snobbery was of that old-fashioned kind which was not wholly devoid of sense. He recognized that an upper class needed to have a purpose; that to have a right to its position, it needed to perform certain social duties and exhibit certain virtues, notably that of personal courage, which he certainly possessed himself. In ordinary social life, Bertie had too much sensitivity to let his class-consciousness show, and above all too much intelligence to let it interfere with his judgement of individuals.

This is shown by the fact that he liked Thomas Bowles, whose origins were odd and certain of whose activities would definitely have seemed to Bertie a touch vulgar. Thomas was born in 1841, as the illegitimate, though much-loved, son of a Liberal politician called Thomas Milner-Gibson. Like Bertie, he started as a public servant, working for some time in the Legacy Department at Somerset House; but the life bored him and he switched to journalism. He became well known as the founder and proprietor of the magazine *Vanity Fair*, the cartoons from which are still to be seen decorating the walls of London's clubs and the dustier of its restaurants. The cartoons, signed 'Spy' or sometimes 'Ape', depict a succession of Victorian gentlemen more or less well known in their day, with a caption that is sometimes jokey, sometimes sycophantic, sometimes merely descriptive. The magazine was funny, cheeky and rather scurrilous. *Vanity Fair* landed Thomas into several scrapes: he was once attacked by an irate gentleman in the street outside his own offices, and blows were exchanged. To be sure, by the time he came to know Bertie in Parliament this sort of thing was in the past. He had already sold *Vanity Fair*, though he retained *The Lady*, another magazine which he founded and which is still in the Bowles family.

Thomas always had an interest in politics; he had first stood for Parliament as early as 1872. His victory at Kings Lynn in 1892 had been strenuous and narrow. His campaign was conducted with energetic showmanship from his sailing yacht, which was moored in the harbour and used as a committee room. He won by only eleven votes; but once in, he made the seat his own until a quarrel with his own party lost it in 1906. He made a considerable mark in Parliament, though he was never to achieve any office or honour. He was combative, witty, and good at thinking on his feet; he was also good at the detailed reading of bills, and a great master of parliamentary procedure, which he already knew well even before entering the House. He was also, even at his most perverse, transparently sincere. The combination of qualities was rare and formidable. It was a time when more attention was paid to the course of debates than is the case today, because it was commoner to break party ranks; and successive governments feared Bowles as a knowledgeable and effective critic of official policy, whether his own party or his opponents were in power. He was passed over for many less able men. No doubt this was partly because he could never resist making any wounding crack that might occur to him, for this is always unpopular with the great and the good; but we believe the reason lay deeper. Despite his charm, bounce and surface gregariousness, Thomas was at bottom a solitary figure. He was in no sense a team man, both because he was too fond of personally showing off, and because he could never conform to any views he did not like which might be arrived at by a majority.

But Thomas, though pleased with himself, was not a selfish man. He was, rather, an almost quixotic altruist. His true motivation in politics was a succession of causes: it was for them, not for himself, that he fought. They were often connected with the sea, which was his enduring passion. He owned a succession of small sailing yachts, always crewed by men from Aldeburgh, then a simple and rugged Suffolk fishing village. (Its subsequent transmutation to a musical festival centre with a faint air of preciousness would have surprised Bowles, and by no means pleased him.) In 1874 he found time in a very busy life to study for and obtain his master mariner's certificate. All his life, he spent as much time as he could at sea, and his sons and daughters were to a considerable extent brought up on his yachts. He was a steadfast believer in the Royal Navy and in its importance to national defence, and it was in this area that he was finally to make a definite contribution to the country's safety in the First World War. His belief in Britain's maritime pre-eminence was also connected with his enthusiasm for free trade. He thought that as long as Britannia ruled the waves, it was possible to perpetuate the trading and industrial dominance she secured following the Industrial Revolution. Economic developments in other countries which were already making this view out of date were closed to him, for he had no knowledge of industry; the sea, and the skill of the British sailors, were to him the key to prosperity as well as to security.

We shall be dealing with each grandfather's career in more detail later; here we are concerned with how they and their families came to know each other. Thomas was at the time a widower; his wife Jessica had died in 1887, leaving him with four children, the youngest only two. From then on he devoted all his spare time to being with them and bringing them up. They were taken with him on his cruises; even when he went calling, in London, he would commonly take one or more of them with him. Sydney remembered being left in the halls of strange houses for long periods with the footmen. When asked to stay in the country, Thomas commonly refused on the grounds that he had to be with his children. This was what he told Bertie when asked to Batsford in 1894 to make a political speech. Bertie of course, who had a large house and a growing family of his own, asked him to bring them along.

The children got on well with their Mitford contemporaries, of whom there were in 1894 already seven – the family was to be rounded off with a flourish by the birth of twins in 1895. Bertie's wife, however, did not take to Thomas, and in all the years they

were to know each other was never to use his Christian name. She
disliked his self-advertisement, distrusted his unconventionality,
and did not appreciate his jokes. Some of her own relations were
quite unconventional enough to be getting on with, and she
certainly thought little of *them*. It has to be admitted that Lady
Clementine Mitford was just a bit stuffy.

In her defence, it has to be mentioned that Thomas's behaviour
to his children must have seemed odd to a normal mother, not to
say unfeeling and a little mean. He did not bother with Christmas
or birthdays, maintaining that it was enough to feed children and
look after them without giving them a lot of superfluous presents.
Party frocks for the girls he also regarded as quite unnecessary; on
nearly all occasions they were dressed in sailor suits like the
boys. There was a terrible row at Batsford one afternoon during
the Bowles family's first visit in 1894. The routine was that the
children joined the grown-ups for tea every day, having changed
from their day clothes into something smarter. Sydney, aged
fourteen, did already possess a black velvet dress, but Dorothy or
'Weenie', aged nine, had nothing to change into. So Joan Mitford,
who although a year or two younger was about Dorothy's size,
took pity on her and lent her a dress to wear for tea. All hell broke
loose; both children were severely scolded by all the parents.
There is no doubt that Clementine's irritation with Joan would
have been given an extra edge by her feeling that it was really that
dreadful Mr Bowles who was to blame for everybody's embarrassment. Of course, she no doubt added to herself – for she was a
good woman, nothing if not fair-minded – what could be expected
of the poor man, trying to bring up children single-handed? Later,
she was to be of assistance to him in recommending a governess.
Yet in a sense Thomas was to have the last laugh on all those who
took this view of his methods. His children, to the end of their
long lives, all revered first him, and, later, his memory; and they
all followed, according to their lights, his practices and his philosophy. In particular they all retained his independence of mind; it
is a bitter paradox that this independence was to lead Sydney into
an admiration for, of all people, Hitler.

During the three years when they were in Parliament together,
Bertie and Thomas were both on what would now be called the
right of the Conservative Party. To be sure, Thomas had also

inherited from his father a radical cast of mind, much in evidence in his writings; it was one day to lead him to change parties. Bertie lacked anything of the sort. It is often illuminating to class English politicians in Civil War terms as Roundhead or Cavalier; types which correspond not with party, or with degree of progressiveness or reaction, but with contrasting forms of political feeling and motivation. Bertie's Northumbrian reverence for tradition, and for feudalism as expressing valour and personal loyalty, make him easy to place as a Cavalier; he cannot be pictured as anything but a King's man. Thomas was an East Anglian Roundhead. His disputatiousness, his loyalty to causes rather than persons, indicate that he would have been happiest with the Independents, perhaps as one of Admiral Blake's captains.

This underlying difference between the two was to surface, but not till long after Bertie had left Parliament. In the meantime they worked together in a parliamentary battle that meant much to them: the unsuccessful resistance to the introduction for the first time of estate duty. This was incorporated in the 1894 budget by the Liberal Chancellor, Sir William Harcourt. The innovation was disliked widely but not, on the whole, very intensely; at any rate the Conservatives never reversed it. As was to be the case in our own day with capital gains tax, it was as if even many of its opponents thought that its hour had come. But this was not Thomas's view, or Bertie's. Thomas was not even reconciled to it by the fact that the money was to be earmarked to strengthen his beloved Navy. He regarded it as being against natural justice to impose a proportionately greater burden on the rich; a view which today seems perverse. He thought it especially unfair to tax landed estates because of the difficulty of finding liquid funds to pay the duty. Whatever we think of his reasoning, we cannot accuse Thomas of self-seeking; he was never a rich man, and in particular he never owned land.

Bertie was certainly a large landowner; but his argument was the rather different one that estate duty was financially unsound because it taxed capital to provide income, thus squandering the nation's capital assets. He admired the pertinacity and skill with which Thomas fought the measure from the backbenches, and in his *Memories*, written long after the two men had ceased to be political allies, he was still very admiring. 'Mr Bowles' interleaved copy of the Bill with every line, every sentence, every word, carefully weighed and annotated was a monument of industry. So profound was this talented man's study of its provisions that no flaw in its harness could escape him. There is no denying that he was Harcourt's great danger . . .' But finally all his industry proved in vain, and it was Bertie who did secure a small amendment in committee, namely the exemption of legacies to universities.

The contrasts between the courtly and cultured landowner and the pugnacious magazine editor are obvious, and it is the contrasts that members of the family who still remember them tend to emphasize. But there were also similarities which may explain the liking they certainly had for each other, whatever reservations (one suspects especially on Bertie's part) may have qualified it.

Both were unquestioningly patriotic, with a patriotism that looked backwards to the knights and yeomen of England rather than forward to imperialistic expansion. Neither had the least use for the Liberal view, in their day associated with Lord John Russell and above all with Gladstone, of British power as a vehicle for moral uplift and the policing of the world. As to their personal qualities, both were highly intelligent and, in their different ways, good company. They had charm, they were amusing, and they were supremely confident men of the world. Both were considered good-looking, in rather the same fair, blue-eyed style. It was Bertie's looks that were outstanding; Thomas was thought by some to be rather too short, especially in the legs. In addition both Thomas and Bertie seem, not to put too fine a point on it, to have been rather more than ordinarily randy. This comes out in some of Thomas's writings, though necessarily veiled in the arch manner common to his times; as to Bertie, the hostess Lady Cunard was later to throw at Tom Mitford the accusation, culled from her much older husband Sir Bache, that his paternal grandfather used to take the Prince of Wales 'wenching'.

Another point they happened to have in common was that both, because of childhood years spent in France, spoke perfect French. In effect they were both bilingual, although Thomas's accent always remained noticeably English. This had more than usual significance in their period, because it was more fashionable than ever before or since for Englishmen to be bad at languages. To mangle French was a particular point of honour. Lytton Strachey recounts that his grandfather, a cultivated and intelligent man who was a friend of the historian Carlyle, scolded a French coachman with the remark, 'Vous avez drivé devilish slow.' If, as Strachey makes out, this was typical of the Victorian gentry, both Bertie and Thomas were conspicuous exceptions. It was Bertie who was the real linguist, knowing perfect German from his childhood tutor and then learning Russian, Chinese and Japanese. Thomas's only foreign language was his French. He used to say, 'You can travel the world with a knowledge of English and French coupled with a *profound ignorance* of German.'

Another similarity which perhaps drew the two of them together was in each case the reason for his knowing French, namely an unconventional childhood. Thomas was illegitimate, which meant that he could not go, like his half-brothers, to an English public school; he was sent instead to France. Bertie was the child of a broken home, something far rarer then than it is today. His mother ran away when he was very young and there was a divorce; she went to live in Italy and remarried, remaining virtually a stranger to her Mitford sons. Bertie, the youngest, was only three when she left, and she was hardly ever spoken of again. When, years later, his first child was born, Bertie did not inform his mother, though she was by then living in Earls Court; she learned of the event from the newspapers. It is unnecessary to suppose that this was caused by any particular resentment on Bertie's part towards his mother; she would simply not have been among the people he thought to inform. He and his brothers were brought up by their father, again to a great extent in France, which was then cheap; and he was sent to Eton at the early age of nine, which would now be impossible and was even then unusual.

It was not customary in the 1890s for people to complain to one another about their childhood insecurities, and these two particular men would perhaps at any time have been rather unlikely to do anything of this sort. But perhaps each spotted in the other, half instinctively, the trace of early uncertainties surmounted.

# PART ONE

## Algernon Bertram Mitford

# I

# Family and Early Life

Bertie Mitford, being keen on his lineage, particularly enjoyed an encounter with a fellow countryman at Spa in Belgium, where he was taking the waters in 1862. After chatting for some time, the gentleman asked his name. 'Dear me,' he said, 'if you are the son of Mr Mitford of Exbury and Lady Georgina Ashburnham, you are descended from perhaps the two oldest Saxon families in England. Sir, you are a remarkable person.' The man was Sir Bernard Burke, of *Burke's Peerage*. Bertie tells this story in his *Memories*, going on, it is true, to give an account of the history of both families which modestly makes out that Sir Bernard's view was exaggerated.

Bertie's mother's family, the Ashburnhams, were Sussex nobility. A Bertram Ashburnham was supposed to have been Warden of the Cinque Ports under King Harold and beheaded by William the Conqueror for his part in resisting him, but this is probably legend. What is certain is that the John Ashburnham who attended on Charles I was an ancestor. He secured as a memento one of the two shirts the King wore so that the spectators would not see him shivering in the January cold and think that he was afraid. Originally stained with a satisfying quantity of the royal blood, Bertie tells us that by his time this shirt had been washed clean by an ignorant and officious housekeeper.

As to the Mitfords, whether or not they were Saxon they were certainly medieval. Belonging to the landed gentry of Northumberland, they remained for centuries locally prominent, without ever becoming nationally distinguished. Tom Mitford used to tease his father and uncles by saying that one never seemed to come across a Mitford in the history books. They, too, seem to have been on the Royalist side during the troubles of the mid-seventeenth century, if not so prominently as poor John Ashburnham who spent the entire Commonwealth period in the Tower. At any rate, Robert Mitford managed in Charles II's reign to recover the castle and small town of Mitford which Henry III had confiscated from an ancestor in 1264; it is a fair guess that this was for services rendered to the restored regime.

Meanwhile John Mitford, third son of the man who pulled off this *coup*, was already in London making his fortune as a merchant. He helped to refound the Royal Exchange in 1667 after the Great Fire, in consequence of which he acquired some original shares in the enterprise. Bertie Mitford's father, and his cousin, tried to prove the family's title to these Royal Exchange shares, which by the nineteenth century would have been very valuable. They failed, being unable to show that there had been no other John Mitford who might have been entitled to them. Proving a negative is notoriously difficult, but it was a disappointment, especially for Bertie's father who was always rather hard up. To be sure, Bertie's daughter Iris was to observe in conversation in the 1960s, 'Our family would certainly have spent it all long ago – but they would have had fun with it.' The exotic garden at Batsford would no doubt have been made even larger and more elaborate. If any of the money had reached Iris herself, it would certainly have gone straight to charity; her 'fun' consisted entirely of good works.

John Mitford the merchant settled permanently in the south, but his descendants were never to lose their links with Northumberland and with their cousins who remained there. His grandson, another John, married Elizabeth or Philadelphia Reveley from that county. (Bertie calls her Elizabeth, as does *Burke's Landed Gentry* for 1939; more modern reference books call her Philadelphia.) This match was indirectly to bring the family a large fortune through Elizabeth's sister's marriage to Thomas Edwards Freeman, the squire of Batsford in Gloucestershire. Two of the sons of John and Elizabeth were to be the first members of the family to achieve prominence.

The elder of the two was William Mitford, Bertram's great-grandfather, who wrote a monumental *History of Greece*, celebrated in its day. The work is now forgotten, though the leather-bound spines of its numerous volumes still contribute to the decor of the

occasional country house library. William was born in 1744 and
lived at Exbury on the Solent, a place which Bertie describes as
an 'earthly paradise'. He was extremely gifted; besides his classical and historical scholarship he was a talented amateur artist
and musician. For some years he was a Member of Parliament.
He was a keen officer in the Hampshire militia, eventually coming
to command it, and for this reason in later years he was always
referred to as the 'Colonel'. Edward Gibbon was a fellow officer in
the militia, and it was Gibbon who persuaded him to write his
*History of Greece*. Gibbon and Mitford used to be compared with
each other as Handel had been with the now forgotten Bononcini.
In each case the reputation survived which deserved to do so.
Mitford's *History* is urbane and readable, but it is not a work of
genius.

The *History* is written from a firmly conservative point of view.
This may have contributed to its eclipse after Macaulay had set the
progressive fashion in history writing which has on the whole
persisted ever since. One admirer, though, was Thomas Carlyle.
Bertie says in *Memories*: 'Mitford's history naturally took the Tory
side in Greek politics: Grote and Thirlwall followed on the
Radical side. One day Thomas Carlyle began talking to me about
my great-grandfather; Carlyle was certainly no Tory, but he
praised the so-called Tory book far above the other two. He said
that Mitford had the talent of clothing the dry bones of history
with living flesh and blood . . .' Carlyle, of course, was *sui generis*:
it is true to say that he was no Tory, but he was hardly much of a
Whig either. We note that Bertie uses the word 'naturally'; it is to
him a matter of course that his ancestor would have written from
the Tory point of view. Like Bertie's own writings, William's
history expressed in literary terms the exact viewpoint of a group
of people who, as long as they hold to that viewpoint, tend to be
inarticulate. Of course members of the Tory gentry, through the
generations, have frequently found a literary voice; but this has
very often meant their taking on at least some of the progressive
ideas of other writers. This did not happen to any literary member
of the Mitford family until modern times.

Similar political views, rigidly held, caused William's brother
John to come to grief in his career. John was born in 1749 and
became an outstanding lawyer, being called to the bar in 1777.

Three years later he published a book, *Mitford on Pleadings*, which was a considerable success, even making him a fair amount of money; it continued to be read for a century afterwards. Bertie tells us that, when he was in the United States in 1873, 'more than one well-known judge and lawyer came up to me wanting to know what relation I was to the *Pleadings*'. The money earned by the book helped John buy a property at Redesdale in Northumberland – an instance of the family's feeling for its ancestral county. The book also set him on the road to success in the legal side of politics. He entered Parliament, becoming successively Solicitor-General, Attorney-General and Speaker. He helped in the abolition of the Penal Laws against Roman Catholics, and the Catholics, in gratitude, subscribed to present him with a golden vase.

This was ironical in view of what was then to happen. John was raised to the peerage as Lord Redesdale and appointed Lord Chancellor of Ireland on the death of Lord Clare. Clare was the political fixer who had two years before bribed and bullied through the Irish Houses of Parliament the Act of Union with Great Britain, which abolished them. When in Ireland, John originated a phrase which has passed into common usage. He said, 'I find that there is in Ireland one law for the rich and another for the poor.' A memoir on John by Francis Hargrave, dated 1845, notes that this 'has been often quoted'. John was at first seen in Dublin as an improvement on Clare, conscientious when Clare had been flippant. But it was soon apparent that a touch of flippancy might have helped John get on better with the Irish barristers, many of whom rather liked their little joke. If he had been more popular, it might have helped him in the trouble that was to follow. For full Catholic emancipation was being promoted, that is to say the granting to Catholics not just of freedom from the Penal Laws which had restricted their right to worship and to hold property, but of all civil rights including the right to vote. John, being a high Tory and a devotee of the Established Church, hated the idea. This is not inconsistent with his previous campaign against the Penal Laws: John had concern for the rights of Catholics as private people, but he had an even stronger political fear of the Roman Catholic Church as an institution. He and his like saw Rome in something of the same light that some (not quite all) of their descendants see Moscow. To grant individual Catholics equality in such matters as the right to own land was one thing; to grant them political influence, especially in Ireland where they were in a large majority, was quite another. So he used his office to block the appointment of Catholics to all positions of responsibility, even that of Justice of the Peace. This caused him to be detested in Ireland, where even most Protestants, at the time, supported Catholic emancipation. It also drew sharp criticism from English Whigs such as Fox and Canning.

The explosion came in 1806 when John Redesdale refused to make Lord Cloncurry a magistrate. Cloncurry had been suspected of treason, but no grounds could be found for an indictment, and he was imprisoned without trial for two years in the Tower of London during a time when the wars against France and the 1798 rising in Ireland had induced Parliament to suspend the right of habeas corpus. John justified his refusal of Cloncurry's magistrature by reference to this suspicion of treason, which the authorities had never dared to test in the courts. There was an outcry; John was humiliatingly overruled, and removed from office. He was never again to leave the backbenches of the House of Lords. People saw him as having disgraced British justice, though he was never to accept this. (It must be remembered in John's defence that the Napoleonic Wars were still in progress. The Second World War was already over when Home Office officials denied a passport to John's collateral descendant Diana and her husband, Sir Oswald Mosley, who had not long before been released from a term of arbitrary imprisonment requiring, like Cloncurry's, a suspension of habeas corpus. Cloncurry's ghost was perhaps amused.)

John Redesdale's enforced retirement under this cloud was soon eased by his inheritance, in 1808, of Batsford and its large estate. His uncle by marriage, Thomas Freeman, died in that year, and Freeman's only descendant, a granddaughter, shortly after him. In the event of her dying childless, as she did, the estate was left to John Redesdale, though he was no blood relation. The property comprised many thousands of acres of Cotswold countryside; David Redesdale's estate of Swinbrook in Oxfordshire, where the seven Mitfords were to be brought up, was what remained after the house itself and most of the land had been sold to pay debts and duties. In memory of Thomas Freeman the family name was, in law, changed to Freeman-Mitford.

John lived until 1830, leaving a son and daughter, both born in his late middle age. Neither was to marry; they set up house together at Batsford and lived in perfect and celibate amity, like characters in the books of the hunting novelist Surtees. John Thomas, Lord Redesdale, owned the Heythrop hounds and was for a long time Master of the Hunt. He was a leader of the High Tory squirearchy that ran Victorian England at just below that top level at which the Whig grandees afforded themselves, as ultimate luxury, certain progressive sentiments. Redesdale was assiduous in local affairs, especially on the Board of Guardians administering the Poor Law which is now so notorious. His groom used to say that if his old horse was given its head it would go straight to Shipston-on-Stour, where the Guardians met. He was known as the Lord Dictator; an Ape cartoon in *Vanity Fair* with this caption shows him as a paunchy, benevolent old fellow in grey tail-coat and gleaming top hat, with a vague resemblance to the guitarist Segovia. Bertie attributes the nickname to Redesdale's legendary strictness in supervising 'certain Parliamentary agents and promoters'. It was pillars of respectability like Redesdale who put a stop to the Eatanswill style of politics described in *Pickwick Papers*.

Redesdale did not by any means spend all his time in Gloucestershire. He was also active in managing the House of Lords in the interests of the Conservative Party. Though rarely mentioned by historians, he was a figure of whom contemporary politicians were well aware. The Duke of Wellington made him a whip; later he became Chairman of Committees. His influence was entirely exerted on behalf of the status quo, as when he successfully resisted attempts to abolish the function of the House of Lords as highest court of appeal. In 1857 he nearly succeeded in getting the Lords to throw out a bill to liberalize divorce, packing the House for the occasion with High Church 'Puseyites'. Lord Palmerston's government was put to a good deal of trouble in countering this move, which stemmed from Redesdale's religious, rather than from his political, conservatism. He was in fact a keen amateur theologian who engaged in polemics in the Anglican interest, venturing in a public correspondence to cross swords with Cardinal Manning himself over papal infallibility and the status of

Holy Communion. In 1877 Disraeli rewarded his long years of parliamentary activity by promoting him two steps in the peerage, making him the first and only Earl Redesdale. He died in 1886, leaving Batsford to Bertie, since of Bertie's elder brothers Percy had died and Henry had left the country and married a German girl by whom he had a daughter. For some reason the family cut him off and he was never forgiven; all mention of him is omitted from Bertie's *Memories*. Henry died in 1910 and was buried in Bad Godesberg.

This, then, is how Bertie was to inherit Batsford from his cousin. However, he did not inherit the title. What happened was that when he was later made a peer, he also took the title Redesdale, causing permanent confusion as to which Lord Redesdale has which number; his son David, for instance, was, strictly speaking, second Lord Redesdale of the second creation, not fourth Lord Redesdale. But we must now go back again and consider his direct ancestors.

William Mitford's eldest son Henry, Bertie's grandfather, was a captain in the Royal Navy at the time of the Napoleonic Wars. He died the victim of one of those ludicrous disasters that used to happen in that service from time to time, and make us wonder how Trafalgar was ever won. In 1803, Captain Henry Mitford was appointed to his first command of a ship; she was HMS *York*. With his navigating officer, he went down to inspect her before commissioning. They found her unseaworthy, and reported the fact. The Admiralty was outraged – not at the condition of the ship, but at Captain Mitford's comments which its officials chose to see as constituting insubordination. They told him to sail, or resign his commission. So of course he sailed, and on Christmas Eve 1803 the *York* went down with all hands in a fog in the North Sea. A single spar was later washed up on the coast. The incident is reminiscent of the sinking, in harbour, of the *Royal George* in 1782 when, in the words of Cowper's poem made memorable by the tune by Handel to which it is sung, 'Kempenfelt went down with twice four hundred men'.

Henry had just married for the second time; he left two daughters by his first marriage, and his second wife, née Mary Leslie Anstruther, was pregnant. A son was born after his death, and christened Henry Reveley Mitford. Mary soon married again, and together with his older half-sisters Henry Reveley was brought up by his grandfather, the historian. Now approaching sixty, Colonel William was becoming with the years more and more crotchety and set in his ways. His two interests were his books and his garden. He continued to study and to write intensively, pausing sometimes to drag a heavy trunk over the floor for exercise, and he would potter about the grounds at Exbury, pruning his shrubs with a horn-handled knife which Bertie was to inherit. Childish prattle was the last thing the Colonel wanted, and he did not, Bertie says, give his grandson a very happy childhood. His older sisters were kind to him, though, as was his great-uncle John, the first Lord Redesdale. John married when already Lord Chancellor of Ireland, in the same year that his nephew Henry went down with his ship. Henry Reveley was consequently a contemporary and lifelong friend of the Chancellor's son, the future Earl, even though William's early marriage and John's late one meant that the two were of different generations.

Henry Reveley Mitford, Bertie's father, grew up to be both amiable and cultured, sharing many of the talents and interests of both his forebears and descendants. He seems to have lacked the toughness of his grandfather, the curmudgeonly old historian, or of his son Bertie. Like them, though, he was musical and fond of painting. He knew a great deal of history, his particular period being France in the seventeenth and eighteenth centuries; and he was an expert on the French portraits of the period. Bertie once suggested to him that if he were transported back to the *salons* of those times he would have known most of the people by sight, and he replied, 'Upon my soul, I believe I should.' So would his descendants Nancy and Diana. Bertie also tells us that his father was good at languages, which from such a linguist means a lot.

Henry Reveley Mitford cut short his time at Oxford to take up a post as attaché to the British Legation in Florence, which before the unification of Italy was an independent capital. Then, as now, it contained a colony of cultivated English people, drawn to the place by a love of the arts or of the climate; some of them, perhaps, were attracted by the somewhat looser conventions which in all generations prevail among people who live abroad. It was among this agreeable society that Henry Reveley met Lady Georgina Ashburnham whose father, the Earl of Ashburnham, owned a Florentine villa. He married her in 1828 and left the Foreign Service, having just inherited the house at Exbury on the Solent after the death of his grandfather. Henry Reveley returned with his wife to England, and lived at Exbury the life of a country squire, with the customary seat on the magistrates' bench. Several children were born to the marriage, of whom three boys survived; twins named Percy and Henry, who were born in 1833, and Bertie, who was born on 24 February 1837.

In 1838 Henry Reveley let the house, and the family left England to live on the continent. Bertie says that this was in order to save money, which is probably true as far as it goes, since life in England was comparatively expensive and small country estates, like that at Exbury, have never been lucrative. However, it is possible that the wish to move originated with Lady Georgina rather than with Henry Reveley, and was prompted by a more positive consideration than the wish to economize. For they went to Frankfurt, and it was at Frankfurt that their friend Francis Molyneux was secretary to the British Legation.

Molyneux was a younger son of the second Earl of Sefton. Like both Henry Reveley and Lady Georgina, he belonged to that cosmopolitan or rather European section of the upper class that spoke French, manned the diplomatic service, and was at home in foreign capitals. He had known the Mitfords for some time, but at some point he and Georgina started a passionate love affair. One would like to know at what point; probably it was after the Mitfords established themselves in Germany. When, in May or June 1838, the family arrived in Frankfurt, Molyneux was there at the hotel to receive them. He habitually took them in his carriage on long drives through the German countryside; sometimes both the Mitfords would come, sometimes just Lady Georgina. He would come to tea with the family at their third-storey flat; he came every day 'whether Mr Mitford was there or not'. We know all this from the Mitfords' maid, who gave evidence at what was then an exceedingly rare event: the court hearing leading to the couple's divorce.

For one day in May 1841, just about three years after the family had arrived in Germany and when they were staying for a while in Wiesbaden, Lady Georgina asked the maid to pack her things. She then kissed the children goodbye and drove off with Molyneux.

Henry Reveley was not at home that afternoon; he returned to find that his wife had left him for ever. He evidently suspected nothing until that moment. Where Molyneux and Georgina went first is uncertain, but in August they booked into the Hyde Park Hotel in London as Mr and Mrs Murray. There they were visited by her brother, Colonel Thomas Ashburnham, who also gave evidence at the divorce. To be precise, the court hearing was an action Henry Reveley brought against Molyneux for 'trespass and criminal conversation' with his wife, as a result of which he received damages of £1,000. The divorce itself had to be effected by a special Act of Parliament, to which the Royal Assent was given on 23 March 1842. Molyneux and Lady Georgina married later that year, and went to live in Italy, probably because in those days no respectable household in London would receive a divorced woman.

Echoes of the scandal persisted for at least a century in the form of a rumour that Francis Molyneux was Bertie's real father. This surfaced as late as 1941, when Debo Mitford was about to marry the then Lord Andrew Cavendish, son of the tenth Duke of Devonshire. The Duke was chatting to a friend in his club about it, and went to get a *Burke's Peerage* to look up the Mitfords. 'If you want to see who they really are,' said the friend, 'look under Sefton.' People love scandalous speculations as to true parentage, and rumours of this kind, once propagated, die hard. They are not of course always untrue, but this one probably is. It would imply that Francis Molyneux was physically intimate with Lady Georgina as early as May 1836.

Bertie's childhood between the ages of five and nine was spent with his father and elder brothers in France; in Trouville for the summer, in Paris for the winter and spring, 'never twice in the same apartments', as he puts it in his *Memories*, though they were always near the Madeleine which was conveniently close both to Henry Reveley's circle of friends and to the Tuileries gardens where the children played marbles with the little French boys. King Louis-Philippe used to take his constitutional there in a long grey overcoat, accompanied always by just one companion. 'That old grey overcoat covered a King,' says Bertie, 'and we looked at it with awe.'

Henry Reveley's friends were not of this opinion; he moved

among the old legitimist aristocracy, to whom Louis-Philippe was a usurper. His very name recalled to them his odious father, Philippe d'Orléans, who had supported the Revolution and voted for the beheading of Louis XVI. They exchanged stories about the vulgarity of Louis-Philippe's middle-class courtiers, and looked down their noses at his dull family. The older ones told riveting tales about the revolutionary Terror, especially one old lady who had been Marie-Antoinette's lady-in-waiting. Others recalled their privations when in exile in London. One gentleman of ancient lineage had set himself up in Soho as a maker of whalebone corsets, another had nourished himself with conveniently cheap meat, which hawkers sold in the London streets, called 'kami' – in English, cats' meat.

Some of the educational practices of those days seem a little odd. Bertie, aged seven, was taken with some fellow pupils at his school to the morgue to see the corpse of a girl who had been stabbed to death by her sweetheart. The dead bodies were naked; a trickle of water played on each to keep it cool. The sight, Bertie says, 'fed me with nightmares for weeks.' Similarly, at Trouville the boys went with their German tutor to watch the animals being killed in the local slaughterhouse.

Trouville was then a fishing village, but it was just beginning the transformation which was to make it a fashionable resort. In at least one year the family stayed on there in the autumn for some time after the smart visitors had left; this was very probably for reasons of economy. Henry Reveley's older sisters used to come along with them, and sometimes his mother, now the widowed Mrs Farrer, would come and take over the household. This was not much fun, for she was Scottish, and enforced the gloomy Sabbatarianism for which Scotland was then famous. It is clear, though, from Bertie's account, that it was of an Episcopalian rather than of a Calvinist nature. On Sundays, while everyone else in Trouville was having an even better time than usual, the old lady made the Mitford family sit through an interminable service conducted by herself, using the Book of Common Prayer. 'She began with the morning service read from beginning to end, including the priestly absolution, which she delivered with peculiar unction; then came the Litany, which the professional cleric omits when the Morning Prayer has been given in its entirety;

then the Communion service.' Presumably the prayers of con-
secration would simply have been read through; Mrs Farrer would
hardly have ventured to dispense the Communion itself, like a
priest. At any rate, this was still not the end. 'By the time most
performers would have been exhausted – not so my grandmother;
she proceeded to deliver one of Blair's sermons, and woe be to us
if we yawned, or fidgeted, or were guilty of inattention!' The fact
that Henry Reveley put up with all this reinforces our suspicion
that he was not possessed of a particularly strong character.

Bertie went to Eton in 1846, as we have mentioned, at the
unusually early age of nine. When he first went, he had a good
start in many ways. Being so young, he was at first kept in the
private quarters at his 'damery' or boys' house. He was looked
after by young Miss Jennie Evans, who was later to inherit the
damery from her father and become the last of the independent
dames; after her day all the houses were taken over by teaching
masters. She used to carry little Bertie upstairs on her back and
generally mother him. By the time he was big enough to be
moved to the boys' part of the house, where Charles Dickens's
son was his neighbour and friend, he already knew the ways of the
school. Indeed even before he went his father, an enthusiastic old
Etonian, had told him exactly what to expect. Another advantage,
at least in psychological terms, lay in the fact that the headmaster,
Dr Edward Hawtrey, had been his father's tutor and was a close
family friend. Hawtrey invited Bertie and his father to lunch on
his first day, and was kind to him throughout his time at Eton.
There was no favouritism in this: the headmaster of Eton was
in any case too remote a figure to affect in any definite way the
career of an individual boy; but it must have been good for his
morale. Unluckily, though, Hawtrey stopped being headmaster
and became provost before Bertie reached the top or headmaster's
division, and he passed his last year and a half under Hawtrey's
successor, whom he found dull.

But in general Eton was made for Bertie and he for it. He ended
his time second in sixth form, captain of his house, and a member
of Pop. He enjoyed the school work and was good at it; the
linguistic facility that was to enable him to master even the most
alien of modern languages worked just as well with Latin and
Greek, and was to be in turn splendidly developed by his detailed

knowledge of them. He also liked games, especially rowing, though these were not yet the object of such a cult as they later became.

In particular they were not yet compulsory, which was fortunate for Algernon Charles Swinburne, the poet. Swinburne was Bertie's first cousin, since their mothers were sisters. They were exactly the same age, but Swinburne went to Eton at the more normal age of twelve so that Bertie, already an old hand, was asked by his parents to look after him. Boys are apt to respond badly to this sort of request, but Bertie took to Swinburne and 'was able to steer [him] through some shoals'. Swinburne was an odd figure, undersized and with a shock of bright red hair inherited from his father, an admiral. 'His language, even at that age, was beautiful, fanciful, and richly varied', and he had a peculiar singsong voice inherited from the Ashburnhams. The two boys used to go for walks together and spin fantasies, often based on Swinburne's voracious reading.

Bertie was at Eton just at the time when its peculiar version of the Victorian public school system was being developed. Before his day was the old Eton of riots, multiple birchings, and savage boxing duels lasting for hours in which it was not unknown for a boy to be killed; the Eton of the picturesque but disorderly procession 'ad Montem' at which money was begged, and sometimes actually extorted, from passers-by, the Eton of the infamous Long Chamber where seventy scholarship boys or Collegers were locked in from dusk to dawn. Shortly before Bertie arrived, Long Chamber had been reduced in size, divided into cubicles, and supplemented by what are still called the New Buildings; during his time Montem was abolished. During and just after his time Eton became, in its essentials, what it is today. The school was late in effecting equivalent reforms to those which Dr Thomas Arnold had enforced at Rugby in the 1820s. Dr Hawtrey began the modernization as headmaster, and later, as provost, he helped his successor to complete it.

If Eton has tolerated more individuality and provided an easier life for its misfits than other public schools, this may be related to the difference between Dr Hawtrey and Dr Arnold. Hawtrey was, in Bertie's words, a 'traveller, man of the world, and a linguist', acquainted with intelligent men in several different countries as well as with fashionable society in his own. It was rather his knowledge of the wide world than any 'muscular Christianity' of Arnold's type which made him see that things must change; that Latin and Greek, learned in insanitary surroundings and inculcated by the birch, no longer sufficed as a preparation for life. He introduced French and mathematics to the curriculum. He had, of course, no thought of abolishing corporal punishment, which he practised with skill, if not with the enthusiasm of his legendary predecessor Dr Keate. The attitude then to beating was quite different from what it is now. Neither the beater nor the beaten regarded it in itself as cruel or degrading. Once, says Bertie, some boys were caught with the materials for making rum punch. Many others then committed offences themselves for the pleasure of seeing the extra-special thrashing that would be given for this serious delinquency. The fact that this meant they would be beaten themselves, presumably less hard, did not deter them. Boys then regarded the business of being beaten almost as an initiation rite; a victim who did not flinch was regarded as coming out with credit. The idea that the beating inherently humiliated the victim, whatever the courage with which he faced it, would have been thought ridiculous. To be upset by a beating was to excite contempt, not sympathy; and the possibility of a sexual element was as yet unsuspected.

Immediately on leaving Eton, Bertie saw Batsford for the first time; he spent four weeks hunting and shooting there with Great Dictator Redesdale before going to Wales to be coached for Oxford by the famous Greek grammarian W. E. Jelf. Jelf was an austere scholar, but Bertie got on well with him. He stayed there from January to October of 1855, studying the great classical authors in considerable volume and in the minutest grammatical detail. This won him the Slade Exhibition to Christ Church.

However, once he reached Oxford Bertie enjoyed life too much to continue on the narrow path of scholarship. At Jelf's, where there were no other distractions, he could concentrate his powerful mind on the task in hand; at Christ Church there were temptations to which he was neither the first nor last to succumb. With high Victorian seriousness he castigates himself in his *Memories* for his 'loafing'. He did benefit, as does everyone at Oxford, from meeting clever people; he records talking at some length to the famous oriental scholar and philologist, Max Müller, at a party in the Christ Church Deanery. But much of his time appears to have been spent boxing, a sport then practised without gloves. There were few of what are now known as 'sporting facilities'; it was in each other's rooms that he and his friends used to spar, and they engaged a battered prizefighter from London to coach them. Bertie defends the bare-knuckle system, then shortly to be superseded: 'There was unquestionably much ugly mauling, but probably less danger than exists in these days of gloves, and hooks on the jaw, and deadly punches over the heart and vital organs.' In general sport at Oxford was then only just beginning to be organized. There were cricket and rowing in the summer, as now, but the winter pastime was hunting. There was as yet very little football. Bertie approves of the later fashion for games, saying that later generations of undergraduates 'are leading cleaner, wholesomer lives than we did'.

When the time approached for his Moderations, Bertie had to cram into six weeks a quantity of reading that ought to have been occupying two years. By ordinary standards he would seem to have succeeded, at least up to a point, for he did achieve a second; but for him, as Slade Exhibitioner, this amounted to failure.

Not long afterwards he accepted a nomination for the Foreign Office, rather than stay for two further years and sit his Greats. He was probably right; once the habit has been acquired, idleness at Oxford is very hard to shake off. Besides, the Foreign Office was in the family. His father had also cut short his time at Oxford to go into it, and his eldest brother, Percy, was a diplomat for a time.

# 2

# Foreign Office

Bertie entered the Foreign Office in February 1858, the month in which he became twenty-one. Neither the typewriter nor carbon paper had been invented, so the junior clerks had to copy all the documents in longhand.

Despite this, he settled down happily enough in the African Department, intending at the first opportunity to get a foreign posting. The department was directing the suppression of the slave trade: information about the ships practising the trade would reach the Foreign Office from the British Consul in New York, and the details were then copied on to slips to be sent round to the Admiralty for action to be taken. Bertie started a register of slavers; he came to have a detective's interest in the work.

It was also at the African Department that Bertie came to know Sir Richard Burton, the great explorer and Arabist. After returning from his discovery of Lake Tanganyika, Burton became fascinated by a controversy over whether there was such a thing as a gorilla. A traveller called du Chaillu had described the animal, but some said it was a fabulous beast. Similar arguments now arise over the Abominable Snowman and the Loch Ness Monster. Burton wanted to go out to Africa to look, but since he was a captain in the Indian Army the only way he could get there was by obtaining a consular appointment to the region. He secured the appointment of Consul to the Spanish colony of Fernando Po, and was sent to the Foreign Office to learn about the area; Bertie was deputed to brief him. The two became friends, and soon Burton half persuaded Bertie to go out to Fernando Po as his deputy. 'Luckily my father put his foot down,' was Bertie's own later comment. As for Burton, he was never to find a gorilla.

Bertie's hours of work were odd by modern standards, and

seem also to have been fairly flexible. The Foreign Office allowed
him plenty of time to do all the many things he enjoyed. The
clerks were not expected in the office till noon at the earliest, while
they normally knocked off at about seven in the evening, except if
there was great pressure of work; then they would often stay very
late. He employed his free mornings taking drawing lessons, or in
fencing and gymnastics; and he led an active and varied social life
in the evenings. As he puts it, 'A clerk in the Foreign Office at that
time carried with him a passport to all that was best in political,
diplomatic, literary and artistic society', and being both bright and
gregarious he used these facilities to the full. He was, for instance,
asked by the French ambassadress to look after a party of smart
young Parisians on their visit to London. One of them was the
Marquis de Gallifet, a young cavalry officer later to become well
known for his merciless reprisals against the Paris 'Communards'
in 1871. It was also at this time that Bertie met, and impressed,
Benjamin Disraeli, who was already a leading Conservative
politician. At one dinner party he sat next to Mrs Disraeli; all of a
sudden she turned round to him and said: 'Dizzy has got his eye
on you.' Time was to show that this was the case. Bertie also
became rather a favourite of the Palmerstons, and frequented
Lady Palmerston's Saturday tea parties – the country weekend
was then unknown – as well as Holland House and other important *salons* of the day. He was musical; as soon as he left
Oxford he was recruited into the orchestra of the Amateur Musical
Society as first cornet. His friend Henry Coke, who recruited him
to his own amateur band, describes him in *Tracks of a Rolling
Stone*, 1905, as 'perhaps the finest amateur cornet and trumpet
player of the day'. In this way he came to know many of the best-
known musicians and singers of the day, notably the soprano
Jenny Lind and the conductor Costa, under whom he played and
who seems to have been as sharp-tongued as Sir Thomas Beecham.
He met Thackeray at dinner with the Pre-Raphaelite artist Sir
John Millais. He also came to know the Prince of Wales, at whose
wedding in 1863 he was a gentleman usher.

In contrast, he also kept up his interest in bare-knuckle fighting,
then already illegal but still popular; he watched a famous 'world
championship' match in 1860 between an Englishman and an
American, held clandestinely at Farnborough and broken up at

the last moment by the police, but later the subject of an anonymous account in *The Times*. At no point in his account is there any hint of fear that his superiors in the Foreign Office might object to his presence at this illegal event, should the police have picked him up. Possibly he thought there was safety in numbers, as the crowd was about twelve thousand; but this is more likely to be a sign that the public service in those days was less pettifogging about unimportant things than it is today.

At the same time, it is hardly necessary to point out, it was also much more reliable about what really mattered. All the then head of the Foreign Office told Bertie on his arrival was this: 'Remember that there are no secrets here; everybody is trusted, and you will find that nothing is hidden from you. But you must hold your tongue.' And it worked. Years later a great European financier, whom he does not name, was to tell Bertie that the British Foreign Office was 'the only one at which we have never been able to buy information'. Nor were there at that time any ideological traitors to give it away free.

Bertie's first foreign assignment was in Russia. It was only a temporary exchange posting for six months, covering the winter of 1863–64, but he made full use of it. For one thing, he learned the language; in less than three months he was speaking Russian fluently enough to hold his own in a conversation with Tsar Alexander himself, though he speaks of his relief when His Majesty reverted to French.

This occurred at a private dinner party, and several people noticed that the Tsar singled out this junior British diplomat for a chat. The probable reason for this is worth recounting, for it shows to what perfection Bertie knew, when talking to the great, how to lace his urbanity with just the right touch of pertness. It was at his first presentation, with a group of other young diplomats. The Tsar afforded a few words' conversation to each. When he said he had been at Oxford:

'Ah!' said his Majesty, '*j'ai été à Oxford. L'orateur public a même prononcé un discours en Latin en mon honneur.*'

'*Dont je suis sûr,*' I answered, '*que votre Majesté n'a pas compris un traître mot.*'

He seems to have paused here because he gave the Emperor time to become nettled.

The clouds gathered on Jupiter's brow and there was thunder in the air. 'Who,' they said as plainly as speech itself, 'is this whipper-snapper who dares to say that I, the Emperor of all the Russias, am an ignoramus that does not understand Latin?'

'*A cause de notre prononciation barbare*,' I continued.

The clouds were dispersed, the sun shone again – all was well with the world. The Emperor laughed heartily at the expense of the public orator, and his '*prononciation barbare*', and kept me talking for some few minutes. (*Memories*.)

The Oxford public orator would in those days, of course, have used what became known as the 'old pronunciation', in which Latin was pronounced in every detail as if it was English. Foreigners found this very strange.

Through contacts provided by his embassy colleagues and London friends Bertie soon came to lead as active a social life as in London, if not quite such a varied one. In the nature of things, he mainly frequented diplomatic circles and the court nobility; the only time he was in the same room with one of the great Russian writers – it was the novelist Turgenev – he was at the other end of a long room, and they never spoke. He found that the Russians were very familiar with the English novelists of the time; Bertie's friend Thackeray was a favourite in particular, and Bertie made up his mind to tell him how much admiration for his work he had found in Russia. Unfortunately, the novelist died before his return.

Visually Russia fascinated Bertie. St Petersburg's graceful palaces were inhabited by a glittering society of handsome people; the military parades and religious ceremonies appealed strongly to one who was always a lover of the stylish and the spectacular. Bertie also visited Moscow, and was impressed in a different way by its more alien attractiveness, darkened by the memory of Ivan the Terrible and the fire which drove Napoleon to retreat.

Politically, Bertie saw nothing special to object to in the Russian system; his assessment of the relevance of liberal objections to the Tsarist despotism is so low that he does not even bother to comment on them. The censorship annoyed him a little, but it was so haphazard as to allow in practice for fairly wide freedom of comment. The ambassador, Bertie says, advised him that all correspondence should go by diplomatic bag, as all letters going through the post office were opened; and the man who taught him Russian was tailed by the authorities, simply because he had previously taught the *Times* correspondent who had just been expelled from Poland. Bertie mentions these things without any sense of indignation. He simply saw them as customs of the country.

The fact is that, like all rooted conservatives, Bertie judged the political conditions in a country not by its rights but by its amenities. He was a person to whom, for instance, the right of a government to censor the press was acceptable, so long as it was not exercised. He tended to discount, just as liberals tend to emphasize, the effect of paper guarantees and democratic constitutions on the actual condition of the people. Even in the matter of the Polish insurrection of 1863, which was just in the last stages of being put down, Bertie comes out on balance on the side of the Russians. He admits that they started it. Knowing that Warsaw was full of disaffection, the imperial government introduced conscription for the Poles in January 1863 and selected for army service those they considered dangerous. This led to a terrorist rebellion rather like that which gained the Irish Free State its independence in 1922, except that it was much more brutal and was, of course, ruthlessly suppressed. Bertie does not gloss over this ruthlessness, only saying rather lamely that many Russians deplored it, and that stories of atrocities against Poles that had reached the West were often exaggerated. In particular, he insists, they were not tortured; flogging, for instance, was used as a judicial punishment but not to extract information. This is a distinction that seemed more real in his day, when flogging was commonplace in both civilian and service life in Britain, than it seems to us.

On the other side, his account of the Poles' behaviour seems more modern.

The Poles were past-masters in the art of exciting dramatic emotion and surrounding base crimes with a political halo. Some scoundrel would be condemned to death for murder, rapine, arson or some other abomination. Immediately he was glorified into a political hero and martyr . . . All Warsaw turned out in deep mourning to do him honour, and witness the sacrifice . . . Popular resentment against the Government was stimulated, and, what was still more important to the agitators, the kind hearts of foreign correspondents were touched . . .

The British Foreign Secretary at the time was Lord Russell, better known as Lord John Russell, a Liberal statesman and former Prime Minister with a penchant for moralistic intervention in international affairs. Russell's detractors, of whom Bertie was one, accused him of 'meddle and muddle'. Russell is one of the few people of whom Bertie speaks in his *Memories* with consistent dislike. He regards him as having so lowered British prestige among the nations as to have led Germany to feel that Britain would not move if Belgium were attacked in 1914, and therefore as having in a sense caused the First World War.

This particular accusation is very far-fetched, but it is certainly true that British statesmen have sometimes made a habit of taking a high moral line in conditions when they then either had to back down, or found they could provide no real help. It can be traced back to Cromwell, and Milton's sonnet about the Waldenses: 'Avenge, O Lord, thy slaughtered saints . . .' It is an expression of the Puritan side of Britain's personality. Russell was a practitioner of this moralism, as Gladstone was to be; much later it was to achieve its finest flowering in the Labour leadership of the 1930s which called both for resistance to Hitler, and for disarmament. It came naturally to the United States, itself an offshoot of the Puritan side of British culture; so Russell also foreshadowed Presidents Wilson, Roosevelt and Carter, the Fourteen Points, the Atlantic Charter, and the phraseological framework of the United Nations.

On the subject of Poland in 1863, Bertie agrees that the state of public opinion in Britain and France compelled some reaction, but thinks this should have been a 'friendly intercession' on behalf of the Poles by both governments in concert. What Lord Russell did was, admittedly in the form of a diplomatically phrased note, to threaten war unless certain concessions were made. Prince Gorchakov, his opposite number, replied in effect that Russell did not know what he was talking about, and the concessions were refused. This forced Russell to retreat, making the French feel considerably let down. In particular, Bertie accuses Russell of ignoring the Russians' historical reasons for fearing the Poles, who had occupied Moscow in the seventeenth century and whose claims were certainly not confined to provinces where they were in a majority. (They were to prove the truth of this when in 1918 they took advantage of the temporary weakness of Russia during its post-revolutionary Civil War and annexed a large Ukrainian-speaking area.)

Shortly afterwards, still during Bertie's time in St Petersburg, the crisis over Schleswig-Holstein blew up. This territory, belonging to the Danish Crown but under complicated legal conditions, was seized by Bismarck's Prussia from the Danes in 1864. It included the deep-water port of Kiel, the long-term importance of which was that it enabled Prussia to create a navy. In the case of Poland, Bertie thought Russell was too belligerent. In the case of Denmark the complaint was that he was not firm enough, because this time, as Bertie saw it, a vital British interest was involved. He thought it very important that Prussia, already clearly moving to unite and dominate Germany, should not acquire Kiel. Russia and France were also basically hostile to Bismarck's intentions, though Bertie cites indications to the effect that France viewed the possibility of a German navy as a potential advantage, balancing British naval preponderance. Lord Russell made his opposition to Prussian designs on Schleswig-Holstein very clear to the whole of Europe. Then, however, he suddenly backed down. Bertie was called out in the middle of a February night, during a howling St Petersburg blizzard, to decipher for the ambassador a telegram instructing him to tell the Russian government that Britain would not interfere on behalf of Denmark. Prince Gorchakov, still smarting from Lord Russell's moralizing about Poland, could not resist rubbing salt into the wound when Lord Napier went to inform him of the change of policy. He said: 'So I can put aside the supposition that England would ever make war for a question of honour.' Pretty words, Bertie comments, for a British ambassador to listen to; but his underlying point is that this particular treaty obligation had a material importance to Britain. Russell was allowing interest as well as honour to go by the board.

Bertie returned to the Foreign Office in May 1864, but remained alert for any opportunity to be sent abroad again. In October of that year, when his holiday was due, he procured a trip to Turkey as a messenger. He greatly enjoyed this visit. He managed, as he always did, to get about a good deal, climbing Mount Ida and admiring the Greek remains of Asia Minor. These were still being actively pillaged for fortifications rather than, as now, carefully excavated and restored. On his way home he stayed at Corfu, which until very recently had been occupied by the British. Bertie's innkeeper told him that their departure had ruined his trade, and that of the whole island. Bertie fell in with an agreeable Russian who, to his distress, pointed out what an important stronghold the island could be and asked, 'What was your Lord Russell about?' Another black mark for that statesman. However, the whole journey took only six weeks, and by the end of November he was back in London at his copying.

# 3

# The Legation in China

He was not to stay for very long. In February of the next year, 1865, someone was suddenly needed for Peking. Bertie volunteered with an alacrity that seems to have surprised his superiors. But it suited their convenience and they agreed to the posting. He was put in touch with the British minister in Peking, Sir Frederic Bruce, who was in London at the time. Bruce was handsome, slow-spoken and shrewd; foreigners of the time used to think of the English diplomat as phlegmatic and devious, and Bruce was just that. He took to Bertie, and gave him a thorough briefing on what to expect in China.

Potentially, the legation in China was rather a dangerous place, though Bertie was never personally to face any violence in China. (Japan was to be another matter.) The general level of law and order was good because the people were disciplined and peaceable, and Bertie tells us that no Chinese would ever have dreamed of going about armed for self-protection. However, foreigners were disliked, especially by the Dowager Empress Tz'u Hsi who was the real ruler of China. The very presence of foreign legations in Peking was an affront to the government's dignity; their acceptance had been imposed by British and French armies as part of a humiliating peace treaty only five years before in 1860, when they captured Peking at the end of a two-year war. Much later, in 1900, the same Dowager Empress, who was as durable as she was disastrous, was to encourage the anti-foreign 'Boxers' actually to attack and besiege the foreign legations; they would only be rescued by another invading army. In the towns foreigners were often shouted at as 'devils', though Bertie tells us that in the countryside the people's attitude to them was rather one of slightly awed curiosity.

Sir Frederic Bruce told Bertie something about his future colleagues, notably Thomas Wade, the chargé d'affaires. Wade was to run the legation until Sir Rutherford Alcock, Bruce's successor, arrived in November. Wade was a considerable Chinese scholar and was in fact, as an Englishman, an important pioneer in this field. He was at that time preparing one of the first Anglo-Chinese linguistic textbooks. Later he was to be Professor of Chinese at Cambridge. He helped devise the so-called Wade-Giles system of transliterating Chinese into Latin script that was until recently standard usage not only in Britain but in many other Western countries. (Mao Tse-tung and Teng Hsiao-ping are Wade-Giles transliterations, as opposed to Mao Dzedong and Deng Xiaoping which conform to the system now replacing it.) Wade was also an outstanding mimic. Bruce mentioned this to Bertie, and told him to be sure to ask Wade 'whether he has added me to his Gallery of Illustration'. He had done so, says Bertie in *Memories*; for naturally, as soon as he came to know Wade well enough, he asked him to 'do' Sir Frederic. Wade told Bertie that he had once been interpreting for Bruce in negotiations with Prince Kung, the official in charge of foreign affairs. Kung was being difficult, and at last Wade, by his own admission, lost his temper. Bruce, however, was quite unperturbed, continuing to puff away at a cheroot. Kung pointed out to Wade that his chief did not appear to be as upset as he was; upon which Wade turned on Bruce and said, 'The Prince says that you are not angry, that it is only I who am excited.' Sir Frederic languidly took the cheroot out of his mouth, and drawled, 'Oh, damme, tell him I'm deyvlish angry', upon which he beamed at Prince Kung and his entourage and resumed smoking. Bertie says the imitation was exact.

Bertie wrote long and detailed letters home, which he was to edit in the form of a book, *An Attaché at Peking*. He published this in 1900 and added an introduction, which gives some political background and makes certain policy suggestions. For instance, Bertie suggests that the Chinese should move their capital from Peking to Nanking, where the Western powers can more conveniently control them. By that much later date, he had become accepted as an authority on Far Eastern affairs, largely on the strength of the popular success of *Tales of Old Japan*. There is no evidence of any great evolution in his political views on China

from what he thought as a young diplomat. At neither date is
there any attempt to see political events from the point of view of
the Chinese. The emphasis is entirely on the rights of the Western
powers in China to trade, and police their trade, and 'teach the
Chinese a lesson' where necessary. It is not only Britain who has
these rights; all Western powers seem to be approved of by Bertie
in the Chinese context, even Wilhelmine Germany of which, in
*Memories* and especially in *Further Memories*, he was to be so
bitterly critical. (But *Memories* and its successor were to be published later still, during the First World War; the evolution of
Bertie's attitude to Germany is a subject to which we shall revert.)
The difference in *An Attaché at Peking* between the introduction
and the letters which form the main body of the book is not that
his attitudes have changed, but that the letters are rarely about
politics at all. They are descriptions of his immediate impressions
and experiences, simply and directly conveyed.

The journey to Peking took three months, but the latter part of
this time included stops of several days at Hong Kong, Canton,
Shanghai and Tientsin, which gave him the opportunity to make
friends among the British officials and traders. So already on
arrival at Peking he had learnt something about China, both from
observation and from his hosts. The old Chinese Empire was
crumbling under the impact of Western ideas which came through
trade, technology and Christian missionary activity; military force
was often used to back Western interests. But the Empire was so
vast, and in practice so decentralized, that the process of decay
was extremely leisurely. For example, at the time of Bertie's arrival, a revolt was going on in another province. But it was
sufficiently distant for Bertie to encounter no disorder on his
journey; and although he did not think much of the Chinese
imperial forces, he does record that they eventually defeated the
rebels. Not that he gives them much credit for this; he regards
them as having entirely depended on European officers.

Altogether his political view of the Chinese is briskly patronizing. He takes for granted the right of Europeans to intervene with
force in protection of trade, or for other purposes which suit them.
It does not cross his mind that the British might have been wrong
in fighting the Opium War of 1839 so that British merchants could
sell the drug to the Chinese people; anyway he believes the harm

in opium to be exaggerated. He mentions with only mild regret the punitive destruction in 1860 of the Emperor's Summer Palace; this was in fact an appalling act of vandalism, and his attitude, for a cultured man, is notably complacent. In another passage, when he is commenting on the event from the political point of view, he makes it clear that his main grounds for condemning the action are that the palace is so far from Peking that the Chinese can ignore the 'lesson'. It would have been better, Bertie thinks, to have destroyed the Imperial Palace in Peking itself.

Peking he found to be 'like a vast curiosity shop with all the dust and dirt which are among the conditions of *bric à brac*'. The city's private affluence and public squalor, in description, exceeds anything that was to be even imagined by J. K. Galbraith. The streets were cluttered and filthy; but the shops and private houses were spotless and meticulously cared for. The dust, blowing in from the Gobi Desert and often reaching his horse's hocks, was the worst Bertie was to encounter anywhere in the world; when the weather was wet it turned to mud. The beggars, some of them actually naked, were a sinister and pathetic sight, and in the summer they stank. Yet he says in his diary (6.9.66) that as he drove out of Peking for the last time, 'I quite envied a coolie whom I saw going in dragging by the tail a dog who had died a natural death to make a meal of him.' This remark is affected and rather unattractive, but it shows that on balance he loved Peking. Partly this was because of the *bric à brac*; it was in Peking that Bertie first began seriously collecting objects, both for himself and for other people. This was to become one of his great interests, influencing the domestic interiors of the family down the generations. Although few of his grandchildren were to share his taste for Gothic, both medieval and Victorian, they admired the eighteenth-century French furniture he also collected; and although most of his oriental objects were subsequently dispersed, a screen with large white Chinese characters on it was to be seen in Nancy's Paris drawing room a century later, looking more at home among her French furniture than a purist might have expected.

There was no Peking equivalent of Bertie's encounter with the Tsar. The Chinese imperial government had been compelled to accept the foreign legations, but that did not mean it felt the necessity of conforming to Western diplomatic usage. The idea of inviting each new diplomat to attend on the head of state could not apply in the case of the Chinese Emperor. On the contrary, he was considered so sacred that on the rare occasions that he left his palace in procession the public, including *a fortiori* the foreign diplomats, was warned to stay away from the streets through which he was to pass. The nearest equivalent to the presenting of credentials occurred when the court official from time to time in charge of the rather ill-regarded task of coping with the foreigners felt like visiting the legation concerned. These occasions provided the opportunity to introduce to him a new diplomat of junior rank, though a new minister would be received at the equivalent of the Foreign Office, an inconvenient building, access to which was through the kitchen.

The dignitary to whom Bertie was presented was the same Prince Kung who had spotted Sir Frederic Bruce's comparative calmness. Kung was the uncle of the young Emperor T'ung Chih, in whose name the Empress Dowager ruled. He arrived at the legation in a sedan chair preceded by two elegant mandarins and with a number of footmen. A man in his late twenties, he was conspicuously pockmarked and shortsighted; 'He has', Bertie says, 'the same trick of screwing up his eyes that I have, and I could not help thinking what a caricature we should have made as we sat opposite each other making faces.' (*An Attaché at Peking*.) He also had a habit of shifting the conversation from the business in hand, especially at awkward moments, on to some object that happened to catch his eye. On this occasion he lighted on the single eyeglass Bertie wore. Spectacles were familiar in China, but a monocle was a novelty. Prince Kung referred to it several times during his conversation with Wade, which was long and apparently amicable, though Bertie did not, of course, understand any of it.

This gave him time to observe. Here is his account, as sharp as it is condescending, of the appearance of one of Prince Kung's companions.

Heng-Chi . . . is a little thin old man . . . and a great dandy. He wore a pearl grey silk dress turned up with blue. His fan case, chopstick-case and other knick-knacks which he wears at his girdle, are richly embroidered, and mounted with seed pearls and a peculiar clouded

pink coral which the Chinese call baby-face coral. His snuff-box is of
the finest Fei Tsui, or emerald green jade, which is worth its weight in
diamonds here, but of all his possessions none is in his eyes more
charming than a large silver Geneva turnip watch which he displays
with much pride. In his boot, which is of black satin, he carries his pipe
with its tiny silver bowl, and a gorgeous Fei Tsui mouthpiece, together
with sweet-meats, pills, and other trifles. His white cap with the red
tassel of office hanging all round it, has a pink coral button (Heng-Chi
is a mandarin of the first button), and the peacock's feather which falls
from it is mounted in more Fei Tsui. To crown all, he wears a pair of
spectacles as big as saucers, with broad silver rims. Never was a little
old man so pleased with himself . . . (*An Attaché at Peking*.)

Next day Heng-Chi invited Bertie, with Wade, to watch a
military parade at six o'clock in the morning. Wade, a former
soldier, had translated the English drill book, and was pleased with
the way the two thousand soldiers performed. Westernization had
not touched the Chinese military music, though, which was
performed by twelve men playing conches and seemed to Bertie a
dismal howl. There was an accident with the artillery: a big gun
was fired while its powder box was still open, and the box
exploded, injuring four men. The lieutenant in charge of the gun
was there and then flogged with a bamboo cane. After the parade
Heng-Chi entertained the diplomats to an elaborate banquet.
Bertie was still rather unfamiliar with Chinese eating habits; he
found it strange to begin with dessert and end with soup, and was
put off by the final complimentary belches of his Chinese table
companions. He enjoyed the food, though; there were more than
sixty different dishes. He tried almost all of them, and liked every
one he tried. To be sure, they were very rich and, he thought,
probably unwholesome. He was particularly struck by the sea
slugs, which reminded him of turtle soup.

During the high summer the legations and all their staff moved
out of Peking to escape the heat, only returning for as short a time
as could be managed on the days when the mail arrived, to deal
with the dispatches. The British ensconced themselves in a Buddhist monastery called the Temple of the Azure Clouds, whose
landscaped grounds with fountain and rockery certainly influenced
the taste in gardens that Bertie was to express at Batsford.

From there Bertie did a good deal of sightseeing, but his main occupation was learning Chinese. He had a teacher, a thin old man who smelt strongly of garlic, and knew no word of any language other than his own; so, since there was at first nothing to be had in the way of a textbook, the initial stages were difficult. However, Wade was at the time working on an Anglo-Chinese textbook, and he let Bertie have the use of the manuscript pages as he prepared them. Bertie studied during the mornings, and then wrote down his lessons on paper fans, which he carried about for the rest of the day. When he became proficient, he talked with his teacher on all sorts of subjects. The teacher told him a good deal about the Chinese arts of medical diagnosis, and prophecy, by means of palmistry and the study of the features. Bertie then scored a great success by telling him of the Western art of phrenology. The idea of there being any significance to the bumps of the head was unknown in China, though very much in harmony with Chinese modes of thought; so Bertie treated his teacher to a reading of his cranial protuberances. How much Bertie actually knew of phrenological lore, and how much he simply made up, is impossible to say; but in any case the teacher was delighted.

By the autumn, when the diplomats returned to Peking, Bertie had acquired a good working knowledge of Chinese. He now began to be assigned to the task of showing visitors around; he was always, he says, glad of the excuse to visit with them the curio shops and the raucous, stinking, but endlessly fascinating bazaar. Sometimes people would come up to him in the street for a chat, curious at the sight of a foreigner. One such, an educated man, asked 'whether it was true that in Europe there were men with holes through their chests and backs whom their servants carried about by passing a bamboo pole through the hole . . .'

He also had the experience of watching the mass execution of fifteen criminals of whom one, a murderer, was beheaded, and the others had the privilege of being strangled, which was considered less of a punishment because the Chinese thought it important to take one's body out of the world in the same state as it had come into it. Perhaps for these reasons the murderer raved and cursed, but two of the other condemned criminals chatted and joked with Bertie. Each had to go through the form of acknowledging the justice of their punishment before the presiding official; then the sentences were performed by the public executioner, in all cases with 'merciful quickness'. Bertie thought the Chinese method of manual strangling with a whipcord was much quicker and more humane than hanging.

He was also present when a Cantonese acquaintance purchased an eight-year-old girl. There was a lengthy session of bargaining between the buyer and the girl's father, in which the girl participated. To Bertie's surprise she supported the buyer, helping him to beat her father down — so keen was she to leave her very poor parents, who probably could not give her enough to eat.

Bertie travelled extensively during his time in China. He made a journey to the Great Wall with some colleagues, returning via the tombs of the Ming emperors. He noted on that occasion that the inhabitants seemed to be both friendlier and more prosperous the further he moved away from Peking. Later, he undertook two extended trips to Mongolia, where he spent some nights in a yurt, the Mongol dwelling, made of poles and felt, which is a cross between a hut and a tent. He spent the high summer of 1866 in a temple 'even more delightful than that of the Azure Clouds', and then, at the end of September, on the orders of the Foreign Office, left for Japan.

# 4

# The Opening of Japan

Bertie arrived in Yokohama in October 1866 in a pelting rain-storm. The people on the waterfront looked dispirited, though satisfactorily outlandish. He noted the minor officials with their swords, sad-coloured robes and lacquer hats, and the coolies with their straw raincoats looking like sodden and animated haycocks. There were a few women about, 'clattering and splashing in high wooden pattens', carrying babies with skin disease. Mount Fuji was hidden in dense clouds.

For the first few days, until lodgings could be found for him, Bertie was put up at the legation which was at the time in Yokohama. On his first night at dinner he met his new colleagues, and some of the officers of the Norfolk Regiment then stationed there. The minister, an 'old China hand', was Sir Harry Parkes, shrewd, sandy-haired and irascible; Bertie's relations with him were to be quite satisfactory, but he did not warm to him as he did to Wade in Peking. Also present was Ernest Satow, later Sir Ernest, an eminent diplomat and an expert on the Japanese language. Satow had started simply as an interpreter, but by the time Bertie arrived he was a fully fledged diplomat, though officially junior to Bertie himself. The two were to become close through shared adventures.

The conversation that first night was about the anti-foreign feeling in the country and the danger from wandering ronins – unemployed samurai – who had several times attacked the lega-tion. That night Bertie was awoken by a terrific banging and ran into the passage, thinking the ronins were attacking; but his encounter with them was not to come till later. This particular alarm was caused by an earthquake.

By the next day the rain had stopped and the sun was shining.

Walking out in the afternoon Bertie saw Mount Fuji, 'snow-capped, rearing its matchless cone heavenward in one gracefully curving slope from the sea level'. From that moment, he tells us, he contracted a 'fever of intoxication' for Japan 'which burns to this day, and will continue to burn in my veins to the end of my life'. The fact that this sentiment is said to have begun precisely with his view of Mount Fuji is almost comically in accordance with Japanese convention.

The real reason why Japan thrilled Bertie, as China never did, was his love of knights in armour. 'This would be but a dull and sorry world without the glorious inheritance of the Middle Ages,' he was to say many years later, in 1911, during a lecture entitled 'Feudalism in Japan', given to the Authors' Club. We shall see how he loved the Tower of London, which later in life it was to be his duty to restore. He valued the chivalry and the pageantry of the Middle Ages, the courage and the adventure, the principle of fealty. He at once spotted the fact that Japan, with all its obvious cultural differences, had some of the spirit of medieval Europe. It was as if he had taken a time machine back to his favourite period; in the lecture just quoted he makes exactly this point, referring to H. G. Wells's novel, *The Time Machine*. Japan was still a feudal country in the sense that medieval Europe had been feudal, whereas China was not, fascinating as it was in its own way. Talk of Chinese 'feudalism' in the nineteenth century is merely confusing; it was a country run by village landlords under an imperial bureaucracy. Superficially it might look like a feudal country, but it lacked the spirit of knightly honour. Chinese soldiers were not knights; the gentry despised them, having already before the birth of Christ abandoned the military profession for the civil service on the grounds that war had become degraded. Personal fealty was not thought important as a general principle. In Japan, though, the pride of the samurai was precisely his willingness to die for his lord; members of other classes respected him for this.

It was not only the samurai who behaved in this way, as a reading of *Tales of Old Japan* makes sufficiently clear; nevertheless it was the samurai who epitomized the feudal spirit of Japan, and one story in Bertie's book, that of the Forty-seven Ronins, is its best illustration. The incident is by no means legendary; it happened at the beginning of the eighteenth century. The forty-seven

were samurai, the retainers of a lord who quarrelled with a man
sent to instruct him in court etiquette. The lord's instructor was
arrogant, provoking the lord to be insolent in return. As a result
the lord had to commit hara-kiri, and all his property was forfeit.
His forty-seven retainers became unattached ronins. After biding
their time, they attacked the house of their lord's enemy and killed
him. Then they themselves waited in a temple for the order to
arrive that they should themselves commit hara-kiri; it came, and
they did so. They had offended against public order and must
die. However, their loyal action made them heroes, for public
opinion and for posterity. The temple where they were buried was
specially venerated, and their graves came to be regarded as a
shrine – a fact that is perhaps even more uniquely Japanese than
the incident itself.

The feudal spirit so admired by Bertie is probably the reason
why the Japanese empire still survives as a constitutional monarchy. The empire, that is the notion that the country should be
unified under one ruler, was part of the great package of Chinese
culture that Japan began adopting in the fifth century AD. In China
the unified empire had been achieved by force, but was endorsed
by popular feeling on the essentially rational grounds that unity
and order are good; the Chinese had reached this position the hard
way over centuries of increasingly ruthless internecine war. The
important thing in China was that there should be an emperor;
who the emperor should be was secondary. If a dynasty failed or
was overthrown, it could be replaced with no more than temporary inconvenience. In China, the empire was an idea.

In Japan, on the other hand, the empire was a family. The
notion that there should be a single ruler became attached to the
country's most powerful line of chiefs, then coloured by the idea
of personal fealty, and finally deepened to an almost religious
veneration. The family consequently achieved the longest run of
continuous sovereignty that any family has had anywhere, from
about AD 400. Since then the emperors have had their share of
reverses; for centuries at a time they have had no real power at all.
But the respect in which they were held was real enough for it to
be always convenient to those who ruled Japan to govern in the
Emperor's name, rather than to supplant him.

The dynasties that did come and go were those of the real

rulers of Japan, the shoguns. The latest dynasty of shoguns was established by Tokugawa Iyeyasu in 1603, and Iyeyasu's descendant, Tokugawa Keiki, was in power when Bertie arrived in Japan. He was to witness Keiki's overthrow by a coalition of daimyos (great nobles). Dissatisfied with the Shogun's response to the Western challenge, the rebels brought the Emperor Mutsu Hito out of reserve. The Emperor was intelligent and open-minded, but above all had very effective advisers. Together they imposed a thoroughgoing modernization, even abolishing the privileges of the very daimyos who had initiated the restoration. All Japanese could see clearly the danger to their independence posed by Western power, but it was the Emperor's prestige that enabled the daimyos to accept necessary change. Much later still, when in 1945 the militarist leaders had led Japan up a blind alley to unconditional surrender under nuclear bombardment, Mutsu Hito's grandson Hirohito was still there, able to sign the document without loss of face. The American General MacArthur found it as convenient to keep him as a symbol of legitimacy as had the shoguns of old. Hirohito was then able to pass more easily than even the English kings to the status of constitutional monarch in a democracy, since his ancestors, for many more centuries than their English equivalents, had become accustomed to enjoying veneration without power.

Fascinating as it was to Bertie, feudal Japan was not an altogether comfortable place. One aspect of Japanese martial pride was that foreigners were not only hated, as in China, but sometimes actually attacked. Bertie always carried a pistol, and kept it beside him on his desk when he was working. No samurai was ever without his deadly sword in the street; and at any moment, irritated by the presence of a foreigner, he might cleave him from neck to waist. The advice given was to shoot to kill as soon as one saw an inch of blade. Though this did not happen very often, some people were unable to stand the constant stress; one student interpreter at the British legation actually killed himself because of it.

During Bertie's first few weeks at the legation things were quiet. Satow guided the newcomer round Yokohama and the surrounding countryside, resplendent in its autumn colours. Bertie was soon installed in his own little house, built of white wood and paper, 'not much bigger than a doll's house, and quite as flimsy'. There were dwarf trees on the verandah and a miniature garden. The legation doctor, Dr Willis, an amiable giant, lived in a similar dwelling next door.

The legation was temporarily housed in Yokohama rather than in the capital Yedo – later Tokyo – because a few years earlier it had been attacked by ronins. Sir Harry Parkes preferred to be in Yedo, so he and Bertie went there to arrange quarters for the legation and its military guard. They found two large bungalows near the temple of Sengakuji, burial place of the Forty-seven Ronins. Early one morning after their return to Yokohama, a fire broke out which destroyed much of the city, including the houses of Bertie and Dr Willis. Bertie only just escaped, losing everything he had, including his dog, which, frightened by the crowd, bolted back into the blazing house.

The political calm soon ended. The Shogun, Tokugawa Iemochi, had died in December, to be succeeded by his cousin, Tokugawa Keiki. Then came another death; that of the Emperor Komei who, secluded in his mysterious court at Kyoto, contracted smallpox and died at the end of January 1867. His successor was the fifteen-year-old Mutsu Hito. In the meanwhile the new Shogun had said he would receive the heads of the foreign legations at Osaka, and in early February Bertie, with Satow, went in a man-of-war to make the arrangements for their chief. This visit was ostensibly for the purpose of arranging points of etiquette and ceremonial; in fact it gave them the opportunity to meet many of the important men in Japan, who were now lining up to form the two sides in a short, sharp civil war.

Japan had been almost entirely cut off from other countries for more than two hundred years by the deliberate policy of the shoguns, starting with the exclusion orders of Tokugawa Iemitsu in 1637–38. The Japanese were entirely happy about this. However, they were not to be left alone. The period of Japan's isolation was a time when ships from Europe and America were travelling the world in ever greater numbers, for trade, for fishing, for adventure and conquest. Inevitably they came to Japan; inevitably there was trouble. It was the United States which decisively ended the isolation in 1854, acting in irritation at the ill-treatment of its shipwrecked whalers and in anticipation of

profits from trade. Commodore Matthew Perry was sent with a
small flotilla to coerce the Shogun into opening his country.
Iemochi, having no navy to protect himself, felt he had to agree.
But this made him unpopular. To the great lords or daimyos the
Shogun was, after all, only the first among themselves. The first
Shogun had been appointed to keep out the Mongols; his full title,
Sei-i-Tai Shogun, meant Barbarian-repulsing Warlord. What was
the good of a Shogun if, far from repulsing barbarians, he let them
in? The imperial court felt similarly, and in about 1860 began very
discreetly canvassing support among the daimyos for a move to
overthrow the Shogun. Everyone had to be cautious. The Bakufu
(the Shogun's government) had spies everywhere; all nobles had
to spend some time in the capital under the eye of the Shogun,
and leave their families, effectively as hostages, when they were
absent. But this did not prevent plans being laid.

By the time Bertie arrived in Japan the parties had been for
several years preparing for conflict. On one side was the Shogun,
with his own formidable Tokugawa clan and the Hatamoto, the
subordinate nobility allied to it; on the other were a number of the
independent daimyos, with the covert backing of the imperial court.
And there in Osaka they all were, waiting to pay their respects,
sincere or not, to the new Shogun. Representatives both of the
Shogun's party and of the discontented clans visited Bertie and
Satow; and all had an axe to grind. The diplomats had to be careful,
especially in talking to those who were against the Shogun. But
they met many of the people who were to play a leading role in the
following decades of change, and gave them information about
European methods of government, including parliamentary practices. Among the ordinary people, as distinct from the samurai, the
diplomats were objects less of resentment than of curiosity. 'The
street in which we lived was so crowded with sightseers as to be
almost impassable, and the hucksters and costers of Osaka set up a
fair trade outside our temple, where they did a roaring trade in
fruit, sweetmeats, cheap toys and the like.' Bertie also did plenty of
shopping of his own among the lacquer and brocade merchants. He
and Satow could not go on these expeditions without officials to
disperse the gaping crowds astounded at their appearance and dress.

Bertie and Parkes visited the Shogun in May 1867. He held
court in the magnificent castle of Osaka, in a stateroom whose

walls were covered in gold leaf and decorated with splendid paintings of birds. He graciously shook hands in European fashion with Parkes and drank the health of Queen Victoria. Bertie considered Tokugawa Keiki the best-looking man in Japan.

The British kept reasonable personal relations with the Shogun but were discreetly expecting his enemies to win the coming struggle. The French took the opposite view. Their minister, Léon Roches, was an ex-soldier. His main experience had been in North Africa and he knew less about the Far East than his British colleagues. More accurate information enabled the British to see that the position of the Shogun and Bakufu was not as strong as it appeared, either in law or in fact. Ultimately the foreigners would anyway need to deal direct with the Emperor, in law the absolute sovereign, because treaties concluded with anyone else could be repudiated. Realizing this, the British did not confine themselves to expecting the downfall of the Shogun; they intrigued to that end. Meanwhile the French and British ministers, who disliked one another, pursued a policy of what we should call one-upmanship. Roches offered a French military mission to train the Shogun's army; then Parkes, to get even, brought over a naval mission to initiate a navy. As Bertie comments, 'Who could have foretold that the foundation of the marvellously successful Japanese army and navy should have its origin in the jealousy of the English and French ministers?'

Of the two policies, the French one, though it was to prove ill-conceived, was easier on the legation staff; it consisted of trying to persuade the Bakufu to grant France a series of monopolies for things like docks and arsenals. The British view, though ultimately correct, was harder to carry out at the time, because it involved making contact with potentially disaffected feudal lords while still keeping good relations with the Bakufu. This was the more tricky in that anti-foreign feeling was, if anything, stronger among the 'outside lords' than in the territory directly controlled by the Shogun. In pursuit of this policy, Bertie and Satow were sent to Kanazawa, capital of the clan of Kaga, in August 1867.

The ruler of Kaga was reputedly the richest clan chief in Japan. His position in the coming conflict was still neutral, and unlike some of the other outside lords he had not entered into any relations with the foreigners on his own account. Parkes wanted to have dealings with him, and in particular he wanted permission to open to foreign trade the conveniently landlocked harbour of Nanao.

It was from Nanao itself that Bertie and Satow set out. With Parkes, they went there with a surveying expedition to northern Japan by three British ships, which also carried officials of the Bakufu to protect and advise. Parkes parleyed with two emissaries of the Kaga clan. The talks went fairly badly, but Parkes said he would send Bertie and Satow to Kanazawa itself, from which they would travel to Osaka to rejoin him. The Kaga negotiators accepted this, if rather unwillingly, but the Bakufu's officials were little short of panic-stricken. From their point of view there was a risk of disaster. The locals might have taken it into their heads to kill the two diplomats, provoking a British punitive expedition. Finally the two started off, after the Bakufu officials had obtained from the Kaga men a written receipt certifying that they were in good health at the time of delivery. A guard of twenty men escorted them.

All went well at first. They alternately walked and rode through beautiful scenery, the inns were good, and the only inconvenience was from the crowds which came to stare at them in every village and town. The negotiations themselves succeeded in establishing friendly communications: in his memoirs Satow mentions the heights of flowery speech to which Bertie rose in talking to the representative of the clan chief. It turned out that he was happy for Nanao to be opened for trade in fact, but feared that if it was officially made an open port the Shogun's government would seize it.

After leaving Kaga Bertie and Satow were nearly murdered. The Japanese officials, after a fierce argument, persuaded them to take a detour round a place called Otsu which was on the direct route to Osaka. Bertie said he would only agree to this if they made a request in writing. It turned out later that a party of Tosa clansmen had been waiting at Otsu, intending to kill the two foreigners. Bertie comments: 'The fun of the thing was that the Japanese officials, in persuading us to change our route, had not the remotest suspicion of what they were saving us from.' Can this be right? One suspects that they knew very well what was planned, and that this was why they were so obdurate. Bertie and Satow had been lucky, for shortly after their return to Osaka they heard news that some samurai had hacked two British sailors to pieces. Later, at Yedo, Bertie saved his own life by scattering cockle shells on the paths of his garden so that anyone approaching made a noise. In this way he was woken by a group of five or six marauders who fled when they saw him and his Chinese servant awake and armed. Another time he saw a headless body lying in a pool of blood; the head had probably been removed, Bertie explains, to be placed on the grave of someone whom the victim had murdered.

Meanwhile the power of the Shogun was fading as he was finding it more difficult to control the clans. Bertie and Satow spent most of December 1867 in Osaka, centre of his power. The purpose of the visit was to prepare for the opening of the place to foreign trade; but many of the important people in Japan were there too, notably representatives of the great clans, so many political discussions took place. It became clear that the most powerful clans were going to insist on a change. The Bakufu was no longer in undisputed control of the capital, Yedo; crucial negotiations were in progress at the imperial court in Kyoto. The turning point came when, in early January, the Emperor felt able to dismiss his bodyguards, who came from a clan allied to the Shogun, and appoint others from the daimyos' party.

The Shogun then arrived from Kyoto with his troops on 7 January. Groups of men in armour turned up in advance; Bertie talked to some of them, finding them 'very civil' and ready to die in the Shogun's cause. Then came the main body, and Bertie's description is worth quoting in full.

A more extravagantly weird picture it would be difficult to imagine. There were some infantry armed with European rifles, but there were also warriors clad in the old armour of the country carrying spears, bows and arrows, falchions, curiously shaped, with sword and dirk, who looked as if they had stepped out of some old pictures of the Gem-Pei wars in the Middle Ages. Their *jimbaoris*, not unlike heralds' tabards, were many coloured as Joseph's coat. Hideous masks of lacquer and iron, fringed with portentous whiskers and moustachios, crested helmets with wigs from which long streamers of horsehair floated to their waists, might strike terror into any enemy. They looked like the hobgoblins of a nightmare. Soon a troop of horsemen appeared. The Japanese all prostrated themselves and bent their heads in reverent awe. In the midst of the troop was the Shogun, accompanied by his faithful adherents, Aidzu and Kuwana. The Prince himself seemed worn and dejected, looking neither right nor left, his head wrapped in a black cloth, taking notice of nothing . . . At the gate all dismounted, according to custom — save only the War Lord himself; he rode in, a solitary horseman.

The differences between the French and English ministers then introduced a rather farcical note into this scene of high medieval drama. Roches had arranged an audience for himself. Hearing this, Parkes insisted on having one too. The upshot was that the Shogun, who clearly had far more pressing worries, received them both together, to the irritation of Roches. Bertie was present, and heard the Shogun claim to have left Kyoto voluntarily to avoid civil war. It was a face-saving formula that deceived nobody.

However, his forces were not to be finally disposed of without a battle, which took place at Fushimi on 29 January. The Shogun's army numbered ten thousand against six thousand, but when it became known that the imperial court supported the clans, groups of Shogun supporters went over to the other side. This even included, rather late in the battle, the commander-in-chief.

The civil war was brief but vicious, entailing a breakdown of law and order; villages were burnt and plundered. Every night Bertie saw the reflection of flames in the sky. So when, the day after Fushimi, the Shogun told the legations he could no longer protect them, the British set out from Osaka for Hiogo. Most went in overcrowded boats, but Bertie was detailed to go by land, in charge of the mounted escort. He lost his way in a blizzard; two men fell off their horses into the cold slime of a ricefield. After several hours he managed to find the high road at a place by a river where some hundreds of Japanese soldiers were waiting to be ferried across. Not knowing who they were, Bertie was apprehensive; but their commander proved to be friendly. In the course of a ceremonious exchange, he apologized for the delay caused to Bertie through the necessity to ferry his troops. Bertie, who was by now good at this sort of thing, then apologized for the inconvenience caused by his own. They eventually reached Hiogo frozen, but all safe.

A few days later they received word from Osaka from the victorious party which made it clear that their safety would have been assured there; whereas it was at Hiogo that they ran into danger. The legations had been assigned a plot of land at Kobe, just outside the Hiogo town gate, for a foreign settlement. The ministers were inspecting this when a force of Bizen clansmen, armed with rifles, came out of the gate commanded by a man called Taki Zenzaburo. They opened an intense barrage of fire on the assembled foreigners. Only one American sailor was wounded, however, because the attackers did not understand how to use the sights of their rifles. After several volleys they marched off, to be pursued, fruitlessly, by the foreign guards.

The new government wanted good relations with the foreigners, and decided to make an example of Taki Zenzaburo. The Emperor himself sentenced him to death in the honourable way reserved for the samurai; that is, he was ordered to commit hara-kiri. One man from each of the seven foreign legations, together with seven Japanese, were asked to witness the event. Parkes sent Bertie, which is how it came about that he was one of the first foreigners ever to witness the solemn and gruesome ceremony. His account of it, in an appendix to *Tales of Old Japan*, brings out the 'pity and terror' that Aristotle said was the content of tragedy.

The hara-kiri ceremony took place in a temple, at ten-thirty in the evening. Bertie and the other legation representatives were escorted through the courtyard, 'crowded with soldiers standing about in knots round large fires, which threw a dim flickering light over the heavy eaves and quaint gable-ends of the sacred building'. They then waited in an inner room for a long time, in dead silence, for none of them felt like speaking. The provisional governor of Hiogo, Ito Shunské, then came in. Bertie already knew him from his negotiations in Osaka; he was soon, as Prince Ito, to become the first Japanese Prime Minister. In the meantime he was representing the Emperor at this ceremony as chief of the Japanese witnesses. He told the foreigners who the Japanese witnesses were to be, and asked if they had any questions to put to the prisoner. When told there were none, he withdrew, and the silent waiting resumed.

At last Bertie and the others were ushered, behind the Japanese, into the main hall of the temple:

A large hall with a high roof supported by dark pillars of wood. From the ceiling hung a profusion of those huge gilt lamps and ornaments peculiar to Buddhist temples. In front of the high altar, where the floor, covered with beautiful white mats, was raised some three or four inches from the ground, was laid a rug of scarlet felt. Tall candles placed at regular intervals gave out a dim mysterious light, just sufficient to let all the proceedings be seen. The seven Japanese took their places on the left of the raised floor, the seven foreigners on the right. No other person was present.

After a few minutes, Taki Zenzaburo, a fine-looking man aged thirty-two, entered in his ceremonial dress with its hempen 'wings'. He was accompanied by his *kaishaku* and by three other officers, all wearing the *jimbaori* or surcoat with gold tissue facings that Bertie compares to a herald's tabard. The *kaishaku* was in a sense the executioner, since he finished the suicide off; but his status, given the general respect accorded to the hara-kiri, was really much more comparable to that of a second in a duel. In this instance he was one of Taki Zenzaburo's pupils in the martial arts, selected for his skill in swordsmanship.

With the *kaishaku* on his left hand, Taki Zenzaburo advanced slowly towards the Japanese witnesses, and the two bowed before them, then drawing near to the foreigners they saluted us in the same way, perhaps even with more deference; in each case the salutation was ceremoniously returned. Slowly, and with great dignity, the condemned man mounted on to the raised floor, prostrated himself before the high altar, and seated himself [that is, knelt in Japanese fashion] on the felt carpet with his back to the high altar, the *kaishaku* crouching on his left-hand side. One of the three attendant officers then came forward, bearing a stand of the kind used in temples for offerings, on which, wrapped in paper, lay the *wakizashi*, the short sword or dirk of the Japanese, nine inches and a half in length, with a point and an edge as sharp as a razor's. This he handed, prostrating himself, to the condemned man, who received it reverently, raising it to his head with both hands, and placed it in front of himself.

After another profound obeisance, Taki Zenzaburo, in a voice which betrayed just so much emotion and hesitation as might be expected from a man who is making a painful confession, but with no sign of either in his face or manner, spoke as follows:

'I, and I alone, unwarrantably gave the order to fire on the foreigners at Kobe, and again as they tried to escape. For this crime I disembowel myself, and I beg you who are present to do me the honour of witnessing the act.'

He bowed again, and let his upper garments slip down around him so that he was naked to the waist. He tucked his sleeves under his knees to prevent himself falling backwards, which would have been dishonourable. He then took the dirk.

He looked at it wistfully, almost affectionately; for a moment he seemed to collect his thoughts for the last time, and then stabbing himself deeply below the waist on the left-hand side, he drew the dirk slowly across to the right side, and, turning it in the wound, gave a slight cut upwards. During this sickeningly painful operation he never moved a muscle of his face. When he drew out the dirk, he leaned forward and stretched out his neck; an expression of pain for the first time crossed his face, but he uttered no sound. At that moment the *kaishaku*, who, still crouching by his side, had been keenly watching his every movement, sprang to his feet, poised his sword for a second in the air; there was a flash, a heavy, ugly thud, a crashing fall; with one blow the head had been severed from the body.

A dead silence followed, broken only by the hideous noise of the blood throbbing out of the inert heap before us, which but a moment before had been a brave and chivalrous man. It was horrible.

In due course the imperial court invited the foreign representatives to call on the Emperor. This was a sign of how far the revolution had already gone; until ten days before, even the great daimyos had not been privileged to see the Emperor face to face. The Shogun himself had to confer with him from behind a lattice curtain; only the imperial family and the court nobility had direct access. The idea, therefore, that this sacred and secluded being should show his face to foreigners, whom many Japanese considered to be descended from cats and dogs, was shocking. Some found it intolerable.

The British legation's audience was arranged for 23 March 1868. They set out in procession. First came a troup of mounted men from the London Metropolitan Police; then Parkes, Satow and two Japanese officials; then a guard of British cavalry. Bertie followed in a palanquin, because his horse had gone lame. Dr Willis and a group of naval officers came next, followed by about fifteen hundred Japanese soldiers. When they came into a narrow street the Metropolitan Policemen were suddenly attacked by two ronins who slashed about them with their swords. The eaves of the houses projecting low over the lane stopped the mounted men from using their lances. One Japanese official then engaged one of the ronins, but stumbled and was wounded; the other official then cut off the ronin's head. The other ronin then aimed at Parkes, missing, and cruelly wounded Satow's horse, before laying about him among the cavalry. Bertie, in his palanquin, had more free-dom of action. He jumped out, confronted the man, who was bleeding from a wound, and managed to get in under his guard and wrench the sword out of his hands. For someone unversed in the martial arts to do this to an uninjured samurai would have been a considerable achievement; not to put too fine a point on it, it would have been impossible. Satow, in his memoirs, does not mention Bertie's feat, merely saying that the man was stopped by Bertie's palanquin and dropped his sword. However, he does explain how Bertie could have managed it, for he makes it clear that, before reaching Bertie, the man had been tripped up by a soldier and bayoneted by several others. He managed to get up and stagger on, but was very severely wounded. Bertie handed him over to the soldiers but he wriggled free from them, though receiving a pistol shot in the face, and tried to escape over a wall. Bertie recaptured him and put him in his palanquin, forcing two protesting shopkeepers to act as bearers since his own were helping to tend the wounded. The Japanese soldiers in the procession had disappeared when the trouble started. Evidently some of them sympathized with the ronins, because Bertie says that they 'only came back having in the distance fired what was something uncommonly like a *feu de joie*'.

The prisoner, and the British wounded, were lodged nearby in a temple. Bertie interrogated the man and came to like him; he thanked Dr Willis for tending to his wounds, and Bertie for bringing him food, saying: 'If only I had known how kind you foreigners are!' He answered Bertie's questions quite readily. The attack was irrational and almost spontaneous, though a Japanese interrogator later elicited the information that three other people were involved. Bertie was greatly impressed with the damage two men could wreak against seventy, commenting: 'It only shows how much mischief a man may do if he does not try to save his own skin.' This has become familiar to the world as the kamikaze spirit.

This time the culprit was not allowed to commit ritual suicide; he was deprived of samurai rank and beheaded by the common executioner. The government also decreed that further attacks on foreigners would be treated in this way. The authorities were naturally horrified, and deeply apologetic; and the visit to the Emperor took place as planned, but three days later. This time the approaches to the palace were guarded by a concentration of picturesquely armoured warriors that effectively prevented any recurrence.

When, after a long wait, Parkes and Bertie were ushered into the presence, the exchange of civilities was in itself unremarkable, though the Emperor himself apologized for the events of three days before. What struck Bertie most was the bizarre sight of the boy Emperor, with his eyebrows shaved and replaced by black lines high on the forehead, his rouged cheeks, his mouth painted in red and gold, and his blackened teeth. He was soon to take the lead in abolishing all this and adopting Western fashions.

The next five months Bertie spent in Osaka conducting single-handed all relations with the new government, since Parkes and the rest of the legation returned to Yokohama to look after the interests of the British community there and to promote trade. This was the time when Bertie felt closest to the Japanese, never speaking any other language or seeing a European face, living on rice and fish from a Japanese cookshop. The work was hard; dispatches had to be composed, translated and copied. On the English side Bertie had no secretarial help, though for the documents in the Japanese language he engaged two secretaries for the cost of whom, later, the Treasury meanly refused to pay. There was also a substantial amount of entertaining to be done, and there were interminable interviews at the Foreign Office. Bertie's main preoccupations were to induce the government to promulgate in the country its stern prohibition of anti-foreign acts, and to procure an easier time for the Japanese Christians. In both these matters, Bertie was reasonably successful, but he became worn out through overwork and it was a relief to return to Yokohama in August and then to settle down in Yedo, soon to become Tokyo.

Thus began a few more peaceful months in the city, calm after the civil war. Apart from showing round the occasional visitor, or sometimes riding over to Yokohama on legation business, Bertie had comparatively little official work. It was at this period that, with Parkes's encouragement, he wrote most of his *Tales of Old Japan*.

However, in August 1869 things livened up. An elaborate reception was held for the Duke of Edinburgh, a younger son of Queen Victoria. This was the first time that a European royal prince had paid a visit to the Emperor; it was important for both sides that the occasion should go well. Bertie was appointed to be the Duke's interpreter, which was no sinecure; he had to learn how to speak the special language of the Japanese court, and how to avoid the smallest solecism in an area where the centuries-old etiquette of Japan was, naturally, at its most elaborate. It was, of course, the sort of thing Bertie particularly enjoyed getting right.

That winter, Bertie's health began to flag seriously. He was recalled home, and finally boarded ship on 1 January 1870; he 'had almost to be carried on board ship by our good Doctor Willis'. Despite a month's holiday in Singapore, he was glad when the Foreign Office granted him a year's leave on his return to London, especially as he had the *Tales* to revise and prepare for publication. He also resumed his active social life in London. The Prince of Wales had founded a new club, the Marlborough; he would not join White's because of restrictions on smoking there. Bertie joined the Marlborough, and resumed his contact with the Prince.

Bertie found that he was for a time the only person in London with first-hand knowledge of Japan. The Japanese were out to borrow money in the City, to finance their future development; and of course the banking fraternity wanted Bertie's opinion on the Japanese government's solvency and reliability. 'They drew the Foreign Office for me, they hunted my lodgings; at length one gentleman, Mr Julius Beer, ran me to earth at my club.' Bertie reassured him, and according to Bertie's account in 'A Tale of Old and New Japan', the country received her first foreign loan. (Lecture delivered on 14 November 1906.)

# 5

# Travels

Early in 1871 Bertie was on his travels again, this time as a private individual. His diplomatic career was in fact at an end; he was not officially to leave the Diplomatic Service until 1873, but he took the decisive step towards ending his career in it when in 1871 he declined an appointment to St Petersburg on grounds of expense. It seems strange to us today that he could be unable to keep up appearances in St Petersburg, where he would after all have had a diplomatic salary, and yet could afford on his small private income to travel, during the next three years, over half the world.

*Tales of Old Japan* appeared in the spring of 1871. Bertie had made an extremely bad deal, as it turned out, in selling the book outright to Macmillan for £240. This left him, after necessary expenses, with little if any profit. The book proved a runaway success, and this is the first example of the rather unfortunate touch he was to show in financial matters; if he had negotiated a royalty he would have had a steady and helpful income from it for the rest of his life. In *Memories*, with rueful and rather self-conscious magnanimity, he thanks Alexander Macmillan for encouraging him and for taking a chance on a new author, adding: 'It is a satisfaction to know that he was no loser by his gamble.'

Bertie did not even wait for the reviews; he took off with some others for the Middle East to visit his old friend Sir Richard Burton, by then British consul in Damascus. Burton was shortly to lose his job under a cloud. Bertie thinks it was at least partly because of the offensiveness of his wife, though Burton was himself both undisciplined and unconventional. He showed Bertie round Damascus as no one else could. He was also, as befitted such a distinguished traveller, a master of the traveller's tale; but of course Bertie, after his time in China and Japan, could now

compete in this field. On one occasion he told Burton of the chief
executioner at Yedo, whom the young samurai used to bribe to
test their swords on corpses. With a good blade, the man could cut
right through three at a blow. 'Ah!' said Burton. 'It has always
been a matter of regret to me that I never quite succeeded in
cutting a man in two. I very nearly did once . . .'

Burton took his guest to see the Countess of Ellenborough,
a famous and mysterious figure who had led a life of adventure
and was now married to an Arab chieftain. She was living in
a European house, furnished according to a rather old-fashioned
English taste; a good-looking but unpretentious old lady in 'quite
inconspicuous Paris fashion' with gracious old-world manners.
The only odd thing about her appearance was that her hair and
eyebrows had been dyed jet black in deference to an Arab superstition about the evil eye.

They also visited Abd el Kader, the great Algerian chieftain
who had resisted the French conquest of his country in the 1830s
and 1840s. In Bertie's youth, in France, he had been a legendary
figure; the French always rather admired him as a chivalrous
enemy, and when he was finally captured in 1847 he was taken to
France where he was enabled to live in some style. Finally he had
been allowed to leave France and given an allowance of £4,000 a
year; he finally settled in Damascus, where in 1860 he was able to
help protect the Maronite Christians from persecution. For this
Napoleon III gave him the Legion of Honour. He also did France
a good turn in 1871, the year Bertie met him; he forbade his son
from leading a renewed revolt against France that would have
taken advantage of the French defeat in the Franco-Prussian War.
Bertie describes going through a dark passage to a pleasant
courtyard with a fountain playing in the centre and a marble
verandah on the outside, and set about with oleanders in great
tubs. Here was Abd el Kader, in Arab dress, with blackened beard
and eyebrows and slightly rouged cheeks. He was studying an old
Arabic scroll which turned out to be a treatise on magic.

During his stay, Burton showed Bertie the first chapters of his
translation of the *Arabian Nights*, telling him that he was the first
person to see it. Bertie is interesting about this aspect of Burton
and also, in describing him, rather interesting about himself.
Burton's *Arabian Nights* had to be privately printed, and his wife

burned his papers after his death including, notably, his translation of *The Perfumed Garden*, the Arabic manual of sexual technique. Much later, just before his death in 1890, Burton was to show *The Perfumed Garden* to Bertie, whose comment was: 'If you really mean to print that, I should advise you to wait till you have resigned and secured your pension.' This delighted Burton who replied, 'Yes, I think I have shocked Mrs Grundy this time.' If the truth must be told, Bertie himself was shocked, and came to the conclusion that the desire to shock was the key to Burton's character. However, Bertie also believed that this was as far as it went. He says: 'Much that he wrote should never have been written; there is no need to specify; at the same time I believe . . . that his life was morally without stain: he was a model husband, and his wife adored him . . .' Bertie adds that he was a kind and amiable man who kept up a façade of ferocity, and that his talk was better than his books. Only his translation of the *Arabian Nights* was a success; 'For that there were adequate if not altogether blameless reasons.' In contrast, the man who wrote of Burton in this rather sniffy manner, Bertie himself, was apparently a persistent womanizer both before and after his marriage. It is all very Victorian. Whatever the personal life of a gentleman of that time, he saw decorum in published material and in conversation as a good thing in itself. We, who no longer share the unspoken assumptions on which this attitude was based, tend to look on it as hypocrisy. Sometimes, no doubt, it was; but Bertie never pretended to plaster sainthood. His aversion to explicitness about sex was more a feeling that to do what *The Perfumed Garden* describes, in passion and in private, is acceptable, whereas to write about it or discuss it in cold blood is, to use the modern expression, sick. It is a point of view.

He had not long returned from this visit when, in May 1871, he received a note from his friend the Duke of Sutherland. The first train was to be allowed into Paris following the end of the civil strife with the revolutionary Paris Commune that had succeeded the Franco-Prussian War. The Duke suggested that the two of them should go there 'to see whether we could be of any use', as Bertie puts it in *Further Memories*, though clearly curiosity was their real motive. The train was delayed at Creil, where Bertie saw the 'scowling and truculent-looking' Prussian soldiers and the sullen populace. This very probably was his impression at the time, but in his further comments Bertie, writing when the First World War was already under way, is noticeably influenced by his view of current events. He says: 'It is a terrible sight to see a great people trampled on and tortured by the savagery of a victorious army; but when that army is a Prussian army – ask the Belgians.' To an extent he rather soon contradicts this, because he goes on to say that, in Paris itself, 'strange to say . . . every Parisian with whom I talked was far more bitter against the Commune than against the Prussians'. Commune supporters were still being arrested and shot, and little piles of clothes that had belonged to casualties in the disturbances were to be seen on the street corners. Bertie witnessed one strange scene in the Place Vendôme, where the column illustrating Napoleon's victories had been knocked down by order of the Commune and was lying broken on a bed of straw. Some soldiers came by with a civilian under arrest; Bertie recognized him as the artist Gustave Courbet, whom he knew by sight and who had been Minister of Fine Arts under the Commune. As he watched, an elderly gentleman dashed up and, before the guards could stop him, knocked Courbet's hat off, shouting: '*Au moins, scélérat, tu te découvriras devant la colonne que tu as fait tomber!*' (At least, villain, you will take off your hat to the column you knocked down.) Courbet picked up his hat and looked rather dazed; the guards grinned but took no action. A sad little incident. By Bertie's account it seems to have been the restaurateurs who were most particularly hostile to the Commune after its fall. The head waiter of the Café Royal was especially rude about Courbet, making out that he would never let him inside the place again; although a year or two later Bertie was to see him welcoming the artist, by then free and famous again, with all his old obsequiousness. The wine waiter at Voisin's restaurant, where the Commune ministers had often eaten, boasted to Bertie that he changed the labels on his wine, charging them for good vintages when they were really given *vin ordinaire*. 'I was quite safe,' said the waiter; 'how could these animals know what was what?' (*J'étais sûr de mon affaire; est-ce qu'ils s'y connaissaient ces animaux-là?*) Bertie was entirely in favour of the reprisals against the supporters of the Commune which were organized by his old acquaintance Gallifet, by then a general who had distinguished himself in the Mexican

war of 1865 and in the Franco-Prussian War. Here again the First
World War intrudes into Bertie's account. If Germany uses
poison gas, he says, so must we; in the same way Gallifet was
right in killing the Communards who had committed so many
crimes, especially the murder of the Archbishop of Paris. But one
specific incident upset Bertie. He was passing the prison of La
Roquette when he happened to see some Communard prisoners
being taken out for execution, watched by a crowd. Next to him
was a pretty young girl of about fifteen in the charge of a maid. A
seriously wounded prisoner was carried out on a litter; he was well
dressed but had a three days' growth of beard and his head was
swathed in bloodstained bandages. The girl cried out 'Papa!' and
fell into the arms of her nurse: the wounded prisoner waved feebly
in reply. 'The poor child stood there shaking from head to foot
and weeping on the bosom of her *bonne* . . .'

In February 1872 the Duke of Sutherland took Bertie on a visit
to Garibaldi, the great fighter for Italian unity. Garibaldi was one
of the heroes of all Europe. Ageing now and infirm, he lived in
retirement on the island of Caprera off the north-eastern corner of
Sardinia. Bertie and the Duke, with Sir William Russell of *The
Times*, were on their way to Egypt. The Duke was an old friend
of Garibaldi, so they made arrangements to call on him on their
way. Garibaldi was sixty-four at the time and living in a plain,
unpretentious house with his third wife, a simple countrywoman
called Francesca, and a crowd of scruffy supporters. He struck
Bertie as charming and unexpectedly gentle. Because of his
military exploits against the Neapolitan monarchy and the papal
forces, people looked on him as a revolutionary firebrand, but that
was not the impression he gave. Nor was he a swashbuckler. 'It
was the combination of this sympathetic kindness with the stern
determination of the born fighter that made him . . . such a king
among men.' Bertie also found in him 'a spice and no more of
Don Quixote'. He had bad rheumatism, and suffered from an old
war wound, so he found it difficult to get about. He hated the
Church, and this feeling was even stronger in his followers. One
of them had painted over the dog kennel the words '*Casa di Pio
Nono*' (the House of Pope Pius IX). Garibaldi was a constitution-
alist and a political moderate, an admirer of the English system.
He told Bertie: 'In England you have the finest form of govern-

ment in the world – a republic in which the President rules by the will of the people, and being hereditary depends on no political cry of the moment.' He added that he only wished that the same state of affairs could apply in Italy. Garibaldi and his foreign guests dined on roast kid, with the followers sitting around the walls watching them, unable to understand the conversation because it was in French. Francesca Garibaldi joined them after they had finished. Bertie slept in a box room where he was kept awake by armies of fleas.

The next year, 1873, Bertie made an extended trip to the United States. There is a story in the family that he did so because he proposed to Lady Clementine Ogilvy, whom he was later to marry, and she turned him down. It was the custom in these circumstances for gentlemen, when crossed in love, to go big-game hunting. In *Memories* he does not mention this unsuccessful proposal, but makes out that the main purpose of the trip was to see a silver mine in the mountains of Utah in which some friends of his, and perhaps he himself, had invested; on the way he also wanted to hunt the American bison or buffalo, whose massacre was then taking place. He began in March with ten days in New York. From New York he set out with two friends, Oliver Montague and Tom Nickalls. They first went to Chicago, a city whose surging growth had hardly been checked even by a disastrous fire in 1871 which had burnt down a third of it. All the damage, says Bertie, had been replaced in eight months' concentrated reconstruction. After a few days they set off for St Louis, where they drank the local champagne; 'I am told that it is greatly admired at Paris, sir,' said his host proudly, to which Bertie replied with diplomatic effusiveness. Always adept at conforming to local standards of good manners, Bertie had already learnt that 'in America the word good is insufficient; you must say that everything is the best; less praise is an insult and an ignorant insult at that.' After St Louis they stopped at Kansas City before going on to the small settlement of Fort Wallace, the base for their buffalo hunt.

The Wild West as recorded by Bertie is both like, and unlike, the versions of it with which we are familiar through Hollywood. There are aspects one recognizes at once, for though it has become a legend, the legend is based on comparatively recent

fact. To be exact there have been two successive legends about
it which now coexist and conflict; first the idealization of the
individual pioneer, whose enterprise was summed up in phrases
like the Frontier Spirit and the American Dream, then the derision
and debunking of his achievements in an excess of collective guilt
about the treatment of the Indians and the environment. John
Wayne, in short, was followed by Sam Peckinpah. Bertie glimpsed
the opening of the West as it was happening, and the interest of
his account lies in its anecdotal directness, and in the fact that
his experiences predate both legends. He admires the pioneers'
energy, and their courage in facing hardship, though as a cultivated European he is patronizing on matters of style. He is
extremely critical of the treatment of the Indians; more ammuni-
tion can be found in his description for the point of view of the
modern breast-beating Western than for the earlier school. What
one catches most strongly from his writing is the haphazardness of
the whole process. People of all kinds and origins, including a
sprinkling who were well educated, would take off in a direction
often decided by pure chance. Bertie encountered an instance of
this in Chicago. A rough-looking individual, chewing black tobacco, climbed into the horse bus that was to take Bertie and his
companions to the St Louis train. He asked where the bus was
headed. On being told, he commented: 'Waal! that's not my road,
but I guess it don't much signify', adding that he was 'bound to go
to the end of the rope, anyways'.

The American West was by no means wholly English-
speaking. Kansas City had a strong German influence, even pos-
sessing a German-language newspaper besides four English ones.
Just outside the town Bertie found a bar kept by 'a very aged
German of whom nothing was to be seen save only a portentously
thick red nose; the rest of him was hidden by a grey military great
coat and cap, which seemed to grow out of a great shock mass of
grizzled hair and snuffy beard, that probably no comb or brush had
disturbed for years.' The bar room, dirty and squalid, was decorated with the portraits of the German Emperor, the Crown Prince
and Bismarck, together with a picture of Napoleon III surrendering
his sword after Sedan; the old man had followed his country's
triumphs from afar. When he found that Bertie could speak his
language, the barkeeper called in his neighbour, the gunsmith,

another German as old and dirty as himself. It turned out from their conversation that the gunsmith, at any rate, could have retired years before in comfort. The two old men remained where they were, partly because they were accustomed to the life, but mainly because of rumours of a buried treasure somewhere nearby: their version of the American Dream.

Fort Wallace, which the travellers reached after a hideously unpleasant train journey lengthened to thirty-two hours because of trouble on the line, turned out to have a remarkably pleasant inn kept by a couple called Ruggles. Mrs Ruggles, in particular, was an educated lady who knew Europe well: it was odd to find her catering for the rough crowd of the Wild West. Fortunately her husband was well able to take care of himself and her. The inn was burgled and Mrs Ruggles lost her jewellery. However Mr Ruggles made inquiries, tracked down the thief and recovered the booty at gunpoint.

The optimism of the Western pioneers, their mixed origins, their independence, their tendency to go off at a tangent, and of course the gunlaw as exemplified by Mr Ruggles's exploit, are all fairly familiar to us as filmgoers. The dirt, even though somewhat played down by Hollywood, is something one was entitled to assume. What is less familiar is the number of people who were plain incompetent.

There was plenty of incompetence in the buffalo-hunting 'outfit' joined by Bertie and his companions. They chose it because it was the only one which claimed to possess a tent. Since there was still a hard frost this seemed a decisive advantage, although the tent turned out to be 'nothing more than a bit of torn canvas stretched on three poles, open to the four winds of heaven'. When they started out the Englishmen were jeered at for their smart appearance and gleaming rifles; Bertie comments, 'It is astonishing how suspicious men of a certain class are of cleanliness; dirt alone is to them workmanlike.' The mockery turned out to be misplaced; though Bertie and his friends did not hit by any means everything they shot at, their comparative accuracy impressed the members of the 'outfit', whose abilities lay in tracking rather than in shooting, and whose weapons were second-rate and none too well looked after. Bertie describes the hunters swaggering into camp 'ragged, unkempt and very very dirty', and 'throwing down their rifles on the iron-hard ground as if they rather wished to break them'. It was not only at shooting that these professionals were surprisingly unskilled. One of them proved unable even to tether a mule properly; his carelessness allowed the party's mules to wander off into the prairie and become lost.

The leader of the hunters was different from the others.

Captain Vogel was a small, lean man, not strongly built but toughened by hard work and a strenuous life. Long elf-locks of fair, sun-bleached hair fell over his shoulders; his beard was thick and tangled. He had bright blue eyes which always seemed to be looking into the distance – a hunter's eyes. His features were regular and showed breeding. He was clad in a nondescript suit of grey rags and a battered old wide-awake; his arms were a heavy three-barrelled rifle – the only one of its kind that I ever saw – and a hunting knife. A strange man, as gentle as a woman, a paragon alone among the hunters of the West, for he neither swore, nor smoked, nor chewed, nor drank spirits, nor gambled; not even when resting during a holiday in some town. As his name implied, he was of German origin, but he had no knowledge of his birth tongue, though he remembered hearing his father and mother speak it when he was a child. Born in the Eastern States he came West many years ago, a sickly youth, condemned by the doctors, and took to hunting in search of health. He found it in the keen air of the prairie. Now sickness and pain were strangers to him, and fatigue had lost its power over him. His little three-year-old mare, his solitary pet, followed him about like a dog. His one ambition was to set up as a farmer somewhere in the Wild Country when he should have saved money enough.

Vogel was a master of tracking: he and his men would between them give an imitation of a buffalo that would induce the herd to accept them; but when he was with Bertie he missed with every shot. Bertie himself killed several buffaloes, bringing the head of one of them back to England; in due course it was to hang at Batsford. One can imagine Vogel in a film, cleaned up a little and played by Gary Cooper or Alan Ladd. Note also Bertie's reference to the fact that the hunter's regular features 'showed breeding'. A remark like this would not be made nowadays, and there might be a temptation, in the overheated atmosphere developed around the Mitfords following the activities of two of Bertie's granddaughters, to regard it as a kind of proto-Nazism. But in Bertie's day the feeling that regular features, in some rather imprecise way, showed 'breeding', was commonplace enough to pass without comment. Nevertheless, a care for breeding and for genetic quality was a constant concern of Bertie's; he often described people in these terms, Japanese grandees as well as Europeans. It ties in with his later interest in the breeding of animals, and perhaps anticipates his respect for the writings of Houston Stewart Chamberlain.

A good deal of the conversation round the campfire concerned the question of the Indians. The hunters, as is perhaps to be expected, disliked the Indians and were afraid of them. Even so, these same hunters thought that the government treated the Indians shamefully, and detested the 'Indian agents' whose job it was to distribute blankets, guns and so on to the inhabitants of the reservations which the tribes were allotted. The agents cheated on the quality of the goods they provided and made large personal fortunes. It fell to Bertie to tell the hunters of the recent massacre by the Modoc Indians of United States peace commissioners led by General Canby. One hunter, whose opinion of the Indian was that his proper place was six feet underground, commented: 'Why don't they call out the hunters? Guess we're used to trackin' varmin.' But even he joined the others in blaming the government far more strongly than the Indians. Bertie comments: 'These men, with whom we were talking, were rough and wild and uncouth, but they were not bad fellows . . . They had a fair right to complain, for they were the most likely men to suffer by the policy of a Government which provoked the savages by robbery, and then furnished them with arms to avenge their outrages.' He adds: 'The Indian agent was surely one of the most striking products of universal suffrage.' This last remark, which is quite normal from a Victorian conservative, shows a sense of values now so alien to fashion that it perhaps requires explanation. What Bertie is saying is that a system based on votes, the majority of which will be those of the unsophisticated, will tend to throw up officials who are on the take. They will be like this because they will be those who know how to pander to the representatives of the populace rather than those who have a tradition of service or inherited self-respect. Even in Bertie's own day this view, although it would strike a chord among some of the ruling classes, was giving way before liberal optimism about human nature. It is essentially that of his great-grandfather William.

On their way to Utah and the silver mine, Bertie and Oliver Montague then went on to Denver, Colorado; the territory of Utah was at the time in United States law a dependency of Colorado, though it was in effect ruled by the Mormon Church and its President, Brigham Young. The balance between the two authorities, neither of which wished to recognize the other, was extremely uneasy, and might at any time have been resolved in a resumption of the Mormon war of 1856.

Denver, in the meantime, seemed pleasant, quiet and orderly; quite different from what New York gossip, and the works of Bret Harte, had led Bertie to expect. Again there was a good hotel, this time kept by a Frenchman who produced authentic French food. Bertie was well aware that the reason for the orderliness was the existence of committees of vigilantes operating lynch law, but he praises the results of the system: '. . . Whereas the Tombs, the famous prison at New York, was full of murderers, who might or might not be punished as politics might dictate, in Denver or Virginia City justice marched with no lame or uncertain foot.' President Grant was in Denver on a visit, and a number of Indians from a nearby reservation were there to meet him. Bertie describes the appearance of their chief, who called himself George Washington:

A small thickset old man, with a most villainous expression, heightened by dabs of blue, red and yellow paint, which gave quite a fiendish look to his cruel mouth and cunning little bear's eyes. Long, straight elf-locks of coarse black hair parted in the middle, and the parting painted vermilion, fell over his shoulders. He wore a chimney-pot hat, decorated with red and yellow streamers, a short blue coat with military buttons; necklaces and other ornaments of coloured beads; two revolvers; leather trousers with tassels all down the sides. His crew were as ugly and as evil-looking as their chief. Some carried bows and arrows in leathern quivers slung at their backs; not one was without a revolver. Looking at their stunted, shapeless bodies, it was hard to say whether they were men or women.

Bertie saw more Indians at Ogden, in the Rockies, where the companions changed trains for Salt Lake City. 'The curious-looking creatures, wrapped in their shoddy blankets, hung about

the railway stations, impassive, unnoticing, impenetrable, as little
moved as if they had been corpses by all that was going on around
them. Had they any feelings? Perhaps, but they never showed
them.'

In Denver Bertie joined up with Captain Forbes, another
Englishman who was interested in finding out the truth about the
silver mine. He also, as he puts it, struck up an alliance with the
Governor of Colorado, McCook, who had business with Brigham
Young, and travelled in the train with them. Bertie was always
good at using his contacts to gain access to important people, and
this was undoubtedly a help in securing a personal interview with
Young. Another travelling companion was Colonel Steinberger of
the United States Army, who had a message for the Mormon
president from the federal government which was apparently
somewhat disobliging.

Bertie devotes a fair amount of space to a description of the
Mormons as he found them, and of Brigham Young. His attitude
combines disdain and disapproval with a good deal of rather
grudging respect. 'No scholar could be won by the Book of
Mormon,' he pronounces; although he acknowledges that the
Latter-Day Saints are growing in numbers and prosperity, he
doubts their ability to convert anyone really intelligent. He is
moved by the Mormons' courage and achievement under ad-
versity, but repelled by what he sees as their vulgarity, and a
strain of cant and cruelty.

The brand-new town of Salt Lake City, by the lake and with
the Wahsatch mountains in the distance, was attractive. But there
was one 'shrieking ugliness, the huge tabernacle with its great
oblong white roof shaped like a dish cover'. The apparently
peaceful scene was deceptive; Salt Lake City was under constant
threat from a regiment of artillery of the United States Army
whose officers, by Bertie's account, would have liked nothing
better than an excuse to blow the Mormons to pieces. Within the
town itself people lived in fear of the Danites, Brigham Young's
law-enforcers who quietly assassinated people on his orders.
Bertie's guide round the town was reputed to be one of these
Danites. Bertie remarked to him, as they walked through the
cemetery, that a good many of the deceased were said on their
gravestones to have been 'found dead in Jordan'. How could so

many people fall in the river, asked Bertie, in a community where no one got drunk? With a 'significant and ghastly grin', the man replied: 'I guess they died with their boots on.'

Brigham Young personally gave permission for Bertie and Forbes to visit the silver mine, and was reasonably gracious to Bertie at his interview, though later, when they went to the Mormon church, he preached an offensive sermon at them. Bertie admires and deplores the prophet in approximately equal measures. He was at the time a well-preserved man already in his seventies, possessed of great magnetism, but with an evident streak of brutality. He lived modestly and Bertie gives him credit for sincerity, saying that he clearly believed completely in the late Joseph Smith and in the genuineness of the Book of Mormon which the angel had given Smith in a vision. Bertie caught a glimpse of some of Young's wives, and those of the other elders; he did not find them attractive. From Utah, Bertie travelled further west. He visited the mines round Virginia City, Nevada, and then proceeded to California where he was astonished by the giant redwood trees of the Yosemite Valley, even more than by the city of San Francisco itself. In San Francisco he took ship, and after a long and rough passage arrived again in his beloved Japan. He travelled around on horseback for a few weeks, this time as a sightseer, though he saw several friends.

From Japan he travelled back across the Pacific to San Francisco. He retraced his steps, again through Virginia City, to Salt Lake City. There he found his friend Colonel Forbes, with whom he set out on another shooting expedition in the Rocky Mountains. The trip was an uncomfortable failure. It was October and already freezing; they had no tents and slept in buffalo skins. After this he returned to New York, and thence to London.

# 6

# The Stanley Connection

The year 1874 was important for Bertie; it was when he finally settled down. He found a job that was both congenial and important; he found an entirely suitable wife; and he bought Lindsey House in Cheyne Walk, Chelsea, where he was to live until he inherited Batsford in 1886.

The job, which will be discussed in the following chapter, was an appointment as Secretary to the Board of Works, in which Bertie did work of lasting importance in the improvement of London parks and the restoration of the Tower of London. The wife was Lady Clementine Ogilvy, second daughter of David, Earl of Airlie. She was attractive, with a rather strong-looking face which betokened considerable firmness of character. Her full figure was to run to fat in middle age. At twenty-one she was sixteen years younger than Bertie, and her antecedents were rather interesting, especially on her mother's side.

Her father was a conventional Scottish aristocrat of strong religious principles. He had gambled in his youth and been, it was hinted, something of a rake; but his worldly-wise mother-in-law had said in a letter at the time of his engagement, 'That he has lived like a monk with the strong passions he appears to have, I never imagined.' All this was in any case long behind him; by the time Bertie met Clementine, Lord Airlie had for many years settled down to a respectable upper-class life. Besides fathering and bringing up his six children, he shot, ran his estates, went about in society and occasionally attended the House of Lords as a representative Scottish peer. He was no fool, but suffered all his life from chronic deafness which made him seem sometimes rather slow on the uptake. His wife Blanche most decidedly outshone him, particularly in company; but he had sufficient dignity and self-confidence not to mind this in the least. He rode her on a loose rein, which was sensible of him, both because she was fundamentally decent and reliable, and also because she was quite exceptionally bright and of a rather uncertain temper which would have reacted badly to close control.

Clementine's mother was a Stanley; to be exact she was one of the nine children of Edward, second Lord Stanley of Alderley. These Stanleys are well documented. Nancy edited two volumes of their ample correspondence; Bertrand Russell, whose mother, Katherine, Lady Amberley, was Blanche's sister, brought out the *Amberley Papers* in two volumes. The family was as unalterably Whiggish in politics as the Mitfords of their time were immovably Tory. They possessed great intelligence and some of them, though without actually achieving much, showed in their lives a notable individuality. They remind one of the later Mitfords, Blanche's descendants, in several ways. Notably, they developed in their family to a very fine art the practice of teasing; for this reason some outsiders regarded them, again like the Mitfords, as being rather heartless. Even their mother, who was accustomed to them, refers to them in a letter as 'this sharp-tongued family'.

Their father, too, noted in at least one of his children a certain conversational fluency; in a letter to his wife after their son Lyulph had badly bitten his tongue while playing football, he writes: 'Poor Lyulph, I hope his tongue is not seriously injured, as it is his main breadwinner. Though we may benefit from his mitigated speech, and you will not be able so frequently to stop the company to listen to his marvels, it must be very disagreeable to him and I hope will soon get well!' From Lord Stanley this was a bit rich, because it was from him that most of the sharpness of tongue had come; but mature conversationalists are apt to be rather impatient of budding ones, and Lord Stanley was well known, not only for his jokes, but for the fact that they were not always kind. His contemporaries called him Ben, after Sir Benjamin Backbite, a character in one of Sheridan's plays. He was, however, a serious politician; though he was insufficiently pushing, and perhaps a little too indolent, ever to reach the very first rank. Lord Palmerston liked and trusted him, for he was a landowning Whig of exactly the same persuasion who disliked the Radicals in his own Liberal Party as much as he disdained the Conservatives; and he was included in most of Palmerston's governments. He was charming and clever, but also very satisfied with himself. He had that typically Whig pride that, if less obtrusive was, once spotted, more offensive than its Tory equivalent. For it was not mere class pride but included also an assumption of moral and intellectual superiority. Lord Stanley's attitude to royalty seems, to anyone less grand, notably casual. He wrote to his wife on 28 July 1861: 'Granville tells me the Queen had mentioned my name as one of the Ministers who might go to Balmoral. As I shall be in the neighbourhood I said I had no objection.' For his colleagues in the House of Lords he had little time, especially for their permanent Conservative majority which was at the time managed, as it happens, by John Thomas, Lord Redesdale, the future Earl. 'I dined yesterday at Greenwich with Lord Redesdale and the Lords, a stupid fish dinner almost all Tories but as I have always excused myself hitherto and this year he has been amiable on Private Business I thought I might as well go.' Beneath his acerbity and supplementing his charm there must have been a basic benevolence, for his children adored him and his clever wife Henrietta Maria remained under his spell until the day he died.

Blanche, born in 1829, was Lord Stanley's second daughter and third child. When one reads Henrietta Maria's account of their courtship at Alderley Park one's heart goes out to both Blanche and the young Lord Airlie: on a superficial level to David, but in a profounder sense to Blanche. He was the one who kissed, to use the French expression, and she the one who offered the cheek; and in addition she possessed a quick wit sharpened by years of verbal sparring in her family. Altogether she held far more of the cards than was fair. For one thing the unfortunate Earl was already noticeably deaf, though Blanche forced him to overcome this disability for her; 'He hears Blanche as she told him she never repeats anything as it made people inattentive,' writes Henrietta Maria Stanley to her husband, finely careless of the sequence of tenses. But at least David Airlie had something that Blanche was denied: the luxury and the intoxication of passion. 'She . . . laments she cares little for him and should so like to be desperately in love,' observes her mother. Before David's arrival at Alderley in August 1851 to pop the question, she showed herself full of doubts. 'She says . . . that she does not think he will like her when he finds how serious and how spirited she is, that if he had any wish to be useful among his own people she might be happy but that a life of amusement with him she could not look forward to. Yet when I say would you like him to be put off she says she knows she would be sorry after.' The thought is unavoidable that this response had something to do with his being an earl with respectable, if considerably encumbered, estates; though even in private conversation between mother and daughter this would only have been understood, not actually mentioned. Henrietta Maria adds: 'She wishes the whole thing had never been, that she likes her present life, is quite happy here and does not wish to marry just now – and yet she will accept him I know. Will she love him after, is it safe to run that risk?'

Clearly it depended on whether the couple could steer adequately between Scylla and Charybdis, between the danger of her driving him away and that of her dominating him to such an extent as to lose her respect for him. In the event these perils were successfully navigated. His adoration of her gave them a good start, though she did not make the proposal easy. Her anxious mother watched them together in the garden. Each had a book, but he was only pretending to read. Henrietta Maria wrote on 3 August: 'I do not know why he does not settle it, Blanche says she gives him every opportunity, but her manner is rather brusque and perhaps he is a little afraid, and she every now and then says very odd things.' Later in the same letter Henrietta Maria goes on: 'She rather talks to him as if he was to be civilized, she keeps giving him little passages to read which he gets through very much as he did the machinery at the Exhibition.' On occasion the worm could turn. David Airlie once said of Bacon's *Essays* that it was a deep book, and Blanche retorted: 'Oh yes, one you would not care to look into.' He answered quietly: 'You seem to think I cannot understand any book, and yet I know that one well.'

Henrietta Maria Stanley was at first seriously worried about the marriage. The ceremony took place in September 1851; three months afterwards she was writing that Blanche was not happy. 'I repeat there is no fault to find with Airlie he is considerate to the last degree and she will be to blame if he changes.' Even nearly three years later, these forebodings have not altogether subsided; 'I do not think Blanche is nearly as amiable in her own home as her husband,' she wrote. But there was infact more to both Blanche and David than met the eye; she was more loyal and sincere, and he was a good deal shrewder, than one might have given them credit for. They had a life to live together, and they buckled down to it. Even his financial problems, which surfaced not long after they married, probably helped, for they overcame them together; they also learned to respect each other in the course of philosophical arguments in which he held his own perfectly adequately. Henrietta Maria writes from Cortachy Castle in November 1851: 'He and Blanche are at opposite ends, she all for beauty and sentiment, he for truth and goodness.' Blanche said she did not like goodness that was not beautiful, and David told her off, accusing her of superficiality derived from German books.

Clementine Ogilvy, Bertie's bride, was not of course born when her parents had this very Victorian difference of opinion, but it represented a contrast between their temperaments that was fundamental enough to be permanent. Clementine entirely preferred her father's point of view; she disapproved of the Stanleys, even flying so far in the face of the facts as to say that she had not a drop of Stanley blood in her veins. Self-scrutiny, to which she was not addicted, would have indicated that this was in itself rather a Stanley remark. She disapproved of her uncles' eccentricities and was impatient with the family jokes. But since the Stanleys were rather like the later Mitfords, it seems right to give a short account of them here.

Edward, Lord Stanley, or 'Ben', has already been described. His wife was Henrietta Maria, daughter of the thirteenth Viscount Dillon. She was quite as bright as her husband and children; but just because her marriage was almost cloudlessly happy, she did not show this fact to a wider public until he died in 1869. (We say *almost* cloudlessly happy; her letters do show that she was at times jealous of her husband's attentions to a certain Lady Jocelyn; but whether or not there was anything in this, it certainly did not affect the Stanleys' marriage or their family life.) Henrietta Maria outlived her husband by twenty-seven years, during which time she became prominent as a pioneer of women's education, helping to found Girton College, Cambridge, and numerous girls' schools. She became more and more formidably outspoken as she grew older.

The eldest and strangest of her nine children was Henry, born in 1827. After showing advanced-radical tendencies in early adulthood, he became a convert to Islam. He went into the Diplomatic Service, but when in Constantinople and Cairo he developed a passion for the Turks and Arabs. He resigned at the age of twenty-six, adopted Arab dress, and spent the next sixteen years wandering about Asia. As long as he could, he kept from his family the news of his actual conversion, as also that of his marriage to a Spanish lady called Fabia. He married her several times; in a Moslem ceremony in Constantinople, a civil one in Geneva, a Church of England one, and finally a Roman Catholic one. None of the ceremonies was valid: she had a husband in Spain, though Henry never knew this. The couple lived together at Alderley when he inherited in 1869, having apparently informed his mother of his marriage at his father's funeral. Henry's parents were horrified by his way of life, and rumours of his conversion to Islam particularly distressed them; they were always relieved by his half-hearted denials. To each other they were very rude about Henry; in 1859 Lord Stanley writes to his wife of a 'paragraph in the *Morning Post* about that wretched fool Henry, saying that he was at Penang living entirely with Mahomedans and dressed in their dress'. His wife, in her reply, 'had seen that paragraph and it made me sick'. Henry had wide interests and an inquiring mind; when only twelve he was already asking for an Arabic grammar. But he was rather gauche and slow, in a family where these traits were not regarded charitably. Bertrand Russell says he was the only one in the family who was 'definitely stupid', but the key to his troubles seems really to have been that he was deaf. When Lady Stanley tells her husband that Lord Airlie suffers from this affliction, the way she puts it is that he is 'quite as deaf as Henry'. Insensibly he became the butt, laughed at rather than laughed with. In the end, when he came into the estate, Henry showed that he had all along possessed the slow-burning resentment of the habitual underdog; he had his brother Lyulph turned off his land by the gamekeeper, refused to give the living at Alderley to his other brother, the Reverend Algernon, and would not allow a memorial to a third, John, to be placed in the church.

His sister Alice was one member of the family with whom Henry always remained on good terms. She was the second child, born in 1828, and was drawn to Henry by the fact that she, too, was regarded by her parents with as much irritation as affection. Henry, alone of the family, always liked Alice's husband, Augustus Fox; in return it was Alice who was the first to agree to receive Fabia, when Henry brought her home after his father's death. Fox was an army major, later colonel, and married Alice in February 1853; they were rather poor until he eventually came into an estate on the death of his kinsman Lord Rivers. 'As they are poor, cubs will come thick and fast,' predicts Lord Stanley's mother in a letter written when she hears that Alice is expecting her first child. 'Don't tell Mr Reynard pray, as he don't understand a joke.' Old Lady Stanley was right about the 'cubs', of whom there were to be nine; the charge of humourlessness stuck as well, and was to be a bad handicap to Fox's relationship with in-laws to most of whom jokes were as the breath of life. Henry probably found Fox a relief.

Blanche came next, in 1829, and after her Maud or Maude – the spelling seems to have been optional – who arrived in 1832. The only one of the girls who never married, she seems, Nancy says, to have been a saint; in any case she was the one who made the most effort to keep on good terms with all her brothers and sisters. She worked tirelessly and effectively to help the poor, notably in the girls' club movement. Once she made a speech to a girls' club in Greek Street, Soho, then a slum; the girls were using make-up, to her displeasure, and she plastered herself with rouge and lipstick, saying, 'Girls, you see how lovely I look tonight; it is all due to artificial methods.' Like many saints Maude cared little for the pleasures of the table. Monsignor Algernon Stanley – see below – remarked to Blanche Airlie that Maude's food was fit for pigs. 'No, Algernon,' his sister corrected him: '*not* fit for pigs.' But her nephew Bertrand Russell liked her because she gave him marrons glâcés, and had a parrot that talked.

The second son, John, was born in 1837. He became a soldier by profession, and had tremendous courage and fighting spirit, though his health was poor. His letters show a natural gift for description, and a certain balance which, in family matters, repeatedly shows up the waspish partisanship of his parents. He is fairer than they are both to Henry and to Augustus Fox. At the age of seventeen he went to fight in the Crimea. His letters home are lurid: 'After the fight [before Sebastopol] were found three spare hands that could not be matched.' From there he was invalided home, but in due course he recovered and went to India, where he arrived in 1857 during the Mutiny. He was appointed one of the aides-de-camp to Lord Canning, the governor general, and became a great favourite of Lady Canning, to whose household he was detailed to make himself useful. In his descriptions of life there John is very rude about the Indians, shocking his liberal parents. They object to his calling the Indians niggers, and generalizing about their faults. He, at the sharp end, stands his ground. On 23 March 1859 he writes: 'Your . . . objection to "niggers" as a term is hardly logical, you say they are the same blood and race originally as we – so are Africans.' Henry's orientalism distressed John greatly; to him, in India, it was a form of 'going native', Islam being, after all, India's second religion. He nevertheless kept his balance on the subject rather better than his parents did. Let Henry bore himself out of his ideas, John advises his mother on 14 September 1859. However, he enjoyed teasing Henry. Sometimes, according to Nancy, when both brothers were staying at Alderley, John would come down early in the morning and dedicate the breakfast to a statuette of the Buddha; this in Henry's eyes polluted it and rendered it uneatable. 'Have you dedicated it all?' Henry asked, to which he received the reply: 'All but the ham, dear boy.' In due course John retired from the Army. He married Mary Stuart Mackenzie of Seaforth and had two daughters. He died at the age of forty-one.

After John came Lyulph, born in 1839. Academically he was much the cleverest, obtaining a first in Greats at Oxford. Lyulph was a keen debater at the Oxford Union, where he always supported radical causes. His father sometimes disapproved, as once when Lyulph spoke in favour of a motion saying that universal suffrage was the only limit to reform. 'It is not true and if we were to see it we should soon repent,' observes Lord Stanley on 18 November 1859. Lyulph's early promise remained unfulfilled; Bertrand Russell thinks that his wit was too caustic for success in politics. He certainly never lacked moral courage. During the First World War, when war fever was intense, he chaired a pacifist meeting addressed by Russell. He married and had a number of children. On Henry's death he inherited the family titles but chose to call himself not Lord Stanley, but Lord Sheffield, a barony which he had inherited through his grandmother.

Kate, born in 1842, came after Lyulph. She married Viscount Amberley, son of the Earl Russell who had been Lord John Russell, and died at the age of thirty-two, shortly followed by her husband. She was a freethinker and an ardent feminist, making speeches for women's suffrage a generation before it became fashionable. The couple left two sons to be brought up by their grandmother. The younger of these was Bertrand Russell, the philosopher, mathematician, socialist, nuclear disarmer and accomplished intellectual tease; perhaps, as regards pure intelligence, the brightest man ever to have inherited an English peerage.

There were two more children. Algernon, born in 1843, was idle at Harrow: he was flogged a lot and learned little. He caught up later, though, taking Holy Orders in the Church of England where he gravitated to the extreme High Church or Anglo-Catholic party, to the distress of his father who refused on this account to give him the living at Alderley. Henry, as we have seen, confirmed this refusal. In due course Algernon entered the Church of Rome and went to the Vatican, where he eventually became Monsignor Stanley, Bishop of Emmaus. The bishopric was *in partibus infidelium*: that is to say in heathen regions, meaning that Emmaus was in effect a phantom see whose pastor could reside comfortably in the Vatican. However, as Bertrand Russell remarks, 'The priest never overpowered the Stanley in him.' When a young relation asked what was the difference between Rome and the Church of England, he is supposed to have replied: 'Dear boy, it is all great nonsense.' He always ate well, even during Lent. A niece visited him in Rome at that time of the year and commented on this, to receive the reply: 'Ah, my child, Holy Mother Church sees to it that we don't starve.' Nancy adds: 'She saw to it like anything, for when this penniless younger son died he was found to have left a very considerable fortune.' The youngest Stanley was Rosalind, born in 1844, who married George Howard. In due course her husband became Earl of Carlisle. Nancy says of her: 'Her husband was wonderfully handsome, and an artist; like Lord Airlie, he did not have the whip-hand of his wife. She seems to have gone to various extremes of opinion and behaviour as intelligent but uneducated women so often do when their husbands fail to control them.' A violent teetotaller, she is accused of having had the wine in the Castle Howard cellar poured down the drains; though this is apparently legend.

A distinctively Stanley family occasion was Henry's funeral after he eventually died in 1903. The interment was performed, following Henry's detailed instructions, according to the rites of Islam. The deceased was buried in a wood at Alderley, standing up and facing Mecca. Monsignor Algernon was not in the least respectful: 'Lived like a dog, buried like a dog,' he commented. As the corpse was lowered feet first into the narrow grave, Lyulph's son Arthur removed his hat. 'Not your hat, you fool,' said Algernon, 'your boots.' (This is Nancy's account. Bertrand Russell in *The Amberley Papers* says Henry was buried in the mosque in Woking by the Turkish ambassador. Whichever version is true as to location, one likes to believe in Algernon's tart remarks.)

This, then, was Clementine's mother's family. We have seen that Clementine herself rejected this part of her heritage. She was not on particularly good terms with her formidable mother, who certainly showed some dislike of Bertie, even writing to her daughter, for years after her marriage, as Lady Clementine Ogilvy. One rumour in the family, not by any means improbable, is that Blanche Airlie was herself having a flirtation with Bertie and resented the switch to her daughter.

Bertie's successful proposal was rather spectacular. He went to an afternoon party at Holland House and found Clementine with another admirer standing by a lily pond. After a while Clementine said: 'That water-lily would be just the thing to wear with my gown at the ball tonight.' Bertie, dressed immaculately in lavender trousers, immediately stepped into the middle of the pond and picked it for her, his trousers soaking and muddy. That night she wore the lily in her brown dress, and when he proposed she accepted.

They were married on 31 December 1874, in the chapel of Cortachy Castle. The choice of season seems odd; Bertie reached Cortachy only just in time to avoid a historic blizzard which halted all trains. However it was a grand affair, celebrated with feasting and bagpipes in the kind of feudal setting most calculated to appeal to him.

# 7

# Office of Works

In the meantime, in May 1874, Bertie had been appointed Secretary to the Board of Works. This was a piece of shrewd talent-spotting by Benjamin Disraeli. Disraeli had just become Prime Minister, and it was the first important civil service post in his gift to become vacant. Mrs Disraeli had been right, all those years before, in telling Bertie that her husband had his eye on him.

The post was in effect that of the permanent head of the Office of Works. Bertie had to report to the First Commissioner of the Board of Works; this post was later renamed Minister of Works, and its holder was a minor member of the government not normally in the cabinet. The department's functions were to look after the parks and government buildings; it was also responsible for the construction of stands and other temporary structures for ceremonial occasions. It was made clear to Bertie at the time of his appointment that he would be expected to make a good many changes; in fact Disraeli's private secretary told Bertie that the place was an Augean stable and needed to be swept out. Bertie did so, though he encountered opposition at first. People in the department had been allowed to do almost nothing, and naturally resisted activation. When Bertie first became Secretary one of the senior clerks told him that the Secretary should never go and see anything, because if he did he would not be in a good position to say 'no'. Bertie changed this; he had both the courage and the tact to say 'no' when he had to, but he wanted also to know when he ought to say 'yes'. Unfortunately the retrograde forces in the department obtained the support of Bertie's political chief. The First Commissioner was Lord Henry Lennox, and he was entirely the wrong man for the job. He was idle; what is more, he was disgruntled. As an old associate of Disraeli's, he had felt himself entitled to a higher appointment. To be exact, he had set his heart on being First Lord of the Admiralty with a seat in the cabinet. He was angry with Disraeli, and said so. When Bertie was briefing Lennox on the estimates he would have to defend in the Commons he would barely listen; fortunately the Members proved lackadaisical enough to let Lennox get away with it.

Lennox obstructed every improvement initiated by Bertie, who finally put his resignation into the hands of the Prime Minister. The result was an inquiry, which upheld Bertie's point of view. Lennox resigned in 1876, and from then on Bertie had a good understanding with all his political chiefs, whether Conservative or Liberal, and was able to get them to absorb their briefs. This was fortunate, because over the years Members of Parliament began to pay more attention to the Board of Works' estimates, especially when Lord Randolph Churchill began gingering up the Conservative opposition to Gladstone's government. Bertie, who liked Lord Randolph, met him in a park one morning at a time when he was attacking the First Commissioner, as Bertie thought, with particular vexatiousness. 'My dear Randolph,' said Bertie, 'for goodness' sake leave my unhappy estimates alone!' 'Very sorry for you, my dear fellow,' answered Lord Randolph, 'but we must harass the government.'

Bertie's achievements during his twelve years at the Office of Works were considerable; much of what he did can be seen to this day. He restored Hampton Court and the Tower of London; he improved the Royal Parks in London; and he masterminded the recasting of Hyde Park Corner.

When one considers what he did one is struck forcibly by Disraeli's great cleverness in choosing him; yet there was also an element of luck, because the Prime Minister who had spotted Bertie as a bright young man can scarcely have known how precisely right the appointment was. For Bertie was not only intelligent, tactful and a good organizer; he also had an instinct for style and quality. Also his preferences in this field were exactly what were required. His aesthetic views are not those of today, in fact some of his pronouncements now read rather oddly; but according to his own canons, which were those of his own time, his eye was sure. He had a particular dislike for the Georgian epoch, which, he says in his essay *A Tragedy in Stone*, 'was fatal to many of our finest antiquities throughout the country. The prevailing *dearth of taste* is shown by the ruthless way in which picturesque old manor-houses of the Tudor and even earlier times were swept away by the score to make room for Grecian temples or Italian villas.' Our italics. The convention now is to suppose that, far from suffering a dearth of taste, the eighteenth century was precisely the most tasteful in world history. Batsford was to be Bertie's revenge on the period; he tore down an eighteenth-century house which prints indicate to have been not only charming but also quite big enough, and replaced it by a cheerless essay in Victorian Tudor. Yet although the aesthetic side of the pronouncement quoted seems perverse, the facts he states are correct. Britain's medieval and Tudor monuments had been allowed to fall into decay during and since the Georgian epoch, and had also been occasionally 'improved' in ways which were not in harmony with their original style. It was good that they were restored by someone who was aesthetically in sympathy with them.

The palace at Hampton Court provided Bertie's first important task; it had been badly neglected. Most of the King's Beasts had fallen from the roof of the great hall; much of the brickwork was rotting away, plastered over and covered with graffiti. The necessary repairs could not be done all at once, but Bertie secured an annual allowance of £500 from the government which in those days was enough to ensure that restoration would take place over the years; he also saw to it that those who worked in the palace were properly organized to deal with outbreaks of fire.

The care of the Royal Parks grew, Bertie says, into a passion with him. The flower garden in Hyde Park had been laid out some time before but was still rather elementary; the trees were overcrowded and the shrubs had been allowed to run wild and degenerate. Bertie took matters smartly in hand and went to the trouble of becoming a very competent amateur botanist, an expert especially on trees and shrubs. He claims to have 'more or less remodelled' all the parks. The area at the lower end of the Serpentine called the Dell was his creation. As he puts it:

When I took over the care of Hyde Park the place where the Dell now is was a shrubbery with open hurdles which was the lair of all the nightbirds and undesirables who haunted the Park after dark. They slept under the bushes and every morning a gang of men had to clear away a mass of filth indescribable. I determined to do away with this scandal. I put up an unclimbable fence, laid the place out as a sub-tropical garden with palms, tree ferns, dracaenas and other beauties, planted the little stream with water-lilies, royal fern and so forth, and made it from an eyesore and a den of horrors into what it now is.

He planted rhododendrons beside Rotten Row, and he greatly extended the flower beds. Hyde Park Corner was then, as always, a place of massive traffic congestion. What was needed was a wider approach to Grosvenor Place, and this was achieved by some levelling off and the moving of Decimus Burton's arch to the top of Constitution Hill. This was one scheme that Disraeli turned down; he did not want to spend the money, and said that to do away with the traffic congestion at Hyde Park Corner would be to destroy one of the sights of London. However, the plan was finally carried out in 1884, and the new arrangement lasted until it too became unable to cope with the traffic, and Hyde Park Corner was changed again in the late 1960s.

Bertie also undertook extensive restoration at Windsor Castle, but the operation which lay closest to his heart was undoubtedly the renovation of the Tower of London. This great complex of buildings, on a site going back to the Romans, can claim to be the most historic in Britain; and it had fascinated Bertie since as a boy he had read Harrison Ainsworth's *The Tower of London*. He describes it, and recounts his efforts at restoring it, in *A Tragedy in Stone*. The architect in charge was Sir John Taylor, to whom Bertie gives the credit, but the administrative mastermind was Bertie. The Tower was in very bad repair: Prince Albert had for a time taken matters in hand, but virtually nothing had been done since his death in 1861.

The first building to be tackled was the chapel of St Peter ad Vincula, under which are buried many of the celebrities executed on Tower Hill or otherwise done to death. With the encourage-ment of Queen Victoria herself, Bertie's department undertook the work. There was, he says, no question of restoration, for there was almost nothing to restore; 'Any semblance of decoration, or even of decent respect for the sanctity of the building, had long been swept away and given place to the painted deal and the plaster of Georgian vandalism.' To us today it might perhaps have seemed quite attractive, but let that pass. The important thing was to save the building itself, which was in imminent danger of collapsing into its own vaults. Queen Victoria had stipulated that the graves under the chapel should be treated with care and that some attempt be made at identifying the bodies. So when Bertie had the foundations opened up, he took with him an archaeologist and an anatomist. Nothing of interest was found under the main body of the church, for the old graves had been disturbed for the burial of anyone who might happen to die within the Tower. But under the chancel they found bodies that they could identify with some confidence. The first were Henry VIII's second wife, Anne Boleyn, 'Protector' Somerset, who had been the guardian of Edward VI, and the Duke of Northumberland, who had organized the revolt on behalf of Lady Jane Grey. They failed to find Lady Jane herself, or Henry VIII's fifth wife, Katherine Howard; but the Duke of Monmouth – Charles II's son, who rebelled against James II – was there. After the repair works were complete, the bodies were reburied in new lead-lined coffins, each bearing the name of the person it was supposed to contain.

After St Peter's, Bertie and his department tackled the rest of the Tower. Much had to be pulled down: 'Every available nook and corner seemed to have been filled with some degraded shanty put up without the slightest regard to the beauty and romantic interest of the place.' To Bertie's mind fortunately, a good many of these accretions, used by the Army and others, were themselves in bad repair, so there was little opposition to their destruction, or that of a large military warehouse that had been erected in place of a part of the Tower that had burned down in 1788. This, and other parts that were in bad shape, were put back more or less as they had been.

Meanwhile he settled in Chelsea with his bride, Clementine. She was not, at first, very clever with money. When they married Bertie gave her an allowance and opened a bank account for her. She overspent it, and was fortified in her habits by seeing to her delight that the balance on her account seemed to get larger every month. The figures were in red – so attractive; no one had told her there was such a thing as an overdraft. Finally Bertie had to pay it off, and explain the facts of financial life. They were a close and happy couple, and children soon started arriving. Six were born during his twelve years at the Office of Works: Frances in 1875, Clement in 1876, David in 1878, Iris in 1879, Bertram in 1880 and John in 1884. (Later, at Batsford, Joan was to be born, in 1887, followed by the twins, Rupert and Daphne, in 1895.) It was a good time for Bertie; besides his work, which he enjoyed, and his family life, he continued the active and varied social existence which he had led as a bachelor. He had dozens of interesting friends. Two, of whom he saw a great deal, because they too lived in Chelsea, were the painter Whistler and the historian Carlyle. Chelsea at that time still felt itself to be a village, apart from the rest of London; Bertie says, 'If in London the last person with whom you are likely to make acquaintance is the man who is living next door to you, in Chelsea it was quite different; we were very neighbourly.'

Whistler was, in his lifetime, quite as famous for his jokes as for his art; he collected some of his unkinder writings in a book called *The Gentle Art of Making Enemies*. He used to call on Bertie and Clementine with some of the papers and letters which were intended to form the raw material for this work and read them out, 'exploding with laughter over his own witticisms'. Bertie says, though, that the best of them were too libellous to publish. Bertie admired Whistler as a painter too, and says it was a pity he was not more appreciated; but one reason for this was that when he got into debt he used to destroy his own works so as to stop them falling into the hands of his creditors. Once Bertie called on him and found him 'boiling with anger surrounded by masterpieces which he had just cut to ribbons in a storm of mad fury . . . and all for a miserable debt of thirty pounds, which, for the moment, he was unable to pay'. Any one of his friends, says Bertie, would have lent him the money, but he was too proud to ask; and what upset Bertie most was that a portrait of Clementine, just finished, was among those destroyed.

One famous conversational sparring partner of Whistler's was Oscar Wilde, and Bertie says that 'a set-to between that big fat man and the little gnome-like Whistler was certainly good to listen to – but the lightweight always carried off the belt'. Bertie agrees that Wilde was clever, but thought him unoriginal and found his appearance absurd. On the last occasion that he saw him, Wilde

. . . was swaggering in the King's Road dressed in a brown frogged coat, rimmed with cheap fur; on his head was an extravagant hat with a brim as much curled as the roof of a Chinese pagoda; the size and flatness of his huge play feet were accentuated by being forced out of a pair of tight trousers carefully strapped over a pair of aggressively varnished boots. Whistler might be vain, but it was the vanity of Puck. The other man was Caliban.

Carlyle was an old friend both of Bertie's family and of Clementine's. He was old now, and his wife Jane, with whom he had had such a proverbially difficult relationship, had died some time before. People tended to be rather afraid of Carlyle, but Bertie was not: he had known him since childhood. He was evidently something of a favourite, since Carlyle allowed him to smoke with him in his study where few other men were permitted to light up. Carlyle was an admirer of *Tales of Old Japan*, telling Bertie that he had read it 'from alpha to omega', though he found that there was too much blood and murder in the stories. Carlyle's conversation seems to have been rather like his extraordinary writing: striking, highly coloured and full of arresting turns of phrase. But when he had finished one of his tirades on some such subject as the Bulgarian atrocities, on which he was quite as indignant as Gladstone, he would guffaw with laughter. On this Bertie notes: 'I call attention to those bursts of laughter. They were very characteristic and very significant. Those who from Froude downwards have recorded much of Carlyle's conversation have given the impression of an ill-natured, discontented man . . . That he held violent opinions expressed in violent language is a fact. But much of his so-called cynicism was, I am convinced, misunderstood.' Bertie found him kind and, in a rough way, considerate.

This period of Bertie's life came to an end in 1886, when Earl Redesdale died. Bertie's father, Henry Reveley, had died in 1883, and of his twin elder brothers Percy had died in 1884, while Henry had cut himself off from the family and gone to live in Germany. So Bertie inherited Batsford, with its large estate and considerable local responsibilities. He had to give up his post at the Office of

Works and move to the country; there was no one else to whom he could delegate his functions in Gloucestershire, and in any case they were functions which, with his love of tradition and the social order, he was temperamentally suited to enjoy. His resignation was genuinely regreted; Gladstone was Prime Minister at the time, and he had come to value Bertie's abilities as highly as had his old opponent, Disraeli. It is easy to see in his letter to Bertie on his resignation more than the usual polite form of words.

I received with very great regret the announcement of your resignation, which at the same time I admit to be no desertion on your part, but to be reasonable and just.

But it will, I fear, be very difficult to fill your place with a person possessed in the same degree with yourself of the varied and high qualifications which it requires.

Queen Victoria, through her secretary Sir Henry Ponsonby, said: 'Her Majesty considers you have done your duty at your Office not only to her entire satisfaction, but also in a manner which has proved to be of great benefit to the public.' This also, surely, is above and beyond the requirements of mere politeness. The fact is that Bertie had been the right man in the right place, and had done an excellent job.

# 8

# Figure of Dignity

So in 1886 Bertie sold his house in Chelsea, and moved to Batsford with Clementine and the six children. He was at once made a magistrate and a deputy to the Lord Lieutenant of Gloucestershire. Magistrates in those days had more than their purely judicial functions; at their meetings at the Quarter Sessions they performed a good many of the duties now in the hands of elected local authorities. These meetings would last for up to three days, and Bertie enjoyed them on the whole:

We put up at the Judges' lodgings at Gloucester, and had the opportunity of discussing business and comparing notes with men from distant parts of the county . . . Quarter Sessions were of the nature of a very pleasant club at which, in addition to the transaction of business, there was all the charm of a delightful social gathering . . . The men who habitually attended Quarter Sessions were all of them able men, cultivated and well read. One dear man, now long since departed, was a little too well read. He was very proud of his scholarship and especially of his knowledge of Cicero – the one classic bore whom, above all others, I disliked. One night I had gone to bed with a bad headache, unable to dine. My friend came to my room after dinner, full of sympathy. He sat down on my bed and quoted Cicero for an hour or more. There was no escape. I lay there and listened in silent patience to excerpts from the treatise *De Amicitia* [On Friendship], wishing that it had never been written, or at any rate that Amicitia would prompt my persecutor to leave me to bear the throbbings of my head in peaceful solitude.

In memory of his cousin Earl Redesdale Bertie erected the Redesdale Hall at Moreton-in-Marsh, of which he was Lord of the Manor; it was completed in 1887, an early sign that he was going to fulfil his local duties not only with punctiliousness but with generosity. At the same time, almost as soon as he inherited, he pulled down the old eighteenth-century house and built the present Victorian Tudor mansion to replace it. This was an expensive operation and seems to us to have been altogether rather a pity. Sydney tells us in *Five Houses*: 'When David, a little boy of eight years old, saw the windows being pulled out of the old house, he went away by himself and cried. He was right to mourn for the good old house and for the fortunes of the family.'

Bertie at once began applying his mind to learning about agriculture. He was not a farmer himself, his land being nearly all let; but times were bad in farming for all those who lived off the land. He looked for suggestions as to how the lot of his tenants, and therefore his own, could be improved. It was one of the tenants, John Timms, who suggested that he should buy a good Shire stallion. As Timms pointed out, there was not a decent carthorse in the whole countryside, and the breeding of good carthorses would both improve cultivation and perhaps also make money. Bertie took up the idea and began going round the sales with John Timms, though in the event it was not a stallion he first bought, but a mare called Chance. This six-year-old animal had won almost all the available prizes, and Bertie became known among horse-lovers not by his own name but as the 'owner of Chance'. He paid the very high price of 520 guineas for her, and soon bought two stallions, both of which were prizewinners. Bertie's Shire stud quickly became one of the most successful in the country; this was partly because of the skill of John Timms and of his son William, but Bertie's own flair had much to do with it. His daughter Daphne, Lady Denham, told us that her father had a particularly sure eye for the excellence of animals. She herself is an expert on dogs, and has been a judge at shows, but she told us: 'I can tell you the difference between a good labrador and a bad one, but I'm not so certain I can pick out the best from the good. My father could.' The Shires made Bertie's name in the horse world, though he got rid of them all after a few years.

During his first years at Batsford Bertie threw himself with enthusiasm into country life and local pursuits, going rather little to London, though he did buy a yacht in 1889 and become elected to the Royal Yacht Squadron. However, in 1892 he was prevailed upon to stand for Parliament for Stratford-on-Avon. The seat was not a safe one for the Conservatives, but he won fairly comfortably; he was helped by the support of the Liberal Unionists in the constituency – Liberals who had split from their own party in distaste at Gladstone's Home Rule policy. Despite this, the Liberals won nationally.

Bertie only stayed in Parliament for three years. Gladstone's successor Rosebery called a General Election in 1895; Bertie went back, as he puts it, 'gleefully to my garden, my horses and my turnips'. He had unsuccessfully fought the introduction of death duties, in conjunction with Thomas Bowles: he had witnessed the bitter struggles over the Irish Home Rule Bill: and he had enjoyed, as most Members do, the sensation of being in on great events. Joseph Chamberlain and Arthur Balfour were the two politicians he seems to have most admired, though he also had great respect for Gladstone and a good personal relationship with Sir William Harcourt, the Chancellor of the Exchequer responsible for death duties. He was not enough of a party man to make a really keen politician; at the Office of Works he had got on equally well with both parties, and this had made him rather too relaxed. At fifty-five he was also rather old to adapt to new habits. He gives the impression in *Memories* that he is glad to have been in Parliament, but that one stretch was enough. He was made a peer in 1902, taking the title of Baron Redesdale.

His greatest interest from now on was his garden. During his spell at the Office of Works he had, as mentioned earlier, become an expert botanist, partly under the influence of Sir Joseph Hooker, the director of Kew Gardens. During the thirty years he was at Batsford he probably spent at least as much on developing the garden and arboretum as he had spent on building his new house. In 1896 he published a book called *The Bamboo Garden*, about the use of bamboos and other exotic plants in an English setting, which was admired by Sir Joseph Hooker and which probably had some influence in encouraging the fashion for exotic plants, though, as Bertie puts it, 'It could only interest those who possess gardens of sufficient importance to grow the plants of which it treats.'

The plants did not suit Clementine's health; she often felt unwell at Batsford, and this was thought to be caused by the alien pollen. However, she put up with it loyally, and in fact she was probably at Batsford more than Bertie, who often went to London on his various commitments. He was made a trustee of the Wallace Collection; he took up photography and became President of the Royal Photographic Society.

Bertie had always been a friend of the Prince of Wales. When the Prince became Edward VII, he made great use of Bertie as a gardening adviser for Windsor Castle, Sandringham and the other royal residences. He also came to stay at Batsford. Not all the King's descendants found that Bertie's gardening advice had been altogether happy. During the Second World War, Batsford was largely occupied by service officers, though the owner, Lord Dulverton, still lived in it as well. King George VI came once on an inspection, and Lord Dulverton showed him the garden.

'Do you have trouble with polygonum?' he asked, in his shy stammer.

'Yes, sir, we do,' answered Lord Dulverton.

'Old Redesdale got my grandfather to plant it at Sandringham, and we can't get rid of it.'

Old age approached for Bertie, and one by one his children grew up and went out into the world. He himself lived a useful and busy life, developing the Batsford garden, breeding animals, studying, writing, and contributing indefatigably to the work of the committees, boards and societies in which he was interested. Among the Cotswold gentry he was liked; they regarded him as one of themselves, for he shared all their country interests and exercised upon them the practised charm of a man of the world. But he was regarded also with a special respect, since he possessed in addition the glamour of a scholar and a traveller. Unfortunately he was all the time quietly overspending his income. Family gossip has it that part of the trouble was embezzlement by a trusted employee. If this was the case, the man was allowed to leave without disgrace, and the matter was hushed up. Sydney maintains that the new house and the elaborate garden improvements were in themselves more than Bertie could afford. We probably need to look no further to explain the money troubles which were to surface a few years before the end of Bertie's life, and which made it impossible for the family to retain Batsford after his death. In

the meantime the façade of his existence was imposing, and there
was no discernible sign that the structure was not entirely solid.
The family was punctilious in its church-going. This was then
usual, but even in the context of their time Bertie, Clementine and
their children seemed particularly devout. Alec Kearsey, husband
of Bertie's eldest daughter Frances (Pussy or Puma), was asked at
a later date whether this was because Bertie was religious. 'It was
entirely Clementine,' he said. 'Bertie was a pagan.' He was not, of
course; he respected his religion and collaborated in its observance
without any sort of hypocrisy. He was simply not what used to be
called an enthusiast.

Bertie was in demand as a lecturer: on Japan, on gardening, on
the history of art. His part in public life was now essentially
ceremonial; he was a figure of dignity, knew it and enjoyed it.
Modern fashion would have it that this function is at least superfluous, if not actually ludicrous; but whether or not one agrees
with that fashion, it was not then in force, and someone like Bertie
could be considered quite entitled to regard himself as genuinely
important. In his case, this does not add up to being pompous.
Bertie was always saved from pomposity, inwardly by his lively
intelligence and outwardly by his beautiful manners. His intelligence kept his outlook fresh and ensured that he was always open
to ideas, while his manners saved him from the habit of arbitrarily
pulling rank that is the rudeness of old age just as impudence is the
rudeness of youth.

As a figure of dignity, he had his successes. One of these was in
1905 at Cowes Week, then a much more important social occasion
than it has since become. The regatta even had a certain political
and diplomatic significance, because not only was Edward VII a
keen yachtsman, but so also were many of his fellow monarchs;
the King's rivalry with his bumptious nephew, Wilhelm II of
Germany, has become famous. Thomas Bowles, as a serious
yachtsman, turned up his nose at Cowes week, as probably did
others of his sort, but nobody missed them. Seamanship came a
bad second to display, and the rich of all Europe converged for the
fun. It was also a time for ceremonial visits from the world's
navies. In 1905, the Entente Cordiale with France was in the
making. This understanding with Britain's traditional enemy was
in accordance with the inclinations of Edward VII, who had

always borne a certain resemblance to the child in the French nursery rhyme who says sweets are worth more than reason:

> *Moi je dis que les bonbons*
> *Valent mieux que la raison.*

France, with its women and champagne, represented 'sweets' to Edward; Germany, home of his own earnest father, land of smug philosophers, represented 'reason'. But the change of alliance would probably have happened even if Edward had been Prince Albert to the life, simply because Germany had been since 1871 the strongest power in Europe, and British policy in Europe has consistently been to support the balance of power by backing the second strongest.

However this might be, the movement towards a French alliance gave special significance to the ceremonial visit of a French naval squadron to Cowes in 1905. A luncheon was given for the French, and Bertie was asked to make a welcoming speech in their language. Probably it was the King who chose him, for he had every reason to know that Bertie's French was perfect, since the two of them had in the past enjoyed together the '*bonbons*' of Paris and Biarritz. Bertie's speech was gracious, apt and well turned; he was proud enough of it to quote it in full in his *Memories*. But one account, that of Lord Suffield in *My Memories*, shows that when it was delivered it actually caused something approaching a sensation.

He spoke so beautifully that the French officers wept, and the Admiral, Caillard, said he could not speak more than a few words in reply. They were all astonished that an Englishman could make a speech in French so eloquent that few Frenchmen could attempt it. I sat just opposite my old friend, and close to the French ambassador, whose eyes, like my own, were full of tears . . . That night, at a party on the French Admiral's ship, Redesdale's speech was almost the sole topic. The Frenchmen could not say enough in praise of him.

We owe this reference to Diana, who comments: 'I wish people cried when I talk French but if they do it's with rage.'

Early in the next year, 1906, Bertie's ability to make himself agreeable in the service of his country was put to more extended use. It was British policy to conclude an alliance with Japan, which had just established itself as the dominant power in the Far East by defeating Russia in the Russo-Japanese War of 1905. The Emperor Mutsu Hito and his advisers had not been idle since Bertie had last met them. They realized that the only way to avoid being overwhelmed by the West was to adopt Western techniques, and to unite the country effectively; also that both these things had to be done fast. The loosely structured feudal Japan had to be scrapped and the whole of society remade. The same independent daimyos who had helped the Emperor defeat the Shogun had to give up their local power and their retainers; it proved necessary to subdue one of them, Satsuma, in a short, sharp war, but the others abdicated voluntarily before the immemorial prestige of the Emperor. That monarch then turned himself into an analogue of a Western sovereign, complete with parliament and ministers, and a nobility with five ranks. Of the models available, that of Bismarck's Germany was preferred, even the court etiquette being based, according to Bertie, largely on that of Berlin. Bertie mentions this without comment; but for us it is easy to see that the Prussian spirit, of all variants of Western culture, was the most likely to appeal to a samurai once he had dropped fealty to his own lord and substituted allegiance to the state. The armed forces were reorganized in a Western style, and armaments industries were established; education was remodelled on the German system; and even the arts gave up their age-old devotion to Chinese styles and began imitating the West instead. This was most notably the case in music. The court adopted European dress. At first Europeans found all this rather quaint, but the Japanese victory over Russia abruptly changed matters. It made Japan suddenly, in all seriousness, a useful ally for the worldwide British Empire. The alliance also suited the Japanese at that time, so it was concluded. Japan was to take part in the First World War on the side of the Allies.

One move made by the British towards clinching the alliance was to offer the Order of the Garter to the Emperor, and to send the King's nephew, Prince Arthur of Connaught, together with a high-powered retinue including Bertie, to present it to him. Besides the admission of the Emperor to Britain's highest order of knighthood three Japanese, Marshals Yamagata and Oyama and Admiral Togo, were given the Order of Merit. Very few foreigners ever receive this honour – they were in fact the first – and although the Order of Merit is not an order of knighthood it is in some ways more of a distinction than the Garter itself, of which Lord Melbourne had remarked with approval that there was 'no damned merit about it'. Bertie was chosen as part of the mission because he was a known expert on Japan and spoke the language.

The mission set off from Marseilles on 12 January 1906, and travelled right round the world; on its way to and from Japan it visited those parts of the British Empire that lay on the route. Bertie's account of it is very fulsome, for of course he loved every minute of the trip. He sees it as crowning the work of Parkes and Satow in Japan; he might have added his own name, though he is of course too modest to do so. The ceremonial, both English and Japanese, deeply appealed to him, as did the fact simply of seeing again the country for which his 'fever of intoxication' had started to burn from the first sight of Mount Fuji. His granddaughters, Nancy and Unity, were both in due course to fall in love with foreign countries, and would have felt much as he did had they helped present the Garter to, respectively, de Gaulle and Hitler. In Nancy's case delight would not have overcome her sardonic spirit, but in Bertie's it most certainly did. His book, *The Garter Mission to Japan*, is unctuous to the point of caricature. To be sure, he himself sees there is something amiss. 'It is not an easy matter to record a succession of entertainments, each perfect of its kind, each marked by the same graceful hospitality, the same cordial enthusiasm. If only in any one of them there had been some small failure, some error of commission or of omission, it would have given to my writing a little of the zest of variety, a little of the spice of criticism.' One takes the point; pageantry can never become high drama. But although Bertie lived at a time when even intelligent people did not sneer as much as they do now, he need not perhaps have set down quite so lovingly every little diplomatic deftness. 'To [General] Sir Thomas Kelly-Kenny [the Emperor] spoke of improving the horses in Japan, the existing breed being too small. The General, ever equal to the occasion, replied that "it is not always the big horses and the big men that do the best work." His Majesty caught the allusion at once, and chuckled with pleasure at the joke.' Few of the jokes in *The Garter Mission to Japan* even reach this level.

To us today, the interest in the book lies perhaps less in the remaining echoes of the old Japan than in the emerging lineaments of the new. Bertie visits the naval shipyard where the Japanese ironclads are being built, or refashioned from captured Russian warships. Bertie cannot understand the technical details – 'to me one lathe is much like another' – but he grasps the essential point of what has been called the 'industrial feudalism' of modern Japan.

Work! Work! Work! Never were men so eager as these Japanese artisans. The presence of an English Prince, with his following of famous admirals and generals, hardly tempts them to glance for a second away from lathe or hammer or file. Not for a moment does the clang of metal upon metal cease . . . It was as if each man felt that upon him and upon his work depended the fate of the Empire. Here is the true spirit of labour, the chivalry of work; the ambition which makes a man determine that at the end of each day *he* shall be able to say to *himself*, 'Well done, good and faithful servant.'

Altogether Bertie feels like Rip Van Winkle. 'I have been asleep, and centuries have passed over my head.' He can hardly any longer find his way about Yokohama. Japanese of the younger generation sometimes turn to him and ask him how it was in their country when he was there before; already those times were referred to as *Mukashi* – 'in ancient days'. One of the displays put on for the mission is a representation of the ceremonial procession of one of the great daimyos – a sight that before the restoration had been commonplace on the main roads of Japan.

The very paraphernalia necessary for the procession was hard to find, and old cupboards in ancient castles, and houses in distant provinces, had to be ransacked in order to bring them to light. Even the stage management was difficult. Few men are left who have seen such a procession after they came to man's estate – none, probably, who have ever had the direction of such a thing. When the leading men came strutting into the park several of the younger generation of Japanese, one of the Princesses in particular, turned to me and said, 'You have often seen such processions in real life; is this a correct representation?' Indeed, it was very correct.

The bystanders did indeed, he explains to the young people, have to bow their heads in the dust as the great man passed, preceded by his professional bullies, carried by his eight bearers and accompanied by his martial arts teacher, his guards, and his attendants in all their barbaric picturesqueness.

Bertie showed during this trip that he was physically tough for his age, just sixty-nine. With the rest of the mission he spent the whole day in the rain taking part in an odd sport in which one chased duck with a kind of butterfly net. This practice had not existed when he was in Japan before, having been invented in the 1870s for the amusement of the imperial family. He was thoroughly soaked, but plied his net with the best of them.

Somewhat naturally, Bertie is relieved that the samurai have been disarmed. No longer need a European walking the streets fear that some ronin might suddenly take it into his head to attack. As the members of the mission watch a ju-jitsu display in which a young girl polishes off an armed assailant, a Japanese general turns to Bertie and says, 'Some of that girl's tricks would have been pretty useful to you in the old days, would they not?' He is also impressed with the Naval Academy, noting the atmosphere of dedication and enthusiasm. It does not, of course, strike him as in any way sinister that the same aggressiveness which used to threaten the individual foreigner is now self-evidently being channelled towards the outside world.

Even though the Japanese had outwardly innovated their practices in the way the authorities wished, the revolution had not yet by any means reached everyone's hearts and minds. This Bertie shows, especially at both extremes of society; etas, the equivalent of India's untouchables, are still despised, and the great daimyos, though deposed, are still revered. Universal conscription on the European model having been introduced, Bertie asks a general whether this applies also to etas. The general says it does, and claims that they have been accepted by their colleagues in the ranks; but he has to admit the small detail that the others refuse to eat with them. As to the deposed daimyos, their former clansmen still venerated them and their families. Bertie came across this when Admiral Togo and General Kuroki, battle-hardened heroes of the war with Russia, met the heir to the house of Satsuma, who was in theory a simple nineteen-year-old naval cadet. 'If his manner with them was perfect and most deferential, theirs with him was no less so, and one could not help feeling that Shimadzu is still a name to conjure with. Long may it remain so!' On the other hand, the class structure was changing in the middle. Bertie gives figures showing that the old military classes, the high-ranking nobles and the samurai, do still predominate among the cadets at the Tokyo Military Academy, but by a surprisingly narrow majority: they account for about 55 per cent, the rest coming mainly from the merchant class.

It is sad when Bertie leaves Japan. He notes, of Admiral Togo and General Kuroki, with whom he made great friends, that 'unless some miracle should happen, I should never see those kind faces again'. He knows that he is getting old, that he has his own responsibilities on the other side of the world. There is nothing affected in his final description of the sight of Mount Fuji as the party steams out of Yokohama to the strains of 'God Save the King', the waves of the assembled Japanese dignitaries and the booming salutes of the naval guns. Every word is from the heart.

Rarely indeed during our stay in Japan had Mount Fuji deigned to show itself. Jealously it had hidden itself behind a veil of snow and rain. But this was a glorious afternoon. There was not a cloud floating in the sky; and when the sun set, the stately mountain stood out in all its majesty, a solemn mysterious mass against the fiery heaven. As it welcomed our coming, so it revealed itself to speed our homeward way. Never did I see it grander or more imposing than on that evening. The great beautiful mountain, matchless in all the world! . . .

But we have to add an irreverent footnote. A few years afterwards Bertie was at an international exhibition with his youngest daughter, Daphne. He found a little Japanese boy, and addressed him in his own language, The child, according to Daphne, did not understand a word he said.

He never did go back to Japan, for he had plenty to do in his own country. His garden and arboretum became ever more elaborate. He made a small lake at great expense and shortly afterwards showed round a lady who was supposed to be a great expert. Her advice was to have the fishpond removed.

He also spent much of his time writing. During the years before the First World War he became interested in a very odd writer indeed: Houston Stewart Chamberlain. Chamberlain was an Englishman who wrote in German; he was an ardent disciple of

Wagner, and married Wagner's daughter, Eva. He came from an English military family, but his poor health when a boy cut short an education which would have fitted him for a career as an army officer, and he received his schooling in France and Germany. He fell in love with Germany, taking to it with the fervour of a convert. During the First World War he took German nationality, following which his own countrymen came to regard him as being beyond the pale. Worse, he was one of the ideological inspirers of the Nazis; one of the theorists whom they had in mind when they glorified the Germanic race and persecuted the Jews. Racist and antisemite; that, in today's thinking, about wraps Chamberlain up, in Germany even more than in Britain. There is still a Chamberlain-strasse in Bayreuth named after him, but otherwise it is as if he had never been.

However, before the First World War Chamberlain was a celebrity. Though highly controversial and never academically respectable, he was one of the most prominent intellectuals in Europe. He wrote books on Kant, Goethe and Wagner, all of which won some renown. But he was best known for his work of historical philosophy, the *Foundations of the Nineteenth Century*, to the English translation of which Bertie contributed a long introduction; he was Chamberlain's own choice for this. He also translated Chamberlain's book on Kant.

To get an idea of the *Foundations*, imagine a Fellow of All Souls, perhaps very slightly drunk but certainly in a state of high excitement, going on all night airing his sympathies and his antipathies, his prejudices, his insights. The great names of the past, rather dim in most people's memory, spring into manic life, admirable or loathsome. Every so often there is a startling illu-mination; often the monologue provokes a desperate desire to argue. The listener is quite uncertain as to the subject in which his fluent companion might actually have earned his degree. History seems most likely, but the books cited, the knowledge pyro-technically displayed, could equally point to a qualification in philo-sophy, politics, classics, even perhaps theology or one of the less exact of the sciences. It happens that Chamberlain's subject, so far as he had one, was botany, although he never actually acquired a degree in it.

Today, if people look at the *Foundations* at all, they probably flip through it in order to pick out the anti-semitic bits or find something extravagant about the merits of the Teutons. In Chamberlain's own day people read the work as a whole, including the parts in which the Jews and Teutons are not mentioned; and this has to be remembered if we are to be fair to Bertie. Chamberlain believed that culture was determined by racial character, that the races associated with the Indo-European or 'Aryan' languages were the best in the world, and that of these races the Teutonic or Germanic people were pre-eminent. It followed that the German Empire, as representing Teutonism, ought to become top country, not just from its own point of view but for the general good. As to Jews, Chamberlain disapproved of them, with reservations indeed but on balance strongly. He thought Jewish habits of thought were apt to undermine the Teutons by playing on their sense of sin; this might ruin the possibility that they would beneficently control the world.

All this provided material for Nazi writers and so contributed to the climate that led to Nazi crimes. But the *Foundations* also contains much to indicate that Hitler's system, as it was actually to be established, would have repelled Chamberlain; that some aspects of it would have seemed to him very un-Teutonic. For there are many passages in which he deplores absolutism. Freedom to him is characteristic of the Teuton, and is one of his main charms. Chamberlain objects to the Roman Catholic Church and to the Holy Roman Empire of the Middle Ages because they were absolutist, in which respect they continued in the tradition of the later Roman Empire which he also deplored. The usual Nazi tendency in medieval history was to take the side of the Empire against the Papacy; to Chamberlain both are equally undesirable. 'From Constantine . . . to Frederick II of Hohenstaufen, no Emperor permitted an atom of personal or national freedom, except when weakness compelled him to make concessions.' As to Roman Catholic dogma, it can neither allow individual free will nor national distinctiveness. 'The genuine nation will never submit to the Imperium' – of either sort. Chamberlain sees the formation of European nations, and the Reformation led by Luther who is one of his great heroes, as part of the upsurge of the Teutonic spirit. Hitler, of course, was to run an 'Imperium' in exactly the sense that Chamberlain deplored. He would also have disliked the anti-Christian, neo-pagan streak in Nazism. He deeply revered the figure of Christ, who was not in his eyes a Jew: and he hoped that a modified Christianity would at last express the religious genius of the Teuton, frustrated up to now by the Roman and Old Testament traditions. The family was very important to Chamberlain; women ought to have an honourable status. He thought that the Greek city states fell because they put the state before the family, whereas the Roman Republic founded the state on the family and therefore proved durable. Chamberlain would have been horrified by such Nazi inventions as the *Lebensborn*, combined brothel and orphanage in which the children of racially approved people were bred as in an intensive farm; he opposed Galton's eugenic theories, and disliked Darwin as well. Early Roman law, which exalted the family, he said was 'just as incomparable and inimitable as Hellenic art. Our ridiculous Germanomania will make no change in that.'

'Ridiculous Germanomania' is an example of the impossibility of ever being able to predict what Chamberlain will say next. He refers also to the Old Testament as 'prototype of the *noble* and yet quarrelsome and revengeful Jew'. (Our italics.) To call the Jews noble, even in conjunction with less amiable characteristics, is not unqualified anti-semitism.

We must not devote any more space to the *Foundations*, but it is necessary to indicate how Bertie, and many of his contemporaries, can have admired the work. It is not consistent or rigorous enough to be called a great book, but it is unfailingly lively. This is what appealed to Bertie. The novelist Edmund Gosse, who at the end of Bertie's life was his friend and literary adviser, writes in the introduction which he provided to Bertie's posthumous *Further Memories*: 'Perhaps the most remarkable fact about Lord Redesdale was the redundant vitality of his character. His nature swarmed with life, like a drop of pond-water under a microscope.' He was, right to the end of his life, ready to respond to intellectual stimulation.

Further, the beliefs expressed by the book were not then considered shocking. Exaltation of the Germanic, Teutonic or Nordic race was fairly general; the quotas for immigrants into the United States were strongly biased towards northern Europe, and nobody thought this odd. The same was true of the wider 'Aryan' grouping; Chamberlain's essential attitudes remained widespread up to the Second World War. L. Austine Waddell, a respected expert on Tibet, refers in the preface to *The Buddhism of Tibet or Lamaism* (1939) to 'the Aryan race, to which the purer Britons belong', and claims to have demonstrated that this race provided 'the originators and chief propagators of the world's civilization, including the higher religions'. It was also permissible, and not unusual, to express dislike of the Jews. Arthur Balfour himself, whose Balfour Declaration was to further the establishment of Israel, is shown by his biographer Kenneth Young (*Balfour*, p. 257) as visiting Bayreuth and agreeing with Cosima Wagner when she was disobliging about the Jewish character.

In his introduction to the *Foundations* Bertie takes issue with Chamberlain on his attitude to the Jews, especially the Ashkenazim. (Like many anti-semites, Chamberlain had a soft spot for the Sephardim.) Bertie's reservations are certainly too measured to satisfy us moderns, accustomed since Hitler to regard anti-semitism as a subject not for disagreement but for horror. Nevertheless they are there.

To the Ashkenazim . . . Chamberlain is as it seems to me unjust . . . They are born financiers and acquisition of money has been their characteristic talent. But of the treasure which they have laid up they have given freely. The charities of the great cities of Europe would be in a sad plight were the support of the Jews to be withdrawn; indeed many noble foundations owe their existence to them. Politically too they have rendered great services . . .

Bertie, like Chamberlain himself, regards race as the basis of history, but he seems to see a future determined not by a Teutonism purged of Jewish influence but by Teuton and Jew in partnership. He admires the Jews precisely because of their racial consciousness. He says he once called on a Jewish friend, who had just seen Disraeli. ' "What did you talk about?" I asked at haphazard. "Oh," said my host, "the usual thing – the Race." ' Disraeli was of course one of Bertie's great heroes as well as his benefactor. Bertie does indeed agree with Chamberlain in disliking the Jewish influence on Christianity, and quotes with approval his remark that, had the Romans not captured Jerusalem, '. . . all freedom of thought and of belief would have vanished from the world'.

To Bertie, Chamberlain had provided for his own kind the same sort of historical explanation and justification as the Jews found in the Old Testament for theirs. This is not the least of the ways in which Bertie's ideas are now right out of fashion; not only because of the way this particular tendency was disgraced by Nazism, but also, perhaps, because it is obscurely felt that the northern European peoples are so generally prosperous that it is somehow not cricket for them to consolidate this prosperity by exercising a racial self-interest that less privileged races can be permitted. As the decline in their power becomes more generally apparent to themselves, this fashion may change.

# 9

# Old Age and Death

Probably through Chamberlain, Bertie came to know the Wagner family: he went several times to the Bayreuth festival which was by then effectively run by the composer's son, Siegfried. To the end of his life, we are told, Siegfried kept a photograph of Bertie on his desk, and Bertie was often invited to the family house, Haus Wahnfried, where Cosima Wagner still presided. Bertie deeply admired Wagner's music. He was musical himself, and he also loved grandeur. He accepted Wagner's claim that the music-dramas of his maturity are not operas, but something higher. 'Wagner was a great magician, and could transport his people whither he liked . . . The book, the music, the scenery, the stage-management, all the invention of that one brain. What a power he wielded! You must journey to Bayreuth to feel its full force. There the master-mind, the singers, the orchestra, and last, not least, the audience, are all in sympathy . . .'

This comes from 'Bayreuth in 1912 – a Sketch', an affectionate description of his last visit to the festival. He writes of Haus Wahnfried: 'In Wahnfried everything speaks to you of Wagner. The design was his: the admirably proportioned rooms were planned and measured by him: every detail was thought out with strenuous care and loving foresight . . . The works of art, the knick-knacks all tell their story.' Bertie's descendants Tom, Diana and Unity, and afterwards Diana's sons Jonathan, Alexander and Max, were to find Wahnfried essentially unchanged when they visited it, though Cosima was by then dead and the hostess was Siegfried's widow, Winifred.

By 1910 the results of Bertie's overspending had caught up with him. The main action he took was similar to that of his father when, so many years before, he had let Exbury. He found a tenant

for Batsford, William Nelson, who moved there with his family.
Bertie moved himself and his family to London, to a large Victorian house in the Pont Street style, resplendent in its external
decoration of red terracotta, on the corner of Kensington Court
and Kensington High Street. The house, externally unchanged, is
now the main part of the Milestone Hotel.

Deprived of his beloved garden, Bertie now devoted himself
more and more to writing, a pursuit to which he was also driven
by a deafness that year by year made social contact more difficult.
*The Bamboo Garden* had already appeared in 1908, and it was
followed in 1912 by the collection of essays *A Tragedy in Stone*. In
1913 the English translation of the *Foundations of the Nineteenth
Century* came out with Bertie's introduction, and in 1914 it was
followed by Bertie's own translation of Chamberlain's book on
Kant. Then, in 1915, came his two-volume *Memories*, by far his
most successful work after *Tales of Old Japan*. Decca was to
regard *Memories* as boring (*Hons and Rebels*), but at the time of its
appearance it was popular. Edmund Gosse called it 'one of the
most successful autobiographies of recent times'. It has certainly
been the main single source for the chapters on Bertie in this book.
Decca eloped at eighteen, so she was only that age, at the most,
when she looked at it. One must also remember the purpose of her
own book, which is to show ardent and idealistic youth shaking
from its feet the dust of a stuffy past. Certainly there are faults
in *Memories*. There is a self-indulgent lack of organization, a
tendency to digress. There is often – though fortunately not
always – an annoying lack of sharpness in Bertie's remarks about
people, that in the case of the great can amount to obsequiousness;
there is a lack of self-analysis. These traits were of Bertie's time,
but the refusal of intimacy is more complete than fashion dictated.
We see in it a family characteristic, since it recurs in full force in
all the literary Mitfords two generations later, when it had become
usual to tell all. Yet *Memories* reads well even today, and it is quite
easy to see why seventy years ago the educated public found a lot
to like in it. The work teems with stories that would have amused
them. The celebrities Bertie knew and described were of more
general interest then than now, because they were nearer the
reader's own time. Some of course have faded more than others;
Carlyle's reputation was then high but has crumbled, whereas

interest in Burton remains great. On Garibaldi, whose legend has obscured the real man and his actual views, Bertie is a corrective. The scenes wear at least as well as the people: Eton in the 1840s, Oxford in the 1850s, Russia and China in the 1860s, the Japanese revolution, the Wild West before Hollywood got at it, and of course London over many decades of Victoria's reign, are made to live again.

But in the meantime war had broken out. Bertie, like many people in all classes, welcomed the war, or at any rate accepted it as a stern necessity. His attitude to Germany in August 1914 seems to have lain somewhere between his position in 1912 and that at the end of his life in 1916, as shown in the posthumous *Further Memories*. In 1912 his admiration of the 'goodly gathering' at Bayreuth was not in the least vitiated by an atmosphere of German patriotism, which must have been fairly obvious. Wahnfried was a centre of such feelings, shared in full measure by the Wagner family. In 1916, perhaps thinking mainly of poison gas and certainly under the influence of the wartime newspapers, he writes (*Further Memories*, p. 79): 'The whole coarse-fibred soul of the German seems to be infected by the very potentialities of all these ghastly new discoveries, which seem to urge him on to new cruelties and new crimes.' He does add that 'in 1870 [the German] knew how to spare'.

Bertie agreed that Britain was morally bound to go to the aid of Belgium, and also that Germany had to be 'stopped'; this is a recurrent theme of the diplomatic parts of *Memories*. But had he quite reached the stage of seeing Germans as having coarse-fibred souls? Perhaps he never really did reach it; in any case his account of Bayreuth in 1912, previously a privately printed 'sketch', is inserted almost unchanged into the second volume of *Memories*. His action in suggesting the second name Valkyrie for his newly born granddaughter Unity glances back at his reverence for Wagner, most German of artists, as well as celebrating the outbreak of the 'just war' against Wagner's country. Nancy, to be sure, says that he justified the choice of name partly on the grounds that the original Valkyries were Scandinavian and not German; but this does not make them any less Wagnerian.

But Bertie never again mentions Houston Stewart Chamberlain. Reference to him, and even to his brother who was a professor of

Japanese in Tokyo, is removed from the version of 'Bayreuth 1912' inserted into *Memories*. It is as if the *Foundations* had never been for Bertie 'a simple delight – the companion of months', had never fulfilled for him 'the highest function of which a teacher is capable, that of awakening thought and driving it into new channels'. This is a matter on which one really would like Bertie to shed some light. He rejected Chamberlain himself as a renegade, that is clear. To what extent, if any, did he cease to respond to his ideas?

Certainly both Bertie's sympathies, and his principles, became instantly engaged in the war. He would not have been able to distinguish between them. England was engaged and England was in the right. To him as a former diplomat, for whom international agreements had been the very reason for his existence, the widely reported surprise of Bethmann-Hollweg that England should go to war about a scrap of paper would have seemed particularly distasteful. One reason for Germany's failure in the first half of the twentieth century does seem precisely to have been its tendency to play what, remembering Alice, one may call the Carpenter to Britain's and America's Walrus; it only pays to follow Machiavelli on the strict condition that one succeeds in concealing the fact. Belief in the theory of *Realpolitik* is perhaps a disqualification for its successful practice. In those days, in any case, very many people, including old sophisticates like Bertie, really believed in absolutes; the absolute sanctity of one's word, the absolute wrongness of any sort of dishonesty or corruption. Hegelian or Marxist ideas that principles are not absolute, but only a manifestation of state or class interests, had not sunk in.

All Bertie's five sons fought in the war from the start; this, in a family like theirs, was a matter of course. They did not wait to be conscripted. Clement was already in the 10th Hussars and Tommy in the Navy; David, despite having lost a lung in the Boer War, joined the Northumberland Fusiliers, Jack entered the Life Guards and Rupert, aged nineteen, went into the Navy. In a statistical sense this family was to be rather lucky, for only one of them was killed. The First World War often wiped out whole families of sons, and it was precisely young officers who were most at risk. Unfortunately the victim was the beloved Clement, on whom Bertie's main hopes for the future of the family were pinned.

Clement fell on 13 May 1915. He was not exactly his father's favourite; that distinction belonged, by all accounts, to the charming scapegrace Jack. But he had a solider distinction, for of all Bertie's sons it was Clement whose qualities he most respected. The loss was cruel, and perhaps especially so as Clement had shortly before won the DSO, to his parents' inexpressible pride and delight. Clement's widow had a daughter, Rosemary, aged five, and was expecting another child who, if a boy, would have been heir to Bertie's title. In the event another girl, Clementine, was born, bringing the succession to David. It came as no joy to him. Pam remembers him and Sydney openly weeping when the news of Clement's death was brought; it was the first time she had seen grown-ups cry.

After Clement's death, Bertie wanted to go back to Batsford. Sir William Nelson, as he was by then (he was created a baronet in 1912), made no difficulties. The lease was brought by agreement to a premature end. Only a small part of the house returned to use, and most of it was to remain under dustsheets until David sold it five years later.

Bertie was now seventy-eight, and his deafness was very severe; but until his death in the following year he carried on all his activities. There was no trace of senility, nor any sign of slackening off. His friend Edmund Gosse has given us a striking description of him at this time in the introduction to *Further Memories* (1917). Gosse says that after his son's death Bertie's 'dominant vitality asserted itself almost with violence, and he seemed to clench his teeth in defiance of the blow to his individuality'. He was sustained until July by the work of revising *Memories*, and then went to Cowes, to live in the Royal Yacht Club while the actual work of moving back to Batsford went on, supervised by Clementine.

It was not an ideal place to be. In wartime there was no sailing, and the club contained only one other resident. Even he left after a while, so that Bertie was entirely alone. In a peacetime July, of course, the place would have been thronged. Bertie started reading Nietzsche, but he did not take to him, observing in a letter to Gosse: 'Here and there I find gems of thought, but one has to wade through a morass of blue mud to get at them.' It is rather an interesting pointer to Bertie's beliefs, or rather his feelings, that he only finds Nietzsche heavy going, not actually objectionable. His devout wife, had she glanced at Nietzsche, would most certainly have reacted more sharply to the great opponent of Christianity. All in all Bertie was bored at Cowes; and he appealed to Gosse to come over and stay with him, not only to chat but also to advise him what to write about now that *Memories* was finally with the publishers. 'You must sharpen my wits, which are blunt enough just now.' Gosse arrived, and spent several fine August days with his host, sitting about on wicker chairs looking at the drab warships which were all the Solent had to show, or going for excursions on foot or by boat. Despite his deafness, Bertie was as lively as ever, 'in a suit picturesquely marine, with his beautiful silver hair escaping from a jaunty yachting cap'. He was irritated when Gosse hinted that at the age of seventy-nine his host might think he had done enough in his life and could settle down to dignified inactivity. This prospect was exactly what Bertie most dreaded. There were a great many things he could no longer do; but writing was still within his powers. Gosse was a writer; what did he suggest? No firm conclusion was reached at Cowes, but their discussion continued by correspondence. Gosse was rather firm in rejecting certain projects he was convinced were unsuitable, notably a study of the Empress Maria Theresa. Bertie did in fact write an essay comparing Maria Theresa with Queen Victoria: just why Gosse thought a full-length study would have been unsuitable he does not make clear, but perhaps he thought the task would prove too demanding. Finally Gosse himself came up with an idea which Bertie seized on. Gosse suggested that Bertie, re-installed at Batsford, 'should compose a volume of essays dealing with things in general, but bound together by a constantly repeated reference to his wild garden of bamboos and the Buddha in his secret grove. The author was to suppose himself seated with a friend on the terrace at the top of the garden, and let the idea of the bamboo run through the whole tissue of reflections and reminiscences like an emerald thread.' To us the idea may seem rather a bad one; but belletristic waffle, to which it seems so inexorably to conduce, was then valued more highly than it is today, and as a suggestion to this particular writer it was exactly right. Gosse showed, in making it, what a good and sensitive friend he was. For the garden was indeed Bertie's most enduring delight, in which it was to be expected that he should wander, thinking his thoughts and mulling over his reminiscences. To put these down on paper, more or less as they occurred to him, should be at least a congenial occupation for the old man, whatever the quality of the actual results. As it turned out, the results were partly good; *Further Memories* is uneven, but it was certainly well worth writing.

In due course he moved back to Batsford, and invited David and his young family into a house on the estate. Now that David was the heir, he would have to learn something about the duties he would inherit; but for the moment, of course, he was still in the Army. Bertie might, one feels, have lived a good while longer; long enough perhaps to show his son the ropes. He was active for his age and deafness was his only disability. But in June 1916 he went fishing and sat on wet grass, catching a feverish chill. He insisted on going to London to attend various meetings, with the result that he became seriously ill. Returning to Batsford he developed hepatitis, and never recovered. He died on 17 August. Clementine went to live at Redesdale Cottage in Northumberland, where her health improved. She lived until 1932, and her descendants loved her in her mellow old age.

# PART TWO
# Thomas Gibson Bowles

# 10

# Mr Milner-Gibson's Indiscretion

One day in 1844 Thomas Milner-Gibson, a Suffolk landowner and politician of the Liberal persuasion, brought home with him a little blond boy, three years old, whom he introduced to his wife Susanna as Thomas Gibson Bowles. He may well have been in a state of some embarrassment, for the child was his illegitimate son. Milner-Gibson was closeted with his wife for quite a time while the boy waited outside in the hall. The story he told her remained a complete mystery for well over a century, except for the name of the boy's mother, said to be Susan Bowles.

Even this was slightly wrong; the name was Susannah. Only the final h distinguishes her name from that of Thomas Milner-Gibson's wife. This fact, and the information that follows, we owe to Julia Budworth, *nee* Bowles, who in 2001 published a life of her father George under the title *Never Forget* (privately printed). Susannah, described by herself as a servant, was born on 24 August 1818, the daughter of William Bowles, a brushmaker, and his wife Mary Ann Daws. She gave birth to Thomas Gibson Bowles on 15 January 1841, at 2 Mount Street, Whitechapel. This small lodging house with at least 13 residents was desperately overcrowded and can hardly have failed to be squalid. Yet Thomas was not the first baby to whom Susannah gave birth in these surroundings. On 24 November 1838, she had been delivered of a girl, Jane Stanley Bowles, at the same address. It is safe to assume that during the time between these two births Susannah worked as a servant in the London house of Thomas Milner-Gibson at 48 Eaton Square and that Thomas Bowles was conceived there. It would then appear, rather remarkably, that Susannah left without telling her master that she was expecting his child. Had she done the same in 1838 when her daughter was born? By analogy, Jane Stanley Bowles's middle name points to the father having been a member of the family of the Earl of Derby, or of Lord Stanley of Alderley. And where was this older baby when Susannah worked for the Milner-Gibsons? Not, we may assume, at 48 Eaton Square. Susannah had parents and an older brother and sister and perhaps Jane was parked with one household or the other, and joined by Thomas when he appeared. Then in 1844 something happened, we do not know what, to make these arrangements impossible. Unable any longer to maintain the discretion she had exercised when leaving the Milner-Gibson household, Susannah approached her former employer and lover for help. In those days, with no Welfare State, it was all she could do. He responded generously, buying a little house in Gravesend for her and her daughter and whisking Thomas away to join his one surviving legitimate child, one-year-old Alice, in Theberton House, Suffolk.

Susanna Milner-Gibson accepted the little boy at once and never made the slightest distinction between him and her own children, except apparently to tell visitors: 'This is Tom Bowles. Be civil to him, or leave the house.' She may even have been quite pleased to have a stepson to mother. The Milner-Gibsons had had bad luck with their family: a son and a daughter had both died young many years before.

The Milner-Gibsons would have more children in due course. Four sons and a daughter, Sydney, were born between 1845 and 1857. The two eldest sons died young but the younger two grew up to become Suffolk squires, Jasper in the Milner-Gibson residence, Theberton House, and George Gery in Hardwick House which he inherited from Susanna Milner-Gibson's father, Sir Thomas Gery Cullum. Alice was to marry and have a family; Sydney, of whom we know Thomas was especially fond, died in 1870. Neither of Thomas's brothers attained any degree of prominence; George's office of High Sheriff of Suffolk seems to have represented their high-water mark. Thomas was the oldest boy of the family, the first whom his father could take sailing and introduce to country sports and politics. He was probably also the brightest. What is certain is that Thomas grew up very close to his father, taking from him an important part of his political attitudes as well as a lifelong passion for the sea.

Milner-Gibson, born in 1806, was one of the leaders of the free trade movement with Richard Cobden and John Bright. He was a Radical, on what we should call the left of the Liberals, at first still known as Whigs. However, he came to these views as a convert, having first entered Parliament for Ipswich in 1837 as a Tory. It was two years later that the free traders convinced him by their arguments; he then resigned his seat and fought the resulting by-election under his new colours, but unsuccessfully. (The modern habit of hanging on to a seat after the views for which the electors voted have been discarded was not, at that time, prevalent.)

Milner-Gibson then joined one of the most successful pressure groups of all time: Cobden's Anti-Corn Law League, which opposed the tariff on imported grains. He became one of its most assiduous campaigners, advocating cheap bread in eloquent and entertaining speeches all over the country. His work for the League earned him a Liberal candidacy in Manchester, the centre of free trade Liberalism, and he re-entered Parliament in July 1841. In 1846, the Conservative Prime Minister Sir Robert Peel repealed the Corn Laws against which Milner-Gibson had so assiduously agitated, but in doing so Peel offended his own party. The backbenchers rebelled, led by Benjamin Disraeli; Peel had to resign, and was succeeded as Prime Minister by the Liberal, Lord John Russell. Russell included in his government several of the leaders of the Anti-Corn Law League, among them Milner-Gibson, who became Vice-President of the Board of Trade for two years. By 1850, he was deeply involved in another cause, agitating for the repeal of the so-called 'taxes on the advancement of knowledge'. This expression referred to the stamp duty on newspapers and advertisements, and the excise duty on paper. In that year he became president of a society devoted to the abolition of these taxes.

Although Milner-Gibson had originally become a Liberal on the single issue of free trade, he quite quickly adopted advanced Radical views on most issues. Those who change their party in politics on one issue often find themselves influenced by their new friends in other matters as well. Within the party, he often found himself at odds with Lord Palmerston, another ex-Conservative Whig and keen free trader, but one whose conversion to Radical attitudes was a good deal less complete.

Milner-Gibson was a convinced opponent of the Crimean War of 1854–56, and this attitude made him unpopular with his constituents as well as with the government. In the election of 1857 both he and John Bright lost their seats, to the delight of another Mitford ancestor, Lord Stanley. 'Gibson . . . cannot be half as mischievous outside Parliament as in,' Stanley wrote to his wife. This remark showed prescience. Milner-Gibson was back in the House in December of the same year as member for Ashton-under-Lyne, and soon, in 1858, caused his party's government to fall. He did this by forcing a major amendment to a bill introduced by Lord Palmerston to amend the law of conspiracy. Palmerston was under pressure from Napoleon III, who was afraid of the activities of Radical refugees in London, having only just escaped with his life from an attack using English-made bombs. Palmerston wanted foreigners who conspired in Britain to commit political assassinations in their own countries to be held guilty of a felony. The Conservatives supported the wrecking amendment simply to get the government out.

However, the Liberals were back in July 1859, under Palmerston as Prime Minister. Palmerston had been furious with Milner-Gibson the year before, but he was not one to harbour a grudge. Feeling that he could not do without this able member of his Radical wing, and with a view also to keeping him out of mischief, he made Milner-Gibson President of the Board of Trade. The appointment suited him, and he kept it for more than seven years, between January 1859 and July 1866. The Whigs who formed the right wing of the Liberal Party still saw him as a dangerous Radical. The Stanleys of Alderley certainly took this view; in 1861 Henrietta Maria wrote to her husband, who was Postmaster-General in the same government, that she had refused an invitation to dinner with the Milner-Gibsons 'as I do not care to make their acquaintance more intimately'. But for Milner-Gibson himself the Board of Trade was a good position in which to further his ideas not only on free trade, but also on the modernization of trading practice. He succeeded in abolishing the 'taxes on the advancement of knowledge'. One project in which he did not succeed was his attempt, in 1864, to make the country go over to the metric system.

In the meantime Thomas Bowles grew up, much loved by his

father and stepmother, who made his childhood happy and secure. It is true that as a boy he did once try to run away to sea, and was 'well on the way to Liverpool' before being found and 'ignominiously brought back'. This incident is told in the preface to his book *Flotsam and Jetsam*, and no further details are given, not even his age at the time of the escapade; but we may be sure that it is, as he says, evidence of his early love of the sea and of a desire for adventure, not any indication that he was unhappy at home. Perhaps it was not from home that he ran away, but from Mr Cobley's preparatory school at Peckham, an institution where he was unhappy and underfed, as was the common lot of boys in preparatory schools. Later, when Thomas became a celebrity, Mr Cobley wrote him a complimentary letter saying that he had always known he would do well; but Thomas still disliked him so much that he sent no reply.

His secondary education, however, he enjoyed. It was an example of good coming out of evil, because one disability imposed by his illegitimacy was that he could not attend any English public school. He was accordingly sent to a school in northern France. Mrs Milner-Gibson may well have suggested this idea, for she loved France. Thomas was successful at school, sometimes winning prizes in French over the heads of fellow pupils to whom the language was native. The master, who liked him, took a rather sporting pleasure when this happened, and used to exclaim: '*Aha! Les anglais vous battent à plate couture.*' Afterwards, Thomas went to King's College, London, but only stayed there about a year; for in 1860, at the age of nineteen, he was nominated by his father to a position as a junior clerk in the Legacy and Succession Duty office at Somerset House. Conveniently, Milner-Gibson had shortly before this been appointed President of the Board of Trade.

The question arises, in any consideration of Thomas Bowles, as to how much he minded being illegitimate. The answer seems to be rather little, but perhaps there was, all the same, a residual discomfort. It cannot be said to have preyed on him, exactly, but his daughter Sydney, in her unpublished autobiographical work *Five Houses*, says that the only member of his family he ever mentioned when she was a girl was his sister Sydney, after whom she was named; and even this was rare. When in her early childhood she heard someone speak to him of his father, says

Sydney, 'I felt a big shock of surprise, for I had never imagined him as having a father or indeed any family; and children are quick to realize when they must not ask questions. The curtain lifted for an instant and fell back again.' On the other hand, his relations with both his father and stepmother remained close and warm to the end of their lives. After her husband's death Mrs Milner-Gibson went to live in Paris where she became more French than the French, and cranky with it. Sydney says in *Five Houses*: 'One day Tap [Thomas] went to lunch in her flat. She removed the cover of the dish and there were revealed delicious-looking chops. She seized the dish, took it to the open window, and threw the chops into the courtyard, exclaiming: "*Quoi? Des chops chez moi? Jamais de la vie!*" Too English. So poor Tap saw his dinner disappear.' That Sydney records this story is, of course, direct evidence that by the time she was grown-up Thomas was talking rather more freely of his family. ('Tap' was what all Thomas's children called him all their lives.)

As to Susannah Bowles: she never married, but long afterwards, in 1859, gave birth to another boy, William Battle Bowles, who grew up to be a solicitor's clerk. He married and gave her two grandchildren, a boy and a girl, of whom the latter had further descendants. Susannah lived until 12 July 1898 when, at the age of nearly 80, she fell down the stone steps into the area of her little house in Ramsgate. She had moved there in 1871. The local newspaper in Ramsgate reported the accident and stated that the victim was the mother of Thomas Gibson Bowles MP. This indicates that Thomas was at the funeral. How closely was he in touch with his mother during her life? Did he see her from time to time when he was a boy? We know that he visited her in his yacht, when he was grown up; there is a reference in his book *Flotsam and Jetsam* to sailing along the Channel 'after visiting my mamma'. This passing reference in a published work was not picked up by anyone until spotted, very much later, by his sharp-eyed granddaughter Julia, who pointed it out to her father George Bowles. One would love to know more about Thomas's visits to Ramsgate. He presumably met his older half-sister, married but childless, and his much younger half-brother, as well as his nephew and niece. Julia Budworth suggests that he also took his friend, the French artist Tissot, of whom a number of pictures of

Ramsgate survive; why else would Tissot have gone to Ramsgate? In that case Tissot very likely met Susannah. If so he did not, alas, paint her picture.

Which is a pity because, as Julia Budworth says in her book, Susannah is always just out of reach. 'There is no known description of her, nothing written by her' – though she was not illiterate, she could sign her name – 'no saying that was particularly hers, no anecdotes, no drawing, painting or photograph of her, no single possession of hers.' Yet we are not quite without clues. She was almost certainly rather small, and blonde; her son Thomas was the only fair-haired child of his father, and was short. Again to judge by her son, she was probably good-looking, with regular features. Thomas Milner-Gibson's regard for her indicates that she had charm; her discretion as regards her pregnancy indicates decency and self-respect. She must have been fairly tough, too, to survive giving birth twice in the slums; and but for her accident she might well have lived many years longer. An indirect indication that Susannah may have been rather fetching is that her daughter, Jane Stanley, married at the age of 45 a pharmacist called George Franks who was only 30, and got away with pretending that she was ten years younger than she really was. They had no children – the menopause is inexorable – but her husband never seems to have seen through the deception, implying that she always looked younger than her age. This may, or may not, be significant, but it contributes to our feeling that Susannah was a useful contributor to the family's DNA.

# 11

# From Civil Servant to Journalist

Thomas found the work of a junior clerk at Somerset House quite as boring as Bertie Mitford, at the same time, was finding the endless copying of dispatches in the Foreign Office. However, the position had its advantages. The pay, though insufficient for the style of life he liked to maintain, was at least regular; and the hours were short. Bertie's social life, it will be recalled, was sometimes inconvenienced by a diplomatic emergency that could keep him at work of an evening. Nothing of the sort happened at Somerset House. The work also gave Thomas a grounding in the practices of public finance, and in certain aspects of the law, which was to be of use to him throughout his public life. It was to lead him, in his seventies, to score an unusual, if not particularly constructive, triumph over the Establishment.

Thomas's hours outside the office were crammed with all sorts of pursuits. For one thing, he was physically very active. Like Bertie, he attended a gymnasium; he also played rackets at the same club as the Prince of Wales, who was his contemporary. He ran competitively, the half-mile being his best distance; and he rode a good deal. In later life he was to say that the two necessities of life were a horse and a boat. Fencing and skating were two other sports which he liked.

Again like Bertie, he was also very sociable, enjoying parties and dinners, in mixed company or with his men friends. He would sometimes drink a good deal. He had a good head for liquor, and seems never to have suffered from hangovers, probably because of his physical fitness. He went often to the theatre and, as theatregoers did in those days, came to know many of the actors and managers. He acted himself, as an amateur, and even wrote a number of plays. All of these are now lost, although one of them was put on by an amateur company in Bristol and was well reviewed.

Only someone of exceptional energy and toughness could cope with the schedule that Thomas set himself; he is said never to have gone to bed before four in the morning. As to this, his biographer, Leonard Naylor, from whose book *The Irrepressible Victorian* most of this information comes, also hints with old-fashioned coyness at a fairly active sex life. 'His great good looks and distinguished bearing fluttered many a feminine heart,' says Naylor, going on to make clear that the fluttering was to continue for most of his long life. As regards unmarried ladies in London society, any attachments would, of course, have been platonic, though not necessarily less alluring for that; but these formed only one small category of the female sex.

All these varied activities not only required stamina; they also cost money, even though amusements of all kinds were certainly less expensive in real terms than they are now. His father gave him an allowance of £90 a year – 'I have often wondered why it was not £100,' Sydney was to comment – and would sometimes give him extra subsidies as well. There is an affectionate entry in his diary for 1865: 'Met the Gov. and got a cheque for £50. Bless his heart. He is always trying to be close with money – but he never is.' Increasingly, also, he began to supplement his income by freelance journalism. In this way he discovered what was to be his true bent. Sometimes he found that his work was conflicting with his social life. At one time, he was to tell his daughter Dorothy, he had his head completely shaved so as to stop himself going to parties. His writing was not confined to articles, and he also published stories and poetry. He wrote a series of poems in honour of Amy Ricardo, great-niece of the economist and future Duchess of Richmond, with whom he was at the time in love; she set them to music. One of these songs found a publisher, though it did not catch on. As to his articles, from the beginning they display an impressive range of interests and knowledge. His main outlet was the *Morning Post*. He met the editor, Sir Algernon Borthwick, and a colleague of his called Coward, on a particularly convivial evening in January 1865 after which 'poor Coward was very sick going home'. The two men encouraged him in his journalism, but Coward advised him to keep his civil service job

— advice which at that exact stage was probably sound. All the same, the newspaper liked his work: by 1866 it was accepting an article almost every day. Naylor lists ten which appeared in ten successive issues, as an example of the range of his capabilities. They were on the casual poor, on electoral reform, on a Surrey meeting of the Liberals, on a meeting about the tax on malt, on the cattle plague, on a meeting against opening museums on Sunday, on Fenianism and the House of Commons, on the medium D. D. Home and spiritualism, on agricultural statistics, and on railway compensation for poor dwellings. At this time Thomas was twenty-five. His facility for writing, and even more his powers of rapidly absorbing and organizing information, were evidently exceptional.

He had an unfailing self-assurance. He decided to ride through Admiralty Arch, something reserved for very important people; when asked by the man in charge of the gate who he was, he fixed him with a confident stare and answered: 'I am Mr Bowles.' He was allowed through. But he was not intolerably brash as a young man, for sometimes he could see himself as others saw him. When he was introduced to the editor of *The Times*, Thomas Delane, he commented in his diary that he was 'very savage with myself all the evening, for I feel I am producing upon him the impression that I am a flashy and conceited young ape . . . Perhaps I am one.' With all his bounce, he had some sensitivity. The combination converted his liveliness into charm: a valuable asset for an inquiring journalist, because it can open, as with a key, doors which must otherwise be battered down.

Thomas was already showing the first signs of that individuality which was later to make him a well-known eccentric. At the time it showed itself mainly in his dress. He designed his own collars, and had his shirts made with a special kind of tail. His jackets had pockets in unusual places. It is the particular nature of this sartorial originality which provides a clue to Thomas's character. It had little to do with display; he was not trying to stand out in a crowd or be a leader of fashion, for if these had been the considerations, why bother with shirt-tails which nobody was ever likely to see? The extra pockets, too, are much more likely to have been designed for convenience than for vanity. It was an early example of something which we shall meet again in his later life and indeed in his children and some of his grandchildren; namely an independence of received ideas springing from a wish to think things out anew from first principles. This is not absolutely to deny Naylor's statement that Thomas was 'a young man proud of being unusual and different'. He quite enjoyed cutting a figure. It is simply that showmanship came second; he was primarily a White Knight rather than a Beau Brummell. Later in life, his preference for his own ideas over received ones was to spread from his dress to his daily timetable, his diet, his health practices, his ablutions and his children's upbringing.

In September 1866 Thomas resigned from the civil service. Coward's cautious advice of the year before was out of date, because Thomas had acquired a real reputation as a journalist and now found it easy to sell any articles that he felt inclined to write. He contributed regularly both to the *Morning Post* and to a well-regarded monthly magazine called *The Owl*, connected with the *Morning Post* in that the newspaper's editor, Sir Algernon Borthwick, was on the magazine's editorial board.

In these circumstances, Thomas's decision to leave Somerset House seems sensible until one considers exactly what he was going to do next. One might have expected him to continue as a freelance journalist, or to line up a staff job on a periodical. On the contrary, he decided, at the age of twenty-six and with virtually no resources, to found and edit a new weekly magazine. His best friend, Frederick Burnaby, suggested the title: *Vanity Fair*. Burnaby was an officer in the Royal Horse Guards or 'Blues'. He also became a contributor to the magazine, providing it with gossip, which occasionally annoyed his brother officers. In due course he was to become Colonel of the Blues, and was killed in action in the Sudan.

*Vanity Fair* succeeded; the temporary setbacks or 'teething troubles' to which all new businesses are subject were mild and soon overcome. Thomas used later to tell his children that nobody should ever stay in a job which bored him, giving his own career as a proof; his daughter Sydney was to pass on this opinion to her grandson Jonathan in the 1950s. Thomas thought that everyone had something which he could do well; he should discover what it was, and do it. In his book of reflections, *Flotsam and Jetsam*, he was to remark: 'The curse of labour . . . is no curse at all, but

rather the only blessing in life . . . Of course, one must have work
that one *can* do, but that is a mere question of choice in a world
where there is so much to do of so many various kinds; and not a
difficult question either, for almost anybody can do anything if
they will but address themselves to it.'

For this idea to be literally true for everybody would require a
good many changes in a good many people; Thomas is generalizing from his own fortunate case, and he probably knows it.
As compared with the Protestant work ethic as normally prop-
ounded, his view can be seen as Pelagian; related, that is, to the
amiable heresy of Pelagius, opponent of St Augustine, who
regarded the fall of man as something that could in principle
be reversed in this life for those who behaved well. It is a more
optimistic idea than the usual version, which underlines the account in Genesis of man's condemnation to earn his bread by
the sweat of his brow: the view which regards labour as a curse
indeed, and good for us just for that reason. But if neither
theologically orthodox nor valid for everybody, Thomas's attitude
might well give hope to a lot of people who do not know what is
in them. The attitude of the Mitfords, with even Decca as more an
apparent exception than a real one, is generally Pelagian. That is,
their strength, and some of their blind spots, are related to an
aversion to that sense of sin, first formulated by the Hebrew
prophets, which Christianity enjoins for everyone, and socialism
prescribes for the well-to-do. Through Sydney, this is clearly
traceable to Thomas Bowles.

*Vanity Fair* certainly started with very little capital, but accounts
differ both as to amount and sources. According to Naylor,
Thomas told his sons that the original sum at his disposal was
£200, half of which he had borrowed. Sydney, in her unpublished
book *Five Houses*, makes it £300; the investors according to
her were Sir Algernon Borthwick, Fred Burnaby and one other.
Following Naylor we can name the other as Charles Waring, an
engineering contractor.

The first issue appeared on 14 November 1868 and had twelve
pages. It contained a good deal of political comment both foreign
and domestic, as well as social news, humour, and arts criticism. It
sold 619 copies. The circulation then fell for several issues until
the advent of the feature which was to become its trademark and

which is the only thing most people know about the magazine: the weekly coloured cartoon. The first of these appeared in February 1869 and was of Disraeli. The cartoon occupied a whole foolscap page. The caption underneath it was often a nickname, either one by which the subject was already widely known, or one invented for the occasion. Sometimes it was a phrase descriptive of the subject's characteristics or activities. Earl Redesdale, for instance, was 'The Great Dictator'; George Whyte-Melville was 'The Novelist of Society', although he is better known as the author of songs in praise of hunting. Sometimes, when more appropriate, or when a nickname or description did not occur to Thomas, the subject's ordinary Christian name would be used, a practice which would then have appeared cheekier than it would now, since Christian names were only used between real intimates. Opposite would be approximately a column of description, including genealogical as well as biographical details, and usually written by Thomas using the name Jehu Junior. The description would normally be outwardly polite, sometimes even sycophantic. But there would often be barbs; for instance in the 5 June 1886 issue, Sir Henry Vivian, MP for Swansea, 'speaks well and ably on the subjects he understands, and, as he dislikes speaking on any others, he rarely addresses the House'. Now and again one of these descriptions would be really interesting; the one of Tennyson on 22 July 1871 gives a view of the poet that still strikes one as shrewd, if in the end rather harsh.

The mere mention of his name awakens in every Englishman an echo of sweet sounds gently rippled into flowing verse, which lies about the chambers of the memory like the low hum of a summer afternoon . . . Nevertheless, Mr Tennyson is perhaps the poet who has done the most to teach us that there is after all no use in poetry. He lacks the blind driving passion and the fierce faith of the very greatest poets. The beautiful and the true seem to act on him, but never to enter into him.

The caricatures themselves were frank, sometimes to the point of rudeness, but almost always lively and well drawn. The first ones were by the Italian Carlo Pellegrini, who signed himself 'Ape', but others soon started appearing by Alfred Thompson, who did not sign, and by the Frenchman James Tissot, who became one of Thomas's most intimate friends. Later the cartoons were mostly by Leslie Ward, who signed himself 'Spy'. A bland description was sometimes accompanied by a vicious cartoon, as for instance the one of Henry, third Duke of Wellington, the Iron Duke's grandson (3 January 1885). The word-picture calls him 'one of the most amiable and unassuming of men' and a 'sound and determined Conservative', and respectfully describes his career in the Army and the House of Commons. The drawing shows an oaf, auburn-bearded, jowly and choleric, with arrogance in every feature of his crimson face.

Sydney was to tell Jonathan that many people thought Thomas was taking an appalling risk with the cartoons. It was thought that the subjects would find them offensive, that some might even sue. But Thomas's instinct was right, and his friends' fears were wrong. The cartoons in fact established the paper, quickly pushing up its circulation well above two thousand. Rather as the great now treasure cartoons of themselves even if they are the savage work of Scarfe or Steadman, people regarded it as a mark of distinction to have been caricatured.

The title of the magazine comes from John Bunyan's *Pilgrim's Progress*. All educated Victorians were acquainted in detail with that towering Puritan allegory, in which Vanity Fair is the place where the pilgrim, Christian, and his companions encounter hucksters dealing in the temptations of this world and in the values of what would now be called the consumer society. The allusion was rubbed in; on the title page was one quotation from *Pilgrim's Progress* – 'We buy the truth' – and on the first page of the text was another: 'That which did not a little amuse the merchandisers was, that these pilgrims set very light by all their wares.' So there was a suggestion of moral superiority in which the reader was included; we are telling you all this about the wicked world, but of course we, and you, are above it all, in the same way that Christian was above the blandishments of the hucksters. Since there can have been few readers who were not in society themselves, in one capacity or another, this was a subtle invitation to eat their cake and have it, too.

By 1870 the magazine was established and making money, but it was still only in its third year. It therefore says a good deal for Thomas's self-confidence, and even more for his confidence in his staff, that he took five months off to cover the siege of Paris for the *Morning Post*. This was the product of a sudden impulse, almost a whim. In September 1870 he was in Southampton after a sailing trip when he learned that the French Army had been routed at Sedan, Napoleon III was in the hands of the King of Prussia, and the Prussians were marching on Paris. Thomas went straight to London to get a passport, and without bothering to inform the *Morning Post* – he knew they would accept his dispatches – arrived in Paris two days after leaving Southampton. He installed himself in a commodious ten-room flat; the place came very cheap in this time of panic. He then began sending his articles to London, where of course the *Morning Post* welcomed them as manna from heaven. Some went, naturally, to *Vanity Fair*.

During Thomas's first few days in Paris he was surprised at life's normality. Some people had fled, but there were still plenty of elegant customers in the cafés on the boulevards. James Tissot turned up to stay with Thomas. The arrival of the tired and demoralized remnants of the French Army from Sedan was the first visible sign that something was amiss. Thomas saw them camping round the Arc de Triomphe in their tents, making soup or polishing their guns. He saw the fortifications arising in the Bois de Boulogne: earthworks and strong palisades. He was once taken for a Prussian because of his blondness; a beggar boy, seeing him sitting in a café, shouted out, '*C'est un Prussien!*' Thomas got up and threatened him with his stick, whereupon he ran away, and nobody else took any notice.

But soon the siege started in earnest. Thomas managed to see plenty of the fighting. He rigged himself up a kind of uniform, which caused a peasant and a French dragoon to arrest him on suspicion of being a Prussian Uhlan. They paid no attention to his pass, which perhaps they could not even read, but took him to the commander of the guard. He was equally suspicious, for he had been warned to look out for a spy, and he only released Thomas after checking with Paris by telegram. Thomas was an eye witness to an important French sortie in which they managed to retake the village of Champigny, which had been partly captured by the Prussians. On this occasion he was in some personal danger, being in the thick of the fighting. He was also present at the last French sortie, that of Buzenval on 19 January 1871. Here he managed to make himself useful, and his accounts in the *Morning Post* and in

*Vanity Fair* show his presence of mind and beneficent bossiness. He came across a farmhouse full of wounded, with only one surgeon trying to cope. The surgeon asked him to go and get some ambulance wagons. 'Of course, I had no kind of authority to do this, but I have already learnt that it does not do here to wait for authority, and people on these occasions are only too glad to be ordered about.' He does not mind admitting that he was sometimes nervous. On one occasion he visited the fort of Rosny during a Prussian bombardment, and stood on open ground talking to two generals. Suddenly he heard a shell approach and fell flat on his face. 'The shell exploded at least thirty yards off, and when I got up, covered with snow, I was disgusted with myself, all the more so because I saw that the generals had not moved.'

In Paris itself he writes at length about the food situation. This seems not, as one might expect, to have got steadily worse, but to have fluctuated, only becoming really serious at a fairly late stage. At first, at any rate, Thomas thinks that many poor people were actually better off than normally, because they were provided with subsidized meals or, if they were really destitute, even free ones. They could also join the National Guard where they had a fairly easy time. It was Thomas, as much as anyone, who spread the stories about the strange meats on which some Parisians lived during the siege. At one moment he says he is 'keeping a sharp eye on my *concierge*'s cat', and later: 'I dined off dog last night. It is much better than horse, but then it was a pet dog and only five months old; very like mutton.' Again: 'I have now dined off camel, antelope, dog, donkey, mule and elephant, which I approve in the order in which I have written them but none of which greatly captivate me.' He approves of the law forbidding the baking of white bread, finding the resulting brown bread 'delicious'. Even at this stage he already took the view, which he was to preach all his life and pass on to his children, that white flour had most of its goodness refined out of it. In his day it was rare to take this view, and the scientific reasons for it had not been established. He was guided by taste and instinct.

His view of the war is entirely pro-French. We today find this unsurprising, following two world wars against Germany, but in 1870 it was by no means universal. Being in Paris, he was of course exclusively exposed to the French viewpoint. He retails stories of Prussian atrocities, but also mentions occasions on which soldiers of the two sides fraternized; on one occasion, some French officers dined with their Prussian opposite numbers, provoking a reprimand and prohibition by the French general. Thomas himself once breakfasted pleasantly in a Paris café with four Prussian officers. The Prussians bombarded Paris, causing 296 mainly civilian casualties in one twelve-day period. This provoked a sharp condemnation from Thomas who called it 'an act of barbarism for which it would be vain to seek a parallel in civilized warfare'. Not any more, unfortunately.

# 12

# Magazine Proprietor

*Vanity Fair* did suffer a slight dip when Thomas was away at the siege of Paris, but it soon more than recovered, and over the years it became an established social diversion and political nuisance. In politics the general tone was aggressively Tory, though Thomas was too quirky for it to be quite predictable. Its most popular feature, after the cartoon, was probably the gossip. Not all of this was hostile or catty; a good deal was neutral, giving notices of coming-of-age parties or even details of gamebags at some of the important shoots. That these should have been thought worth recording in a London periodical shows how prominent, in those days, were the concerns of the landed gentry. Some of *Vanity Fair*'s gossip is actually deferential; although here one has to remember that since many day-to-day references are forgotten, what seems to us deferential quite often meant, and understood, as sarcastic. Again, just as unrelieved din dulls the ears, so an atmosphere of sustained satire, like that of, say, *Private Eye*, actually lessens the impact on the individual victim. A reference in *Private Eye* that is merely rude is hardly noticeable; to strike home it has to reach a very high degree of outrageousness. *Vanity Fair* could cause a given amount of offence with much greater economy of vituperative effort. Often people did indeed take offence, and Thomas used to get into hot water. Sometimes a victim would ask his club to ban *Vanity Fair* from its premises. As a rule, Thomas would get to hear of the move, and publish it, with the name of the proposer, in a subsequent number; he was also usually able to say that the move had been defeated.

One person who now and then disliked items in the magazine was the Prince of Wales, who would show his displeasure in various small ways. Once he refused to meet Lord Ronald Gower, because he wrote for *Vanity Fair*, although Gower's pieces were wholly unrelated to the gossip column. Gower was a known homosexual, and this may have been the real reason why the Prince disliked him. All the same, the ostensible reason was his connection with *Vanity Fair* and the Prince let this be known, to Thomas's fury. Another item that must have annoyed the royal family was the review of an all too sugary life of the Prince Consort by Theodore Martin, published in 1875. The book, Thomas said, was 'deplorable'; the fact that the press had given it favourable notices showed journalists to be guilty of servility. The book was 'calculated not only to lower the idea of the sovereign's personality, but to awaken notions that should be allowed to sleep'. In particular, readers of the book 'are allowed to gather at every turn that the Royal Family of England look rather to Germany than to England as their home'. On another occasion, *Vanity Fair* criticized the Prince of Wales for becoming Grand Master of the freemasons; this was rather odd coming from Thomas, who was a freemason himself. The Prince, he said, 'would do well to hold himself aloof from such vanities.'

*Vanity Fair* seems rarely, if ever, to have been sued for libel. There was, however, an occasion in 1884 when an enraged reader physically attacked Thomas and fought with him in the street. The attacker was Lord Marcus Beresford, who curiously enough was the brother of one of Thomas's closest friends, the future Admiral Lord Charles Beresford. Lord Charles never seems to have held it against Thomas that he quarrelled with his brother. The background to the incident was that Lord Marcus had been appointed by a certain Colonel Trevelyan as trustee for an annual maintenance payment to his estranged wife. The money was not being paid, with the result that Mrs Trevelyan was virtually destitute. She had taken to the bottle, been in the workhouse, and found herself in prison for making a disturbance outside Lord Marcus's house. Colonel Trevelyan held that she was in breach of certain conditions under which the money was granted, and that Lord Marcus's relationship with Mrs Trevelyan was more than that of a normal trustee. *Vanity Fair* published a highly coloured article about Mrs Trevelyan's sufferings. Why, it asked, 'if Lord Marcus was her trustee, does he not force Colonel Trevelyan to keep his wife from starvation?' This was followed by a letter in the next issue, signed 'E.O.P', which was more explicit still, saying that Beresford was, 'we may suppose, too much occupied in more congenial pursuits to trouble himself about the lady in whom, perhaps, he once took a more lively interest'.

This last crack stung Lord Marcus into action. Armed with a stick, he went round in a cab to the *Vanity Fair* office, at which he was told that Thomas had not yet arrived, so he sat down to wait for two hours, a circumstance that did nothing to improve his temper. He also had a group of his friends present. In the meantime, one of the *Vanity Fair* clerks went to warn Thomas that Lord Marcus was outside the office, and in truculent mood. When Thomas reached the office there was a fist fight in which, if anything, Thomas seems to have had the best of it, though the position was obscured by partisans of Lord Marcus at one point restraining Thomas, and clerks from the *Vanity Fair* office at another point holding back Lord Marcus. It is worth noting that the partisans of each protagonist confined themselves to restraint and perhaps verbal support, thus respecting the conventions of single combat. A Welsh doctor, up in London for the day, happened to be present at the scene; he said that he saw a stick used, though was uncertain by whom. Thomas sued Lord Marcus for assault, and the Welsh doctor is thought to have helped secure Lord Marcus's acquittal. Perhaps it is more likely that the jury was influenced by Thomas's evident skill, and relish, in defending himself and hitting back. The suspicion may even have arisen that he rather enjoyed the whole affair. The court was thronged with spectators, including Mrs Trevelyan, and the press, of course, had a field day. On the whole, as was perhaps to be expected, they were on Thomas's side.

But there was much more to *Vanity Fair* than gossip; Thomas was not only passionately interested in politics, but also had a keen eye for just about everything else that was going on, whether in literature, art, theatre or sport. His *bête noir* was Gladstone, and in the 7 October 1871 issue he wrote:

If Mr Gladstone is not as thick skinned as a rhinoceros, he must surely have been deeply hurt at the tone of the Irish press in reference to his late speech at Aberdeen. That speech is characterized with true Irish energy as 'bitter, untruthful and malicious'. . . . And yet with all this the Irish nation appears to have boundless faith in Mr Gladstone . . . because he is subject to sudden and miraculous conversions. He was one of the stoutest defenders of the Established Church in Ireland – he was one of the most determined foes of the Ballot – what is he now? Only let old Father Time have fair play, and with a little pressure, Mr Gladstone will come round to anything that anybody wants of him – anybody, that is, who is strong enough to threaten.

This is a fair sample; and it was, of course, prophetic, since Gladstone was indeed to become converted to the cause of Irish Home Rule. Thomas regarded Gladstone as a consummate hypocrite, his high-mindedness as a cunningly constructed mask for self-interest and lust for power. Disraeli once said something to the effect that he did not so much mind Gladstone always having the ace of trumps up his sleeve as his invariable claim that it was the Almighty who put it there. These were Thomas's sentiments. He accused Gladstone, as the right has always accused the left, of invariably preferring foreign interests to those of his own country. On a pettier level, he taunted him with being an abject snob. In 1874 he wrote: Gladstone 'is . . . a middle-class man who falls down flat on his face before a title. A Tory Minister could do no more than he has done either for the aristocracy or for the cause of nepotism.' This was written before the days of Lord Salisbury and Arthur Balfour, against whom thirty years later he was to make the same accusation, more damagingly.

Thomas's denunciation of Gladstone was at its most intense at the time of General Charles Gordon's disastrous expedition to Khartoum, ending in his death in 1885. Thomas knew Gordon and considered him 'the most notable living Englishman'. Gordon was also a great favourite with the public. Very many people besides Thomas regarded his abandonment as shameful, and Gladstone was regarded by some as a murderer. An embarrassing incident took place at a children's party in the British embassy in Paris. A small girl called Violet Freeman was there with her brother; their father worked at the embassy. When Mrs Gladstone was announced Violet's brother seized her by the arm and whispered: 'Under the table! Quick!' The two dived under the cloth. Naturally the ambassadress noticed their absence, and soon found them cowering in their hiding place. As they got up rather shamefacedly, she asked what they had been up to. 'Well,' said Violet's brother, 'we know Mr Gladstone is a murderer, and we were afraid Mrs Gladstone might be one, too.' Mrs Gladstone had been well within earshot, and the ambassadress turned to her. 'Home politics!' she said, apologetically. Violet grew up to be a great friend of Sydney's, and we shall meet her later as Mrs Hammersley, an important figure in the lives of all the seven Mitfords as confidante, playmate, correspondent, fan, critic and occasional butt. *Vanity Fair* did a great deal to contribute to the atmosphere which caused the Freeman children to conceal themselves. On 2 January 1886, for instance, it said:

A column and a half of the newspapers yesterday were taken up by a list of the idiots who had written or telegraphed to congratulate Mr Gladstone on the attainment of his seventy-sixth birthday. I am sure I am very glad that Mr Gladstone is seventy-six. I should be better pleased if he were ninety-six, or for that matter, a hundred and six, for the older he is the sooner we are likely to see the termination of the most mischievous career of modern times.

This seems petty and rather spiteful. Bertie, who opposed Gladstone quite as much as did Thomas, is more gracious; in *Memories* he credits Gladstone with 'a marvellous power over language' and adding, of Gladstone's last Home Rule bill: 'The Niagara of words, the overpowering cataract of eloquence, stupefied and dismayed, but it did not convince me.' (Vol. 2 p. 550.) *Memories* was written in Bertie's old age, but even in his prime we do not think he would have expressed himself as Thomas did.

One original political feature of *Vanity Fair* in its earlier years was called 'Both Sides'. In this, a question of the day was debated, for and against, by named supporters and opponents, and the arguments were presented opposite each other in double columns. Most of the questions dealt with are, of course, by now of interest only to academic historians, if even to them. But sometimes one finds arguments that are still trotted out today. On 5 August 1871, under the heading 'Should a life annuity of £15,000 be granted to Prince Arthur?', we might be reading about a controversy of our own time, though no government today would dare to recommend a payment of, say, £300,000 a year to a junior member of the royal family, which would be more or less equivalent. Mr

Gladstone, Mr Disraeli, and Colonel Beresford, 'as spokesmen of 289 members of the House of Commons', say 'yes', that is both government and opposition. Mr P. A. Taylor, Mr Dixon and Sir W. Lawson, as spokesmen of fifty-one presumably Radical Liberal members of the House of Commons, say 'no'. Gladstone and Co. point out that 'Her Majesty on ascending the throne relinquished the possession of a large estate, and the civil list was a settlement in lieu thereof, and one not to her Majesty's advantage', and the republicans reply: 'If this institution of royalty is necessary, the people have already found money enough for it.' The government considers that £15,000 is moderate because it is less than the average income of the House of Lords, the Radicals talk about the existence 'side by side with these enormous incomes of that poverty which we are all seeking to remove'; and so on. Another 'Both Sides' earlier in the same year, on 29 July, deals with a proposal to introduce the metric system; this controversy was still alive despite Milner-Gibson's failure to make the change in the 1860s.

Early in 1885 Thomas launched a magazine for women, *The Lady*. It was second in the field, the *Queen* being already in existence, but it was a success and made money from the start. It has also proved astonishingly durable, still remaining as a private concern in the ownership of two of Thomas's grandchildren. It has also changed remarkably slowly in appearance, and very little in essence, though its main function is by now as a medium for small advertisements; it is the *Dalton's Weekly* of the gentry.

One friend who gave Thomas some advice on the initial advertising of *The Lady* was Lewis Carroll, in real life the Reverend Charles Lutwidge Dodgson, mathematics don at Christ Church. A letter from Dodgson to Thomas, dated 12 January 1885, makes quite a shrewd point. 'I would suggest the omission of the dogma, "To look beautiful is one of the first duties of a lady" . . . The maid does not need to be thus counselled; and to the elderly, whose charms are matters of history, such words are a mockery.'

Dodgson was rather an unexpected friend of Thomas; in most ways he could scarcely have been more different. About nineteen years Thomas's senior, he was a shy, unworldly man who found refuge from the terrors of society in deeply conventional views, a strong religious faith, and the scrupulous practice of celibacy. Had he lived in a Roman Catholic country, he would probably have been a monk. The cloistered existence of a Victorian academic suited him, though he gave up lecturing undergraduates as soon as he decently could, and had early in life discovered that keeping order in a class of boys in a secondary school was beyond him. The contrast between Dodgson and the sociable, worldly and far from celibate Thomas was considerable. Dodgson even hated the sea which Thomas loved so much. His 'Sea Dirge' was entirely sincere:

> Pour some salt water over the floor,
> Ugly I'm sure you'll allow it to be:
> Suppose it extended a mile or more,
> That would be like the sea.

But it is obvious why they liked each other. They both loved jokes and they made each other laugh.

Possibly Dodgson's only worldly amusement was the theatre, which he loved and attended regularly, though he was worried that some productions were not suitable for the fair sex. He suggested in 1877 that Thomas should publish a '*Vanity Fair* play-bill', 'with a list of all amusements to which ladies might safely be taken, and a warning against objectionable plays'. Thomas did nothing about this; even in those days, the idea would have made him a laughing stock. On at least one occasion there was difficulty between them. Dodgson was a fanatical opponent of smoking, whereas Thomas believed tobacco to be 'the harmless, necessary friend to all', as he wrote in *Vanity Fair* on 3 January 1885. One evening in 1879 Thomas was staying with Dodgson in Christ Church, and when they got back to his rooms after dinner he asked if he could smoke a pipe. His politeness in asking did not turn aside Dodgson's wrath. 'You know I don't allow smoking here,' said his host, and turned him out to have his pipe on the cold, dark stairs, where another don called Strong found him disconsolately puffing away. Strong took him away to his own rooms and entertained him for the rest of the evening. Thomas took no umbrage; he was unconventional enough to respect the eccentricity of others. The two remained good friends. In 1891, Dodgson gave Sydney, then eleven years old, a copy of

*Alice's Adventures Underground*, the first version of *Alice in Wonderland*. Stuck in the front is a tiny envelope containing a very Carrollian letter beginning as follows:

My *dear* Sydney,

I *am* so sorry, and so ashamed! Do you know, I didn't even know of your *existence*? And it was *such* a surprise to hear that you had sent me your love! It felt just as if Nobody had suddenly come into the room, and had given me a kiss! (That's a thing that happens to me, *most* days, just now.) If only I had known you were existing, I should have sent you *heaps* of love, long ago. And, now I come to think of it, I ought to have sent you the love, without being so particular about whether you existed or not. In *some* ways, you know, people that *don't* exist, are much nicer than those that do . . .

# 13

# A Master Mariner and His Reflections

A key to Thomas Bowles's character and beliefs lay in his love of the sea. When he was a boy, his father taught him to handle sailing ships as an expert and navigate like a professional. All his life he was at his happiest with seafaring men, whether the fishermen of the Suffolk coast whom he came to know as a boy, or the ratings and officers of the Royal Navy whose cause, as a politician, he was so consistently to champion. 'They who go down to the sea in ships' were the only people whom, as a class, Thomas really respected. He became an expert on sea law and naval strategy, and thought that sailing was unrivalled both as a hobby and as a means of forming character.

He was first of all a practical seaman, obtaining his master mariner's certificate in 1874. He worked hard for the examination and was delighted by his success. It was, in fact, remarkable to have achieved it in such a busy life, for there was a large quantity of information to absorb. In *Flotsam and Jetsam* he alludes to his time sitting the examination, saying that he has

. . . passed the last two days at St Katherine's Docks engrossed in calculating problems of navigation and nautical astronomy. It will add nothing to my stature and I know it. But yet I have already faced two pent-up days of meridian and ex-meridian altitudes, azimuths, amplitudes and Napier's diagrams, and am going to face the Board of Trade knows how many more, merely for a bit of paper, which will be of no use, heavenly or earthly, to me when I get it . . .

The last remark is not to be taken at face value. It was not only for his own private satisfaction that he wanted the certificate, but also in order that the seafarers whose opinion he so much valued should accept him as one of them. In the sense that his gainful occupation was always on land, he would never be anything but an amateur sailor; but he made very sure that he would have the skills of a professional, and the proof of those skills in the form of a qualification.

His yacht in 1874 and for some years after was the *Billy Baby*, crewed by three men from Aldeburgh of whom the skipper was Ned Kersey. The yachts would change from time to time, but Ned was a fixture, remaining in Thomas's service for more than forty years; he would be in charge of the yacht all the year round, hiring other Aldeburgh men as necessary when a cruise was planned. Every now and then someone would drop out and a replacement would be taken on, reluctantly as far as Thomas and Ned were concerned, from some other port. This tended not to be a success. The beauty of Aldeburgh was that it was a fishing port, and a small one, where Ned Kersey knew all the men and their families. Fishermen, Thomas thought, were real sailors, uncorrupted by contact with fashionable yacht owners, for whom Thomas felt great contempt. Part of the value of the master's certificate was that it provided documentary proof that he was superior to them. In *Flotsam and Jetsam* he wrote extolling his three North Sea fishermen in the *Billy Baby*. '. . . three men who have passed their lives among stern realities, who are ready and brave, true and intelligent, and who have not been demoralized by a daily consumption of platitude and sophistry. Not from Cowes are they, nor like the men of Cowes, who have been demoralized thus and by other means, but fresh from the Dogger, with all their rough honesty upon them.'

*Flotsam and Jetsam* is put together from the thoughts which occurred to him on various cruises from 1874 to 1882, when it was published. Naylor dismisses it as a 'light-hearted effort', but it is more than that, though it is discursive and uneven. Thomas by no means confines himself to his thoughts about the sea and ships. He writes also of politics and society and religion and just about everything under the sun. It is an opportunity to see his mind at rest and reflective. His journalistic writings and polemics show it in action, engaged on various causes and taking various stands, often ephemeral in interest and not always mutually compatible. *Flotsam and Jetsam* articulates his beliefs as a coherent philosophy of life and shows that he is something more than a showman and run-of-the-mill eccentric. It gives some idea of the nature of his conversation, which Sydney regards as having taught her more than her lessons did, and of which so many different people were to remember the instructiveness and the sparkle.

At the beginning of the book, before setting off on his 1874 cruises, he has been reading John Stuart Mill's autobiography, and this starts him off on a rumination about man's essential solitude. A real man, he says, is always alone in the world. If he thinks he has found a mate in any true sense, he is suffering from an illusion. Mill thought he had found a mate, 'and labours touchingly to prove her such; but to my mind he fails as touchingly'. It is not that Thomas regards all relationships between people as illusory. He accepts hierarchy, that is relationships between higher and lower, and also what he calls 'trusteeship'. On hierarchy (not the word he uses), he thinks that a man's character marks out for him 'a little platform of his own just broad enough for the sole of his foot. Another cannot stand *there* with him, though many be above and some perhaps below. If he be the real man, that place is his and his alone: he is a separate being and principle, and as such he can have no companion.' This is the same insight as was to be expressed by Robert Ardrey: 'I do not have to be number one to be happy; number six will do.' Fiercely as he loves freedom, Thomas does not fall for anarchism. That each man is unique does not imply that all men are kings. As to trusteeship, this for him covers family relationships and ought also to govern commercial ones, and he sees it as having nothing to do with self-interest. He apostrophizes Jeremy Bentham, apostle of Utilitarianism:

Jeremy, thou wast a noodle . . . Here is Ned, for instance, roused at three in the morning, and now striving all he knows to make out that black buoy. Yes, I do pay him a salary . . . but is he not a trustee for his old mother at Aldeburgh, to whom he is going to send a post-office order for one pound ten this very day, and also for his young woman, whom he intends some day to endow with the scanty bliss of a seaman's marital attentions – nay, even for the fabricator of those sea boots and the Chinaman grower of that tea which makes me shudder, but which he gulps down with so much gusto? All for self? What, even his young woman? Then self has no longer a meaning, and we are stumbling as usual over words.

This is not really a refutation of Bentham. It is rather a plea for human relationships to be regarded not as purely mechanical or mathematical.

Thomas rejoices in the British climate. 'Here, while I have been looking from my deck at this decayed, sordid town of Poole, have I seen in ten minutes at least half a dozen different cities in it, each with its particular tone of beauty, and all various. They say it is like Venice, wherein they are wrong, for it is far better and more beautiful to look at . . .' We have already noted Thomas's view that labour is not really a curse but a blessing. What is a curse, in his view, is not work as such but monotony, and the feeling, which monotonous work engenders, that work should be alternated not with other occupations but with rest. He hated the concept of the holiday:

It is an utter blunder to suppose that men do their work well in inverse proportion to its amount. The capacity of man for work is almost unlimited; but then it must be work of a varying kind, each kind holding its proper place. To expect any human creature to work nine hours a day making pins' heads is one form of insanity – to expect to relieve him by half a Saturday of stagnation, a Sunday of church, and eight hours at the seaside for half-a-crown is another.

Work for Thomas ought to be the occasion of *striving* and where possible also of *risk*. His love of striving leads him to express a point of view very close to that which makes Goethe see the continuing willingness to strive, not to be content, as qualification for the salvation of his Faust. We are also reminded of Tennyson's Ulysses: 'To strive, to seek, to find, and not to yield.' But he likes striving less because it is meritorious than because it is fun:

What moments are there like those when, bracing your nerves and setting your teeth, you rejoice as a giant refreshed, to run the race before you and feel the distance disappearing beneath your feet? Not the triumph of the victory, still less the repose on the other side of the goal – for that is but a kind of death between the races in which alone you feel that you really live.

Again, he believes that pictures of vessels at sea should not show them, as is customary, under full sail and with a fair breeze, but 'close-hauled in a gale of wind, beating up for port against a head sea'. In yet another passage he says:

When the soldier-spirit burns in a man, he thinks it sufficient to be Napoleon; if he is in philanthropic mood, he conceives that he may do as much as Howard; if a statesman, he may reach as high as Sully or Pitt; if an artist, as far as Michael Angelo [sic]; if a poet, he would emulate Dante or Shakespeare. Yet these men are themselves the proof that this is not enough. *They* reached at something higher than themselves . . . Is this not . . . an argument, if any were needed, to prove the necessity for that mysterious presentiment of the Best which we call God?

He enjoys the flow of adrenaline, noting after a river collision: 'Feeling injured and being angry for five minutes' is 'one of the greatest luxuries I know'. Fear is another luxury: '. . . there is nothing in existence equal to the sweetness of sailing within an ace of the greatest possible danger and yet coming off untouched'. He believes it is a mistake in contemporary clergy to cast doubt on the existence of hell. 'If a religion does not make you feel that it has enabled you to sail close round destruction and yet to weather it, men will content themselves with natural philosophy.'

He makes no bones about the joys of chasing women, and, in accordance with his preference for striving even over achievement, it is in particular the chase that he extols.

I have often asked myself which is the most pleasing stage in a successful love-making, whether the going forth to the encounter when as yet one knows not what one's fate will be in it; the first encouragements, so slight and delicate as to be imperceptible to all but one's own eye; the open avowal mutually given and received; or the final admitted lover-state. The common theory is that this last stage is the best because it gives the least trouble and anxiety; yet I should say that the first stage is by far better, precisely because it gives the most . . .

In more sedate mood, he savours the pleasures of the table. Putting in at Dieppe, he finds that at the Hôtel Royal, everyone turns out to welcome him when he goes to dine there, and

. . . asked me affectionately all round after my health and my doings, and provided me with a *sauce hollandaise*, which was like eating the kingdom of heaven. I remember an old French gourmet once said to me '*Jeune homme, quand vous aurez épuisé les délices de l'amour, des affaires, de la politique et de la religion, vous finirez comme moi par vous rabattre sur la cuisine*'. [Young man, when you have exhausted the pleasures of love, business, politics and religion you will, like me, end by falling back on those of the table.] I began to fancy I must have already arrived at that stage.

Certainly, the gastronomic delights across the Channel were always a strong reason for traversing it. Food was important to Thomas. He by no means shared the puritanical aversion to thinking and talking about food that made Victorian Britain proverbial throughout Europe as a gastronomic wasteland.

But eupeptic though Thomas was, he was also compassionate and had a lively social conscience, though of a type more typical of his time than of ours. He fully recognized that there was an obligation to be charitable: 'Shall we say, when the wretched cries for alms, that we have paid our poor-rate?' he asks. 'Are we to reply that his claim to a living share of the earth's fruits is a claim on the whole of society, and that we have discharged our quota? Not so.' This rejects, on grounds not of meanness but of generosity, the logic that now underlies the welfare state. It is a demand for the inclusion of a sincerely felt impulse in the duty to our neighbour, thus essentially an insistence on the involvement of the individual will. It is as far as possible from Beatrice Webb's feeling that giving only has merit when we do *not* want to do it, let alone Marx's idea that it is better when the workers are treated badly, since it will excite their collective spirit to overturn the system. Quite as clearly as these two, however, he saw what was wrong with laissez-faire capitalism: the fact that the employer's only obligation to his workpeople was to pay their wages, that there was no commitment to look after them in sickness and old age, as there had been in feudal times.

Is it not strange that men should be found who can amass a fortune out of the blood and bone of their fellows, and who yet thoroughly believe that they have no duties to fulfil towards them? I know a good dozen who . . . have taken from . . . thousands that lifetime of toil, which is all the toiler's wealth, and who will calmly stand by and see the executioner Hunger step in to make an end of what little life there is left in them . . . Surely, this is breaking the bargain.

Here is the voice of Tory radicalism; the argument that was to be picked up by socialists such as R. H. Tawney. As might be expected, Thomas was particularly angry when it was an injury to the interests of sailors that offended his social conscience. The authorities had recently turned Greenwich Hospital from a home for old sailors to a college for naval officers, and he was indignant, seeing it as 'the perpetual old shameful tale of taking from him that hath not and giving to him that hath. Thus did they three hundred years ago with those lands of the Church which had equally been set apart for ever to the pious uses of God and the poor.'

He deplores the English class system.

How thoroughly the belief – once so strong – has died out, that Englishmen are all men of the same nation, brothers of the same family, bound to stick together against the world if need be! We are now, it appears, brothers only of those of our 'class'. The 'gentlemen' are of one race, the middling classes of another, the working classes of yet another . . . And then the gentlemen and the other 'classes' make themselves up into infinite subdivisions, each of which is as alien to the other as all are to each . . . I have heard of a house in that condition.

He means, of course, the house divided against itself, which the Bible says will fall. It is a shock to find him, as early as 1882, describing what Belloc was to call Britain's 'hoary social curse' as strongly as this: but it must be remembered that Britain had long been at peace, and long periods of safety always accentuate internal divisions that can vanish quickly at the appearance of an external enemy, in men as in prairie dogs. His distaste for these divisions, and the unthinking snobbery that accompanied them, was accentuated by his great respect for working people, particularly his Aldeburgh seamen. They are not uneducated, he says, but

. . . thoroughly well educated; their whole powers, mental and physical, are cultivated and developed by them in the very highest degree for the work they have to do in life . . . When members of Parliament know as much of history and statesmanship as ploughmen do of ploughing; when ministers can conduct a negotiation as safely as a hansom cab-driver guides his cab, or a bargeman his lighter; when parsons have brought their light to shine before men as bright and as true under all circumstances as a few common sailors keep the Varne or the Owers in all weathers; when judges steer as true a course by the law as Ned will by the compass; and when ladies have learnt to wear their dresses as well as their sempstresses stitch them – then I shall listen with more patience to them when they talk of others being uneducated.

But it is as individuals that he respects people, workers included; he is deeply distrustful of human beings in groups. Not for him Hegel's 'idea' or Marx's class-consciousness which are supposed to inspire men in the mass to achieve progress. On the contrary, he holds that membership of a group causes people to behave worse than as individuals.

A man hesitates to be a liar, a traitor, a thief or a spoiler purely on his own account, and taking all his own risks; but he will readily lie as the editor of a newspaper, betray his country in complicity with a party, steal money as the financier of a company, or remove his neighbour's landmark in the ranks of an army . . . We seem to think that when we follow a multitude to do evil, the evil thereby becomes good.

This aversion to collectivism was a constant in his thinking; it was much later to make him leave the Conservative Party when it had been, as he saw it, corrupted by the ideas of Joseph Chamberlain. Just how any fairness could be achieved without some form of collective action was a question which this archetypal individualist was never properly to face. No wonder he was happiest on the sea, sailing wherever he felt inclined in the company of his valued and familiar crew, feeling under his feet the movement of the vessel he, himself, had made sure was well found, his keen blue eyes now studying his familiar instruments, now scanning the wide horizon.

# 14

# Marriage, Children and Bereavement

In the early 1870s Thomas seriously courted Jessica Cavendish-Bentinck, a cousin of the Duke of Portland; but in 1874 she married Sir Henry Tatton Sykes ('rich old Sir Tatton of Yorkshire,' as Sydney describes him). He was to marry not this Jessica, but another. One day, probably in 1874, when Thomas was cruising in the *Billy Baby* in Southampton Water, he called on the governor of the Netley Military Hospital, Major-General Charles Evans-Gordon. The General was a widower with a grown-up family of seven; besides five sons there were two daughters, who were both at home. The elder, Frances, ran the General's household. The younger, Jessica, was in her early twenties: tall, slim and fair-haired, she was musical and able, as so many Victorian young ladies were, to sing romantic songs and accompany herself prettily on the piano. Thomas fell in love with her on that first visit and began paying court; it soon became apparent that she returned his affection.

The Evans-Gordons claimed some connection with the sixth Viscount Kenmure, who was executed after the failure of the 1745 rebellion and lost his titles through attainder. The original name was Gordon; Evans was attached in a later generation. The General and his sons did not exactly smile on Thomas's suit. It need not be supposed that this was wholly due to family pride, although Thomas may not have seemed a particularly creditable connection, being a parvenu and born out of wedlock to boot. Their objections probably had most to do with Thomas's personal manner. Success had certainly by that time increased his natural ebullience; the manner which was to annoy Lady Clementine Mitford was well on the way to developing. He never lost his power to charm, but became rude when views were expressed with which he did not agree. His own views, too, were often odd. 'Don't . . . talk . . . such . . . RUBBISH,' was a remark, Sydney tells us, 'that he often made in a loud voice, so that people looked around.' This description is of a later period in his life, it is true, but Thomas was already Thomas. The conventional gentility of an old military family was not an environment where he would have been likely to fit in, especially as prospective son-in-law. Consistency of behaviour and conventionality of views were expected there; Thomas's charm and originality were at best at a discount, his want of tact a mortal sin. He may well, on occasion, have contradicted the General himself. At one time he was actually forbidden to enter the house.

However, both Thomas and Jessica were determined on the match. She was of age, he was able to support her, and there was nothing her family could do except give way, and put as good a face on it as they were able. The marriage took place in 1876. Jessica took some time to forgive her family for their opposition, and relations were cool at first with some, at least, of them. However, what rift there was healed in due course. Sydney recalls that her uncle Henry Evans-Gordon's four daughters were great friends of her childhood. The youngest, Margaret, 'was such a rare wit that we began bursting with laughter almost before she opened her mouth'. Margaret was to marry Arthur, Lord Stanley of Alderley, son of Lyulph; that this humorist should marry into the Stanley family is an example of what biologists call assortative mating.

Thomas and Jessica were very happy and deeply in love. They settled at Cleeve Lodge, in Kensington near the Albert Hall, a pleasant and spacious Regency house with nearly an acre of garden. At one time Thomas kept chickens there, to the distress of their neighbour, the Duchess of Grafton, who wrote complaining that his cock's crowing got on her nerves. His lengthy reply detailed a number of reasons why he did not think it could be his cock that was annoying the Duchess, and ended by saying that he was confirmed in his belief by the fact that the bird had been killed and eaten three months before. Cleeve Lodge is the first of Sydney's *Five Houses*, her manuscript which we have found the most useful source of information about Thomas's life as a family man. Four children were born. First came two boys,

George and Geoffrey, then two girls. Sydney, the elder, was named after Sydney Milner-Gibson, Thomas's much loved half-sister, who had died at the age of nineteen. The other was Dorothy, or Weenie; to later generations Aunt Weenie, a nickname so invariably used that we did not discover her Christian name until after we had started research on this book.

Jessica was not really cut out for maternity, either physically or temperamentally. In a letter of June 1880, not long after she had given birth to Sydney, she tells Thomas: 'To leave all and follow you is my desire, no consideration comes really before that. It is you who wish to place children, household, and many things first in my heart and I who have always rebelled against them, and told you that . . . I married you to be with you.' It was his political career that she followed with most interest; she advised him on his speaking technique, recommending that his impromptu remarks should be truly impromptu and that he should try to be 'himself'. She also expressed views on his magazines. On one occasion in 1886 she is 'glad you have postponed the *Lady*'s demise by making her 3d. . . . *Of course* your mere presence gives a different and better tone to your business. I only wonder that it gets on anything like so well as it does the months and months you are away from it.' She was delicate; quite often her letters show her as suffering from some unspecified ailment, or recovering from it. Once she expresses a complaint at renewed pregnancy. The letter is undated, but it must have been written when she first knew she was carrying either Geoffrey or more probably Sydney. A lady friend, she says, had told her that the conception 'was sure to happen . . . from your coming to see me so very soon after my confinement. Of course I knew that it was dangerous so I told you, but it would certainly have happened sooner or later. I never had any faith in you about it. Only if you could have managed to wait two or three months I might have been able to take other precautions for myself which I dare not do so soon.' George, Geoffrey and Sydney were all born within four years, though after Sydney's arrival in 1880 Jessica does seem to have persuaded Thomas to be more circumspect, because there was an interval of five years before Dorothy's birth in 1885.

Had she needed to look after the children herself, Jessica might have found it hard to cope. As it was, Sydney remembers her as

kind, if rather remote, and her letters reveal her as affectionate
and solicitous. Sydney pictures her in her drawing room, rather
overfurnished in Victorian chinoiserie; usually she reclined on a
sofa. She died when Sydney was seven, but even before then
Sydney testifies that of their two parents it was Thomas who took
the main part in the children's life and upbringing. The day-to-
day care, of course, was in the hands of nurses and governesses,
but they were expected to follow certain directions which he
devised. One governess was to become important: Rita Shell, to
be known as Tello. By a strange coincidence, her father had
been Henry Reveley Mitford's bailiff at Exbury on the Solent,
and the family came to know her in 1880 or 1881 when they were
renting a house called Inchmery, in a part of the New Forest
belonging to the Exbury estate. (Sydney was born at Inchmery.)
Rita Shell would then have been in her late teens, a tall, serious,
attractive girl, educated for some reason in Germany and highly
accomplished. She was, Sydney says, 'the friend of all'; Jessica in
one of her letters describes her as a 'treasure'. She left some time
before Jessica's death, to be succeeded by a 'nonentity' (Sydney
again), but this was not to be the end of her part in the family's
life.

It was a fifth pregnancy that killed Jessica on 12 June 1887, at
the age of thirty-five. Sydney says that she did not really want yet
another child; no doubt she knew that her health might not permit
it. One wonders what exactly was chronically wrong with her.
From Sydney we hear of the sofa, not the sickbed. Could her
being 'delicate' have sprung partly from an attitude of mind? If it
did, it is noteworthy that Thomas, with his firm belief in what
would now be called the power of positive thinking, did not try
harder to bounce her out of it. This is no doubt because he was
not only in love with this stately, languid creature, but also
slightly in awe of her — too much so to subject her to the
beneficent bossiness with which he was normally so free, especially in matters of health. He never tried to persuade her to
follow the health rules he followed himself and applied to the
children; he never encouraged her, for instance, to accompany him
on his morning rides in Hyde Park. There was a tendency in those
times to regard poor health as interesting and attractive; the
attitude was lampooned, as in W. S. Gilbert's song about the pale

young curate, but it would not have been lampooned if it had not existed. In women, neurasthenia appeared to some Victorians as a manifestation of the Eternal Feminine.

Jessica's attitude to the fifth pregnancy was outwardly cheerful. She writes on 14 February 1887: 'I am not well and although my ideas on this subject have passed into a joke with you I believe this time that I am in for Number 5 . . . Once I am over the first part I don't care and you I know would be glad if I am right.' But the same letter of April that talks of a cough also mentions 'my other trouble'. (A tendency to haemorrhage?) In any case she fell seriously ill at Cleeve Lodge one day in early June 1887 and called a doctor, who on his own responsibility and while Thomas was at the office performed an abortion to save her life. Thomas returned and, in a rage, turned the doctor out of the house. She died a few days later. We shall never know if she could have been saved; either, as Thomas evidently thought, by not having the operation, or, once it had been performed, by the doctor being permitted to care for her. Certainly the event confirmed Thomas's suspicion of the medical profession. Someone of a more intro-verted nature might have blamed himself, either for expelling the doctor or for getting Jessica pregnant again. This was not Thomas's way; he blamed the doctor instead.

His grief was unaffected and unmitigated. Sydney records that she was sent in to see him in his room and that he, usually so welcoming to all his children, was like a stranger and did not want her. She remembered the funeral to the end of her life as a terrible experience, always recalled to her by the smell of stephanotis. Shortly afterwards Thomas sold Cleeve Lodge and moved with his family to the country. The fact that he was able to do this and run his magazines from outside London, in the days before the telephone was available, is clear evidence of the stability and smooth organization which his business had achieved. Sydney thinks he moved from London because of grief at his wife's death, but in fact he was already contemplating the move before this happened. Jessica, in a letter of 14 March 1887, approves the idea of letting Cleeve Lodge and taking a house in the country for three years. The fact that he sold the house rather than merely letting it may indeed have been caused by her death.

*

Even before Jessica's death, the pattern of life of Thomas and the children was well established. Sydney describes it in *Five Houses*, and Dorothy in two articles published in *The Times*. As with his clothes when he was a young man, he had it all worked out. In Sydney's words:

The early hours of the day were devoted to what he called getting rid of his body; exercise in the open air, food, dressing and bath. The rest of the day could then be devoted to things of the mind. At six he got up and made himself a tiny cup of Turkish coffee and then worked until nine, when his horse was at the door and he went for a ride in the Row until half past ten. We children would hear him come in, and I would be sent for to 'help him to dress' and to rush down to tell Etienne, our French cook: 'Breakfast in twenty minutes.' In the summer his breakfast was laid under a tree in the garden; and one of us was always present to run, if necessary, with some message of praise or blame to Etienne. It was very seldom that we were given a taste of anything (our breakfast was at the more usual hour of eight o'clock) but we had pleasant conversation. For me it was a break in lessons. But no lessons or anything else were ever allowed to stand in the way of Tap's requirements . . . The breakfast was delicious, or, if it were not, Etienne would know the reason why. There was generally a grilled cutlet, or a dish of eggs scrambled *au jus* or with tomatoes, and a dish of vegetables. With this he drank China tea . . .

This meal was lunch as well as breakfast; Thomas ate no more until dinner in the evening.

As to the children's regime, Thomas caused to be hung up in the nursery a varnished and printed card with a number of rules of which Sydney could remember five:

1. The window is to be open day and night six inches at the top.
2. The children are to have no medicine of any sort.
3. The children are not allowed to eat pig, rabbit, hare or shell-fish.
4. The children are not to eat between meals.
5. The children are to be rinsed in clean water before getting out of their bath.

The nurses, says Sydney, 'paid as little attention as they dared to these rules'. The first rule, the open window, would today be thought unremarkable, if somewhat spartan, but it was then unusual. There was in particular a feeling that it was unhealthy to 'let in the night air', although Florence Nightingale had sensibly pointed out, according to Sydney, that it is the only air there is at night. The prejudice may have been related to a superstition which was current in Elizabethan times that moonbeams could be harmful; the expression 'moonstruck' is a survival of this.

The rule against medicine was, Sydney says, thought by the nurses to be almost impious. She herself fully agreed with it and was to follow it with her own children. She comments: 'It was the usual custom then to give every child "a good dose" once a week; and the foundations of much ill-health were thereby laid. I am afraid our nurses, and perhaps my mother too, did occasionally disobey this order, as I can remember a stuff called Fluid Magnesia. But we were at any rate spared the horror of Gregory and Liquorice powders.'

The rule against eating pig and so on is a summary of the Jewish dietary regime incorporated in the laws of Moses, which Thomas had himself begun to observe some time before. The family even went to a kosher butcher. Thomas respected the Jews, and believed that their diet had given them the necessary health to survive persecution through the centuries. He also believed that the rules originated in ancient Egypt, since Moses is said in the Bible to have been brought up by Pharaoh's daughter and to have been 'learned in all the knowledge of the Egyptians'. He felt that observation of the laws of Moses might enable one to escape diseases whose origins were so far unknown – a theory which today seems ironical in one who was always a defender and partisan of tobacco.

The rule against eating between meals would, of course, have been to the taste of the nurses; it is the only one of the group which is entirely conventional. On the other hand, the injunction to rinse the children after their bath was never, to Sydney's recollection, obeyed. It is of a piece with Thomas's passion for cleanliness, and distrust of mere superficial washing, which made him take Turkish baths every week, when he could. He thought, as Dorothy recalled in her first *Times* article, that in a conventional bath 'you soaked the dirt off yourself and then sponged it on again'. He passed this feeling on to his children. Sydney was mildly shocked when Jonathan, aged about fourteen, told her he had never had a Turkish bath. 'Oh, darling, haven't you really? I must speak to your mother.'

These five are only a selection from Thomas's rules. There was, as Sydney makes clear elsewhere, another important one: namely that no child should ever be forced to eat something he or she did not want. This was also to be enjoined by Sydney in her household and carried to considerable lengths; legend has it that Unity subsisted on nothing but milk, chocolate and bananas for a whole year. Diana also prescribed it with her children, sometimes managing to override the feelings of those in direct charge, though sometimes failing, for the forced feeding of children remained almost as fashionable in the 1930s as in the 1880s. Thomas's opposition to it fits in with the underlying principle of his health theories which was that nature knows best. 'Trust the Good Body' was his slogan; if a child does not want something, it is for a good, instinctive reason.

The family had no regular orthodox doctor of medicine, at any rate after Jessica's death. Their usual attendant was a Swede called Kellgren who was indeed known as Doctor, but by pure courtesy, for he had no degree. He was primarily what would now be called an osteopath, although he seems not to have learned from the school of osteopathy as it was already developing in the United States. Besides manipulating the joints, he gave massage. He also prescribed exercises on the Swedish system. He was something of a faith healer, and sometimes practised the laying on of hands. One technique of his recalls the Christian Scientists; he used to rally the patient by assuring him that his illness was imaginary. Sydney says: ' "You are awfully vell," was a great saying of his; rather annoying when we felt awfully ill.' At a later date Sydney was to become familiar with Dr Kellgren's large house in Eaton Square:

In the big drawing-room was his 'gym'. It was a strange and peculiar sight. There was various apparatus round the walls, and a number of hard couches covered in red velvet. The room was full of patients in dressing gowns; and Dr Kellgren's assistants, after consulting a 'pre-scription' written out by him, approached with a polite bow and put the patient through various exercises and a certain amount of massage. To see the old and inevitably fat striving to touch the floor with finger-tips, or hanging on to a ladder, and all at the orders of a smart young man looking more like a cavalry officer than a doctor, was somewhat odd. But how good for them! . . .

After the exercise and massage Dr Kellgren would come in and say, with a bow to the patient, that he would 'take your stomach in the next room'. 'One soon found out that, on arrival in Dr Kellgren's room, the loudest shrieks were of no avail; as he was stone deaf . . .' or at any rate affected deafness for these occasions. As one patient put it to Sydney, 'he seized my vitals like a rat'. Sydney says that he effected marvellous cures and was a born healer; 'His methods were sensible and natural, and the exercises and rubbings could only possibly do good and not harm.' According to Dorothy, Thomas used to spend an hour every day with a 'Swedish manipulator'; this would have been either Kellgren or, more likely, one of his assistants. In Sydney's account these visits were not daily but roughly once a week. Kellgren may have been something of a charlatan, and Thomas himself something of a crank; but it can also be said that they seem somehow to have got their priorities right, because all four children, and Thomas himself, were to live to old age in good health. This was the source of Sydney's ideas about the 'Good Body', laughed at by Nancy and Decca. But in *Five Houses* she is quite unrepentant, saying of orthodox doctors: 'Today, I believe, they have come to some of the same conclusions as the old quack and follow many of his ideas for which they persecuted him when he was alive.'

Thomas did not buy another house when he sold Cleeve Lodge. Instead the family went for a time to live in a furnished house in Hampshire. There they were rejoined by Rita Shell as governess; 'Miss Shell' was soon corrupted by Dorothy to Mittelle, and thence to Tello, the name by which the Bowles family and their descendants were to call her ever afterwards and which we shall use from now on. Sydney says that Thomas wrote to Tello at her current post to ask her to come back, but what really seems to have happened is much more unusual, not to say intriguing; she wrote to him, very soon after Jessica's death, offering to return. There is at any rate a letter from her to Thomas dated 25 June; the year is not given but it can only be 1887, so it was sent less than a fortnight after Jessica died. It says:

'I am glad to have your letter this morning, and to know that you are willing for me to return. I thank you for what you say, but I assure you I have considered everything, and am sure I shall not regret the step I am taking.' She goes on to ask him to write to her current employer as 'I am particularly anxious it should be quite understood that my offer to return to you has not originated through my not liking it here.' She adds that the exact time of her return must suit the convenience of her employer. The wording of this letter does without question imply that the initiative had come from Tello. It looks as if she wrote to Thomas alluding to the worry he must feel at having to bring up four young children as a widower; and offering to return if this could be of any help to him. Thomas consulted Sydney; she tells us that he twice asked her whether she preferred to be taught by Tello or by her successor, Miss Shales – not the 'nonentity' who had replaced Tello, but another. Sydney says that some inner contradiction made her say that she preferred Miss Shales, but she resolved that if asked a third time she would opt for Tello. He never did ask her, and she regretted not having given her real opinion. Perhaps the boys were also asked at their boarding school and they chose Tello explicitly: perhaps Thomas just decided to follow his own judgement. Whatever the details, she returned. One may suppose that besides her affection for the children and sympathy with them in their bereavement she was already a little in love with Thomas. Had she originally left the family's service because she felt she was becoming interested in him?

The furnished house in Hampshire was only a temporary expedient, for soon the family moved to Wilbury in Wiltshire, a beautiful country house built in Palladian style in the eighteenth century. It belonged to Thomas's friend Sir Henry Malet, who wrote for *Vanity Fair*. One of Sir Henry's ancestors had bought it with a fortune amassed in India at the time of Warren Hastings. Thomas agreed with Sir Henry that he should come with his family whenever it suited him, sharing the house and the expenses. So they all moved in; Thomas, the four children, Tello, a maid and a manservant. For Sir Henry it was an expedient to help him with his money problems. He possessed three thousand acres around Wilbury, but was short of funds, especially at that time when agriculture was in a depressed state. The arrangement must

have suited both parties, for it was to go on for years; Wilbury
was Sydney's home during much of her late childhood and early
adolescence. In due course Thomas was to become rather tired of
the Malets, or rather of Lady Malet, who was quite a trial, and he
tended to move into Wilbury when they were not there and he
could have the house to himself. Wilbury's beauty and the mag-
nificence of its furnishings made a deep impression on Sydney
and helped to form her taste.

Everyone liked Sir Henry, but Lady Malet was another matter.
Sydney remembers her as 'rather my idea of what Emma Hamilton must have been when Nelson knew her, only less beautiful and
attractive. She was very fat, with a fine skin and eyes, untidy, lazy,
and decidedly queer. She spent most of her day lying on a sofa in
the Blue Room, attired in loose garments with lace.' She was not
delicate, like Jessica, just inactive. She henpecked Sir Henry and
was a bad housekeeper, often accusing the servants of dishonesty
and accordingly suffering frequent changes of staff. She rather
preferred animals to humans; she would cause her horses to be
tethered near the drive to watch the comings and goings, on the
grounds that they must be bored in the stables. Like many ladies
of the period, Lady Malet dabbled in the spirit world. Over the
doors of the beautiful little drawing room, decorated in bright
blue and gold, with its colourful Aubusson carpet and elaborately
framed rococo mirror, were two oval spaces in which paintings by
Boucher or Fragonard would have been appropriate. But Lady
Malet had put in two rather dismal pictures that were, if not
strictly by her, at least by her hand. They consisted, says Sydney,
of 'amateurish white leaves on a grey ground, with an ill-drawn
lily inserted here and there. Her hand, she said, was guided by a
spirit, and these drawings were the result.' Sydney tried to like the
spirit paintings, for she was impressed by their supernatural origin,
but failed. Even as a child she felt them to be out of place in the
room.

The butler at Wilbury was called Malpas. He used to stand on
one leg in the dining room, and when asked by Lady Malet why
he did this, he replied: 'Because the storks do it.' He could be a
terrible bore. One morning, as Thomas was sitting alone at his
accustomed late breakfast, Malpas began to recount, gratuitously
and in considerable detail, the entire history of his family.

Eventually Thomas could bear it no longer and snapped: 'Oh, go away, Malpas!'

The butler obeyed, but turned at the door to add, in hurt but resolute tones: 'And I have a cousin in Australia.'

Malpas also had definite ideas on how to welcome callers. When a neighbouring couple called Mr and Mrs Stevens came to visit, he put a bottle of Stephens' ink on each of the occasional tables to make them feel at home, recalled Dorothy in her second *Times* article, in 1963.

Malpas sometimes tried the patience of the grown-ups, but more annoying to Sydney was the Malets' daughter Vera, who, being about Sydney's age, was marked out as her playmate. Vera liked newts and frogs, which she kept in the outhouses; she also frequented the eighteenth-century ornamental grotto and the dark passage which led from there out on to the side of the hill. Here in the gloom, among rotting beech leaves and dead birds, Vera liked to play with her frogs and talk about ghosts. Sydney avoided these pursuits whenever she could, since she neither took to Vera's amphibians nor shared her taste for the 'Gothick'. One prank of Vera's did amuse her, however. There really was supposed to be a ghost at Wilbury, a lady with a little dog. She was said to walk up the back stairs with her throat cut, dripping blood in which the dog, following behind, made footprints. There were marks upon the back stairs, impossible to scrub out, alleged to represent these footprints. Sydney says: 'Vera throve on this story. It was constantly in her mind. There were several paintings of ladies with dogs in the dining room and billiard-room; and, after considering them all carefully, we finally decided on a pale woman in a green silk dress holding a tiny spaniel . . . From a study of her we ran to the back stairs to examine the marks.' But one day they went further. Vera had a nosebleed, and this gave a marvellous opportunity for touching up. 'With three fingers carefully steeped in her flowing gore she made the marks of a little dog's feet all up the stairs. It was most successful, and we were proud of it. Of course a deadly secrecy was enjoined, or the whole story of the lady and her dog might fall into disrepute.'

Sydney was a very different type of child from Vera. She was a daydreamer, rather bookish and also distinctly squeamish. She liked discussion, especially with Thomas who always treated his children exactly as if they were grown up; she enjoyed her lessons with Tello; and she liked telling herself stories. Often these had to do with one of the pictures in the house, of which her favourite was a large picture representing Sir Charles Malet, the nabob ancestor of Sir Henry who had bought Wilbury, attending a Durbar. Sir Charles and a small group of Englishmen were standing before a magnificent Indian ruler on his throne flanked by courtiers in glittering robes, their turbans adorned with jewelled osprey feathers. Sir Charles, in blue coat and white breeches and with his hair in a tail, seemed to be presenting something to the ruler. Attendants with huge fans surrounded the scene. 'With this picture opposite me at meals,' says Sydney, 'I could forget Lady Malet and Vera and my private sorrows and find myself with Sir Charles Malet at the Durbar; in fact sometimes I was Sir Charles himself presenting a scroll in the name of my Government.' She preferred it to the picture on the opposite wall which showed a slaughtered deer with its tongue hanging out, together with other dead game and a quantity of fruit. There were no stories to be had out of this picture, which only made her sad and uneasy, so she always tried to arrange matters so that she faced the other one. We may imagine that Sydney, lost in contemplation of the Durbar, was not always quick to reply when addressed at mealtimes, and that the vagueness for which she was to become known first became noticeable at Wilbury.

It was only in the afternoons that Sydney was Vera's victim, as she puts it. On weekday mornings she would ride every day with Thomas the four miles to Grateley station and back in order to fetch the morning papers which had arrived from London. Though the route lay over soft downland turf, Thomas did not like the horses to break into a canter, but kept to an exceptionally fast trot, with little Sydney, as she puts it, 'rising quicker and quicker in the saddle like a pea on a drum'. She rode side-saddle in habit, boots and bowler hat: the attire was tight and uncomfortable. On Sundays the routine was different, for there were no newspapers. Thomas had found a Turkish bath. It belonged to a neighbour, Major Poore, who had rigged it up in one of his outhouses, so this was their Sunday destination. Sometimes Thomas would leave Sydney behind to go to church with Lady Malet and Tello, but more often he would take her along. While he basked in the cleansing steam, Sydney had a second breakfast with Major Poore and his large family, of whom Sydney's friend was Nina, later to be Duchess of Hamilton and known as the 'Animals' Friend'. A strict vegetarian, she led the campaign for the compulsory introduction of the humane killer in slaughterhouses. On returning from the ride, whether to Grateley or to Major Poore's, Sydney would be expected to attend Thomas at his breakfast, as at Cleeve Lodge. There would then be a couple of hours of lessons before lunch. But although Sydney is very respectful about Tello's teaching, she regards her time with Thomas as the part of the day during which she learned most. During their rides, and while she sat with him as he had his breakfast, Thomas would talk to Sydney about everything under the sun, including his projects for his own career. His great wish at this time was still to get into Parliament; but during this first time at Wilbury in 1888 he felt that his life was too much disrupted by Jessica's death for him to undertake another candidacy just yet. Instead, his mind was turning more and more to the idea of buying a yacht and embarking on an extended cruise with the entire family. This, in August 1888, is exactly what he did; for the best part of the next year, the Bowles family home was to be a ship.

# 15

# Cruise of the *Nereid*

The vessel was the *Nereid*, a schooner of 150 tons according to Sydney, though Dorothy, in her first *Times* article, gives 200 tons; she depended entirely on sail, for there was no auxiliary engine. Thomas had been to immense trouble to find and choose her. His main complaint on this search was the tendency of those who wished to sell their yachts to concentrate on inessentials such as the decoration of the cabins or the quality of the furniture. The sellers would send him 'beautiful plans of their vessels with the very cushions of the sofas drawn thereon in fascinating relief'. On the other hand they 'never dwelt greatly on the nautical outfit'. In their meticulous inventories there was always a sugar duster but by no means always a second anchor cable. (All this, according to Diana, was still true after the Second World War when she and her husband were looking for a yacht to buy.) Finally Thomas found *Nereid*, and the more he saw her the better he liked her. He gave her a typically thorough going over.

I had her hauled up and all her ballast out. I crawled under her false keel, and clambered about her from her garboard-strake to her planksheer, looking for wrinkles and weeps in her copper, and finding none. I questioned the housing and hounding of her masts and the remote corners of her stanchions with my clasp-knife. I tested her timbers and her shelf with an auger. I explored her limber-channels and smelt down to her keelson. I overhauled her tanks, looked over her running gear, and noted what of it was perished and faded and long in the jaw; and finally I inspected her sails, ground tackle and boats.

He was satisfied, and the transaction was effected. His precautions were to turn out to have been extremely wise.

*Nereid*, with her successor *Hoyden*, constitute between them the third of Sydney's *Five Houses*, and she describes the wild excitement of the children at the first sight of her at Southampton. Ned Kersey had collected a crew of ten Aldeburgh fishermen, and they scrubbed and polished until everything was shipshape. In late July 1888 the children arrived on the quay, with Tello and Miss Griffin, Dorothy's nurse, and their possessions; these last were packed not in trunks but in wooden boxes which could be thrown away, since there was no room on board to stow luggage. They also brought their terrier, Smiler, who was later to suffer death in the harbour of Haifa by jumping overboard from the dinghy where he was tethered and hanging himself with the rope. A boat came alongside rowed by four sailors in blue jerseys with '*Nereid*' embroidered on the front, which took them to the yacht. Once on board they all rushed to explore. Remembering the moment, Sydney comments: 'The best thing about a sailing ship is the beautiful cleanness. The deck is of pure white wood; all the brass is shining; and all is kept so wonderfully clean.' She further comments: 'It seems to me that cleanness and luxury are interchangeable terms. There is no luxury where there is dirt: and where everything is shiningly clean there is luxury.' But even in old age, remembering *Nereid* and the magical occasion of first seeing her, Sydney's habit of cool appraisal remains at work. She remembers thinking that the varnished wood was rather ugly. The skylight in the cabin she shared with Tello sometimes leaked, though 'we hardly dared speak of this to Tap as it was one of the things that made him angry. His ship was supposed to be watertight . . .' although here she adds, tolerantly, 'and so she was in the main.'

Thomas himself also wrote about the *Nereid*'s cruise, a full-length book called the *Log of the Nereid*. It even found a public: the popular novelist Ouida, a political fan of Thomas's, mentions it in a letter to him. But as a piece of writing it does not show Thomas at his best. It is like a home movie, facetious, self-indulgent and sentimental. Dorothy, aged three, is made its heroine; always referred to as 'Weenie', she is supposed to be the captain of the ship. The other children are referred to as First Lieutenant Sydney and Quartermasters George and Geoffrey, but they come over as comparatively shadowy figures. Dorothy's lisps, pouts and imperious childishness seemed funny at the time, but they do not go well into cold print. There was at the time a literary fashion for baby talk; Lewis Carroll's *Sylvie and Bruno*, which is wrecked by it, was published in the same year as the *Log*, 1889. However, the celebration of Dorothy as a spoilt child gives a most misleading impression of the extent to which she was in fact spoilt. The *Log* itself goes a good way to correct this, if it is read carefully. It is for instance said that Dorothy, at teatime, 'is too often deposed from command by a coup d'etat, and sent to her Wailing-Place . . .' and later that she has found in Smiler, the dog, 'one creature in the ship who does not give himself absurd airs of superior bigness and wisdom, and whom she can order about and tyrannize over generally'. Certainly Thomas was amused by Dorothy, and so no doubt were the sailors: she seems to have been fairly precocious and conscious of her own charm. But none of this by any means implies that any of them stood any real nonsense. They could at any time call on her nurse, whose entire duty was to control her. More important, it does not mean, as has been suggested, that the other three children had their noses out of joint. They were all of schoolroom age, and they were in the charge of Tello, not of the nurse. George at eleven, Geoffrey at nine and Sydney at eight were already treated by Thomas in most respects as adults. Sydney, it will be remembered, had been his confidante and companion on his daily rides at Wilbury. She was more likely to be participating in the petting of 'Weenie' than wishing to be petted herself; no schoolchild likes to be treated as a baby.

On 1 August the *Nereid* put out to sea, sailing across the Channel to Dieppe. Bill Knight, the steward and cook, went ashore to get some milk and came back, saying, 'It's a job to make 'em understand here. They don't speak the same language as we do, not by a long way.' Thomas and Sydney both praise Bill's cooking; like Etienne before him, he had Thomas to coach and criticize him. After Dieppe they sailed north to Portsmouth and to Cowes, where the regatta was just over. They then cruised in leisurely fashion down the coast to Dartmouth, for whose less fashionable but perhaps jollier regatta they were just in time.

Annual regattas were then held at most coastal towns. At Dartmouth there were not only sailing races, but also rowing and athletics and all kinds of other sporting events, including a grand display of boxing. There was a lavish funfair; though Thomas found the steam organs of the merry-go-rounds 'afflicting', and Sydney comments that the bands were 'fearfully discordant'. The funfair included all the sideshows then considered indispensable; 'giants, dwarfs, skeleton men, headless women, and sheep with six legs', says Thomas. There were also fireworks; altogether it was a splendid send-off for the family's long voyage.

One or two little difficulties had to be settled before they could actually sail. One of the sailors wanted to go back to Aldeburgh, and his replacement let Thomas down, so that eventually they sailed one hand short. Miss Griffin, the nurse, also gave notice; she did not want to be away for so long. However, one of the sailors, Tom Cable, had a sister called Jenny. A telegram was sent to Aldeburgh, and she consented to come along as nurse, in which capacity she remained with the family for many years.

They set off southwards on 1 September, and soon ran into a strong wind and a heavy sea, with the vessel going 'seven knots, comfortably enough, but plunging a good deal', as Thomas puts it breezily. The children did not mind, but both Tello and Jenny Cable were prostrate with seasickness, with the result that Thomas had to put Dorothy to bed, struggling with her clothes, which he understood less than perfectly, and occasionally falling over with her, to her great delight. This interrupted his navigation: 'When you want to get a meridian altitude of Aldebaran, it is awkward to have to leave your sextant and star to take care of each other in order to find out which end of a petticoat comes off first, and how on earth suspenders are cast adrift from stockings.' But by 12 September they were in a dead calm; the weather was beautiful, and Thomas took advantage of the time to allow the three elder children up on deck at night and teach them the constellations. Water and food began to run short. They killed a dolphin, which replenished their fresh meat; Ned Kersey nailed up its tail on the jib boom in the form of wings, according to an old seaman's superstition that this would bring the wind. Whether or not because of the dolphin's tail, a wind did soon come, and in due course became a gale. They made Gibraltar on 22 September.

Their voyage continued in a leisurely way eastwards through the Mediterranean. Thomas liked Algiers both for its French food and for its magnificent Turkish bath, where he was bathed and 'shampooed', by which he means massaged, 'in a manner so complete and so refreshing as those can have no idea of who only know Turkish baths and shampooing from English experience'. The family also made friends with the crew of an Austrian man-of-war. They dallied for a time at Malta. Thomas's comments on Maltese politics are of interest even now. Malta, he says, is the 'Paradise of Small Politicians'. People who have failed at various callings begin to clamour; and 'clamour, as everybody knows, is politics'; and instead of settling it by 'half a dozen £5 notes judiciously, or even injudiciously, distributed', the British start taking notice of the matter as a crisis and grant a constitution, 'the remedy for everything since the time of the Abbé Sieyès'. There are elections, then 'debates and orations, and everybody starts a newspaper'. The governor, and lieutenant-governor, proceed quietly about their business of doing things while the politicians are talking about them. 'But this', Thomas foresees, 'will be mended in time.' Then they sailed past the coast of Libya to Alexandria, where they landed on 8 November.

Alexandria did not appeal to Thomas. It 'has no character at all. It is neither eastern nor western, but a mass of Oriental and Occidental rubbish, painful and puzzling, without a rule or a principle to be discovered anywhere.' The social conditions shocked his conscience. Furthermore, he was irritated by the disappearance of nearly all the four thousand Turkish baths that had once existed, according to him, in the city: the inability of the poor to afford them, and the greed of land speculators, had combined to destroy them. He did, however, find one which suited him, for which the money had been given by a beneficent sheikh. English philanthropists, he thought, ought to do the same for London and the manufacturing towns. The women's Turkish bath, to which he sent the girls, was, Sydney found, dirty; she disliked the sight of the naked women. Worst of all, she and Dorothy both caught lice in their hair.

As always, Thomas made friends with the officers of the naval ships in Alexandria, in particular those of HMS *Phaeton*, to the stern of which the *Nereid* was tied. He would ply them with technical questions which it seems they could not always answer. But this time he only stayed two days, for he was impatient to visit Syria and see the Holy Land. Too impatient, as it nearly turned out; for soon after setting out the *Nereid* ran into a storm of such fury that even Thomas describes it as 'a most anxious and trying experience' and admits that they were 'all in some danger'. Sydney, who says that it was nearly the end of them all, attributes it entirely to Thomas's obstinacy; very bad weather was forecast and the officers of the *Phaeton* had pressed him to delay. They had, though, lent him their chart of the Bay of Acre, which he had carefully traced; Thomas might take risks, but he also prepared himself well.

Once at sea, the warning indicators proliferated. The barometer fell, and birds began behaving oddly; a rook and a duck both took refuge on the *Nereid*. Then the lightning flashes started, and finally the ever-worsening squalls, constantly changing direction. The sea was running too high for accurate calculation of position, and Thomas's sextant became virtually unusable through spray. He would have given a good deal, he says, 'for just thirty seconds of the comparatively high and steady platform of a thousand-ton ship'. He laid the vessel to during the night and waited for daylight, hoping for a let-up; but in the morning the conditions were, if anything, worse. The storm was blowing them straight towards the Syrian coast. For two days it continued; and then, to Thomas's concern, the coast loomed up, indistinct but ominous, through the driving rain. The *Nereid* could not be allowed to drift on, or she would smash against the rocks with the loss of all on board. Thomas therefore caused one small sail to be hoisted, and they tacked into the storm and away from the shore, desperately trying to gain time. The strain might have been too much for the yacht, but Thomas's care and precautions paid off. The ship held, but for the loss of one spar. With the aid of the copied chart, they made the shelter of Haifa. Later he was to learn that the same storm, thought to be the worst for a generation, had not only wrecked a good many ships up and down the Syrian coast, but had prevented HMS *Phaeton* from putting out to sea. Thomas resolved, when back in Alexandria, to offer the *Phaeton* a tow.

Sydney remembers the storm as being not so much frightening as uncomfortable and tedious. Cooking was impossible, so Bill Knight played dominoes with the children. There was no daylight, for every skylight was obscured by its wooden cover; the main cabin had an oil lamp which swung wildly with the ship; 'We seemed to climb a succession of mountains and slide down the other side. Occasionally a big gust of wind rushed through the stuffy cabin as the companion top was lifted for a second to allow Tap to come down and study the chart. Dressed in oilskins and seaboots he was wet and glistening all over. We could see he did not want to be bothered with questions and so we remained silent.' Thomas, preoccupied as he was, noticed this; the children, he says, 'have been neither sick nor sorry through all this trying time' but, except for Dorothy, 'they have been a little quiet'.

The family recuperated for about a fortnight in the monastery of Mount Carmel, which struck Sydney as spacious and beautifully clean. The monks were kind and hospitable, but spoke no English; communication had to be through one of them, Father Felix, who knew French. He could also snap his fingers so loudly that it sounded like a pistol shot; this amused Dorothy in particular. While they were there, the monastery was visited by a party of Cook's tourists, prototype of the modern package tour. The Cook's tour was an institution particularly repugnant to Thomas, the arch-individualist; he himself had already rejected the assistance of Cook's when in Alexandria. He suggested to one member of the party that they might give up one or two of the places they were visiting and stay a day or two. They refused; they had to catch the steamer from Jaffa on a particular date, and then go on to Nazareth. The proverbial American who does Europe in a week was already on his way.

After this the Bowles family sailed up to Beirut, which Thomas found to be without interest: 'a smaller, dirtier, worse Alexandria'. He left the *Nereid* at anchor there, and paid a short visit to Damascus, where he saw all the sights and met a number of cultivated Arabs. One of them he records as using 'sons of Crusaders' as a term of disparagement. This amuses Thomas when he thinks of how proud Englishmen are of descent from a Crusader. He visited two Turkish baths in Damascus, pronouncing that city 'supreme' in this important matter.

The family then took a steamer from Beirut to Jaffa, leaving the *Nereid* behind because Thomas considered Jaffa to be an unsafe place to take a sailing vessel. From there they visited Jerusalem and its Holy Places. There was no railway, so the family travelled for eleven hours in a diligence: 'and dead tired we were when we arrived,' says Sydney.

Jerusalem struck Thomas as 'a miserable village which would be horrible of aspect were it not for the bright sky, and the sun, and the traditions that surround it'. Sydney remembers the Dome of the Mosque of Omar and the Church of the Holy Sepulchre 'where we were taken by stages to the Holy Places until at last we came to the place of the Sepulchre itself, a blaze of candles, and red and gold. I think we children expected something more, some kind of miraculous appearance.' At the Wailing Wall Sydney says they 'strongly disapproved of such a public exhibition of woe'.

Thomas, on the other hand, finds 'The Wailing Wall' a 'touching sight', though he goes on to say that he does not see what the Jews have got to wail about. For one thing they did not found Jerusalem, and only ruled it for five hundred of its three thousand years of history. For another, 'If they have been expelled from Jerusalem, they are the rulers of London, Paris and Berlin . . . and I cannot believe that they hold themselves to be worse off for the change. Nor shall I believe it till I see the great house of Rothschild abandon London in order to set up as bankers in Jerusalem . . .' He is very disparaging about the Jewish refugees from Russia. 'There is, I suppose, no human animal more utterly devoid of all dignity and nobility, none that bears an aspect at once so abject and so dangerous as the lower class of Russian Jews who have recently overrun the Holy City.' He talks of 'their pale, womanly faces, rendered loathsome by a long, greasy curled lock in front of each ear; their narrow shoulders, bent carriage, filthy gaberdines, and furtive glances . . .' But he recognizes that these poor people are the remnants of a murderous persecution, and slates the Russian government for using them 'as a convenient pretext for fastening grievances on the Turkish authorities. Holy Russia first expels her Jews and then protects them. It is ingenious and characteristic.'

Too much can be – and has been – made of this diatribe. It does not imply that Thomas had a prejudice against Jews as such; had such a prejudice existed, it would have been reflected in *Vanity Fair* and elsewhere, and nothing of the sort can be discerned. All that happened was that he saw a group of people who seemed to him to be unattractive, and said so. The passage is also imbued with disapproval of their persecutors, for Thomas adds: 'If the Jews do not appear to advantage in Jerusalem, neither do the Christians', and details contemptuously the tedious and interminable squabbles over trifles of the various churches: the setting up by Catholics and Orthodox of – for instance – rival Gardens of Gethsemane, and the futile and meddlesome attempt of the Protestant missionary societies to make converts. Thomas's sympathies are with the Turkish authorities, whom he sees as making a reasonable job of their task of keeping order between the bickering men of God.

Back on board the *Nereid* in Beirut, Thomas comments: 'Nobody knows how comfortable a good ship is till they have left it for a time.' Renewed contact with his Aldeburgh crew was equally refreshing. One of them said, in his forthright East Anglian fashion: 'Well, if this here's what they calls the Holy Land, give me Orfordness.' He was mainly referring to the weather, which had once more turned unfavourable, so that the Austrian consul advised Thomas to return to Alexandria by steamer. Again he disregarded this advice, but this time he was right; the weather became good again, and they reached Alexandria without trouble.

There they renewed their acquaintance with the crew of HMS *Phaeton*. One of the sailors on board was a very good tailor, and he made sailor suits, complete with caps, for all the children, and for Tello and Jenny Cable as well. The clothes were correct in every detail, except that the women and girls, instead of trousers, had skirts stitched by Jenny Cable. The sailor clothes were afterwards, as Sydney attests, to be a 'sore trial' to them, as in the incident when they first visited the Mitfords at Batsford, but at first they were very proud of them, 'and much did we despise those poor children who wore "sailor suits" made in a shop'.

After a visit to Cairo where they were all together, the family split up. Thomas met his old flame Lady Sykes with Sir Tatton and their son Mark, who was ten; and he and George joined the Sykes family for a month-long trip up the Nile. At Assiout George sprained his ankle badly. An English doctor who was there advised that it should be rested, to which George agreed as he was in considerable pain; but Thomas disregarded the doctor, made George walk on it, and secured the services of an Egyptian masseur who, using a traditional technique which 'most closely resembles in many respects that of Dr Kellgren', cured him in less than two days. The masseur 'was a charming old man. He had certainly never seen a dead body cut up or worked in a hospital; but he had learnt from his father a knowledge of the living frame and of the way to handle it in certain cases, which the College of Surgeons might do well to consider, and to acquire – if it can.' The Turkish bath at Assiout was also excellent. Primarily, of course, the party was sightseeing and visiting the antiquities; and Thomas expresses admiration not only of the ancient Egyptians but also of those of the classical period. He finds the ancient religion both profound and modest, and discerns under its apparent polytheism a belief in one divine principle. He admires the ancient Egyptian practice of mummification and ancestor worship and considers that it contributed to public order. As to Roman Egypt, he regards it, perhaps somewhat oddly, as a glory for the country that 'there is scarce a dogma engrafted on Christianity, from the Athanasian creed downwards, which had not its origin on the banks of the Nile'. The squabbles of the early Christians perhaps appealed to his disputatious side.

While Thomas and George were on this trip, the others stayed in Alexandria where the *Nereid* was tied up to the *Phaeton*. Sydney says that all the officers spoilt them, and there was one young lieutenant who came particularly often.

When I was lying on my bunk I heard him come aboard, and then he would go to the piano and play and sing. The song was 'Queen of my Heart' from the opera *Dorothy*, and these were the words of its chorus:-

> From daylight a hint we might borrow
> For prudence may come with the light
> So why should we wait till tomorrow
> When you're Queen of my Heart tonight?

So I think Tello was Queen of his heart. She must have been attractive then, tall and handsome, clever and sympathetic.

The lieutenant used to come and sit with the family on a sandy beach, and most of his attention was devoted to Tello. This surprised Sydney, because she had a little tortoise which, she fancied, poked its head out of its shell when she called it. Surely this should have interested him more than boring adult chat with

Tello? But Sydney had an admirer of her own, an American admiral who gave her a bracelet which he told her she was never to remove. She never did: 'It is still on my arm as I write, nearly sixty years later.'

The *Nereid* left Alexandria on 27 February. On 6 March she ran into a cyclone, which drove the family off their course, but they made Malta on the twelfth. There they caught up with Thomas's accumulated mail of nine months, and he found, not altogether surprisingly, that it was advisable to go straight home. The family therefore left the *Nereid* for Ned and the crew to sail her home, and took a P & O steamer. Thomas found it 'not easy to feel quite safe in a steamboat with other people in command, after having been accustomed so long to the security of a good sailing vessel, and one's own navigation; but, of course, one must occasionally take risks'.

# 16

# Member of Parliament

Thomas does not say what the urgent business was which made him come home in a hurry, but it was probably a firm offer for the purchase of *Vanity Fair*. It is certain that Thomas sold the magazine for £20,000 to Arthur H. Evans at the end of March 1889, that is, virtually as soon as he came home. He was, we may conjecture, getting rather bored with *Vanity Fair*, otherwise, it is hard to imagine how he would have kept away from it for the period of his cruise, nearly twice as long as his absence at the siege of Paris. His editor and staff had kept things going during his absence, as they had in 1870–71, but he could not count on this sort of luck holding for ever.

There was a positive reason, as well as this negative one, for wanting to be rid of *Vanity Fair*. Thomas wanted now, at last, to be a participant in politics, not just a commentator from the sidelines. For this he needed to reduce his business commitments and increase his financial resources, and the sale of *Vanity Fair* did both at a stroke.

*The Lady*, of course, was different; there was no question of his selling that. It was deliberately kept bland and uncontroversial, it only needed the very minimum of attention from him, and its profits were satisfactory. Added to the proceeds of *Vanity Fair*, they justify Sydney's remark that from then on Thomas was a rich man. This is true in the sense that he always had enough to fulfil his commitments, and enough over to pay for his amusements. It was in those days necessary to be well-off in order to pursue a political career; Members of Parliament were unpaid, and indeed Thomas was to campaign, vainly, against paying them when the reform was introduced in 1910.

Thomas had already stood for Parliament a number of times,

always in the Conservative interest. As early as 1874 he fought Darlington; then he contested Banbury in 1880, which he might have won had it not been for a strong general swing to the Liberals. In January 1883 he was adopted as candidate for the not very hopeful seat of Salford. He nursed this constituency conscientiously, but in vain. His campaign taught him the art of public speaking, which does not always come easily to journalists, any more than coherent writing always comes easily to orators. Meetings were more important in those days than they are now that television provides all the politics, and more, that most people want. The Victorians went to public political meetings in large numbers; an audience of eight thousand heard Thomas at the St James's Hall, Manchester, in May 1884, speak against Gladstone's policy in the Sudan. The speech was cheered to the echo, but nevertheless Thomas failed to be selected two years later for South Manchester. 'I hardly knew whether to be sorry or glad that you have not been chosen,' said Jessica in a letter of June 1886, adding that he would have enjoyed the fight, but no Tory was likely to win in that constituency.

His first real chance at a seat in Parliament came when in 1891 he was adopted by the Conservatives of the Norfolk port of King's Lynn. Though held by the Liberals, the seat was a winnable marginal. It was also in East Anglia, which was his home area. He secured the adoption despite making it clear to his party workers that he would never follow the party line on any matter if it conflicted with his own judgement.

It is quite possible that I may occasionally, if I am returned, have to give votes that the more tractable members of my party may not altogether like, for, although I am more or less of a party man, above all I am an Englishman, and I aspire to be a statesman, and I will vote for what I believe to be the interests of England according to the true dictates of statesmanship, even though my own party should say me nay.

No one could say that he had not been warned. The trouble is that while it sounds splendid in the abstract to choose a candidate with this kind of sturdy independence, when it comes to an actual argument it can look different, especially when, as was to be the case with Thomas, rebellion against the party becomes habitual and flagrant.

The next general election came about in June 1892, and Thomas, individual as ever, fought the campaign from his yacht, the *Hoyden*. He had sold *Nereid* in 1889; she had arrived in indifferent shape at Cowes after Ned and the crew had taken her through some bad weather. He therefore had the *Hoyden* constructed at Lowestoft to his own specifications in the style of a fishing smack, displacing 100 tons. Sydney describes her as slow and comfortable, and they sailed in her every year, though no further than France. For the election Thomas had her tied up in King's Lynn harbour. He lived in the *Hoyden* with his family – or rather with Sydney and Dorothy, for the boys were away at boarding school – and made it also the main committee room from which he set out to woo the three thousand electors. It was thought necessary to canvass every one of them; Thomas would do no canvassing himself, but the two little girls in sailor suits and pigtails did plenty of it: to their misery, as Sydney says. Apart from that they found the election great fun, especially the polling day itself. 'We were seated with Tap in a big landau drawn by two black horses belonging to the local undertaker. The whole thing was smothered in yellow ribbon (our colour), and we drove round all day from one committee-room to another, greeted everywhere by excited and enthusiastic supporters.' But the election was close, and as evening drew near this came to be realized, and optimism waned. A few fights broke out, and Thomas made the girls go back to the *Hoyden* rather than accompany him to the count. 'My governess and I sat on deck waiting in the cold, and listening to the sound of distant cheering and shouting. At last, about midnight, an approaching roar was heard. Tap was being brought down to the docks by his triumphant supporters.' He was in by eleven votes.

At the age of fifty-one he was older than most new members, but he was exceptionally well prepared. He had been writing on current affairs virtually all his adult life. He had sufficient appetite for detail to be able to back his views with solid argument, coupled with a talent for coining the telling phrase. In addition, he already knew more about parliamentary procedure than most Members of Parliament. Six months before he was elected, in January 1892, Henry Chaplin, the President of the Board of Agriculture, wrote to him asking to consult him privately on proposed new procedural rules. 'There are some points on which I should like to talk to you – for you are well versed in parliamentary law and procedure.' Chaplin had been a Member of Parliament for twenty-three years.

Thomas's main area of expertise – and the area where, in his off-beat way, he was to produce some concrete political achievement – was in naval affairs and particularly in naval law. As early as 1878 he had produced a pamphlet, *Maritime Warfare*, attacking the provisions of the Declaration of Paris of 1856, which determined the international law of the sea in time of war. His particular objection to the Declaration related to a provision whereby a combatant ship was in duty bound to let enemy goods proceed, if carried in a neutral ship, unless they constituted contraband of war. At the time of the Boer War he was to argue that this provision, which stopped the trade of the Afrikaaner Republics from being throttled, lengthened the war and caused many extra casualties.

The sea was not the only area of Thomas's interest, in fact as time went on there were fewer and fewer subjects which he left alone; but it was his nautical side which provided the cartoonists and parliamentary sketch writers of *Punch* with a clue on how to treat this increasingly conspicuous backbencher. He appeared frequently in *Punch* as 'The Cap'en', in pirate dress with pistol and bandanna; quite soon the magazine's cartoonist, for some obscure reason, started drawing him with a peg-leg and a hook for a hand. Visitors to the gallery used to be surprised at seeing him with all his limbs complete. Inside and outside Parliament he was a well-known card. On one occasion he left his umbrella at the Carlton Club, and returned to find that it had disappeared. He went to the Club Secretary and asked him to put up a notice: 'Will the nobleman who stole Mr Bowles's umbrella kindly return it.' When the Secretary demurred, Thomas reminded him that the Carlton called itself a club for noblemen and gentlemen, and that no gentleman would have stolen his umbrella. Not that he claimed the status of gentleman for himself. When a cab driver, disappointed with his tip, asked him if he called himself a gentleman, he replied that he did not call himself anything so expensive. His conversation, by all accounts, was brilliant. Much later a cabinet minister was to tell Sydney: 'I owe all my career to your father, who persuaded me to turn my attention entirely to national finance of which he said most Members of Parliament were ignorant.' Sydney unfortunately does not name this man, but says he later became Chancellor of the Exchequer. He may have been one of those who used to meet Thomas during his regular rides in Rotten Row, Hyde Park, for which his new residence in Lowndes Square was as convenient as Cleeve Lodge had been. Sydney would come with him and hear many political discussions, sometimes being shamed by Thomas's 'rude vehemence'. But this characteristic, embarrassing to his child, did not put people off coming to hear his views. A similar testimonial to Thomas at an earlier stage is found in an account by F. E. Smith, later the Earl of Birkenhead, of a visit he paid to the United States during the First World War. He met in Chicago a former secretary of Thomas's, Samuel Insull, by then a millionaire. Smith writes: '. . . Mr Insull of Chicago, millionaire and man of affairs, attributes nine-tenths of all the education he ever had' to Thomas. (Insull was later to be the centre of a spectacular fraud case, although we can scarcely blame Thomas for this.) Sir George Clerk, British ambassador to Turkey whom Diana met on a visit to Constantinople in 1930, and on a less pleasant occasion in 1940, told her he still remembered Thomas's conversational prowess from hearing him as a young man.

The first subject with which Thomas dealt at length in Parliament was the question of the territory of the Pamir range. Russia had just invaded and, in effect, annexed this area bounded by Tibet, Afghanistan and Kashmir. Thomas complained in May 1893 that papers containing official information about this had been withheld from the House, and moved that they be released to it. The area, he said, was one of the most interesting countries in the world. It lay at an altitude often to fifteen thousand feet and was claimed by China and Afghanistan as well as by Russia. He quoted various authorities to show that, far from being unproductive, it was a flourishing and fertile country. If there was to be a boundary commission, China and Afghanistan should be represented on it; and although Britain had as such no rights in the area, it was wrong that it be left to secret diplomacy. It had been through relying on secret diplomacy that the first Afghan War had arisen. Sir Edward Grey, in reply, said that if the information was released the Russians might take this as an unfriendly act; and that in any case Thomas's description of the Pamir country had referred entirely to its condition in the summer. But Thomas was beginning to establish himself as a well-informed opponent of bureaucratic reticence. He also showed a geopolitical grasp rare in his contemporaries, in that the importance of the Pamirs to Russia's control of Afghanistan and the security of the Indian subcontinent is much clearer now than it was then.

Foreign affairs are always a minority interest among British politicians. It was over the proposal to introduce progressive death duties in 1894 that Thomas first really made his mark in Parliament. We have seen how it was in his persistent and well-researched attack on this proposal that he became for a time the comrade in arms of Bertie Mitford. The expertise of his campaign was acknowledged by the Chancellor of the Exchequer, Sir William Harcourt, in a letter to him the following February, which referred to 'your mastery of figures – of which I have formidable experience'. The electors of King's Lynn seem to have been little affected either way by his performance, for in the 1895 General Election, at which the Liberals were ousted and a Conservative government under Lord Salisbury was returned, he increased his majority only to sixty-nine.

In the next year, 1896, he became concerned with a matter that for the first time put him at odds with his own party leaders and in the same camp as the hated, and by now aged, Gladstone. The Turkish Armenians had rebelled against the Sultan. The army had easily put down the rebellion, which was on a very small scale, but the Turkish population had massacred six thousand Armenians in revenge. The Great Powers, including Britain, made a joint protest, accusing the Sultan's government of organizing the atrocities. Thomas thought this was unwise and that Turkey should be supported, as being a necessary protection against the irruption of Russia into the Near East and possibly later into British India. In particular he thought that Britain should hand back Cyprus to the Turks, as had been envisaged in the Cyprus Convention of 1878. Thomas eventually withdrew his critical parliamentary motion, but in October 1896 he went on a long fact-finding trip to Greece and Turkey, being entertained by the Sultan and granted an extended interview. The Sultan struck him as gracious but care-worn; it was clear that he experienced great difficulties in running his unwieldy empire. He convinced Thomas that he was genuinely trying to effect reforms; Thomas advised him to carry out a few reforms thoroughly rather than try everything at once and leave it incomplete. The Sultan pleaded bad communications and shortage of money, and feared that if, for instance, he allowed the Christian minority to carry arms, it would lead to a backlash from the Moslems like that of the Ku Klux Klan in the United States. Thomas pleaded the Sultan's case to Lord Salisbury, but in vain; Britain continued to stand with the other Great Powers. It was Thomas's first major difference with his party's leadership. It was not to be his last.

At some time during the cruise of the *Nereid* Tello became pregnant, and a son, John Stewart, was born to her not long after her return. She could not very well remain as governess but Thomas supported her, installed her in a London house and gave her a job on *The Lady*, she rose to be its editor after about three years. She also in due course bore three more sons, of whom Thomas was the father, and remained on friendly terms not only with him but with his children throughout their lives. Why did he never marry her? Had he done so immediately they returned to London it would have legitimized the first child, and no one would have objected – certainly not his existing children. The most likely explanation is that the first child was not his, but that of the naval lieutenant who serenaded Tello in Alexandria and distracted her attention from Sydney's tortoise. In this case it may well be that Thomas at that stage merely stood by Tello out of friendship, and that his own love affair with her did not start until after the first child was born. The idea that the two of them were furtively coupling during the *Nereid* cruise does in fact seem somewhat unlikely. Lovemaking on board the *Nereid* itself would have been impossible without everyone knowing, as anyone who has spent some time on board a small yacht will agree; and that would have been the last thing either Thomas or Tello would have wanted. It would have shocked the crew and bewildered the children. There would have been some opportunities in port, but had anything been going on between them Thomas would surely have arranged matters so that when on land they were together as much as possible. Far from going out of his way to achieve this, he went gallivanting off without her to Upper Egypt, giving the musical lieutenant his opportunity. As to why he did not marry Tello at some later stage, when he undoubtedly did have an extended affair with her, it is said in the family that another of his mistresses, a married lady herself, forbade it. Whatever the truth of the matter, Tello was always to remain as Sydney describes her in her first period as governess, 'a friend to all', and Thomas treated her and all her children as a second family, though Tello never told them that he was their father, or anything more to her than family friend and former employer.

As to Thomas's original family, they spent a certain period after the *Nereid* cruise moving about. They were sometimes at Wilbury under the arrangement with Sir Henry Malet, and every summer they would sail to France in the *Hoyden*. But business required Thomas to be in London frequently as well as to visit his constituency at King's Lynn, and he never went anywhere for more than a day or two without the children. At King's Lynn they would usually stay at the Globe Hotel. He was not an easy guest. Dorothy relates that early one morning, when staying there, he woke his family and the rest of the hotel with loud shouts of 'Fire!' She continues: 'We ran out to ask where the fire was. My father, still shouting "Fire!", said that was what he wanted to know as he had asked for one in his sitting room at 6 a.m.' In London they would at first stay at Claridges, which was not at all like it is now. Sydney describes it as 'a comfortable and homely hotel situated in four or five not very large houses in Brook Street. There were no public rooms, but each guest had his bedroom and sitting-room, solidly and comfortably furnished. The food was excellent, the staff well-trained.' It was already expensive, but Thomas could afford it, thanks to *The Lady*. However, as soon as he became a Member of Parliament in 1892 he needed his own London residence. At first he took a succession of furnished houses, not always very pleasant. Sydney mentions one in particular, 'a horrid dark house in Hertford Street, which is a horrid dark street. The song of the year was "After the Ball", and the very sound of this sad tune at the [barrel-] organ which came every Thursday was enough to cause tears.' They had at the time 'a dreadful governess who used to fight with me and then make it up in a theatrical manner'. Thomas dismissed her as soon as he found out what was going on, but she stayed for some time, possibly more than a year.

Finally, in 1894, Thomas found 25 Lowndes Square. It was not beautiful, but it suited them: it had a good drawing room for Thomas, and another big room for the girls' lessons, with a piano and a 'grubby kind of conservatory' at one end. Thomas felt that Sydney, now fourteen and still suffering from the hysterical governess, was old enough to start doing the housekeeping. He put her in charge of the servants, and gave her the account books and even his cheque book in which she would prepare the cheques for his signature. This arrangement was to last for the ten years until she left to get married to David Mitford, when Dorothy took over for the two years before she herself married. The experience was to prove valuable to Sydney, especially when she was first married. She and her husband were, both then and later, some-times short of money, but it would always be mitigated by Sydney's efficiency at managing the household. The responsibility laid on her by Thomas had its pleasant side. She enjoyed Tuesday afternoons, when she sallied forth from Lowndes Square with Dorothy and the governess to the Army and Navy Stores, list in hand, to order the week's groceries. Afterwards they took the lift up to the top floor for tea, which was a treat. On the way the lift man would announce the departments on each floor in a sing-song voice, his pitch rising with his lift from bass at the ground floor to a clear tenor at the third. Sydney would always remember his rigmarole word for word, with its exact intonation. Keeping the accounts, too, was a task Sydney accomplished without difficulty. What she did find trying was having to manage the servants, of whom there were about six, two of them men. These last paid little attention to their teenage mistress. They were often 'dirty, drunk and generally disreputable', although they took care to behave themselves when Thomas was there. Sydney was too diffident, or perhaps too proud, to call him in to assist. She did, however, make a resolution in this period never to employ men-servants in any household of her own. She was to keep to this; she and David never employed a butler or footman, always par-lourmaids. On one occasion Sydney did complain to Thomas that a particular footman, also called Thomas, was appallingly stupid. 'My dear,' said her father, 'of course he is stupid. If he were not stupid he would be Prime Minister of England or a Marshal of France.'

We have already alluded to the first visit of the Bowles family to Batsford, which took place in the winter of 1894–95. Bertie Mitford asked Thomas to come and speak for him at a meeting, and he agreed, but asked if his children could come; he may even more or less have made it a condition. Bertie made no difficulties; he was hospitable, his new house at Batsford was extremely commodious, and he himself had a large family, some of whom were of compatible ages. So Thomas went along with Geoffrey, Sydney and Dorothy; George, for some reason, did not come this time.

This first visit left an enduring impression upon Sydney. A smart waggonette and pair met them at the station, complete with coachman and footmen in top hats and white breeches. After a long drive in the dark they arrived.

The big door opened and a flood of warm light came through it; and, opposite the door, burned a great fire of logs standing upright in the fireplace . . . The peculiar thing about this hall was its smell – the most delicious and special odour. It seemed compounded of wood-fire, beeswax-polish, and . . . rare spices; and, if I had come across this smell in the desert, I should have been at once transported back to the hall at Batsford.

They were ushered next door, into the library, where they were greeted by Bertie and Clementine. Their daughters Frances and Iris were there as well, 'and, with his back to the fire, standing half on the fender, and wearing an old brown velveteen coat such as keepers wore in those days, stood a wonderful figure of a young man. It was David, aged 17. So, when I was 14 and he was 17, I fell in love with him. Certainly I fell out again, and we did not marry for nine years after that.' The romantic note, in Sydney's writing, is often followed in this way by a slight cold douche. She continues to describe her future in-laws, aged fifty-seven and forty-one, as they first appeared to her. Bertie 'was the best looking *old* man I ever saw, with pure white hair and glittering . . . blue eyes, together with a bony rather hooked nose and a good figure, though not very tall . . . Lady Clementine had a fine presence and much personality. She was beautiful in her youth but, like all middle-aged women then, was too fat. She had nine children, and therefore she had some reason for having lost her youthful figure.' In fact Lady Clementine had then only seven children; the twins which made up her total of nine were to be born in September 1895.

What with the two good-looking daughters, and the glamorous David, Sydney 'tried to put my best foot foremost and show at my best in this glorious company'. But Thomas was not much help. 'Lady Clementine asked Tap if the children dined downstairs, and he said "Oh, yes." We could see, with a little dismay, that she had expected him to say "Oh, no." ' In the end it was arranged that nine-year-old Dorothy should have supper upstairs, and Geoffrey and Sydney should go down. Bertie took her arm as they went in to the enormous dinner which was usual in the big houses of those days, and consisted of soup, fish, entree, joint, game and dessert. 'No human being could eat so much and remain slim and healthy,' Sydney comments, and adds that in practice people would often take very little of a course or refuse it entirely. Thomas was a pioneer in opposition to the practice of overeating, and the fact that he was in Bertie's house for the first time did not stop him airing his views. 'All was going well with Tap behaving himself in a seemly manner when our host was heard to press one of the guests, a gross old man, to have some more, saying "It will do you good." Tap leaned across the table and called out: "My dear Sir, the part of your dinner that does you the most good is the part that you *don't* eat." ' He was, no doubt, only trying to be helpful; and the rest of the dinner passed off happily. Afterwards Geoffrey and Sydney played the piano and sang songs, 'the only accomplishment in which I seemed to excel these wonderful Mitfords, and one which they seemed to enjoy'. Geoffrey specialized in sea songs like 'Tom Bowling', while Sydney sang the American songs that were then in fashion and known as 'nigger songs'.

The political meeting took place a day or two later at Broadway, eight miles away. It was after dinner, and the evening was rather spoilt for Sydney because a fishbone had lodged in her throat. 'When I got back to my room I managed to get it out with a button-hook, for which I was much praised.' The meeting was a quiet affair, and 'seemed much less good to me than our big roaring meetings at Lynn'.

All in all, the Mitfords must have taken to the Bowles family, despite Thomas's quirks and Lady Clementine's conventionality, for they went fairly often after that. It was at this time that Thomas dismissed the hysterical governess. He consulted Lady Clementine, who knew of the perfect replacement. Her name was Miss Loraine, and she was 'old and a dragon, a disciplinarian, a teacher of manners'. Sydney acknowledges that she and Dorothy needed such a personality at the time, although for Sydney herself, already in charge of the household, it must have been confusing to be expected to tell off the butler at one moment and submit to Miss Loraine at the next. Thomas put up with Miss Loraine, though not altogether willingly. She forbade such things as Sydney's habit of stretching herself during meals, which Thomas, on the whole, had encouraged: 'Very good for you, my child.' The practice may have accorded with the precepts of Dr Kellgren, but even Thomas saw that a girl had to learn some deportment. Miss Loraine stayed with the family for two years, between 1895 and 1897. If Thomas was not altogether sorry to see her go, she had at any rate, in Sydney's words, 'found a pair of savages and . . . helped to turn us into human beings'. Mathematics, even arithmetic, were, according to Sydney, beyond Miss Loraine's powers, but she 'was a very good teacher of French grammar and she made me play Beethoven'. Beethoven, that is, rather than the songs and popular music which Sydney liked to play, exactly as her mother had done. Sydney had great musical facility, and until her old age, when Parkinson's disease made it impossible, was fond of gathering her children and descendants round the piano for a sing-song. Her playing was no doubt the better for Miss Loraine having forced her to learn some of the classics; it would have helped her to do justice to her favourites, 'Grace Darling' and 'Soldiers of the Queen', as well as to the 'Death of Nelson' which always brought tears to her eyes. Towards the end of her life, too, we remember her very competently sightreading '*Als die gold'ne Abendsonne*', a song about one of Hitler's regiments marching into a little German town. Unity had brought the music home.

Thomas's morning routine remained much as at Cleeve Lodge, except that now Sydney would accompany him on his morning rides in the park. She gives an affectionate description of a fine May morning in the late 1890s:

The sun comes in early through the flowery chintz curtains and, in the distance, we hear the Guards band faint and far away but ever coming nearer. We jump out of bed, put on dressing-gowns, and throw wide open the window to see the Guards pass. Soon they come swinging along, the band playing *The Belle of New York* or *The Quaker Girl* and the men glancing up to see if the maids are looking out of the windows at the tops of the houses – and of course they are. The Regiment marches on into the park. It is about eight o'clock, time to get up . . . The plane trees in the Square are putting on leaf and it will be hot. I put on my thick cloth riding-skirt with breeches underneath, and my thinnest coat which is of black flannel with a white pin-stripe, and I tie my white silk stock. Then we go down to breakfast with our governess. Punctually at nine Tap comes for me to walk round to the Mews behind the house to give carrots to the horses and see them bridled, or sometimes they are brought round to the door. Many other horses are waiting at other doors, their grooms walking them up and down.

The row was crowded, and the ride there was 'like an amusing party taking place every day'. They always came home by eleven, for Thomas's breakfast and Sydney's lessons.

Sundays of course were very different; the famous British Sunday, famous all over Europe for its gloom, was at the time in full force. There was no riding in the Row. Instead, if they had a governess who insisted, the girls went to church. Thomas never went, though Sydney insists, perhaps somewhat defensively, that he was 'very far from being a man without a religion'. Certainly he knew his Bible well, but his worship of God was too individual to fit easily into the assumptions of any church. Then, at midday, the family put on their best clothes and went into the park for a walk. So did all London; the occasion was known as Church Parade, because a great many of the walkers were returning from church. It was a little like a walking version of the daily ride in the Row, except that there were more people; the proportion of people known to the Bowles family being accordingly lower, it was less of a party.

Sunday afternoons were the time to pay calls. If Thomas was not in the mood to do so, the girls found that the time hung heavy; if he was, they had other worries. Sydney does not mention people calling on them: no doubt this was because there was no hostess to preside. It was usually men who called on their women friends, who 'sat at home hopefully, with a large tea-table covered with cakes and sandwiches, ready to "receive"'. Thomas frequented several hostesses, but he had a peculiarity; he always took his daughters with him, and the boys too when they were home from school. This was all right when there were children in the house, as at the Sykeses: Mark Sykes had remained a friend of George's after their trip together up the Nile. But otherwise the ladies, Sydney thinks, 'must have been much put out by the arrival of two little girls with hearty appetites at their afternoon tea-parties where they were hoping to entertain politicians and writers and to form a kind of salon'. In the earlier years, at any rate, the girls would be dressed in their sailor costumes, made now at Gieves, the forces' tailor, but still to the correct naval specifications except for the skirt. Thomas had no idea that the children might be in the way, but they themselves soon began to notice 'that some topics were discussed in an undertone, and we looked away and pretended not to hear'.

One hostess, Mrs Bischoffsheim, told Thomas plainly that she did not want the girls, so when they went there he would leave them in the hall, sitting in the footmen's beehive basket chairs and reading their papers. There was a 'comic paper called *Ally Sloper's Half Holiday*, and a sporting print known familiarly as "*The Pink'Un*"'. The trouble was that now and then a well-meaning guest would come and tell Mrs Bischoffsheim that there were two children sitting in the hall, and she would have to ask them in; this did not please them, as they knew quite well that they were not welcome. When Sydney was about sixteen this particular ordeal ceased, because she took such offence at something Mrs Bischoffsheim said that she begged Thomas never to take her there again. Oddly enough it was a compliment, if rather a rough one. The hostess looked Sydney up and down and said: 'H'm. She won't hang fire long.' The acknowledgement of her good looks, already becoming noticeable, was more than offset for Sydney by the manner of appraisal, for all the world as if she were a horse. Thomas would be by turns amusing and acutely embarrassing, or indeed both at once. One hostess was called Mrs Crackenthorpe, and her husband was Montague Cookson Crackenthorpe. Thomas thought the name funny, and while waiting on their doorstep he would do a little dance while singing 'Montague Cook – Montague Cook – Montague Cookson Crackenthorpe'. This would cause the girls to get fits of the giggles, the more agonizing in that at any moment the Crackenthorpe butler might catch Thomas at this performance. Much as he amused his children, there were many ways in which he made them squirm. At Sydney's very first grown-up dinner party, when she was seventeen, she was mortified to hear her hostess say in a vexed tone: 'There! Mr Bowles has taken all the peas again.' On one summer evening he was guest of honour of the mayor of Hammersmith in the town hall; the invitation may have been at short notice, or perhaps he had forgotten to tell Sydney, but in any case he could not find her. So he called out of the window to Dorothy who, dressed of course in sailor clothes, was walking the dogs in the Lowndes Square garden, grubby as only a London garden in those days of coal smuts could be. He whisked her off to the dinner without giving her time even to wash, let alone change. 'Elegant ladies in beautiful gowns, gloves and tiaras were surprised when the Mayor offered me his arm and sat me at his right hand at the top table.' She remembered little more owing to her glass being repeatedly filled with champagne. Her age at the time of this incident is uncertain, but she cannot have been more than seventeen at the very most and was probably considerably younger. When she did reach the age of seventeen, even Thomas saw that Dorothy was getting too old for sailor clothes, and as part of her outfitting took her to a shop to buy her a bonnet. He settled in a chair and asked if the blue bonnet in the window would suit a lady of forty.

'Admirably,' replied the assistant.

To which Thomas said: 'Then it will not do for my daughter aged seventeen. Good afternoon, Ma'am.'

His methods of getting to know people at sea could also be mortifying. On one occasion he had rowed himself and the family alongside a man-of-war and asked, 'Is Captain Johnson on board?'

Back came the reply: 'No Captain Johnson here, sir. Captain Wells.'

'Oh, of course,' said Thomas, 'I mean Captain Wells,' and asked to see him.

Soon, says Sydney, Captain Wells was their good friend; 'but this method of approach embarrassed us dreadfully'.

This incident occurred during one of their regular annual cruises in the *Hoyden*, which occupied much of Parliament's summer recess. The girls came along every year until they married. They always went to France, usually to Trouville and Deauville on the Normandy coast. Trouville, just beginning to be 'discovered' when Bertie was a small boy, was by then a well-known resort. It was there they got to know the fashionable artist Helleu, who was to be an intimate family friend. Helleu is almost forgotten now, for we associate the nineties with the Impressionists, but he was at that time very well known. His portraits are fresh and lively, as are his pictures of ships. He painted several pictures of young Sydney at this time. Helleu, like Thomas, was a yachtsman, and in the summer would base himself in Trouville harbour, living in his yacht, the *Etoile*, with his wife and two children. Rather as Thomas had used the *Hoyden* as his committee room at King's Lynn, Helleu made his yacht into a studio where he would paint the *beau monde* who came in the summer, or do the then fashionable dry-point etching on a sheet of copper. A favourite sitter was Consuelo, Duchess of Marlborough, née Vanderbilt. After they became friends, he and Thomas would usually tie up alongside each other. Each liked the other's company; Helleu was as much of a humorist as Thomas. He used to say of his wife that he had married her for her hair, which was of a rich auburn colour, and Sydney records him quoting La Rochefoucauld: 'When a piece of good fortune befalls you, look at the face of your best friend – you will see a grimace on it.' He worked fast and kept his sitters amused by a flow of chat interlarded with compliments on their appearance. Sydney often sat for him and his compliments 'gave me a very good conceit of myself'. Diana, too, was later to be on the receiving end of these compliments. Helleu had an artist's delight in the appearance of things. One windy day Sydney was looking over his shoulder as he was painting the yachts in the harbour, all dressed in their flags for the occasion of the Grand Prix de Deauville. Helleu said: '*Ah, que je suis heureux! Je suis au bal avec les drapeaux.*' Sydney and Dorothy used to enjoy the scene at Deauville races, enhanced by spectacular floral decorations, though conscious that their own standard of dress was not up to that of the Frenchwomen. Helleu's darkly handsome daughter Ellen, a little younger than Dorothy, seemed very elegant. 'The dresses which had been thought very pretty in London looked positively dreadful at Deauville,' says Sydney; not the first English girl to have this feeling, which Nancy would have endorsed. She remembers Thomas waiting patiently for the two of them as each did up the other's long hair with masses of pins in front of the only available long mirror.

Through Helleu they came to know two other well-known artists. One was Boldini, a fashionable portraitist whose reputation has remained, perhaps, higher than that of Helleu. People referred to him as '*le monstre*', and Sydney thought him an old horror. He was catty about his friend Helleu; talking of his pictures of the Duchess of Marlborough, Boldini used to say there were many Helleus at Blenheim – in the passages. The other was the cartoonist Sem, whom she calls 'a dear little fellow'. Their company was relaxing to Thomas as they talked amusingly, but never of politics. They obviously liked this English '*député*', although thinking him rather serious. Their main interest, naturally, was in the graphic arts, and artists. As might be expected, their tastes were not those of today; of those of their contemporaries respected in our own times, the only one they admired unreservedly was Degas. In one minor respect Helleu's taste was actually in advance of his time, and that was in interior decoration. Sydney says that his Paris drawing room, which doubled as his studio, was full of furniture upholstered in white, anticipating by a generation the fashion for white furniture initiated by Syrie Maugham between the wars and known as the 'white furniture traffic'.

As time went on, Thomas certainly did not become any less quirky. We shall be noting this in the next chapters as regards his public activities; his private habits remained the same as he became older, only perhaps more so. He often used to take a house in Scotland for part of the summer, and according to Dorothy, in her second *Times* article, he rigged up, outside one of these, a Turkish bath in some empty dog kennels. One kennel was filled with bricks which were heated by a stove. 'When they were hot enough, in went Tap. Later he emerged to be drenched by buckets of cold water, thrown from the roof by the butler.' The trouble was that the kennels were situated near the front door, in full view of it; so callers were often treated to the sight of Thomas, naked as the day he was born, undergoing his improvised shower. Another health rule which he certainly practised at the end of his life, although it is uncertain when he began it, was one of the forms of *neti*, the cleansing of the nasal passages as practised by some devotees of yoga. Every day he would take a bowl of tepid water, lightly salted so as to bring the osmotic pressure roughly in balance with that of the body, and breathe it in through the nose, then expel it. Pam says he told her how to do this when she was a small girl. It is supposed to prevent colds. It would be interesting to know where he got the idea from.

Life in Lowndes Square continued in the same way as the girls grew up, interspersed with the visits to Scotland and the annual trips in the *Hoyden*. Sydney married David Mitford in 1904, when she was twenty-four. Thomas lent the *Hoyden* to the young couple for their honeymoon cruise, complete with Ned Kersey, though the crew was not as satisfactory as in former times. Sydney wrote to Thomas, on 5 September 1904: 'We have had some trouble with our boys – the first was a dirty little beast and the second had no soul above a whelk-pot which he was always attending to when Ned wanted him . . . he has been dismissed too . . . Ned says it is very different from his day when you threw a boy overboard and left him there for half an hour for nothing at all.' Presumably this was an example of Ned's salty humour.

Sydney's marriage did not seriously disturb Thomas; he gave David a job on *The Lady*, and they settled down in Graham Street and started their family. Dorothy took over Thomas's household; she was nineteen and just as competent as her sister. However, she had her difficulties, and they were, exactly as Sydney's had been, with the male staff. The butler was inefficient, and the Armenian chef, though an excellent cook, was extremely tiresome. Thomas often used to give him notice, but he refused to leave. Once he chased the butler with a large saucepan full of hot potatoes. 'Finally Tap said: "We must shut up the house in order to get rid of Ohannes. We will go to China." We dismissed the household and installed a policeman and his wife as caretakers. On the day of the departure I waited for my father in a four-wheeled cab piled with luggage. Thomas walked slowly to the cab, put his head through the window, and said "It is raining, my dear Piggy. We won't go." And we never did.' (*The Times*.)

However, in a couple of years Dorothy began seriously courting, and it began to look as if she would get married too. This worried Thomas; he had no other daughter to take over the housekeeping, and he would miss her as well. This was also the time of the intrigue against him in his constituency, supported by Conservative Central Office, which was to lose him his seat at King's Lynn; it was not a good time for Thomas. Dorothy's admirer, Percy Bailey, was a young officer in the 12th Lancers, a good cavalry regiment; his antecedents were impeccable, yet Thomas grumbled. He did not want her to follow the drum, he said; and when Percy took her to the Savoy for dinner, he expressed objection to her 'roistering in taverns'. However, there was nothing for it but to agree to the match, though his temper was not improved by the fact that, during the months before she married, Dorothy rather neglected the housekeeping. On his drive with her to the church, Thomas, suddenly struck by his sadness at losing her, mitigated it by bringing up this point. 'He became very melancholy and wearily remarked that he would now never know what he owed the Aylesbury Dairy.'

# 17

# Disenchantment

One common pleasure that Thomas enjoyed more than most people was saying 'I told you so.' He was able to do this in 1900 in a renewed attack on the Declaration of Paris of 1858, because it was quite evident that the renunciation of the right of search, to which Britain had consented in 1858, was hampering the prosecution of the Boer War. As he puts it in his pamphlet, if it were not for that change in international law all merchandise belonging to the Boer republics could be seized, including all the gold production from the Transvaal being shipped to Europe in exchange for arms. The pamphlet had no effect at the time, but it was in due course to bear fruit.

It was now, however, that Thomas's political career began to go wrong. Superficially, one might think that it was his misfortune that the Conservatives came to form the government in 1895. The record would seem to show that he was better fitted for opposition than to be a loyal member or follower of a government. But was this really the case? He was a phrase-maker and a clever debater, but that is by no means all he was. He was also indefatigably industrious, capable of tackling any amount of small print. This aptitude for detailed work, combined with his other abilities, would undoubtedly have made him an outstanding minister, perhaps surpassing his father, who was in so many ways like him. Perhaps Lord Salisbury and his successor Arthur Balfour ought to have made a real effort to harness his talents. The point was often made in the press at the time, and certainly, if such an effort had been made and had succeeded, the government, besides gaining an effective minister, would also have been spared from the attacks of probably the most damaging of the critics who harassed it from its own backbenches.

There is another side to this, though. Thomas's differences with the government were real and substantial, and clearly destined to grow. For the Conservative government and party were moving towards protectionism, which he opposed as much as his father had, despite a momentary flirtation in the eighties with 'fair trading'. It was a part of a generally collectivist mood that was emerging in the party, a collectivism based on the interests of manufacturing industry seen as a sort of cooperative to which, when necessary, the interests of the consumer had to be sacrificed. This was to be the dominant sentiment in Europe between the wars, cutting across ideological and national boundaries, and it is still very much alive. The closed system of Stalin's Russia, Mussolini's corporatism and Hitler's autarky with exchange control were all virulent expressions of it, and in Britain it was to take the milder forms of imperial preference and Keynesianism. Before the First World War the trends which were to lead in these directions and away from free trade could already clearly be seen. Industry was in difficulties from foreign competition, and the idea of putting national sentiment and national power to work in propping it up was beginning to look seductive. To Thomas, not only a free trader but also an extreme individualist, collectivism was as repugnant as protection. He never had any conception of the problems and requirements of manufacturing industry, and was as far as it is possible to be from the view that production, as such, is a sign of strength. He would have sympathized with the modern trend towards 'deindustrialization'.

But this was still in the far future, and in the meantime the tendency was strongly the other way. British industry was a fact; millions depended on it for their livelihood. It had been first in the field, but foreigners were now competing. They could not always be defeated by price, especially since social conditions abroad were as a rule such as to facilitate competition by sweated labour. Very well; protection must be introduced to secure the market, and a policy of imperialism must be pursued to extend it.

It was Joseph Chamberlain, the former Radical mayor of Birmingham, who had brought these attitudes and policies with him into the Conservative Party; and the section of the party which he led was becoming more and more influential, making the old landed interest accommodate it. Thomas eventually came to hate Chamberlain as much as he had once hated Gladstone, and Chamberlain was an important member of the government team. So while Thomas as a minister might, indeed, have made a great contribution, it can equally be said that he might have only done this for a period, before a resignation which he would have made very sure was spectacular.

For he was a resigner. In 1901 Balfour appointed him a member of a committee to look into the defences of the naval base at Gibraltar. It had been set up as a result of a pamphlet written by Thomas himself in the previous year, *Gibraltar – a National Danger*. In it he said that the dry docks then being built in Gibraltar were in the wrong place; work ought to be stopped and the installations constructed on the east side of the Rock, out of the range of Spanish guns. Balfour was impressed by this argument, and formed the Gibraltar Committee to look into it and report; it was logical that Thomas should be a member. The inquiry was completed in a month, and on all important matters the committee was as one. But Thomas objected to some details in the report, so he suddenly and for no substantial reason resigned. It was all very well for the journalist Spencer Leigh Hughes to comment in the *Morning Leader* shortly afterwards that Thomas 'is one of the few interesting members of this Parliament . . . which was born moribund', that he was 'always up to something' and 'as mobile and ubiquitous as a Boer leader'; all very well, too, to laugh at Balfour for having been driven by his resignation from the committee 'into a display of temper most unladylike'. Balfour had his faults; if not exactly effeminate, as Leigh Hughes hints, he was perhaps a little languid. But he also had a government to run, and a government must be a team. If Thomas could thus flounce out of the Gibraltar Committee, then he might similarly flounce out of a cabinet. Leigh Hughes goes on to be facetious about Thomas having perhaps been left out of the government because he was not tall enough, and then, more to the point, to speculate that he might have been included had he been a member of Lord Salisbury's Cecil family – Balfour was Salisbury's nephew – or the clique of Birmingham-based MPs who were the 'family' of Joseph Chamberlain. Thomas was later to mock a great deal at both Cecil and Chamberlain supporters. On balance, Balfour would probably have done better to try Thomas out when he first became Prime

Minister. One person who certainly wanted to take the chance was
Joseph Chamberlain himself. Chamberlain approached him twice,
once directly, once through an associate; the second time was after
the tariff reform movement started and Thomas had made clear
his rooted opposition to it. Thomas was to reveal these approaches
in a speech at the General Election in 1906, when Chamberlain
was playing a leading and open part in driving him from the
House of Commons.

After the Gibraltar Committee investigation had been completed, in April 1901, Thomas delayed his return to England to
take a trip to Seville, where he met the Duke of Marlborough and
his young nephew, Winston Churchill, who was newly elected to
the House of Commons. Thomas had admired his father, Lord
Randolph Churchill, whose 'ginger group' within the Conservative Party *Vanity Fair* had supported in 1880. Now, in Seville,
Winston Churchill read Thomas the maiden speech he proposed
to deliver, and Thomas was sufficiently impressed to predict
in his diary a great future for him. When the speech was delivered, Thomas helped Churchill out of a rather tight corner:
Churchill describes it in *My Early Life*. He and Thomas were
sitting next to each other, and Lloyd George was speaking from
the opposite benches to an amendment he had moved. Churchill
was to be called next. Naturally he had seen to it that his speech
would have followed on perfectly well from the amendment,
which was moderately phrased, but unfortunately Lloyd George
announced that he did not intend to move it after all, and proceeded to speak on the main question, getting more and more
carried away by his own Welsh *hwyl*. Churchill, who was never in
all his long career to be particularly happy with the necessity of
speaking impromptu, and normally learned his speeches by heart,
was desperately scribbling remarks by which he might start his
speech when called, so that it should follow on from what Lloyd
George was saying. Each of his notes 'became in turn obsolete. A
sense of alarm and even despair crept across me. I repressed it
with an inward gasp. Then Mr Bowles whispered: "You might
say 'Instead of making his violent speech without moving his
moderate amendment, he had better have moved his moderate
amendment without making his violent speech.'" Manna in the
wilderness was not more welcome! It fell only just in time.' Lloyd

George sat down, and Churchill used Thomas's suggested remark, which won a general cheer, after which Churchill 'got through it all right'. The incident is a tiny one, and it is only Churchill's subsequent fame that makes it worth mentioning; but it shows Thomas's debating faculty at work, as well as providing an instance of how kind he could be to a young colleague in temporary difficulties.

To the government he became more and more of a nuisance. On 6 August 1902 he made a speech on the Appropriation Bill that was by common consent brilliant, attacking in particular a clause which lengthened the temporary borrowing powers of the Chancellor of the Exchequer. The press generally praised the speech, but in their comments one or two ominous notes could be discerned. The Conservative *Morning Post* was admiring, to be sure, but the most fulsome tribute was in the *Daily News*, whose tendency was Liberal. It is never a good sign for a politician if he is too much approved of by the press of the opposing party, as from now on began to be the case. Nor was the article in the *Daily News* exactly reassuring in the parallel it drew: it said that Thomas's irony was 'more searching than anything which the House has heard since Disraeli set himself to destroy Sir Robert Peel'. The *Liverpool Post* was also complimentary, but hinted that thwarted personal ambition might just be a factor; it said that Thomas's was the only speech that really commanded the attention of the House, but added that 'underneath his remarks was the suggestion that if the Government had only included Mr Bowles then it would be the best of all possible governments'.

Relations cooled further. In 1903 Thomas's name was dropped from the Public Accounts Committee. The *Daily News* protested, on the grounds that Thomas 'is by far the most important member of the committee. He has devoted continuous time and labour to it; he has discovered many gross instances of financial laxity; he has been a veritable watchdog of the public and the House in their struggle with the slipshod extravagance of the Executive.' He was reappointed to the committee the next year, but resigned in 1905.

He now began opposing the Government more and more frequently. It was natural that he should vote, on 9 February 1904, for a Liberal motion condemning any policy of protective tariffs; this was in accordance with his deep and conscientious beliefs. So, it might be said, was his opposition to the government's policy with regard to the introduction of Chinese indentured labour into the Transvaal. The labourers were volunteers for a period of three years, and objections by local people compelled the authorities to enclose them in isolated compounds; this provoked the accusation of slavery by the Liberal opposition, and it would certainly have touched the chord of libertarianism in Thomas. But he was uncharacteristically naive if he did not suspect that the Liberals were raising this matter as a political stunt, as was proved by the fact that when they came to power in 1906 they did nothing to change the system. And why did he vote for an opposition motion to reduce the Army by ten thousand men? Four more times that year he voted against the government, and finally the local Conservatives at King's Lynn, encouraged by Central Office, decided they had had enough. On 20 January 1905, while he was absent in Egypt, they adopted another candidate for the next election in his stead. They can hardly have hoped that Thomas would take this lying down, and the party leaders in London, at any rate, were probably resigned to losing the seat at the next election; but Thomas had become such a nuisance that the loss was considered worthwhile. Besides his adverse speeches and votes he was a ready coiner of the damaging quip; it was he who first called the Balfour government the 'Hotel Cecil' because of its alleged domination by the Cecil family. This epithet caught on, and did the government no good at all.

It is decidedly, and we think significantly, uncharacteristic of Thomas that he should not have been aware of the move against him in his constituency and counteracted it. Already ten months before, in February 1904, two Members of Parliament who were close supporters of Joseph Chamberlain, stung by a particularly vicious attack by Thomas on their man, had sent a telegram to the mayor of King's Lynn asking when the town would be represented by a gentleman; a clear sign to local people that their member was not to be considered sacrosanct. Thomas might have fought back in the constituency association, where he could certainly have mustered plenty of personal supporters. Alternatively, he might have crossed the floor of the House as his father had done long ago, resigning his seat and fighting a by-election as a Liberal, which the actual result at the subsequent General

Election suggests he would have won. But changing parties is a big step for any politician to take, and Thomas, already well into his sixties, had been a Conservative, and a strongly partisan one, for a very long time indeed. Going over to the Liberals would mean severing a whole host of sentimental and personal ties, built up over a lifetime. He would be joining the party of the pro-Boers, the party of death duties, the party of Gladstone! He was to do it, but the process involved a period of indecision in which the initiative was left in other hands.

Thomas stood as an independent at the election, and went down fighting. The new candidate, Alan Burgoyne, knew perfectly well what he was up against, admitting at his adoption meeting that Bowles was 'one of the finest orators in England' and might have achieved high office had he not started to oppose most of the government's policies. In later speeches Burgoyne turned nasty, accusing Thomas of being motivated by selfishness and conceit. This, indeed, was how a good many people saw him, including from this time onwards the Mitford family, to whom, since Sydney's marriage in 1904, he was now linked. Lady Clementine, or Lady Redesdale as she now was, asked Thomas, probably at the time of the election of 1910, for what party he was standing. He thumped himself on the chest and replied: 'Bowles.' This became a familiar anecdote in the family, and Bertie's daughter Daphne was to bring it up as an instance of Thomas's egotism. In a way it is; but there can also be seen in it a kind of forlorn bravado, a retreat into clowning. Another less shrewd crack by Burgoyne, alluding to Thomas's age, was that he 'appeared to be smitten with incipient second childhood'. This is belied by his electioneering performance, in particular by one speech in which he excoriated Joseph Chamberlain. Chamberlain had endorsed Burgoyne as candidate in a letter describing Thomas as a false friend who had stabbed his party in the back. This gave Thomas an opening, for Chamberlain had abandoned the Liberal Party, as well as most of the policies of his early career, and had not proved an easy colleague to Balfour. Thomas said:

Mr Chamberlain started as a Republican, which, indeed, gave him his opportunity of abandoning his first political associate Sir Charles Dilke. He was then a Free Trader of the most pronounced type, a

Radical of the most violent description, an apostle of Ransom, and a name of such fear that at the word Chamberlain the fine ladies of London hastened to lock up their spoons. He is now a Protectionist and a Conservative, and though still a revolutionary, to some extent a consort of the aristocracy.

Thomas said he had always mistrusted him. 'I remembered that he had deserted Mr Gladstone. I remembered the phrase in *Othello* – "She did deceive her father, and may thee".' After revealing Chamberlain's earlier approaches to himself to join the government, he repudiates the accusation of false friendship and back-stabbing.

My opposition has always been open, always avowed. It has been made to the faces of those I have opposed, on the floor of the House, before the assembled senators of the country. It has been made in plain language. It has been supported by argument. This is no false friendship, nor stabbing in the back.

I will tell you my idea of a false friend and a back-stabber. To sweat the workman for personal profit, and fawn on him for political profit; to promise old age pensions for votes, and, having got the votes, to refuse the pensions; to intrigue against your own leader in his own cabinet and, because he rejects your insane proposals, to resign at a critical moment; to drive out of the cabinet by secret intrigue every man of position, capacity and repute; to insist that an abjectly incapable son shall be made Chancellor of the Exchequer as the price of abstention from opposition, and, having got this, nevertheless to blackmail for two and a half years the Government you have abandoned; at the end of that time to procure the insulting rejection by the representatives of the party of a resolution approving your leader's policy; and to follow this up by openly flouting and insulting that leader with charges of humiliating and disgracing the party, while at the same time beslavering him with professions of affection – this is false friendship; this is stabbing in the back.

It was a caricature, but a recognizable one, of Chamberlain's career, expressed with damning effectiveness. But it is the very end of this speech that leads us, rereading it today, into uneasy thoughts:

With all his talents, though Mr Chamberlain has occasionally got the support of selfish interests, he has never won the affection or the trust of any party. He who, had he been honest and true, might have been a leader, can never be but what he always was – a wrecker. This is what makes him so bitter – that he feels that he is the most conspicuous failure of the nineteenth century – that he who could never endure to be second, will nevertheless never become first . . .

We shall never know if this was true of Chamberlain, because what ended his political career was, in the event, a permanently incapacitating stroke. It can however, with one important change, be all too readily applied to Thomas himself. He can easily be depicted as being bitter through having become a wrecker instead of a leader. But it would be wrong to say this was because he was not honest and true. The trouble was precisely that he was these things, that he stuck to his beliefs of a lifetime, rather than compromise them. In the end, politics is a nastier business than he could ever bring himself to see. It is not in real life but only in legend and rhetoric that honesty and truth, as such, are qualifications for political leadership.

This speech against Chamberlain made quite a stir, and not only inside the constituency. It earned him, he claimed, a thousand letters, postcards and telegrams in support. The *Daily News* described it as 'an amazing piece of invective', comparable to Hazlitt: 'It belongs indeed to the day when satire was fiercely candid as well as delightfully literary.' But it did not win him the seat, which went to the Liberal, a retired naval lieutenant called Carlyon Bellairs. Not only was the Conservative vote split, but there was in that election a countrywide Liberal landslide. In this context, Thomas's result was notable. The vote was:

| | |
|---|---|
| Bellairs (Liberal) | 1,506 |
| Bowles (Independent) | 1,164 |
| Burgoyne (Conservative) | 772 |

When, besides the Liberal landslide, it is remembered how very marginal the seat was during Thomas's first two elections, it seems remarkable that the combined vote for Burgoyne and Thomas of 1,936 was so comfortably higher than the Liberal vote. Only really sizeable personal support for Thomas can explain it. The result was still the end of him as a serious politician, though he was again to enter Parliament briefly, as a Liberal. He was however to remain very active in public affairs as a voluble outrider. He was also ultimately to score two successes against the Establishment: one was spectacular but in the end rather useless, while the other was quieter and of more specialized interest, but quite possibly saved the country in the First World War.

# 18

# Elderly Gadfly

Thomas was sixty-five when he lost his seat, the age at which it is now considered appropriate for a man to retire; but retirement was the last thing he had in mind. It was a consolation that the Balfour government had been swept out of office. A parallel springs to mind, from 1974, when Edward Heath was defeated partly through Enoch Powell's activities. Powell later disclosed that, on hearing the news when under his shower, 'I sang a Te Deum.' We do not know whether Thomas did anything analogous in his Turkish bath, but his sentiments must have been similar. Just as Powell was to regard Harold Wilson's Labour Party as the only hope to get Britain out of the Common Market, Thomas thought, and stated in an open letter dated July 1906, that 'Sir Henry Campbell-Bannerman's Government and the Liberal Party now alone stand between the country and the catastrophe of Protection'. He now joined the Liberal Party, addressing many meetings all over the country and writing frequently to the press, especially on the subject of national finance. He also, purely to annoy, opposed Arthur Balfour in the City of London, where the seat was vacated for Balfour following the loss of his own seat in the débâcle of the General Election. The City was so safe for the Conservatives that normally Balfour would have been returned unopposed, so Thomas put him to the trouble of fighting a by-election.

The contest may have been hopeless, but Thomas was at the top of his form as a speaker. It is worth quoting one comment, by James Douglas in the *Morning Leader*, not so much because it is complimentary as because it catches the particular nature of his speaking style: 'His oratory is an assault. He does not persuade; he carries you by cold storm. His eloquence is frigidly clear, fluently laconic, barbed with sarcasm or feathered with derision, void of sentiment, emotion, imagination or moral splendour – absolutely lean, bare, bony logic.' This verbal puritanism is very Anglo-Saxon, very East Anglian; the high flights of the Celt are foreign to it, but it can be as effective in debate as Cromwell's Ironsides in battle.

He was to fight several more elections, but only succeeded in getting back to Parliament once, and that for less than a year. He was re-elected for King's Lynn in February 1910 as a Liberal, but lost again in December. Thomas cannot have been much happier with the Liberal Party of 1910, with its radical budget and determination to curb the power of the House of Lords, than he was with the Conservative Party of 1906. The main political battles were being fought between men with whom he had no sympathy and over matters in which he had little interest.

The most important thing he did, and it may well have been the most important achievement of his life, was to frustrate the setting up of an international court of appeal to override national courts in the matter of naval prizes. The significance of this was that if, in time of war, the British Navy captured a vessel and the British courts decided that its cargo should be impounded, the other party could in certain circumstances appeal against the decision to the international court. Since the British Navy was then the most powerful in the world, it was clearly to Britain's disadvantage that law be substituted for force in naval matters. It is true that international law, then as now, would always in practice have to give way to force; that if in time of war Britain felt the need to override some adverse decision of the new court she would be physically capable of doing so. But this would be a gift to enemy propaganda and a needless irritation to many neutrals. The proposal to set up the court was made, and agreed, by the Second Peace Conference at The Hague in 1907, and it was worked out in detail. Rather as the United Nations Security Council has its permanent and its temporary members, the court was to consist of eight permanent members, one from each of the countries then adjudged Great Powers – they included, of course, Germany and Austria-Hungary – and others to be chosen by rotation, to a total of fifteen. As far as Great Britain was concerned, the proposal needed parliamentary ratification. There was opposition: *The Times*, notably, pronounced against the proposal in September 1907. Nor was it, for the time being, put before Parliament. But the Foreign Office was dead set on it, and it was clearly only a matter of time before a determined attempt would again be made to ratify. In 1909 came the Declaration of London, tending in the same direction; and this, too, would clearly come before Parliament sooner rather than later. Thomas used the time available to him to write a book, *Sea Law and Sea Power*. This closely reasoned argument against the innovations came out in 1910. It did not come a moment too soon, because in the same year the Naval Prize Bill was introduced in the House of Commons, passing in 1911. Thomas's activity redoubled; he persuaded Arthur Balfour to speak with him against the bill at a large meeting in the City of London in June 1911. The last hope was the House of Lords, and even though that body had just been deprived by the Parliament Act of the right to do more than delay a bill by two years, if it threw it out the bill might not be reintroduced.

This, in fact, is what happened. Thomas's arguments were put forward in his book with expertise and passion; they found no real rejoinder, especially at a time when the danger of war was becoming more and more apparent. The House of Commons, with its government majority handled by the whips, docilely followed the dictates of officialdom; had it not been for Thomas's book and the campaign which he orchestrated, there is little doubt that inertia and ignorance would have allowed the Prize Bill free passage through the Lords as well. The outcome of the First World War might well have been different in this event. The blockade of Germany would have been rendered impossible, or possible only at a cost in adverse propaganda that might well have been sufficient to keep the United States neutral.

Thomas now turned his attention from the law of the sea to his other main area of expertise, public finance. He took on the authorities single-handed in a test case on a point of principle, and beat them. The case was *Bowles v. the Bank of England*, and as a result of it the government was forced both to speed up its budget procedures and to pass a special Act of Parliament, which became popularly known as the Bowles Act but which he himself preferred to call the Bowles Evasion Act. It was, in its way, quite an achievement: it induced officialdom to smarten up its procedures and taught it that it cannot always have everything its own way.

The point raised by Thomas was, however, essentially trivial, and it is easy to see why his opponents regarded his action as intolerably vexatious, letting this be seen in several passages during the legal proceedings, especially at the beginning before they realized what they were up against. It had long been the practice, as it still is, for regular income payments such as dividends and most interest to be paid to the recipient after deduction of income tax at the standard rate. This made the payer of the income responsible for passing to the Exchequer the tax deducted and for providing to the recipient evidence that this had been done, evidence that the recipient would then take into account when making his own tax returns. This practice was prescribed by the law, but at the time it entailed an irregularity which, up to then, had always seemed unimportant. Income tax was authorized year by year, and each Finance Act only sanctioned it for the year with which it dealt. The law under which tax was deducted, the Income Tax Act 1842, only applied to tax properly sanctioned and imposed by Act of Parliament. Accordingly, any tax deducted from income during the period when there was no Finance Act yet in force was illegally deducted. Of course it suited everyone that this practice should be winked at. The government would be sure of getting its money punctually and independently of the parliamentary timetable; the company or authority which paid the income, similarly, was accorded an accustomed routine which was easy to follow, and for the taxpayer, though he might be out of his money a little earlier than otherwise, this was offset by the simplicity and predictability of the arrangement. What happened was that before the end of the previous year the House of Commons' Committee of Ways and Means would pass a resolution fixing the rate of income tax which would then, later, be included in the year's Finance Act. It was on the authority of this resolution that the payers of income deducted tax. The trouble was that the resolution was not an Act of Parliament; and the whole English government system, from Magna Carta onwards, was predicated on the fact that an Act of Parliament was necessary before taxation was levied.

What prompted Thomas to make his move was the fact that the

period between the beginning of each financial year and the
passing of its Finance Act had been growing ever longer. In one
year, 1909, the Finance Act was not passed at all during the
financial year with which it dealt; it only became law on 29 April
1910. This was, to be sure, a special case; it was the historic budget
introduced by Lloyd George as Chancellor of the Exchequer
which the House of Lords, contrary to long-established constitutional custom, had ventured to reject, thus calling down upon
itself the curbing of its powers in the Parliament Act of 1910. But
in other years, too, the budget procedures had at that time become
very leisurely. The Finance Acts for 1910 and 1911 were passed
respectively in November and December. That for 1912 went
through in August, but Thomas is certainly right in attributing
this acceleration to a desire to thwart his own legal action which
was at the time in progress.

His first move in his campaign against this technically unlawful
taxation was an unsuccessful action against the Attorney-General
in 1911. This concerned what was then called supertax, subsequently to be renamed surtax and later still additional rate tax.
This was then, as now, the responsibility of a body called the
Special Commissioners. Thomas contested their right to demand
returns of income for supertax purposes before the Finance Act
had been passed. Mr Justice Parker, who was also to try the case
against the Bank of England, dismissed this earlier case. He ruled
that the law did entitle the Special Commissioners to demand
returns of income since these only constituted preliminary work to
determine what tax would be payable. But he added: 'It must not
be understood that I am expressing any opinion as to how far
the Special Commissioners have power, before the tax for any
financial year is actually imposed, to go beyond the preliminary
work.' Thomas saw this as conveying the clearest of hints that the
actual collection of tax not sanctioned by Act of Parliament was
indeed illegal, and that an action hingeing directly on this specific
point would succeed.

He shifted his line of attack from supertax and from the Special
Commissioners. Income tax deducted at source, which then constituted four-fifths of all income tax collected, provided not only a
much larger target but also a much less mobile one, in the sense
that it could be reliably predicted when the income would arrive

and stocks could be bought in the certain knowledge that there would be an income payment at a particular date before the Finance Act was passed, the deduction from which would therefore be illegal. So on 31 May 1912 Thomas bought £65,500 5½ per cent Irish Land Stock at 77½, on which a six-monthly interest payment was due on 1 July. Thomas knew quite well that the Finance Act would not be through on this date. As with all government stocks, the body responsible for the payment of the interest was the Bank of England, which, though it was then privately owned, was yet in very close touch with the Treasury and charged with the management of the National Debt. He could have chosen any company or other entity which paid dividends or interest, but his choice of the Bank was obviously a suitable one. It was conspicuous; it was respectable to the point of pomposity. It was also the agent of the government which was really to blame for the irregularity, yet, being privately owned, it was not subject to any of those immunities behind which government authorities could shelter under the legal maxim, 'The King can do no wrong.' Perhaps Thomas ought to have purchased stock in the Bank of England itself, rather than Irish Land Stock, for as it was the Bank was able to argue with some show of conviction that it was only acting as agent for the Irish Land Fund. However, this did not in the event do it any good.

Thomas had the time of his life. He decided to employ no barrister, but to argue his case in person. He felt that he could do this because the case turned on constitutional law and on the law of Parliament. 'Of the former I had long been an assiduous student; with the latter I had contracted a detailed and as I believed an unusual acquaintance, as a Member of the House of Commons and of its Committee of Public Accounts,' he says in his preface to his book *Bowles v. the Bank of England*. This was true; he also had no intention of missing any of the fun.

He first tried for an injunction to stop the Bank deducting the income tax from the first payment of interest, due on 1 July. The amounts involved were as follows. Income tax was at the rate of 1s 2d in the pound, or 5.83 per cent. The gross half-yearly interest on Thomas's stock, due on 1 July, was £900 12s 6d, on which the income tax was £52 10s 8d. 'I have no doubt', he said in an affidavit dated 26 June 1912, 'that unless restrained from doing so the defendant Bank of England [will make this deduction] in respect of income tax which has not in fact been imposed by law . . .'

Dr Edwin Freshfield, the Bank's solicitor, did not deny this in his affidavits in reply. His main point was that it had been the Bank's practice, since the passing of the Income Tax Act 1842 which provided for deduction, to deduct income tax 'in reliance upon and in obedience to a resolution of the House of Commons foreshadowing the introduction and passing of an act of Parliament imposing income tax for the year at the rate specified in such resolution', adding that '2,400 dividend warrants have been printed for the purpose of paying the interest' on the Irish Land Stock. He next made a point which was a tactical error, though it was clearly one which the officials of the Bank who instructed him would have emphasized. 'It will be a matter of great public inconvenience and occasion great labour to the Defendants' officials if the said interest has to be paid without deduction of income tax. The Dividend Warrants cannot now be altered and supplementary cheques will have to be drawn in favour of each holder.' He appealed to common sense; if Parliament did impose income tax at the rate mentioned in the resolution, 'the Plaintiff will become liable to bear income tax in respect of his said interest and to the precise amount which he seeks in this action to have the Defendants restrained from deducting and he will have gained nothing at all by this action'.

This was true, but irrelevant. Thomas made mincemeat of Dr Freshfield's affidavit. He quoted the 1897 edition of Erskine May, the authority on parliamentary law, which described as 'remarkable' the effect given to a vote of the Commons in tax-gathering in anticipation of the relevant statute, adding: 'It is obvious that the practice is not strictly legal.' Freshfield had said the resolution on which the Bank relied for its deduction 'foreshadowed' the Finance Act, and Thomas jumped on the word: 'My Lord, are we to be levied upon a foreshadow? Are we to be assessed and taxed by virtue of a mere foreshadow?' Then he turned to the question of convenience. The reason why this was an unwise one for the Bank to make so much of was that it had nothing whatever to do with the law, and amounted to asking the judge to bend the law so that certain people should be saved trouble. This type of request irritates the judiciary. Thomas was in top form: 'Really, my Lord, is it not a little trifling with the courts to suggest that because 2,400 dividend warrants with an unlawful deduction of income tax have been printed, this court should hesitate, or ought to hesitate, to stop an infringement of the law?' And again:

Is the Bank of England not prepared to undertake some inconvenience and some labour in order to comply with the law of the land, the law dating from Magna Carta, and ending with the Bill of Rights? Is the Bank of England prepared to come to this court and say: 'We ask this Court to allow us to break the law because it would inconvenience us and occasion great labour for our clerks?' Well, my Lord, I should think the clerks are there for the purpose of undertaking labour; and that whatever inconvenience may be imposed on the Bank of England in order to cause it to comply with the law should be cheerfully assumed by that great institution . . .

He quoted from Magna Carta, from a law of Edward I, from the Petition of Right of 1628 and from the Bill of Rights of 1689. The amount at issue may only have been £52 10s 8d, but it was still more than the £1 that Hampden objected to paying Charles I for ship money, in the dispute that was to lead up to the English Civil War. The fact was that nobody should be made to pay tax which was not covered by a valid Act of Parliament, complete in all its stages. He did not initially succeed in having the deduction stopped, and the action dragged on until the summer recess; the law officers of the Crown now wanted to become involved, and they had not the time to spare. But, ominously for the Bank, Mr Justice Parker certainly showed no sign of finding in their favour. On the contrary, he ordered the £52 10s 8d to be paid into court.

When hearings resumed in October Thomas raised more pre-cedents, this time going right back to King Alfred. Now it was the Attorney General, Sir Rufus Isaacs, who took the lead on the other side. At one moment the question arose as to whether the point to be decided was confined to income tax, or whether it also covered customs. The Judge said: 'If the question in relation to Customs ever arises from a subject of the Crown, somebody will very likely be here to represent the Crown upon it.' Sir Rufus answered wryly: 'My Lord, I am not quite sure that another Mr Bowles will ever arise.' Essentially all he could produce was another argument of convenience, this time from the point of view of the Treasury: 'It is obvious . . . that there would be an inconvenience and a loss to the King's revenue if steps were not taken to collect the money which would become payable before the Statute is passed, and that no doubt is why the practice has sprung up . . .' And again, 'There is no difficulty, I agree, if you have to follow a gentleman like Mr Bowles, but there are many people from whom you would never get tax unless you managed to deduct it at the source.' He managed to find in a later edition of Erskine May than that which Thomas had quoted a remark to the effect that 'an anticipatory authority is imported by usage to the resolutions of the committee of ways and means which impose or alter taxation', but the phrase 'by usage' in effect removes the force of this. He and his colleagues went on for days making as good a case as they could – in fact some of their submissions are worth reading as an example of how much lawyers can make out of a weak case. It was no use. The Judge's remarks tended more and more in Thomas's favour, and in the end he found for him with costs. He got his 52 10s 8d, which he then had to pay to the Inland Revenue in due course. To his irritation – and it is an irritation many subsequent litigants have shared – he only received so-called 'taxed' costs of £308, whereas the action had cost him £446. He wrote a letter of complaint to the Prime Minister, Herbert Asquith, but got nowhere. As a matter of fact his main expense was not costs, but a loss of more than £2,000 on the capital value of the Irish Land Stock. It had been well worth it: the greatest tease of a lifetime.

Yet it was not just a tease. The Bowles Evasion Act – his nickname for it is entirely appropriate – contained important restrictions, even though, as he sourly put it, 'Mr Austen Chamberlain and his fellow-leaders of the Opposition Front Bench showed a strange and unexpected sympathy for the novel device it embodied.' No wonder: Austen Chamberlain, Joseph's son, as shadow Chancellor, was also interested in easing procedure for which he himself might one day have to be responsible. The bill was enacted on 25 April 1913. It gave provisional taxing power to resolutions of the House of Commons, but only for four months, and only for taxes that had existed before, not for new ones. It therefore obliged governments to pass their Finance Acts by

August at the latest, thus putting a stop to the very long delays to which Thomas had objected.

What was he to do now? He toyed with the idea of another spectacular lawsuit. It was proposed to start paying Members of Parliament a salary, as the Chartists of 1848 had demanded. Thomas was strongly opposed to it, and asserted it to be essentially illegal, something that was believed by others beside himself. However, it was obvious that if it was wanted strongly enough by King, Lords and Commons, something would be done to make it legal. Even if he had instituted a test case and won, the measure would have been introduced somehow by an equivalent of the Bowles Evasion Act. We need not question his sincerity when he said that it was not a question of expense which deterred him. By the age of seventy-two he had acquired enough experience of public affairs to know when something was clearly not going to work. He confined himself to protesting.

He embarked on one more enterprise: the *Candid Review*. This was a quarterly magazine, thick and substantial, with as much reading matter in each number as a novel. It carried no advertisements; more remarkably, all the articles were unsigned. Many of them were by Thomas himself; at least one was by Bertie. It was on Lord Lyons, the British minister to the United States at the time of the American Civil War. The *Candid Review* was designed to circulate among what are now known as opinion formers, and to an extent it probably did so. The anonymity of its articles ensured that its contributors, other than Thomas himself, would rarely be journalists or other writers trying to make a name; they would tend rather to be serving officers or senior officials or others closely in touch with actual affairs, who had points they wished to make but were precluded from making under their own names. The trouble is, of course, that this same anonymity makes it impossible to know just how authoritative any item was.

Thomas brought out twelve issues, from February 1914 to November 1916. He then, finally, gave up; the labour was becoming too much, even for him. Had it achieved anything? Thomas professed to think so: 'Our labours have been attended with some measure of success,' he said in the last number. 'Something has been done', notably towards the more efficient prosecution of the First World War. Privately, we know from Sydney that Thomas thought the war a folly; and he also thought it was being fought the wrong way, that Britain should never commit large armies to the continent. What actual effect the *Candid Review* had on opinion and events can only be guessed at, but certainly no attention was paid to Thomas's main point.

The closing of the *Candid Review* marks Thomas's retirement, at the age of seventy-six. He had earned it. Earlier in the year, on 21 July, he had been guest of honour at a great dinner at which senior naval officers and others thanked him for his services to the Navy, and in particular for his part in nullifying the Declaration of London. His old friend Admiral Lord Charles Beresford was in the chair, brother to that Lord Marcus Beresford with whom Thomas had traded punches outside the *Vanity Fair* offices so long before. In his speech Lord Charles said that Thomas's book on sea power had become a textbook, 'not only in naval schools but among lawyers'. Another admiral, Sir Hedworth Meux, expressed his regret that neither the Prime Minister, Herbert Asquith, nor the Foreign Secretary, Sir Edward Grey, was present to admit their mistake over the Declaration of London and to thank Thomas for his service in getting rid of it. Thomas must have enjoyed this remark. His reply showed him in typical form. After detailing his agitation against the Naval Prize Bill, he congratulated the House of Lords, who 'to their everlasting glory, saved the country from the last surrender of its rights. They thereby rendered impossible the convocation of that fantastic Hague International Prize Court composed of defaulting Dagoes and negro neologists, which otherwise would have been erected, and would at this moment be judging every capture and act of Jellicoe and Beatty and of every other officer under their orders.' He would not have been enamoured of the United Nations.

Thomas passed the very last years of his life peacefully and, for an old man, in good health. He went from time to time to see his children and their families. David offered him a pleasant and commodious house on his estate, Wychwood Lodge. There he could have been near Sydney and also not far from Dorothy, who lived near Stow-on-the-Wold; but Thomas would have none of it. Quoting Wordsworth, he said: 'Two voices are there, one is of the sea and the other of the mountains; and I hear neither at the

Lodge.' He had no great personal sadness at the end of his life; his sons George and Geoffrey, naturally both of them naval officers, survived the war, and both his daughters were happily and suitably married. He was, though, only partly satisfied with his life's work. In 1918 he received from the Librarian of Congress in Washington DC a routine letter asking for information on his date of birth and his publications. Having a good deal of time to spare, he wrote at some length. Naylor rightly regards this letter as 'almost a political testament'. In it Thomas puts the sea at the very centre of his political ideas and aims:

Having frequented and followed the Sea, though unfortunately only as an amateur, from my childhood up, I learnt from its rough yet tender lessons that it is still, as ever, our Mother, our Nurse and our Teacher, and Sea Power our only defence. I applied myself to the task of becoming . . . a good seaman as well in its practical as in its intellectual and political meaning.

He became a master mariner and always had his own ship with a crew of Aldeburgh fishermen – 'the best seamen I know for foul weather'. He goes on:

I saw that if I had any business in life it was to teach my fellow countrymen what the Sea and History had taught me. I tried to do so. In 1887 I published *Maritime Warfare*. I sought to enter Parliament, failed often, and at last did so, in the hope that there, at least, I should be able to give the Message of the Sea . . .

I failed signally. For that I could never get a hearing . . . On Parliamentary Procedure I was endured. In Finance I achieved something. On constitutional questions and in the frays of Party I sometimes got a hearing. But never on the Sea and all it means. Nor was it until by the common consent and common efforts of all leaders, all wirepullers and all caucuses united against me, I was proscribed from Parliament, that I got the message of the Sea in some sort listened to. Then I did at least destroy the Declaration of London, which would else have destroyed our Sea Power in this war quite completely. For which thank God . . .'

As to his date of birth, Thomas says that no man knows this except by hearsay and that a man is 'as good as his arteries and his activities, his rightness and truth and courage'. However, he adds:

'I have now, in the desire to satisfy you, made investigations into the past which I have long neglected . . . I believe that I was born in London on the 18th January, 1841. I am no more certain of it than I am of the birthday of Julius Caesar. But that is what I think.'

In the summer of 1921 he went on holiday to Algeciras, in Spain near Gibraltar, where he quite unexpectedly and peacefully died. The British admiral in command at Gibraltar sent his own barge to convey Thomas's body along the coast to the Rock, and attended his funeral there in full dress uniform. When George Bowles thanked the admiral for these attentions he received the reply: 'When a distinguished Englishman dies it is the least I can do.' To the Navy, Thomas was one of its own.

# PART THREE

# The Mitford Childhood

# 19

# David and Sydney

David was born on 13 March 1878, Bertie's third child and second son. He was an active little boy who preferred to be out of doors and took early to field sports, most especially to shooting. He was strikingly handsome, with a long, regular face and his father's luminous blue eyes.

He had, at times, a wicked temper; on one occasion which was never forgotten he threatened his father with a red-hot poker from the fire, and would have burned him badly had not the French tutor, Monsieur Cuvelier, dexterously snatched it from him. Monsieur Cuvelier was a small, wiry man, immensely proud of his time in the French Army during the Franco-Prussian War of 1870. He was known in the family as '*Douze Temps*', because he enjoyed demonstrating the twelve movements of rifle drill. In later years he became a French master at Eton, and lived there after his retirement; he used to invite Tom to tea when he was at the school. He often came to stay with David at Asthall. Sometimes David's brothers Tommy and Jack would be there, and they would all become boys again; to the astonishment of the children their father and uncles would make Monsieur Cuvelier re-enact a scene from the Franco-Prussian War in which he had carried a comrade to safety by fording a river. One after the other they would leap on to the old man's back and make him carry them around the room. Since they were all about twice his size it made a bizarre sight. The young David liked Monsieur Cuvelier, but did not take to lessons in general and was bored by reading. Initially this was probably simply because, as a healthy boy, he preferred to be out with gun or rod. He was not alone in this; in fact none of Bertie's nine children inherited his intellectual interests. They learned what they were told to learn, including near-perfect

French from Monsieur Cuvelier; but the intellectual curiosity without which education beyond the secondary level has no reality never appeared in them, even though it was Bertie's most enduring characteristic.

This is strange, because they were all quite intelligent. David, in particular, possessed a distinct way with words; Nancy's originality of perception and phrase can without any doubt be traced back to him. It did not come from Sydney, although she was a natural writer, which David was not. Of the two Sydney was also much the more logical and consistent. It was from her that the Mitfords inherited their ability to express themselves clearly and in a sustained manner. A revelation in preparing this present book has been the quality of Sydney's unpublished writings. But though this material has, particularly for us who knew her, an evocative and special charm, and although it is shrewd and in places funny, it completely lacks the Mitford iridescence – the stylistic fantasy, the queer, sudden illuminations. This iridescence is Nancy's particular quality. It comes straight from David, and it is a paradox that this man, who was in most ways so conventionally masculine, had a mind that was entirely intuitive, non-logical: the kind of mind often thought of as feminine. Changing one's mind is said to be a woman's prerogative; no woman has changed her mind as suddenly or as repeatedly as David, though at any given moment his views appeared solid as a rock. (It is curious that adherents of the pseudo-science of astrology have the opportunity to nod their heads at all this and say but of course, he was a typical Pisces subject.) The 'masculine' side of the Mitford mind comes from Sydney, who was much more inner-directed, less swayed by immediate emotion; who could structure an argument or a piece of writing, and found it satisfying and almost restful to keep detailed financial accounts.

David was a natural comic; Nancy's jokes, including those at David's expense, are often patterned on jokes made by him. Debo emphasized this to us in interview, as does Diana in *A Life of Contrasts*. Unfortunately neither, when it came to the point, could give us the stream of remembered witticisms for which we hoped. Debo did, however, remember that when David went shopping, which was always at the Army and Navy Stores, he claimed that he had to get there by 9 a.m. punctually in order to avoid 'inconveniently shaped women'. He also did indeed use the word 'sewer' to describe someone he did not like. This had nothing to do with drains; it was an Anglo-Indian insult picked up perhaps in Ceylon.

He had three particular aversions. One was unpunctuality. Nancy is entirely true to life in *Love in a Cold Climate* when she makes Uncle Matthew growl: 'Twenty-three and a quarter minutes past; in precisely six and three-quarter minutes the damned fella will be late.' He trained his children early, and punctuality has always been one of their virtues. His second aversion was stickiness; traces of jammy hands on a surface he had to touch sent him into a rage. His third was spilling, or any untidy eating. Diana tells us:

Meals in the dining-room were an ordeal when he was at home and had it not been for prestige reasons I would have preferred to stay upstairs with Nanny. However quietly one sat, however far from him, he saw in an instant if a drop or a crumb was spilt . . . When despite one's efforts something was spilt he roared with rage. At the end of his life, forty years after the days I am describing, he was still the same. Once we were lunching at a London hotel in a vast restaurant; he was nearly blind; yet several tables away he spied a little boy: 'Look at that degraded child throwing its food over the good table cloth,' said Farve.

Degraded was a favourite word, with David as with his daughters; 'good', as here in 'good table cloth', was another characteristic turn of phrase.

As a small boy David was sensitive and sentimental. Sydney tells us that when the old house at Batsford was pulled down to make way for Bertie's Victorian-Tudor Valhalla, David at the age of nine watched the demolition from a hiding place and cried by himself. Her comment is that he was right to weep for the modest old house; the family fortune began to decline with Bertie's new building. David was himself, however, to commit his father's error over again on a smaller scale when he built Swinbrook.

Bertie sent David, not to his beloved Eton, but to Radley. This was because he thought that David would behave badly and hinder Clement in his Eton career. At least this was the impression David received; his parents, he was given to understand, were allotting a second-rate education to a second-rate person. It was partly for this reason that he hated Radley. Not only did his studies continue to bore him, but he also disliked the team games that constituted the outdoor aspect of school life. He reacted strongly against the school spirit based on football and cricket, the exhortations to 'play up and play the game', the pretensions of the pavilion and the sweaty comradeship of the scrum. This whole ethic of team games, enshrined in quantities of school stories now unread, had been decisively imprinted on most men of David's class by the public schools. It accompanied and in part replaced the older upper-class love of field sports. We remember that Bertie, who belonged to an earlier generation, approved of the fact that since his day the team games spirit had taken over at Oxford University. David might well have felt like commenting that it was all very well for his father to talk, never having suffered under the games cult; except that this was the kind of reaction which David was too respectful towards his parents ever to have formulated, even in his own mind. In any case he found team games unpleasant. He lacked the natural talent that could have enabled him without effort to shine at them; and he would not make the effort that might have made up for his want of skill. This slacking, especially in someone obviously rather strong, made him fall foul of the games-playing stars of Radley; they in turn did not appeal to him as they strutted about in their coloured caps and scarves. This type of boy hero dominated the public schools between 1880 and 1940, encouraged by the philistine majority among the masters; its dominance gradually died out after the Second World War. Harold Nicolson satirized the type in his character J. D. Marstock in *Some People*. We are certain that David's memory of these dismal young magnates was the real reason why he did not want to send his daughters to boarding school. Eton was in his eyes tolerable; Bertie had loved it and Clement enjoyed it, so his only son Tom must certainly go there. But he felt that a girls' public school would be more like Radley, and Radley in caricature at that. He is supposed to have said that hockey would give a girl bad legs, and perhaps he did say it. If so, it was not a sign of ignorance or eccentricity. The underlying thought was rather that no daughter of his should suffer under, or herself become, a female Marstock.

When David grew up he would have liked to go into the Army,

but Bertie found him a job tea planting in Ceylon. The plantation belonged to Charles Yorke, uncle of Henry Yorke, who wrote novels under the name Henry Green and was to be a great friend of Diana. We know rather little about the time David spent there, and to what extent he enjoyed the life. He used to tell his children stories; on one occasion his bearer warned him in the nick of time that his cook was approaching and about to knife him in the back, upon which he turned round, disarmed the man and shook him like a rat. Bertie visited him there, as he records in *Memories*, but all that seems to interest him is the temples; he only mentions David in passing.

At all events David returned home after a few years, and the outbreak of the Boer War in 1899 gave him the opportunity to join the Army; his regiment was the Northumberland Fusiliers, and he joined up in the ranks. His elder brother Clement also fought, in the 10th Hussars, and so did his uncle David, eighth Earl of Airlie, who was to be killed leading a cavalry charge.

David's letters home at this period give a very clear picture of him. They show him as impulsive, naive and rather humble, with a touching idealism. There is no trace of the humour we have mentioned, which was perhaps a later development and was anyway always more evident in his conversation than in his rather rare letters. He enjoyed soldiering. The dangers and discomforts did not put him off his wish to make it his life; perhaps they even confirmed it. He wrote to his mother on 12 March 1900: 'I believe if Father tried I could get a commission in the army, after this it would not be very difficult, and then I would have the profession I always wanted. What do you think?' He had possibly had a talk on the subject with General Brabazon, who a few days earlier had appointed him as his orderly. The appointment delighted David, who wrote to his father: 'Am I not lucky? I get to know things which I did not know before . . . I don't know who worked this but one of your friends whom you asked to look after me is at the bottom of it.' Soon afterwards they went to the front, and David received a flesh wound, in the calf. He wrote on what looks like lavatory paper to his father from the hospital at Bloemfontein: 'I have no news of home, no tobacco, no money, nothing. It is the first time I have ever had to go without anything and oddly enough it does not worry me much.' Later in the same letter he shows himself a prey to the self-doubt which we believe was very much one of his characteristics: 'I have seen a lot of soldiering lately, so much so that it has rather put me off taking a commission. I have seen the terrible responsibility of an officer and I have seen men's lives lost by an officer making a small mistake, and I have rather come to the conclusion that a man has no right to go into the army if he does not feel competent . . . I only wish I had you here to talk it over with and advise me.' He recovered soon, and resumed his duties with General Brabazon, but only for a time, for he writes to his sister Iris on 3 August 1900: 'I went up to say goodbye to the dear General this afternoon. He was very kind to me as he always has been – he said he hoped we should soldier together again some day – dear man. He has had bad luck all through the campaign. If I could turn into just such another soldier, a "Brab of the 4th", I should be proud and contented. He is a soldier and a gentleman, and that is the most you can say for any man.'

In the event the military profession, as far as peacetime soldiering was concerned, would be denied him. In due course he was wounded very seriously in the chest, and a lung had to be removed; this rendered him unfit for military service except in the emergency of the First World War. It is said that while he was in hospital with his wound he dictated a love letter to Sydney, to be delivered to her in the event of his death, which means, of course, in the event of its no longer being of any use; but the gesture was a charming and romantic one. At all events he recovered and was sent home. No doubt the weeks of pain in hospital, and the possibility of dying, had concentrated his mind, made him realize his feelings for Sydney, and given him the resolution ultimately to declare them.

Sydney had grown up to be tall and good-looking: some considered her a beauty, with her light brown hair, blue eyes, regular features and slim figure. She had rather a strange mouth, though, which turned down sharply at the corners and gave her, even in youth, a slightly censorious look. This did express one side, though only one side, of a complex character. Her diary for 1898, the year she came out, shows a love of company, a readiness to be frivolous and even at times flirtatious. An undercurrent of seriousness is however already discernible, expressed in a tend-

William Mitford, historian

Henry Reveley Mitford

Lady Clementine Mitford

Algernon Bertram Mitford

Bertie Redesdale's nine children at Batsford, c. 1895. *Standing, left to right:* David and Bertram. *Seated, left to right:* Joan, Iris holding Daphne, Clement, John, Frances holding Rupert

Thomas Gibson Bowles

Sydney Mitford, *née* Bowles, c. 1900

David and Sydney as apaches

Nancy with hoop

Diana, Nancy, Pam, Tom with chickens

*Left to right:* Tom, Nancy and Unity, Sydney, Pam, David and Diana, 1917

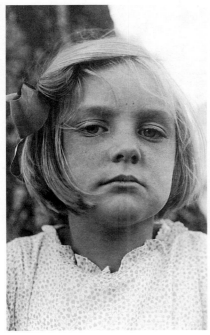

Unity aged seven

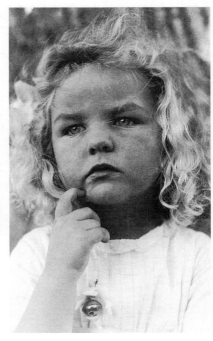

Decca aged four

Sydney and David

Diana as Empress Poppaea

David prospecting

Diana on Mosley's motorboat in
the Mediterranean

Mosley steering

(*Above*) Bryan Guinness in Sicily, 1929

(*Above right*) Pam with Togo Watney, 1928

Decca

ency to give good advice to her friends. It was perhaps this, coupled with the rather severe classicism of her features, that induced Helleu to nickname Sydney 'La Loi'. One is reminded of Max Beerbohm's cartoon 'Literature, Mr Philip Guedalla and the Law', in which the popular historian is represented being torn between two female figures, literature being a curvaceous wanton, the law gaunt and stern. Sydney always monitors her own likes and dislikes, even her loves. Again and again in this typical young girl's diary the artless narrative seems to be intruded on by the sober middle-aged lady she was to become. 'Anyone who reads this would think I was a sentimental vain foolish little ass, whose head is particularly easily turned.' But under the surface she knew her own 'faults and shortcomings . . . I hate them in myself and I hate them in other people. I hate vanity and self-satisfaction and people who detail all that the last young man said to them, and how he looked and how she looked and how she answered . . .' Sydney will herself sometimes give way to vanity, in the privacy of her diary, but never without slapping herself on the wrist for it: 'I get a good many compliments one way and another . . . Oh but I get dozens of them. I get them in the look of the man in the street, and the man in the hansom who turns round to squint at me under the blind. Oh Sydney you conceited *pig* to write such things down. What girl just come out with *any* looks and a well-known father doesn't get dozens of compliments?'

Her first party as a debutante was at the Duchess of Devonshire's. She enjoyed it, but was very far from being dazzled. 'I didn't feel the least bit nervous or shy. I don't see why I should, but still I didn't.' They arrived at about ten-thirty and were among the first; no doubt Thomas, as an inveterate early riser, would have wanted to get away early. In the bend of the stairs was a 'heavenly Hungarian band which inspired me like wine'. At the top were the Duke and Duchess, 'the latter I thought too awful for words, dreadfully painted with a hideous set grin on her face. The Duke stood just behind and looked half asleep, and very bored.' But she admired the Duchess's diamonds. She was taken round the magnificent rooms by Lord Rowton, pioneer of housing charities and a friend of Thomas, before meeting a number of her friends from Prince's ice rink. She left with Thomas at about midnight.

Her upbringing had matured her early; she had already for

years been in charge of her father's household. She also, in a
sense, had to be her own mother, having no older female relation
in the house. Thomas would chaperone her at dances, and there
was a governess; nevertheless, if Sydney had been so minded, she
could have got away with much that a girl with a watchful mother
could not. She was not so minded. On one occasion she replies to
a young man's letter 'asking him not to write again as Tap
wouldn't like it, and perhaps it isn't quite fair to do a thing I
know Tap wouldn't approve of. In fact it isn't at all fair. So I have
stopped it. But I didn't the least want to, as I enjoy getting letters
from people I like.'

When she worried Thomas, as sometimes happened, it did not
so much concern her morals or her respectability; on that score, he
was probably well aware that she had her head screwed on. Very
much the politician, though, and preoccupied with his public
controversies, he was sensitive to the danger of his children
causing quarrels in private life. He did not like it when Sydney
drew caricatures and sent them to people; this made enemies, he
said, despite his experience with *Vanity Fair* having been happier
than the Jeremiahs had predicted. He fretted about a doggerel
poem she sent to a friend, Claude Napier, who frequented Prince's
skating rink where she went. It was entitled 'The Halls of Bliss'
and starts:

> One evening I strolled into Prince's
> Having nothing whatever to do
> And thinking perhaps to meet there
> A casual acquaintance or two.
>
> I walked to the desk with my shilling
> And asked in loud tones for some skates
> 'And a lesson too, please, from Kurten,
> For Wiedemann everyone hates . . .'

Claude Napier showed the verses around; Thomas came to see a
copy and was worried that Wiedemann might sue Sydney for
libel. So Sydney got the original back and it is in the diary, 'his
copy . . . handled by his own nice hands!' However, in the album
left by her friend Janet Tooth there is a copy of a much longer
version, in what is presumably Claude Napier's handwriting and

signed by him; he seems to have appropriated Sydney's verses and added some stanzas of his own. Janet Tooth was a neighbour of Sydney's in Lowndes Square. A stunning blonde, she skated to professional standards and won many awards. (Her daughter, Mrs R. A. Howard, was kind enough to show us this album.)

Prince's was a great meeting place; it was in fact very much part of the social scene, as the press of the time shows. Sydney went there often. She enjoyed skating, and seems to have become quite good at it; at the end of the 1898 diary the family go to spend Christmas in Paris, where they find the skating standard lower than in London and she and Dorothy 'made quite a sensation' dancing together. David, too, was a keen skater; Decca was later to say that when he was not skating he was thinking about skating, and Unity was to note his irritation at being unable to skate on a visit to Berlin.

It will be remembered that riding in the Row with Thomas seemed to Sydney like a regular daily party; but it was not, perhaps, as much fun as Prince's, where she went without Thomas. At any rate, the rides in the Row are scarcely mentioned in this diary, whereas Prince's is one of its main subjects, during the periods when Sydney is in London. It is there she meets the friends whom she judges in her cool, mature way; Cicely Haig, for instance, her best friend among the girls, because she is a very good skater and 'not silly about any particular boy, like all the other little geese at Prince's'. It is there, also, that Sydney meets Grenander.

Grenander, a Swede, was one of the professionals at the rink. Sydney loves watching him practise for the figure skating championships in his costume of black silk tights and coat trimmed with astrakhan. She is unable to watch the championship itself because on the same day, 22 February, Dorothy is acting in a play. However, to Sydney's delight Grenander wins the championship, so she does two drawings of him: one conventional one of him doing a figure in his championship costume, with the caption '*Veni Vidi Vici*', and one hideous caricature. Dorothy shows both to him and, delighted, he snatches them.

Soon Sydney admits to herself that she fancies him. A chunk of the diary is missing at this point, probably removed by her, although later entries show that nothing can actually have gone on outside her own mind. Her speculations have gone far, however, for the next page after the gap starts:

. . . know for instance that if I were married to Grenander he would pall on me dreadfully in about a year – at least I think he would, of course he might not. He never palls on me now, I love being with him, I would do almost anything he asked me. I would let him call me Sydney, I would even let him kiss me, I almost think. (Oh Sydney, you are shocking.) All the same if he asked me to marry him I don't think I would dream of saying yes – but then of course there not being the smallest chance of it, what's the good of thinking of that?

One day she broke her ankle at the rink. Someone gave her sal volatile. Grenander rallied round and made an attempt, seemingly rather a successful one, to set it. It hurt, but 'was I sorry for myself? No. On the contrary I was as happy as a Queen. Because the man who for the moment possesses my fickle affections was beside me and doing the best he could for me.' Tears started to her eyes but she managed not to wince or cry out. 'Everyone said how plucky I was. I shouldn't have been plucky if he had not been there.' Grenander and another friend, Admiral Maxse, then took her round to Dr Kellgren. He pronounced her fibula broken. Kellgren was, to judge by her account in *Five Houses* (which does not mention Grenander), very much himself. He reset it but put on no bandage or splint.

'I said to him "But then supposing I move it by mistake in the night?"'

'He roared with laughter (he was a great laugher) and said: "You vill not do that. It vill hurt too much."'

She was not laid up for long.

On a later occasion, in April, she managed to have a nice long chat with Grenander. She and George were alone in the house, George being on vacation from Cambridge where he was an undergraduate. Sydney invited Grenander and a Cambridge acquaintance to tea. George and the other Cambridge man talked Cambridge gossip, 'So of course Gren was left to me. Q.E.D.'

But for the summer months Grenander is forgotten, overlaid with other impressions. At Whitsun the Bowles family go to stay at Batsford; the famous singing star, Clara Butt, is there recovering from a slight accident, a fall from a dog cart. 'She really is a delightful creature and her voice! — words fail to describe it . . . This splendid creature is 6 ft 2 in high and weighs 14 stone, though not the least fat. We were all her devoted slaves, Tap included, and he is frightfully difficult to please.' Then in May Week she and Dorothy go to visit George in Cambridge. Dorothy is ill one day 'but I Kellgrenized her as best I could', and she recovers. George has a friend he expects Sydney to fall for, but she does not do so. Once this person 'has the cheek to take my hand which was on his arm. I hate people who behave like that, *unless* I want them to. I mean I wouldn't have minded Mortimer. Oh I daresay I should though.' She lectures some of the young men a little. One of them does not want to go into the Church as his father wishes, and believes Latin and Greek to be useless unless one is going to teach them. 'So I told him I thought him excessively stupid to talk like that and that I hoped he would work because otherwise he could never hope to do anything worth doing.' She visits Girton, the women's college, to which there is some idea of her going, an idea she quite favours. (Nothing came of it.)

The family spent a long time in Scotland that year, from 8 August to 14 October. They settled with all their staff, except a cook whom they hired locally, at Birsemhor Lodge, Aboyne. On the way they spent a night at a hotel in Aberdeen where there was 'the usual row between Tap and the hotel servants'. Grenander is now mentioned again, but as a name from the past: 'It seems such ages since I was really smitten. I believe Grenander must have been the last.' Now, however, she is ready to fall for a boy called Charlie Gordon, with 'piercing blue eyes and lots of curly dark hair, but a slightly weak mouth'. Again the appraisal, the summing up on both sides of the ledger. She is also attracted to Eustace Heaven. At Lady Granville's ball she would rather sit out with Eustace than dance with anyone else. She is pleased with her outfit at this ball: 'The enormous magpie and cherries which formed the coiffure were really rather becoming.'

But she learns the faithlessness of man — Eustace Heaven is paying equal court to Sybil Bass. As in some light opera, the two girls plot together; each will say the other loves him. However, there is no dénouement; somehow Sydney and he drift back together. She likes him best when he is not flirting, she tells him severely during the course of a long walk on the shores of a lake. There is a Proustian touch here; she notes that during this conversation she was 'pulling to pieces a spray of some very pretty tree with red berries on it' (mountain ash?). 'I know that I shall always remember that scene when I see red berries. It is quite the nearest I have been to a real real flirtation.' She learns to shoot, and to play golf and cricket. There are picnics, bicycle rides and long walks in the purple mountains. All her life Sydney was to have a feeling for Scotland and its scenery. There is a moment of embarrassment one Sunday when Sydney goes with the Heavens to the Roman Catholic church where they worship. She and Violet Heaven are provoked by a rather absurd sermon into an irresistible fit of the giggles. The priest, as they think, catches them at it and roars that they are insulting God and His holy angels. 'I was simply burning with shame,' says Sydney, but 'all the same I knew I hadn't been insulting God and His Holy angels . . . for I had naturally tried my very best to stop.'

There is an undated entry in November where Sydney takes herself to task for allowing her diary to be a chronicle of the state of her own and others' hearts. She is reading the memoirs of Saint-Simon and ought, she thinks, 'to try and copy his style and detail the events of our court, so as to be of some interest to posterity'. But she has not much opportunity of observing the movements of the 'inmates' of the court, 'which wouldn't be very interesting if they were observed I think'.

Then comes a sensation. On 28 November she records that someone has told her Grenander is in love with her. 'What joy would that knowledge have given me six months ago! But since Aboyne I am older and wiser and I know that Grenander's being really in love with me, even if I were in love with him, would bring unhappiness to both of us.' The news brings a great deal of self-examination. 'Now, diary, you see how much I admire and like this man, and I now believe he loves me. Yet if he were to ask me to marry him I would say no. If he were English, and in every way a man of my own station, I know I would say yes . . . So now, Sydney, your mercenary and worldly soul is laid bare . . . I can't write any more for despising myself.'

Finally, after the end of the year, she rereads her diary. She has enjoyed her first year as a grown-up and is sorry that it is over;

but 'what an awful ass I have been! Fancy thinking myself in love with Claude Napier! . . . a perfect baby . . . Of course Grenander still goes on. You see there is some background for my affection for him, because he is such an exceptionally good sort.'

This cool compliment does not lead the reader to expect that Sydney's crush on Grenander would go on for very long: nor did it. In due course she fell in love passionately with a young man called Edward Meade, always known as Jimmy. Jimmy was, it appears, attractive to women and fond of flirting. When she realized this Sydney broke off whatever understanding there may have been between them; it never amounted to an engagement. She is said to have been heartbroken; there is a story that tears were streaming down her cheeks as she walked up the aisle to get married to David and that this was due to the fact that she still longed for Jimmy Meade. Even if Sydney did cry at her wedding, it need not have had anything to do with Jimmy, but the fact that this was said shows how contemporaries viewed the matter. Certainly the affair had no lasting effect on her. At first it may have been David who was in love, rather than Sydney; but she was fond of him, and seems to have fallen in love after marriage. The story of this marriage's partial break-up for reasons of politics, when they were both already getting old, is as odd as it is poignant.

# 20

# Early Married Life

After their marriage David and Sydney settled down in London at a small house at 1 Graham Street (now Graham Terrace). They were sufficiently hard up to put Sydney's housekeeping experience and ability to the test, although they lived at a standard which today we should regard as more than comfortable. Children steadily appeared; their first house was small, but they managed in 1914 to move to a larger one in Victoria Road, Kensington, when Unity, the fifth, was expected. They even had a country place, the Old Mill Cottage on the outskirts of High Wycombe; this belonged to Sydney. They would go there in the summer and let their London house, for there was always a market for summer lettings from people who wanted somewhere for the 'Season'. The Mitfords always had an adequate number of servants; the world was still not much changed from what it was a generation earlier when the hero of the *Diary of a Nobody*, a simple bank clerk, had as a matter of course a cook and a maid. In particular the children always had a nanny and, from a fairly early date, a nurserymaid as well. In addition there were a cook, kitchenmaid, parlourmaid and housemaid. However, the Mitfords belonged to a class whose expectations in those days were high. Their friends and relations thought that David and Sydney were brave to the point of rashness in starting a family on so little. They had perhaps about £1,000 a year: the equivalent of more than £20,000 in today's currency.

Their income came mostly from Thomas Bowles, who gave David a job on *The Lady* as office manager, and also paid Sydney a small allowance. David disliked office life, was bored by London, and only really enjoyed himself when out of doors. But he stuck to it for ten years, and did his best, grateful for Thomas's kindness. The offices of *The Lady* were where they are now, in Bedford Street, Covent Garden. The pleasant old building, still mercifully not redeveloped, harboured a fair number of rats. David's solution was original; he acquired not a cat or a terrier but a mongoose, with which he staged rat hunts. These satisfied his sporting instincts and were, no doubt, a welcome diversion for the rest of the staff. George Bowles, Thomas's elder son, was already in overall charge of *The Lady*, and the two brothers-in-law became friends for life. This friendship is an example of the way in which David could sometimes not only appreciate intelligent people, but also secure their appreciation in return. For George was a man of parts; at Cambridge he had been editor of *Grania* and president of the Union. He was to summarize and develop his father's political ideas in a book called *The Strength of England*, and he was also an excellent amateur guitarist and an expert conjuror and member of the Magic Circle. Had David been a fool or a bore, George had no need to put up with him.

David would have been better prepared for what was in fact to be his future, if his own father had given him a house on his estate and sent him to be trained in agriculture or estate management. But he was the second son, and there was no intention to leave him any land of his own. Younger sons were not meant to hang around. He had liked the Army, but his loss of a lung in the Boer War meant that this profession was closed to him.

In any case his letters to his mother, during the first year or so of his marriage, show him to be in a dream of happiness. He also emerges as sensitive and affectionate, artlessly delighted about the impending birth of his first child, Nancy. He writes from Thomas's house in Lowndes Square on 9 May 1904: 'I knew how pleased you would be to hear our secret – It is such a joy to us – Of course you know what a pleasure it is but I never dreamt of such happiness. I had never any idea of what it would be like. Now I hardly think of anything else . . . We think we shall get into our house next week. I shall be *so* glad – You can't think how pretty my Sydney has made it, it is perfect.' Then on 17 November: 'It has been a year of the greatest happiness to me, and I am afraid that in my happiness I forget others who have not been so happy although they deserve it far more . . . Even if I don't deserve it I *am* grateful.' Nancy was born on 28 November, and next day David writes: 'She is in splendid spirits I cannot tell you how sweet and brave she has been all through. She wanted a boy but is very pleased as things are. The baby is splendid, 9½ lbs at birth, and the prettiest little child you could see.' Then on the thirtieth he tells his mother that Sydney is going on well, but 'I shall be very glad when I can see in her face that she is really more comfortable'. A subsequent letter says that the name is not quite settled, but he expects it will be Ruby. (We wonder how Nancy would have liked this.)

The household was from the start subjected by Sydney to her father's health rules. Her slogan, like his, was 'Trust the good body.' None of her children was vaccinated, although this was already by way of being compulsory; Sydney took advantage, as Diana was later to do with her children, of a provision in the law exempting the children of those with a conscientious objection. Sydney banned as far as possible the use of all medicine; she would only call the doctor in severe emergencies. When he did come, and prescribed some 'mixture' or other, it was either not obtained at all or left unused in a cupboard. It has to be said that Sydney's disbelief in doctors was fortified by one particular experience. Pam caught polio in 1911, at the age of three; in those days this disease, when it did not actually kill, usually left patients severely crippled for life. Sydney consulted six doctors in turn, with no effect; she then called in her father's osteopath, 'Dr' Kellgren. Under his treatment Pam recovered almost completely; she could ride to hounds, swim, skate and even ski. To this day Pam attributes her recovery entirely to Kellgren's massage and exercises. It was of course a time when others, besides Kellgren, were trying out methods of physiotherapy to help against polio; he was not unique. But such treatment was still rare. Sydney was always to apply Kellgren's methods for injuries. Decca, in *Hons and Rebels*, says that when she broke her arm Sydney removed the bandages that the doctor had applied when he set the fracture; she then made Decca do exercises to prevent the arm becoming stiff. The treatment was that which had so rapidly cured Sydney's broken ankle long before, and it worked just as well on Decca, though leaving her rather double-jointed.

Sydney also imposed on the household the dietary laws of Moses, but David, from the start, refused to comply; he would not be deprived of his bacon and sausages. One may surmise that there were words about this at the beginning between David and Sydney, but if so the matter was settled long before the children were conscious. The meat of the pig was provided, but only for the master of the house and of course for guests. This increased the yearning of the children for it; Tom was to write triumphantly from his preparatory school: 'We have sossages every Sunday', no doubt in order to enhance his sisters' envy and perhaps gently tease his mother. Nancy remembers: 'Whiffs of fried bacon from my father's breakfast and the sight of him tucking into sausage rolls or sausages and mash, cold gammon and cranberry sauce, pork chops with apple sauce, pigs' thinkers and trotters and Bath chaps were daily tortures; the occasional sucking-pig which crackled into the dining-room hardly bears contemplating, even now.' The sucking pig, one suspects, is an invention, but we get the point. Shellfish, too, became a craving. When Diana married and became free of the Mosaic laws, all she could at first think of to ask her cook to prepare for dinner was dressed crab; night after night she ordered it. The bread in the Mitford household was a great speciality. In latter years Sydney tended to make it herself; the recipe came from Thomas's German cook Dina, and the flour was wholemeal and stoneground. This bread, crusty and irresistible even when stale, is enshrined in a leaflet called 'Lady Redesdale's Bread Recipe', obtainable to this day in the Chatsworth food-shop.

All his life David was a total abstainer from alcohol. This was not on grounds of health or moral principle; he just never liked the taste of drink. He was not proud of his abstinence; in fact, on festive occasions, he disliked drawing attention to it for fear of seeming a killjoy. When he inherited from his father he acquired a gold cup which his father had had made from the medals he had won for his Shire horses. David used it specifically so that the fact that he was drinking water should not be too conspicuous. There was always wine in the house, which was provided when there were visitors. One might expect that in the circumstances this would be chosen by Sydney, but the tradition that the man takes care of the drink was too strong. David delegated the choosing to the wine merchants, Berry Brothers; they seem to have performed satisfactorily.

David insisted upon supervising Nancy's birth; there is a story that he personally administered the anaesthetic. He was present at the births of all of his seven children, anticipating by many decades the vogue for paternal participation in childbirth. We have seen how delighted he was with the baby; he called her Blob-Nose or Koko, starting a relationship that by the time she grew up was to become, as Debo recalls, 'a constant knock-about turn'. Nancy's caricatures of her father, especially the early ones such as General Murgatroyd in *Highland Fling*, were both meant by her and accepted by him as part of this. David certainly served as the model for Uncle Matthew, the best known of his literary avatars, but there is also a sense in which he consciously colluded in the creation.

Under Thomas's influence, Sydney engaged as nanny the daughter of Ned Kersey, whose name was Lily, soon corrupted to Ninny. If Aldeburgh men were the best sailors, it followed that Aldeburgh girls were the best nannies. Lily was untrained, but so had Jenny Cable been. Nancy was to be rather hard on Lily in retrospect, although she did not remember her directly, holding her 'partly responsible for my great nastiness to the others'. She had, as nannies will, transferred her affections to Pam when she was born on 25 November 1907. Sydney told Nancy later that she used to hear her saying, 'Oh Ninny, how I wish you could still love me!' In the end, according to Nancy, it was her great sadness at this that induced her parents to send Lily away in October 1908.

In *The Water Beetle* Nancy also blames Lily for having 'laid the foundations of the low stamina which has always been a handicap in life'. This was always to be a grievance. In conversation and in letters it was not Lily she blamed but her mother, particularly for not calling in doctors often enough. Nancy in fact absorbed much of her mother's scepticism about doctors, even before her own last terrible illness which was to seem to prove the point in appalling fashion. However, she liked blaming her mother for things. When Nancy was a baby she had, apparently, something wrong with her urinary tract that made micturition painful, and it remained untreated. She used to wonder whether this stopped her having children. Again, in 1961, she wrote to Diana wondering where Debo got her 'abounding energy'. 'One tiny dollop of it would have changed my whole life,' she adds. 'Of course the dentist says

I was starved when I was five and having our mater I guess that may be true.' This may refer to Sydney's refusal to allow the children to be forced to eat, but it is more likely to be based on the under-provision of food that sometimes occurred in Sydney's extreme old age, of which Nancy complains in other letters.

Nancy was certainly short of energy in middle life. In Paris she usually went to bed early and did not wake till nine or rise till eleven. However, Diana says this was not true when Nancy was young. 'When she came out she often danced all night and hunted all day and danced again. She stayed in countless country houses and someone who really lacked energy would have collapsed after these exertions.'

As to Nancy's childhood, which she implies in *The Water Beetle* was short of affection, a very different light is shed on it by a letter to her from Sydney dated 20 July 1952: 'You were terribly spoilt as a little child, and by all. It was Puma's idea.' Puma, more often known as Pussy, was David's eldest sister, Frances Kearsey. 'She said you must never hear an angry word and you never did, but you used to get in tremendous rages, often shaming us in the street – but the angry word was not allowed. So! Puma adored you and in fact until Pam was born you reigned supreme, but after that Lillie [*sic*] didn't like you any more, and that was very bad for you, however she soon departed.' More constructive was the advice of Nancy's formidable great-grandmother, Blanche, Lady Airlie, to whom Sydney took her for inspection when she was four. 'How is the child progressing in French?' asked the old lady. Sydney admitted that she had not begun to learn it, upon which Lady Airlie pronounced: 'There is nothing so inferior as a gentlewoman who has no French.' Sydney thereupon engaged a French governess.

As nanny, Lily Kersey was succeeded by Norah Evans, of whom nothing is known but her name, and who left in March 1910. Tom was born in her time. Her successor was a figure remembered in legend as the Unkind Nanny. Tom and Diana were born respectively on 2 January 1909 and 17 June 1910. Tom's birth delighted Sydney, who would always have preferred to have boys; but by the same token Diana's arrival rather disappointed her. Another boy would have been so tidy, two of each. The Unkind Nanny, during whose brief reign Diana was born, depressed Sydney further by observing: 'She's too beautiful; she can't live long.' Tinged with gloom though it was, this was the first of many compliments Diana has received all her life, right into old age; she herself thinks the remark absurd on the grounds that no new-born baby can be anything but repulsive to look at. To the man in the street this is perhaps so, but nurses and midwives think the view as odd as the claim that all Chinese look alike. All it shows is that the Unkind Nanny knew about babies' looks, for Diana was by common consent to be the beauty of the family. Penelope Betjeman recalls her as the best-looking girl of her whole generation. Debo was to say of her on television, 'She's the only one of us who's got a face.' It is the long Mitford face, very like David's. Debo herself has Sydney's face. Common consent, to be sure, does not mean universal consent; some have always preferred Debo's looks to Diana's, while Pam, with the startling blue eyes inherited from David and Bertie, also has her partisans.

In any case the Unkind Nanny's remark passed into family legend. The prediction of an early grave was to be useful to Diana. Now and then she could stop her elders from teasing her by saying: 'You know I can't live long; you'll be sorry.' One of their taunts was based on the fact that Diana was born after the death of Edward VII so that she, unlike them, had only lived in one reign. Pam remembers watching from the window of Bertie's house in Kensington Gore as all the crowned heads of Europe went by for Edward VII's funeral procession.

Four months after Diana's birth, some time in October 1910, the Unkind Nanny was sacked. According to Diana, her parents discovered that she used to knock Nancy's head against a wooden bedpost. Nancy claims not to have remembered this, or even to know what form the Nanny's unkindness was supposed to have taken: 'Did the Nanny beat us or starve us or merely refuse to laugh at our jokes?' She does, however, remember the dismissal, which was effected by David, Sydney having retired to bed. 'There was a confrontation in the nursery as of two mastodons,' says Nancy, adding that during it she herself felt entirely on the side of the nanny.

Her successor was chosen with great care. For several weeks there was only a nurserymaid, and a number of applicants came and went. Finally, however, Laura Dicks, to be known as Blor, applied for the post. She was thin, pale, fine-featured, with curly reddish brown hair and a kindly expression. Sydney liked her on sight, but wondered, looking at her, if she was physically capable of coping with four children even though she was only thirty-nine. The same thought occurred independently to Blor herself. However, the sight of Diana as a baby decided her. Like the Unkind Nanny, she knew a face when she saw one. 'Oh! what a lovely baby!' she exclaimed, and signed on for life. Nancy, just short of six years old, was reading *Ivanhoe* in the nursery when Blor arrived for the first time, and Blor showed a tact unusual in nannies; she did not interrupt her. 'I remember every word of *Ivanhoe*, which I have never read since, but have no recollection of the advent of Blor,' says Nancy. 'No doubt it seemed at once as though she had been with us for ever.'

It was about the best thing that ever happened to the family. Nancy, in most matters so sharp and critical, can in her essay 'Blor' (*The Water Beetle*) find nothing whatever to say about her that is not complimentary. Diana and Decca, otherwise not always at one, coincide with each other and with Nancy in their love of Blor. Jonathan (the author) remembers her well a generation later, exactly as described by Nancy except that her hair was no longer brown but a pure and ethereal white, and her face covered by a mesh of delicate wrinkles. She had a characteristic nervous tic – a sort of sniff which was also partly a hiccough, partly a little asthmatic gasp. On this Decca and Debo based their nickname for her, 'M'Hinket'. She wore spectacles with thin silver frames, and looked altogether as different as possible from Jonathan's own stout Nanny Higgs with her double chin and thick horn-rims. Blor was a great one for gently taking her charges down a peg: 'Nobody's going to look at *you*', she used to say, not a bad phrase to cool down the exuberant child or encourage the shy one. Her main virtue, to be severely tested over the years, was fairness. Both these traits probably came from her puritan upbringing. Her father, a blacksmith who made wrought-iron gates and lived in Egham, was a devout Congregationalist who taught her from her earliest years to follow in all matters her conscience rather than her sympathies. But she departed from the nonconformist image in that she was not in the least dour; she had natural charm and humour. Nancy, who admits, or to be more accurate proclaims, that she herself was vile to the others, thinks she would have been much worse but for Blor. 'My mother's scoldings and my father's whippings had little effect, but Blor at least made me feel ashamed of myself.'

Diana has made it clear in interview that she thinks this mention of whippings is untrue. In her autobiography she presents her father's fierceness as being real enough, but entirely verbal. According to Diana, '. . . not only did he make us scream with laughter at his lovely jokes but . . . he was very affectionate. Certainly he had a quick temper, and would often rage, but we were never punished', except sometimes by being sent to bed early. Decca does say she was beaten for bullying Debo, but she implies that this was exceptional. *Hons and Rebels*, contains a remark with a very significant qualification. Discussing the family background of herself and her first husband, Esmond Romilly, she says both experienced lunacy and Esmond underwent brutality. As regards brutality, then, she specifically confines the allegation to Esmond's childhood, clearly indicating that there was no brutality in her own.

Shortly before the sacking of the Unkind Nanny, Nancy began going to the Frances Holland day school, which she was to attend until 1914. Rather oddly, she never makes any mention of this, but she must have enjoyed it because she was later to write that to go to school was the dream of her life, and she certainly liked camping with the Girl Guides when she was older. But David and Sydney, like many people in those days, did not consider boarding school suitable for girls. Tello and the 'old dragon', despite the intervening nonentities, had taught Sydney quite satisfactorily; so it was not unreasonable to think that governesses could educate her daughters. This view was proved correct.

Pam and Tom used to go every week to the dancing class of Miss Vacani, who taught the children of royalty and the gentry their first halting dance steps from before the First World War until well after the Second. Pam, after her polio attack, was at a disadvantage; in particular she could not hop on her right leg, so the polka was out. She was kept firmly in the back row and not often attended to. But Tom was one of Miss Vacani's favourites, in his green shoes with large silver buckles.

In 1912 David staked out claims totalling 40 acres on a new gold field in northern Ontario. It was not necessarily a stupid speculation, for there was gold in the vicinity; Sir Harry Oakes, who had the next door parcel of land, made millions out of it, before being murdered in the Bahamas. But David never found much on his land. He and Sydney went out there towards the end of 1913 for the first time; they lived in a small but solid house made of logs – not a shack, Sydney insists in her unpublished life of Unity. It was, she makes clear in a roundabout way, the place where Unity was conceived; an odd coincidence, for the place is called Swastika.

Unity was born on 8 August 1914, just after war was declared. Nancy remembers the soldiers marching to the war past Bertie's house where the family was staying over the time of Unity's birth; their drab khaki was very different from the sumptuous ceremonial uniforms at the old King's funeral procession watched from the same window four years earlier. The new baby was christened Unity Valkyrie. Each name celebrated the start of the war in its way; Unity expressed Sydney's vain hope that it would be short, and Valkyrie, war-maiden, was, as we have seen, at Bertie's suggestion. Bertie would certainly not have been pleased, at this time, to know that in later life Unity would adopt for her second name the German spelling, Walküre, or that the start of another war with Germany would so shatter her world as to make her put a bullet in her brain. As a war-maiden, she was scarcely to come up to scratch.

David, as we have seen, rejoined the Northumberland Fusiliers at the beginning of the war, despite having lost a lung. He was not supposed to be at the front, but he went to France, serving behind the lines as a dispatch rider. In practice he came under fire several times and was mentioned in dispatches. On at least one occasion Sydney was able to join him in Paris for a period of leave, and they visited Helleu, who turned his sharp artist's gaze upon David in his uniform, with his tanned face and bright blue eyes, and observed that he was khaki from head to foot: 'Only the eyes are not khaki.'

The shattering news of Clement's death in May 1915 arrived when David was home on leave with his family at High Wycombe. Clement was greatly loved, above all by his parents but also by his brothers and sisters; Daphne, Lady Denham, the sole survivor of Bertie's children, remembers his kindness to this day, and he was Nancy's favourite uncle. David never resented that Clement was so consistently preferred to himself, but concluded early in life that this preference was just. He at once obtained a compassionate extension to his leave and went with Sydney to Bertie.

David went back to the war, but returned unexpectedly on leave again in August to Victoria Road. Sydney and the children were at the seaside staying with Thomas at Bournhill Cottage, a house he had rented on the Solent. If David hoped for a little peace this time he was disappointed. The cook greeted David with the news that Bournhill Cottage had burned down and could not tell him whether all, or indeed any, of his family had escaped alive. Fortunately they all soon turned up, none the worse except for the loss of Diana's teddy bear. The fire had occurred two nights before. It had been an adventure for the children, sitting on the lawn in front of the blazing house with the grown-ups hurrying to and fro, saving what they could. Tom, already at six a polite little boy, called out 'Good morning, Mr Caddick', to the butler as he bustled past with a load of dining-room silver, and was surprised not to get an answer. At dawn they set off for Eaglehurst, the house of Thomas's neighbour Marconi, the radio pioneer. They had sometimes been to tea with the Marconi family, who now made them welcome. Following the family's nocturnal arousal, the day seemed endless, and they stayed the next night with the Marconis before taking the train back to London. Pam had reason to feel a little smug; she had smelt burning, and said so to the nurserymaid who was putting her to bed. The nurserymaid, believing perhaps that Pam was making an excuse so as to stay up a little longer, had paid no attention.

Soon after this they had to move out of London. David's army pay was less than he had earned at *The Lady*, and Thomas further reduced their income, writing to Sydney that increased taxation forced him to economize, and that he had decided to cut her allowance. This rather amused her as being typical of her father, and she told the story as a joke in later years, but at the time it was decidedly inconvenient. However, Bertie came to the rescue by making available Malcolm House, near Batsford, so the family moved there, letting both Victoria Road and the Old Mill Cottage. Sydney disliked this move, but the children found it to be for the better; for the first time, says Diana, they were living in the real country. For her the summer of 1916 was enlivened by seeing a vision. 'At least I said I had seen one, and the others believed me and made me describe it so often that I hardly know now whether it was a dream or whether I saw it with my mind's eye. It was the conventional sort of vision where heavens open and angels appear in a golden light. Nancy, Pam and Tom flew to Sydney to complain, "Oh, Muv, it's *so* unfair, Diana's seen a *vision*." '

It was during August 1916 that Bertie died. Clementine, walking in the garden at Batsford, found Pam and Diana, and on an impulse took the little girls to see their grandfather, who was suffering from the jaundice that was the final stage of his last illness. He was sitting up in bed in a vast, dim room with the blinds down. Diana found his appearance frightening. 'A thin, bright yellow face; a shock of white hair standing on end. I do not remember what he said to us; I could not take my eyes off his face.' Pam, less shocked, remembers that he told her she would not like what he was drinking; it was the whey from a junket. She too noticed that his 'lovely white hair' was standing on end.

Malcolm House was right next door to the church, and on the day of the funeral the bell tolled loud and insistent. The Batsford gardeners had filled the grave with so many flowers that no earth was to be seen and Diana, creeping unseen into the churchyard with Pam and Tom on the day before, received such a powerful image of the bright colours that for years afterwards when she heard of a death she pictured a grave lined with flowers.

# 21

# Batsford

Bertie's death, following that of Clement, meant that David became Lord Redesdale and inherited Batsford. During 1916 the family moved there from Malcolm House. The Army authorities accommodated David's new responsibilities to the extent of giving him the post of Assistant Provost Marshal at Oxford, which was within easy distance of his family. He had rooms, of all places, in Christ Church, where his children enjoyed visiting him and playing his pianola; he used to come over to Batsford once a week on his motorcycle, and stay a couple of hours. With the estates, unfortunately, came crippling debts. Retrenchment had come much too late. It was obvious that the big house would have to be sold, along with much of the land.

In the meantime even David, whom his daughters were to accuse of always selling his property at the worst time, realized that it would be mad not to hold on at least for the duration of the war; so the great mock-Tudor pile with its elaborately planned gardens and arboretum became the family home for the next four years. Sydney was unable to afford more than a skeleton staff, so they did not use all the rooms.

Their situation was slightly helped by adopting the same expedient as had Sir Henry Malet when he shared Wilbury with Thomas Bowles. A neighbour in Victoria Road was Ronald Norman, brother of Montague Norman who was later to be governor of the Bank of England. Ronald Norman and his wife, Lady Florence, wanted to get their four children out of London for the duration of the war, so they lodged them at Batsford. The two families got on better than Sydney had got on with Vera Malet. Sibell and Mark, the older two, were of an age to play with Pam, Tom and Diana. Their parents, cultivated and indulgent,

would often visit them; Diana found them surprisingly different
from her own. Mary, the youngest, went up to her mother and
deliberately knocked a coffee cup out of her hand; Diana, knowing her own mother, held her breath for an explosion, but Lady
Florence only said, 'Oh, darling, was that an accident?' As to
Ronald Norman, Diana, accompanied by Sibell, actually saw him
sitting in an armchair reading.

'I said to Sibell, "Does your father often read?"

' "Oh yes," she replied.

' "I've never heard of a man reading," I said.'

She judged all men by reference to her own father.

Despite being more than half under dustsheets Batsford was
now a lively place, perhaps livelier than it had been since Bertie
built it. We interviewed Pam together with her aunt Daphne,
youngest of Bertie's children, and it became clear how much freer
David's children were than his brothers and sisters. 'We were not
allowed to play with the village children,' said Daphne. 'Oh, *we*
were,' said Pam, making it clear that the only time she got into
trouble for this was when she stayed out after dark and caused an
anxious search. Daphne's generation had been walked up and
down in the garden for exercise, watched by a nurserymaid; Pam's
had been allowed to play in it at will. Much the same was true
indoors. When David was at home the family played hide-and-
seek all over the house, bringing all five staircases into use. Diana
remembers 'the sound of footsteps thumping down the corridor, a
distant scuffle and scream and Farve's triumphant roar when he
caught someone'. Even Clementine Redesdale would join in the
rough games; as grandmothers will, she adopted a far more
relaxed attitude to David's children than she had to her own, and
though in appearance old for her age she had also become less
'delicate' than when she was younger. On Bertie's death she had
moved up to Redesdale Cottage, but she often came to Batsford to
stay and had the children to visit her. Her heavy figure did not
deter her from playing hide-and-seek, and once she fell flat on her
back. It was thought that only the bun on the back of her head
saved her from concussion.

Sydney took to bee-keeping, and Pam remembers her taking
the swarms and tending the hives assisted by Miss Mirams, the
governess, both wearing masks. The surplus honey was taken to

London, and sold whenever Sydney had the occasion to go. Miss Mirams was a good teacher, the best the family were to have; the runner-up was probably Miss Hussey, of whom more later. Miss Mirams's competence is proved by the fact that when Tom went to his preparatory school he started a form above the bottom. Blor was a help to her. A nanny would often be at odds with the governess, unwilling to share her power with the newcomer. Blor was, Nancy tells us, never like this, but always backed the authority of Miss Mirams and of her successors and encouraged the children to do their work. Thanks both to Miss Mirams and to Sydney's own teaching of the children, all the children were at this time educationally extended except perhaps Pam. She had been held back by her early attack of polio, and was well below the standard of Nancy, who was three years older and had school experience. She was therefore taught with Tom and Diana, respectively two and three years younger. But Pam at this time nevertheless scored at least one minor coup, of which she still enjoys the benefits. A big fete was held in the Batsford grounds in aid of a local convalescent home for the war-wounded. Among the attractions was a white elephant stall which Sydney, thinking it rather bare, impulsively enriched with knick-knacks from the house. She included a small rare Buddha from Bertie's collection, no more than a rather ugly little curio in Sydney's eyes but valuable even then. Pam bought it for sixpence and still possesses it. David bought another for the same sum, and rescued a precious oriental vase, but many valuable objects were lost on this occasion, no doubt to surface later to the profit of shrewd dealers and sharp-eyed collectors. Sydney never lost this habit of helping with fetes by giving away the family's possessions, either at Batsford or later at Asthall; not only antique ornaments, but even some of the children's toys, were requisitioned. 'We soon learned to hide our possessions when a fete loomed up,' says Diana. At Asthall, Decca lost two woolly animals in this way; they were soon found in the village, though, and the buyers were delighted to exchange the threadbare objects for new ones.

Nancy decided that the Batsford fete should be graced by a play, entrance fee sixpence a head, in which the children were to perform with contemporaries from the village. They rehearsed under the direction of Georgie Gordon, Sydney's much younger first cousin, but the producer had an uphill task. Nancy and a village boy took the main parts, those of a farmer and his wife; the other Mitfords, to Nancy's great satisfaction, were made to play her children. Diana remembers only the first line, belonging to the boy: 'It was "Phew, wife, the heat is tremendous." Nancy's partner pronounced this as Few, Woife, and he gave every subsequent syllable exactly equal value, so that it sounded utterly unlike somebody talking in real life.' They worked at the play for weeks, and two days before the fete they had their dress rehearsal in front of Sydney. The cast was excited at the dressing up, but their delivery was incurably wooden and Georgie had to prompt continually. At the end, says Diana, there was a worrying silence, then Sydney spoke out firmly. She forbade them to do their play, explaining that it was too bad.

Georgie Gordon remembers the family well, both at Batsford and subsequently at Asthall. Sydney seemed, by comparison with her dynamic younger sister Dorothy Bailey, 'quieter and vaguer'; the verdict on the play must have come as all the more of a bombshell. 'Vague' is a word that observers were to apply to Sydney all her life; there was, as it were, an almost invariable mist around her which only occasionally cleared to reveal the iron mountain at its heart. Towards the end of her life deafness, as well as the mellowing of old age, made the mist more and more impenetrable. But at Batsford she would often interrupt her reverie. Under the vague manner was an alert and intelligent woman.

As to the children at this period, it is the two eldest that Georgie Gordon remembers best. Nancy was 'dark and different-looking', almost always buried in a book. Pam seemed solitary, and often rather out of things; at any rate Georgie remembers her remarking, not in a mood of self-pity but rather as an interesting fact, 'Nobody talks to me', adding: 'I go for walks by myself; the other day I was so lucky, I found a penny.' Pam's own memories of Batsford are happy. She and Diana, particularly, had secret houses and stores of food and endless games. There were times when she felt it prudent to get away from Nancy; as the second child, she bore the brunt of her legendary teasing. Yet of course Nancy could also be so funny and delightful that she and the others were attracted. It was the attraction of the flame for the moth.

Already while they were at Batsford the children were beginning to show the distinctive way of talking that others were often to regard as affected. It has tended to be congenial to male homosexuals of the 'camp' variety, and was definitely a reason why Brian Howard, as an Oxford undergraduate, was to extol Nancy to Harold Acton as a 'delicious creature'. The voice was a little like Howard's own; Howard probably thought he had found a kind of soul-mate. Distinctive in itself, the family voice became more so than ever when it was used to wheedle and persuade. Tom, aged seven, invented what he called his 'artful scheme of happiness' for getting anything he might want. We quote Diana again: 'He looked long and lovingly at the desired object, and when this had been noticed he began to speak. "Oh, what a lovely box; I don't think I've ever seen such a lovely little box in all my life. Oh, how I wish I could find one like it! Do you think I *ever* could? *Oh* (to the owner) you *are* lucky." He made his voice positively sag with desire.' Readers of an astringent turn will probably react with Belloc's lines: 'Alas that such affected tricks/ Should flourish in a child of six.' However, this way of talking, this *sagging* of the voice, was to become generally characteristic. A gloomy and exaggerated version of it was to arise in the form of Boudledidge, the private language concocted by Unity and Decca. Later in life the manner tended to express appreciation rather than to aim at material gain. During the war Evelyn Waugh took Nancy to lunch at the Hyde Park Hotel; there was toast on the table in little silver racks. 'Oh!' she exclaimed in tones of rapture: '*Toast!*' The Mitfords have always retained the habit, reminiscent of the Artful Scheme of Happiness, of wrapping up any request for a favour, however simple, with elaborate injunctions not to think of doing it if it gives the least trouble. Unity once wrote from Germany asking Diana to get her some material from Gorringe's, a well-known draper in Buckingham Palace Road; 'but only if you are literally in Gorringe's', she said, twice, in the course of a rigmarole covering half a page. Debo wrote to Diana shortly after Christmas 1943: 'Darling-Honks, Oh Honks oh Honks the gifts, I am completely o'ercome by their glory I can't think what to thank for first. The underclothes Honks, the stockings, all the Honnish things for Em, well I must say I never saw such a parcel. The coupons Honks, you must have spent so many I can hardly bear to think of you going quite naked which is what you'll surely have to do . . .' and so on.

Even to their children, Diana and Debo always expressed themselves in this way. Where other adults might content themselves with at most a perfunctory 'Be an angel and fetch . . .' they would carry on for some time about how unbelievably saintly and unprecedentedly adorable one would be if one could possibly . . . and so on. On one occasion it was all rather too much for Diana's son, Alexander Mosley. 'Come on, Mum,' he said resignedly. 'Spit it out.' Her son Desmond Guinness also caught the habit for a time. During his National Service, he once absentmindedly told the officers' mess steward who had just brought him a drink that he was sweet. 'I'm sweet, I am,' he overheard the man tell his colleague. That the Mitfords should in many people's opinion be affected has never prevented them from suffering when they encounter what they regard as affectation in others, including any attempt by an English person to pronounce foreign languages properly. Diana says of Lord Berners in Italy that 'he never embarrassed with a good accent like some of one's compatriots', and Nancy, in *Love in a Cold Climate*, has Polly saying of her husband: 'He can talk all those terribly affected languages (Darling! Italian! You'd die!).'

To return to Tom, in 1918 he went away to his preparatory school, Lockers Park. Miss Mirams was rather worried; she knew about boys. The Mitford voice, the intonation, the words they used, all seemed to her affected and for Tom dangerously so. She confided her fears to Sydney. He ought, she said, not to say things like 'How *amusing*.' 'Boys never say how *amusing*,' said Miss Mirams; especially in that tone of voice, was the implication.

She was quite right; yet she need not have worried. Tom was lucky; he seems never to have suffered from homesickness, bullying, bad food or other features of preparatory school life. This was unusual. Quite a few boys enjoy their public school, but few are on record as liking their preparatory school. Tom did so from the very first day. The 'sossages', of course, though no doubt gristly and overcooked and certainly inferior to those that other boys had at home, were a bonus; but by themselves they hardly explain his contentment. In fact we learn from Rosemary Bailey, Clement's daughter, that she and the Mitfords' other cousins looked forward to visiting them precisely because the food, despite the Mosaic restrictions, was so particularly good; the comedown to school food should have been that much more marked. Tom does not seem to have noticed it. He was a hearty and comparatively undiscriminating eater: 'Isn't Pam *wonderful*,' he used to say, 'the way she refuses food.' He would then eat her helping. As to more important matters, even at the age of nine Tom was urbane, quick-witted and totally self-possessed. He had sufficient presence to avoid being teased, and he never seems to have had the least trouble in organizing himself in all necessary ways, or in moderating the family speech mannerisms to a level where they were acceptable. Occasionally he would 'get the swish' for some misdemeanour, but these experiences, like all others, were surmounted with no trouble and recounted in tidy and well-expressed letters home. He was quite popular, without being in any way a schoolboy hero; good enough at games to enjoy them; and normally near the top of his class. Innate temperament apart, what was his secret?

His parents' love was one factor, heightened in David's case by what can only be called respect. Given David's image, it may be thought rather surprising that it was not he rather than Miss Mirams who had uttered the advice to avoid calling things 'amusing', indeed that he had allowed the habit to grow up in the first place. The David of legend would surely have checked the Mitford mannerisms with some roughness. But David had no trace of the conventional public school man's heartiness, the kind of machismo that used to go with team games and prompted Oxford rugger men to throw aesthetes into Mercury – the pond in Tom Quad, Christ Church. All David ever put into Mercury were a few rainbow trout, when he lived in Tom Quad as an army officer. He was not intellectual, but he was never anti-intellectual. His children did indeed say of him that Jack London's *White Fang* was the only book he had ever read, and that he never again felt the need to read another. But he was never contemptuous of the things of the mind; on the contrary, his attitude towards them was always notably humble. A view has grown up about David that he was a raging philistine; this is untrue though he would sometimes growl at modern art. Uncle Matthew's admiration for Davey Warbeck in *The Pursuit of Love*, which admittedly comes as a surprise to the Radlett children, is nevertheless one of the touches that is truest to the original. David regarded his own erudite father with something like awe. What is more remarkable, and we suggest rather touching, is that he also recognized and respected the intellectual leanings of his own children when they began to emerge. This applied to Nancy, but above all to the adored Tom. Diana tells us that when Batsford was sold in 1919 David asked Tom, aged ten at the time, which books in the library should be sold and which kept. Presumably others were consulted as well, but this shows that David already respected Tom's judgement, using him almost as he used Berry Brothers to restock his cellar. Literature, like wine, was not for David, but he made sure it was available for those who appreciated it.

David's admiration helped Tom to become unusually self-confident, as did Blor's solid affection and the benefits of Miss Mirams's good teaching. To be sure, had he been an only child these factors alone might have simply made the transition to school life more painful, and thus done more harm than good. But Tom's home was no bed of roses. He knew all about bullying and teasing and other aspects of the social life of children; he had learnt from his sisters and his playmates the Normans, and, thanks notably to Nancy, he had learnt in a hard school. He was no stranger to being mocked, or indeed to being physically hurt; he had learnt to stand up for himself or, where necessary, to ride with the punch.

One particular game, which must have been invented about the time of the Treaty of Versailles, took the form of a kind of tableau. Nancy thought the name of Czechoslovakia, just then being carved out of the old Austrian Empire, was irresistibly funny. We are used to it now, but it is possible to cast one's mind back, and see her point. She invented for herself a persona, a 'Czechish lady doctor', who would express in a heavy foreign accent her longing for 'Moi Czecho'. The lady doctor's voice became the first of the Mitfords' private family languages. Nancy would shepherd Pam, Tom and Diana somewhere out of the way. Tom would be made into a patient brought to the lady doctor by Diana, his mother, for examination; Pam would be in attendance as nurse. Nancy would lie Tom down, look at his chest and start up in consternation.

'Air you his mozzair?' she would ask Diana, her eyes wide with simulated concern.

Diana nodded.

'Opairation!' said Nancy, 'at wonce!' She would then add in a stage whisper: 'Eat weel be *agonee*!'

Tom, as patient, was supposed to have overheard this by accident. 'Agonee for me?'

Nancy reassured him with heavy-handed and theatrical false-hood. 'No, no, for the poor old woman in the 'ospital.'

The operation would take the form of a painful knuckling in the chest. The characters, other than that of the doctor, could of course be changed round at Nancy's whim. The victim would on occasion be Pam or Diana; but it was usually Tom. At least once he attempted to organize his sisters to resist Nancy; there is in existence a piece of paper, written childishly in pencil, headed 'Leag against Nancy head Tom'.

The lady doctor's voice was to prove durable; Nancy used it both in conversation and in letters, especially but not only to her sisters, to the end of her life. Chiefly it was a foreign accent, but there were certain other features like a tendency to tack -ling on the end of proper names. Pam's nickname 'Woman' thus acquired its variant 'Woomling'. Of Pam, Nancy would say, 'Oh she ees wondairful', and sometimes she refers to her as 'Wondairful' or 'Wondair'. 'Oh she ees wondairful' is sometimes shortened in Nancy's letters to 'Oh she ees', a turn of phrase which may have foxed some researchers. Nancy herself became 'Naunceling'. A phrase that Nancy often used was 'A leetle beet mud', when she wanted to throw doubt on someone's possession of perfect mental health.

One by one the children progressed from the nursery to the schoolroom, which meant meals in the dining room. We have noted that this promotion entailed more honour than pleasure because of David's phobias against making a mess at table and in particular against stickiness. Another taboo was on David's wire-less, to him a marvellous invention and and object of great sanctity. To interfere with it was to incur a blasting. These things always remained in the minds of David's children. When in April 1941 Jonathan and his brother Desmond went to stay with David on the island of Inchkenneth, Diana wrote to Jonathan to say she hoped the two of them were not putting honey on David's wireless. He liked this; 'She knows me,' he grunted complacently.

Another characteristic of David's was his liking for cups of cold tea. He would ask for, or himself make, a cup of tea which would of course be too hot to drink at once. He would leave it to cool on the mantelpiece of the room where he happened to be. Occasionally there would be more than one of these, cooling in various rooms. He called them his 'suckments'. The word was invented by his brother Jack, who had the same habit. The tea would often be cold when he returned to it, but he would drink it quite happily. Sometimes a maid would spot a cup full of stone-cold tea, the milk congealing on the top in a beige scum. Her natural inclination would be to clear it away. When this had occurred once or twice, David started locking his cooling teacups in the safe. He did this, let it be noted, rather than scold the maid. All his life David was exceptionally polite to servants; in return for this they loved him. Sydney, too, had the respect and affection of those who worked for her. As a rule they stayed for a lifetime.

Perhaps the Czech lady doctor's exploits were partly founded on the fact that Diana had her appendix removed at Batsford. Towards the end of the war she began getting bad pains; finally the operation was performed on the spot, in one of the visitors' rooms. The others were sent away for a few days to David's sister Joan Farrer and her family; they remembered the prophecy that she could not live long and did not expect to see her again alive, but she awoke from the anaesthetic in a huge brocade bed. Her recovery was hastened, she says, by the beauty of her surroundings and the fuss everyone made of her, especially Pam who bought her a magnificent paintbox. During the same year, on 11 September 1917, another girl was born, called Jessica after Sydney's mother.

Mention of Joan Farrer reminds us that we ought not to omit the uncles and aunts. At Batsford, and indeed later at Asthall and Swinbrook and until the time when politics were to cause division in the family, there was a lot of coming and going between the Mitfords and their near relations. David was one of a family of nine, and Sydney one of four, so they were numerous.

The favourite at Batsford was not an aunt but a great-aunt: Lady Blanche Hozier, known as Aunt Natty. She was Clementine

Redesdale's sister and the mother of another Clementine who was married to Winston Churchill; and it is whispered in the family that Bertie, her brother-in-law, once had an affair with her. Nobody can know if this is true, but one would not necessarily put it past either of them. Aunt Natty resembled her sister in being stately and rather fat, but there the likeness ended. Even in old age Aunt Natty was distinctly 'fast'; she even wore a coloured ribbon with her widow's weeds, something Clementine Redesdale would never have dreamt of doing. David put her up at Batsford, at first in the big house, then in a Queen Anne house in the village; before the war she had lived at Dieppe, which she liked because of the gambling. Diana says: 'She never dressed till lunchtime, but used to throw a cape over her flowing nightgown and walk about the village.' She caught Tom and Diana staring at her feet and fat white ankles, stockingless in her bedroom slippers: this seemed curious in those days when no child ever saw a grown-up's legs except in stockings, let alone those of a dignified old lady. Aunt Natty used to tell endless stories to the children, mostly about her own childhood. They enjoyed these, but mostly they liked Aunt Natty because she was, in Diana's words, 'the first unprincipled grown-up who came our way'. She had brought over her Scotch terrier from France hidden under her cloak, so as to evade the quarantine restrictions. Diana tells the story:

'Just as she was walking through the Customs he wriggled.

' "Madam," said the Customs man, "have you got a dog under your arm?"

' "Certainly not!" said Aunt Natty.

' "Well, Madam, then what's that there moving then?"

' "So I flung open the other side of my cloak and said: 'Cannot you believe the word of an Englishwoman?' and I walked through." '

This story shocked Sydney, as did sayings like 'I love privilege.' Clementine Redesdale also thought this outrageous. Altogether, if Clementine had, as she claimed, not a drop of Stanley blood in her veins, Aunt Natty seems to have had little else. Like her Stanley ancestors, too, Lady Blanche Hozier wrote a good letter; and this enables us to get a glimpse of Batsford in 1917 through her eyes, for three letters from there to a friend survive. 'Yesterday,' she writes on 11 June 1917,

. . . as I went into the little church in the park . . . I saw outside the churchyard gate Sydney's dog, and Nancy's dog (one I gave her) and three dolls – all resting quietly near each other in the grass, waiting for their owners to come out from church. Unity, a dear little girl of nearly three, is brought into church just before the last hymn, which she stands up and sings; 'God Save the King' she listens to with wrapt [sic] attention – then, runs out.

Thomas Bowles was staying at the time; 'brilliant in conversation – we talked till nearly 11 last night. I was tired – but did not think about it till I came to bed.' In her next letter, of 14 June, she notes Thomas's odd hours, which must have given the Batsford servants some trouble but which, of course, Sydney would never have thought of attempting to modify. 'Mr Bowles only eats with us at dinner – any time after 5 a.m. he rings for his *café au lait* and rolls – is out by 6 – breakfast at 11.30, tea at 3.30. He comes and talks to us while we are at luncheon and tells the three schoolroom children stories.' She mentions the club for convalescent soldiers for which the Batsford fete was given; Sydney went to wash up there one afternoon a week, and on certain other days detailed two of her servants to lend a hand. Lady Blanche also notes the excellence of the library at Batsford, 'inherited and added to by Bertie'. The third of these letters is written on 1 September 1917, by which time Sydney was 'expecting her sixth baby any minute' and Blanche had moved into 'such delightful rooms in an old Queen Anne house, furnished for me with such love and taste'. She says Sydney is 'good – unselfish – beautiful – and she and her husband the greatest lovers'. Such testimony means a good deal from someone who was sharp-eyed and sharp-tongued, and indeed proved herself so in references to other people in these same letters. Diana says the children liked Great-Aunt Natty more than all their uncles and aunts put together.

All of these were alive except Clement. Bertram, known as Uncle Tommy, married late, during Asthall days, though he had already been going out with his wife Dorothy before the war. They never had children. He had been a sailor and a great traveller. He had served in the Royal Navy during the war, earning the DSO, and then been naval attaché in Copenhagen for three years. After this he settled down in Swinbrook as a farmer, putting into practice various advanced theories of cultivation. He and David were very close, and the children loved his travellers' tales. He claimed once to have tasted what turned out to be human flesh.

The next brother was Uncle Jack, whom his brothers called Jicksy. He was a rolling stone; in January 1914 he had been married to a German-Jewish heiress, Marie-Anne Friedländer-Fuld, but the marriage had ended after a few weeks. He had been a great favourite of his father, who even forgave him as a boy for ruining one of his guns by leaving it out in the snow. David used to tell this story, which Diana says would 'electrify' the children. David's own guns were his most sacred possession; 'The notion that one of us children could leave one of Farve's guns lying out in the snow was simply too terrifying to think about.' Jack was for some time secretary of the Marlborough Club in London. He usually spent Christmas with David and his family.

Lastly there was Uncle Rupert, with his twin Aunt Daphne the youngest of Bertie's children. He was, among other things, an actor in films between the wars. He died in 1939 and his only son is the present Lord Redesdale.

Of David's sisters, there were Frances, always called Puma or Aunt Pussy, and her husband Alec Kearsey and daughter Clementine, known as Pussette. Pussy was popular with the children.

The next was Iris, Bertie's favourite daughter, who looked after him a good deal in old age and whom he often took on his travels. Iris had striking, rather faunlike good looks, but she never married. All her working life was spent with the Officers' Families' Fund, of which she became general secretary in return for a tiny pittance. Charity, and practical good works, were her life; but she was also shrewd and funny. She took some hand in the care of Rosemary and Clementine, Clement's daughters, when their mother Lady Helen remarried and went out to the Sudan with her new husband. She looked after her brother Jack in his last years.

Joan, the next sister, was married to Denis Farrer and had six children whom the Mitfords knew well; mutual visits were frequent, and Robin Farrer, whose real name was Joan, was to be a particular friend of Unity's. Denis Farrer was a grandson by her second marriage of Bertie's grandmother, the Scottish Mrs Farrer who had taken charge of Henry Reveley's household and spoilt little Bertie's seaside Sundays with her interminable services. He and Joan were therefore half-second-cousins, once removed. Joan, by many accounts, had something in her of that earlier Mrs Farrer. Her youngest sister, Daphne, remembers her as a 'terror'; the Mitford children were wary of her. So, seemingly, was their father. Of Joan's husband, David is supposed to have said:

'He'd be all right if he wasn't married to that ghastly woman.'

'But I thought he was married to your sister.'

'He is,' assented David.

This is not to be taken as meaning that the two families were ever on bad terms; quite the contrary.

Daphne, the youngest sister, was (and is) a striking beauty. She was married in 1914 to the first Lord Denham; their son is the chief Conservative whip in the House of Lords. Especially before her marriage, she used often to stay with her family; her main interest then, as now, was dogs, of which she became a breeder. She remembers at Batsford being impressed at finding Diana, one frosty morning, taking the trouble to break up the ice on the dogs' drinking water. It is the kind of thing she would remember. The only one of Bertie's children still living, her memory is clear and her help has been invaluable.

As to Sydney's brothers and her sister, they were all strongly marked, as she was herself, with their father's influence. Throughout their lives they were always to revert to him whenever they met, to wonder how he would react to this or that event. George ran *The Lady*, of which Thomas had left him a 43 per cent interest, his other three children having 19 per cent each. We have mentioned his writing, music and conjuring. He was a Member of Parliament for a short time. *The Lady*'s success continued under his management and he found time to exercise many other interests. Diana remembers him excavating a Saxon barrow near Asthall with care and enthusiasm, presenting the rather fragmentary results to the Ashmolean Museum in Oxford. He took his wife to see his finds. 'Only that little heap?' she said. Usually he disliked the country, which he thought was 'all mud and blood'.

If George inherited the practical side of Thomas's character, it was Geoffrey who inherited that independence of received ideas which was perhaps his most interesting gift. He had been, like George, a commander in the Navy during the First World War, and afterwards settled down to a life in which his main occupation seems to have been writing letters to the papers. He was always poor, and rather ascetic; he never married. A keen and expert sailor, at the end of his life he devised a new style of rigging for sailing ships, which excited some interest. He took a sporadic interest in politics: Decca remembers him making a speech for the Conservatives in Oxfordshire. He stood for King's Lynn as an Independent in 1945, reviving memories of his father by electioneering from his yacht, but lost his deposit. Geoffrey's main preoccupation, though, was natural food; in this he followed his father, but went much further. Many of his ideas, such as his opposition to artificial fertilizers, are identical to those of modern 'macrobiotics', and he was also what would now be called an environmentalist. Pasteurization of milk as well as refinement of flour, and its contamination by preservatives, were to him examples of 'murdered food'. If he were alive today he would greet with enthusiasm the growth of the health food movement, of which he was certainly a precursor and perhaps a pioneer.

Lastly there was Sydney's sister Dorothy, still known as Weenie, or Aunt Weenie to the children. She and her husband Percy lived with their family near the Mitfords at Maugersbury, near Stow-on-the-Wold. She was a woman of great energy; Debo, who loved staying with her, says she often got up at four in the morning, and Georgie Gordon testifies to the contrast of her obvious practicality with Sydney's apparent vagueness. All agree on her kindness, and Jonathan remembers her charm. Her son Richard was to marry Rosemary, Clement's elder daughter, whose numerous children are therefore descended, like the Mitfords, both from Bertie and from Thomas.

This is perhaps the place to introduce Mrs Hammersley, a lifelong friend of Sydney's who was to play a greater part in the life of the whole family than any uncle or aunt. She had been born Violet Freeman, and spent her early life in the embassy in Paris where her father worked; we have mentioned how she and her brother hid under the table when Mrs Gladstone came to a children's tea party there. Her family became friendly with that of Thomas

Bowles when they moved to a house in Lowndes Square, and she sometimes went with the Bowles family on their yachting trips to France. She married a banker who was much older than herself; he died in 1913 and his bank failed, leaving her a widow with young children, not destitute exactly, but in straitened circumstances. In Diana's words she was 'loved by us all for her cleverness and pessimism'. She was an intellectual and the friend of many writers, beginning with Somerset Maugham who was a childhood friend; she was also an accomplished amateur pianist. However, she was also the prey to frequent depressions. She certainly looked depressed, with her black widow's weeds and her long saturnine face with great dark, heavy-lidded eyes; but if anyone cheered her up it was the Mitfords. They called her Mrs Ham, the Widow, or the Wid. When Unity was a small child she had a familiar, known as Madam, of the type some children think up, to whom she attributed any little crimes she might have committed. Mrs Hammersley asked her one day what Madam looked like; Unity looked up at her solemnly and described her, point by point, coinciding exactly with Mrs Hammersley's own appearance. She kept in touch with most of the family all her long life; her correspondence with them, especially with Nancy, makes particularly good reading. They teased her constantly; she loved it, and played up to it. She told Diana in one letter, dated 14 March 1955, that she had nourished a nest of vipers in her bosom, the Mitfords. 'So loving and benign, *seemingly* . . . I dearly wish you were sitting here for a chat, though I suppose it would have ended up with a back chat and scoffing of the sisters at their – Poor, old and pale Mrs Ham.'

Batsford, with the Gloucestershire land surrounding it, was finally sold in 1919. The postwar boom was getting underway, so this first and largest sale of David's property was made at a time when prices were at least respectable. He might have done better to hang on another year, but the Rothschilds used to have a saying: 'Tops and bottoms are made for fools.' Those who want to wait for exactly the best moment to sell, or to buy, are liable to have to wait for ever; and though prices did rise, they soon fell more. David retained his land in Oxfordshire, where conditions were good for his two favourite pastimes, shooting and fishing. The Windrush is a famous trout river, and the rolling hills and copses around Swinbrook were particularly suitable for the rearing and killing of pheasants. To house his family he bought Asthall Manor, a Jacobean house, rambling and commodious, adjoining one of his farms and next door to the village church. Diana says he never intended to stay there long, always planning to build his own house on the hill above Swinbrook. But by the time his new house was finally built the children had come to love Asthall as their home.

# 22

# Asthall

The family was at Asthall Manor for only six years, but they are the classic years of the Mitford childhood. It was this period above all that was to form the raw material for Nancy's art. The Batsford time preceding it was less dominated by David's presence, because it included the later years of the war when he was away at work in the Army; it also lacked the two youngest children, since Decca was not yet two when Batsford was sold and Debo was not even born. Later, at Swinbrook, the family grew up, left one by one, and started administering the shocks that were to change David and Sydney from a self-confident couple belonging to an earlier and more stable age into vulnerable inhabitants of the twentieth century. At Asthall the characters in the story were complete and functioning. David with his jokes, rages and idiosyncrasies, and Sydney with her health theories, her stately vagueness and her censoriousness, were in unquestioned control. The children dreamed intermittently of escape, but at this stage the outside world was indeed a dream. Asthall reality was rock-solid; it was not till later that it was to become legend. There was Nancy with her sharp turn of phrase, her literary tastes, her interest in modern art and fashion, her bright undergraduate friends; there too was Pam with her country skills; there in school holidays was Tom with his music and his omnivorous reading. There was Diana, another avid reader, her beauty growing slowly apparent within the chrysalis of adolescence; Unity with her bounce, her juvenile poetry and her talent for drawing; Decca with her verbal felicity and wicked charm; and Debo, lover of hens and horses. It was perhaps rather odd that Nancy, particularly, did not leave home until the year after Asthall was sold, for she was already twenty-three when this happened.

There are facets of their life which Nancy does not evoke at all.

Bryan Guinness, in an unpublished review of Decca's *Hons and Rebels*, sees the Redesdales as benevolent parents with pastoral tastes who brought up their children according to the precepts of Jean-Jacques Rousseau, to be familiar with farming, the practical care of animals and the slow, kindly rhythms of the countryside. This view does indeed express a facet of their existence; if it is a partial one, it is no more partial than Nancy's. Suppose Nancy, instead of being herself, had been say Richard Jefferies. The very idea would have caused her to emit a peacock shriek, but just suppose. She might then have written a novel entirely unlike *The Pursuit of Love*, though based just as recognizably on the family as it actually was, simply highlighting and suppressing differently.

Bryan, himself, always had these tastes, and saw what he wanted to see; he was courting Diana, and screened out from his mind, as suitors will, anything that did not accord with his inclinations. But he saw nothing that was not actually there. It is a fact that the children, as part of their education, were encouraged to farm. Each was given a smallholding; they sold the produce, often direct to the kitchen but also sometimes to the butcher. 'I kept chickens, pigs and even calves in a supreme effort to make money,' says Diana, and so did the other girls, though it was not possible for Tom, away at school most of the time. Nancy gave it up at a certain point, but was to find the experience useful much later, during the war, when she kept hens in the garden of her house at 12 Blomfield Road. She even had a hen for a time in Paris, which rather surprised visitors who saw it wandering round her drawing room. Sydney herself was a more serious smallholder. She no longer kept bees as at Batsford, but ran a chicken farm whose net profits, according to Decca, about paid the wages of the governess. On one point the pastoral approach would have been correct, whereas Nancy introduced a distortion which by passing into the language has twisted the picture of the Mitford childhood. The family cult word 'hon' had nothing to do with 'honourable' but was a version of 'hen'.

The children paid David a small rent for their plots. One year Pam pointed out to her father that she ought to be invited to the dinner for the tenant farmers. David at first tried to refuse, but after all she was renting land from him and was therefore a tenant too. At the dinner the farmer sitting next to her asked her what her rent was and it turned out that, area for area, she was paying about twice as much as he was. 'You ought to ask for a reduction,' he said. To David's irritation, she did so; but here, too, her point was taken, and after some argument she got her rent reduced. Pam also remembers Nancy's supreme and irritating competence, learnt perhaps in the Girl Guides, at managing the annual bonfire for the autumn leaves and other rubbish. Her plot and those of Pam and Diana were side by side, and while her younger sisters were desperately rearranging their dead heaps, still smoking sparsely from earlier attempts, or watching the pale deceptive flames of the newspaper and vainly hoping the sticks would take fire, Nancy would crouch, looking like a triumphant witch, before a healthy blaze, triumphantly singing: 'Bürning, bürning, merrily bürning!' The 'u' in 'burning' was pronounced in the French way, or like German 'ü'; it was the voice of the Czechish lady doctor.

The children also kept a great variety of pets. They loved them dearly and were miserable when they died. But even Diana, one of the softest-hearted of the sisters, records that the farm animals she reared were different. 'I did not mind when these creatures were sold to the butcher. It was what they were *for*.' Sometimes a farm animal would of course become promoted to be a pet, as was the case with Decca's sheep Miranda, and a goat of Unity's. Again as in *The Pursuit of Love*, David would get in a rage when one of these pets misbehaved itself in the house, and ban it; afterwards succumbing to the technique which he himself called Thin Ending (that is, inserting the thin end of the wedge), when its owner would plead to be able to bring it in just this once.

Another major omission by Nancy is the importance of music to the Mitfords; she even describes the Radletts, their fictional equivalents, as 'utterly unmusical'. In truth the Mitfords, taken as a whole, were more musical than otherwise, though to a very varied degree. They would regularly gather round the piano to sing to Sydney's accompaniment. Like her mother, Sydney loved songs, especially those of her generation and a little earlier. One was a stirring number called 'Grace Darling':

> 'Twas on the Longstone Lighthouse
> There dwelt an English maid,
> Pure as the air around her,
> Of danger ne'er afraid.

Grace rowed out in a storm and rescued a shipwrecked crew. Spirituals and 'nigger minstrel' songs also featured, as well as hymns: not so much the Anglican hymns they sang every Sunday in church, as the Congregationalist hymns, often much more stirring, that Blor taught them. These included 'Shall we gather at the river', which is of course very widely known, but also and above all one about the Parable of the Lost Sheep starting 'There were ninety and nine that safely lay in the shelter of the fold', which Jonathan knows because Diana taught it to him in childhood, though even his nonconformist friends seem to have forgotten it and he failed to find it in a Methodist hymn book. It deserves resuscitation. Had the musical *The Mitford Girls* tried to be historically authentic, this hymn would certainly have featured in it, as would for example, 'Lady, dressed in jade,/Hold me tight at the masquerade . . .', as well as a good many of Moore's Irish Melodies, and 'The Death of Nelson'. It used to be said of Sydney that she had a song for every occasion.

We do not make any claim that the Mitfords' standard of singing was exceptional. Indeed one guest, Tom's friend Nigel Birch, was overheard murmuring to himself: 'No very outstanding voices.' But at least all sang in tune, and Sydney's playing was reliable. All the children were taught the piano, as was, to be sure, usual in families of their type. At Batsford Sydney excused them from practising, indeed forbade it, when Mrs Hammersley came to stay. 'She is musical,' Sydney explained.

Nancy admitted in later life that her taste extended to the *Hundred Best Tunes*; but she must have had some ear, for she took up the ukulele in early adulthood. Of the girls, it was Diana who progressed furthest with the piano, becoming good enough to stand in for a time as church organist. In this capacity she had surreptitious fun with the voluntaries, finding that 'anything, even "Swanee" and "Ramona", was suitable provided it was played slowly enough to sound holy'. In the thirties, both she and Unity were to play the accordion; they took one or two lessons in Munich.

The family did, however, contain one real musician, and that was Tom. For a time he seriously considered becoming a professional pianist, and he grew up to be recognized as one of the outstanding amateurs of his time. As a young man he was sought after by Lord Berners and other musical friends as a partner for duets. His talent showed itself early, as musical talent often does; and its significance for the rest of the family was that it gave them the opportunity to hear serious music. It was Diana, the sister who was closest to him in age and temperament, who took this opportunity; Nancy was uninterested, Pam busy out of doors, and the others, at this stage, rather too young. The piano was in the library which formed the ground floor of an extension, with bedrooms above, all converted from what had been a barn and therefore detached from the house, though a corridor was built to it. Tom could practise without disturbing David, who, like Uncle Matthew, preferred to listen on his gramophone to Galli Curci or some other favourite singer. The sisters also used the library a great deal, partly because they liked reading and partly because their parents did not disturb them there. When Tom came home for the holidays with a school friend, one of the first things he would do would be to offer to play for him; Diana would come along and listen too. This began when Tom was at Lockers Park: when James Lees-Milne, aged ten or eleven, came to stay it was all that Tom offered him in the way of entertainment.

The whole family used to go to Stratford-on-Avon. Three or four times a year, says Diana, they went there to watch the Shakespeare plays 'in the nice, hideous old theatre before the fire'. Their behaviour was not always impeccable; Diana admits that she and Nancy 'so often began to shake with silent laughter that Muv forbade us to sit together'. This was partly because of what seemed to them to be the extreme old age of the actors. 'It was not quite easy to see good old Baliol Holloway as the ne'er lust-wearied Antony, or his elderly leading lady as a *lass* unparalleled.' But they came to know Shakespeare.

The Asthall library, thanks to Bertie and to little Tom's guidance of his father at the Batsford sale, contained a good collection. All the children were permitted to read any book, provided they put it back where it belonged; and all, or almost all, took advantage of this. The books Bertie wrote himself tended to be disregarded. Pam was the exception here: she read all Bertie's works, being particularly fascinated by *Tales of Old Japan*, and of all the seven children she was the one who first, as it were, rediscovered their paternal grandfather and admired him as a character. But it was Nancy and Tom who became generally well read, followed by Diana and in some areas Unity.

All this entitles us to say that the Mitford household was a cultured one. Its peculiarity, and one of the clues to what was to happen to its members, was that it had an unintellectual head. Had David been like his father, whose outlook he inherited, he would have discussed with his children, in the light of that outlook, the ideas they found in the novels, histories, travel books and philosophical works on his shelves. This would have provided them with his view of the world in verbally explicit form. As it was, Asthall values were imposed by unexplained edict or, more continuously, by example. In so far as either parent discussed political, religious or other general principles with the children this was done by Sydney, who precisely at this period was possibly less reflective and certainly less articulate than at any time before or since, being a busy wife and mother concerned with detailed and day-to-day responsibilities, including the teaching of the younger ones.

The general view of the Mitford girls' education has been conditioned above all by Nancy's novels. The Radlett daughters, in *The Pursuit of Love*, are said to have done practically no lessons, but to have learnt a flashy cleverness while reading in the library, which contained, as did that of the Mitfords, the collection formed by a cultivated grandfather. This left them 'incapable of solid hard work' and meant that they 'completely lacked any form of mental discipline'. It would be easier to know just what Nancy intended by this passage if she was more consistent. Nancy is putting it in the mouth of her narrator, Fanny, who later marries a don and is supposed to be in these matters rather an old stick. On one interpretation, then, the sentiment could easily represent simply Fanny's opinion, not Nancy's own. But this may not be right. Some of Fanny's remarks are definitely to be taken as Nancy speaking; perhaps this is one of them. Nancy tells us in her essay on Blor that she longed to go to school; here she is getting in a dig at her parents, and particularly at Sydney who masterminded the girls' education. During most of her life Nancy was cool towards her mother, and she certainly gave her no more credit for her ideas in the field of education than for her health theories. But the impression that the Mitford girls were uneducated is wrong. Nancy herself, later in life, was to prove just how wrong by undertaking accurate research for her histories. Of the others, Decca was to be indefatigable as a journalistic investigator and was also to undergo the course in Marxist studies prescribed to members of the American Communist Party; Diana edited a literary monthly for six years; and Debo, latterly, has proved herself a meticulous chronicler of the history of Chatsworth. In other words, no fewer than four out of the six sisters have proved themselves by no means 'incapable of solid hard work' of a literary nature. Rather more, surely, than the national average.

The false impression persists, though; John Atkins (*Six Novelists Look at Society*) says that Nancy's childhood was 'as intellectually restricted as that of a slum child', and other commentators have often said the same sort of thing. Decca reinforced the legend. In *Hons and Rebels* she makes out that the family's governesses were at best nitwits and natural victims, at worst delinquents. This impression emerges, it is true, from stories that only the solemn could believe are meant to be taken as the literal truth. The trouble is that a number of rather solemn people have found occasion to write about the Mitfords. One of these stories in particular has been surprisingly influential despite being not merely unbelievable but actually impossible. Unity is supposed to have left her grass snake wrapped round the lavatory chain so as to frighten her governess, causing the wretched woman to faint with fright. This is retailed as a fact by David Pryce-Jones in *Unity Mitford — a Quest*, and was censoriously referred to in a review of the book by Dame Rebecca West as an example of Unity's cruelty. It is of course fictional. No live snake would stay wrapped around a lavatory chain for five seconds. This and other stories of Decca's, whether or not they have been literally believed, added weight to Nancy's insinuation that their education was a farce. The governesses did, it is true, come and go rather; Diana thinks there were altogether about fifteen, counting French teachers who would come for a few weeks in the holidays. Diana also makes it clear that 'none of them was exactly a Hobbes'.

The point is, though, that they worked within a framework, the Parents' National Education Union (PNEU) system. This organization, founded by Charlotte Mason, caters for parents who educate their children at home. At the end of each summer and Michaelmas term it sent examination papers which the children would sit, exactly as at school; their efforts would then be sent to London for marking. This was done systematically, and we have the testimony of Amy Hussey, in a letter to Sir Oswald Mosley, 19 November, 1976, that the 'actual lesson work was usually very well done'. Miss Hussey was probably the best of the governesses apart from Miss Mirams; she was certainly the one of whom the girls were fondest. She came for two periods of about two years each, first to Asthall from 1922 to 1924 and then to Swinbrook from 1931 to 1933. Known as Steegson, she had a cousin called Alan. The children invented a romance and used to sing these words to the tune of 'Lady Dressed in Jade': 'Steegson, dressed in jade,/Hold Alan at the masquerade.' This, with rather a frown, Sydney would just tolerate, but the second verse was banned: 'Steegson, dressed in nothing at all,/Hold Alan at the Chelsea Arts Ball.'

The comings and goings of the governesses mattered less than one might think because one person was permanently in charge of the home education – Sydney. Except for Nancy and Pam, Sydney educated all the children herself up to the age of eight; 'I suppose this is the most interesting and useful thing I did in my life,' she says in her unpublished memoir of Unity. This means that Sydney shares with Miss Mirams the credit for the good educational standard with which Tom entered his preparatory school. Decca, too, says in *Hons and Rebels* that she remembers lessons with her mother better than later ones with governesses. She remembers the patriotic history book *Our Island Story*, now presumably obsolete because the British point of view is out of fashion with teachers. Sydney and Decca both describe the teaching method of 'narration', in which the teacher reads the child a passage from a book and the child repeats what he has remembered. Unity once claimed to have remembered nothing.

'What,' said Sydney, 'not one word?'

'Very well,' said Unity: '*the*.' This is Sydney's account; Decca tells the story with herself as the forgetful child. At any rate Decca appears to think that 'narration' was an invention of Sydney's; it was in fact a regular part of the PNEU method.

Many years afterwards, Sydney was to write to Nancy on 17 April 1960 commenting on the reviews of *Hons and Rebels*: 'I get lots of blame for not sending you all to school, but am quite unrepentant.' We think she was right. But in her memoir on Unity, she wonders rather sadly if her early teaching gave her children some bent towards politics: 'Certainly at the time such a thing never entered my head,' she adds. Is there, then, nothing at Asthall that might have foreshadowed the family's behaviour in the thirties? Perhaps there is, but the subject must be approached with caution if it is not to cause considerable misunderstanding. David and Sydney were firm Conservatives; it went with their position, and even more with being children of their respective fathers. However Blor, like many nonconformists, was an equally firm Liberal, as was her family. What must be underlined here is that she never obtruded her views or argued; still less did she ever try to influence the children. The idea would not have occurred to her, any more than the possibility occurred to David or Sydney. She was not a political person, and they knew it. But her personal qualities were such as to make her views on all matters significant, especially the fact that, unlike so many puritans, she had not a trace of hypocrisy but kept to the high moral principles in which she believed. She was a person of dignity and charm, shrewdness and the best sort of simplicity. In one respect her life at Asthall was not happy; there was no Congregationalist church in the vicinity, so she asked if she could take Holy Communion in the Anglican church. Mr Ward, the vicar, had to refuse; he would have been able to allow it had she consented to be confirmed into the Church of England, but this was out of the question for her. Today, no doubt, she would have had no problem; the dissolution of religious belief has also entailed the dissolution of theological barriers between denominations. But in those days these differences were taken seriously.

The children came to know most of Blor's family. She used to take them every year to seaside lodgings at Bexhill, belonging to a friend of hers who was also a Congregationalist; from there the party would visit her twin sister, whom they all liked but whose uncanny likeness to the beloved Blor used to give Diana nightmares. The sister was married to an ironmonger and had bright daughters, both of whom, Diana says, later became headmistresses. The Mitfords also knew Blor's father, the smith, who grew black pansies and, according to Nancy, 'looked like God the father with a long white beard'. There were other brothers and sisters who 'were all clever and had successful careers'. (Nancy again.) These people need not have uttered one politically tendentious word in front of the Mitford children; they were kind, intelligent and openminded, which was enough to ensure that Congregationalism and Liberalism were words with positive connotations. The darker side of puritanism was not in evidence. On the contrary; far from Blor's family being in any way canting or hypocritical, it was the Mitfords' own parents whose religious sincerity seemed open to doubt, and whose political views, increasingly, seemed blinkered, backward-looking and essentially selfish. Nancy is probably right when she doubts that her parents ever had a conventionally religious thought, and adds that they went to church to support the state. They went regularly every Sunday while in the country where they had an example to set, but not in London, said Diana in an interview. Under the short-lived influence of an Anglo-Catholic governess, Diana went through a period of religious devotion when she was eleven. She became worried about her parents' souls. 'True, they went to church on Sundays; but did they *believe*? Uncle George said that Muv went to church as a patriotic duty; if this were true it would be fatal.' It was true; George Bowles knew what he was talking about. In religion, as in other matters, his sister was influenced by their father, Thomas, and had inherited a certain scepticism. 'No religion is *wholly* bad,' Thomas used to say in a tone implying that most religions were nevertheless apt to be largely bad. As to David, he was unconcerned with the content, as contrasted with the form, of religion because he was not interested in general principles. The church was there, part of the familiar set-up, and it was one's duty to attend it. This attitude is seen through in two minutes by an intelligent adolescent as he tests the solidity of his conceptual and moral environment.

The religious results of this were, to be sure, unremarkable; some of the Mitfords retained their Christian faith and some did not. One who did was Nancy; though she was quite the reverse of devout, she was, deep down, a believer to the end of her life. None became nonconformist; the inner fervour of the Free Churches was declining as rapidly as was that of the Church of England, and Congregationalism remained simply a characteristic of sweet old Blor. What was important was that the Redesdales' Conservatism and churchgoing came to seem to their children to be merely conventional; and this at a time when the social and economic conditions upheld by Conservatives were beginning to seem more and more questionable — and to be more and more questioned. Diana testifies that by 1929 she was very anti-Tory. She was then married, but the clear assumption is that her views were already formed beforehand. The same was true of Nancy, who was to become a Labour supporter in the thirties and consorted a good deal with intelligent undergraduates.

The question above all which divided parents from children at that time was the question of Germany. There is a tendency nowadays to think that soldiers returning from the First World War were all determined that there should be peace and reconciliation, all full of memories of playing football against the Germans on Christmas Day, and of fury against their own sanguinary generals. This is based on the fact that an articulate minority did indeed think along these lines; many of them were writers, like Robert Graves or Siegfried Sassoon. The majority thought differently. In particular David, who would scarcely even read a book, let alone write one, was violent against the Germans. Certainly, he would have said, nothing of the sort must be allowed to happen again; but the way to stop it is not to pamper the filthy Hun, but to crush him. David experienced the war and had the right, he supposed, to pronounce on these matters. The Hun was barbarous, untrustworthy, afraid of cold steel, and either at your throat or at your feet. David was supported in this matter by the memory of his revered father, who also hated Germany at the end of his life; although Bertie's attitude was in fact rather complicated, this would not have appeared in conversation. David, like most of those who are utterly honest, believed everything he was told; he was always to be a sucker for propaganda and fell for that of Lord Northcliffe just as he was later, temporarily, to fall for that of Goebbels.

Only dimly noticed by him, there was in the twenties a reaction among opinion formers against hatred of the former enemy. Peace-time, and the defeat of Germany, meant that the Germans were no longer the actual foe, but only one of several possible ones and not necessarily the most dangerous. And why, indeed, should there be enemies at all? There was a growing dislike of war, and of the excessive patriotism that began to be seen as leading to war. Some of the atrocity stories were disproved; a book by Lord Ponsonby, published in 1927, did much in this direction. The play *Young England*, a jingoistic work expressing the views that prevailed before and during the First World War, was put on in London in the early thirties. It became a wild success, but as a camp joke; people went many times, and learned to shout the dated and pompous lines in time with the actors. The older Mitford children took the new attitude, and so did their friends. At Asthall, as to a considerable extent in the world outside, this was a difference between the generations.

The children knew better than to provoke their father on this or any political subject, for David could indeed be a frightening figure. It is as a corrective that we have emphasized his gentle side; but it would be wrong to forget for a moment that it coexisted with a truly explosive temper. Jonathan only remembers the remains of this, when David was already old, but even then there could be a sort of malevolent implacability about him that one dreaded to arouse, lurking under his usual manner which was genial, if rather gruff. One example of his fury became celebrated in the family. It occurred in 1920, when he got wind of the fact that Michael Bowles, son of Sydney's brother George, had conceived a romantic affection for Diana. Michael was sixteen at the time and Diana was ten, and the whole innocent flirtation rather reminds one of her later friend Lord Berners's mysterious little verse:

> Sacred to the memory
> Of dear little Emily,
> At once the pride,
> And the shame of her family.
> Led astray by a bishop,
> When barely eleven,
> She's perfectly certain
> Of going to heaven.

Not that poor Michael could even remotely be accused of having led Diana astray. He was a romantic, sensitive schoolboy, unhappy at Marlborough, and had been conducting a clandestine correspondence with Diana through Mabel, the Redesdales' parlourmaid. When David found out he set off for Marlborough, some say armed with a horsewhip. Michael had wind of his coming and asked a friend if he could hide in his study because his uncle was on the way with the intention of killing him. He hid successfully, and David left without finding him. This may have been a pity; David's record was in fact almost wholly non-violent, and certainly the idea of attacking his nephew at his school, risking scandal, humiliation and subsequent ridicule, seems far-fetched. At worst there might have been a nasty scene. Much later in life Michael told Diana that the memory of the incident had preyed on him for years; but certainly George Bowles never took the matter seriously or reproached David, for whom his affection remained as firm as ever.

Nancy was to tell a television interviewer that her father's trouble at this time was not having enough to do. Certainly the responsibilities of an agricultural landlord, as such, were unable to expand enough to fill the time available, despite Professor North-cote Parkinson's claim that all work does this. But he was on the County Council, and took his duties seriously; he also kept himself busy with field sports, notably shooting in the winter and fishing in the summer.

Shooting was a passion with David. He was a crack shot, and celebrated as such; in the season he would often be asked to shoots around the country. At home he reared pheasants in large num-bers; Diana says he chose the site for Swinbrook House to be near his pheasants. But like many people who shoot, he was a per-fectionist, and unpunctuality or incompetence in others put him in a black rage. On shooting mornings the children kept well out of the way.

'Where's that hog Forester?' he shouted once.

'Here I am,' Major Forester replied; he was only doing up his bootlace. He was offended, and never came again.

Diana recalls: 'Once when I was standing with him waiting for driven partridges Farve's loader . . . was slow. Farve took both guns and laid them reverently on the stubble; then he picked up the loader and shook him. It was done in deathly silence. Farve never spoke out shooting for fear of turning the birds.' This incident shocked the children, who did not speak to their father for two days. 'When he was obviously not minding we relented.'

On this occasion the loader was a substitute; normally the important task was performed by James Turner, the chauffeur, who was never remiss. He loved shooting as much as his employer, enjoyed driving him to grand shoots, and took pride in his performance. He also cared for David's cars as if they were children. David was really fond of Turner, and the affection was returned. The two men understood and appreciated each other like comrades in arms. Eventually Turner left and went to work for Diana when she married Bryan Guinness; the move was part of one of David's economy drives. David, Sydney was to think, never quite got over losing Turner; and as to Turner, for several years after his new employer had become Lord Moyne, when Turner referred to 'His Lordship' he was still as likely to mean David as Bryan.

If shooting often put David into an unpleasant mood, fishing, by Diana's account, brought out his happiest side.

Early in June the cry of 'The Mayfly's up' set Farve in excitement . . . For weeks he had been oiling his lines and looking for his flies; he had also fished, with a wet fly. I often went with him. According to Farve, if one trod on a twig, or sneezed, even a hundred yards from the bank, every trout heard it and swam away for miles, even perhaps to a stretch of water belonging to somebody else. I hardly breathed during our fishing expeditions; I loved being with him, and considered it an honour being allowed to go.

During mayfly time there would be a pleasant house party with carefully chosen men guests; the atmosphere was informal, relaxed and congenial. Again, just as in *Love in a Cold Climate*, there was at Asthall an annual visit by a 'chub fuddler', who would strew the river with some compound to bring to the surface the coarse fish that competed with the trout. Pam was to read out Nancy's description on television with the assurance that it was exactly true to life: 'He came, he walked along the river bank, and sowed upon its waters some magic seed, which soon bore magic fruit, for up to the surface, flapping, swooning, fainting, choking, thoroughly and undoubtedly fuddled, came hundreds upon hundreds of chub', to be collected by the villagers for the table, or for rendering into manure.

On Sundays in the winter the family usually went coursing. Uncle Tommy would come to lunch bringing his whippet, which with a lurcher of David's would chase the hares. Diana again:

We were cursed by Farve if we did not keep in line; one struggled and hopped through turnips or kale or over the prickly stubble. When a hare got up there were cries of 'Loo after it!'; the lurcher and whippet were slipped and they streaked after the hare, which doubled and twisted and usually got away. Sometimes it was caught; the first one went into Farve's hare pocket, and subsequent ones were given to us to carry. Uncle Tommy and Farve used to say: 'Wasn't that a beautiful sight?' and stand for a while leaning on their thumbsticks while the dogs got their breath . . .

Hunting was the blood sport that David practised least. There were of course horses, and the children hunted regularly with the Heythrop, but neither David nor Sydney went out. This disappointed the groom, Charles Hooper, known as Choops, of whom Josh in *The Portrait of Love* is a portrait. Hooper had come with the family from Batsford and the children were fond of him. He once said to them: 'If only I could get her ladyship up on a horse, perhaps his lordship would play the man.' The idea of David's manhood being in question seemed very funny to the children; to be a man, for them, was to be like David. They themselves all, in various degrees, enjoyed hunting, and among the keenest was Nancy. She remembers how it felt in the following passage from *The Pursuit of Love*:

For three hours that day I forgot everything except my body and my pony's body; the rushing, the scrambling, the splashing, struggling up the hills, sliding down them again, the rugging, the bucketing, the earth and the sky. I forgot everything, I could hardly have told you my name. That must be a great hold that hunting has over people, especially stupid people; it enforces an absolute concentration, both mental and physical.

Jonathan remembers his surprise, in the late forties, at seeing Nancy in her Dior skirt catch and hold a pony with complete assurance. 'I was brought up in the country, you see,' this elegant and urban figure reminded him.

# 23

# Growing Up

David sold Asthall in the autumn of 1926. Swinbrook was not yet
ready, but he bought a large London house, 26 Rutland Gate, with
the mews garage and flat behind it. He had six daughters; four of
them still had to 'come out' and all six might well need a white
wedding, so it seemed sensible and perhaps even, in the end,
economical to acquire a house large enough for a party. But the
family did not move in there at once. David himself stayed at
Swinbrook to see to the building of the new house, and the rest
of the family, including Blor and the governess, went to Paris.
Sydney's friends, the Helleus, had found them a modest hotel
where they could stay, it was thought, more economically than if
they had been living in their own house in London. The rate of
exchange made France cheap for English people at most times
between the wars, as it had in Bertie's childhood. The girls quickly
made themselves at home in the hotel. They had brought with
them a family of desert rats, the only pets they were allowed that
were not subject to quarantine restrictions. It is odd that this was
the case, for desert rats, being mammals; are of course subject
to rabies, and today their reimportation into Britain would be
prohibited.

Nancy and Pam were by this time grown up, and had a number
of friends of their age in Paris. Nancy, in particular, knew the
granddaughter of the British ambassador, so they used to go to the
embassy, sometimes taking Diana. Diana herself, aged sixteen,
attended a small day school called the Cours Fénelon in the Rue
de la Pompe.

For the Christmas holidays of 1926–27 the family returned to
the new house at Rutland Gate, which Nancy and Diana both
found charming. Both of them were at that time just beginning to

notice how houses looked; in Diana's case, particularly, interior decoration was to become one of her preoccupations and skills. In Paris, Diana had admired the house of the British military attaché, General Clive, a typical eighteenth-century dwelling 'between courtyard and garden', and Helleu's white flat. As to Rutland Gate, Sydney had taken care to appropriate for it all the best furniture from Asthall. The only ugly room in the Rutland Gate-house, they all thought, was David's business room on the ground floor for which he had chosen the curtain material. Diana describes that as 'a frightful sort of sham tapestry covered in dingy leaves and berries'. But this, which might have served as a warning, did not persuade Sydney to go over and see what David was doing at Swinbrook. Uncle Tommy was reassuring; he reported that David was providing 'the best of everything for everybody'. But what could the bluff sailor be expected to know about such matters?

It really is very odd, as she herself later was the first to agree, that Sydney never took a hand in the planning or decoration of Swinbrook. She knew perfectly well that David had no pretensions to taste. He made almost a virtue of this. Every year he would buy her a Christmas present in the Army and Navy Stores and every year he would tell the assistant: 'After Christmas a lady will come in and change this.' And every year, sure enough, Sydney did come in and change it. How could she trust David, unaided, to build and decorate a house? Several times he tried to show her the plans and discuss his ideas; she always waved them away. So he stayed by himself at Swinbrook, watching his dream take shape and getting letters from Nancy addressed to Builder Redesdale, South Lawn, Swinbrook – South Lawn being the name, disliked by David, of the small farmhouse which the new house was to replace. There were to be a garage and stables, greenhouses, and even a squash court, which must have been for Tom as no one else in the family played. Each child was to have a bedroom, and the family would move in during the autumn. In the meantime David could not wait to see their happy faces when they saw the paradise he was providing.

It happens that the arrival at Swinbrook coincided with, or only briefly preceded, great changes in the lives of all the children down to and including Unity. It was very shortly after it that

Nancy, already twenty-four, left definitively to share a flat in London. Tom left Eton at this time, and went to Vienna to study German and music. A year after the move Diana married Bryan Guinness and set up house with him in Wiltshire and London; this provided an alternative centre not controlled by 'grown-ups', something much more important then than now because parents were much more restrictive. Finally, Unity went to boarding school at the age of fourteen. It therefore, in the end, turned out to be only the two youngest, Decca and Debo, who lived continuously at Swinbrook for any length of time. It is convenient to take all the five older children in turn, and trace their stories up to this point, starting with Nancy.

It is important not to confuse Nancy at Asthall with Decca at Swinbrook. Her discontent at home was not fundamental, nor was there any rancour in it; it was fitful and superficial, expressing itself in small rebellions and minor pranks. In most ways life there suited her quite well, though the side of her to which it appealed was not uppermost in later life. She enjoyed hunting, and quite liked being a Girl Guide.

Also, Nancy was by no means as confined to home as some commentators seem to think. Even her dream of boarding school was realized, for a short time. At the age of sixteen she went to a 'finishing school' at Hatherop Castle. From there, in April 1922, she went on an extended continental trip with some of the other girls, to Paris and then to Italy. She had been to Paris before; David, though one of his stock characteristics was his dislike of 'abroad', did take the children now and then. He had a healthy mistrust of the Paris traffic, already conducted on the lines of an inadequately stewarded *grand prix*. Once he was standing at the Etoile with his family, intending to see the Arc de Triomphe; after waiting in vain for a break in the swirling and screeching traffic he hailed a taxi, and told the astonished driver to take the party over to the arch. (The subway did not then exist.) On her trip with the Hatherop girls, too, Nancy found the traffic a cause for concern. 'I expect one of us must be run over. I escaped certain death by a very little several times yesterday,' she wrote to her mother. Harold Acton, in his 'memoir' on Nancy, quotes copiously from the letters she wrote home; these are fresh, bubbling and blissfully happy. Everything seems to appeal to her except the actual travelling, for between Paris and Florence she was 'only kept alive by a huge dose of brandy'. 'Why doesn't one always live in hotels?' she writes from Paris. 'There are dozens of sweet little boys here (hall boys) perfect pets, I shall give them my chocs.' In Venice, too, she loves the hotel life, and explains: 'There is an atmosphere of excitement, of latent danger in an hotel . . . Locking my door at night is a never-failing joy, as is going in the lift (I can work it myself now). Then the feeling that when you are out all your things may . . . be stolen causes pleasant thrills to frequent the marrow.' The Florence hotel, it is true, is less pleasing: there are fleas. But she enthuses over the art galleries and the Duomo and the pageant on Easter Sunday. She regrets having been round none of the art galleries in London except the Tate: 'This must be remedied! I never knew there were really lovely pictures in London . . . I don't think it is too late to develop a taste for pictures at 17, do you?' She is already thinking a lot about clothes and personal ornaments; of all the sisters, she was always to be the one that cared most for fashion. She bargains fiercely for a coral necklace in Florence. In Venice she buys a Spanish hair comb: 'I really look quite old in it, a femme du monde you know . . .'

It was at Hatherop that Nancy became a Girl Guide. 'Guiding' was part of the Hatherop system; Nancy took to it rather readily and, as her letters show, enjoyed camping with the others. After she left Hatherop, she suggested to Sydney that she might start a company for the village, with Pam and Diana as patrol leaders. Sydney thought this rather a good idea, so the scheme was put into effect. Diana protested bitterly, but Pam acquiesced, so her protests were overridden; though Sydney did promise that if after a year she still hated it she could give it up. Diana goes on:

It turned out to be all I had feared, and more. Ten of the village girls were told they had got to join, and Pam and I picked sides for our patrols. (No damned merit went into the choice of the patrol leaders.) We were all fitted out in stiff blue drill dresses, black stockings and shoes and hard round felt hats. Nancy, as captain, had a different and rather becoming hat turned up at one side with a cockade. We stumped about at the end of the garden, trying to light damp things with three matches and run a hundred yards in twenty seconds.

Or they held competitions to see who could collect the most useful things, with Sydney as the judge, and generally did the things Girl Guides do, concentrating particularly on first aid techniques with bandages and tourniquets. But why, Diana was to reflect in later years, were they not taught something useful, like cooking? She discussed this with her friend Lady Mersey, who replied: 'They did teach us. Boiled cod.'

For Diana the year limped by, seemingly interminable, but it did finally come to an end. As soon as it was up, she told Sydney she still hated being a Girl Guide and supposed she could there-fore leave. To her bitter indignation, Sydney refused; of course Diana couldn't leave, just as it was doing the village girls so much good. David took the same view, and poor Diana was forced to soldier on. However, the company died a natural death in a few months because Nancy grew out of it.

Possibly one of the attractions of being a Girl Guide to Nancy was in fact the uniform – 'you get to wear a smart uniform', as the poster used to promise aspiring traffic wardens. She was also a mistress of disguise. Every Christmas the family put on fancy dress for dinner; not only the children, but Sydney and David and all uncles, aunts and cousins who were present. There was a well-filled chest out of which they selected costumes. Always it was Nancy who showed the most imagination. Twice she used this talent to perpetrate a practical joke. The first time was during the General Strike, in early May 1926. The family ran a canteen for the volunteers who were driving lorries. It was a time for 'muck-ing in', when people engaged in various projects to assist in the national emergency. The canteen was run in shifts, but Pam was by far the most efficient at it and it was regarded as her enterprise. Very early one morning she was alone, waiting for the all-night lorry drivers. A filthy, leering tramp walked in, demanding a cup of tea. As Pam started to oblige, the dreadful creature came round the counter and actually touched her. Pam tore herself away, then fell over and twisted her ankle; the tramp turned out to be Nancy in disguise. Nancy's other practical joke was even more im-pressive; it occurred when Asthall was up for sale. Having stuffed her bosom with a pillow and got herself up as a fashionably dressed lady of a certain age, she knocked at the door and asked to see round the house. Mabel the parlourmaid let her in, while

Annie the housemaid showed her the upstairs rooms; neither of them guessed who it was, though they saw Nancy every day. Finally she made her way to the nursery, where she bent over a reluctant Decca with a view to giving her a slobbering kiss. At this moment, however, she herself could no longer hold in her laughter, or the pillow.

It must be remembered that by this time Nancy was grown up, in her twenties. She had 'come out', been presented at court; she was going to dances in London and from time to time asking young friends to stay, Oxford undergraduates as often as not. The Girl Guides episode, Diana thinks, was in Sydney's mind something to occupy her during the time before her first London season. Diana testifies that it was not wholly sufficient for the purpose. 'In spite of the Guides, Nancy and I became great friends. During the winter, except on hunting days, we used to sit together aching with boredom . . . The animals were no longer enough.' Nor, though, for Nancy, was the conventional London life of balls and parties. Harold Acton is right to draw attention to the passage from Nancy's novel *Pigeon Pie* in which it is said of Sophia, the central figure: 'She was not shy and she had high spirits, but she was never a romper and therefore never attained much popularity with the very young.' This is self-analysis: it is equally true of Pam, Tom and Diana. Not, however, of Unity, who was a quintessential romper and introduced romping into the family. Nancy's humour was verbal and, with her disguises, histrionic; but it was not boisterous. Among her dancing partners and the girls of her age she was popular, on the whole, only among those who had a certain intelligence.

One who liked her was the Anglo-American aesthete Brian Howard, then at Oxford. Slim, dark and good-looking with brilliant black eyes, there was a sort of desperation about him; he rode to hounds with great daring, as well as shocking people with his aggressively effeminate manner. But he had genuine talents: for poetry, for painting, for publicity. Two lines of his verse, at least, deserve to survive: 'The greens are colding and give one the vertigo / Or ever the dull spoon digs at them.' He has continued to be remembered; Marie-Jacqueline Lancaster actually devoted a full-length biography to him entitled *Portrait of a Failure*, and in Martin Green's *Children of the Sun* he receives much of the credit, or blame, for the downfall of the British Empire. (This, true or not, would have delighted Howard.) He and Harold Acton had been together at Eton, where they had edited the *Eton Candle*. This was one of the one-issue magazines known as 'ephemerals' produced every Fourth of June, and was undoubtedly the most famous ephemeral ever. The editors secured contributions from Aldous Huxley and Sacheverell Sitwell, both already well-known writers. It was in tune with the literary avant-garde, and very much noticed outside Eton, even securing a reprint.

'Ephemeral': the word is all too apt for Brian Howard, a butterfly of sombre brilliance with the self-directed sting of a scorpion. Howard came to know Nancy and admire her; telling Acton that she was 'a delicious creature, quite pyrotechnical my dear, and sometimes even profound, and would you believe it, she's hidden among the cabbages of the Cotswolds'. Acton wonders how Howard and David coped with each other, if they were allowed to meet. They did meet, and coped with each other perfectly well. Howard came to a fancy dress ball at Asthall in doublet and hose, and Diana, aged fifteen, remembers dancing with him. Howard did not spend all his waking hours provoking people, any more than David spent all his in a rage.

Many other Oxford undergraduates visited Asthall. They tended on the whole, though with many exceptions, to be more or less 'aesthetes'. Mark Ogilvie-Grant was one, but not an extremist like Brian Howard. He was favoured by David as well as by Nancy because he liked shooting, and did it well enough; he was also able and willing to get up in the morning. David tended to pronounce his Christian name in an affectionate bark as 'Muck'. One morning Mark was politely downstairs at eight o'clock despite a slight hangover. David strode in, in high good humour. Greeting his guest breezily, he went to the sideboard and lifted the lid from a silver dish. 'Brains for breakfast, Muck,' he observed, 'pigs' thinkers.' Mark's gastric stability was precarious; this overturned it. He turned a shade paler and hurried quietly from the dining room. The incident made Nancy shriek. Mark always remained one of Nancy's best friends and was a very important correspondent. It was thought at one time that they might become engaged, but their relationship was never in fact of this sort.

At Asthall Nancy was already writing little stories to amuse the others. One of them, we know from Diana, was about a certain Lady Caraway Something-or-other who fell in love with a man called Seed. Unable to stand the idea of being Lady Caraway Seed, she forced her betrothed to work very hard and be given a peerage. Nancy also invented the pathetic little poem which she put in *The Pursuit of Love*:

> A little houseless match,
> It has no roof, no thatch.
> It lies alone, it makes no moan,
> That little, houseless match.

Exactly like Linda in Nancy's book, Debo reached the stage when she could not see a match on a table without her eyes welling with tears.

Pam, known frequently from an early age as Woman, was also 'out' by the time the family left Asthall. Of all the seven, she had the hardest time as a child. It will be recalled that she had had polio when small. Worse than this, though, was her position in the family: the simple fact that she was second, three years younger than Nancy, which exposed her to the worst of Nancy's ill-treatment. As we have seen, Nancy claims to have resented her as soon as she was born. What is more, Nancy was wickedly charming and persuasive; as time passed and the others became conscious she tended to make them side with her against Pam, when it was not one of them whom she felt like persecuting. Though none of Nancy's juniors was unscathed by what she was herself to describe as 'my great unkindness to the others', Pam was the first and most frequent victim.

We should not, though, fall into the error of supposing that Pam's childhood was unhappy. Her parents loved her, and she had the excellent Blor. Of all the children except perhaps Debo, she most enjoyed the country environment and her animals. She was not without her defences and her means of evasion. We have seen that she would go off for solitary walks at Batsford, or play houses with little Diana. As against Nancy, she early learned to keep her head down; and in any case she, too, used to laugh at Nancy's jokes, some of the earliest of which she still remembers. Rather than retaliate or compete, she developed an armour which in later life became a special kind of dignity; the reticence which is a consistent family characteristic became her strongest shield. She did not tease back; if she practised verbal aggression it would be more in the nature of a lecture than a tease. Many people take refuge from fact in fantasy; Pam's escape was the other way, back into fact from a fantasy world in which she was at a disadvantage. 'The trivial round, the common task', in the words of the hymn, really did furnish all she chose to ask, undoubtedly because in this area she was always more effective than Nancy. She became the practical one of the family; the one who ran the canteen in the General Strike, and in later life the best at cooking and farming. Verbal fireworks were not for her; she had been burned by them too much and too early. Her avoidance of them was to make her seem, in this family, something of a freak; but perhaps it would be truer to say that she was the only one who was not a freak. In after years Nancy was to observe in a letter that Pam had been to London for the white sales: 'How can she be my sister, I've never been to a white sale in my life.' She is supposed by the others to have an infallible memory for food. Jonathan once heard Debo introduce her to someone: 'This is my sister Pam. She's just arrived from Switzerland and she'll tell you all there was to eat in the French dining cars.' We have mentioned dressing up for the Asthall Christmas, at which Nancy so invariably shone. Pam was at the opposite pole. Every year as the chest was being ransacked for costumes Pam would wander in, rather late from tending her chickens, and select the same purple dress. Her blonde hair in a plait, she would be the Lady Rowena from *Ivanhoe*.

Sydney's first cousin, Georgie Gordon, remembers an occasion at Asthall when some of Nancy's Oxford friends were present. She forgets their names, but one of them must have been Brian Howard. They were playing a game where each player thinks of a word, his successor following with another which starts with the letter of the alphabet following its final letter. There was, of course, an accent on the recondite and the precious; someone said 'Chrysoprase'. After this it was Pam's turn, and she called out 'Fish!' Brian – it can surely have been no one else – turned to Nancy and said in a stage whisper: 'My dear! Your sister is *macabre*.'

A few months before Diana became engaged to Bryan Guinness,

in 1928, Pam accepted a proposal from a member of another brewing family. He was Oliver Watney, always known as Togo: a tall, dark young man with a stoop, rather deficient in vitality because he was plagued by chronic tuberculosis, not then curable. He lived not far from the Redesdales at Cornbury, built in Charles II's reign by the historian and Chancellor, Lord Clarendon. Togo gave Pam a replica of King Alfred's jewel that, Nancy thought and said, looked like a chicken's mess; even such a lifelong poultry fancier as Pam did not think this quip agreeable, but Nancy saved it up for *The Pursuit of Love*.

Poor Togo had only proposed, it seems, because his father had encouraged him to do so; then his father died of a heart attack and his mother started trying to talk him out of the engagement. Under her influence the idea did begin to seem rather daunting. For one thing there were all those sharp, noisy sisters. He went on an extended cruise for his health. Soon after his return he went to see Pam and she gave him back his engagement ring. Everyone in the Mitford family was indignant with Togo, but fortunately Pam was not in love with him, as she was to be with the dynamic man she married. The wedding presents had to be returned; Tom delivered many of them, driving round London in his little car. It was all an embarrassment, but Pam was in fact thoroughly relieved. She went off with David and Sydney to Swastika for the summer to prospect. As usual, gold was found only in negligible quantities. Afterwards, in 1930, Bryan and Diana offered Pam the job of running the farm at Biddesden which they had just bought. In the circumstances a new start was sensible, and Pam was by no means without farming knowledge. She stayed at Biddesden for four years, longer in the event than Diana. As to the 'chicken's mess', Pam later gave it to Unity because she liked it; and Unity later presented it to Hitler.

Tom, at all stages, presents a problem. A reviewer of *Hons and Rebels* remarks of him that he was 'overshadowed in the books as in life'. He was overshadowed in the books at the time the reviewer was writing, though Diana's book, which had not then been written, helps correct the picture. He was never overshadowed in life. On the contrary, Tom was a pivotal figure in the family until he was killed in 1945, and any view of the Mitford story which leaves this out of account is irredeemably distorted. He was, however, not a natural writer or an outstandingly quotable wit. His letters are clear, when he is young rather precociously so, and written in an easy and educated style; but they are not funny like Nancy's. He saw the point of jokes; after his death Diana often said to Jonathan how much he would have laughed at something and the younger sisters used to enjoy making him giggle, or what they called 'blither'. Later he developed his own brand of rather donnish humour. His mind was rather a literal one, more matter-of-fact than those of most of his sisters, but it was well stocked and well organized. He was, though, a serious man, who avoided publicity; his death, even though he was already thirty-six, came too early for him to have achieved eminence in the fields in which he was likely to reach it. Had Tom survived it is possible that he would have become a well-known barrister or judge; just conceivably he might have stayed in the Army after the war and risen to a high rank there, but he had started, perhaps, too late for that to be feasible. His tastes in literature tended noticeably towards the solid; in his maturity, at least, they ran to philosophy and history rather than to the novel. Kant and Schopenhauer were favourite authors, and in one letter he mentions in passing that he is reading Gibbon for the third time. The poetic, emotional side of him was expressed through music. Those who did not know him sometimes thought him cold and proud; he was not indiscriminately gregarious, any more than Nancy was. But he was quite recognizably a masculine variation on the family theme.

We have seen that he had the rare good fortune to enjoy his preparatory school. He went to Eton in January 1922, and liked it even more, as his letters show clearly. He was above average in all his school work; rather unusually for a member of his family, his School Certificate results show his best subject to have been mathematics. It is rare to find anyone tackling the problematic age of adolescence with such ease and control as Tom. Nothing seems to have given him a moment's worry. He was even able to get up in the morning; Old Etonians of a certain age will see the significance of a letter he wrote to his parents on 27 March 1922, in which he says that he is writing in bitter cold before Early School, a class that took place every morning at seven-thirty. Lesser mortals than Tom found it difficult to be in time for it, let alone to write letters before setting off. He passed the tenderfoot exam and became a Boy Scout: 'It was very easy.' At the thought of the 'Trials' at the end of his first term he was not apprehensive, like many people, but 'exited [*sic*]'. One is almost glad to find this thirteen-year-old paragon making a spelling mistake. He enjoyed the Officers' Training Corps, as it was then known, rather quickly becoming a lance corporal and showing a talent for sharpshooting.

As a musician he blossomed, though for a time he gave the piano a rest and learned the flute instead, playing this instrument in the school orchestra. He also took lessons in harmony. In due course he returned to the piano – he never really stopped practising it – and won the school music prize in December 1926, a full year before he left the school. When he was not playing, Tom liked reading and also arguing. One might have thought that in this family enough arguments would have arisen spontaneously, but evidently he wanted more. Richer than his sisters because of his Eton allowance, he would pay them a shilling an hour to argue; by the standards of a child of those days it was a lot of money. It was logical that a boy who would pay to argue should be destined, when he grew up, to become a barrister and be paid for doing it. However, he sometimes had his doubts, as in a letter to Diana of 13 February 1927: 'Couldn't you get hold of some very musical American or Frenchman who is also very rich . . . and get him to engage me as a musical companion at a fat salary (like David and Saul), so that I needn't go to the ruddy [blanks in the original] and blasted bar?' But Tom was not always indoors in the holidays; in the summer he played in the tennis tournaments arranged by their cousins and other neighbours, while in the winter he hunted, though not as enthusiastically as Nancy, or shot.

At a certain point Tom's housemaster gave him the rare privilege of having a piano in his room; this took up most of the space, making it uncomfortable for his sisters when they crowded in, bickering like starlings, before setting off for tea in the town. Tom loved his sisters and they made him laugh. Once, at the Old Boys' dinner at his house, he sat next to another boy's mother, who was rather large, and she described going down to Asthall as a prospective buyer. To his delight she told him that one of the young ones had invited her to skip.

As at other times, there was at Eton in Tom's day a certain amount of what was then known as 'the love that dares not speak its name', though it dares now, all right. Tom rather fancied a boy called Milton. Once in the car, when the family was passing a signpost to Milton-under-Wychwood, he is supposed to have murmured: '*Lucky* Wychwood!' Tom gossiped on the subject to Diana, though not of course to his parents; so the girls knew all about it. Once Tom brought a friend home to stay. The house was full, so Sydney asked if the friend would mind sharing with Tom. She was a little surprised when one after the other all her daughters filed out of the room, doubled up with silent mirth.

After Tom left Eton he went in January 1928 to Vienna, to learn German and study music. As at Lockers Park and Eton he worked systematically and made progress; here again his letters are full of assurances that he is enjoying himself. He was to speak German better than any member of the family; Putzi Hanfstaengl told Jonathan this, many years later. For exercise there he skated, like his parents; in the summer he would play tennis.

He found out that a friend of his, David Streatfeild, was in Austria, and by getting his mother to write to his friend's father traced him to Burgenland, 'where he lives with this Hungarian in a huge empty castle'. Tom was invited to stay there for a few days in February, and the visit was a great success. The Hungarian, Janos Almasy, became a friend of Tom's for life, and later also of Unity. The castle was Schloss Bernstein. 'It is really in Hungary,' said Tom in a letter, 'but since the war in Austria as they moved the border a few miles.' It was immensely old. 'I have never seen a view to approach it, and being on the very top of a small but steep hill, it looks out in every direction.' By 9 March Tom has decided he would like to go permanently to Bernstein as paying guest. He writes to his parents for permission. Almasy 'is about 40 I believe, or possibly a little less, and extremely clever. I have asked one or two people about him and they all speak well of him.' If David wants to find out for himself, he can ask David Streatfeild's father. Tom agrees that it will be more expensive, but says he will be more comfortable and better looked after; and 'money does trickle away so in a town'. The Redesdales agreed to the arrangement.

\*

Boarding school was far from being the dream of Diana's life, as it had been of Nancy's; on the contrary, it was her nightmare: 'The thought of being sent away from home was enough to give me a temperature.' Needless to say, this gave Nancy an irresistible opening for a tease. She used to tell Diana she had been discussing her with David and Sydney, and it had been agreed that school would do her good. Diana did not really think that her parents would discuss her future with Nancy, but such was her worry at the prospect that she never failed to rise to the bait. It was not until the age of thirty that Diana was to undergo experience of institutionalization, in the form of her years in Holloway Prison. Diana's objection to the idea of boarding school, all her life, has been rooted, visceral. To be in the power of bossy people, to be ordered about not for a tease, as by Captain Nancy, but in earnest: this has always been her dread. She is like a certain sort of upper-class socialist or anarchist in this; except that he, unlike her, would usually associate this kind of unpleasantness above all with Fascism.

Diana was also becoming restless at home. She longed to be grown up and independent; not necessarily rich, but free to enjoy conversation with intelligent people in pleasant surroundings. All her life she has particularly enjoyed chatting, as did Nancy. They loved chatting together, but were not always enough for each other. Tom and his friends were a help when they arrived for the holidays, but Mrs Ham, on her visits, did almost more harm than good; her account of her brilliant friends, the Huxleys or Logan Pearsall Smith, only tantalized Diana the more.

Tom, though only there in the holidays, was even more important to Diana than was Nancy. With only eighteen months between them he was, she says, almost like a twin. They would walk together and discuss everything under the sun. His brilliance on the piano had the unfortunate effect of making her give it up when she was sixteen because the contrast with him was too painful; she had violin lessons for a while, but this was not a success either. Her musical standards had outrun her abilities. Henceforth she would only perform, and then rather rarely, for singing when her sons were small. In the thirties she had a brief flirtation with the accordion before giving it up as altogether too embarrassing; the fact that she ever played this hearty instrument illustrates the difference between the Germans she got to know in her Nazi period and her English friends. Diana also missed Tom when he went back to school because he had enormous influence with their father and could be her advocate. It was with Tom that Diana would often be asked to stay in the holidays at Chartwell with the Churchills; Winston Churchill's wife Clementine, Aunt Natty's daughter, was David's first cousin. Diana Churchill was of an age with Tom, and Randolph with Diana, of whom he was to remain a lifelong friend. She even claims that he was never rude to her, an uncommon distinction by all accounts; but she did at times undergo the inconvenience of his habit of telephoning very late at night. One morning at 3 a.m., a year or two after he had died, Diana's telephone rang, and before she was properly awake the thought flashed through her mind: 'Randolph!' When Tom and Diana first visited the Churchills, Winston was Chancellor of the Exchequer in the Baldwin government. Ironically, in view of later events, it was there that Diana first became interested in politics, through hearing the subject discussed by experts. Once Winston, though he had by then rejoined the Conservative Party, expressed eloquent praise for Lloyd George. This fascinated Diana more than Winston can have intended, because she says that, had she had a vote in 1931, she would have cast it for a Lloyd George Liberal.

The visit to Paris after the sale of Asthall was important in Diana's development. The Cours Fénelon, to which she was sent, was a good school; she says she learned more there in six months than she had at Asthall in six years. She was one of a class of a dozen girls who were taught in the mornings by a Mademoiselle Foucauld, and then lectured and questioned in the afternoons by professors from the Sorbonne. Diana disappointed the other girls during the ball games they played in the yard during break; being English she was expected to be good at them, but she dropped all her catches. Most of her children and some of her grandchildren were also to be like this, to the scorn and despair of their respective playmates. She remembers the unrelieved stuffiness of the classroom. 'On the 15th October Mlle Foucauld spent the whole morning with a hammer and nails, nailing sausages of red stuff round the window frames. Once the sausages were in position the windows could not be opened again until they were ripped off the

following spring.' The French of Mademoiselle Foucauld's generation were like this. Nancy used to tell of an old country lady
who was furious with some English officers, billeted on her
shortly after the Liberation, because they would keep opening the
windows of their bedrooms. She left them little notes saying, '*Je ne
suis pas chargée de chauffer la Picardie*' – it is not up to me to heat
Picardy.

For part of the next Christmas holidays Diana stayed with the
Churchills at Chartwell, and then travelled back with Winston and
Randolph to Paris; they were going on to Rome to visit Mussolini,
whom at that time Winston Churchill admired. Diana noticed
Winston's kind sympathy with Randolph, who was sick on the
boat; 'Nobody pitied us if we were sick on the Channel,' she
comments. This term the family was not in Paris, so she stayed
with two old ladies who had a flat near her school. The Helleus
also lived nearby, as did her violin teacher; she could visit both on
foot.

It was the first time she had had any freedom. She comments:

In London we could not so much as go to Harrods from Rutland Gate
by ourselves – a distance of two or three hundred yards. This
meant . . . that either one had to find a sister willing to go, or coax
Nanny out, or else stay at home . . . We took it as a matter of course;
most of the girls we knew followed the same rule . . . At Asthall it was
different; we were supposed to ride two together, but we could walk
wherever we liked.

She sometimes took advantage of her Paris freedom to go to
the cinema with a young man, telling her landladies that she was
sitting for Helleu or having a violin lesson. She did in fact see a
good deal of Helleu, who drew her often, admired her beauty, and
taught her to appreciate pictures. He and his wife also used to feed
her; she was at an age when one is always hungry, and her old
landladies were sparing with their food. But towards the end of
her time in Paris Helleu fell ill and died. In misery, she wrote to
James Lees-Milne (19 March 1927): 'I shall never see him again,
never hear his voice saying "Sweetheart, *comme tu es belle*", never
ring at his door and hear him come to open it with a happy step.'

Diana made a bad mistake in Paris; that of keeping a diary.
It proved as fatal to her as President Nixon's habit of taping

himself. Sydney found the diary lying about in Rutland Gate when Diana was back there during the Easter holidays, and read it. The cinema visits were mentioned. Sydney was horrified and so was David. What had the girl been up to? Plans were hurriedly changed – there was no question of her going back. In deep disgrace, she was put back into the schoolroom. Swinbrook was not yet ready; she was sent with the three youngest girls, in charge of Blor and the current governess, to a cottage by the sea in Devon. There were not enough books to read, and she suffered 'the terrible, deathly essence of boredom'. It was there that the incident occurred on which the story of Unity's snake may be based. Diana had a snake which escaped in the bathroom. Nobody was particularly frightened.

But at last came the time when the house at Swinbrook was ready, so they moved in. Diana only lived there for just over a year, and for much of that time she was actually in London or staying away. For part of the summer holidays of 1927 she was at Chartwell. As usual there were some very interesting guests: the artist Sickert; Sir Edward Marsh, who was well known between the wars as an art expert and patron; and Churchill's scientist friend, Professor Lindemann. Marsh christened Diana Artemis, to distinguish her from Diana Churchill. Lindemann, in his cold, remote way, seems to have taken rather a fancy to Diana. Always close to Churchill, he was to become his scientific adviser during the war and ultimately to be raised to the peerage as Lord Cherwell. A prominent advocate of obliteration bombing, he was one of those whose hatred of Germans became, in the rage of conflict, virtually genocidal; a mirror image, almost, of Hitler's determination to wipe out the Jews. Lindemann was not yet anti-German, because when Diana admitted she was bored it was actually he who advised her to learn German and read Schopenhauer in the original. Odd advice, one might think, to an adolescent girl, but then Lindemann was an odd man. It was not just a whim; he reverted to the subject at the end of the visit when they said goodbye. 'Come and see me next term at Christ Church,' he said, 'and tell me how you are getting on with your German.' Diana took the idea seriously enough to put it to her father, who forbade it straight away. Tom was at that time learning German in Vienna; but Tom was a boy.

That autumn Diana started to go to dances, and the following year she 'came out' and went to many more. She used often to go with her namesake Diana Churchill, one year older, and since Rutland Gate was let she would sometimes stay at 11 Downing Street (Churchill was at this time Chancellor of the Exchequer). One of her parents or Mrs Churchill would accompany her to each dance, but she nevertheless managed sometimes to slip away for a time to a night club, the charm of such escapades being entirely that they were forbidden. This time, however, she was never found out.

Unity, always known as Bobo, was a sensitive child. When small she was introverted, and as she grew up she became boisterous. Her mother says that as a little girl 'she was shy and easily upset. If anything was said at meals that she did not like or that caused her embarrassment she just slipped quietly off her chair and disappeared under the table until such time as she felt ready to face the world again. It was an understood thing that no one took any notice.'

Unity drew well; among her works was a collage representing Hannibal crossing the Alps which she gave to Hitler. She also showed a rather precocious talent for rhyming. Some of her juvenile poetry is quite passable, but her bent was for the serious rather than, as Nancy's was, for the comic, and serious juvenilia are not very quotable.

Both Sydney, and Decca in interview with David Pryce-Jones, mention her great facility for learning poetry by heart; Sydney says: 'Keats, Shelley, Byron and Blake were her poets, especially Blake.' Unity was also an avid reader of fiction; Decca says she liked the Brontës and Poe. She admired the paintings of Hieronymus Bosch. Decca also mentions Huxley and Waugh, but Waugh must have been later and so probably was Huxley. Synthesizing Sydney and Decca, then, we have the early nineteenth-century poets, with the accent on Blake; and Poe and the Brontës. It all adds up to a picture of a quintessential romantic. Like many romantics, Unity was by turns dreamy and unruly. Her graduation from Sydney's teaching to the schoolroom about coincided with Miss Hussey's first spell as governess, and Sydney remembers that she would often find Unity waiting outside her room, sent by Miss Hussey to confess some misdemeanour and be ticked off. It was

Miss Hussey who first suggested that Unity ought to go to boarding school, where she eventually went in 1929. She and her cousin Christopher Bailey, who was the same age, used to encourage each other in naughtiness; once, aged six, the two of them ate all the strawberries in the greenhouse that were being kept for some special occasion. This incident became celebrated.

Sydney also records a political speech Unity wrote when she was ten, at the time of the 1924 General Election. It seems to cast a shadow before it:

Ladies and Gentlemen,

I bring you here today to see the state of our country. It is like a book which I expect you have mostly read, *Gulliver's Travels*. Our country is like Gulliver, in the hands of a lot of tiny men, tied down and cannot help herself, so it is in our hands to see that she is rightly governed. Remember, ladies and gentlemen, that every vote helps its cause. You are, as it were, between two destructions, Labour and Liberal.

The image of Gulliver bound relates to Fascist thinking. The Nation, the Folk, the true and decent people, were seen as tied down by the 'tiny men' of democratic politics. Oswald Mosley was often to talk like this, and Unity's view of Nazi Germany was precisely that it was a Gulliver whose bonds had been miraculously untied. The image also ties in with philosophical and literary romanticism, the idea of the human spirit bursting the bonds imposed by the reactionary and the pettifogging.

Too much should not be made of Unity's wilfulness, because neither Sydney nor Blor ever had much trouble with her. Unlike Diana, who was small in childhood but suddenly grew fast in adolescence, Unity was always rather big, which increased her shyness. Sydney says she was 'very tall and very straight and she had two thick plaits of golden hair and a severe and serious expression'. Nancy, helpful as ever, christened her 'Hideous', and Decca remembers her as a shaggy Viking or Little John. She used to fix David at table with a baleful stare from her intense blue eyes and make him roar with irritation; this delighted Decca, who took it as proof that David could not stand the power of the human eye. The best single adjective to describe her at this age is probably the French *farouche*, conveying diffidence covered by sulky aggression. Children often pass through a stage like this. But it was not unmanageability that prompted David and Sydney to send Unity to school, rather that she badgered them to let her go. Finally, in January 1929, her wish was granted and she went to St Margaret's, Bushey.

# 24

# Swinbrook

Poor David! Swinbrook House had been his dream for many years, and he had given great thought to it with the idea that it should please his family; but he got little enough thanks. 'We all thought the house monstrous,' says Diana, and Nancy wrote to a friend from Rutland Gate in June 1928: 'I really feel ashamed to have any guests [at Swinbrook] and one simply couldn't have anybody artistic to stay there lest they sicked in the hall.' If today a visitor to Swinbrook might think this rather steep, it is because we are rendered punch-drunk by the architectural horrors of the modern age. We, who have seen the Centre Pompidou, the Barbican Scheme and the Czechoslovak Embassy in Notting Hill Gate, find David's effort entirely harmless; compared to these it even, in Lewis Carroll's words, 'Seems, to one's bewildered fancy/To have partially succeeded.' Swinbrook is an unremarkable, rather insipid square building in Cotswold stone, such as councillors might have erected between the wars as a cottage hospital, or dons as a modest extension to an Oxford college. But when Swinbrook was built real monstrosities were as yet rare; Le Corbusier had not long enunciated his appalling doctrine that a house was a machine to live in, and compared with what was then around David's creation did seem dreadfully redolent of what John Betjeman was to call 'Ghastly Good Taste'. Certainly it lacks the period charm of Asthall. What was perhaps even more to the point, it was inconvenient. David's children did, as promised, each have a room, but they were allowed no fires in them so they were always cold, as was most of the house. It was at Swinbrook that the linen cupboard became a favourite resort because of its hot pipes: the 'Hons' Cupboard' of *The Pursuit of Love*. In addition, and perhaps worse, there was no library; the books were kept in

David's business room, where the children were not always welcome and browsing was in any event uncongenial. The piano, too, was in Sydney's drawing room which everybody used, making it difficult for Tom to settle down to undisturbed practising. For confidential chatting there was the squash court, rarely applied to its true purpose, but this was a dismal and spartan retreat. Only one of David's children ever came to love Swinbrook and that was, oddly enough, Debo, later to become most renowned of them all for decorative taste. To this day she retains for it a warm, defensive affection, not because it was attractive but because she spent her childhood there.

Clearly David must have minded the children's disapproval, especially as it was shared by Sydney. Diana thinks his feelings were hurt more than he ever admitted. Even from his own point of view, the move from Asthall proved on balance a mistake. It may have been more convenient for supervising the rearing of the pheasants, but it was a move far away from the river, putting an end to the fishing parties which had made him so happy in the mayfly season.

The cost was certainly more than he could afford. David's finances are a mystery to us, as Diana says they always were to her; the point is that they were also, essentially, a mystery to himself, and a worry for this reason. His feelings on the subject bore only a fitful relation to the facts. Most of the time he thought he was much poorer than he was; often he would conceive a wild desire to 'cash up', when he would sell whatever he could lay his hands on at almost any price. First to go were his father's oriental objects; then came his French furniture and china. When they were grown up his daughters, sons-in-law or grandchildren would sometimes pick these things up at auction rather cheaply. He was to sell Swinbrook with virtually all his estate at just about the bottom of the market in 1936. Sometimes David felt he was richer than he actually was; he would then talk to someone in his club, and on the basis of what he was told make some odd investment. The ideas were sometimes bizarre; one of them was a plan to beautify wirelesses by encasing them in papier-mâché containers of what were supposed to be beautiful and tasteful design. The project ended in tears; its originator sued David, unsuccessfully as it turned out, for slander. David had said the man, a South

American, was not a marquis. There were other schemes to get rich quick: the land at Swastika was one. As to ordinary spending, the family in many ways lived extremely well. David never failed to buy a new car every year: particularly when Turner was still his driver, those in the know would virtually queue up to buy these cars when they were sold second-hand after a year of being driven with expert care and tended like antiques. It was like buying a new car at a third of the price and being spared the bother of running it in. What seems certain is that David's major extravagance was the building of Swinbrook, aggravated from the point of view of cash availability by the simultaneous purchase of Rutland Gate, though this was at least a sensible investment. It was during and after this period that the occasional economy drives began; the first of these on record was the temporary move to the Paris hotel. The sale of Batsford and the Gloucestershire land had left the family finances stable, despite the papier-mâché wireless covers; the Swinbrook venture ended this stability and put them into inexorable de-cline. One sign of this was that Rutland Gate was frequently let, rendering it unavailable for the entertaining for which it was bought, as for example at the time of Diana's wedding reception. When this happened the family usually retained as a *pied à terre* the mews flat over the garage behind; they always referred to this as the 'Garage', and it was kept after the house was sold. Sydney was always a help with her methodical housekeeping, her shrewd poultry farming and her small but steady income from holding 19 per cent of *The Lady*; her cumulative effect over the years was probably appreciable. However, Sydney's efforts can never at any given moment have seemed of more than very marginal value, and from this time on David was permanently worried about money.

For the next few years life passed happily enough, though every now and then there was a Homeric row. Tom's friend James Lees-Milne was at the centre of one of them. The children, and Lees-Milne, were expressing a wish for reconciliation with Ger-many; Lees-Milne attacked an anti-German film about Edith Cavell. Suddenly David exploded and ordered him out of the house, himself stalking out of the room. There was an appalled silence, and Lees-Milne hurriedly packed his things and went outside to his motorcycle. It was raining hard and the machine would not start, so Lees-Milne crept back into the house for help.

He met the parlourmaid, Mabel, who hustled him upstairs saying he could leave early in the morning. At about six he went downstairs with the intention of leaving, but David saw him; as usual, he had been up since five. David had forgotten, it seemed, about the previous night's row: at any rate he greeted him with a cheerful 'Good morning, Jim.' Lees-Milne might perhaps have stayed, but felt it better all the same to leave. (This incident, in a very different form, is recounted in Lees-Milne's autobiography, *Another Self*. He makes it happen at Asthall rather than Swinbrook, and says it was his first visit to the family, whom he had in fact been visiting regularly since he was with Tom at Lockers Park. He even says that the sisters chanted unfeelingly that he ought to go, though in real life they were horrified and embarrassed. His account is exceedingly *ben trovato*, sufficiently so to be repeated almost verbatim by Harold Acton, but departs in nearly all respects from the sisters' recollection. The above is based in essence on a letter from Diana.)

The younger sisters had their own games, their own fantasies. They invented not one but two private languages. Boudledidge was the odder of them, shared between Unity and Decca; it had to be uttered while making a miserable, frowning and rather costive-looking grimace with the mouth pulled sharply down to one side. Hopeless yearning was the keynote, together of course with deadly seriousness. The language itself was English with the vowels distorted, the consonants softened and extra syllables inserted, the word 'boudledidge' being itself derived on this system from 'pallish', the language of the pals or boudles. 'Dear old pals, jolly old pals,' the sisters would sing; or in Boudledidge 'Deedr oudle boud-d-d-dles, juddledy oudle boud-d-d-dles.' Unity never forgot Boudledidge, even after her suicide attempt. In about 1943, at the breakfast table, there was a packet of the cereal called Force. 'What's Force in Boudledidge?' asked Jonathan, on a whim. Unity shut her eyes for a second and a look of enormous sadness came over her face as she pushed down her mouth to one side. 'Vudz!' she moaned. The sadness was not real, though she was a sad enough person by then; it was ritual. The other language, Honnish, was easier; it was the language of Decca and Debo. Hon meant hen, and the language was based on Oxfordshire country speech.

Life for the younger sisters was probably on balance more

culturally restricted than it had been for their elders at Asthall. The lack of the old barn in which the older children had read and argued and played was clearly a disadvantage, and perhaps a crucial one. It might be said to explain why Decca's literary gifts, equal in their way to those of Nancy, expressed themselves so differently. Too much should not be made of this. Decca's writings, like Nancy's, proclaim that her education was bad but prove that it was good. In certain ways Swinbrook provided more than Asthall had. There were visits from the older ones, and there was plenty of conversation with their bright friends who came to stay or visit. Evelyn Waugh was an example. David thought him a sewer, at least so Evelyn said, years later, in his letter of condolence to Nancy on her father's death; but *Vile Bodies* contains for all time a private joke between him and Decca. She had a beloved if overfed sheep called Miranda; Unity had a goat. So in Decca's usage 'sheepish' meant everything pleasant, 'goatlike' everything nasty; Unity used the same words in the opposite sense. *Vile Bodies* contains a passage where 'sheepish' is used to mean good, then, a little later, 'goatlike' occurs to mean bad. It reads rather oddly. Another clever visitor who got on with Decca was Roy Harrod, later to be an eminent economist and the author of a life of Keynes. He was a young don who had been a friend of Bryan's at Oxford, though already a senior member of the university. Legend has it that he won his first-class degree by writing four brilliantly concise essays on one sheet of paper in his tiny writing. Harrod was the subject of Decca's first known literary effort, a thriller which began with him lying on the floor equipped with a long, white bloodstained beard.

Then again, the children were often away from Swinbrook. Diana was important here, for Unity, Decca and Debo used to go and stay with her and Bryan Guinness after their marriage. At their house, Biddesden, there was a well-stocked library – Bryan at once saw to that; there were bright people in plenty, and there was good conversation. Decca's account of Biddesden in *Hons and Rebels* has to be read in the light of her Marxist commitment and of the aversion she felt for Diana in later years. She talks of the comfort of the house, never mentioning its beauty; comfort is a matter of economics, belonging to what Marx calls the base of

society, while beauty is only a matter of the comparatively unimportant superstructure. She also says that Diana herself was
silent and supercilious. This, we feel who know Diana, is likely to
be at most a half-truth. Diana has never been a silent person, and
we cannot conceive of her refraining from laughter, as Decca says
she did, in order to preserve her face for old age. Even deafness
has not inhibited her love of chat and particularly of jokes. It
is true that her face has always been rather immobile except at
moments of great animation. But at this time Diana was a young
adult, enjoying her new freedom from childhood restrictions. Did
she perhaps pay less attention to Decca than previously? Diana
denies it, saying that she chatted endlessly to Decca, particularly
about books. But till then, Decca had always been for Diana
something of a knockabout turn, and she used to get her to do
recitations in Boudledidge. After her marriage this kind of thing
amused Diana less, and Decca perhaps felt rejected. The sister, we
suspect, on whom the atmosphere of Biddesden life worked most
strongly was Unity. The ease of Diana's performance as hostess
brought Unity under her influence; the charm of Biddesden
worked its magic on a character which, unlike Decca's, responded
intensely to the visual. She remained under Diana's spell when it
was working in a very different direction.

Unity, as we have seen, went to boarding school. The first she
went to, St Margaret's, let her out after a few days to be bridesmaid at Diana's wedding. The Farrer girls, Joan's daughters, were
at St Margaret's; so were Rosemary and Clementine, Clement's
daughters. Of Unity, Sydney writes that she was 'extremely
happy, though her conduct they said was bad'. It was very much
a church school, having in fact been founded for the daughters of
clergymen, who still formed a sizeable element. So the authorities
were offended when Unity refused to be confirmed, announcing
that she was an atheist. This particular crime cannot really be
called insubordination, though it certainly seemed like it. Nor was
it done to annoy, though it did. To someone of Unity's temperament, serious and sincere under the boisterousness, loss of faith
was an important matter; she would scorn to go along with
confirmation for the sake of peace. But to the school it was all of
a piece with being a generally bad citizen. Unity also refused to

join the Girl Guides. Quite often Sydney used to be summoned to see the formidable headmistress, Miss Boys. The last straw, Sydney says, was when Unity added the word 'rot' to the line 'A garden is a lovesome thing, God wot', making 'God what rot.' Decca says that this was delivered as a recital in front of the whole school at speech day; David Pryce-Jones shows that this is certainly untrue, and also that the remark was probably not original. This does not mean that it was the sort of thing that a girl would have expected to say to a teacher with impunity. In any case, after the end of the Michaelmas term 1930, it was made clear that she would not be welcomed back at St Margaret's. Sydney says: 'I visited the headmistress, who explained to me that many girls left school at 16 and Unity could well be one of them.' This puts paid to the legend, told to Pryce-Jones by more than one of his informants, that it was David who visited the headmistress and that in the course of the interview he was grossly and personally offensive. This was always improbable; David could be irascible, but he was never ill-bred. The existence of the legend shows, however, that Unity left behind among the others a pungent image of rebelliousness such as the law-abiding enjoy embellishing as compensation for their own conformism. Her later notoriety helped in perpetuating this image, and perhaps also in touching it up. But Unity had enjoyed herself at St Margaret's; Sydney says she was 'really heartbroken to leave', regarding it as a 'tribute to the school that she remembered it with the greatest affection', visiting it from time to time in after years. David Pryce-Jones mentions one such visit, in 1938, when she wore a swastika badge and was asked to take it off. This is likely. In the late thirties she was rarely without her swastika, which had been given to her by Hitler himself and carried his facsimile signature on the back. It was a part of her normal apparel; she would not have worn it specifically as a provocation.

During the Swinbrook years David and Sydney spent at least half of their time in London or High Wycombe. Debo was the only one of the children who passed throughout the same sort of uncomplicated country life at Swinbrook with horses and pets that the others had spent at Batsford and Asthall; Decca too had her animals, but she soon developed other interests. As when Sydney wrote about her first visit to Germany, Decca described this period later, at a time when she had become politically committed; *Hons and Rebels* and *A Fine Old Conflict* must be read with this in mind. Some degree of commitment was already there, to be sure; she took in the *Daily Worker*, decorated her room with hammers and sickles, and devoured the *Brown Book of the Hitler Terror*, she had pillow fights with Unity on her visits, each shouting their political slogans. But Decca's Communism was still only an interest and enthusiasm, not a dedication, and certainly neither David nor Sydney had the least idea of the alienation that was to follow. Sydney's main worry at this time was her daughters' obsession with matters risqué or mildly improper. They thought a lot about the White Slave Trade, always expecting to be whisked off to Buenos Aires. Leo d'Erlanger was a highly respectable young banker who lived near their house in Rutland Gate and raised his hat to them politely as he passed in the street in black coat and pinstripe trousers. He knew Nancy slightly. Decca and Debo were convinced that he was high up in the White Slave Trade and christened him the White Slaver. At High Wycombe, in the Mill Cottage, Sydney would raise her eyes mildly and gaze out of the window if the subject turned towards matters of which she disapproved. Mr Mason, the miller, would be pottering about the yard on his business. 'Mr Mason! Here you come!' Sydney would say firmly, a sign that she wanted the subject changed. This was the period when Diana's divorce, Unity's flamboyantly proclaimed Nazism, and later Decca's elopement each in turn shocked their parents and shook their self-confidence. As we consider David and Sydney through these years they seem to shrink as their daughters grow. They had new nicknames: The Poor Old Male and The Poor Old Female, or TPOM and TPOF. Decca used to shake her father's elbow as he was drinking his tea, to give him palsy practice for when he was old. As it happened it was not David but Sydney who was to suffer from Parkinson's disease in old age. There was, however, a considerable difference between the two of them. Both were out of their depth in the waters into which their daughters plunged them; but it was David who was ultimately swept away. Sydney learned, in her fashion, to swim, although she swam very much against the current.

The Poor Old Female was also shortened to The Fem. On one occasion Sydney rang up Mrs Ham, and absent-mindedly called her by the children's nickname: 'Hello, Wid.'

Mrs Ham was not in the least disconcerted. 'Hello, Fem,' she returned, in her hollow voice.

Finally David sold Swinbrook and almost all his remaining land in 1936. It was a bad sale, for agricultural prices were low; but besides wanting to 'cash up' David had ascertained that Tom would never be particularly interested in life as a country gentleman; his preference was for London, his preoccupation with his career at the bar.

# PART FOUR

## Youth

# 25

# Nancy in the Thirties

Nancy was still loosely based at home after the move to Swinbrook, but in practice she spent most of her time away from it. She
had a friend called Evelyn Gardner, who had recently married
Evelyn Waugh. People called them the 'he-Evelyn' and the 'she-
Evelyn'. In June 1929 the Evelyns offered Nancy a room in their
London house; anticipating the vogue of the seventies, they lived
in Canonbury Square. Decca wrote to Pam in Canada, where she
was with her parents at Swastika looking for gold, to say that
Nancy was in London with a friend called Evelyn. They would be
doing all their own housework, like Pam and Sydney in Canada.
The arrangement did not last long; it ended when the first Mrs
Waugh left her husband in the next month. Nancy took the he-
Evelyn's part. Evelyn Waugh became not only a friend for life but
also an important help with her writing. He and Nancy corresponded till his death; she was never too proud to accept his advice on
points of style, and it was he who suggested the titles both of *The
Pursuit of Love* and of *Voltaire in Love*. Nancy found writing easy;
dangerously easy in a sense. Jokes seemed to well out of her and
style came naturally. But such fluency can throw up mistakes, and
Evelyn helped her remove them. The two were deeply fond of
each other; they would not have been themselves if they had not
got in many mutual digs, often in print, but they made each other
laugh.

Nancy's first novel was *Highland Fling*. She wrote part of it
staying in Paris with Bryan and Diana; she was also 'desperately
trying to finish it' during a three-week stay with her grandmother
at Redesdale Cottage over the New Year 1929–30. She adds that
she has had to alter it quite a lot, 'as it is so like Evelyn's in a lot of
little ways, such a bore'. Decca remembers her also writing parts

of it at Swinbrook; she used to read out extracts to the young ones to make them laugh. David was in it as General Murgatroyd, and Decca says that some of the uncles and aunts were there too. We can perhaps identify Uncle George Bowles: there is a long-winded old admiral who goes on about the merits of blockade. In real life George Bowles was usually thought to be good company, but the admiral's views were certainly his. They were also those of Sydney's other brother, Geoffrey; they derived from Thomas. As to General Murgatroyd, Decca makes out that he was David, larger than lifesize. We disagree. To the extent that he does remind one of David, it is David seen through the wrong end of a telescope, a distinctly poor thing when compared to Uncle Matthew in the mature novels. He resembles a clockwork figure who is occasionally wound up at Nancy's whim and then left to run down. She takes care always to put the young people in the book, her own generation, in a position of advantage. The book is about a shooting house party in a Scottish castle. A young couple are standing in for the hosts, and General Murgatroyd is simply in charge of the sport. The poor man's day at the butts is ruined by what seems to us, at least, the bad manners of a precious young fellow guest, Albert Gates. Unable to vent his irritation in any other way, the general picks up his loader and shakes him. The reference is to David's notorious shaking of his loader, years before; but it is of course unfair, for David's grudge had at least been against the loader himself.

Albert Gates suffers from the fact that Evelyn Waugh was to do him so much better in the shape of Ambrose Silk and Anthony Blanche. In real life he would probably have been homosexual, whereas in the book he is loved by Jane Dacre and eventually gets engaged to her. Nancy's unhappy engagement with Hamish Erskine was just starting at the time. Albert is not Hamish, but Jane with her ups and downs, her uncertainties, her reticence, has something of Nancy. Nancy was in love with Hamish for at least three years; he was no doubt flattered and amused, but that was all.

Hamish, the younger son of Lord Rosslyn, was five years younger than Nancy. David and Sydney both disapproved of him. Sydney wrote to Diana on 1 June 1930 that she hoped she and Bryan would try to stop them marrying, 'and make them wait until he has at any rate some work. If they marry in a runaway manner,

Farve will I am sure stop Nancy's allowance. If it might be happy
for Nancy I would never bother about the money part of it, but I
don't see how it can end in anything but trouble and sorrow, the
man being what he is. Except from Nancy I have never heard a
good opinion of him.' Nancy used to write about Hamish to Mark
Ogilvie-Grant, who was in Egypt at the time. In a letter of 19
February 1930, quoted by Harold Acton, she writes that she has just
been reading André Maurois's life of Byron. 'Byron is so like
Hamish in character, the other day Hamish said to me in tones of
deepest satisfaction, "You haven't known a single happy moment
since we met have you." Very true as a matter of fact, what he
would really like would be for me to die and a few others and then
he'd be able to say "I bring death on all who love me." ' The affair
started in late 1929 and ended in the summer of 1933. Nancy did in
fact once try to kill herself by putting her head in a gas oven. 'It is a
lovely sensation just like taking anaesthetic so I shan't be sorry any
more for school-mistresses who are found dead in that way, but just
in the middle I thought that Romie [Gilbey] who I was staying with
might have a miscarriage which would be disappointing for her so
I got back to bed and was sick,' she told Mark Ogilvie-Grant. He
perhaps cast doubt on the story, for she wrote later: 'The gas story
is quite true, it made Robert [Byron] laugh so much.'

Not everything went wrong with Nancy at this time. Most of her
letters are cheerful, such as one to Mark Ogilvie-Grant dated 10
December 1930: 'I have just been lunching with your mame and
inadvertently gave her a letter of yours to read in which a lift boy is
described as a Driberg's delight. "What is a Driberg's delight, Dear
Mark has such an amusing gift for describing people!" ' Mark's
mother would not have understood the allusion to the sexual
proclivities of Tom Driberg, the gossip columnist and politician.
*Highland Fling* did quite well for a first novel, and *The Lady* hired
Nancy to write weekly articles for five guineas a week. Previously
the magazine had enabled her to make money in a more unusual
way. Her clothes, like those of most of the female members of the
family, used to be made by Gladys, Sydney's lady's maid; all Nancy
had to pay for was the material. Nancy answered the advertisement
of a doctor's wife in *The Lady* who wanted second-hand clothes;
Nancy sold her clothes for more than they had cost her, and the
doctor's wife raved over their quality and price and kept asking for

more. Whether Sydney knew of this we are not sure. It was clearly a reason for Nancy to stay at home, but relations with her parents were not easy. In her 10 December letter to Mark Ogilvie-Grant she tells him that she now makes it a point of honour to be out for every meal, and again on 15 March 1931: 'They have been simply too odious lately, and had a fearful row the other day ending up by accusing me of drinking. I must say I do go to awful sorts of parties so I'm not surprised they are in a state, but if one can't be happy one must be amused don't you agree.' She was already twenty-six at the time – rather old to be lectured like this. Why did she not leave? Clearly for reasons of cash. Her allowance was tiny, and her articles did not bring in much. If she had needed to pay rent there would have been virtually nothing left, especially as Hamish was expensive. He not only drank, but gambled. She stayed at home and vented her irritation on General Murgatroyd. About this time she had a proposal from a rich merchant banker, but she did not love him and would not marry him, despite seeing how convenient his money would be. Her description in *The Pursuit of Love* of Linda's loveless first marriage is in part a speculation on how this marriage, if it had occurred, might have turned out.

Eventually she did move away from her parents in early 1933, when Diana divorced. Diana gave her a room at 2 Eaton Square, always known in the family as the Eatonry; she kept this room till she married Peter Rodd in November of the same year. David and Sydney were very unhappy with Diana following her divorce; Debo says that she and Decca were not allowed anywhere near the Eatonry. In theory they also disapproved of Nancy living there; in practice, they were no doubt quite glad to have her finally out of the way. It was during this time that she wrote a little story, entirely for private publication: 'Two Old Ladies of Eaton Square'. Nancy and Diana are the two crones; their greatest friend is an old gentleman in a butter-coloured wig, who lives at the other end of the square (Mark Ogilvie-Grant). For a time he is faithless to the old ladies and abandons them for a pretty young lady in Eaton Terrace (Anne Armstrong-Jones, later Countess of Rosse, Lord Snowdon's mother). At the end they get him back.

Nancy's sojourn at Eaton Square shows that Nancy was not so anti-Fascist as she later became. Diana was in the first flush of her conversion, and would not have tolerated any really serious criticism. Nancy teased her about politics in a good-natured way, as she was later to tease Unity and Decca. A character called the 'Little Leader' occurs in the story about the Old Ladies, and Nancy takes a crack at him. The point, though, is that she does it in fun. She says, for instance, that when the Little Leader called on the Old Ladies, 'it was proof of the trust he had for the ladies that he came armed only with two revolvers, a bowie-knife and a bar of Ex Lax the delicious chocolate laxative.' The laxative was a reference to Mussolini's Fascists, who used to dose their opponents with castor oil. Diana took it in perfectly good part.

Finally Hamish brought his understanding with Nancy to an end; he made Diana do the dirty work, as he was unable to face Nancy himself. Almost immediately she found someone else. He was Peter Rodd, son of Lord Rennell, who had been a particularly successful ambassador to Italy, where Peter had spent much of his childhood. He proposed to Nancy, Diana thinks, only about a week after she had broken the news of Hamish's decision. Nancy accepted at once, conditionally. She wrote to Debo: 'Can you keep a secret? It is a very important one, as nobody knows about it, not even William [Unity] or TPOF [Sydney] . . . Well, I am perhaps going to be married to a very divine person called Peter Rodd.' The trouble was that they had no money. 'But if we can get some we shall marry and if we can't we shan't and that's why it's an important secret because if we don't it's a bore if everyone knows.' Always known as Prod, he was rather short, blond, and good-looking in a square sort of way. Nancy's sisters were never kind about him; like Blor, only in an opposite sense, he unites Diana and Decca. Decca referred to him in the television programme about Nancy as 'the old tollgater'; she meant that he used to drone on about the tollgates on the English roads, all of which he used to list from his photographic memory. Diana says he was 'a handsome and clever man, who despite his undoubted intelligence and even charm managed to be an excruciating bore, buttonholing one and inexorably imparting information upon subjects one was only too happy to know nothing about'. Poor Peter! On the few occasions that Jonathan met him as a schoolboy, he struck him as genial and generous. Did he bore Nancy? Harold Acton evidently feels he must have done, but concedes that, if so, she was far too loyal to admit it. In *The Pursuit of Love* she has Linda's first husband, Tony Kroesig, informing people 'how many harbourmasters there were in the British Isles', though in other respects Tony has nothing to do with Peter. The only direct evidence we have indicates that, far from boring Nancy, Peter made her laugh. Many years afterwards, after he died in 1968, when they had long been divorced and even longer separated, Nancy wrote to Diana on 13 August: 'Peter's last words were "Oh God I am finished – see you presently" which Francis thinks may mean that he was really a believer but I think more likely a typical Proddish joke of the sort one loved him for . . . I can't remember from old days I don't suppose we ever mentioned the subject.' What attracted her to him was that he seemed so confident and knowledgeable; he had been everywhere and seen everything, and he was always just about to do something spectacular. He was also a brilliant natural linguist.

In politics he was inclined to the left, but in an erratic way; when he and Nancy were first engaged they even bought black shirts and went to some Fascist meetings. This phase did not last long, but *Wigs on the Green*, Nancy's third book, cannot be fully understood unless we bear in mind that it did take place.

Nancy's letters show that she was in love and radiantly happy. Peter seems to have appealed very temporarily to the same seriousness that Sir Oswald Mosley had stirred in Diana, that Hitler was about to evoke in Unity and Esmond Romilly in Decca. For there is a sense in which Peter appeared to be what Esmond Romilly, in particular, actually was. They married in November 1933, and went to live at Strand-on-the-Green. David gave Nancy a small allowance, but they were poor; Peter's freelance journalism and other activities brought in very little and Nancy did not earn much from her writings. *Christmas Pudding*, her second novel, had appeared in 1932. It is better than *Highland Fling*, though equally lightweight; the reader has less of a feeling that she is trying to work out her own personal frustrations. One quotation throws light on the political attitude of Nancy's contemporaries. Of a Conservative MP in the book she writes: 'To hear him talk about Bolshevik Russia was a revelation to Paul, who took it for granted that Communism was now universally regarded as a high, though possibly boring, ideal.' This is rather close, *mutatis mutandis*, to St Augustine's youthful wish for God to make him chaste, but not yet. David Caute, in his study *The Fellow Travellers*, shows that many left-wingers used to admire Stalin's Russia from afar rather than actually go there. But Nancy is not talking about fellow travellers. She is noting something more diffuse but also more fundamental: the fact that quietly, without their behaviour necessarily changing much or at all, the more intelligent and idealistic young members of her class had transferred their moral allegiance from the imperatives of Christianity to those of socialism in the widest sense of the word. Of course the behaviour of some of them certainly did change; some turned into the Cambridge spies, others fought for the Republicans in the Spanish Civil War, others again turned into 'committed writers'. But it is the existence of this general atmosphere, captured in passing by this quotation from Nancy, which explains why there grew up in the thirties a predisposition to think the best, rather than the worst, of Soviet Russia. This entailed thinking the worst, rather than the best, of its Fascist adversaries, even though the appeal of those adversaries to a smaller minority was partly due to rather similar feelings.

*Wigs on the Green* came out in 1935, and this time a certain seriousness underlies the froth. Just as *Highland Fling* included an attempt to cut Nancy's father down to size at a time when he was annoying her, so *Wigs on the Green* was in part an attempt to reduce Unity's activities, and by extension those of Diana, to manageable proportions. They were in fact more manageable than they became immediately afterwards: Unity was not yet a personal friend of Hitler when the book was being written. Even a year later, *Wigs on the Green* might have been a different book. Possibly it might not have been written at all; Nancy knew what she could do and what she could not. She instinctively avoided choosing targets for satire that were too demanding. For example, she never took on Diana directly. What is more, she removed from *Wigs on the Green* certain passages that Diana thought damaging to Mosley. This did not placate Diana, who felt that when Mosley and his supporters were being attacked in real street fights she could not have much to do with a sister who was publicly laughing at them. Nancy never came to Wootton Lodge, where Diana lived from 1936 to 1939.

She wrote to Unity on 21 June 1935, just before the book came out; her mocking tone does not conceal the fact that she was dreadfully worried, especially about Diana.

Darling Head of Bone and Heart of Stone,

Oh dear oh dear the book comes out on Tuesday. Oh dear, I won't let Rodd give a party for it, or John Sutro either, who wants to. Oh dear I wish I had, never been born into such a family of fanatics. Oh dear . . .

*Please* don't read the book if it's going to stone you up against me . . .

Oh dear *do* write me a kind and non-stony-heart letter to say you don't mind it *nearly* as much as you expected, in fact you *like* it, in fact after *I Face the Stars* it is your favourite book even more favourite than mine comf [*sic*].

Oh dear I am going to Oxford with Nardie [Diana] tomorrow, our last day together I suppose before the clouds of her displeasure burst over me. She doesn't know yet that it's coming out on Tuesday. Oh dear I have spent days trying to write her diplomatic letters about it. Oh dear I wish I had called it mine uncomf now because uncomf is what I feel . . .

So now don't get together with Nardie and ban me forever or I shall die . . . I did take out some absolutely wonderful jokes you know and all the bits about the Captain. OH! DEAR!

In an earlier letter, written on 23 April 1935, Nancy claims, 'Your Bowd [Decca] read *Wigs on the G.* and said that it quite inclined her to join the movement. I swear that's true, so please don't stone up . . .'

Diana's dislike of *Wigs on the Green*, and Decca's subsequent enthusiasm about it, have combined to make people think of it as a simple satire on Unity and British Fascism. The case is more complex than this, for Eugenia Malmains, the fictional Unity, is not wholly a figure of fun. We find her saying things that Nancy believed herself. Eugenia is made four years younger than Unity; her parents are dead and she lives with her grandparents, known like David and Sydney as TPOM and TPOF. This reduction of Unity's age and increase in that of her parents certainly makes all of them a little sillier. Eugenia has become converted to 'Social Unionism', a sort of Fascism, whose leader is called the Captain. She starts a branch in the village, and organizes a pageant of Social

Unionism. So far so good. But we get our first surprise when Eugenia lists the events the pageant is to show: 'The March on Rome, the Death of Horst Wessel, the Burning of the Reichstag, *the Presidential election of Roosevelt*'. (Our italics.) The point is that Fascists used often to cite Roosevelt's New Deal as a model. Economic activism of this sort was advocated by Mosley, and Hitler's measures to end the slump in Germany were on the same lines. To include Roosevelt's election in Eugenia's pageant concedes a point to the people at whom Nancy is supposed to be laughing.

The second surprise is Eugenia's speech: 'The rich have betrayed their trust, preferring the fetid atmosphere of cocktail-bars and nightclubs to the sanity of a useful country life.' This ties in exactly with Nancy's sentiments as expressed in the introductions to the two volumes of letters of the Stanley family, as we shall see. And again: 'The great families of England herd together in luxury flats and expend their patrimony in the divorce courts.' Another remark worth noting is made by one of the young men in whom there is a touch, perhaps, of Peter Rodd: 'Western civilization is old and tired, the dark ages are practically upon us anyhow, and I should prefer that they march in with trumpet and flag than that they should creep upon us to the tap of a typewriter.' This, too, is Nancy – in one particular mood. But in general Peter and Nancy at this time 'considered themselves Socialists', as Harold Acton puts it; the hint of condescension is fair. It was their socialism, such as it was, that decided David to send them out to fetch Decca back when in February 1937 she eloped with Esmond Romilly. He thought they might talk Decca's language. Tom would really have been a better choice; he was the one who was to make friends with the Romillys after their marriage. The Rodds went out to St Jean de Luz, argued with Decca, and returned empty-handed.

Not long after this Nancy's cousin Edward, Lord Stanley of Alderley, commissioned her to edit the Stanley family letters. He was Lyulph's grandson and his mother, *née* Margaret Evans-Gordon, was Jessica Bowles's niece, so he was twice Nancy's cousin; he was also a lifelong friend. The letters appeared in two parts: *The Ladies of Alderley*, covering the period up to 'Ben' Stanley's marriage, and *The Stanleys of Alderley*, comprising the time up to his death. Nancy's introductions show how her feeling for people like herself combined with a socialistic view on political right and wrong with which it sat uneasily. That is, she felt she ought to disapprove of those people whom she found congenial. The living mind, especially a mind like Nancy's, can quite well believe things which are inconsistent with each other. One trick is to think of the two contradictory propositions not both at once, but each in turn. This is fine in conversation but looks odd in print, so another way is to say that what is wrong at one period of history may be right at another. This is what Nancy does in these introductions. She excuses the Victorian upper class from having a social conscience in the modern sense on the grounds that the idea had not been brought to their attention. Now that the concept of a social conscience has been widely publicized, anyone behaving with the self-confidence of the Victorians would have to be brutally insensitive. Victorian self-confidence has now gone; but it has been followed not by generosity and sympathy, rather by mean-spirited fear. It is like the Fall of Man; there is, as it were, a tree of socialist knowledge of which the Victorian Stanleys have not eaten, but Nancy's own generation has done so and from now on the concept of *noblesse oblige* cannot be honest or consistent unless it envisages the abandonment of privilege.

But let her speak for herself. The introduction to *The Ladies* starts as follows:

Here is the picture of a dead world, past and gone. We who are being herded in this terrible twentieth century towards, we suppose, a brave new world, may care to examine that other world, to peer into the picture and to see how human beings behave when they neither drive nor are driven, but live in peace . . . The minor nobility of England a hundred years ago . . . could live their lives, develop their personalities and cultivate their talents in perfect security. Secure in their financial situation, they could indulge the natural wish for a large family without thought for the future. Secure in their domestic relations, husband and wife could build up the fabric of marriage without considering the possibility of a divorce. Secure in their religious beliefs and in the knowledge of immortality, they were able to regard this life as an incident rather than as the whole experience of man. Above all, secure in their Whig outlook, they never questioned the fact that each individual has his allotted place in the realm and that their own allotted place was among the ruling, the leisured and the moneyed classes. This peace and this security, which are today outside the experience of any but the rich and heedless dolt, had been enjoyed by their ancestors for hundreds of years, were to them the natural order of things, and, like the music of the spheres, went unheard because too familiar. Now that the music has stopped its echo must have a nostalgic charm . . .

The introduction to *The Stanleys* goes further; the music to which the peers and people danced was the source, not just of contentment, but of political success and greatness.

The people have liked in the past, and they still like, to be governed by sensible men of ample means; not to put too fine a point upon it, they like a lord. They also like to be governed in a fine and flourishing manner, they expect education in their masters and a knowledge of history, and they are gratified by classical quotations, which they prefer to American slang. During the whole of the 19th Century the English and their rulers were in perfect accord, they understood and trusted the integrity of each other's aims and methods, and consequently the country was enabled to achieve a greatness, not only material, but spiritual, which has never been equalled in the history of the world . . .

This disregards the fact that the British Empire was founded at least as much on the inventiveness of manufacturers and the shrewdness of traders as on the solid social fabric sustained by the landed aristocracy. For all that, it is certainly a part of the truth; a nation at one with itself is best able to take advantage of its opportunities. Nancy then turns to her own day:

These sensible men, are they by any chance afraid, afraid of losing their ample means? These lords, divorced from the land which was the reason of their being, do they fly . . . into the arms of alien creeds; and worse still, do they begin to hate and fear the people? The segregation of classes, which has resulted from the abandonment of the now impoverished land by its former owners . . . has been most harmful to the aristocracy; they are losing their hitherto intimate knowledge of, and trust in, the people. The English are like a fine and nervous horse, which, ridden with good heart, can surmount any obstacle, but which, when out of sympathy with its timid rider, will shy at the shadow of an ice cream cart or the distant growling of a dachshund.

So much for Hitler and Mussolini. The following passage, however, is a puzzle:

The frontiers of our great Empire should be opened to all in trouble, the sorrows of the world must be our sorrows and the wrongs must be put right by us . . . The proudest title we can acquire is that of 'a nation of governesses.' We are the only adult nation and until the others come of age we must be their governesses, lecture them at all times, put iodine on their knees when they fall down and graze them; when we see them torturing a kitten we must slap them hard and take away the kitten.

As happens a number of times in Nancy's writings, it seems impossible to tell just what she is up to here. Teasing, of course; but from exactly what standpoint? There certainly was a strong unspoken assumption in British policy which could be expressed in such terms as 'We are the only adult nation': it was the idea behind the replacement of Empire with Commonwealth. Colonies were said to be 'getting ready for independence', for all the world as if they were children preparing for their 'O' levels. On the whole Nancy probably felt like this. But in expressing the feeling in such absurd terms Nancy was lampooning it. Did she mean to, or not?

In May 1939 Nancy went for a few weeks to Perpignan to help the Republican refugees from the Spanish Civil War, which had just ended. Peter was already there, as were one or two other English people. She knew no Spanish, and had never been a social worker; but she helped in all the ways she could. She was to use this episode in *The Pursuit of Love*. She was naturally very sorry for the refugees, most of whom were no doubt ordinary people caught up in a terrible fear, but among whom there were certainly some with crimes on their personal conscience. For a familiar pro-Republican source, see Hemingway's *For Whom the Bell Tolls*, in which village revolutionaries force the leading figures to jump off a cliff; in many places similar things had happened, and the Franco forces contained many exasperated relations of the victims, bent on revenge.

Like Linda in *The Pursuit of Love*, Nancy had to help get some refugees on board a ship for Mexico. It was no picnic; an adverse gale kept the vessel out of Port Vendres where it had been supposed to dock, and the refugees had to be redirected to Sète. In a letter to her mother she wrote:

I was up all yesterday night as the embarkation went on until 6 a.m. and the people on the quay had to be fed and the babies given their bottles. There were 200 babies under two and 12 women are to have babies on board. One poor shell-shocked man went mad and had to be given an anaesthetic and taken off . . . The boat sailed at twelve yesterday, the pathetic little band on board played first God Save the King, for us, then the Marseillaise and the Spanish National Anthem. Then the poor things gave three Vivas for España which they will never see again . . . And now there still remain over 300,000 poor things to be dealt with, 500,000 counting the women, and more arriving all the time.

But though she worked hard, Nancy was unable as ever to resist a tease, and announced that Unity might turn up to help. The horror this aroused among the Quakers and leftists can be imagined.

Later in 1939 the Second World War broke out, and Nancy wrote her fourth book, *Pigeon Pie*. One short passage in it seems worth quoting here to show how the world seemed to Nancy at this moment. Sophia, the female protagonist, thinks to herself: 'The world is not a bad place, it is a pity to have to die. But, of course, it is only a good place for a very few people. Think of Dachau, think of China and Czechoslovakia and Spain. We must die now, and there must be a new world.'

# 26

# Diana's First Marriage

During the season of 1928, Diana and Bryan Guinness became interested in each other; the friendship blossomed and turned into love. Bryan was twenty-two, the son of Colonel Walter Guinness, the Minister of Agriculture, who was later to be created Lord Moyne; Colonel Guinness was also a director of the Guinness Brewery and brother of the chairman. Bryan himself was at the time reading for the Bar. He was slim and sensitive, and the remains of adolescent diffidence combined in him with the beginnings of adult disillusionment to set him apart from the normal run of dancing partners, although dancing happened to be something he did exceptionally well. He was very well read, and possessed a genuine poetic talent, evocative and apt. He rode horses, but strictly as a diversion, and had none of the enthusiasm for field sports which would make him too reminiscent of the boring side of country life. Nor did he enjoy team games; like Pam, he had suffered from polio when younger and in any case lacked what he himself describes as 'an eye for a moving ball'. To Diana, he seemed to promise and to embody all that life of which she had dreamed at Asthall: a life of intelligent conversation illuminated by jokes and enlivened by personal gossip which had no need whatever to be especially kind, as long as it was funny. She envisaged, it is clear, something like Huxley's *Crome Yellow*, or the calmer parts of *Point Counter Point*.

The attraction was mutual, but it concealed a core of misunderstanding. Bryan saw in Diana a fresh, unspoilt girl, excellently educated, bright without at that stage seeming too sharp, and stunningly beautiful. The surface pleasantness of society already palled on him; he spotted the cynicism underneath. One of his poems, 'The Party', starts: 'Here friendship founders in a sea of friends,/And harsh-lipp'd *bubbly* cannot make amends.' Diana seemed not to belong to this morally empty world; she was a country girl. If her vision of their future approximated to scenes from Aldous Huxley, his derived from Tolstoy. He was a Levin seeking his Kitty; though he was, of course, himself conscious of no such consideration, but simply fell in love.

There was indeed something in Diana that set her apart from 'society', but it was something more positive than mere freshness and something that was still entirely in potential. For all her sparkling gregariousness, deep within her was the urge of Lermontov's lonely sailing boat which 'Rebellious, demands storms/As if in storms there is peace.' Already she had, in diffuse but quite discernible form, a social conscience, a feeling that things needed to change. She was not alone in this; it was very widespread. In her case, it took the form of a vaguely Liberal stance in politics; if she admired any political figure, it was Lloyd George. Bryan would have had little against this. His mistake, as things turned out, was to assume that in Diana's case these feelings could be kept fastidious, and canalized into rural withdrawal. Once aroused, this side of Diana was to be content with nothing short of revolution. She was a political animal with a potential for extremism. But how was Bryan to know this, when she did not yet know it herself?

In July 1928, Bryan proposed marriage and Diana accepted. She told Sydney, whose immediate response was to refuse. They must wait two years; well, one year anyway. They were both much too young.

Events were to justify Sydney's doubt. A note she has left makes it clear that she was not merely acting instinctively to preserve the status quo; she thought Bryan, as well as Diana, too immature to marry. Accompanied by Blor, Diana was allowed to go to stay with Bryan's family in Sussex, where the 'medieval' house of Bailiffscourt was being built, from old materials found on the site or brought from elsewhere, beside the thirteenth-century chapel of the Bailiff from the Abbey of Seez in Normandy. It was the creation of Bryan's mother, Lady Evelyn Guinness, who had a passion for the Gothic style. Against all the odds, her project came off, in the sense that Bailiffscourt is rather beautiful. Now an hotel, it is a place of contemplative charm, quite lacking the fierceness of the Middle Ages as they actually were; but the genuinely old materials make it look absolutely authentic. While the house was being built, the family lived in a group of wooden huts. It was a fine summer, and everybody got on well; Diana took to Bryan's family, and they to her. She particularly lost her heart to Lady Evelyn, whom she came to love in rather the same way as in childhood she had loved Great-Aunt Natty, her first unprincipled grown-up. Lady Evelyn was very far from being unprincipled, but she had an even more charming attribute – that of being almost infinitely indulgent. When Bryan was at Oxford, she had worried about his underspending his allowance; she must have been about the only parent in Oxford history, or indeed in the history of universities as a whole, to be concerned in this direction about the finances of a student son. She was equally indulgent to her other children. For Bryan's younger brother Murtogh an entire staircase in their London house was fitted with a fabulous wooden slide ending in the front hall. Murtogh himself could go down it standing up. Once, at a reception, a small tobogganist is said to have shot between the legs of the Prime Minister's wife as she entered the house.

Lady Evelyn was entirely on the side of Bryan and Diana getting married as soon as possible. However, she did not want to write to David, claiming that she would not dare. If anything, this added to her charm: not only was she on their side, she was as diffident as they were. It meant, though, that nothing could be done before the return of her husband, Walter, who was cruising on his yacht and not expected back till September. In the meantime, Bryan came to Swinbrook for a return visit, which was equally successful. David was on his best behaviour, and Bryan liked the whole family. Always a lover of children, he got on especially well with Decca and Debo.

Then Bryan's father came back, and Diana was again asked to stay, this time in another house he owned, Heath House in Hampstead. Walter impressed her as kind but rather remote. Evelyn Waugh in his *Thirties Diary* has a neat summary of the difference between him and David. He writes on 3 July 1930:

A very good example of the difference between Guinness and Mitford minds. M—— observed to be hopelessly drunk at the Redesdales' dance. Lord Redesdale, on having this explained to him: 'Drunk. Don't be absurd. Girls simply don't get drunk. And even if they did, no one would mention it.'

Colonel Guinness in similar circumstances: 'Does she often get drunk?'

'Almost continually.'

'How very interesting. What does she drink?'

For Walter had the scientific spirit of inquiry; he was a keen amateur anthropologist as well as a politician. Diana was a little in awe of him, but he liked her, immediately agreeing to write to David. The Redesdales made no difficulties when it came to the point; Sydney suppressed her doubts. The date was fixed for 30 January 1929.

It was to be a grand affair at St Margaret's, Westminster. Hundreds of wedding presents arrived. In those days wedding presents were more numerous than they are today, and the system of lists at shops, which now helps ensure that couples receive more or less what they want, had not been developed. Of the flood of gifts that arrived, some were beautiful or useful, but many were neither. The wedding party was to be at Grosvenor Place, because Rutland Gate was let; so it was there that the presents were assembled.

Lady Evelyn looked at them reflectively.

'The glass will be the easiest,' she said. 'It only needs a good kick.' She said silver was much more of a problem. 'Walter and I had such luck, *all* ours was stolen when we were on our honeymoon.' (*A Life of Contrasts*)

The 'good kick' delighted Nancy, who put it into *Highland Fling*.

Diana was married from a house in Wilton Crescent belonging to Lord Dulverton, the buyer of Batsford who was a friend of David. As she was getting ready, Diana fussed about her veil, which was difficult to arrange. Soon she would have to leave for the church, already filling with a congregation agog for the sight of the bride. For David, punctuality was an obsession; Diana knew he was beginning to suffer. As she fretted, Blor uttered her habitual words of comfort: 'Never mind, darling; nobody's going to look at you.'

Diana's marriage transformed her at the age of eighteen from a child, to be admonished and chaperoned, to a fully-fledged adult. She and Bryan went for their honeymoon first to his parents' flat in Paris, in the Rue de Poitiers, and then on to Sicily, which gave Diana her first experience of the Mediterranean, of Greek ruins in the clear sun and almond trees blossoming in February. On their return to London they settled in at 10 Buckingham Street, now Buckingham Gate. Bryan was in due course called to the bar.

They settled down to a pleasant life in London, and were mentioned from time to time in gossip columns which soon put them down as 'bright young people'. Their friend Evelyn Waugh used to laugh rather at this expression, applying it to those of their contemporaries who were particularly sober. 'Bright young Roy Harrod', he would sometimes say of the serious academic economist, or 'bright young Henry Yorke'. Henry Yorke was an Eton friend of Bryan's. Under the name Henry Green he became one of the best writers of the period. A master, even one may say a pioneer, of realistic dialogue, he specialized in quiet and sometimes savage comedy with overtones of poetic mystery. His books always appealed to a minority, but they will never be altogether forgotten. Henry also ran Pontifex, his family's engineering firm in Leeds, and his book *Living* shows that he observed labour relations there with uncanny sensitivity. There is a luminosity about his work that recalls Chekhov. Evelyn Waugh respected it deeply. 'I have talent,' he once said. 'Henry has genius.' Henry made disaster seem funny: it was the way he coped with the melancholia of which he was rarely free, and which seemed to be symbolized by the black city suits and overcoats which he always wore, even in the country. 'Bright young Henry Yorke' was indeed good for a laugh.

As to Evelyn himself, he used to revisit Oxford while Bryan was still an undergraduate and he quickly became a great friend of Diana as well. He saw the Guinnesses continually, especially after his own marriage broke up in July 1929. Diana remembers that 'he was by way of being shattered by [the break-up], but I must admit he showed no signs of it. Possibly his pride suffered, but never was anyone more amusing and high-spirited.' The Waughs' break-up had displaced Nancy from the room she had taken in Evelyn's house; she, too, now saw a lot of Bryan and Diana.

Not long after they had returned to Buckingham Street, they went to Berlin to see the legendary decadence of the night life.

Brian Howard was one of those who encouraged them to take this trip: 'It is the gayest town in Europe,' he told Diana. A little later, in May 1929, they stayed with Bryan's parents in their house at Bury St Edmunds. This was Walter's constituency, and there was electioneering to be done for the General Election that month. Diana testifies that, privately, she was strongly anti-Tory and could not have voted for her father-in-law, but she was in any case under age and did not live in the constituency, so the point was wholly academic. As a matter of fact, although she did not like Walter Guinness's party, she admired him personally.

At about this time Diana came to know Lady Cunard, who was to be a loyal friend. Born in the United States and christened Maud, she disliked being reminded of her American origins and, by the time Diana met her, had for years dropped Maud and become Emerald. She is best remembered as a hostess, though she disliked the tag. The rising young photographer Cecil Beaton sent her a complimentary copy of his *Book of Beauty*; after leafing through it, she threw it in the fire, saying: 'He calls me a *hostess*; that shows he's a low fellow.' (Andrew Barrow, *Gossip*, p. 53.) She did entertain a lot, and her parties were often attended by the eminent. Her husband, much older than herself, had been Sir Bache Cunard of the shipping family; in his lifetime he had stayed mostly in the country, and by now he was dead. She had a peculiarly inconsequential style of conversation; Lord Berners once said of her, 'Emerald hasn't really got a sense of humour; she just says whatever comes into her head and waits to see if other people laugh.' But she knew like the conductor of an orchestra how to make her famous guests give of their best at her table, yet harmonize with the rest of the company in good general conversation. It was thus in a sense as one conductor admiring another that she was for years in love with Sir Thomas Beecham.

It was at the opera that Bryan and Diana met Lady Cunard. She had arranged a large dinner party at her house, 7 Grosvenor Square, with spare places for people she would meet at the opera. Diana found herself sitting next to Lytton Strachey. 'We became instant friends,' she says. 'He was everything I loved best; brilliantly clever and willing to talk for hour upon hour.' He only had three years to live, as it was to turn out; but during that time he became a very close friend. Tall, limp and weedy, with a brown beard and bespectacled spaniel eyes under a high forehead, his appearance is familiar to us now from photographs and from Henry Lamb's portrait in the Tate Gallery, but when he was alive what people noticed about him was his voice. The Mitford voice was often said to be affected, because of its drawl and exaggerated emphasis. Lytton's voice had some of this, but its speciality was rises and falls of pitch. His remarks would often end in a squeak. Sometimes what he said was funny mainly because of this. The architect George Kennedy once remembered what had seemed at the time a superb joke made by Lytton, and began repeating it back to him – do you remember, wasn't it priceless when you said – and suddenly, too late, realized that the entire point of the remark had been the voice. 'What *is* coconut matting,' Lytton had said. 'Is it *really* made of coconut?' Unable to imitate him back to himself, George Kennedy said the words in a normal voice, and Lytton looked at him as if he had lost his reason.

Lytton asked Bryan and Diana to stay with him at Ham Spray where he lived with the artist Dora Carrington and her husband Ralph Partridge. Carrington, as she was always called, loved Lytton so much that she would be unable to face life when he died. He was fond of her, but such sexual drive as he possessed was directed at men. Interest in her was to revive in the sixties with the publication of her letters and of Michael Holroyd's biography of Strachey. It reached the Duke of Windsor in his retirement near Paris. 'You actually *knew* Carrington?' he asked Diana. Carrington did the cooking at Ham Spray with more panache than dependability. It was this that brought her and Diana close, because on their first visit to Ham Spray Diana was poisoned by Carrington's rabbit pie, and had to stay there in bed for two days. For most of that time Carrington chatted with her in her room. It is noteworthy how many intelligent people have, throughout her life, been willing to spend hours talking with Diana.

Bryan and Diana lived at Buckingham Street less in practice than in theory. They spent most weekends, and part of the summer, at Pool Place, a modern villa on the edge of the sea near Bailiffscourt, which was lent to them during the first two years of their marriage. Decca and Debo, with Blor in charge, came to stay there with them. In the autumn of the same year, they again borrowed Bryan's father's flat in the Rue de Poitiers, and both

Nancy and Evelyn Waugh came to stay. Nancy, Evelyn and Bryan were all writing books. Evelyn's was his second novel, *Vile Bodies*, which was to be dedicated to Bryan and Diana; Bryan's was *Singing Out of Tune* and Nancy's was *Highland Fling*, both their first. Bryan's book contains a certain amount about a divorce; this is based on that of Evelyn, not on his own which was not to occur until 1933. Diana read while the three of them wrote; she was expecting Jonathan, who was born in the following March. Evelyn's companionship helped Diana over the dull months of waiting; as a full-time writer, his hours were his own, and he came most days for chatting when Bryan was working at the Temple. Once at this time, Evelyn and Diana were travelling in a taxi along Pont Street, a thoroughfare whose high, flamboyant Victorian style with elaborate stone and ceramic ornamentation was thought the last word in hideousness. Diana said something about this, and Evelyn assured her that the baby she was carrying would certainly live in Pont Street, if only to annoy her. After the birth, in the summer of 1930, Diana started going to a great many parties and seeing large numbers of people. This made Evelyn unhappy with her; he wanted her more to himself. He began seeing much less of her and Bryan, and he finally refused point-blank to come and stay with them in Ireland. It was a form of jealousy, as he himself as good as admitted in a letter to her at the end of his life. Clearly he was, in a wholly platonic way, a little in love with Diana. She did not realize this at the time, regretted not seeing him and wondered what she had done to annoy. They did, however, meet again after the war, and corresponded at the end of his life. It happens that the last letter he ever wrote was addressed to Diana. With Nancy, on the other hand, Evelyn remained continuously in touch.

Bryan and Diana staged a spoof exhibition of paintings at their house in Buckingham Street. The idea, and most of the paintings, were Brian Howard's. The artist was given the name 'Bruno Hat'. Howard painted some twenty pictures on cork bathmats, in surrealist style; one was an 'Adoration of the Magi' in which each of the figures, instead of a head, had three finger-like antennae. The style struck Diana as being 'something between Picasso and Miro; rather decorative', but we see in it also more than a little of John Banting, another artist friend. Banting was in the Bruno

Hat secret; Brian Howard painted most of the pictures in his studio, while Banting himself painted one or two. Evelyn Waugh wrote a preface to the catalogue, entitled 'Approach to Hat'. Bruno Hat was supposed to be an avant-garde artist, tragically crippled and of German extraction. Tom Mitford impersonated him at the opening party, sitting in a wheelchair and sporting a black wig and moustache. He was supposed to know no English.

It worked; not only did their friends come, but also the art critics. Lytton Strachey bought a picture to please Diana, and she stuck a red spot on it. He, of course, was aware of what was going on, but it appears that one or two other pictures were sold to people not in on the secret, and Bryan thought the joke might get out of control. He told the story to the press, so that by the next day everyone knew it was a hoax.

It made the papers in a big way; almost all comment was friendly, although one review was rather sour and pompous. Perhaps Bryan had been wise to bring the deception to an end when he did; journalists, like the rest of us, dislike being made fools of. Diana thinks that for Brian Howard the joke was not altogether a joke, and that he was inwardly disappointed not to have been discovered as an unknown master.

Walter Guinness then enabled Bryan to choose and buy a country house of his own; Biddesden House, near Andover, a couple of hundred yards over the border into Wiltshire. There was a farm amounting to two hundred acres and, when the tenant agreed to leave, Pam was engaged to run it. Biddesden is one of the more attractive results of Marlborough's victories during the reign of Queen Anne. The great commander-in-chief was rewarded with the grandiose pile of Blenheim Palace, but his subordinates also received recognition. Major-General John Richmond Webb was one of them. He built Biddesden, apparently to his own design, of brick ornamented with what were originally triumphal trophies in stone. These have weathered, however, into a state where this fact is scarcely apparent. He added a castellated tower for a bell he brought back from the siege of the city of Lille. In the hall, Webb hung a huge picture by Wootton of himself on a horse with a battle in the background; horse and man are life-size, and very splendid he looks in his red uniform with brown full-bottomed wig. Though no 'stately home', the house is very lovely and Diana says, 'Three times I have had the great good fortune to live in a beautiful house; the first was Biddesden.' It was the first time, too, that she could decorate a house herself, which was something at which she was always very good; Buckingham Street had suffered rather from the fact that it was partly got ready during her honeymoon, without Diana's supervision, and at least one supplier had used his own initiative rather too freely. That very slump which was soon to act on Diana's slumbering political consciousness made fine furniture available quite cheaply. Diana lacked experience, but she had a sure eye; and most of her friends thought her efforts worthy of the house. Certainly the view in the Mitford family was that Biddesden was all that Swinbrook was not. David was one of the few people not to like it; he felt creepy there, only entering the house with reluctance and preferring to stay outside in the car. General Webb is indeed supposed to haunt the house when his equestrian picture is removed, but it was firmly in place at the time, so David's malaise remains unexplained.

John Betjeman used to come frequently to Biddesden; he was always to remain a friend of the Mitfords, though his opinion of Paris was the direct opposite of Nancy's. 'It's so ugly,' he used to say, 'and the food is so nasty.' The Parisian architectural style offended one who loved Gothic and Victorian much more than anything in between, and French cuisine repelled his insular palate. He was a great friend of Bryan and Diana, but at this time was rather keen on Pam — Miss Pam as he called her. The little poem he wrote her was probably not in the authorities' minds when they granted him the Poet Laureateship, but it is worth remembering since it incorporates the first known use of the phrase 'the Mitford girls'.

> The Mitford Girls, the Mitford Girls,
> I love them for their sins,
> The younger ones like *Cavalcade*,
> The old like Maskelyn's.
>
> Sophistication, blessed Dame,
> Sure they have heard thy call,
> Yes, even gentle Pamela,
> Most rural of them all.

(*Cavalcade* was a musical comedy by Noël Coward; Maskelyn was a conjuror who had his own hall for daily performances.) Pam was at that time running the farm at Biddesden; she made a reasonable go of it on the whole, though times were very bad and nearly all farms lost money. One mistake she made went the rounds of the Mitfords. She bid at a farm sale for what looked like a very fine cow; but when she got it back to Biddesden, as she put it, 'the brute was bagless'. Nancy used this in *Wigs on the Green*.

John Betjeman loved singing hymns. A very High Church Anglican, his religion was deep and sincere, but his nature compelled him to include some mockery in all his beliefs. He used to encourage hymn singing at dinner at Biddesden. However, this could not happen until May, the parlourmaid, had finished serving, for she disapproved.

May Amende had come to Bryan and Diana from the employment of his grandfather and his parents, as Turner had come from David and Sydney. Lady Evelyn, like Sydney, never had menservants but preferred parlourmaids; Bryan and May liked each other, so she went with him. May was older than her new employers, and felt that in certain respects, as in the matter of hymns, it was incumbent on her to keep them slightly in order. Few who visited Biddesden at that time fail to remember May's interventions, delivered respectfully but firmly in a rather quavering, ladylike voice, the voice of respectability. She played the role of straight man to the rather numerous comics. 'Oh, *sir*!' she would reproach them.

George Kennedy, a well-known architect of the time and an older friend of Bryan's, was engaged to build a small domed gazebo in flint and brick, with a swimming pool below. He was funny, erudite and charming. The artist Henry Lamb also used to come to Biddesden; his wife was a friend of Nancy's. Lytton Strachey's niece Julia, a young writer, was another friend; her husband was Stephen Tomlin, the sculptor, who made for the garden at Biddesden a large female statue in lead. Diana considers Stephen Tomlin as the best talker of the Bloomsbury school.

Another talker and mimic was the film producer John Sutro, chubby and ebullient. He has always remained the same. Jonathan was at a dance once; a waltz was playing, and he was thinking of nothing much, when he felt a hand on his shoulder and heard a heavy Central European voice. 'In Wienna, in ze olt days, ve really knew how to voltz.' Steeling himself to a bout of tedious foreign reminiscence, Jonathan turned round and, of course, it was John, eyes shining, mouth wide open and tongue slightly protruding in his characteristic motionless laugh.

Robert Byron, another friend, became an expert on Byzantine art. His name made the Greeks love him, for they always assumed that he was a descendant of the poet. Ash-blond and rather fierce, he used to place a handkerchief on his head and do an imitation of Queen Victoria in her lace bonnet: he had her face. Diana once took him in her party to a debutante dance, where to her great embarrassment he insisted on being Queen Victoria throughout.

The Sitwells came to Biddesden, all three of them, writers now under a cloud because their style does not appeal to this generation, but literary lions of the time; they may come back into fashion if some television producer makes a series out of Osbert's four-volume autobiography. The critic and historian Peter Quennell was there. He remembers Biddesden as rather '*comme il faut*'; perhaps this quality seemed surprising because the hosts were so young. Raymond Mortimer was there sometimes; he was to be one of the best critics of his generation, and became in due course, like Evelyn Waugh, an unofficial proofreader and literary adviser to Nancy. Harold Acton also went to Biddesden often. Tall and courtly, he had a slow manner of speaking rendered individual and all the more delightful by barely perceptible Italianate voice patterns. Diana particularly prized his readings of his own poems, whose subtle merits she found indescribably enhanced when they were declaimed in his special voice. Brian Howard came, of course. A London acquaintance who never actually came to Biddesden was Tom Driberg, whom Diana remembers as clever and good company but rather gloomy. High Church, very left-wing and indefatigably homosexual, he became a gossip columnist and used his talents to sabotage the reputation of the upper classes. Later he became a Labour politician. Among other visitors were the painters Augustus John and Adrian Daintrey; the photographer Cecil Beaton; and the artistic all-rounder Lord Berners, though Diana's real friendship with him belongs to a slightly later period. Some of these achieved more than others, but they were all clever people.

We have emphasized the fact that many of Bryan's and Diana's friends were good talkers; this perhaps irritates the reader, for even if their conversation was fun at the time, who can remember it now? It has to be mentioned all the same, because it was so important to Diana. She had achieved what at Swinbrook and Asthall she had dreamed about: a life with intelligent friends.

Misery was caused in early 1932 by the deaths of Lytton and Carrington, but Lytton was still his old self when he loyally visited Diana in bed at Buckingham Street, where in September 1931 she had just given birth to Desmond. Though he disliked babies, he did remember that they were supposed to be bald; yet Desmond had long black hair, and he remarked on the fact.

'Oh,' said the nurse, 'that will all come off.'

'Is it a wig?' he asked, with his special squeak.

Back at Biddesden, Diana found that Carrington had painted a *trompe l'oeil* in a blank window. It is still there; a maid in a green uniform peeling an apple, with a cat looking on. Today, the maid's uniform and cap look dated, almost like fancy dress. Soon afterwards Lytton fell ill, and he died in January of inoperable cancer. Carrington later shot herself; she could not live without him. All the efforts of her friends and of Ralph Partridge, her kind and clever husband, were useless. It was a spontaneous act, in effect, of *suttee* – the Hindu rite of widow burning. People in the West often do not understand this impulse; Carrington's first attempt, using her car exhaust, was frustrated by her husband. She recovered, and her second attempt succeeded. Unity, too, was to be officiously brought back to life after a serious attempt tying in not with *suttee* but with the equally non-Western concept of hara-kiri.

Bryan and Diana left Buckingham Street and bought a house on the river in Chelsea, 96 Cheyne Walk; it was part of Lindsey House, where Bertie had lived in the 1870s. Augustus John and John Banting both painted Diana's portrait. The Guinnesses gave a great ball in Cheyne Walk in June 1932, which many people remember because it was evidently a very good party. Diana says:

We invited everyone we knew, young and old, poor and rich, clever and silly. It was a warm night and the garden looked twice its real size with the trees lit from beneath. A few things about this party dwell in my memory: myself managing to propel Augustus John, rather the worse for wear, out of the house into a taxi; Winston Churchill inveighing against a large picture by Stanley Spencer of Cookham war memorial which hung on the staircase, and Eddie Marsh defending it against his onslaught. I wore a pale grey dress of chiffon and tulle, and all the diamonds I could lay my hands on. We danced until day broke, a pink and orange sunrise which gilded the river.

Nine months later, Diana petitioned for divorce. She had fallen for Sir Oswald Mosley, who had just founded the British Union of Fascists. She fell simultaneously for his ideas and for his person. It was the passion of Juliet and at the same time it was the conversion of St Paul; emotion and conviction were inextricable.

Mosley was a married man with children; Diana had no thought of breaking up his home. But she herself must be free of ties, to love him as she could but above all to serve him, to serve his cause of Fascism which, he convinced her, was the only way to save the country. That the country needed saving was not for her in doubt. All the dances, all the fun in the world could not prevent it being borne in on her that there was a slump; the thought of the poverty and dereliction surrounding her small world was something which she could not ignore. Decca, coming up to adolescence, was feeling the same. In her way, so was Nancy, but she was an artist, unanalytical. No one in Parliament seemed to have the capacity or the will to do anything adequate. Labour had failed; it had run away from the very crisis of capitalism for which it had claimed to be preparing. The Tories, complacent with the enormous majority they had won in 1931, seemed to be doing just as little in their incarnation as the 'National Government' with the pathetic Labour renegade, Ramsay MacDonald, as Prime Minister in name but in fact as mascot. Even Diana's father-in-law, Walter Guinness, seemed to Diana to be sceptical about his own party's performance. Mosley, the most attractive man she had ever met, convinced her that he had a clear answer to all this; a matter on which, be it noted, many much more experienced people than Diana agreed. This was so not only at the time; it was still being said long afterwards, when Mosley had been already irrevocably discredited by his Fascism. R. H. S. Crossman, as ardent an anti-Fascist as anyone, was to write: 'Mosley was spurned by

Whitehall, Fleet Street, and every party leader at Westminster, simply and solely because he was right.' There can be two views on whether this was in fact true; we have learnt that Mosley's essentially Keynesian views on counter-cyclical action in the economy carry their own dangers in the real world. The point we are making is that it was not just the illusion of one infatuated girl.

Diana's friends at the time, of course, non-political almost to a man, did not follow the argument. The conspicuous thing to them was the word, Fascism; and let us note that non-political people often see the wood where those with a closer interest in political argument only see the trees. The image of Fascism, of course, was not what it has since become. The word is now a synonym for political evil; it is an insult, not a technical term. At the time it was not that, but Fascism was certainly regarded by most English people as unsavoury: a foreign import, simplistic, anti-democratic and extreme. It might have a certain crude glamour, but this very affair, the ensnaring (as it seemed) of Diana by Mosley, was surely a case in point, an example of a fundamental amorality, nihilism marching behind a brass band. From Diana's point of view, Mosley and his beliefs lent each other credibility; to most of her friends, on the contrary, each made the other more suspect. It seemed very much as if the fairy princess had been carried off by the demon king.

# 27

# Mosley and Fascism

With the advantage of over fifty years' hindsight, we can now see that it was not like this at all. What happened when Diana met Mosley was essentially a change within her. In a sense, she finally grew up – acquired, that is, the whole of an adult self of which she had before possessed only a part; although had she not found the right partner, the change might not have occurred. It is in the context of the whole family that this becomes clear, for Decca was to undergo a very similar experience at an earlier age, and Unity was to be subject to a sublimated version. Nancy as well was to play a modified but quite recognizable variation on the theme, in her case when already approaching middle age; but there are signs that if her husband, Peter Rodd, had been a more suitable object for this special kind of passion, he, too, could have awakened it. What was it?

It seems to have been a need to link personal love to a general cause; a feeling that love for a man is incomplete unless coupled with support of an ideal. Once the man and his cause are found, each promotes the other. Love for the man brings belief in his cause, belief in the cause makes the man attractive as a fighter for it. It is all profoundly *romantic*; not in the sentimental, vaguely approving sense that the word is applied to a hearts-and-flowers novel or an old-fashioned Hollywood film, but in a much darker sense. It is the kind of thing that the Romantic movement of the early nineteenth century was about; for the Romantics thought at least as much about politics as about love. Byron campaigned for Greece, Lamartine was prominent in the French Second Republic, even old Wordsworth thought it 'very Heaven' to be young at the start of the French Revolution when fine words were being spun and the guillotine sharpened. The supreme hero of the early

Romantic movement, we should remember, was Napoleon. It was in this kind of way that the Mitfords intertwined politics and love. At his worst, the Romantic does what Bertrand Russell once said he does, that is he liberates the tiger from its cage and admires the graceful leaps with which it devours the spectators. But at his best, he believes in love as a liberating force and liberation as the prelude to achievement.

It is in this light that we must see what happened to Diana. No demon king carried her off; she was simply suffused with love and idealism. She always saw certain dangers. She writes to Roy Harrod (undated, summer 1933):

Is it not preferable that in a movement such as this one, that might so easily become barbaric, there should be some civilized persons throwing in their weight with the inevitable boxers, old soldiers, suffragettes and oddments? . . . The Leader is so clever and in his way so civilized and English that it could not be comparable to the German movement. But if everyone of sensibility, charm and intelligence shuns him, there is definitely a danger that he will come to regard these virtues as vicious and the possessors of them as enemies.

As to Mosley, he fell for Diana as heavily as she for him; but behind the façade of single-mindedness and ruthless determination, Mosley was a complex and sensitive man. He remained deeply attached to his wife Cynthia. Fate may be thought to have intervened here: she contracted appendicitis, peritonitis set in, and she died in her husband's arms. He had been constantly at her bedside. Antibiotics would have saved her, but they were not then available. Cynthia's death occurred in May 1933. Those who wanted to think so said that she died of a broken heart, but in fact it seems to have been blind chance. Nicholas Mosley shows in his book about his father, *The Rules of the Game*, that Cynthia was worried about Diana, but the marriage had a record of weathering Mosley's infidelities. Mosley and Cynthia had the difficult, up-and-down relationship that many couples have who are fond of each other even though not altogether compatible; the evidence is that this muddled and imperfect marriage would have continued. In a sense, it did continue. For a would-be dictator, let alone a demon king, Mosley showed unexpected delicacy; that, and an indecisiveness, a shrinking from change, which in the political field was exactly the sort of thing he denounced. His programmes, that is, usually laid emphasis on action, decision, the fearless march into the future. He did not carry off Diana; to be precise, he did not move her into his house at Denham. He kept that establishment going for his children, and himself spent much time there, not only for their sakes but because he was having an affair with their aunt Baba. Lady Alexandra Metcalfe, wife of the Prince of Wales's equerry 'Fruity' Metcalfe, seems to have rationalized this as a way of keeping Mosley away from 'the Horror', as she and her sister Lady Ravensdale called Diana. Lady Ravensdale even told Fruity that for Cynthia's sake he had to allow his wife to carry on with Mosley. (Jan Dalley, *Diana Mosley*, p. 144.) The plan failed. Diana, of course, knew of Mosley's double life, and it says something for her cool confidence that she did sometimes go to Denham, even stay for the weekend.

When Mosley did marry Diana, in 1936, the fact was kept secret for two further years, partly perhaps so that he could continue to enjoy Lady Alexandra's favours: but also for another special reason, which we shall come to. Even when the marriage was finally made public in 1938, Mosley still did not end the separate establishment for the children of his first marriage, though how far his double love-life can have continued is doubtful. In any case none of this had any effect on Diana's attachment to Mosley following her simultaneous love and conversion. She had found a man, and a cause, that satisfied entirely the new faculty that showed itself in her, and the result was a completely happy marriage. The glow of that attachment was to keep the two of them contented through struggle, rejection, prison, and long years of frustration and vilification. In order to understand how this could have been, we need to try to picture to ourselves both Mosley and Fascism, not as they appear today, but as they appeared to her in 1933.

Mosley was, by any standards, a remarkable man. His detractors have agreed on this point with his admirers. It is attested by his achievements before he became a Fascist; it is confirmed by the hatred which he still excited long after he had ceased to be of any danger to anyone. He was hated to a degree that could only mean that in some sense he was still feared. In the last few years of his life this feeling seemed to be abating, but it flared up at his death, at the age of eighty-four, in a blaze of press virulence. He

remained in a strange way a credible figure long after he had
visibly ceased to be an effective one.

Among all the Fascist leaders in the countries of Europe
between the wars, not excluding Hitler and Mussolini themselves,
Mosley was by a long way the one with the most impressive
political career behind him from his pre-Fascist days. He was also
unusual among them in that his origins were within the governing
class. To be precise, his family was of the Staffordshire landed
gentry, Tory squires not unlike the Mitfords, except that they
lacked the diplomatic, cosmopolitan aspect. They were richer than
most such families because part of Manchester was built on land
they possessed. Mosley fought in the First World War with the
16th Lancers. He left his regiment temporarily to act as an
observer with the Royal Flying Corps; after several flights behind
enemy lines, he returned home to train as a pilot. His machine
crashed; he broke his leg badly. Before his wound had properly
healed, he was sent back to the front with his own regiment, and
in the trenches the injured leg became septic. Surgery saved the
leg, but left it several inches shorter than the other and the foot
deformed. He was thereafter always slightly lame, which did not
prevent him representing his country at fencing several times in
the 1930s. He had been school fencing champion at Winchester.

During the latter half of the First World War he worked for a
time at the Ministry of Munitions and at the Foreign Office; he
began reading and thinking, and he discovered a political voca-
tion. His first concern, which never left him, was a passionate
determination that nothing like the First World War should ever
happen again; he identified with the young men, sent to their
deaths by their elders, whose survivors were to build a new world.
Mosley entered the House of Commons in 1918 as member for
Harrow; at twenty-two he was the youngest member. Speaking
and debating did not at first come easily, but he was a quick
learner. In May 1920 he married Lady Cynthia Curzon, daughter
of the Foreign Secretary. Much has been made of the idea that this
marriage gave him an entry into the centre of the Conservative
establishment, and had he been an ambitious backbencher of the
normal type, it might indeed have helped. As it was, it had not
the least effect, for he was moving away from, not towards, the
Conservative leadership; and Cynthia was to follow him loyally.

He in fact broke with his party six months after his marriage, over the question of Ireland. Lloyd George's coalition government, which the Conservatives supported, was facing the Sinn Fein rebellion that was to lead to Irish independence two years later. Faced with a determined guerrilla campaign, it was practising torture and indiscriminate reprisals against civilians. Mosley denounced this strongly and crossed the floor of the House. At the same time, he was also speaking out against the massacre of 379 unarmed Indians at Amritsar in the previous year by British troops.

Having broken with the Conservatives in the Commons, Mosley continued sitting as an Independent. Enough Conservative voters supported him to ensure his re-election in 1922. For two years after that he allied himself loosely with the Liberals. Had he lived in Queen Victoria's reign, he would, no doubt, have found a permanent home with them; but liberalism was no longer the radical alternative, and it was the Labour Party which he joined in April 1924.

The first seat he fought as a Labour candidate was Ladywood in Birmingham. Birmingham was at the time a Conservative city controlled by the caucus which Joseph Chamberlain had set up and against which Thomas Bowles used to inveigh. The Conservative member for Ladywood was Joseph Chamberlain's son, Neville. Mosley did not win, but achieved a swing in his favour against a strong national swing to the Conservatives. During the next two years, outside Parliament, Mosley studied economics and worked out the first of his systematic programmes to solve the national economic problem, the so-called Birmingham Proposals in March 1925. These were produced with the aid of others, in particular John Strachey; but they were based on an insight of Mosley's own, expressed during a tour of the Liverpool slums in 1924. 'This is damnable,' he told the journalist who took him round. 'The rehousing of the working classes ought in itself to find work for the whole of the unemployed for the next ten years.' (Robert Skidelsky, *Oswald Mosley*.) Mosley was one of the first to see the willing hands of the unemployed as a wasted national resource. This insight of course occurred to others as well; it was to become part of a new 'Keynesian' orthodoxy, Maynard Keynes's articles having provided the academic basis for it. What Mosley did, with Strachey, was to introduce this thinking into Labour Party counsels and work out some of its policy implications. After the war it was quietly to achieve the status of orthodoxy. By that time, the detestation of Mosley on other grounds made it difficult for anyone in active politics to admit his part in pioneering it, though historians commonly make it clear enough.

Mosley re-entered Parliament in January 1927 as member for Smethwick, after a spectacularly virulent by-election campaign, in which the Conservative newspapers denounced him as a rich playboy socialist. Mosley was pleasure-loving, but he worked hard as well. The press bias was so blatant that the voters reacted against it, and he won easily. This experience was perhaps to lead him to underestimate the effect of the much more sustained press and media hostility against him in later years.

His abrasive style in the campaign earned him disapproval in political circles; especially, of course, among Conservatives. His parliamentary performances, too, shone with exactly the kind of brilliance that causes the most lasting resentment among the dull. 'Partly it was his habit of subjecting loose arguments to relentless cross-examination in the manner of a prosecuting counsel. Partly it was his facility for the clever, but cutting, phrase.' (Skidelsky, *Oswald Mosley*.) None of this hindered his political advancement at the time, and had he remained within the democratic system, it would have been forgiven, as was Disraeli's dandified sarcasm. In Mosley's case, though, it meant that later on many a mediocrity had the opportunity to repay, with complete impunity, a personal humiliation in debate.

The 1929 General Election returned Labour as the largest party, with the Liberals holding the balance of power between them and the Conservatives. Mosley was returned for Smethwick, and his wife Cynthia for Stoke-on-Trent. Ramsay MacDonald, the Labour leader, became Prime Minister for the second time. He had campaigned on the issue of unemployment, and he now appointed Mosley Chancellor of the Duchy of Lancaster with special responsibilities in this area, deputed to assist J. H. Thomas, the Lord Privy Seal and in effect Minister of Unemployment.

The government was torn between a desire for change and a hankering after respectability. In normal times it would have rubbed along all right. The trouble was that the times were not normal, for the year was 1929 and the Great Depression struck. To be precise, it began to strike; for depressions do not come on all at once. Wall Street crashed in 1929, and this started a process under which economies all over the world deteriorated year by year, steadily and rapidly. The deterioration became serious in 1930. Mosley advocated various schemes such as early pensions and an emergency road building programme. All foundered on departmental or civil service objections. Thomas was no help; the worry of the situation drove him to drink, not action. Finally, Mosley lost patience. He appealed over Thomas's head to the cabinet, and prepared a document, the Mosley Memorandum, which was submitted in February 1930. It was rejected; MacDonald, as Skidelsky puts it, 'wanted the appearance of activity. Mosley wanted the reality.' Mosley wanted to reorganize the government so that it contained what amounted to a war cabinet, for the emergency was to him the equivalent of being at war. He proposed what is now known as a 'think tank' of experts; there was to be immediate relief for unemployment coupled with a scientifically conceived plan by the authorities to modernize industry.

But the government still adhered to the old economic orthodoxies: free trade, a balanced budget and sound money (what we now call Thatcherism). The Chancellor of the Exchequer, Philip Snowden, was certain that the answer to depression was further retrenchment. The Mosley memorandum was not a detailed programme; it was a framework of ideas within which the requisite research, and subsequent action, could be undertaken. But its whole thrust was towards state responsibility, state action, *dirigisme*. It would have been accepted by any Labour government after 1945, but the Labour Party of 1931 lacked the courage of its convictions. It had a utopian desire for a new and fairer world, but it accepted the doctrines of the existing world as to what was practicable.

Mosley resigned from the government. His resignation speech, on 28 May 1930, was memorable: brilliantly conceived and delivered, and in total contrast to the fumbling effort of the Prime Minister which had preceded it. Congratulations poured in from all quarters. He ought of course to have waited, consolidated, built on his success, but he evidently felt there was no time. He took the fight to the grass roots of the Labour Party; but getting the Labour Party to change its policy is a task for a period

not of months, but of decades. He received an ovation at the Party
Conference for his sentiments, but no action on his proposals. He
tried to drum up support where he could: a number of younger
Conservatives as well as Labour members were expressing interest. But early in 1931 he launched his New Party, a venture many
of whose features remind one of the modern SDP. This would
probably not have got far off the ground anyway, but Mosley was
incapacitated by pneumonia and pleurisy during the whole of
March, exactly the time when the launch was going forward.
The Labour Party expelled him, not surprisingly, on 10 March.
Cynthia did her best to stand in for him, addressing meetings
which were systematically disrupted. At the General Election in
October 1931 no New Party candidate was returned. Ramsay
MacDonald had shortly before formed a national government in
coalition with the Conservatives; the Labour Party disowned him,
but he remained as Prime Minister. His National Government,
essentially based on the Conservative Party with himself and a few
other National Labour members, reduced Labour to a rump. The
only substantial thing the new government did was to go off the
gold standard, thus permitting the pound to float downwards. This
initiated a painfully slow climb out of the depression. Many people
saw the danger of a revolution; Mosley now saw the only hope in
it. In October 1932 he founded the British Union of Fascists.
Cynthia, after a brief hesitation, accepted the task of leading the
women's section; but as we have seen, she died in May 1933.

Mosley's adoption of Fascism was not purely reasoned and
logical. He was attracted by it temperamentally, just as he was
repelled by the slow, obstructive processes of democratic politics.
Perceptive outsiders had seen this in him for some time. In *Point
Counter Point* Aldous Huxley has a Fascist leader who is clearly
based on Mosley, as is indicated by his name, Everard Webley; yet
this book was published in 1929, three years before the founding
of the British Union of Fascists. Mosley believed in leadership
rather than committees. He believed in discipline; he believed in
renewal through the war generation; he believed that the running
of society was best looked at as a technical problem rather than as
a moral one; he was an elitist, but believed in an elite chosen by
function rather than class. He could never have moved towards
Communism – as his friend Strachey did with very similar ideas –

partly because he was extremely nationalistic and a believer in military strength, but mainly because he did not think the capitalist system was inherently evil, only that it was working badly.

Within the democratic game Mosley had everything to play for. He chose to give it all up, on the grounds that the game itself, the democratic system, seemed to him to offer no hope. Old interests remained entrenched, old power structures must always impose their own logic. His position on this bore a certain relationship to that now held by Tony Benn; at the very end of his life, Mosley expressed a wish to meet Benn, with whose parents he had been friendly in the Labour Party. In his old age he certainly had a good many private meetings with people in public affairs, but this was one that, for whatever reason, never took place. However, the interest the former Fascist showed in the leader of the left was not one of mere curiosity. There was a fellow feeling, at least on Mosley's side. Mosley remained in many ways a man of the left; he was a believer in state action, an egalitarian in the sense that he was utterly opposed to class distinction; he wanted a radical change in the system. It is true that during the last forty years of Mosley's life, when the salient point about him was to be the extent to which he was hated, right across the spectrum, it was the left who hated him most. Nevertheless, the right had hated him first, essentially as a traitor to his class. He used sometimes to quote Mirabeau as saying that aristocrats hated any friend of the people, but pursued with especial bitterness any aristocrat who was a friend of the people.

It was later to become apparent that both Diana, and Mosley himself, had put themselves outside the respectable politics that attract most respectable people. In particular, the very adoption of the name Fascism and of Fascist methods meant that there was an inevitable confrontation with the Jews, a community which up to the founding of the British Union of Fascists, and even for some time afterwards, Mosley seems never to have mentioned. The rival Imperial Fascist League of Arnold Leese used to sneer at Mosley's party for being 'kosher Fascists', and the *Jewish Chronicle* even welcomed the formation of the British Union of Fascists as being a Fascist party that was not anti-semitic. The honeymoon was short-lived enough, but during it there was a sharp distinction between

Mosley's Fascism and Hitler's Nazism. Nazism was fundamentally and doctrinally anti-semitic; Mosley was not. The Nazis themselves saw this distinction; Julius Streicher's anti-semitic fortnightly *Der Stürmer* even complained that Mosley was the tool of the Jews. (Quoted in David Pryce-Jones's, *Unity Mitford*.) However, on other matters the BUF had considerable fellow feeling for the Nazis because their political opponents were the same as Mosley's: Communism because of its destructiveness and its subservience to a foreign power, democracy because of its perceived incapacity. Hitler had come to power on a rather similar revolutionary programme to that advocated by Mosley: recovery from the slump through isolation from the world financial system, a managed economy, projects of public works. Mosley's attitude to the Nazis at this time was thus one of curiosity and friendly interest, tempered with criticism on some issues, including the racial theory. Mosley always held that a policy of racial purity was inconsistent with maintaining the British Empire. But on balance, his feelings towards Hitler were positive, and this needs to be borne in mind when we consider what next happened to Diana; as also to Unity. For in June 1933, without her parents at first knowing, Unity joined the British Union of Fascists and from then on was very close to Diana. The freedom and fun of Eaton Square, when one was eighteen, was a decisive counter-attraction to the restrictions of home; and there was the excitement of a cause.

The trouble was that the Fascist cause was very explicitly a revolutionary one; neither Unity nor Diana was in this period ever to appreciate the extent to which the amenities of their country, which they took entirely for granted, depended on a solid social structure manned by respectable people who might have seemed, or even been, dull. Long before the war enabled Fascism to be stigmatized as unpatriotic, it was hated and feared by exactly these respectable people, and especially at the very highest level by members of the government and senior civil servants. Robert Skidelsky, Mosley's biographer, found in his researches that under the National Government of Ramsay MacDonald, whose assumptions were very definitely right-wing: 'In all the Cabinet and Home Office papers dealing with Fascist activities there is hardly a remark to be found favourable to Mosley and his movement; rather a great solicitude for the rights and sensibilities of those he was attacking.' In the academic part of the Establishment, especially Oxford and Cambridge, there was more sympathy for Communism than for Fascism. Among the general public anti-Fascism was not considered as obligatory as it became during and after the war; educated people, though, feared Fascism deeply. It seemed to glorify, if not violence as such, then personal toughness, marching in step behind banners, and idealistic obedience. It seemed to be against thought, against argument; the thinkers and arguers therefore hated it.

A factor in this attitude was Mosley's meeting at Olympia on 1 June 1934, and the organized Communist attempt to stop it happening. The meeting took place during the one and only time that Mosley had the benefit of serious press support – that of the Rothermere papers, the *Daily Mail* and the *Evening News*. It was partly this backing that had the effect of arousing curiosity in all sorts of circles, including Establishment ones; quite a large number of MPs and similar figures came out of interest.

Exactly what happened at Olympia is difficult to establish. Often the same event, noted by different eye witnesses, is given different interpretations. What is certain is that the interrupters were carefully organized by the Communist Party for at least three weeks beforehand. Four columns of people marched on the hall, and some five hundred people infiltrated inside it. They sat together in different groups, each of which in turn shouted inter-ruptions. Stewards would then eject one group, upon which the next one would start shouting and be ejected in its turn. The stewards certainly beat many people unnecessarily badly; but plenty of Fascists were hurt as well. Years later, in the 1970s, Jonathan made friends with a man, old by that time and solidly Conservative, who worked for a private organization keeping an eye on some of the extreme left groups that masterminded strikes and disruptions. One day this man needed to get into a private meeting organized by a Trotskyite group. Having no ticket, he went up to the people at the door, rolled up his trouser leg and showed an old wound on his calf. 'I haven't got a ticket,' he told them, 'but I got this at Olympia.' He was let in at once. 'I did get it at Olympia,' he told Jonathan with a chuckle, 'but I didn't tell them what side I got it on.' Many of the interrupters were

armed. Philip Toynbee and Esmond Romilly were runaway public schoolboys, Communist sympathizers, whose experiences at
Olympia properly belong to a later chapter. They came along to
help break up the meeting and bought knuckledusters especially
for the purpose.

The important thing about Olympia, though, is not exactly
what happened or whose fault it was, but the effect of the publicity
battle afterwards. There is no doubt that the anti-Fascists got the
best of it. Nearly all the media were already anti-Fascist, so it was
the anti-Mosley eye witnesses whose accounts were selected and
highlighted. The BBC played a trick clearly designed to sink him;
he was invited to broadcast his account of events, but not told that
an opponent was to speak afterwards. When he wished to answer
certain points made by the opponent, he was refused, and the BBC
never allowed him to appear again until 1968.

The media boycotted Mosley and his ideas from that time on;
his opinions were rarely considered newsworthy, and his meetings
were only reported for the violence at them. Rothermere withdrew his support, for another effect of Olympia was to hasten the
confrontation between Mosley and the Jews. According to Mosley,
Jewish advertisers told Lord Rothermere that they would remove
their custom if he continued to support Fascism. In addition, the
Communist Party had used fear of Fascism to persuade many
Jews to come and help smash up the Olympia meeting, so there
was a noticeably large number of Jews among the interrupters. On
the other side, many real anti-semites joined Mosley, who made
no attempt to exclude them. They included William Joyce ('Lord
Haw-Haw'), the Irish-American hanged in 1945 for his wartime
broadcasts to Britain from Berlin. Mosley expelled him in 1937,
after which he formed a more extreme movement, the National
Socialist League; but while he was in the British Union of Fascists
he used his undoubted ability to make it more anti-Jewish.

Mosley himself later attributed his 'quarrel with the Jews', as he
always called it, to his wish to avoid another war with Germany
and their desire for Britain to engage in one on behalf of their co-
religionists. The quarrel actually started before this had become a
factor. His friendly interest in Nazism excited Jewish suspicion,
and Jews were numerous not only in the Communist Party but in
the international banking community, which Mosley blamed for

keeping Britain attached to the world trading system and sub-jecting its workers to sweated competition. By May 1935, Mosley had been offensive enough about the Jews for Julius Streicher to change his attitude; Streicher sent a telegram of congratulations following a speech at Leicester, to which Mosley replied: 'The power of Jewish corruption must be destroyed in all countries before peace and justice can be successfully achieved in Europe.'

Pryce-Jones cites this telegram as a sign of generalized anti-semitism. It certainly shows that Mosley at that time was hostile to the Jews; but as to whether he was anti-semitic, there was in the early seventies a controversy between him and certain com-mentators. It generated more heat than light because on each side the expression 'anti-semitic' was used in a different sense, so that each in its own terms was right. Mosley's critics used 'anti-semitic' to mean 'anti-Jewish', as in modern usage it generally does. They found it easy to show that Mosley had attacked the Jews fre-quently and with venom. He himself had used the term 'anti-semitism' in this sense, and admitted to it, when he was questioned by Norman Birkett after his wartime arrest. Yet Mosley had a point. There was a type of anti-semitism to which he never subscribed, namely the view that the Jews were a morally inferior race, a kind of criminal tribe inherently worse than the rest of us. This was the view of Gobineau and other racialist writers includ-ing, with reservations, Houston Stewart Chamberlain; it was what Hitler believed. The Nuremberg laws banning marriage between Jew and Gentile were a product of it, as ultimately was the holocaust. Mosley never believed anything of this sort. Whatever the terms in which he attacked the Jews, his grounds were not racial but political. His record before, as well as after, his anti-Jewish period makes this quite clear. There was always a vital difference between him and Hitler. For Hitler a Jew, however well-intentioned, could never fully renounce his Jewishness; for Mosley he could do so. In the context, people naturally consider what was about to be done to the Jews by Hitler, the man with whom Mosley wanted peace and some of whose language about the Jews he was using. Mosley will probably never be forgiven for this association. However, it is only fair to draw attention to the distinction between the two.

# 28

# Diana's Other Life

Decca has said, and there is something in it, that the split between the older and the younger Mitfords was in some measure that between the twenties and the thirties, between aestheticism and political commitment; one might also say between Eliot and the early Auden, or even between the schoolboy magazines, Harold Acton's *Eton Candle* and Esmond Romilly's *Out of Bounds*. That there was a change in atmosphere between the two decades is generally acknowledged. Osbert Lancaster's *Drayneflete Revealed* epitomizes it by the change in his modern poet 'William Tipple', who in the twenties is writing about 'Dido on her lilo / *À sa proie attachée*', and in the thirties switches to 'Maxi my friend from the Mariahilferstrasse' and his fate at the hands of a Fascist tram conductor. Decca's idea was that down to and including Diana the Mitfords were of the twenties, essentially aesthetes; then from Unity downwards they were of the thirties, politically committed. It is fair enough that this should leave out the animal lovers Pam and Debo, but apart from this it is not neat; Unity was always a great lover of art, especially of the art that makes one dream: Bosch, Boecklin and Douanier Rousseau. Our main reservation concerns Diana, about whom it seems to be almost exactly half true. She was of course up to her neck in political commitment, so to that extent Decca is wrong; yet not only had she always been an aesthete, but during her time as a Fascist she never stopped being one. She never gave up the non-political side of her life, never stopped frequenting art galleries, concerts and the opera, never lost her preoccupation with the beautifying of houses. This puzzles those to whom the only noun that the adjective 'Fascist' can appropriately qualify is 'thug', but it is nevertheless the case. The fact that it was possible shows how very different the atmosphere was then from what it is now. As we have seen, it was not yet compulsory in polite circles to hate Fascism; Communists and their supporters were trying to make it so, and as the danger of war became more apparent there also emerged a quite separate anti-Fascist wave that was based on patriotism. However, the general view of Fascism in the early thirties was still only that it was foreign and not quite nice. The Fascists themselves had branches all over the place — Philip Toynbee was shocked to see three uniformed blackshirts in Hull — and there was a considerable throughput of members in all classes, together with a penumbra of sympathizers. The war had not yet taken place, and the Nazi persecution of the Jews had not yet grown to a holocaust, so it was natural that people should not yet be conditioned by these two events.

Diana was not socially boycotted in the thirties, then; to an extent she dropped out herself. While still at Eaton Square, she completely subordinated her movements to Mosley's visits, which often came at very short notice. She therefore almost stopped accepting dinner invitations, except from friends so intimate that they would understand her cancelling at the last minute in the event of Mosley turning up. Later, at Wootton, she of course dropped out still further, since she had moved 150 miles from London.

She kept most of her friends, however, including those who happened to be Jewish. People thought her, perhaps, a bit mad, and sometimes there were strains on her friendships. 'What a bully you are,' she wrote to Roy Harrod on 25 June 1936. 'I thought we had a divine day and not a hint of dread politics. As you know, I feel *very* strongly about these things so very likely it shines out of me willy nilly.' At the time of her divorce she received a good deal of friendly advice not to do it; Roy had been one of the most persistent of these advisers. But few of the people who expressed themselves in this way actually broke with her. We have mentioned the view that she was the fairy princess carried off by the demon king; it soon became apparent that insofar as this analogy was true it took rather the form of Pluto's abduction of Proserpine, for Diana lived much of her time in, as it were, the non-political uplands. She had no wish to obtrude her views; if attacked she would defend them, but in polite society anyone attacking another on politics puts himself in the wrong, and fellow guests who disliked Diana's views would normally have tended for this reason to keep their feelings to themselves. When she was challenged, she always had the skill to reply in such a way as to put herself in the right, at least for the occasion and in the context of required behaviour. Unity was another matter completely; she was neither so reticent nor so imperturbable. She enjoyed shocking people, and went through life rather as a rogue neutron disturbs the balance of one atom after another, leaving a trail of people with outraged susceptibilities.

Lady Cunard remained a great friend of Diana's, squeezing happily into the small dining room at Eaton Square, which could accommodate just six people on red velvet banquettes. 'Diana's dining room is very nice, once you get in', she used to say, hinting at regret that Diana no longer had the space to invite people in what she considered suitable numbers. Nevertheless she said to Chips Channon, future Conservative MP and diarist: 'Better be nice to Diana, after I've gone who will you have but her?' Most of the other friends she had known before her divorce also went on seeing her. Henry Yorke was quite firm: 'You are not going to go out of our lives,' he said, and indeed she did not, for he and his wife were to stay several times with her at Wootton Lodge and after the war at Crowood. John Sutro also kept in touch. He gave a Roman fancy dress party in a private room at the Savoy, at which Diana came as Poppaea, and John himself was a marvellous Nero, like a great naughty baby in a toga. Looking at the photographs, it is true that one cannot believe this Nero capable of hurting a fly. (But perhaps someone who knew him would not have believed it of Nero himself? A friend of Nero might well have dismissed Suetonius as easily as Unity dismissed those who wrote against Hitler, or Decca the reports of the Moscow Trials. After all, Suetonius and the other contemporary historians all hated the Roman Empire of the populace and wanted the Republic of the upper classes.)

Another person whom Diana saw often at this period was Tom's old friend Nigel Birch. He was to become a prominent Conservative politician, resigning from Harold Macmillan's government in 1959 together with Enoch Powell and Peter Thorneycroft in protest against the abandonment of financial orthodoxy. He used sometimes to go to the cinema with Diana; some of the Hollywood love scenes would embarrass him and he would hide his eyes or 'cover up', leaving it to Diana to tell him when he could look again. He was funny and rather a tease; Diana wrote of him to Jonathan on 7 January 1971: 'I believe Nigel calls himself Lord Rhyl pronounced RILE, a perfect name for him.'

John Betjeman also remained a close friend of both Diana and Nancy; in fact they played a part in bringing about his marriage. He fell in love with Penelope Chetwode, daughter of Field Marshal Lord Chetwode who had been Commander-in-Chief in India. She was a formidably unconventional debutante who was less interested in young men than in Indian art, in which she has since become a renowned expert. Her mother had advised her to slap the face of anyone who made a pass at her, and now and then she followed this precept to the letter; people became rather frightened of her. She did not slap John, but was all the same a little uncertain in her response to him and went away to stay with an uncle in the South of France. It was Nancy and Diana who encouraged John not to give up, who made him chase after her, woo her and eventually win her. John and Penelope were to be friends for life to all the Mitfords, seeing a great deal of Diana and Mosley when they were in Wiltshire after the war, within easy reach of Wantage, where the Betjemans lived.

Diana's greatest non-political friend at this period and later was Lord Berners. Older than Diana, he took on for her some of the attributes of a father and even more those of a teacher; on his side there seems no doubt that his affection had a romantic content, though his tastes did not lie in the direction of women. She herself says that knowing Berners was to her almost the equivalent of going to a university. Lord David Cecil said once that Berners was the best-read man he had ever met; and from Cecil this was a high compliment, for he was a famous academic whose lectures on English literature were celebrated at Oxford. Diana had already absorbed a certain amount of, as it were, higher education from Lytton Strachey; but she knew him for a shorter time than Berners and was with him far less. Berners and she loved each other and made each other laugh; but underneath the affection and amusement of their talk there was a solid undercurrent of information passing from him to her. Never has learning been such fun.

She had met Berners through Lady Cunard and they had quickly become firm friends; he went both to Biddesden and Cheyne Walk. He was one of the funniest people of his generation, as well as one of the most talented. He wrote, painted and composed all to professional standard. He had a beautiful Palladian house at Faringdon in Berkshire and a house overlooking the Roman Forum; he specialized in terse anecdotes, often hardly more than remarks, which he would accompany with a dry little cough to do duty for a laugh. He was bald and rotund and his wide mouth under a small moustache seemed always to be slightly smiling; perhaps it was. To Jonathan and Desmond he was 'The Man Who Sat on the Piano', because he once played them the Dead March in *Saul* and substituted for its last chord the satisfying chromatic crash produced by seating himself heavily on the keyboard. This was rather characteristic in that many of his jokes and teases were based on the intrusion into a conventional or structured world of a sudden burst of underlying chaos. His book *The Camel*, the funniest of his brief and delightful novels, contains a marvellous setpiece scene in the dining room of a tranquil country vicarage. The bishop has come to Sunday lunch, and the maid brings in a substantial dish with a domed silver lid. The vicar is proud of his skill at carving a joint, and lovingly sharpens his knife; his wife and the bishop look on. With the confident dexterity of a conjuror the vicar whips the lid from the dish, to find instead of his leg of mutton the rotting corpse of a small dog. It was rather in this spirit that Berners used to touch up photographs, often of royalty, so that their expressions became lascivious, vicious or vacant. The idea of chaos intruding on order is of course characteristic of the surrealists, and it comes as no surprise that Berners was a friend of Salvador Dali, in whose work it is a recurrent theme. When Dali came to London for the surrealist exhibition in 1936, Berners regaled him with a performance on the piano that was considerably more elaborate than merely sitting on it. He invited the artist to tea; a fine silver teaset had been laid out, there were thin cucumber sandwiches and conventional English guests. There was also a plate of chocolate eclairs. At a signal from Berners a footman opened the lid of the piano and carefully laid the chocolate eclairs on the keyboard. Berners sat on the piano stool and played a fugue so vigorous that he was soon covered in cream and chocolate. Without a word he rose, left the room, changed his clothes, and started pouring the tea in the usual way. The other guests were evidently bewildered; Dali himself was deeply impressed.

It was through Diana that Berners came to know all the Mitfords. Like John Betjeman, he had a particularly soft spot for Pam. Sometimes, entirely to annoy Diana, he would claim that Pam was his favourite. Once he expressed this preference, when somebody objected that Pam lacked the Mitford shriek. 'Not at all,' he returned: 'she has a tenor shriek.'

It must have been the greatest possible contrast to the 1933 Nazi congress at Nuremberg when, shortly after it, Diana went to stay with Lord Berners in Rome for a month. After the excitement it was a time of calm, of beauty – and of instruction. During this long period he imparted to her, almost without her knowing, great quantities of information, recommended books, and commented in his sharp original way on everything under the sun. The Forum was in effect Berners's private garden, for few other people went there. Berners's food was superb, except on one day when the chef's canaries escaped from their cages and sat twittering on the surrounding trees; that day he was too busy coaxing them back into their cages to be able to cook anything. In the mornings Berners would compose at the piano, while in the afternoons he would show Diana the sights of Rome, which he knew intimately. Diana found the Romans handsome, catty and frivolous; Mussolini was in power, but politics seems not to have been discussed with any acrimony, though not everyone was in favour of him.

In England Berners lived, as mentioned earlier, at Faringdon House, whose front gate is next to the church. Irritated at one time with the canon who had the living, Berners is supposed to have hung on this gate a notice saying, 'Fire the Canon'. He went in for notices quite a bit; there was one on the bottom half of the dining room door saying 'Dogs Not Allowed', and another in the porch, announcing in the most elaborate possible Victorian lettering 'Mangling Done Here'. Penelope Betjeman's white horse was sometimes led into the drawing room to stand among the eighteenth-century furniture, wearing special soft shoes for the benefit of the Aubusson carpet. There was a flock of astonishing pigeons flying about the grounds, white and pink and blue and yellow and green; the result not of any special knack with bird genetics, but of the regular application of dye. The coloured pigeons were the idea of Robert Heber-Percy, Berners's devoted friend who lived with him for years and in due course inherited the house. Berners was depressed and his friend thought it would cheer him up, which it did, and the rainbow-coloured flock still exists. Robert Heber-Percy was and is another friend of all the Mitfords; darkly good-looking in a rather Mephistophelean way, he was always known as the Mad Boy. He was for a short time married. Years after this union had broken up, Jonathan was told by a friend of his former wife: 'Poor thing, she was married to someone completely mad, in and out of asylums you know.' Such are the dangers of nicknames.

Berners entered also into the political side of Diana's life. With Robert Heber-Percy he went to the Olympia meeting; he had even composed a march for the British Union of Fascists which was played at that meeting, though one of the papers rather woundingly described it as a 'dreary little tune'. It was not that Berners was in any way Fascist; he once told Mosley: 'You'll never win because you've taken on both the Jews and the buggers.' His interest in the movement was ironical, humorous, arising partly from his friendship with Diana and partly from his streak of savage and almost nihilistic melancholy. Diana may in fact have been so fascinating for him simply because she was both exquisitely civilized and in thrall to a dark and raucous creed; if there was one thing he loved more consistently than anything else, it was incongruity. Nazism, too, he treated as a joke. He went once to Munich to spend some time with Diana and Unity. The leader of the Nazi girl students, who was a friend of theirs, was called Rotraut Sperk and Lord Berners thought her name rather funny. He composed in her honour a little rhyme in German, as follows:

> *Rotraut Sperk, du kleine Nette,*
> *Bleib' bei mir im Ruhebette.*
> *Du bist ein schönes Gotteswerk,*
> *Du allerliebste Rotraut Sperk.*

(Rotraut Sperk, you nice little thing, stay with me on the daybed. You are a lovely work of God, darling Rotraut Sperk.) The point of this is that the Nazi press, in its endless stories of lascivious Jews seducing poor and innocent Gentile girls, very often had them doing it on a *Ruhebett*, or daybed.

Another non-political friend of Diana's from this time onwards was the art collector Edward James. He had inherited a fortune and a good eye, and his collection of the work of the surrealists, before they were fashionable, is one of the world's finest; it is particularly strong on Dali, who was a friend of his, and on Magritte. James married the Viennese dancer Tilly Losch, with whom Tom was in love for some time; she cuckolded and exploited her adoring husband until his love turned to bitterness and he petitioned for divorce. The case was marred, but also made into the talk of London, by her extravagant allegations from the witness box. The court believed Edward. Before this happened, Edward brought over to London the Paris-based White Russian artist Pavel Tchelitchew to design the sets and costumes for a ballet, *Errante*, in which Tilly Losch danced. Tchelitchew is best known in England for his portraits of Edith Sitwell, who was very fond of him; he also painted Diana, Jonathan and Desmond in 1934. He found the children hard to cope with during the sittings, for children were creatures to whom he was not accustomed, and his rudimentary English was a hindrance. 'Boys! Boys! Be good!' he used to beg in his Franco-Russian accent. The futile plea became a family catchphrase. The picture is a lovely one and a good likeness of the boys, though Diana has been made rather too gaunt and childlike. 'A Russian peasant,' Mosley used to complain. Edward also brought into Diana's life Kurt Weill, whose *Threepenny Opera* Diana had heard, and admired, in Berlin; his wife, the singer Lotte Lenya, used to come too. He was Jewish, and they had fled from Germany, yet Diana invited them to dinner, and they consented quite happily to come.

Another of Diana's non-political friends of the thirties was the singer Olga Lynn. 'You can only kiss half of me,' she used to say to Diana; for she was half Jewish. Once, in 1938 at the time of the *Anschluss*, she was travelling in a train with a friend, and they were talking of the Nazi regime. In the same carriage were two small fair-haired boys with their nanny; suddenly the elder of the two broke into her conversation.

'My Mummy thinks Hitler's right,' he said.

'Then,' answered Olga Lynn, 'I think I know who your Mummy is.'

She did, of course; it was Diana, and the boy on the train was Jonathan.

# 29

# Pam and Tom: I

Pam gave up managing Bryan Guinness's farm at Biddesden during 1934; by 22 March 1935, in her page in Diana's *All About Everybody* (see p. 374), she writes under 'occupation': 'I have none.' Her favourite pastime at this time is travelling, and she believes in the equality of the sexes. There are some quirks, even apparent inconsistencies, in her entry: she thinks love is more important than money, yet puts desire of possessions as her besetting sin. Her hero in real life is Romeo (real life? we ask – but we get the point) yet her heroine is 'Ornty', her Aunt Iris, a saintly spinster whose entire life was given up to the Officers' Families' Fund for which she worked as secretary.

Pam visited Unity in Munich in June 1935, then returned for a longer time in September and October for the *Oktoberfest*. On the second visit Unity introduced her to Hitler. She found him, she told us, 'very ordinary, like an old farmer in his khaki suit'. She was in the Osteria Bavaria with Unity and a Dutch couple. They had lunch, and in due course the waitress told them that Hitler was arriving. 'Get over to the door for a sight of him,' said Unity. Pam complied, joining a crowd of saluting admirers. Hitler passed through into the garden with his party, and as he went by looked straight into her eyes of startling blue; she says it was obvious that he noticed her. In due course, an adjutant came over and asked if Pam was Unity's sister, then invited them both to lunch with Hitler. It was their second lunch that day. He seated them on either side of him, and asked Pam what she had been doing. When she told him she had driven from the Carpathians he said it was dangerous for a young woman to motor alone on the continent. The encounter was entirely pleasant, entirely friendly, entirely ordinary.

Decca joined her sisters a few days later and she enjoyed herself with Pam, Unity and her boyfriend, Erik; Pam testifies that politics was never mentioned, and there was no further meeting with Hitler.

Rather more than a year after this, on 29 December 1936, Pam married a very remarkable man: Derek Jackson. David is supposed to have referred to his sons-in-law as 'The man Mosley, the boy Romilly, and the bore Rodd'. The remark has the air of being apocryphal and it is in any case incomplete, for it omits Derek, who married Pam a few months before Esmond married Decca. Debo was rather keen on Derek; she is said to have fainted when she heard of his engagement to Pam.

By profession he was a physicist and an outstandingly good one; Professor Lindemann had spotted him as a young man and brought him to Oxford, where he was in due course to become Professor of Spectroscopy. 'He bought me like you might buy a promising yearling,' Derek used to say. The reference to blood-stock was in character; Derek was an expert amateur jockey who sometimes rode in the Grand National. Decca, in *Hons and Rebels*, omits Derek's science and simply says that Pam married a jockey; this is funny as an 'in-joke', but must as such be lost on those of her readers who do not know the facts. It is like describing Ingres as a famous violinist. Science was Derek's passion as well as his profession; alone or with collaborators he produced fifty-seven learned papers between 1928 and 1981. His first success as a young man was in using spectroscopic methods to determine the magnetic moment of the element caesium, approximately at first and then more precisely; he then moved on to other elements. His long career was mainly devoted to developing methods of interpreting the 'hyperfine structures' in spectra which can give information about atoms. For the layman to evaluate his work is impossible, but it is certain that the professionals respected it. Besides his professorship, he became a Fellow of the Royal Society and later an officer of the Legion of Honour in France; and the biographical memoir written for the Royal Society by his main pre-war collaborator, Dr H. G. Kuhn, shows what he did, though in terms that we have largely to take on trust. Derek's science always came first with him. At important moments in his research he would sacrifice his whole social life to it; race meetings and dinner parties would be abandoned, sometimes without notice.

Derek, like Lindemann, was extremely rich. In the latter thirties he owned two racehorses which he called Niton and Xenon, after two rather recondite elements. Jonathan once remarked to him: 'Funny that you should have called your horses after two inert gases.' To this he replied reproachfully, giving his characteristic little grunt like a soft whinny: 'They are *noble* gases.' (The gases are indeed sometimes called noble, sometimes inert – for all the world like backwoods peers.)

Derek had an identical twin, Vivian. Eugenia's horse, in *Wigs on the Green*, was called Vivian Jackson after him. The twins were the sons of Sir Charles Jackson, a Welshman who had been one of the founders of the *News of the World*; shares in it constituted a large part of the twins' fortune. They were educated at Rugby, an establishment always referred to by Derek as 'Bugry'. Vivian, too, was a physicist and a spectroscopist, though in his case he applied himself to astrophysics and worked in London. One year the twins' guardian (their father had died while they were still quite young) offered to release some money to buy them an expensive Christmas present: they chose a spectrograph. Derek used it at Oxford and later in France. Vivian, too, was a keen and successful amateur rider. Both were dark, green-eyed and – we were about to say rather small, but Derek denied this, claiming to be a 'man of medium height'. His stature was, in fact, about equal to the national average of the time, dragged down as it was by malnutrition in the industrial slums. Vivian and Derek would get into heated arguments with others in which they would always take the same side, punctuating their remarks with 'I agree with Derek' or 'I agree with Vivian'. Mosley used to describe his first encounter with the Jackson twins, which took place in the Gargoyle night-club. There was a demonstration of fencing there one evening, and some of the performers were Mosley's friends. The twins barracked them rudely and Mosley told them in sharp tones to stop. They promptly invited him to 'come outside'. The Gargoyle Club was upstairs, and as he travelled down with them in a slow lift, towering above them, one of them proposed that they should all shake hands. Mosley complied, and they were firm friends from then on.

The very day after Derek married Pam, Vivian was killed in a sledging accident. It was the worst bereavement that Derek could have suffered. In later life he confided to Diana that of all the Wagnerian *leitmotive* the one with which he most associated himself was the *Wälsungen Wehe*, which represents the grief of Siegmund and Sieglinde, twins and lovers, at their separation through Siegmund's death. Oddly enough, the twins' entries in *All About Everybody* (see p. 374) do not altogether coincide. It is Vivian who admits to the besetting sin which the record, however, shows to have also been that of Derek, namely fickleness. Derek's entry for himself under this heading is enigmatic; it is 'inertia'. This may of course have merely meant idleness. He was in fact the reverse of idle, but some people think themselves lazy when they are not. In physics, though, inertia does not mean motionlessness: a moving body, too, has inertia. The more inertia a moving body has, the more difficult it is to stop or deflect it. So Derek might mean that his besetting sin was obstinacy, blind pursuit of a line. If so, there was a good deal in it, for he could in some moods be arrogant to a degree that made many people find him intolerable. Derek did sometimes use scientific terms, even to his lay friends, in their scientific meaning, so he may have been admitting to inertia in this rather recondite sense.

However this may be, Derek certainly shared Vivian's fickleness. He had already had one wife before Pam – she was Poppet, daughter of the artist Augustus John. He was to have four more. But he spent fourteen years with Pam, and after their divorce they soon became great friends again and remained so to the end of his life.

Derek loved dogs as much as he loved horses. If one can identify the link between him and Pam it was this, for she, Debo and Unity have always been the dog lovers of the family. 'One can no more imagine Pam or Debo without a dog than Nancy or Tom with one,' Diana told us in a recent letter, though Nancy did for a time have a bulldog called Millie, and Tom once had a poodle which was the gift of a girlfriend. When Pam and Derek were staying in the United States, they had a competition every morning as to which of them would wake first and sing good morning to their dachshunds in England.

In politics Derek was flamboyantly reactionary, but on grounds of friendship he also often expressed support for Mosley, to whose egalitarian social policy he loyally closed his eyes. But the extent to which he would air his political sympathies had very strict limits. In the company of anyone whom they might really offend, he was careful to refrain. In 1933 he acquired a new collaborator, Dr Kuhn, who had just come over from Nazi Germany as a refugee. Dr Kuhn was, he says, rather alarmed when he heard that Derek was a friend of Mosley and almost a Fascist. But 'next day when I met Jackson, my worries soon vanished. He was most courteous and considerate, and we soon got involved in an interesting, amicable discussion of the work planned.' The two in fact became great friends, and their collaboration was a success; it lasted until the war.

During the war, when Derek was in the Royal Air Force and won both the DFC and the AFC, he went far further than mere support of Mosley, shocking the other officers in the mess by pronouncements that were outspokenly Nazi. But he did this precisely with the purpose of shocking, which was always one of his greatest pleasures. With the same end in view, he used sometimes to extol the joys of homosexuality. 'They sent me to Berlin when I was young to teach me to like women,' he said. 'So I picked up a blonde on the street, and when we got upstairs, thank God, it was a boy.' In the right company this anecdote could cause quite a stir – more so then than now.

The only subjects Derek thought worth studying were the sciences, and even among those he was scornful about biology and not too sure about chemistry. As for social science, the very expression was for him a contradiction in terms. In general he felt that no knowledge was worth anything unless it could be completely objective. Of history he said: 'Read a French textbook and it will be pro-French; an English one will be pro-English. Whoever heard of a chemistry textbook that was pro-iron and anti-zinc?' He had no time for linguists. When visiting German physics professors used to come to Oxford he claimed that it was only he and the other scientists who could speak to them. For the Oxford scientists, Derek used to claim, were just as competent in the German language as any Reader in German literature, whereas the linguists were at sea in the science. Derek himself spoke fluent French and German, but had his own ideas on how foreign languages should be spoken. A taxi driver in France once told him he talked with a strong accent, and he chose to take this as a compliment, recounting it afterwards to Jonathan with great pride: a *strong* accent, that was the thing to have – nothing wishy-washy. He practised a special sort of boasting, blatant and direct; it was not designed to impress so much as to be either amusing or annoying, as people might choose to take it. If someone was amused by it, Derek would accept him as an ally; but anyone whom it annoyed could expect more of the same, and probably a dose of rather rough teasing. This boasting sounded just the same in other languages as it did in English; an Austrian lady whom Jonathan met heard Derek announcing to a group of bewildered Viennese: '*Ich bin steinreich, bildschön und weltberühmt.*' (I am rich as Croesus, pretty as a picture and world-famous.) It was like an earlier incident with the Heythrop Hunt, to which Derek had brought a guest. A hunt official 'capped' the guest – that is, asked him for a subscription for the day.

'That's all right,' said Derek, 'he's with me.'

'And why should I know you?' asked the man; a mistake, for Derek was a generous subscriber to the Heythrop.

In some moods Derek might have become violently enraged, but he just said: 'Because I'm so pretty.' (At least this is the story; but it is only fair to add that when Jonathan once taxed Derek with it, he demurred: 'I didn't say that *I* was pretty, but that my horse was.')

Pam and Derek moved into Derek's Oxfordshire house, Rignell, a modern house of Cotswold stone. It had a swimming pool and lavish stabling for the all-important horses. When Vivian came to stay, Derek would forget the time, so deep were they in discussion. Pam remembers leaving the twins over their port in the dining room. In due course she grew tired and went to bed, lulled to sleep by their excited voices which she could just hear from the dining room below. At about four in the morning she woke with a start; they were still at it.

Pam was embarrassed when she travelled with Derek by train, for he had two peculiarities. One was a hatred of Pullman cars, since he liked an enclosed compartment (first-class, it goes without saying). Another was a propensity to pull the communication cord. The fine for 'improper use' was then £5, which he could well afford. It sometimes happened that the only first-class accommodation available was of the Pullman type. Having got in under voluble protest, he would pull the communication cord as soon as the train was clear of the station, demanding a carriage to be attached of the kind he preferred. On one occasion, for this or another reason, he pulled the cord. The train stopped and the guard came to see what was the matter. 'I'll tell you what's the matter,' said Derek, 'your communication cord is filthy – look what it's done to my glove.'

What of Tom? He was called to the Bar, and practised his profession quietly and competently, taking fairly long holidays; he was quite often with Unity in Germany, or with other members of his family. He introduced her to his friend Janos Almasy, and she frequently went to stay at Bernstein; and also to Janos's neighbours, the Erdödys, at Kohfidisch. Their friends there were the two young Countesses Erdödy, one known as Baby and the other, somewhat confusingly, as Jimmy. Diana thinks Tom was at one time rather in love with Baby Erdödy. All these people became close friends of the whole family; when Unity in her correspondence talks of going to Burgenland, the Austrian province which contains both Bernstein and Kohfidisch, she can mean either place or both in turn. Tom took Bryan Guinness to Bernstein in August 1931; Diana did not come, as she was about to give birth to Desmond. Bryan's letter of thanks after this visit contains a reference to Janos's abiding interest in the occult: 'I do hope you have had good news of your brother; and that your dream proved without foundations of any kind, other than what were logical apprehensions.' The brother, Laszlo, was an explorer. Ralph Fiennes was to play him, much bandaged, in the film *The English Patient*. When he was not having ominous dreams, Janos was generally casting someone's horoscope.

He and Unity became increasingly close friends up to 1939, and in that year, and possibly earlier as well, they seem to have had a love affair. It is true that Unity was very friendly as well with Janos's wife Marie, but she was confined by polio to a wheelchair and friends say she did not object to his other relationships. Certainly, Unity stayed for long periods at Bernstein, and Janos was frequently with her in Munich. Once they stayed together in Venice. Her last letter to him is dated 1 September 1939, the day German troops entered Poland; it starts 'My darling', which seems to imply a close relationship, and 'darling' occurs twice more, which was not typical of Unity's letters to friends. She says: 'I am horrified to hear that the critical day is the 7th because I can't bear it if the crisis drags on until then. Surely, we must know what England is going to do sooner than that.' She was right, of course, and Janos's astrological calculations wrong; Britain declared war on the 3rd.

On the surface, Janos was at the time definitely pro-Nazi. For one thing, love affair or not, Unity would otherwise never have been as close a friend as we know her to have been. 'Wasn't the *Führerrede* this morning *wonderful*,' she says in the same letter, referring to Hitler's speech announcing the invasion of Poland; she would hardly have written like this to a merely non-political friend. More positively, on 20 April 1939, Hitler's birthday, Janos held an oath-taking ceremony for Nazi political leaders in the courtyard of Bernstein; Unity was present. We know from Diana, too, that Janos supported the German annexation of Austria, and she is definite that Janos seemed an enthusiastic Nazi. However, all this need show is an ability to run with the hare and hunt with the hounds. Janos was a world-weary Central European aristocrat. Nazism, we may speculate, seemed to him rather vulgar in some ways; yet in this twentieth century of collapse and revolution, the century of the common man, vulgarity in some form was unavoidable, and the Nazis at least seemed people with whom one could deal. The alternative was Communism, the end of everything.

To return to Tom, in the thirties he had a number of love affairs; during the war he was to shock James Lees-Milne by the cold-blooded way in which he talked about women, but this was probably simply his mood of the moment. He can hardly have been as cynical as he pretended, for he could be genuinely and deeply depressed when crossed in love. At other times he rather enjoyed it when his younger sisters teased him about 'committing it'. In the context this meant adultery, or fornication as the case might be, though the Mitfords also regularly used the phrase 'commit it' with 'suicide' understood. When in February 1939 Tom saw Decca off at the station on her departure for the United States, he and she teased each other on this subject for the last time. Blor was worrying about her underclothes. Tom told Decca she had to wash them every night. He *happened to know* American girls always did this. Clearly, said Decca, feigning shock, he had been committing it again. Tom was certainly very fond of the Austrian dancer Tilly Losch, later Lady Carnarvon, who in 1934 engaged in an acrimonious divorce suit from her husband, Edward James. He might well have been named in this suit, but was not; Edward James was a friend of Diana's and perhaps left Tom's name out of it in consideration for her feelings. He was not short of other material. Sydney certainly thought Tom was serious about Tilly, and Tilly's friend Rudolf Kommer, English representative of the impresario Max Reinhardt, thought that, of all Tilly's lovers, Tom was the one with whom she would have been happiest.

Tom was impressed by the performance of Nazism, and deeply so by Hitler personally, but never embraced the creed wholeheartedly because he could not swallow the race theories. He had too many good friends who were Jews, and professional clients as well; his knowledge of German would sometimes enable him to understand the gist of what his East End Jewish clients were saying when they spoke Yiddish among themselves. He had, that is, a more personal contact with Jews than did his sisters; he knew better what they were really like. Philosophically, too, he was a Kantian; no morality could satisfy him which included the condemnation of someone purely because he belonged to a particular group. This of course set up contradictions, of which there are clear traces in Diana's and Unity's letters to each other. Unity introduced Tom to Hitler on 8 June 1935, yet she had wanted to avoid doing so. She took Tom to the Osteria Bavaria, obviously at his request, but did so at a time earlier than Hitler's usual one, her intention being to get Tom out of the restaurant before Hitler arrived, if he did. But for once in his life Hitler came at 1.45, and asked them over. Unity wrote: 'Although I didn't want him to meet him I am quite pleased now. He *adored* the Führer — he almost got into a frenzy like us sometimes, though I expect he will have cooled down by the time he gets home — and I am sure the Führer liked him, and found him intelligent to talk to. So I really think no harm is done.' What had she feared? That Tom might offend Hitler in some way? Or that he might take against him and quarrel with her and Diana, or be an adverse influence with their parents? In any case, it is certain that Hitler did like him; for in

September 1936, when Diana was in Berlin making preparations
for her forthcoming wedding to Mosley, she was invited on the
spur of the moment to dinner with Hitler. She wrote to Unity on
17 September 1936:

He was so wonderful and really seemed pleased we had gone [to the
Parteitag (Party Conference)] every day . . . He asked after Tom and
I said 'Der Judenknecht ist fast Nazionalsozialist [sic] geworden' [The
lackey of the Jews has almost become a National Socialist] and he
roared with laughter and said, 'Ihr Bruder ist ein fabelhafter Junge'
[Your brother is a splendid boy] twice over. Isn't Tom lucky.

This was probably what prompted Unity to write to Diana on 2
January 1937, with a 'new last verse' to the hymn 'There were
Ninety and Nine', making Tom out to be the lost sheep which
Hitler has retrieved:

> And up from the mountains Communist-ridden,
> Up from the Jewish mud,
> There arose a cry to the Reichskanzlei,
>    Sieg Heil! I have found my Tud!
> And the Nazis echoed around the throne,
>    Sieg Heil! for the Führer brings back his own! (bis.)

Unity invented several of these Nazi parodies; there was another,
'The Last Swastika of Summer', which went quite well to the tune
of 'The Last Rose of Summer' because the word 'rose' in Moore's
Irish melody is sung over three notes. Apart from the title, the
words have been forgotten.

Tom was at first hostile to Mosley because he had caused
Diana's divorce. However, later he became friends with him.
This can be dated from February 1938, because on the twenty-
first of that month Unity writes to Diana saying how pleased she is
at the 'Versöhnung' (reconciliation) between the two men. Tom's
views were clear enough; James Lees-Milne had several discussions with him during the war. He saw Fascism as an efficient
form of government which he would have liked his own country
to adopt, thinking that the performance of Hitler and Mussolini
before the war proved this point. He felt, therefore, that Mosley
had the answer to Britain's problems. He was not as fixedly against
the idea of fighting Hitler as were Diana and Unity; nevertheless,

his personal fondness for Germany made him unwilling at the end
of the war to participate in the invasion of Germany itself, so he
volunteered for Burma, where he would instead be fighting the
Japanese.

Before the war Tom was the great go-between, the diplomat,
the only member of the family who was always on speaking terms
with all the others. He worked away at his law cases, in his spare
time he read the classics, and we know that he had an interest in
angels and devils and in the occult, caught almost certainly from
Janos. There is no sign that Tom's interest in these matters was
other than purely academic and superficial, and we have found no
papers relating to it. But Mrs R. A. Howard, who visited Bernstein
in connection with a forthcoming biography of Janos Almasy's
brother Laszlo, uncovered what may be a discreet tease by Tom
on his friend. A good deal of planchette was played at Bernstein,
which has no fewer than three ghosts, and Mrs Howard examined
the record of the spirit communications using the expertise she had
acquired when working on ciphers during the war. One of them
was so close to the first chapter of Dickens's *A Christmas Carol* as
effectively to preclude coincidence. It must have been planted,
presumably by an Englishman who had read Dickens. Tom kept
most things in his head, and was so discreet in his letters as sometimes to give one the impression that he was deliberately trying to
leave no trace in his life's journey. He continued to play the piano,
and sometimes came together with other amateur pianists of
similar character such as Mrs Hammersley, Lord Berners or Lady
Rosebery to play duets or trios.

His unique achievement was to get on with Decca's husband,
Esmond Romilly. When Decca and he were living at Rotherhithe
she saw other members of her family but had to be discreet about
it; Tom she could actually bring home. Had she and Esmond
known that at this time Tom joined Mosley's movement, they
might have taken a very different attitude. In the event, Esmond
was never to know it, and Decca did not find out about it until
Diana, provoked by various remarks of Decca's to which she took
exception, revealed it in Julian Jebb's television programme about
Nancy in 1981. We need not suppose Tom to have been in any
way hypocritical when he went to see the Romillys, merely tactful.
They would have known very well that he opposed socialism and

Communism. But there was no reason for him to obtrude his support of Mosley. This would have made relations impossible. Tom, it is clear, admired the warrior in Esmond; in fact his liking for Esmond sprang from the same tastes as his interest in Fascism. Esmond could like Tom in return because he lacked any trace of the public school pomposity to which he objected. Tom was neither hearty nor hectoring; less so, in all probability, than Esmond himself. Inwardly, of course, he was supremely self-confident, and James Lees-Milne records a ruthlessness in argument. However, ruthlessness as such never offended Esmond; if anything he admired it. What maddened him was pretentiousness.

Tom was uninterested in the country: animals and farming left him cold and field sports did not attract him, though he would sometimes go out for a day's shooting. When David felt the need to sell Swinbrook, he asked Tom if he would eventually become interested in the place; had he said yes, David would have kept it, in whole or in part. But the answer was no, so David went ahead. Tom's interests were the law, music, philosophy and love; after he joined the Territorial Army, soldiering was increasingly added to them.

# 30

# The Lure of Germany

Dr Ernst Hanfstaengl, always known as Putzi, was one of Hitler's earliest supporters. A shambling, lantern-jawed Bavarian of very great height and huge frame, he was one of the first of the civilian middle class to join the Nazis. He had money from a print shop, or small gallery, which his family owned in Munich; because it had a branch in New York, some of this money was in American dollars. Comparatively small dollar subventions from him, during the chaotic time of the great inflation of 1923, kept the infant Nazi movement alive and allowed it to buy its own newspaper. The Nazis had larger contributors later but none, probably, more useful to their movement's survival. Hitler had fled to Putzi's house in Uffing, near Munich, injured in the shoulder, after the failure of his 1923 *putsch* with General Ludendorff. Putzi's wife and his sister Erna looked after Hitler for three days, and it was from there that he was taken off to Landsberg prison where in the next eighteen months he was to write *Mein Kampf*. Some people called Putzi Hitler's court jester, and there was something of this in the relationship, though he himself threw the jibe at his enemy Goebbels, whom he called a 'little Rigoletto'. (Diana, *A Life of Contrasts*.) He was gifted, erudite and in a way winning, but he was one of those people whom it is difficult to take quite seriously and rather tempting to tease. The Nazis in the early days came to know that he was physically timid. Sometimes one of them would rush into the room and blurt out that the 'Reds' were coming for them, so poor Putzi would let himself be bundled into a car and driven dangerously around the Munich streets on squealing tyres. The danger from the 'Reds' during the years of struggle was not imaginary: both Communists and Socialists had their own para-military forces, by no means less violent than Hitler's notorious brown-shifted SA, and both sides suffered a regular quota of fatal casualties, the song-writing student Horst Wessel being only one of many.

Hitler, it seems, was genuinely fond of Putzi; he particularly enjoyed hearing him play the piano. Putzi worshipped him, but hated some of the other Nazi leaders. Partly this was a matter of class snobbery, but no doubt he also sensed that his idol, Hitler, thought him rather a joke. Since it would have been against human nature to blame himself for this, it had to be the fault of others. He particularly disliked Goebbels and Alfred Rosenberg; and Goebbels, at any rate, came to reciprocate the feeling and was a dangerous enemy. In Putzi's memoirs, dictated to Brian Connell (*Hitler, the Missing Years*), he makes out that he tried to civilize Hitler, and this was no doubt how he saw it, after the event at least. It was natural that he should be particularly suspicious of Goebbels, because Goebbels was one of the few to be, like himself, a man with an academic education, combining this with greater ability and a far stronger character. That there should be good reasons to dislike someone does not mean that one necessarily dislikes them entirely for those good reasons.

Putzi looked and moved rather like someone who has been artificially stuck together. Not a Frankenstein monster, for that would imply ugliness, and Putzi was not ugly, just supremely awkward-looking – an enormous puppet on slack strings. Jonathan got to know him after the war and liked him. He had a well-stocked mind and discussed philosophy and aesthetics as well as politics. He still held to Hitler's basic ideology, including his racial feelings, and criticized Hitler's policy entirely cogently on this basis; about Hitler himself he was bitter with the bitterness of love betrayed, having parted company from him before the war in circumstances uniquely farcical. Hitler was a homosexual, he told Jonathan, and described in scabrous detail what he probably did with his young men. This seemed a sensational revelation, and Jonathan naturally probed. 'You must understand,' said Putzi, 'I merely deduce this from knowing him so well. I see it, here, in my mind,' he added, tapping his overhanging forehead. Putzi was kind, hospitable and funny, in 1950 as in 1933, but there was about him something deeply and irredeemably absurd.

When Hitler came to power, he put Putzi in charge of his

party's foreign press bureau; it was an important appointment, because it involved trying to counter the awkward revelations about the regime that were appearing in the world newspapers. The choice of Putzi was perhaps odd in a way, but there were reasons for it; he spoke fluent English, for his mother was American, and he had connections abroad. Committed Nazis with these qualifications were rare: Ribbentrop spoke good English, but he and Baldur von Schirach were the only top leaders to do so. Putzi came to London in the spring of 1933 to spread the word; besides the press he made sure of meeting some private individuals to create propaganda by word of mouth. The whole operation, as compared at any rate with the same sort of thing organized by Communists, was amateurish and haphazard. It had of course nothing to do with the German embassy, still less with the secret service. Putzi found considerable scepticism and polite hostility, but at that stage a good many people were at least willing to listen.

This, then, was the curious man whom Diana found at the house of Mrs Richard Guinness, wife of a distant cousin of Bryan's. He played the piano and he talked about Hitler in a state of high excitement. Diana comments: 'I had often met drawing-room communists who breathed fire and slaughter; he was my first drawing-room nazi.' Fire and slaughter? Perhaps; but whatever the words, the manner would have been rather reassuring, the phrases delivered between deep and rasping breaths by a great clumsy character of a man, obviously unable personally to harm a fly. Diana argued with him; why did the regime persecute the Jews?

'Oh, the Jews, the Jews, that's all one ever hears in London, what about the Jews,' shouted Hanfstaengl. If the Jews wanted to leave the new Germany, they should get out; they were only 1 per cent of the population anyway, and Hitler would build a wonderful new Germany for the other 99 per cent. 'He boomed on all evening,' says Diana, but he also issued a challenge: those present should come to Germany and see for themselves what lies the newspapers were telling. To Diana, in particular, he made an offer that, if she came, he would introduce her to Hitler. Diana made up her mind to go; and go she did, in the summer, to Munich. She took Unity with her.

Let it be noted that they did not go under government auspices. Visitors to Russia or China, to this day, have to get in touch with the authorities and are assigned official guides; everything they see is closely supervised. It is right to criticize the gullibility of people who draw general conclusions from their experience of a country when that experience is thus doctored and doled out. This particular criticism cannot be levelled at Diana and Unity. Though the revolution was hardly seven months old, they simply went as ordinary visitors, first sightseeing round Bavaria with Nigel Birch and Lord Hinchingbrooke. (Hinchingbrooke was to become well-known as a backbench Conservative MP.) They saw no distress, no obvious fear. No one came up to them, as a wretched waiter was to do to Decca when she visited Hungary in 1956, to ask them to smuggle out a letter. It was only when Diana and Unity felt like it that they made contact with Putzi.

He turned out to be a touch less influential than he had implied, and the meeting with Hitler did not materialize. But he took them to the Party Congress, or Parteitag, at Nuremberg. Misled by the fact that *Tag* in German is the word for day as well as that for congress, Diana expected the occasion to last one day only; in fact it lasted four. Putzi looked after them with great kindness; Unity's letters show that she fell, temporarily, rather in love with him. He took the sisters, with an American lady he was also looking after, to all the speeches and parades; he made them laugh, he kept up a constant flow of chat. Diana was impressed by the German organizing ability which could house and feed so many people from all over the country; many of them had to live in tents. The Congress was more spontaneous, less drilled, than those of later years; but Diana's comment on the subject is nevertheless not altogether apposite. She says: 'There was not much in the English papers about the Parteitag; when they mentioned it at all it was to describe it as "militaristic", though it was not even as militaristic as a torch-light tattoo in England.' The point, though, is surely that it was a good deal more militaristic than a British party conference. It was a matter of speeches and parades, not debates. Diana goes on:

A feeling of excited triumph was in the air, and when Hitler appeared an almost electric shock passed through the multitude. In other years, the whole thing had become an established political circus marvellously synchronized and with permanent installations to contain the million or so performers; in 1933, it was a thanksgiving by revolutionaries for the success of their revolution . . . There were almost no foreigners; later on the diplomats and assorted guests came, but not in 1933. By a strange chance, Unity and the American lady and I witnessed this demonstration of hope in a nation that had known collective despair.

Compared to this experience, it seemed pedantic to worry about the tribulations of a few Jews. It is doubtful whether either Diana or Unity gave them a thought. When they were to think of them, it was as enemies of this fine and beautiful thing, this Nazism, this continental embodiment of all that Diana's beloved Mosley was going to do for his own country, still sunk in despair and depression as Germany had been so shortly before. Both sisters were profoundly impressed, and thenceforward they were to regard stories of Nazi crimes either as unimportant and exceptional episodes, or as downright lies. Of course this was wrong; all we are claiming is that at the time it was understandable. The claim for understandability is made often enough for Marxist intellectuals who refused to credit Stalin's atrocities until Khrushchev admitted some of them. Also it should be remembered that the mass holocaust was in 1933 still in the future, whereas the massacre of the so-called kulaks – in reality ordinary peasants to the number of ten million, as Stalin later admitted to Churchill – was in the recent past.

But Nazi concentration camps had already been set up, brutality was already being practised on Jews, and this was known in England well enough. When David and Sydney found out that Diana had taken Unity to the Parteitag they were furious. David wrote to Diana on 7 September 1933:

I suppose you know without being told how absolutely horrified Muv and I were to think of you and Bobo accepting any form of hospitality from people we regard as a murderous gang of pests.

That you should associate yourself with such people is a source of utter misery to both of us – but of course, beyond telling you this (which you already know) we can do nothing. What we can do, and what we intend to do, is to try and keep Bobo out of it all.

Diana was already in her parents' bad books following her divorce, and her adherence to the British Union of Fascists. She, of course, was now twenty-three and independent, but Unity was only nineteen, still a minor. However, David and Sydney's objections came too late. Unity was captivated. 'After this', says Sydney, 'she thought of nothing but of when she could return to Germany', and adds, somewhat lamely, 'There was no reason why she should not.' This is strictly true, since many young people used to go there, especially to Munich; but in the light of David's letter just quoted it is a climb down. Unity was extremely persistent when she wanted to be, and badgered her parents until they gave in.

In May 1934, then, Unity went back to Munich by herself to learn German at the house of Baroness Laroche, who kept a boarding house for foreign girls. She told Sydney later that the baroness 'was very anti-Nazi when I first went there, and later on very pro-Nazi'. She was a member of the new poor who had come down in the world following the First World War; her happiest memories were of being presented at the Imperial Palace in Vienna, and of speaking to the Emperor Franz Josef himself at the house of one of the princesses. A good many such ladies of the old German and Austrian upper classes used to take in young foreigners who wanted to learn some German and pick up some culture; Munich was a centre for it, like Paris and Florence, and the rather artificial exchange rate made it cheap for the English. Unity got on well with Baroness Laroche, despite her opposition to the regime. A very good teacher was found for her called Fräulein Baum, a Silesian who, unlike the baroness, was an enthusiastic Nazi. The food at the baroness's, Unity said, was delicious; this was always a consideration with her as she had a good appetite and, on occasion, what is now known as a weight problem.

Altogether Unity had a lovely time that spring and summer of 1934. She went to the Hanfstaengl shop and met Putzi's big blonde sister Erna. 'She is enormously fat,' she wrote to Diana. 'I took to her tremendously though.' Erna was to become a great friend. Putzi had told Diana and Unity: 'Erna is a good girl.' When Unity met her she thought this very funny and christened her 'the good girl', the name by which the whole Mitford family were to know her. After the war, when Jonathan met Erna, she said: 'We had a terrible diet after the war during the hunger years; you see how fat I am? It is malnutrition.' When this was retailed to Diana, she loved it. Unity used sometimes to go and stay with Erna. In a letter to Diana dated 25 January 1935 she wrote: 'The Good Girl was too extraordinary, she did her morning exercises *quite* naked with me in the room.' Unity was very much in touch with Nazi headquarters, the Brown House; once they sent to her a young English girl whose parents had cut off her allowance because she had gone Fascist; she put her up for the night on the floor of her room. It was not only the Redesdales who had problems at the time with Fascist-minded offspring. But Unity had plenty of non-political English friends as well, such as the other girls at the baroness's, and the artist Derek Hill, who was studying in Munich at the time and with whom she used to go sightseeing and walking in the mountains.

It was Derek Hill who gave Unity her first glimpse of Hitler since the Party Congress, and much closer, too. For a dictator, Hitler was curiously casual in his habits, far more so than even democratic heads of governments are nowadays, let alone dictators. This was so most especially when he was in Munich, where he spent much of his time. He liked a particular restaurant, the Osteria Bavaria. This was a good solid establishment at the top of the middle range, by no means grand. He would have lunch there and sit for an hour or two chatting. When the weather was fine, he sat out at a table in the garden. Another haunt was a café, the Carlton Teeraum. He was not in any way incognito; he would simply go to these places like anyone else, accompanied by whoever of his entourage he happened to have with him. He would spend a substantial part of his afternoons and evenings in this way. Fear of assassination never seems to have crossed his mind. Decca says she formed a project to meet him through Unity and then kill him with a revolver; as she rightly says, this would have been perfectly easy. In any case, Derek Hill with his mother and aunt were at the Carlton Teeraum at about 6 p.m. on 11 June when Hitler came in. Derek, knowing that this would fascinate Unity, at once went to the telephone and rang her up. 'Of course', she told Diana in a letter written the next day, 'I jumped straight into a taxi, in which in my excitement I left my camera which I was going to take to the shop. I went and sat down with them, and there was the Führer opposite. The aunt said "You're trembling with excitement", and sure enough I was, so much so that Derek had to drink my chocolate for me because I couldn't hold the cup.'

In the same letter, Unity asks Diana about the great Fascist meeting at Olympia. Diana had been ill and had to miss it; 'Too awful for you,' commiserates Unity. 'It does sound such heaven.' She adds: 'Do write and tell whether you think Olympia was a success? Does the Leader think so? I suppose all these absurd attacks in the papers are bound to do the Party a certain amount of harm. The accounts in the German papers are marvellous.'

Not long after Olympia, on 30 June, Hitler staged what has become known as the 'Night of the Long Knives' – the brutal massacre of Roehm and other leaders of the SA, together with General Schleicher and some others. Hitler claimed to have uncovered a plot; there is now a view that the army saw the SA as a threat to society and secured Hitler's elimination of the SA leadership as the price of their future collaboration. Had this been so, one would have thought they would have demanded not just the removal of the SA's leadership, but the organization's actual disbandment, which did not happen. There is, however, evidence that if there was a plot, by no means all those killed were in it. The most likely explanation is that Hitler, like any alert gangster, simply took ruthless pre-emptive action against an independent power centre in the party on the basis of rather vague indications that a plot might be impending. Though on a much smaller scale, it has a family resemblance to Stalin's purges. As in Russia, most of the victims died protesting their innocence. Roehm was arrested by Hitler personally. Unity wrote to Diana on 1 July describing events in Munich:

I heard rumours after dinner and immediately went into the town, where there were printed accounts of it stuck up in the chief squares. I couldn't believe it at first. I went to the Brown House, but the street was guarded by SS men so I couldn't get near. I waited in a huge crowd in a square near for two hours, they were all waiting to see Hitler and Goebbels come away from the Brown House. While we stood there, several huge columns of SS, SA and Stahlhelm marched past us to the Brown House, and huge lorries full of sandbags with SS or Reichswehr sitting on top, and there were SS men dashing about the whole time on motorbikes or cars . . . Then word was passed round that Hitler and Goebbels had left by a back entrance and were already flying to Berlin, so I came home.

Her own attitude is perfectly clear.

I am so terribly sorry for the Führer – you know Roehm was his oldest friend and comrade, the only one that called him '*du*' in public . . . It must have been so dreadful for Hitler when he arrested Roehm himself and tore off his decorations. Then he went to arrest Heines and found him in bed with a boy. Did that get into the English papers? *Poor* Hitler.

Not long after this, Sydney visited Unity. She writes: 'In common with most people in England, I took a rather contemptuous interest in the doings in Germany . . . Why did Germany put all her trust in this one man and what kind of man was he? From the time that the first German war ended, I believed that the victors had behaved badly and madly to the defeated.' Sydney gives her reasons for this in two pages, mostly quotations from Keynes's correspondence. The Germans had tried to get the Versailles treaty altered by peaceful means; now at last they turned to a man who might get something done by a show of strength.

And so when I went to Germany in 1934 to visit Unity, I was hoping to see Hitler. Anyhow, what was this insignificant-looking man with a funny moustache and an untidy lock of hair, dressed in an old mackintosh? . . .

It was my first visit to Germany. I had always heard and fully agreed that everything French was charming . . . By contrast, everything German was said to be heavy, ugly, tasteless and altogether lacking in charm. As in so many things which turn out when you look into them to be quite untrue, I found very great beauty and charm in Germany. Nothing I thought could be lovelier than the little baroque theatre in Bayreuth . . . The lovely white, gold, pale blue and pink churches seem to me to be admirably fitted to the worship of God in happiness.

It was certainly her father, Thomas Bowles, who had indoctrinated Sydney with the view that everything German was tasteless: Central European culture was a closed book to him, hence his quirky recommendation of a 'profound ignorance', of the German language (see p. xxvi).

She continues: 'The chief thing I remember about my first visit to Munich, after admiring the beautiful town, was the daily struggle I had with Unity over giving the Nazi salute at the Feldherrnhalle', where there was an inscription to mark those who had died in the 1923 *putsch* and two SS men always on guard. 'Everyone who passed this spot in the very crowded street, raised the right arm in the Nazi salute, even people in cars or on bicycles. I did not feel called upon to do it, being English . . . In the end, I used to take the other half of the street, and we met again at the other side, with great laughter.'

It was not till later that Sydney came to support Hitler. For the moment she was just an interested visitor, still trying to restrain Unity's immoderate enthusiasm. However, she was a person who always thought for herself and made up her mind according to what she thought she saw. Her prejudices were always provisional. This was why, to Decca's astonishment, she was later to get on well with her second husband, a Marxist lawyer of Jewish origin.

Unity returned to Swinbrook for the summer holidays. Tom went to the Bayreuth festival, and for a tease sent her a postcard saying that he had had supper there with Hitler and Goering. She believed him and was 'miserable for days and frightfully *eifersüchtig* [jealous], and then I discovered it wasn't true so I'm furious with him . . .'

She went back to Munich early with the idea of going to the Parteitag again; Diana joined her there. To their disgust, Putzi refused to take them, saying that he had been criticized the year before for taking women in make-up, and anyway he had no tickets to give away. Probably his influence was on the decline. Unity was not to be put off; they would go there on their own. Diana went along, but feared that they would have to sit up all night in the Nuremberg station waiting room. When they arrived at Nuremberg, it really looked as if this might be the case; the city was crammed. Unity did not mind, but feared that Diana might. '*Do* be glad we came,' she kept saying. However, as so often happens in these situations, luck was with them. They got talking in a beer garden with an old man who was wearing the gold party badge which testified that he was one of the first hundred thousand members. He turned out in fact to have party card number 100: '*Parteigenosse Nummer Hundert*', they called him. He fixed them up with beds in a little inn and tickets for everything.

During the autumn term, Diana decided to learn German too.

Unity found her a flat, and moved in with her there; and together they followed a special course for foreigners at the university. Diana loved Munich, its faint smell of brewing and cheap cigars, its heavily subsidized opera which cost nearly nothing to attend, its cheerful population made healthy by the proximity of the mountains for cheap Sunday skiing. When Unity thought Hitler would be at the Osteria Bavaria, she used to insist on going with Diana to lunch there. Diana says she seemed to know by instinct when he was likely to be at the Osteria; some of David Pryce-Jones's informants, talking of a somewhat later period, also make this point and conclude that she must have had some contact in his entourage. There need be little mystery about this, because by then she had come to know Hitler's adjutants through Hitler himself, and all she needed to do was ring them up. It is all the same interesting that she already had this 'instinct' before she had any such inside contact. Diana's explanation is plausible: 'She followed his doings in the newspapers, chatted to the doorman at the Brown House, looked to see if there was a policeman in the Prinzregentenplatz where he had his flat.' When they did see him in the Osteria Bavaria it was liable to mean a wasted afternoon, because of what Diana calls his Spanish hours. He never arrived before two o'clock at the very earliest, and often not before three, driving up with an adjutant and a few friends or assistants in two black Mercedes cars. Unity then insisted on staying in the restaurant until he left, perhaps an hour and a half later, so as to see him go by her table. Hitler noticed her; one of the waitresses told her that he had asked who she was.

'Did he?' said Unity. 'I hope you said an English Fascist and not just an English student.'

In January 1935, when Unity went back to Munich for the spring term, she was accompanied by David, who put up at an hotel. She moved into a hostel for girl students, always referred to by her as 'the Heim'. She had evidently been working on David in the summer and Christmas holidays, because her diary and letters show that he was mixing happily with everybody, English and German; affectionate and impulsive, he was in a mood to enter his daughter's world. He liked Putzi, and 'got on wonderfully with the Sturmführers', she wrote to Diana on 19 January 1935. She took him to the Osteria Bavaria, and Hitler was there; 'Farve has been completely won over to him and admits himself to have been in the wrong until now.' Later in the same letter she writes: 'I am sending you with this letter one of the sacks of Saar earth that are being sold in the streets today . . . Do plant it in your little garden, it will be a part of Germany, or plant it in a pot with a flower. Farve has taken some back to plant at Swinbrook.' It was the time of the Saar plebiscite when that area, claimed by France but under provisional League of Nations control, was given the opportunity to vote for France, Germany or continued international administration. The Saarlanders, being Germans, voted over-whelmingly for Germany; this surprised some foreign observers, who expected that no population would voluntarily vote for sub-jection to Nazi despotism. Unity was of course delighted. After David left she settled down to a happy life, working at her German, seeing friends, sometimes spending the day in the freezing streets collecting for a Nazi charity. Brian Howard was in Munich for Fasching, or carnival; Unity was fond of him despite political disagreements, and saw a good deal of him and of his mother, who was also there for a few days. It was partly over him that she quar-relled with her teacher, Fräulein Baum. 'I have discovered Baum is a little worm,' she wrote to Diana on 8 February. Baum had gos-siped to a mutual friend, about Unity herself, about Howard and about Diana. Among the things she said were that Unity had a 'real affair' with Erik Widemann, an SS man who worked in a photo-graph shop. She was merely anticipating here, for Erik or Erich was to be Unity's steady boyfriend for some years; but the very fact that this was on the cards must have made Baum's gossip all the more irritating. Baum also revealed Diana's relationship with Mosley, and said that Brian was a Jew and a Communist. This is interesting, because although Brian was not Jewish – Martin Green, in *Children of the Sun*, has been into this matter – it was generally thought in England that he was; and although he was not a Communist, his sympathies were left-wing. Baum must have had her sources, probably her other English pupils. But Unity would not believe such things about a friend. Neither Baum nor Unity was aware of what was almost certainly Howard's real reason for being in Munich, which was to pick up boys.

Unity had become a regular customer both of the Carlton Teeraum and especially the Osteria Bavaria, and she often saw

Hitler, who would sometimes give her a friendly nod, an event always noted with delight in her diary. It was on 9 February that he went further. The night before she had been to a fancy dress dance for the foreign students. She spent much of the time with Brian. Presumably she cramped his style, but he squired her loyally enough. She had, however, been up till 3 a.m.; she would not have been hung-over, as she never drank much, but she was certainly tired and did not feel like working that Saturday morning. Her friend Rosemary Macindoe came and gossiped to her in her bedroom, and finally she wandered along to the Osteria Bavaria for a late lunch at 2.30.

What then happened she described in a letter to her father. She wrote to David rather than Sydney because, as Sydney herself makes clear, 'in those days she was more sure of his sympathy than of mine'. Later this position was to be sharply reversed.

Forgy darling,

Yesterday was the most wonderful and beautiful day of my life. I will try and describe it to you, though I can as yet hardly write.

I went alone to lunch at the Osteria and sat at the little table by the stove where we sat . . . last time you were there. At about three, when I had finished my lunch, the Führer came and sat down at his usual table with two other men . . . About ten minutes after he arrived, he spoke to the manager, and the manager came over to me and said: 'The Führer would like to speak to you'. I got up and went over to him and he stood up and saluted and shook hands and introduced me to the others and asked me to sit down next to him.

I sat and talked to him for about half an hour . . . Rosa (the fat waitress) came and whispered to me: 'Shall I bring you a post-card?' So I said yes, really to please her . . . I was rather embarrassed to ask him to sign it . . . and I said I hoped he wouldn't think it very American of me.

He made me write my name on a piece of paper (which I did as you may believe very shakily) and then he wrote on the card: '*Frl. Unity Mitford, ʒur freundlichen Erinnerung an Deutschland und Adolf Hitler*'. Tom will tell you what it means. [Roughly, Miss Unity Mitford, as a friendly memento of Germany and Adolf Hitler; the exact nuance is impossible to translate succintly, being more like 'in order that she may have a friendly recollection of . . .'] I can't tell you all the things we talked about . . . I told him he ought to come to England and he said he would love to but he was afraid there would be a revolution if he did. He asked me if I had ever been to Bayreuth and I said no but I should like to, and he said to one of the other men that they must remember that the next time there is a [festival] there.

He said that he felt he knew London well from his architectural studies and . . . believed it to be the best town, as a town, in the world. He thinks *Cavalcade* is the best film he ever saw.

He talked about the war, he said . . . that international Jews must never again be allowed to make two Nordic races fight against one another. I said no, next time we must fight together.

He talked of the roads, the new buildings that were being put up in Nuremberg for the Parteitag, and other things.

In the end he had to go. He kept the bit of paper with my name on. Rosa told me it was the first time he had ever invited someone he didn't know to sit at his table like that. He had also apparently said that my lunch was to go on his bill.

So, Forgy, after all that you can imagine what I feel like. I am so happy that I wouldn't mind a bit dying. I suppose I am the luckiest girl in the world. I certainly never did anything to deserve such an honour.

A very nice thing was that two very poor girls, who really work themselves to the bone for him – the 'Hungry Girl' and the girl you met in Café Hag – were sitting at another table. After he had gone, they waited outside for me and shook my hand for ages and congratulated me . . . If I had been them, I would have been furious that a foreigner who had never done a hand's turn for him had such wonderful luck . . .

You may think that this is hysterical. I'm sure Muv will, but when you remember that at any rate for me, he is the greatest man of all time, you must admit that I am lucky even to have set eyes on him, let alone to have sat and talked to him.

On 11 February Unity wrote to her mother:

One of the chief things that struck me about him was his simplicity. He talked so ordinarily that one couldn't be nervous. And for the most powerful man in the world to have remained so simple and utterly unconceited, is surely a miracle and a sign of his super-humanity.

Oh dear, I still can't quite believe in Saturday, although I have my signed postcard as proof. While I was sitting next to him, it seemed quite real and ordinary, but after he was gone, it was like some quite unbelievable dream. I suppose to your balanced mind it doesn't seem anything much. However, I think even you will admit that it *was* interesting, even exciting, particularly as he has never done that before.

We do not think that either of these letters shows any sign of an abnormal mental state. She is certainly not self-centred, as obsessed people often are; there is regard for others in the account of the two 'poor girls'. She is self-possessed enough to talk to Hitler normally and naturally; her hand may shake when she writes her name, but otherwise she embarks on a friendly conversation, deeply honoured but not overawed.

As to Hitler, he must have found her entertaining; for otherwise it is inconceivable that this dictator, this absolute ruler, would have wanted to see her again. In the event he met and conversed with her on 140 days in a period of less than five years. This figure is easy to arrive at, because she kept a five-year diary for the period 1935–39, and every time she talks to him the entry is in red ink, making it stand out conveniently. She is strict with herself, too; occasions when he merely nods to her or greets her or shakes hands do not get the red ink treatment. The idea that he might have seen so much of her simply because she was some sort of admiring 'groupie' does not wash; mere admiration was something of which he had plenty. Hitler may at times have used her as a channel for controlled and unofficial leaks, but he did not take up with her for this reason, for at first he knew nothing about her background; Schaub, his adjutant, makes out in an article in *Revue* magazine (1950) that he did not even know she was English when he invited her to his table. She learned to be extremely tight-lipped with journalists as to the details of what Hitler said to her; to private individuals she merely argued his case, often in ways more apt to shock than to convince. Again, it is certain that there was no love affair, contrary to what the French press, particularly, was fond of saying. Hitler was living with Eva Braun during the period in question, as Unity knew quite well. Some of Pryce-Jones's informants make out that there was jealousy between Unity and Eva, but Diana discounts this, as does Sydney on the basis of what Unity told her later. Diana says: 'At a Parteitag we were given seats next to Fräulein Braun, and thought her pretty and charming.' Unity, in Sydney's account, confirms this and adds that Eva Braun was 'always friendly to them, and beautifully dressed. When she heard Eva Braun address the Führer as "*du*", she realized then that there was probably more between them than appeared, but . . . if the matter was not to be made public, she would obviously not speak of it.' Unity's own love life was quite straightforward and Hitler had no part in it; the story in Nerin Gun's book on Eva Braun that Unity was seen on a sofa necking with Hitler in Haus Wahnfried, at Bayreuth, is of interest only as showing the sort of thing that people invent. It has been circumstantially denied by Frau Winifred Wagner. Unity's boyfriend for most of the Hitler years was Erik Widemann, usually known as Erich, which is the more common German form of the name. In 1939 we are fairly sure she had a brief love affair with Tom's friend Janos Almasy. She and Hitler were alone together rather rarely, and then only for tea, when she wanted to tell him something private. She stayed with him once or twice, if one can call it that, in a sleeper on his special train; his habit of taking her on train journeys accounts for her nickname among his entourage of '*Mitfahrt*' (literally journey together, conveying the idea of travelling companion). She never spent a night either at his Munich flat or in his house at Berchtesgaden. There was a false report that she spent the night of 6–7 May 1939 at Berchtesgaden: Giles Romilly rang her from the *Daily Express* to request confirmation and she asked him to deny it, as she told her mother in a letter dated 8 May 1939. He failed to get the denial into print, because the false report is given as fact both by Pryce-Jones and by Andrew Barrow in his *Gossip 1920–1970*. Unity's diary makes it circumstantially clear that she was in Munich that weekend.

Unity's secret was that she could talk to Hitler without false flattery or underlying fear. She was a genuine admirer, not a courtier or sycophant; she was prepared to argue with him, and sometimes did so. Members of his entourage were surprised to notice that, far from irritating him, this put him into a good humour. Of course, she was also an attentive listener, but then so were all who surrounded him. Her speciality was not listening but commenting, discussing, even answering back; in short, chatting. Hitler enjoyed conversation, but had reached a position where normal conversation was hard to come by. People were frightened of him, because his anger could be literally deadly; or on the other hand, they had their own axes to grind. The ordinary human contact that another absolute ruler, the caliph Haroun Al-Rashid, could only get by wandering the streets of Baghdad in heavy disguise, was provided for Hitler by this unusual foreign girl.

As to Hitler's effect on Unity, it has to be remembered that he had charm and humour. The man who ruined Europe, the man who initiated the holocaust, still had charm and humour. In fact, his attractiveness was his stock in trade; without it he would have remained a failed art student. There seems now to be a generally perceived moral duty to portray Hitler as a ranting buffoon; to record that he could be good company, we are given to understand, is to insult the memory of his victims. This is inherently a non sequitur. It is certainly everyone's duty to ensure that nothing like Hitlerism is allowed to happen again, but for this purpose Hitler must be remembered as he actually was; indeed as people like Lloyd George found him to be. No one like Chaplin's *Great Dictator* or Brecht's *Arturo Ui*, or indeed like the mauve-faced automaton portrayed by Derek Jacobi in the film about Unity, would ever come anywhere near the possession of enough power to have millions of people massacred.

Diana was almost as much under Hitler's spell as was Unity and her account in *A Life of Contrasts* is interesting.

Hitler was the most unselfconscious politician I have ever come across. He never sought to impress, he never bothered to act a part. If he felt morose, he was morose. If he was in high spirits, he talked brilliantly and sometimes did wonderfully comic imitations. Once when I was there, he was shown a photograph in a paper of Mussolini. The Duce was on horseback, he had just been presented with a sword, and he lifted it high above his head in a dramatic gesture. Hitler, after 'being' Mussolini, added, 'of course, if somebody gave me a sword, I shouldn't know what to do with it. I should just say, "here, Schaub, take this sword".'

But there was more to Hitler's charm than this. Incredible as it may sound, he excited protective, almost motherly instincts by a sort of helpless look, and this at the height of his power. Diana says that 'what one might call the chivalrous attitude towards Hitler' seemed particularly marked in Goering. There is one place where, to this day, one can get a feeling of this aspect of Hitler's appeal – in Leni Riefenstahl's film about the 1934 Parteitag, *Triumph of the Will*. There is a moment when Hitler gets out of his aircraft and looks around him for the welcoming party; he seems, for that moment, helpless and vulnerable, the Little Man. That apparent vulnerability can exercise mass attractiveness is, of course, well known. In the case of Hitler, who was also possessed of strong dominance and almost hypnotic powers of persuasion, this faculty helped him by, as it were, disarming those he confronted before they were overwhelmed.

There are several passages in the correspondence between Diana and Unity in which they refer to Hitler as looking 'sweet' or 'beloved'. This was the effect he had on them. This lovable man was then in due course to have enormous numbers of innocent people slaughtered.

Life would be simpler if someone capable of ordering mass murder could never show an attractive side.

# 31

# Hitler, the Family Friend

Hitler soon invited Unity over to his table again, this time in the Carlton Teeraum. She was accompanied by her friend Mary Woodisse, an English student in Munich who was also, through Unity, to see quite a lot of Hitler, though unlike Unity she was quiet and retiring. On 2 March she lunched again at the Osteria with Mary, and this time they met Goebbels, who Unity noted was 'very gay, and laughs a lot'. She patched up her relationship with Fräulein Baum after a fashion. On 11 March, again at the Osteria Bavaria, Unity introduced Diana to Hitler. They all talked for an hour and a half, and he invited them to the Bayreuth festival in the following year, 1936.

During the 1935 Easter holidays Unity met a clever, good-looking, unremarkable young man called Donald Maclean, the future traitor and spy. They stayed for a weekend in the same country house, and Maclean filled in a page of *All About Everybody*. This was a little book in which people invited their friends each to fill in a blank page with answers to various printed questions, some of them rather arch or trivial, but nevertheless giving an impression of the person at that time. Under the name and date, the questions were:

What is your occupation?
What occupation would you choose if you had unlimited choice?
Do you believe in the equality of the sexes?
Which would you rather have, love or money?
What is your favourite pastime?
What is your besetting sin?
Do you consider yourself good-looking?
Do you believe in love at first sight?

How many love affairs have you had?

Do you advocate polygamy?

What is your age?

Do you believe in marrying young?

Who is your hero in real life?

Who is your heroine in real life?

Who is your favourite film actor?

Who is your favourite film actress?

Maclean was a twenty-one-year-old student; he would like to be a dancer if he had unlimited choice; he did not believe in the equality of sexes; he thought love more important than money; his favourite pastime was ping-pong, his besetting sin prurience. He thought he was quite good-looking, he believed in love at first sight and in polygamy, but would not say how many love affairs he had had. He believed in marrying young, his hero and heroine were respectively Rabelais and Catherine de Medici, and his favourite actor and actress were Peter Lorre and Anna Sten. Diana, as well as Unity, had an *All About Everybody*.

Unity went back to Munich; Sydney came out to visit her, and had tea with Hitler at the Carlton Teeraum, with Unity acting as interpreter. She did not enjoy this; in a letter to Diana dated 25 April 1935 she wrote: 'Whenever I translated anything for either of them, it always sounded stupid translated . . . I fear the whole thing was wasted on Muv, she is just the same as before. Having so little feeling, she doesn't feel his goodness and wonderfulness radiating out like we do, and like even Farve did.' The same month, Mosley came, and Hitler asked Unity to meet him. Having no idea of the relationship between Mosley and Diana, he was surprised to find Unity and he knew each other. It was a large lunch party; Goebbels and his wife were there, and Ribbentrop, and Winifred Wagner, the composer's English-born daughter-in-law who ran the Bayreuth festival and was to become a close friend of the Mitfords. Werlin, a director of Daimler-Benz who had been at Hitler's table when Unity first met him, went to visit England and had tea at the House of Lords with David, Sydney and Tom. He was impressed: '*England ist ewig*,' he kept saying. (England is everlasting.) Tom wrote to Unity saying he had found Werlin 'really delightful. He can hardly speak English so I talked with him most of the time and he told me what a high opinion Hitler has of you and how unusually intelligent he [Hitler] thinks you are. He also told me the story of the introduction, how he pretended to know you and didn't really, etc., when Hitler told him to go to your table and fetch you.' We know that it was in fact Herr Deutelmoser, the proprietor of the Osteria Bavaria, who asked Unity to go over, so presumably Werlin had cold feet and delegated the task. On 3 June, Unity again lunched at Hitler's flat with Diana and Mary Woodisse. She wrote to Sydney: 'We had a most lovely lunch, none of which of course the Führer ate.' Hitler was a vegetarian, though he would eat eggs, and he only drank mineral water. For his guests he would order food to be sent round from the Walterspiel restaurant. 'The Führer was absolutely wonderfully sweet and showed me his new Böcklin picture with great pride.' Later in the same letter: 'Today has been wonderful and hot. I spent four hours with Max and Stadelmann on a big grassy meadow near the aerodrome. It is extraordinary the way they have no work to do – just sitting around all day in their uniforms . . .'

Later in June, Unity did something really disastrous. Already in May the English press had cottoned on to the fact that there was a story in her; the first mention seems to have been a photograph of her in the *Sunday Express* with the caption 'She Adores Hitler'. This, says Sydney, was the first of what turned later into a press persecution. It was a persecution that was to continue without mercy when Unity was helpless and incurably ill. But by her action on 18 June 1935 she did ask for it.

It seems to have been on little more than a whim that she wrote a letter to *Der Stürmer*. (Her diary entry is simply: 'Write letters, one to *Stürmer*.') This was a low-brow weekly that specialized in anti-semitic smears, often about the defilement of German womanhood by the base sexual desires of Jews. It was an anti-semitic version of those English Sunday papers which peddle sex stories, with a vulgar prurience thinly disguised under a pretence of shock. Its owner and editor was the notorious Julius Streicher. To this periodical, Unity wrote as follows:

Dear *Stürmer*,

As a British woman fascist, I should like to express my admiration for you.

I have lived in Munich for a year and read the *Stürmer* every week.

If only we had such a newspaper in England! The English have no notion of the Jewish danger. English Jews are always described as 'decent'. Perhaps the Jews in England are more clever with their propaganda than in other countries. I cannot tell, but it is a certain fact that our struggle is extremely hard. Our worst Jews work only behind the scenes. They never come into the open, and therefore we cannot show them to the British public in their true dreadfulness. We hope, however, that you will see that we will soon win against the world enemy, in spite of all his cunning.

We think with joy of the day when we shall be able to say with might and authority: England for the English! Out with the Jews!

With German greeting, Heil Hitler!

Unity Mitford.

P.S. If you find room in your newspaper for this letter, please publish my whole name. I do not want to sign UM but I want everyone to know that I am a Jew hater.

Streicher found room for it all right, though not till late July. He gave it a full page and accompanied it with a large photograph of Unity. But as soon as he received the letter he got in touch with her. He invited her to the Hesselberg, near Nuremberg, for the midsummer festival there. It was a gathering based on folklore and folk dancing featuring a big bonfire, which the Nazis had taken over as an annual celebration; it took place on the night of 22 June and the following day. Streicher picked Unity up in Munich, took her sightseeing round Würzburg, and then on to Dinkelsbühl where she was to stay the night. She wrote afterwards to her mother: 'At 9.30 p.m. we started for the high hill . . . We drove in a column, seven giant black Mercedes rushing through the night, all full of men in uniform, all open, I the only woman. When we reached the top of the hill, we marched through the crowd, band playing, between cordons of SA men with torches, to the speakers' stand.' Streicher addressed the throng with its massed torches, and to Unity's surprise he spoke about her, quoting her still unpublished letter, and presented her with a bouquet. 'It was all so unexpected, I can still hardly believe it.' Next day, in the blazing sun, she was back in a seat near the stand, and Streicher asked her to say a few words. Completely unprepared, she did so, hoping for a lasting friendship between Germany and Britain, and expressing her admiration for Streicher.

Sydney and David were annoyed by the press reports which resulted from this escapade, as also from a major interview about the British Union of Fascists that Unity gave to the *Münchener Zeitung*; they had been going to see Unity in Germany but cancelled their trip. David wrote an angry letter to Unity. She defended herself to Sydney: 'I couldn't refuse Streicher's invitation, could I, firstly for politeness' sake, secondly because, naturally, I longed to go. When once there, I couldn't refuse the bouquet offered to me, nor could I refuse to go to the microphone when he called for me.' It was lucky for Unity that the *Stürmer* letter was not yet published. By the time it was, Unity was in England and could soften up her parents in person, something at which the evidence suggests she was rather good, though she had a job with David. She wrote to Diana from High Wycombe on 26 July 1935 that their father was 'in a vile temper for several reasons. Partly because his car broke down, and partly because I brought the pup into the house, but mostly because of my letter in the *Stürmer*.' This was reported in the *Evening Standard* that day, and in three morning papers on the twenty-seventh. Unity received piles of letters; she answered those that were admiring and ignored the critical ones. There were two from her sisters. Nancy was uneasily mocking: 'Call me early, Goering dear, for I'm to be Queen of the May. Fantasia! Fantasia!' Decca wrote at the end of an affectionate letter that she loved her Boud in spite of what she had done, but making it clear that she disapproved.

During October 1935 Unity was ill with a throat infection. At first, her friend Erik looked after her; then he had to go away and David came out. When she recovered, he went with her to Berlin, and she sent Sydney on the twenty-first of that month an account which must have made her mother laugh.

Forgy is in despair because he can't skate. He is now quite determined to hate his stay here, which is a pity. He refuses to take the least interest in anything and pines for home. He had much better have let me come alone, like I planned. I must say one thing, he is very good tempered.

He worries all the waiters and servants dreadfully. You see they can mostly speak a little English and he will talk to them as if they were English, and on the train he suddenly said to the dining car man 'I don't think much of your permanent way, but the rolling stock is a pretty good going on. These cigarettes are killing me by inches!' Then he fires questions at them like 'Do they sell Brambles here?' [his kind of hat] or he tells them about her ladyship and expects them to know it's you. The poor things are so confused, I think they think he's a bit cracked.

In the meantime, it was Diana's turn to demonstrate in public for what she believed. It happened quite by chance, on 27 October. She happened to be walking in Hyde Park when she saw a meeting, and went over to see what was happening. It was a demonstration organized by the British Non-Sectarian Anti-Nazi Council, and among the speakers was Clement Attlee, leader of the Labour Party. She listened; and in due course a resolution was put to the meeting that there should be a boycott of goods from Nazi Germany. All those in favour? A forest of hands went up. Those against? Suddenly something got into Diana; she put up her hand, the only person to do so. Then the band played the National Anthem – this would not happen at a modern left-wing demonstration – and again Diana's hand went up in a Fascist salute. The crowd jeered and began to turn nasty. Two young members of Mosley's movement happened to be there, and escorted Diana away before she could be hurt. This was the only time Diana ever did anything of this sort; it was more typical of Unity.

In April 1936 Sydney took Unity, Decca and Debo on a 'Hellenic' cruise, really a Mediterranean cruise with lectures, organized by the travel agent Sir Henry Lunn. By Decca's account, the girls were rather a handful, but Sydney seems not to have noticed. Besides the Greek scholars and other lecturers there were several fairly well-known people on board, including the Duke and Duchess of Atholl. The Duchess of Atholl, though a Conservative MP, was later to be known as the Red Duchess because of her fervent support of the Spanish Republicans. The ship, the *Laetitia*, went to Corsica, then to various places in Greece, then to Constantinople, and then back for more stops in Greece. That was followed by two days at sea. To amuse the passengers on the first of these days, 18 April, Sir Henry thought he would take advantage of the presence of the notorious Unity Mitford. He organized a debate on the motion 'That the dis-advantages of the system of government in Italy and Germany outweigh the advantages claimed for them'. This motion was moved by a certain Mr Hirst, and Sir Henry Lunn spoke in favour of it. Then Unity led for the opposition, followed by a King's Counsel whose name she did not catch, but who seconded her. Then the debate was open: Sydney, the Duke of Atholl and others spoke, and the Duchess of Atholl wound up. The anti-Nazi motion was passed by a large majority. Afterwards at dinner, the Duchess sent round to Unity the following note:

May I say how well I think you delivered your speech today? It was so unaffected and so sincere.

If I said anything which you did not like, I hope you will believe that I did so out of no personal feeling against you or anyone else. But as a Member of Parliament at a time of great national anxiety, I feel it my duty to try to make known what I believe to be facts . . . which it is important for our people to know.

We see this as an apology for a biased summing up. In terms of debating practice, the Duchess ought, as she well knew, to have been impartial between the two sides, and not to have introduced new points to which there would be no chance to reply. As to the Duke, whose speech Sydney had considered to be rather against the motion than for it, he sent round a glass of champagne for Unity with his wife's note. This account is mainly based on that of Sydney, but it is corrected by reference to Unity's diary con-cerning the order in which people spoke. Sydney remembers the Duchess as proposing the motion, which in itself indicates that she made the most memorable of the anti-Nazi speeches.

On 23 April they landed at Malaga, from where they went to see Granada. Decca says that a crowd of Spaniards got in a rage when they saw Unity's swastika badge and tried to attack her; then other members of the cruise managed to get her away from them and back to the cars. This seems to be a little exaggerated. The relevant part of Unity's diary entry tells of visiting the Generalife Palace and the Alhambra, both of which she admires. They lunch, they look at the cathedral, they start back for Malaga at four and arrive at seven. Sydney, however, does note that 'the crowds in the towns seemed hostile to us and our cars, and pushed their clenched fists up against our windows'. It was three months before the outbreak of the Civil War, so this was a small sign of the revolutionary agitation which was to induce the Army to rise in revolt; the whole group of rich foreigners was the target, not one girl's badge. We think Decca is after the lapse of time confusing Granada with Tetuan, where Sydney records that she herself advised Unity to remove her swastika badge because 'it aroused too much interest'.

One further small point about this cruise may be worth mentioning. Pryce-Jones talked to Sir Henry Lunn's son Peter, who was helping his father run the cruise. According to Peter Lunn, Decca had told him that Unity said her nightly prayers to a photograph of Hitler, and he added that Unity had confirmed this to him. The 20 April entry in Unity's diary says: 'Tease Peter Lunn.' The two Bouds, then, were collaborating here.

Meanwhile, in Britain, Mosley and his Fascists were subjected to a complete boycott by the media, in the sense that they reported only the disorder at his meetings, not the contents of his speeches. This had nothing directly to do with Mosley's public rapprochement with the Nazis, although that, and Unity's much-publicized *Stürmer* letter written 'as a British woman fascist', did him no good at all. The boycott really goes back to the Olympia meeting. In 1936 the Public Order Act was passed, banning political uniforms – a sign that Mosley's whole style was distasteful to the British Establishment. Mosley and some of his lieutenants drew crowds of people to their speeches, and apart from organized disrupters it is clear that the atmosphere at the meetings was friendly; but Mosley was realist enough to know that this itself would never get him the breakthrough that he needed. To reach that large majority who never went to meetings, he needed money enough to start a daily paper of his own as well as a string of other periodicals over the whole range from sensational to intellectual, to finance candidates, and to pay constituency agents. Labour had the trade unions to support them, and the Conservatives had business interests: the Fascists had nothing anywhere near comparable. W. E. D. Allen, a former MP in the advertising business, suggested to Mosley a deal that might have helped.

The thirties were the heyday of radio advertising. Then as now, the BBC carried no advertisements; then as now, there was an almost insatiable demand, especially among young people, for programmes of popular music – the expression 'pop' had not been coined, but the demand was there. Under the sternly high-minded Lord Reith there was nothing remotely equivalent to the modern Radio 1, which itself was started in direct response to Radio Caroline and the 'pop pirates' of the sixties. Two foreign stations were filling some of the demand, beaming popular programmes to Britain and accepting advertisements; one was Radio Luxembourg, which is still of course with us, and the other was Radio Normandie, which made an enormous fortune for Captain Leonard Plugge, MP, the man who obtained the concession for it from the French government.

The plan was to found a radio station of this sort, broadcasting from outside the country. The broadcasts were to be entirely non-political, but the Allens would receive a share of the advertising revenues, of which Mosley would obtain a percentage. Allen had secured the services of Peter Eckersley, a BBC engineer of extremely high qualifications whom Lord Reith had sacked, rather typically, because he became divorced. Allen had good Irish connections and his first hope was for a concession from the Irish Free State; this came to nothing. There was also a scientific adviser, whose profession was that of industrial chemist; his main function would be in the second stage, when a vertical trust would be set up to make 'own brand' goods which the radio station would promote. When this man was introduced to Diana, she was told that he had invented a compound to take the rim off a bath. Diana was a bit slow. 'But surely one *needs* a rim on a bath,' was her comment. 'Wouldn't it otherwise be rather sharp if one wanted to sit on the edge?' Her life had been too sheltered for her to realize that scum forms a rim. 'I got to know what a rim on a bath was later, all right,' she told us. 'In Holloway.'

The question was where they should set up their station. The Channel Island of Sark was interested, but had, of course, no wavelength to dispose of. Then they tried Hitler's Germany. The case they put did not depend on political solidarity, but was rather a matter of tempting the Germans with the prospect of earning foreign currency as the French did. Ohnesorge, the German

Postmaster General, expressed interest, and negotiations got under way. Diana played a key role as interpreter between Mosley and the Germans, and also as negotiator on Mosley's behalf. She says: 'A lot of the time I simply had to go to Berlin and wait about.' On 2 December 1936 she writes to Unity from a hotel in Berlin: 'I did not mean to write, but I am so bored and miserable that I feel I must. I have been here a week tomorrow and I have been alone the entire time . . . I thought I would come back on Sunday, but now it looks more like being *next* Sunday.' Two months later she was back in Berlin, though this time it was more fun. To Unity she wrote again on 16 February 1937: 'We went to Mozart's *Gärtnerin aus Liebe* which is charming and darling the *most* lovely scenery by Benno von Arent, really divine, like Cec [Cecil Beaton] or Olivette [Oliver Messel] but rather more solid.' Professor Benno von Arent was a stage designer who, as a member of Hitler's social circle, became with his wife a friend of both Diana and Unity. He was to spend nine years in the Gulag Archipelago as a war criminal, though all he is ever known to have done is design stage sets. Diana goes on: 'It is wonderful being here and not having to wait by the telephone; I have actually been to the picture gallery among other things.' Her numerous visits to Berlin at this time were all connected with the radio business; for fun, she went to Munich. Of course the whole scheme had to be kept deadly secret; if the Fascist connection was suspected before the station was on the air, advertisers might be discouraged. Negotiations did, however, go slowly forward. At first, the main obstacle was the question of a wavelength in the medium band; to give up one of the ones they had would have been a sacrifice for the Germans. After the Anschluss, the takeover of Austria in March 1938, this problem was solved because Germany had the Austrian wavelengths at its disposal. *'Sie haben Ihre Welle,'* said Ohnesorge to Diana, *'und zwar eine sehr schöne.'* (You have your wavelength, and a very nice one, too.) Unity seems to have taken part in these negotiations once only, and then at the highest level after they were essentially completed. She wrote to Diana on 4 June 1938 that Hitler 'thinks the whole thing is OK, he has spoken with the Minister and there will be no more *Verhandlung* [negotiation] necessary'. Work began soon on a transmitter beamed to Britain from the North Sea island of

Borkum; it was designed jointly by Peter Eckersley and his German counterpart. During the war it was used for broadcasting German propaganda.

Ultimately, events ensured that the only successful thing about these negotiations was their confidentiality. It was mostly to preserve this state of affairs that Mosley and Diana decided to keep secret their marriage, which took place on 6 October 1936. Had she been in Germany as his wife and bearing his name, all sorts of people might have guessed too soon at some connection between the radio company and Mosley. The scheme was of course perfectly legal; it was also a pure business transaction involving no element of subsidy from the Germans, who in fact drove a somewhat harder bargain than the French had done with Captain Plugge. All the same, premature press publicity would have wrecked it. When Diana's marriage with Mosley was finally announced on the birth of their son Alexander in November 1938, Mosley said that he had not wanted to expose Diana to the public strain of being his wife; this rather thin explanation was accepted by all without question. However, there was a problem as to how a marriage between two people so much in the public eye as Mosley and Diana could possibly be kept secret. For this purpose, Diana made use of her personal friendship with the Nazi leaders; it was the only important use either she or Unity were to make of this, unless we count Hitler's help in securing Unity a flat in Munich in 1939.

The marriage ceremony took place in Berlin. Diana and Unity were staying at the Goebbels's house near the Reichskanzlei, and Mosley with one or two friends in the Hotel Kaiserhof. By making her writing small, Unity fits more than usual into the 6 October space in her diary:

Frau Dr, Diana and I drive to Hermann Goeringstrasse about 11.30, I in my car to Kaiserhof to pick up Leader . . . to Hermann Goeringstrasse. The Führer and Doktor [Goebbels] arrive 02.30 . . . The Standesbeamte performs the ceremony. Bill [Allen] and I are witnesses. All sit and talk afterwards, then Frau Dr and I drive to Schwanenwerder [the Goebbels's home], the others follow, the Führer last. Lunch there . . . then a *Dolmetscher* [interpreter] arrives and the Führer and the Leader go and talk alone . . .

Hitler gave them a dinner at the Reichskanzlei, after which he set off for Munich in his special train, taking Unity along. There had been a little contretemps beforehand, though. When Diana was in the registrar's office making the preliminary arrangements, she had given all her personal information including the names of her parents. David's Christian name had made the official look up sharply. 'David?' he queried, for David in Germany is regarded as an exclusively Jewish name. Perhaps the marriage might contravene the Nuremberg laws against the mixing of races. The adjutant accompanying Diana assured him that it was all right – in England a David could often be perfectly Aryan.

The press silence was total: very few people knew of the marriage until it was announced two years later. Mosley did not even tell his mother, which was unkind because she idolized him and was at the time a person of firm religious conviction and profound respectability, who suffered from the idea that her son was living in sin. This shows to what lengths he would go to keep the marriage secret. Diana did tell her parents, under a vow of secrecy; but because of this secrecy, to her disappointment, they forbade Debo to visit her at Wootton Lodge. Unity wrote to Diana on 26 March 1937:

Yes, I did know that Muv isn't going to allow Debo to come and stay with you, I had it all out with her before I left. The poor thing was quite distraught about it and . . . did hope you would understand . . . only suddenly it came over her that she couldn't let Debo, being so young, go to stay with you when the whole world *thinks* you are living in sin although you aren't really.

The marriage did thaw out David and Sydney's relationship with Mosley – before he and Diana were married they had greatly disapproved of him, because they saw him as having broken up Diana's first marriage. Sydney was in due course to become great friends with him, though David, until his extreme old age, remained somewhat disapproving. This was because the approaching war caused a strong reaction in David against anyone desiring peace with what had again become the filthy Hun. Debo did once go to Wootton on the quiet, nevertheless; it was in August 1938. Mosley had never met her before; he was peacefully fishing in the lake, accompanied by Diana, Jonathan and Desmond, when Debo arrived with two men friends, one of them Lord Andrew Cavendish whom she later married. Diana wrote to Unity on 18 August: 'They stayed literally ten minutes and then scrammed. They all looked as if they had seen a ghost, Debo said they were frightened they might be shot at.'

Diana and Mosley had moved in 1936 to Wootton Lodge, over the Staffordshire border from Ashbourne; they rented it and she gave up Eaton Square. Wootton was the second of her 'beautiful houses' mentioned in *A Life of Contrasts*. It was an imposing seventeenth-century stone house with a wide stone staircase up to the front door. At the back, it was perched on a rock. It had a charming sunken garden, leading down to two lakes stocked with trout. 'I am so happy to live in such a lovely house. You will adore it,' Diana wrote to Unity on 26 June 1936. 'I am in paradise; and as many roses to pick as you want.' The landscape was wild and romantic: the Weaver Hill was visible in the distance. Jonathan, aged six, was struck with the name 'Lodge', for knowing that lodges are found at the gates of large houses, he imagined that Wootton had once been the gatehouse of some unimaginably enormous mansion at the end of a marathon drive. Where this huge pile could have been, he never worked out.

In the meantime, Unity continued to spend most of her time in Germany, based in Munich. After she had become fluent in German she had no regular subject to study, nor did she attempt to take a job; life was cheap there because of the special exchange rate, and when she was in England she lived with her family, so she got by on her allowance. She worked at one period translating part of *Mein Kampf*, we do not know what has happened to this translation, and the whole of *Mein Kampf* was anyway available in English. Naturally there were all sorts of rumours and speculation as to what she was up to; the answer, so far as we can see, is nothing much. It was not that she just hung around waiting for her meetings with Hitler; she had plenty of friends, and she was a sightseer, opera-goer and film fan. Certainly, there are times when her diary expressed disappointment about not seeing Hitler, but this does not happen sufficiently often for one to be able to call her obsessed on the subject. On one occasion, Hitler discussed Mosley's movement with Unity. Unity writes to Diana on 8 April 1937: 'He said very emphatically that he thought it *might* have proved a fatal mistake in England to call them Fascists and Blackshirts instead of something typically English, and suggested that if he had been starting a party in England he would have gone back to Cromwell and perhaps called his S.A. "Ironsides".'

Did Unity ever denounce anyone to Hitler? That people should have suspected this is at the same time natural and fundamentally illogical. For denunciations there certainly were in this ruthless dictatorship. The people were kept content, and Hitler himself was surrounded by a charmed circle, but persecution took place, and there were disappearances and arbitrary arrests; and among the social elite there were many, Gentiles as well as Jews, who were hostile to Hitler and justifiably afraid of him. The question, though, is whether Unity told on people. Pryce-Jones retails a rumour that she denounced a Prince Lippe-Biesterfeld who is supposed to have been arrested after criticizing the Nazis in front of Unity at a dinner party. He does not establish even that the Prince was at the dinner party concerned. If he was there, his arrest might have had nothing to do with the dinner party, and if there was a denunciation, it could have been made by another guest. The prospect of Unity having anything to do with the Prince's arrest recedes so fast that the rumour seems hardly worth mentioning. Certainly, Unity would have been a dead loss as an *agent provocateur*. Her open enthusiasm for Nazism was hardly designed to lead people on – it would have been more likely to shut them up. Not that it always did so: later, on 18 March 1939, she wrote to Diana of a dress show in Munich: 'The entire Munich *Adel* [nobility] was there, and it felt *exactly* like an underground Gunpowder Treason and Plot meeting . . . I sighed with relief when we left.'

But Unity was the essentially innocent instigator of one rather sad little affair, the downfall of Putzi Hanfstaengl. Hitler showed in this matter one of the faults which rendered him unfit for the status of world leader – his frivolity. The reader may think that even to mention frivolity in connection with Hitler is to white-wash him. Of course his frivolity becomes lost in the enormous magnitude of his crimes; yet it does, perhaps, have a significance even in connection with those very crimes. For the Putzi incident was an example of the petty cruelty that can be a sign of some-thing worse.

It started on 6 February 1937. Unity, Diana and their cousin

Clementine Mitford were in Berlin and Hitler asked them round to the Reichskanzlei. A number of other people were there. They had tea, then dinner, then saw two films. Afterwards, according to Unity's diary, she and Diana chatted with the Führer. 'He plans wonderfully funny joke on Putzi.' Clementine, now Lady Beit, remembers the occasion but was not in on the discussion, which could hardly have interested her as she did not know Putzi.

What happened was that, some time previously, Putzi had said to Unity that now the party was in power it was a pity that there was no struggle any more, except in Spain. He envied those who were fighting for Franco. Unity repeated this to Hitler; it seemed harmless enough. Hitler said: 'I'll tell you what we'll do, we'll let him fight for Franco if that is what he wants.' He outlined the practical joke. Putzi would be told to report to a military airport for orders for a special, secret job for the party. A pilot would take him up; then, in mid-air, would hand him his orders revealing that he was going to be dropped behind the Republican lines in Spain for a secret mission. After circling round a few times, Putzi would be dropped again at Munich, none the worse except for a little scare. Diana and Unity laughed with Hitler, not really thinking the scheme would be carried out.

It was carried out, though, exactly as planned. Putzi reported to the airport, the pilot gave him his sealed orders, and then dropped him again. But the effect was shattering on a timid man who was by now well aware of the seamy side of Nazism and worried at the personal danger to himself now that he had so obviously lost his influence. When he opened the papers, he at once came to the conclusion that this was an elaborate plot to murder him. He pleaded with the pilot: 'Fortunately,' as he put it to Jonathan afterwards, 'the pilot was a Bavarian.' We cannot know exactly what the pilot told him, but when he landed at the airport, Putzi thought he was faking engine trouble in defiance of orders and in response to his plea. Putzi took the first train out of Germany to Switzerland, from where he travelled after a few weeks to London and holed himself up in a mews flat, terrified that the Nazis were after him.

This happened when Unity was over in England to be with her family during the crisis over Decca's elopement, and Putzi was in Switzerland by the time she got back on 23 March. She spent the next two days in Nuremberg with the Streicher family looking round the new grounds for the Parteitag, seeing *Die Fledermaus* with Frau Streicher and her son Elmar, lunching, dining, chatting and singing with the family. Nothing sinister or distasteful happened; it is too often supposed that someone unpleasant like Streicher is unpleasant all the time, but life is not like that. 'I stayed three nights in Nuremberg and spent the whole time with the lovely Gauleiter,' she wrote to Diana on 26–27 March. The only irritating presence was Elmar Streicher, who, though he played the mouth organ beautifully, struck Unity as ignorantly pompous. 'Elmar makes the most amazing statements about England (he was there for a few weeks last year) and he is always believed in preference to me . . . He seems to make one long speech the whole time, if I were his father I would shut him up.' So it was not until 26 March, Good Friday, that she rang up Erna Hanfstaengl and heard what had happened. She hurried off to have tea with her to discuss what could be done. 'It's all so dreadful,' she notes in her diary; and to Diana, in the same letter just quoted, she said that Erna had not slept for worry in the last three weeks. Erna did, however, cheer up enough to give a big Easter lunch for Frank Buchman of the Oxford Group (later Moral Rearmament) and two of his supporters. She then, Unity thinks in a letter to Diana of 30 March, went to visit Putzi in Zürich. It was Diana who tried to do something about it, though not till May, on one of her visits to Berlin. She saw Goering and told him the whole story. On 28 May she wrote to Unity:

I saw *von und ʒu* [a nickname for Goering] and he asked me to go and see the two-headed man [Putzi] and persuade him to go back, and then they wouldn't do anything to him. I said we were there when the joke was invented, so he said well then you can promise it was only a joke and I give my word as an officer that nothing will happen to him and he will get a *wissenschaftliche Stellung*. [Scientific post: one wonders what Goering had in mind, or whether Diana misheard him.] When I got back I rang him up but I doubt if he will see me. I shall do my best, mostly for Gooders' [Erna's] sake and also because he may do harm, although I feel he is too mad to be taken much notice of. *Von und ʒu* sent you his love and said he wouldn't like to think of a Parteitag without us. Wasn't it sweet of him.

Putzi did see her, but it was no use. She wrote to Unity on 8 June:

I saw the two-headed man in London and darling he was quite mad and he said 'if you were really there when they thought of the trick, of course you would have come and said so long ago. It has taken them five months to think of this lie for you to tell me. Of course, there is not a word of truth in it, the truth is they wanted to *bring* me *um* [kill me] and they didn't manage it, so now they pretend it was a joke. In any case, *alle diese Schweine sind für mich erledigt.* [I'm finished with all these swine.] He simply screamed at me. I begged him to be *anständig* [decent] for Erna's sake and he shrieked '*Was heisst anständig?* [What do you mean – decent?] They have never been *anständig* to me,' etc., etc.

From his point of view, it was impossible to believe the whole thing was a joke. To think that his enemies had poisoned the mind of his hero, Hitler, to the point of ordering his assassination, at least left him a big man, a Roehm. To admit to himself that, on the contrary, he had been elbowed aside to be made a figure of fun, would have been to enter a psychological wilderness. By the time Pryce-Jones interviewed him, he had persuaded himself that Unity had denounced him to Hitler, but he cannot have believed this at the time for he saw her on several occasions in London, and her behaviour is utterly inconsistent with the theory. The first time they met was quite by chance. Unity described the encounter in a letter to Diana of 7 July 1937:

I had to drive Debo to Nancy's house, where she was staying the night. As I pulled up by the gate, what should I see but a huge two-headed figure in a dinner jacket walking along towards us. I rushed at him affectionately but he was very stand-offish. Debo said she had never seen a lady pursue a man like I did. Anyway, I managed to say what I wanted to say but was answered with a flood of invective about Him. But all the same, I couldn't help but feel sorry for him, he looked so broken somehow.

It was in fact lucky for Putzi that things turned out as they did. Had Hitler not played on him this callous practical joke, or had he returned at Goering's invitation, he would certainly have been arraigned at Nuremberg. Probably he would have been jailed as a minor war criminal. As it was, he was taken to the United States during the war and treated rather well: Roosevelt and Churchill themselves found time to question him about Hitler's past and character. Their dialogue has been published in the form of a book, *Catoctin Conversations*. He returned to Germany and spent a serene old age in his pleasant house near the warm, shallow Staffelsee. Some of the villagers, he told Jonathan in 1950, had even started addressing him again by the title he had acquired as a Nazi government functionary, calling him Herr Hofrat. By believing what he did, he could keep his pride.

The Mitfords' old family friend Mrs Ham visited Unity in Munich in April 1937, and the two of them got arrested. It is worth giving Unity's description in full, for it shows how Unity's attitude to Mrs Ham was that of the whole family: affection, comic exasperation and a particular sort of teasing. It ties in exactly with Nancy's letters to Mrs Ham. She wrote to Diana on 22 April:

The Wid is being killingly funny but I must say I have had about enough of her now. I am being very unkind and brutal to her as I have discovered that is the best way to treat her. Don't you agree? Of course, all her plans for her journey have gone wrong and she thinks of nothing else and is *always* asking for advice, which I refuse to give her, she went to mass this morning to pray about it. One very funny thing has happened to us. On the morning of the *Geburtstag* [Hitler's birthday, 20 April] there was a military parade on the Oberwiesenfeld, and as I had forgotten to ask for tickets the Wid and I just went and walked about and watched it from a distance. Some armoured cars passed us and I made as if to photo them but they were going too quick. Immediately a hoard [*sic*] of Grüne Polizei rushed up, and one of them jumped in the car and made me drive to the Gestapo. Mrs Ham, protesting her innocence in broken German, was made to come, too. At the Gestapo we were kept in *Schutzhaft* [protective detention] for two hours while they developed my film. Mrs H. was killingly funny the whole time. Wasn't it wonderfully funny that I should happen to be arrested just when she was there . . . She is killing with Erna, they adore each other; at least she adores Erna . . . Erna and I dragged Mrs Ham to the wrestling and she sat most of the time with her eyes shut.

For poor Mrs Hammersley, the arrest must have been terrifying. This passage is perhaps the most striking example in all Unity's correspondence of her complete unawareness that the Nazis were in any way dangerous.

By the end of 1937, both Unity and Diana were referring to Hitler in their letters to each other as Wolf, the name he went by to his real intimates; but they did not use it to his face, Diana tells us. The name survives in the only place in Germany still called after Hitler – Wolfsburg, home of the Volkswagen or People's Car that was designed by Porsche to provide a car which ordinary people could afford. Porsche designed what was essentially the post-war beetle, and Hitler's entourage suggested that the place where it was to be made should be called Hitlerstadt. He demurred, but agreed to Wolfsburg. (Professor Benno von Arent told Jonathan this in 1955.) Had the British occupying authorities known of the name's connection with Hitler, they would, no doubt, have changed it, but they evidently did not, and no one has bothered about the matter since.

The Goebbels family became friends of Unity and Diana, though they really liked Magda Goebbels better than her husband. It was her part they took when, as sometimes happened, there was an apparent rift between the two. On 14 August 1937 Diana writes at length describing a 'wonderfully typical day' at Schwanenwerder; the party plays Animal, Vegetable and Mineral and then Analogies, which Diana teaches them.

The lovely part of the day was a *wonderful* film called *Entscheidende Tage* and it is *only* real-life films, of the war, the Versailles treaty, the revolution here, the coming of the Führer, 1923 Parteitag, meetings, Schlageter being shot, Jews, Nazis, the 1929 Parteitag, *Machtübernahme* [seizure of power], *Aufbau* [reconstruction], 1936 Parteitag. It was *pure* heaven, except that the Doktor schimpfed [complained] all the way through at the man who had spent 8 months making it. I must say, he was perfectly right because it was an awful muddle and terribly hard to know what was going on. The Doktor said he himself didn't know half the time although he lived it all. So it has got to be entirely altered, but darling the *material* is simply thrilling.

Next year there was an idea that Magda might come and visit the Mitfords in England: 'We must make her, while they still have Rutland Gate,' writes Diana to Unity on 31 May 1938. At that time, Magda had just had a daughter. 'She is to be called Hertha! Magda loathes the name, but the Führer chose it for her.'

# 32

# Decca, Discontent and Elopement

When Decca was a child she used to say to her father, 'Farve, can you give me a pound?' 'Certainly not.' 'Try-dear-try,' she would reply, as if it was all one word. Whenever anyone did give her any money she put it into a bank account at Drummond's, which was quite openly called her Running Away Money and was a family joke, on the level of her handkerchief called the Maid of All Work, which she used for every type of wiping or mopping and refused to have laundered. She also had an old dog to which she would give a good-natured pinch, saying, 'This cold weather — carries so many old people away.' This kind of thing made everybody laugh. She was a great one for special relationships. She and Unity were the two Bouds with their language, she and Debo the two Hons with theirs, and later she and Nancy took to calling each other Susan.

It was adolescence, not childhood, that was the problem for Decca. Very attractive children can find it hard to cope with the changes in what is required of them when the old tricks suddenly stop working. Decca was also bored. She was not of course the only one; we remember Diana moping at Asthall with Nancy and suffering the deadly essence of boredom when kept at home in disgrace. But Decca says she felt the same thing from the age of thirteen. Tom was a help, studying for his law examinations at Swinbrook. He was a good companion and an educative one; arguments and conversations with him, the books he recommended, all helped to keep boredom at bay. Decca admits that the boredom arose largely within herself. Sydney was always taking them on trips: to Europe for sightseeing or winter sports, to the English seaside. But Decca hated the strict supervision, the chaperonage, the prohibition against talking to strangers or seeing a film of which Sydney did not approve. She felt confined and cut off. The contrast with Nancy, on her trip with the Hatherop girls to Paris and Florence, is complete. She, we remember, loved every minute of it, and did not feel in the least enclosed. Times had admittedly changed in the intervening decade, but the difference was mainly a personal one between Nancy and Decca. Nancy liked buildings and pictures; she was an avid sightseer. Decca was not. Travel, to her, was only genuine if it resulted in human contact with the inhabitants.

It was the same desire for human comradeship that made her yearn to go to boarding school, devouring school stories and hanging on Unity's words during the holidays as she related her pranks and adventures. Her parents refused to send her, precisely because of Unity's experiences which had not, they thought, been a good advertisement. She and Debo did for a time go to day school, Oakdene near High Wycombe, at a time when they were living at the Old Mill Cottage because Swinbrook was let. Decca loved it as much as Debo hated it. But it only lasted a term. Sydney was sorry for Decca, and understood her. It was adolescence that was the trouble; in the meantime, she set to work with what palliatives she could. But the trips abroad and other entertainments were not in Decca's case effective, nor was the conventional period in Paris to learn French.

Like Nancy and Diana, but at an earlier age than either, Decca developed a social conscience; and in her case it was more intensely felt simply because she had not, as they had, the distraction of caring also about culture. Both Nancy and Diana appreciated architecture and interior decoration and were interested in art: Diana was also passionately fond of music. None of this seems to have applied to Decca at any time in her life. Nancy, the socialist, and Diana, the Fascist, came to disagree on almost every political point, but they were at one in assuming that, whoever was to end up on top, cultural values must be preserved. This is not logically incompatible with a sense of social justice, but in practice it renders it less single-minded. In Decca's case, there was no obstacle of this sort to her moving right over to the Communist position. She could of course have gone the other way. It was the Nazis, not the Communists, who sang '*Wir werden weiter marschieren/Bis alles in Scherben fällt*' (We shall march on/

Till everything falls in pieces). Decca's leftward move was not just in a spirit of contradiction to Unity. She testifies in *A Fine Old Conflict* that her interest in politics seems in fact to have predated Unity's, even though she was three years younger. She was aware of the Depression, of hunger marches, of pacifism, at a time when Unity's interest was concentrated on her poetry and painting, art for art's sake. Where Diana's nagging feeling that all was not well with society could find an outlet in her beloved Mosley who would make everything right, and where Unity was glamorized by Diana and thus by Mosley at one remove, Decca had at the beginning no figure equivalent to Mosley, and her elder sisters were part of the old world with which she was so discontented. Having no person from whom to hope for a solution, she had to turn to political literature; and compassion has always been best verbalized by the left. The destructiveness of the Russian Revolution, insofar as it was real to her at all, came over simply as the smashing of oppression; she was increasingly attracted by its proclaimed ideals. As to Stalin's current behaviour, reports on these horrors came from sources which she found inherently suspect. She could write them off as capitalist propaganda, in a mirror image of the pro-Nazi selectivity of her sisters.

Decca's move to the left began in early adolescence with an interest in pacifism. War was nothing but mass murder, and the glorification of war was a gigantic crime. But her reading soon moved on to socialism and Marxism. The mass murder that is war was not caused by some explosion of madness or by an inherent human tendency towards belligerence; particular people – members of the ruling class, like her own parents – were to blame for organizing it in their own selfish interests. By what right were they richer than others, by what right did they order them about? Thus her chafing at restrictions and boredom in her own life was given a focus; her resentment was not mere personal rebellion but had an objective reason. It was a positive duty. She did not lose her sense of fun, nor did she in any way try to hide her feelings. In fact she made a joke of her beliefs for the others. She even had a sort of ally in Nancy, for she and Peter Rodd had begun to profess socialism. But Nancy made Decca rather impatient because it soon became clear that she would not actually do anything for the cause. In her turn, Nancy could not resist laughing at Decca, which was particularly insulting. Nancy, adult and under nobody's control, could perfectly well have worked for socialism, if only by canvassing for the Labour Party; but she simply could not be bothered. This same Nancy was insinuating that Decca's own beliefs were a mere adolescent phase, a pose like her own! She would show her; she would show them all. With Unity, Decca retained a boisterous friendliness, decorating her room at Swinbrook with Communist emblems to balance Unity's swastikas and picture of Hitler. They shouted slogans at each other in a spirit of competition rather than hostility rather as if they were supporting rival football teams.

Decca's Communism was much less playful than the rest of the family thought at the time; events proved that soon enough. But as compared with her subsequent account, it was also a great deal more fitful. Unity's diary shows that on 23 March 1935, she and Decca went together to the Black House, Mosley's headquarters, to buy a black shirt for Diana. Was it likely that a really firm anti-Fascist would have gone on this expedition? Also, between 24 September and 4 October that year Decca was in Munich with Unity and also with Pam for the Oktoberfest. She lunched several times at the Osteria Bavaria and at least once went to the Brown House. Most of the time was spent sightseeing, boating and so on. Pam testifies that Decca seemed to enjoy herself and that there was no hint of political uneasiness. Hitler, as it happens, never turned up at the Osteria when Decca was there, otherwise they would have met. This nearly happened on her first day, 24 September; they went to the Osteria and, as Unity's diary puts it, 'The Führer is coming, then they ring up to say he can't.'

This shows that Decca's political views were not yet set. Had she expressed herself in any definite way against Nazism, Unity would never have risked her meeting Hitler and perhaps offending him. She was, we note, apprehensive about Tom meeting Hitler; as regards Decca, there is no sign of this. Also, Decca was able to have a perfectly pleasant time in Nazi Germany not only with the non-political Pam, but also with Unity and indeed Erik, neither of whose views were in any way kept hidden. Had she already felt the visceral horror of Nazism that she later professed, their heartfelt support for the regime would have rendered her visit emotionally impossible; she would have been half the time in a rage and the other half in tears. This is not to say that she liked Nazism; her reaction to Unity's *Stürmer* letter earlier that summer proves directly that she disapproved of it. But the reaction was a measured one. She remained, we remember, Unity's Boud in spite of all. This about sums it up; their special friendship was stronger than the incipient political strains.

The page of *All About Everybody* that Decca filled in shows similarity to Unity's page. She would, given unlimited choice, be a pirate; Unity would be a gangster or airman. Both believed in the equality of the sexes – Diana did not – and both preferred love to money. Naturally, Decca did not have Hitler as hero in real life, as Unity did; but her choice of Julius Caesar was also Mosley's. Her heroine was Mary Read, a girl pirate; Unity's was Joan of Arc. The main contrast between the Bouds was in their besetting sins, a matter in which many people who filled in *All About Everybody* show considerable self-knowledge. Unity's was 'boasting', Decca's was 'fury'. This illuminates the scenery of Decca's hag-ridden adolescence as a flash of lightning reveals a nocturnal landscape. It is a key to Unity's character, too.

Decca's outward life at this time was conventional. She came out in 1935 and did a season, which she did not enjoy; unlike Nancy, she was a 'romper' of a sort, as she was to prove, but she did not take to the conventional type of romping, at debutante dances and similar occasions. Unity had most certainly romped when she had come out, taking her pet rat to dances, flaunting a spectacular fake tiara, and purloining writing paper from Buckingham Palace on which to write to her friends. Decca had enjoyed hearing about all this, but did nothing like it.

Decca already admired her second cousin Esmond Romilly, who was a little younger than herself. She had not met him, but his activities had been reported in the newspapers since he had run away from his school, Wellington, in 1934. Just when she first knew of him cannot be exactly pinpointed; what is certain is that he cast a long shadow before him.

Esmond was Aunt Natty's grandchild, son of Clementine Churchill's sister Nelly. He had something of Aunt Natty's confident and patrician delinquency; we remember how shamelessly she browbeat the customs officer in the matter of the smuggled dog. Esmond's unscrupulousness was of this sort. He had assurance and a natural gift for straightforward self-expression, together with a firm belief that the end justifies the means. His courage was flawless, of the type of which people say 'He has no nerves'; he was a natural dominant, a confident gambler, a warrior. He had all the fiercer attributes that young scions of the upper classes were supposed to have in order to run the Empire. He was, however, in rebellion against the whole set-up. He was made for Decca and she for him, even sharing her indifference to visual beauty. Philip Toynbee says of the bedsitting rooms where he lived, that there was never any question of his decorating them with pictures; he never even seems to have had any books. Toynbee's book *Friends Apart* is a valuable memoir of Esmond.

At his preparatory school Esmond had been a romantic right-winger, a Jacobite; according to Robert Skidelsky, he was at one time a supporter of Mosley. His elder brother Giles was at the time already a Communist, and this amused their uncle, Winston Churchill, who called them the Red Rose and the White Rose. At Wellington Esmond soon changed his views and joined his brother on the left. Early in 1934, at the age of fifteen, he ran away, but running away was not enough for him; he would attack and subvert the whole public school system, the whole apparatus of discipline, prefects, fagging, the whole ethos of empire-building. In their place he would elevate belief in pacifism, Communism, and the brotherhood of man. It was perverse, it was zany, but in its way it was rather splendid.

He set himself up with some dismal-sounding left-wing intellectuals in a 'progressive' bookshop in Parton Street, Bloomsbury. There he created a magazine which was in a sense to the political thirties what the *Eton Candle* of Harold Acton and Brian Howard had been to the precious twenties. It was called *Out of Bounds* and was designed to be distributed among public schoolboys with a view to turning them against the system. He sent round a circular declaring in ringing tones that the magazine opposed reaction, militarism and fascism in the public schools. It did not, as would probably be the case today, advocate the schools' abolition, though it asserted that they were based on propaganda that adapted them to an evil and outdated social system. It opposed the Officers' Training Corps and the claim to be building character, as well as rules said to be suitable only for very young children.

The magazine made more scandals than conversions. It was distributed rather unevenly, since it depended on the efficiency and dedication of the representatives Esmond found in the various schools. Still, it caused a certain stir in several of them. John Mortimer tells us that when he was at Harrow a circular from Esmond transformed him into 'a one-boy Communist cell'. The representative at Rugby was Philip Toynbee, for a few weeks in the summer term of 1934. Encouraged in his discontent by the message of the magazine, he ran away to Parton Street to join Esmond. Toynbee was a distant cousin of both Decca and Esmond. Unsurprisingly, the common ancestors of all three were the Stanleys: Toynbee's grandmother was Rosalind, Countess of Carlisle. His father was Professor Arnold Toynbee, author of *A Study of History*. He was seventeen, two years older than Esmond.

Toynbee returned to Rugby to be conventionally expelled. However, during his four days at Parton Street, Mosley held his meeting at Olympia; and Toynbee, with Esmond, responded to the Communist Party's call to break it up. They bought knuckledusters at an ironmonger in Drury Lane; trying them on was great fun. On the day they carried a Communist streamer on two poles, then dropped it when the mounted police advanced. They got into the hall itself. Just before Mosley spoke, four interrupters chanted a hostile slogan. A number of stewards tried to eject them; Esmond and Toynbee attacked the stewards and were thrown out by different gates, having got separated in the mêlée. Esmond was apparently unhurt but Toynbee was roughed up fairly severely. He appears not to have had a chance to use his knuckleduster but was hit hard enough to make him cry, as well as getting a few bruises. Once in the street he was taken in charge by the Communists who had arranged the attack on the meeting; they had provided a first-aid post where he was patched up. His tears embarrassed him and he went home as soon as he could get away.

Shortly after this, Esmond consented to go back to school; his parents sent him to the co-educational public school Bedales, an establishment with advanced views and comparatively lax discipline. He quite liked the place, but found that after his period of independence he could not really fit in there, so at the end of the term he was back at Parton Street producing *Out of Bounds*, ready for the autumn. Toynbee joined him in his bedsitting room some time after Christmas. One night, the two of them got into trouble. After a fight with two men who made a pass at them in a café, they returned to Esmond's bedsitting room, where between them they consumed a bottle of whisky Esmond had received in payment for an article. They then went to call on Esmond's mother. A taxi to Pimlico, and there they were, beating on her door, reeling and riotous. She lost her head and called the police.

They were hauled up in court next morning. Toynbee was merely fined, being over eighteen; but Esmond was adjudged to be beyond his parents' control, and sent to a remand home, where he stayed for six weeks. This is the kind of thing now commonly referred to as a 'short, sharp shock'. He suffered; some of the older boys were genuinely savage. He emerged just as wild as before, and bitter as well. A cousin called Dorothy Allhusen volunteered to be responsible for him on his release; she could, of course, not pretend to be able actually to control him, but at least she provided a place where he could go and stay.

He went to her after his release from the remand home, and in collaboration with his elder brother Giles, wrote a book called *Out of Bounds*, which told the story of the magazine and of themselves. Giles was now at Oxford; he shared Esmond's views, but had stayed at Wellington. After their book came out, Esmond became a commercial traveller in silk stockings. When calling on a household, his method rather resembled Thomas Bowles's way of getting to know the captain of a ship. 'Captain Romilly?' he would ask of whoever opened the door. When he was told there was no Captain Romilly, he would push through and announce that he was Captain Romilly. He then got another job as a salesman, this time of advertising space for the magazine *World Film News*.

In July 1936 the Spanish generals revolted against the Republic, because the Popular Front government was failing to put down, seemed even to some to be encouraging, a growing amount of revolutionary disorder. When members of one of the government police forces actually murdered a right-wing MP, the generals moved, and the Spanish Civil War started. This was in essence a purely Spanish affair, but it occurred when all Europe was in a politically excited state. The world Communist movement, and Soviet Russia itself, backed the Republic because it was providing so favourable a terrain for social revolution; Mussolini, Hitler and Salazar of Portugal backed the generals for the same reason in reverse, and in the hope of securing a new ally. The League of Nations soon decreed 'non-intervention'. Britain tried on the whole to keep to this policy, but France, under a Popular Front government, helped the Republic as much as it dared. In any case, the Communists and Fascists, both as individuals and through the countries they respectively controlled, made a farce of non-intervention.

All these events started happening over the next few months, but to Esmond the matter seemed crystal clear as soon as the war broke out. To him, as to George Orwell and so many others, the Republic meant democracy, decency and hope; the generals meant Fascism, reaction and oppression. He was one of the very first to join the International Brigade that the Communists organized. He who had refused to join the Officers' Training Corps at Wellington hastened to become a soldier. Later a good many Englishmen were to join the Brigade, enough to form a battalion; among them was Giles Romilly. But at this early stage there was only a section of twelve Englishmen, who were attached to the German-speaking Thaelmann battalion.

Soon Esmond was sent to the front, and he took part in the successful defence of Madrid against the first Nationalist onslaughts in the autumn and winter of 1936. He fought in several encounters; then came a sharp engagement at Boadilla del Monte in which the entire English section was wiped out, except Esmond and one other. He went down with dysentery and returned home on sick leave in January 1937; here he had the painful duty of visiting the families of his dead comrades. Toynbee found him changed: thinner from his dysentery and rather sad and thoughtful. He talked about the disorganization of the war: Madrid would not have been saved but for the Communists, yet their dull authoritarianism would spoil the beautiful anarchic Spanish character. Toynbee himself, a committed party member at the time, was a little cast down by this; he himself had gone on a trip to Spain as a student delegate and wrote in his diary an enthusiastic passage, reproduced in *Friends Apart*, in which he exults in the unmilitary appearance of the soldiers in the Barcelona streets, and notes with affection the endless initials painted on the trains –

UGT for the socialist trade unions, CNT for the anarchist ones. He feels the city belongs to his side. We are reminded of Orwell's *Homage to Catalonia*, but Toynbee's joy at seeing the slovenly uniforms of Barcelona also rather reminds us of Unity's pleasure in the smart ones of Munich. Later Esmond recounted his experiences in a book, *Boadilla*, which excited attention at the other end of the family spectrum. Diana wrote to Unity on 24 January 1938: 'I have just read *Boadilla* and it made me be on the Government side in Spain for about three days. It is fascinating but of course very young; he can tell a story well.'

Even before he went to Spain, Esmond had become one of Decca's heroes. By the winter of 1935–36 her boredom at home had become more acute than ever; she and Debo were the only ones still there. At least Debo still had lessons to fill her day; Decca just sat around. Much of the time she was reading the *Brown Book of the Hitler Terror*, an account of Nazi atrocities which emanated from a group of German Communists in Paris led by Willi Münzenberg. One of its participants was Arthur Koestler, who writes about this part of his life in *The Invisible Writing*. Where they could, Münzenberg's team recounted facts; but where this seemed desirable they also embroidered and even invented. This was one of the ways in which Nazis and Communists used inadvertently to help each other in the thirties: by telling lies about each other which, being lies, could be convincingly discredited, they rendered each other's real atrocities harder to believe. The *Broom Brown Book* was, of course, gospel truth to Decca; it was her *Foxe's Book of Martyrs*. But her *Pilgrim's Progress* was *Out of Bounds*, the book by the Romilly brothers about their magazine. Esmond emerged from this a soulmate as well as a hero. He had much the same background. He, too, had been a Conservative as a child. He, too, had first swallowed, then rejected, the version of the world put about by his parents, and for the same reasons. He and Giles, too, had been teased by their family when they were converted to Communism; Uncle Winston's nickname of 'Red Rose' for Giles seemed similar to Nancy's gibe about Decca being a ballroom Communist. Esmond's parents, Decca read, had suggested that if he was a Communist he might think of helping with the housework; Sydney had similarly remarked to Decca herself that she should think a Communist would be tidier and make less work for the servants.

The Spanish Civil War struck Decca exactly as it had struck Esmond. She formed a wish to go to Spain herself, to fight, to agitate, even to be a nurse; to do *something*. It gave a focus to her old, vague intention to run away; now she had somewhere specific to run away to. Then she heard that Esmond had gone there. Once again he had acted where she had only dreamed. However, she did take part in one political demonstration that winter, and though it was in itself ineffectual it led her, indirectly, to Esmond. It was, oddly enough, a manifestation by young left-wingers in favour of Edward VIII; for the abdication crisis was just then brewing up and support for the King was something Communists and Fascists had in common. 'Stand By the King!' Mosley's paper, *Action*, was demanding at about the same time. The demonstration was organized by a left-wing friend of Decca's called Peter Nevile, who knew the Romilly brothers and introduced Decca to Giles. Giles was himself about to enlist for Spain, and he had various contacts. He was sympathetic, of course, and though he himself offered no concrete help to Decca, he did tell Esmond about her. Esmond was intrigued to hear of this unexpected sister of Unity Mitford. Resigned for the moment, Decca went off with her family to stay at Downie Park, a house lent them by David's cousin, the Earl of Airlie, near where he lived, Cortachy in Scotland. By her account, Decca sulked and moped. Unity's diary, telegraphic though it is, gives a rather different impression. The house party was a large one and would seem to have been lively. Mrs Ham was there. Decca participates in the party games, reads aloud to Unity while she is doing 'my picture' (presumably one of her collages), goes to the cinema and chats. Unity also wrote from there to Diana on 2 January 1937; there is no mention of Decca being in a bad mood, though perhaps Unity simply did not notice, for her main interest in this letter is Tom's supposed conversion to Nazism. Sydney writes in her account of Unity that 'it was a very cheerful Christmas with two dances and all kinds of joys', but she does seem to have noticed that Decca needed taking out of herself; she began discussing plans to take her and Debo on a world cruise.

But just before the family left Scotland, Decca received an invitation to stay with Dorothy Allhusen at Havering House, near Marlborough; she was Decca's cousin as well as Esmond's, again through the Stanleys. This was exciting; as Esmond's unofficial guardian Mrs Allhusen was sure to have news of him, and he might even be there himself. Filled with this secret hope, she set off southwards in Unity's car with Sydney. They visited Edinburgh Castle, stayed the night at Redesdale Cottage, saw round Durham Cathedral, which Unity found '*wunderschön*', and then stayed with their cousins at Castle Howard. Unity wrote to Diana from Rutland Gate on her return, on 16 January, that Castle Howard 'is the most amazing place I ever saw, full of Van Dycks, Rubens, Tintorettos, Breughels, etc., also vast collections of Greek and Roman statues, and the house is about like Blenheim . . .' All this Decca saw with half an eye, trailing round politely with the others.

Eventually, Decca went off for the weekend to Dorothy Allhusen's. When she arrived in the comfortable house, so much better heated than Swinbrook, Mrs Allhusen announced the expected arrival of Esmond. Little did she know the effect this would produce on Decca. Sydney was shortly to write to Nancy: 'It was wrong indeed of her to ask them together, she knows Esmond if anyone does.' Sydney was, of course, writing under stress and in a state of worry, but cooler reflection would have shown that she was being unfair. Esmond certainly had a record of wildness and uncontrollability, but his misdeeds had never, until then, included abduction; they had not concerned women at all. Mrs Allhusen had no reason to be apprehensive, precisely because she *did* know Esmond.

Even now it was not abduction as such that seems to have intrigued him so much as taking a smash at authority, at his class, at his family; also, specifically, at the Mitfords. There was Unity; there was Diana, known to be involved with Mosley; there was David who was openly friendly about Hitler. What a lark it would be to help her get away from them! The fact that Decca was also pretty and funny was an uncovenanted bonus; he would probably have been almost as keen to get her away from her family if she had not attracted him at all.

She did attract him, of course; in fact it was probably love at first sight with him. (With Decca it had actually been love before first sight.) Nevertheless he did not declare his feelings until after they had run away together.

Nancy's wedding to Peter Rodd, 1933

Pam's wedding to Derek Jackson, December 1936.
*First row, left to right:* Sydney Redesdale, Derek Jackson, Pamela Jackson,
David Redesdale. *Second row, left to right:* Diana Mosley, Stella Jackson,
Nancy Rodd, Dorothy Bailey, Tom Mitford. *Third row, left to right:* Daphne
Mason, Bertram Mitford, Iris Mitford, Dorothy Mitford. *Fourth row,
left to right:* Jack Mason, Madeleine Bowles

Esmond and Decca

House on Inchkenneth

Unity at Hesselberg speaking to 200,000 people, 1935

Unity celebrates King George V's
Silver Jubilee in Germany, 1935

Diana and Tom

A flower from Julius Streicher, 1935

Unity, Diana and friends

Decca and Erik Widemann, 1935

Unity in her room at the students' hostel

Debo's wedding to Lord Andrew Cavendish, 1941. *Standing, left to right:*
Sydney, the Duke of Devonshire, David, Lord Andrew Cavendish,
the Marquess of Hartington, the Duchess of Devonshire

David, Unity, Sydney; wartime, at Old Mill Cottage, Swinbrook

Sydney at Inchkenneth with her goats, c. 1955

Jonathan and Catherine Guinness

as did Peter Rodd. It was Peter who suggested what to do. Since Decca at nineteen was under age, David could make her a Ward in Chancery, relinquishing guardianship to a judge. Then anyone marrying her without permission would be in contempt of court and risk prison. To stop the marriage, it was the best move; all the same it was a disastrous one. In practice the marriage was neither stopped, nor greatly delayed; but the threat of prison soured relations between Decca and her parents and made Esmond seem right when he portrayed them to her as enemies.

Yet Sydney immediately made it clear to the young lovers that family opposition was not absolute. She wrote to Nancy on 1 March: 'Farve has made her a Ward in Chancery which will make it difficult for them to marry in a hurry, but I am writing to tell her that they shall certainly marry later if they still wish to.' This might have shown Decca that her family was not unconditionally hostile, only temporarily shocked; though in the euphoria of her great adventure, and confronted by the legal move, we understand her ignoring the overture at the time. It is rather a pity she did not mention it when she came to write *Hons and Rebels*; the omission makes her parents seem malevolent, when they were really just distraught. Sydney wrote to Nancy again on the third: 'The papers . . . have surpassed themselves as one might have expected . . . Farve and I have been terribly down, I never saw Farve like it before, he had lost his buoyancy but I am thankful to say he is a great deal better. Diana, Bobo and Tom have been much here and have helped so much.'

By now the story had hit the papers. It was made for them: peer's daughter, young warrior, stuffy and obstructive parents – an archetypal romance, not a dry eye in the house. The *Daily Express* scooped the story on 1 March, splashing it on its front page with a photograph of Decca and Debo. But it spoiled its success by making out that it was Debo who had run away. Debo did well out of this mistake; she sued the *Daily Express* for libel and won £1,000. But the newspaper which really fell down on the story was the *News Chronicle*, which employed Esmond. It did carry Esmond's 'exclusive' story, but not till 4 March.

In the meantime the authorities had traced Decca to Bilbao and the consulate there asked her to return. It seems that she refused at first, but later agreed to leave with Esmond for St Jean de Luz, just over the French border. A Royal Navy destroyer, HMS *Echo*, was in the area to pick up British people who wanted to be evacuated before the expected Nationalist offensive in the area. The idea got about that this ship was sent simply to evacuate Decca and Esmond, and a question was asked in Parliament about it. Toynbee repeats this *canard*. In fact Decca and Esmond were only two of 157 people taken on board. Nor is it true, as Toynbee also says, that the ship had originally intended to take them right back to England, but that Esmond confronted the commander and made him drop them at St Jean de Luz. It must have been known before they left Bilbao that they were going to St Jean, because Nancy and Peter were there to meet them. The Rodds picked them up in a motor boat, says the *Daily Telegraph* of 11 March 1937. Decca, the newspaper adds, was smiling, but Esmond was angry. He stopped reporters talking to Decca and told them: 'She will go and grow beetroots for the rest of her life.' The four had dinner, then left St Jean de Luz together by train; they were expected to go straight to London, says the *Telegraph*, presumably because Peter had told them this. But in fact Decca and Esmond got off the train at Bayonne, and the Rodds returned empty-handed.

In Bayonne Decca and Esmond had a problem, for their livelihood depended on Esmond being in Spain. It was as a Spanish 'stringer' that he was accredited to the *News Chronicle*, and reports filed from Bayonne did not qualify. However, he got a job with the local representative of Reuter's News Agency, translating the radio reports from the Basque front. He also started work on his book, *Boadilla*.

Sydney says in her memoir on Unity that she received fairly frequent letters from Decca in Bayonne. Towards the end of March she went out to see her and Esmond. 'I was there for one day,' she says, 'and we were all friendly and had luncheon together and I promised to do all possible to arrange their marriage.' Diana wrote to Unity on 30 March 1937: 'I suppose they will let them be married, and I suppose it is better so.' The judge gave his permission, and the wedding took place at the British consulate in Bayonne on 18 May. Sydney and Mrs Romilly went out; Sydney brought with her a dress for Decca and they spent the morning getting her a coat and hat. 'She looked lovely,' says Sydney, 'and by that time, I had quite forgiven them both.' The mothers took Esmond, Decca and a party of their friends from the consulate to a wedding lunch, which was delayed because Sydney and Mrs Romilly made their taxi take a roundabout route to avoid the press; they lost the married couple and all the guests. 'Time went on, the Feast was ready, but no-one came. We were nearly in tears, when Nelly [Romilly] boldly announced she would go out in the town and find them.' She did, and the late lunch was as convivial as could be wished.

# 33

# Approach to War

In *The Pursuit of Love* Nancy makes her heroine say: 'It's rather sad to belong, as we do, to a lost generation. I'm sure in history the two wars will count as one war and that we shall be squashed out of it altogether . . .' It is possible to see what she meant, for the two wars, in their Western theatre, were between substantially the same contestants for essentially the same war aims (the Far East was different). The question at issue, which was half settled at the end of the First World War and fully decided at the end of the Second, was whether or not Germany should dominate Europe and so become for a century or two the leading power in the world. The two wars determined, at staggering cost, that this possible stage in history should not occur. To our distant descendants, an account almost as bald and brief as this of the two world wars could possibly seem sufficient.

This view of the time between the wars has by no means yet been reached, but people today are nevertheless beginning to forget a number of things that to those alive at the time were self-evident. The Treaty of Versailles was the starting point of the period, forming the basic condition of international politics for twenty years. The treaty was presented to world opinion as being based on moral principles and as *fair*. The main principle was that of self-determination. Austria was broken up, Poland recreated and Italy enlarged in obedience to this; the fact that this arrangement left a good many German speakers as members of minorities under foreign rule, there and elsewhere, seemed to imply that self-determination was for everyone except Germans. In this and other ways, the treaty's fairness seemed to many people to be more a matter of theory than of practice. Vera Brittain's *Testament of Youth*, Harold Nicolson's *Peacemaking 1918* and Maynard

Keynes's *The Economic Consequences of the Peace* are only three of many contemporary works in which one can find this attitude to the treaty, and many people felt like this. There is a school of thought nowadays that says Britain ought to have gone to war with Hitler in 1936 over his reoccupation of the Rhineland, under the treaty provisions still closed to German troops though the French had withdrawn. But those who deplored Versailles would have regarded a war on this issue as an outrage; the country would have been torn apart.

When it came to Czechoslovakia and Poland, opinion was more evenly divided, but self-determination still provided a case for Hitler. There were upwards of three million German speakers under the rule of the Czechs: the so-called Sudeten Germans formed a majority of the population in the districts round the edge of the country bordering Germany and Austria. Many Germans had also been put under Polish rule, and the allotment to Poland of West Prussia, even though it did have a Polish majority, was resented because it cut off German East Prussia from the rest of the country. All this is now fading from our minds, because in the light of the 1945 settlement we begin to wonder what the fuss was all about. Had the Germans in Poland and Czechoslovakia known the end result of their agitations, they would, no doubt, have been delighted to accommodate to their new rulers; for this end result was to be forcible expulsion and partial massacre. They can perhaps be excused for not seeing this in advance.

Unity was not sophisticated or knowledgeable, and she was hopelessly partisan, but her letters of the time transport us back to this other world. She saw it selectively, but what she saw was there. The ethnic Germans of Czechoslovakia and Poland did see themselves as unjustly cut off from the Reich, and the people of German-speaking Austria, transformed into a small country by its severance from the rest of the former Austrian Empire, felt the same way. These are matters on which, to judge by all serious accounts of the period, Unity's views reflect the actual truth. Unity wrote to Winston Churchill in March 1938, at the time of the Anschluss, giving the facts on Austria as she saw them. He replied first by telegram: 'Thank you dear Unity for your clearly written letter which I am answering in a few days.' Then came a letter dated 12 March: 'There can be no doubt that a fair plebiscite would have shown that a large majority of the people of Austria loathe the idea of coming under Nazi rule. It was because Herr Hitler feared the free expression of opinion that we are compelled to witness the present dastardly outrage.'

The telegram was affectionate, but the letter can only be called arrogant. Unity soon found out that it was untrue, for she saw the scenes of wild mass enthusiasm which accompanied Hitler's entry into Vienna on 14 March. She arrived that morning in Munich with a friend; with only a quarter of an hour to spare they caught the 7.45 train to Vienna. The diary says: 'Arrive in Vienna 4, 1½ hours late. Taxi to hotel Kaiserin Elizabeth . . . Hear that the Führer has already arrived. Taxi to Ring. *Huge* crowd outside Hotel Imperial cheering and singing. HE comes out on balcony.'

Next day, she saw Hitler and they shook hands; Sydney quotes Hitler as saying later, 'They said England would be there to stop me, but the only English person I saw was on my side.' In May, she went to stay with the Erdödy family at Kohfidisch. From there, she wrote to Sydney: 'All is very much changed here and everyone very enthusiastic . . . The gardeners and village people no longer greet one with "Kuss'die Hand" but with "*Heil Hitler*" and never get tired of saying it. The whole village is covered with flags . . .' The reaction in town and country, which Unity saw with her own eyes, made her see Churchill's letter as a bark rather than an argument.

Mosley, of course, was at the opposite pole from Churchill. He thought Britain's interests were best served by allowing Hitler a completely free hand in Eastern Europe. The trouble with this policy was that a strengthened Germany might, when it suited it, then turn on Britain as it was in fact to turn on its Soviet ally. Mosley did in a sense cater for this risk by playing up the necessity of arming to the teeth, especially in the air. In the matter of re-armament, he agreed with Churchill. He also forbade his supporters from fighting for Franco in the Spanish Civil War, in contrast to the Communists who actively recruited volunteers to fight for the Republic. His slogan was 'Mind Britain's Business', and most people would now agree that neither side in that war was Britain's business. But to apply the maxim to the Second World War was not realistic, given Hitler's character. It was Hitler, not anyone in England, who made nonsense of Mosley's hopes and ensured the final triumph of Churchill. Hitler seems, at any rate with part of his mind, to have had a genuine wish for friendship with Britain; but his disregard of English susceptibilities was so complete that this wish cannot have had a very high priority with him.

Did Unity help Hitler to misunderstand British public opinion? We think not. She used to tell Hitler many stories showing that her support of him was not exactly popular. On 10 April 1938, for instance, when walking through Hyde Park, she heard a demonstration and went over to it. It turned out to be organized by the Labour Party on behalf of the Spanish Republic. Some way from where she was standing listening to Sir Stafford Cripps, a counter-demonstration by a few Fascists took place. They were not members of Mosley's British Union of Fascists; they were carrying a swastika flag, which identifies them as belonging to Arnold Leese's Imperial Fascist League. (Mosley's movement always used its own symbol, the flash and circle.) There was a fight, after which two men were taken to hospital. Someone spotted Unity's swastika badge; although she was not very near the Imperial Fascists, it was perhaps natural that he should connect her with them. He tore it off her lapel and she hit him. A woman shouted 'Go back to Germany', and Unity hit her too. The crowd then turned on her with the idea of ducking her in the Serpentine. The police moved in, however, and she was helped by two bystanders, Joe Allen and Edward Warburton, who escorted her to a bus stop. Warburton got on the bus with her, and took her to the Hyde Park Hotel for a cup of tea; a few days later she invited him back to tea at Rutland Gate. He was a Mosley supporter, as it happened.

'Press ring up all evening,' says the diary, and the significant thing about the incident was indeed the press reaction to it. The *Stürmer* letter had not been forgotten. Some commentators let it be understood that they wished Unity had been ducked, or otherwise injured. Though violence committed by Fascists was frequently cited as a reason to disapprove of them, violence offered to them was welcomed. The cartoonist Low was plainly disappointed that she got away. 'Miss Fatuity Again,' he headed his cartoon, describing her as a 'special Society nuisance who nearly started a revolution in Hyde Park by saying Hitler was nice, snapped just before she was thrown into the Serpentine.' But the English press did not worry Unity. 'My fan mail about Hyde Park', she wrote Diana from Munich on 27 April 1938, 'has been too wonderful for words, and I have even had letters from America.' She added that 'the best and killingest' was from their friend Franz von Pfeffer, an ex-officer who had been active in the right-wing Freikorps in the twenties. He had written: 'I heard about the fight you had in Hyde Park, and since I, naturally, assume that you acquitted yourself with honour, this is to wish you well. *Heil Hitler!*' The day after she wrote this letter, Hitler gave Unity two swastika badges, each with his signature engraved on the back, to replace the one she had lost.

After Austria came Czechoslovakia. During 1938 the agitation among the Sudeten German minority in that country was building up towards the crisis that was temporarily resolved at Munich in October. With two young men, Philip Spranklin and Bill Rueff, Unity did a short tour in Czechoslovakia; Spranklin was a British Fascist who lived in Munich. Their first stop was Eger, then a German-speaking town just over the border. There they made contact with the local members of the Sudeten Deutsche Partei, which was by then effectively Nazi. They were shown round the town, Unity wrote to Sydney, by a middle-aged lady who had known Bertie in Marienbad (Marianske Lazne). Next day, they went to Karlsbad (Karlovy Vary). Philip Spranklin knew the local MP, Senator Wollner Unity found Wollner 'a perfectly heavenly man, rather like the Leader to look at, only huger', as she wrote in a letter to Diana on 29 May that year. Wollner gave the three of them seats on the platform at a meeting he addressed. 'He is a *wonderful* speaker, one of the best I ever heard, most of the audience cried and I must say I did almost,' she wrote to Diana. Later, Unity dined with the journalist Ward Price, who was alone in Karlsbad. Again from her letter to Diana: 'He had toothache and had to drink masses of brandy, and the more he drank, the more flattering his compliments became.' Next day, Wollner accompanied Unity and her companions on a drive into the country, and this is Unity's description as given in a letter to Sydney on the twenty-eighth:

The Czechs plan to abandon that particular part of Sudetendeutschland when war comes . . . In preparation, they have mined every bridge and every important building . . . so that they will leave nothing but ruins behind them when they retreat . . . Every bridge and railway is patrolled, and one can quite clearly see the dynamite packed underneath and the fuses sticking out ready to be lit . . . When we came to the line of defence there were camouflaged tanks in the road and machine guns on every hillock. We were stopped and searched numberless times . . . In every village there was a notice to say, among other things, that everyone must be indoors by 8 p.m., that more than two people may not carry on a conversation, and that anyone who goes into the woods will be shot . . . As a looker-on, one can hardly bear the injustice and cruelty, and the idea that England might side with the Czechs is too loathsome for words . . . I would like every Englishman to do the drive I did yesterday, and talk to the people I talked to.

Sefton Delmer, writing in the *Daily Express* on 30 May, confirms this account of Czech war preparations and adds, 'From what I saw in my journey across Germany, I did not get the impression that the Germans are preparing for war right now.' This view of peaceful Germans and belligerent Czechs, which now seems so bizarre and perverse, was therefore not just a product of Unity's imagination; Delmer, if not always wholly reliable, never favoured the Nazis.

From Karlsbad, Unity drove with her two companions to Prague; they were again stopped and searched several times on the way. They put up at the Hotel Pension Cerveny, where they met John Lepper, an English writer and journalist who had been in the International Brigade and knew Decca and Esmond. 'The boys go out with him in the evenings,' she wrote to Diana. 'Bill tells me that Philip says awful things about the Nazis but this may be an exaggeration.'

Unity herself spent a good deal of time with the international press. On the day after her arrival she lunched with Ward Price and Yeats Brown; the French journalist Jules Sauerwein joined them afterwards. Ward Price was annoyed; he had published an interview with Henlein, the leader of the Sudeten Germans, which had then been repudiated. Unity comments in a letter to Diana: 'I must say it is regrettable that they should have double-crossed Wardie, who is the only friend we have among the journalists.' She met him also for tea that day, together with 'a lot of acquaintances – Peter Rodd, Edward Stanley, Robin Campbell and Lucy Byron's husband. They are all convinced there is to be a war, and have arrived like vultures from all quarters.'

One journalist she appears not to have seen, though, is Sefton Delmer, who in the same dispatch just quoted says: 'Just to make us all feel thoroughly uncomfortable in these exciting circumstances, the Hon. Unity Mitford walked tall and blonde among the crowd, a forbidden Hitler swastika badge in her button-hole. "They booted me in London for wearing it, I'd like to see them try it here."' The possible dates for this encounter are 28 and 29 May. The diary, though telegraphic, is fairly comprehensive as to Unity's movements on both dates. Delmer is not mentioned nor is the Esplanade Hotel, where in his memoirs he says the conversation took place.

Unity and her companions started back for Karlsbad, with Senator Wollner in the car. At Kamenne Zehrovice, about 30 kilometres from Prague, they were stopped and their cases were searched. This time, though, they were detained and taken to a police station; officials were sent for from Prague to question them. It was possibly Wollner's presence which caused the arrest. Unity, Spranklin and Rueff had been stopped and searched on the drive to Prague through the same area, but not detained. However, the group clearly became of much greater interest when it included a Sudeten German senator as well as a foreigner of known Nazi sympathies. Unity's diary says: 'We are then endlessly questioned and searched and at last I am taken to a room where a woman searches all my clothes.' She was made to strip. 'At last after 4½ hours we are allowed to go.' Some papers were taken from her, as well as her camera and films. As British subjects are supposed to do when in trouble, she rang up the consulate in Prague, who told her of the British legation's worry about her wearing her swastika badge. Shortly afterwards she and the others were released, but at the consulate's suggestion she sent in a written complaint. This was conveyed to the Czechs, who eventually replied that they had warned her as a known Nazi not to drive through the area. (Unity nowhere mentions having

received any such warning.) They added that everything confiscated had been handed back; this was true with the exception of
her camera. Her swastika badge had not been taken or even, it
seems, noticed until near the end of the interrogation. Hitler
himself replaced the camera as soon as Unity got back to Munich.
She writes to Diana on 4 June 1938: 'Bertha has just come in with
a parcel for me, and it is a most *wonderful* Leica from the Führer,
in place of the camera the Czechs took, with an awfully funny
note from him.'

While Unity was in Czechoslovakia, Diana was in Berlin. She
went to a party given by a French diplomat's wife, and met André
François-Poncet, the French ambassador, whom she describes to
Unity in a letter of 31 May:

He was fascinating, we talked for ages but I am afraid he hated me. He
was zittering [trembling] like anything and obviously thinks there will
soon be a war. I said 'Well what would you do about the Sudetendeutsch, if you were in charge here?' and he replied that the Führer
had done enough now and should rest on his laurels. People are odd,
aren't they, I mean the implication that it is all a question of prestige
and not one of *Vaterlandsliebe* [love of country].

In July, Unity went to the Bayreuth festival and saw Hitler a
number of times. She dined with him on 25 July, and her letter to
Diana of 28 July gives a picture of him ranting, the only example
of it in her correspondence.

The Führer got into quite a rage twice; the first time with Kannenberg,
for whom I felt heartily sorry! The second time, however, was a
tremendous one and was over Reichsminister Gürtner and the new
laws he is making. He got angrier and angrier, and at last he thundered
– you know how he can – like a machine-gun – '*Das nächste Mal, wenn
die Richter so einen Mann freilassen, so lasse ich ihn von meiner Leib-
standarte verhaften und ins Konzentrationslager schicken; und dann werden
wir sehen, welches am stärksten ist*, the letter of Herr Gürtner's law *oder
meine Maschinengewehre!*' [Next time the judges let go someone like
that, I shall have him arrested by my personal bodyguard and sent to a
concentration camp; and then we shall see who is stronger, the letter of
Herr Gürtner's law or my machine guns!] It was wonderful. Everyone
was silent for quite a time after that.

No doubt they were. Nothing that we have found in her papers more epitomizes Unity's special view of Hitler than her account of this sinister outburst.

At Bayreuth she caught influenza, which Hitler inadvertently made much worse. To Diana she wrote on 4 August in pencil:

I felt queer Friday night on coming home very late from the Führer's, after *Walküre*. The Führer, however, had said he would take me with him to Breslau, and, of course, I would rather have died than miss that. So on Saturday, I stayed in bed till 5, and then go up and packed, and the *Sonderzug* [special train] left at 7. By the time it started I felt like death, and dreaded being called to dinner . . . However, when I was with the Führer, I felt sort of stimulated like one does, and he was in a sweet mood . . . Of course, eating was agony and yet I had to because I couldn't say I was ill. Luckily, the Führer had to have a *Besprechung* [talk] with an officer after dinner so I got to bed early, feeling frightfully sick. We arrived at Breslau at the unearthly hour of 7.30 a.m. We drove in *Kolonne* [procession] to a hotel which had been *abgesperrt* [closed off] . . . We walked to the square where the march-past was to be, which was next door to the hotel. Already the sun was almost unbearably hot − before 8 a.m. − so you can imagine what the next 4 hours were like, and I had a high temperature. We sat on the front row of the *Tribüne*, just behind the Führer's little jutting-out box. Behind us were Wollner and other Sudetendeutsch leaders. I think Wollner was terrifically impressed that I had come with the Führer . . . Well then the Führer arrived and the march-past began − 150,000 people . . . they marched in three columns, the middle one going in the opposite direction from the other two. At first came the Reichs-deutsche from the various *Gaus* [areas], then the Sudetendeutsche. I never expect to see such scenes again as when the Sudetendeutsch women arrived. You will have read about it in the papers but the accounts I saw seemed to bear no relation to what actually happened. Really everyone was crying, and I thought they would never sort out the muddle when the marchers broke ranks and surrounded the Führer once more, and they were all sobbing and stretching out their hands and some of them managed to shout in chorus, '*Lieber Führer, wann kommen Sie zu uns?*' [Dear Führer, when are you coming to us?] and '*Führer, wir schwören Dir auf's Neu, wir bleiben Dir auf ewig treu.*' [Führer, we swear to you again, we shall always be faithful to you.] Henlein stood beside the Führer and it must have been his greatest day.

She could then go to the hotel and lie down for a while, but was not too ill to notice that one of Hitler's secretaries who had been detailed off to accompany her 'was in her element, as she is very pretty and very loud and coy with the *Umgebung* and *Begleitung* [Hitler's circle and escort] and calls them all "*du*", from Sepp Dietrich to the chauffeurs'. Unity then had to get up and watch demonstrations of gymnastics and mass dancing. 'We had to leave early so as to get to the *Flugplatz* [airport] before the Führer, our planes left at 8, I didn't go in the Führer's because I was suddenly terrified I would give him my flu.' They landed at Nuremberg and were driven to Bayreuth; a car was sent to take her to dinner, but this time she really did feel too ill to go. She was developing pneumonia.

Before leaving for Berlin, Hitler sent flowers, and left word with Winifred Wagner to look after Unity. She wrote to Sydney on 3 August: 'Frau Wagner came to see me this morning which seemed like an oasis in the desert as I had felt rather forsaken since the Führer left. She brought the biggest and most beautiful bunch of garden flowers I ever saw . . . She is such a nice motherly person. It seems that the Führer . . . said the doctor's bills were to go to him.' Sydney at once flew out to be with Unity, who had been moved into a private clinic. Pryce-Jones says that this was after she had been discovered pouring her medicine out of the window; we detect Sydney's influence. But this was powerless against the notorious Dr Morell, whom Hitler sent to look after her. In Sydney's account there is a characteristic diatribe against Morell.

I was horrified to see him giving her perhaps ten or fifteen different injections in a day . . . However, it was no new thing for me to be opposed to a doctor's treatment . . . It was strange that Hitler should have had so much faith in Dr Morell and his terrible injections . . . In the end, his health was completely undermined by the hateful stuff that was continually pumped into him by the assiduous Dr Morell . . . The Führer sent her a telegram to beg her to do everything Dr Morell ordered. It would, therefore, be useless for me to object.

All she could do was to cheer Unity up by reading aloud to her from Hardy's *Under the Greenwood Tree* and Kipling's *Kim*.

Unity also received letters from her sisters. Nancy wrote on 9 August:

I am awfully sorry you are ill . . . I remember being ill in Napoli and a doctor laid his bearded face on my bosom which was his old world way of taking my temp. I thought luckily that it was only part of my delirium.

I am getting on well with my German. I know Herrschaft Tish and pfui Pfennig, gemutlicht and rashenshender, six words that would get one a long way if made good use of. Oh and mit mir. Did Muv enjoy her flight? She must be enchanted by the injections you describe. I fear that modern science means o to her.

Well, head of bone, heart of stone – Here is a little poem to show you what a lot of German I know . . .

The poem concludes:

> And rashenshender we do all day
> (Tish, Tish and a merry go round)
> For my lover he is a geboren Malay.

'Rashenshender' is Nancy's version of *Rassenschänder*, someone who commits *Rassenschande*, racial disgrace or, in other words, inter-racial sex. On the same day Diana wrote that she was 'frightfully jealous of you having been at Breslau, even in the *Times* one could see how wonderful it must have been.'

In due course David came out too, and finally Unity recovered. Sydney returned home, leaving David with her. Despite Hitler's instructions, David managed to pay Unity's medical bills, as Sydney put it, 'without hurting anyone's feelings'. Unity and David went to Munich where they lunched with Hitler. 'Farve really does adore him in the same way we do, and treasures every word and every expression,' she writes to Diana on 12 September.

Sydney returned next month and they all went to the Nuremberg Parteitag with Robert Byron. Tom had been coming but had influenza, so Byron came instead. He never pretended to be anything but anti-Nazi – once in her diary Unity refers to him as Red Robert – but he was a close family friend. Sydney describes the spectacle admiringly and at length, though she also says: 'One can understand why the Germans prefer to wear uniform as their other clothes are so badly made.' David, Sydney and Unity went to a party Hitler gave for the foreign guests, and were invited to go to his rooms after the party. They stayed alone with him for half an hour, Unity interpreting. Finally, in response to the roars of the crowd outside, Hitler excused himself with the words: 'I must go now. This tyrant must show himself.' Sydney wished afterwards that she could have talked to him about the danger of war. She did, however, manage to make a point about this danger to General Reichenau, a cousin of Baroness Laroche, whom Unity invited with his wife to dine with them in the guest house. He said: 'The question really is, will the English fight?' Sydney replied: 'Yes, they will fight, and if necessary for ten years, at sea.' This warning caused evident consternation. It could have been Thomas Bowles speaking.

Hitler's closing speech on 12 September promised help to the Sudeten Germans and seemed to bring war close; Robert Byron left that night, so as to be sure of getting away. That day Unity wrote to Diana: 'All the journalists here, headed by Wardie and Sauerwein, are going about with long faces "giving it 24 hours" and discussing possibilities of getting back to England. Wardie, of course, is full of every curl being of international importance and considers I hold the fate of Europe in my hands. Isn't he wonderful.' In fact the Munich settlement followed in the next month. Just before it was finalized, on 7 October, Sydney wrote to Unity: 'The Col. [Percy Bailey] and Weenie have been here 2 days, he getting nearly ready to go to Czechoslovakia with the British Legion and he is simply adoring it . . . he has got a kit bag and wonderful blue uniform and is completely happy. Tommy and Jack are going too, and all hugely looking forward to it.' She adds that Tom, by whom she is sending this letter, 'is against the Peace and has nearly joined the war party, I fear! Please talk to him.' After the settlement, Diana wrote to Unity on 26 October that Mosley 'had a wonderful campaign during the crisis and huge crowds . . . I think most of our class wanted to fight, but not the workers.'

Sydney says that during 1938 Unity grew up: 'She became more serious and discreet.' Diana said much the same thing in interview, and Unity's letters tend to confirm it. She spoke at a debating society on 17 November that year; Dr Sigismund Fitzrandolph of the German Embassy helped her with suggestions for her speech, as did Mosley. But an article of hers that the *Daily Mirror* published on 18 March 1939 appears to have been her own unaided work. It was headed 'What Miss Mitford Would Like to See'. '*We* don't agree with her,' the newspaper assured its readers. Between Unity's delivery of the article and its publication Hitler had moved into the Czech lands, a fact that effectively sabotaged Unity's case; for this invasion was Hitler's first seizure of territory not inhabited by Germans. The inhabitants of Prague most certainly did not cheer as had those of Vienna, and Hitler was in open and obvious breach of his word. It was the event which most powerfully tilted British opinion towards war, convincing many former appeasers that they had been 'had'. (Lord Hailsham was one; see his autobiography.) The article's appearance at this bad moment should not blind us to the fact that it is a rather well written, a simple, straightforward polemic.

Unity begins by pointing out that Germany has signed a pact with Britain in 1935 voluntarily limiting its naval power to 35 per cent of that of the Royal Navy. This shows that Germany never wishes to go to war with England again. Hitler rejects the Kaiser's policy of rivalry with England. 'Every German knows that the future of the Reich lies, not in a large overseas colonial empire, but in an entirely different direction . . . in which there is no reason at all why she should come into conflict with British interests.'

She goes on to say that Hitler's racial theory precludes any wish to weaken England. 'Germans believe . . . that the future of Europe stands or falls with the Nordic race. And they believe that enmity between the two great Nordic countries would mean its virtual suicide.' English and German people get on together, she says. 'Even during the September crisis [over Munich], when it was touch and go whether the British Government would take sides with the Czechs against them, Germans never became unfriendly towards English people, though they were naturally puzzled at the attitude of England's rulers.'

She quotes the British ambassador to Germany, Sir Nevile Henderson, to the effect that the real interests of the two countries are complementary to one another. She goes on: 'With Germany, the greatest Continental Power, allied to Britain, the greatest

Colonial Power, another world war would become an impossibility . . . The German Army, the British Navy and the two Air Forces combined would police the world and keep "peace in our time".' The article ends with a quotation from Hitler to the effect that no German wishes to cause the British Empire any difficulties.

The grand design as outlined by Unity would have meant taking the gigantic risk of abolishing the balance of power policy in Europe that had served Britain for centuries, and handing over control of the continent to a dictator who had shown proof of unreliability as well as signs of instability. But we do not have to agree with her article to recognize that it is a far cry from the *Stürmer* letter. She does not even mention the Jews. On this subject, though, she had already begun to encounter difficulties of a kind which maturity must force any doctrinaire racist to face. In other words, she met something that even to her appeared as a hard case. She wrote to Diana on 18 July 1938:

You remember my little friend from Vienna who you said was like an Indian, and his pretty blonde fiancée who asked the Führer for an autograph in the Osteria. Well, yesterday she telephoned and said could she come and see me for five minutes, but her fiancé mustn't know anything about it. So, this morning she came . . . Heinz, her fiancé, was a member of the SS in Vienna – I believe since 1932. He was a tremendously enthusiastic Nazi, and really risked everything for the cause during the Schuschnigg regime. Well, it seems that just after the *Machtübernahme* [in the context she obviously means the Anschluss with Austria] his father, also a member of the *Partei*, who had brought him up to be very *national-denkend* [nationalistically minded], told him that both his (Heinz's) mother's parents were Jewish. Of course, poor Heinz was completely *erledigt* [shattered] when he heard it and wanted to shoot himself at once, which it seems to me would have been the best way out. Though, officially, he doesn't count as a Jew as both the grandparents were baptized. But for Heinz, being a real Nazi '*aus Überzeugung*' [through conviction], that naturally made no difference. His father made him promise not to do anything until they had a reply to their *Ersuch* [request] to the Führer, but so far there has been no reply, and in the meanwhile, of course, he is having what is practically a nervous breakdown. Well, it seems that there are several half-Jews who have . . . been allowed to remain in the Party on account of special *Verdienste* [services]. So they hope that he also will, though of course this will anyhow, from his point of view, have ruined his life.

Unity told the fiancée that if she gave her a personal letter for Hitler, she would pass it on to him; we do not know if this happened or, if so, with what result.

Unity's attitude is to us extraordinary, notably the remark that if Heinz had shot himself at once that would have been the best way out. However, Unity was not recommending something she was unprepared to do herself, as she was to prove when war broke out. She might well have shot herself if she had discovered that her own mother was Jewish. To the really fanatical Nazi, Jewish blood was such a contamination that to discover one possessed it might indeed make it impossible to live with oneself. The view is an inherently sick one, but within its limits Unity shows human sympathy and a willingness to help. She is not being callous; according to the lights she and Heinz shared, she is even being humane. David Pryce-Jones sees the kernel of the holocaust in the fact that Unity was later on to view a number of flats whose Jewish occupants were leaving Munich and, according to him, ignored these people. There is something in this: such insensitivity is certainly a worrying symptom. Yet it does not go to the heart of the matter. Ideological perversion is what twists people into committing human sacrifice for the victim's own good, or that of humanity. Torquemada burning people to save their souls, the Reverend Jim Jones dosing his flock with cyanide to send them to heaven, Stalin slaughtering ten million people because, as he told Churchill, though it was terrible, it was 'absolutely necessary for Russia': these are the models. Unity's perverted sympathy with poor Heinz is truly sinister; the connection with genocide is clear.

In the same long letter, there is a reference to Unity's dislike of the Italians, and even of Mussolini; something which we had not suspected, but which comes clearly enough out of the material. Once she was disparaging about Italy in Hitler's presence and some of his companions ticked her off; Hitler defended her, though he was careful not to endorse her views. Since that time, her anti-Italian feeling became a private joke between her and Hitler. Later, in the letter of 18 July just quoted, Unity writes:

At lunch, a man who was there said the Osteria was just like an Italian Osteria, *mur viel sauberer* [only much cleaner]. At that, the Führer looked at me out of the corner of his eye and then started to blither quite uncontrollably, and when he had sufficiently regained his composure he said, '*Das hört sie gern*' [she likes to hear that]. I think the man was amazed.

The six months between March 1939, when Hitler invaded the Czech lands, and September of the same year when he invaded Poland, and Britain and France declared war, give an odd impression as we read our documentation. In May, Hitler made arrangements for Unity to be found a flat of her own in Munich through the *Wohnungsamt* (housing office). In arranging this, Pryce-Jones sees Hitler as practising a deception on her, because in the same month he ordered the German Army to prepare for the invasion of Poland, which Britain and France had guaranteed. Talk of deception is wrong, but there was certainly an inconsistency. Hitler was explicit with both Unity and Diana about the danger of war between Britain and Germany; he never pretended to be going to respect the guarantee to Poland. He hoped that Britain would not declare war, but feared she would. 'We will always keep up Anglo-German friendship, whatever the English Government may do,' he told Unity; she quoted this in a letter to David on 15 May 1939. Yet he gave no serious thought to what would happen to her if war came; all his plans for her assumed peace. He arranged for her flat, talked of whom they should invite to the Parteitag that September, and so on. To us, the war seems exclusively his fault, if only because it would have been so easy to put off the invasion of Poland for a year or two to allow international opinion to acclimatize itself to what he had already done. The ball was at his feet and at no one else's. Did he know this? Sometimes he gives the impression of passivity in the grip of irresistible forces. He could still make Unity laugh; in a letter to Diana of 15 May she says he told her that he had made a new speed limit '*zum Schutz der deutschen Landwirtschaft*' (for the protection of German agriculture), because of a time when she and Diana had crashed into a manure cart.

Unity herself had a very clear plan in case of war: she would kill herself. She told several people this, including Diana who tells us that, but for her husband and children, she herself might have done the same thing. But Diana would have done it from a rather different motive. Unity could not bear a war because her loyalties were now at least half German. Diana remained entirely British, tied to her country by her husband, family and home. Her depression came from knowing that war meant ruin for Mosley.

On 29 March Unity wrote to Diana following a lunch with Hitler. 'He held my hand most of the time and looked sweet and said *"Kind!"* [child] in his sympathetic way because he was so sorry about England and Germany being such enemies. However, he said nothing but wonderful things about England and he completely gave me faith again that it will all come right in the end.' And again on 15 May:

I had lunch with W. on Thursday and Friday and he was sweet. I do think I have been lucky — I left England nine weeks ago and have seen him nine times, and during that time I was 2½ weeks in Burgenland and Hungary. Also, he has . . . said particularly wonderful things. On Thursday . . . Wagner said to me, *'Sie sind so still'* [You are so silent], and Wolf took my hand and said in his wonderful voice (you know what I mean) *'Das arme Kind ist unglücklich'* [The poor child is unhappy], and then he turned to me, with the *sweetest* look in his eyes, and said: *'Kind, Sie müssen es nicht so tragisch nehmen.'* [Child, you needn't take it so tragically.] So then as you can imagine I felt that none of it mattered any more, just for the moment, but I felt I could *kill* the Umbrella [Chamberlain].

Depression came over Unity in waves that spring and summer; sometimes her mind was on other things, sometimes she could think that this crisis, like that of the previous autumn, would disappear, but often she felt very low. So did Diana, but she had Mosley. Erna Hanfstaengl, still a great friend, put Unity up for more than two months; she was worried about her health and encouraged her to go to Berlin to see the famous Dr Sauerbruch. He prescribed massage and exercise, telling her that she was overweight. Unity repeated this to Hitler, and he thumped the table and said: 'If he says that again, I'll take the National Prize away from him.' Erna arranged for her to take singing lessons with a Spaniard called Raventos. But Unity's last attempt to help Erna reconcile Hitler with Putzi, though it began hopefully, ended in failure and lost her Erna's friendship at a time when she needed friends. To Diana she wrote on 18 March 1939: 'It is lovely staying here with Erna but she is very strict and makes me wash the bath out, etc . . . The only boring thing is that she schimpfs [complains] as much as ever, and shrieks at me as if I were responsible for it all. She trots around stark naked in the morning . . .' Later, writing on 5 April, she said she proposed to take Erna to England. She would 'plant' her on Diana for ten days. 'She will erziehen [educate] you like she does me, you will find you are a different person by the end!' She also arranged for Erna to stay with Sydney. But then she wrote to Diana on 31 May:

The Good Girl always said she could get the two-headed man back if she could see W. first. Well, last week I was lunching with W. and we came to talk of our two-headed friend and so I summoned up all my courage and asked if he would see her. He was perfectly sweet and said yes . . . However . . . over the weekend . . . she and her friend kept saying to each other, of course it won't come off . . . I couldn't sleep for fury.

But when the day arrived, 30 May, 'Gooders put on her Sunday best and off we went trembling with excitement. Imagine, she hadn't seen him for 15 years! I stayed in the hall while they discussed the whole affair and then I joined them for tea. It seems it went off very well.' But Erna then gave Unity a letter for Hitler, which she gave him over tea in his flat on 9 June. We shall never know what was in this letter, but after reading a few sentences he tore it up and burned it, forbidding Unity ever to see Erna again. Unity's diary says: 'I am miserable at having had to give it to him but he is *sweet* and says he will give me furniture for my sitting room.' (He in fact seems to have forgotten this promise; at any rate it was not honoured during the few months of peace which remained.) Unity left Erna's and moved to an hotel, after which she went to England as planned, but without Erna.

It ought perhaps to be mentioned here that Erna, in an interview with David Pryce-Jones, gave him a very odd version of this story in which Erna's proposed journey to England was not in order to stay with Sydney and Diana, but to see Churchill on the invitation of his son Randolph. Unity is supposed to have been present when Randolph suggested this. It appears to be fantasy.

There is quite a lot in Unity's letters and diary about Erna's proposed trip to England, but no mention of Randolph Churchill.

In the meantime, Hitler had helped Unity to find a flat. Writing to Diana on 5 June she says: 'Well, today's exciting news is that I have a *Wohnung* [flat]. Wolf told Wagner [Adolf Wagner, Gauleiter of Munich] that they were to find one for me . . . So, today a young man from the Ministerium took me round to look at some . . . At last, we found the *perfect* [Unity's italics] *Wohnung* in Schwabing, in a modern block of flats . . . It belongs to a young Jewish couple who are going abroad.' With them she dealt, it seems, perfectly amicably; at any rate she bought a cupboard from them, she told Sydney in a letter written on 28 July. On the surface, then, the amenities were preserved between Unity and the owners. Yet just to let drop that they were 'going abroad' now comes over, looking back, as distinctly chilling.

Between 12 June and 7 July she was in her own country with her parents, playing rummy with her father, seeing everyone including aunts, uncles and cousins, not all of whom at all approved of her. She saw Putzi on 23 June and told him what had happened. She also saw some political friends such as Major-General J. F. C. Fuller, and went along to Earl's Court with Mosley and Diana when they discussed arrangements for Mosley's big peace rally. She even went with Sydney to the Conservative college at Ashridge, where she stayed the night of 30 June between lectures on world affairs.

Hitler invited Unity and Diana to Bayreuth again for the last time; Unity found two bouquets awaiting her, one from the local Gauleiter, and one from the mayor. She and Diana saw a good deal of Hitler, as well as of other Nazi leaders and the Wagner family. She also met Lady Kemsley during the interval of *Parsifal*, and they talked about Decca, Unity tells Sydney on 28 July. 'She seems to be fond of her, who wouldn't be.' Unity had met two other friends of Decca as well. 'What funny places I do meet her odd friends in – first Prag [*sic*], then Bayreuth.'

On 2 August, the day before they left, Hitler told the sisters straight out that he expected war. Unity's diary quotes him as telling them '*Wenn kein Wunder geschieht, sehe ich alles sehr schwarz. Und an Wunder glaube ich nicht.*' (If there is no miracle I see the outlook as very black. And I do not believe in miracles.) Diana told him that Mosley would go on campaigning for peace as

long as this was legal; Hitler's comment was: 'If he does, he may
be assassinated like Jaurès in 1914.' After they left, Unity told
Diana again that she would kill herself if there was war. Afterwards they watched a performance of *Götterdämmerung*, and
Diana remembers: 'Never had the glorious music seemed to me
so doom-laden . . . I knew well what Unity, sitting beside me,
was thinking. I left her next day, death in my heart.' (*A Life of
Contrasts*.)

Unity got back to Munich on the third. Outwardly, her normal
life continued; she read and wrote, decorated and furnished her
new flat, went to the cinema and followed the international
situation. She saw Hitler on 4 and 5 August, both times at the
Osteria; on the fourth he was 'fascinating about his new buildings', on the fifth he was 'sweet'. This was the last time she saw
him before the war. Her diary and letters do not convey any
feeling of isolation until the very last few days. Janos came to stay
for a day or two as, later, did Edda and Carmencita Wrede, two
young princesses who were identical twins and half Spanish. On
her birthday, 8 August, she wrote to her mother saying that her
flat is 'perfect joy and heaven . . . and I am simply longing for
you all to come out and stay with me (only one at a time, of
course, there's no room for more) . . . You simply can't think
how wonderfully well and healthy all the rushing and carrying up
and down stairs and sweating has made me feel . . .' Is she, here,
laying it on a little too thick? She would certainly have wanted to
reassure her parents as to her state of mind. On the fourteenth she
is again in apparent good spirits, writing to Diana to ask if she is
coming out before the Parteitag, with or without Jonathan and
Desmond. There had evidently been a rift between Goebbels and
his wife, for she adds: 'They report, from Salzburg, that Magda
and the Doctor are completely *versöhnt* [reconciled] and have gone
off on a second honeymoon.' It seems from a later letter, of 18
August, that Diana had planned to come on the twenty-eighth
with Jonathan and Desmond and Vivien Mosley, her stepdaugh-
ter. Unity also describes two evenings out. 'Debo's friend Mr
Douglas Home [William Douglas Home, the playwright] and
a . . . clergyman friend of his have been here for two days, I
shewed them round a bit and I dined with them at Walterspiel . . .
Last night we all went, with the English Consul and his wife, to

Platzl.' But there were sinister portents. Petrol was getting rather short; for this reason she would be unable to get to Burgenland before the Parteitag, as she had intended. So was food: some of her friends brought her butter and eggs from the country.

On 22 August Unity notes in her diary: 'Hear the wonderful news about the Pact with Russia.' This reaction is interesting, because it shows that anti-Communism, as such, played little part in Unity's political feelings. She simply saw the pact as a hope for peace; surely Britain and France would not declare war now that saving Poland had become a clear impossibility. But two days later she writes to Diana: 'I wish I could make out . . . whether there is going to be a war or not. When I heard about the pact with Russia, I thought *not*. However, now it looks worse than ever. It's nearly three weeks since I saw W. I wish he would come.' More and more people were getting called up: the Wrede twins, trained nurses who had experienced the siege of Toledo in the Spanish Civil War, left for Berlin on the twenty-fifth expecting to get their papers. On the same day Unity went for a chat, evidently inconclusive, with the consul, Wolstan Weld-Forester. On the twenty-seventh she wrote to Diana:

I feel awfully cut off, since all the foreigners and even journalists left – not that I knew any of them, but the feeling of security is gone. Tomorrow, I shall go round and see if the Consul is still there. He is quite a nice chap. It seems as if I haven't seen anyone for days, except for my singing master and his wife. Max rang up to say he had some butter for me, I went round to the *Führerbau* in the afternoon to fetch it, only to find he had been called up. My *Tapezierer* [upholsterer] was also called up, in the middle of the night, so I shan't get my new curtains . . . On thinking things over – I have done nothing else the last few days – I thought I might disappear into the mountains in Tyrol perhaps, if war is declared. Of course, the other thing seems the easiest way out, but it seems silly not to wait and see how things turn out, it might all be over in a few weeks, like Gen. Fuller predicts . . .

To Sydney, too, she writes on the same day that she may go to the Tyrol, 'as I think to stay here would make too many difficulties for everybody'. No mention here of 'the other thing'; she did not talk of this to her parents. She went to see the consul again on the twenty-ninth: 'Visit the Consul, chat to him,' she says in the diary.

This is unlikely to have had anything to do with a wish to leave Germany; her basic intention was to kill herself, which would have been more difficult in England where she would be surrounded by her family. Her last moment of real happiness, perhaps, was when she received two birthday presents from Decca; they arrived three weeks late, on 31 August. To Sydney she wrote on 1 September: 'Please thank her a million times when you write – I don't like to write as she always said not to' – because of Esmond? – 'and anyway, I don't know her address.'

The next day she wrote to Diana:

Your letter of the 30th just arrived. You can't think how thrilling it is every time I hear the letterbox click, as I always expect every letter to be the last that will get through . . .

In case you didn't hear the Führer's speech, this is what he said about England. '*Ich habe England immer wieder eine Freundschaft und, wenn notwendig, das engste Zusammengehen angeboten. Aber Liebe kann nicht nur von einer Seite angeboten werden, sie muss von der anderen ihre Erwiderung finden.*' [Again and again, I have offered England friendship and, when necessary, the closest collaboration. But love cannot be offered from one side only, it must find a return from the other.]

I tried to ring you up last night but was a few hours too late – no more calls to England allowed.

Last night, we had blackout for the first time . . .

I fear I shan't see the Führer again. Nardy, if anything should happen to me, and the English press try to make some untrue story out of it against W., you will see to it that the truth is known won't you . . .

Next morning, Sunday 3 September, the British consulate telephoned Unity to tell her there was a telegram for her. She went round; she was given the news that Britain was about to declare war. She sat straight down to write a letter to her parents:

Darling Muv and Farve,

I came round to the Consulate to get your telegram and hear that war has been declared. So this is to say good-bye. The Consul will kindly take this to England and send it to you. I send my best love to you all and particularly to my Boud when you write. Perhaps when this war is over, everyone will be friends again, and there will be the friendship between Germany and England which we have so hoped for.

I hope you will see the Führer often when it is over.

With very best love and blessings,

Bobo.

Fondest love to Blor.

And I *do* hope Tom will be all right.

Returning to her flat, she telephoned Rudi von Simolin, asking her if she was coming to Munich that day. Rudi was a girl of about her own age with whom she had made friends at Erna's. 'Not till Monday,' replied Rudi; 'why don't you go to the Burgenland until all this dies down?' Unity declined to do so; she said goodbye and abruptly put down the telephone, Rudi recounted in a letter to Janos of 5 September.

Unity then went to Adolf Wagner, Gauleiter of Munich, at the Bavarian Interior Ministry. She knew Wagner well; his office, like that of the British consul, was open that Sunday because of the international crisis. In a state of evident agitation, she asked, 'Shall I be interned?' He reassured her that she would not, and promised also that he would see that she had some petrol for her car. She asked him, if anything happened to her, to see that she was buried in Munich with her photograph of Hitler and her party badge. Wagner was worried about what she might do, and made arrangements for her to be followed. She went to call on Frau Raventos, wife of her singing teacher. She gave her 1,000 marks, asking her to give the money to the British consul because her father had sent it to her and she did not need it any more; and a letter, seemingly containing keys, addressed to Rudi von Simolin. Frau Raventos thought her distraught and upset. Finally, Unity turned up again at Wagner's office, this time in a state of complete calm and apparent normality. She handed him a large envelope and took her leave. The envelope contained a Nazi party badge, a signed photograph of Hitler with a personal dedication, and a letter to Hitler.

Unity then walked straight round to the Englischer Garten, in her handbag the little automatic pistol she had bought in Belgium some time before. As soon as she thought she was alone, she fired a shot into the ground, then put the pistol to her right temple and fired again.

# PART FIVE

# War and After

# 34

# The Semi-attached Couple

David sold Swinbrook and the estate in 1936. He only got a low price, but all the same the proceeds began burning a hole in his pocket. Two years later a man in the Marlborough Club, source of most of his odd investments in the past, asked if anyone was interested in buying a small island in the Inner Hebrides, and David said he might be. The island was Inchkenneth, and Sydney and Unity went to look at it. They loved it at first sight, and David bought it, giving it to Tom.

Inchkenneth is a small island like a crustacean with a jointed tail, lying low in the sound between the great frowning hulks which are Mull and Ulva. It is greener than either, covered mainly with short grass and having little bracken and almost no heather. It has a ruined chapel, a large plain house and a cottage, a walled garden, a single oatfield and a modest jetty. Its 'tail' is a curved string of mysterious hillocks known as the Humpies, each sloping and grassy on one side and precipitous on the other. It was an odd purchase; the upkeep of such a place is never cheap, certainly not for a couple like the Redesdales who would always need a boatman, and getting to it was always described by Nancy as 'The Worst Journey in the World', the title of Cherry-Garrard's book on her hero Scott of the Antarctic. The journey involved a night train to Oban, an hour or two over to Mull on a steamer called the *Lochinvar*, though hardly young; a drive across Mull; then a short crossing in a motor boat. The place, once reached, is one of the most beautiful in the world. Both of us, Jonathan and Catherine, have been under its spell. We have clambered among the varied rocks, red and black and grey, sandstone, basalt and granite: we have fished for mackerel or cuddy in the dark sea. It rains a great deal, but somehow that does not matter at Inchkenneth, only making it more beautiful when the sun comes out.

David and Sydney were at Inchkenneth when war broke out. They were worried about Unity in Germany — sufficiently worried for David to send her 1,500 marks for emergencies — about £75 in those days — and to write begging her to come back. The money got through; the 1,000 marks Unity gave to Frau Raventos was what remained of it. From the last days of August the posts were interrupted and telephoning was impossible. They sent a telegram to Unity at the British consulate, but heard nothing for nearly a month.

At last, on 2 October when they were in London, a letter dated 18 September arrived from Teddy Almasy, Janos's brother, in neutral Budapest; he said that Unity was ill in hospital and being well looked after, but did not say what the trouble was. Incredible as it may seem, the Germans had made the matter a *geheime Reichssache* or state secret, presumably on Hitler's personal orders. This was stupid from their point of view, because it allowed rumours to circulate which were discreditable to them, such as that Unity had been murdered by the SS or put in a concentration camp. All the Almasys could do was send one or two more reassuring but totally noncommittal telegrams. Towards the end of the month the *Sunday Pictorial* rang Sydney at 2 a.m. to ask for confirmation of a story that Unity had died in hospital; she told the newspaper she did not believe it. Reports trickled through from other press sources, and from the Foreign Office, that Unity was alive. Then, says Sydney: 'On Christmas Eve the telephone rang from Berne and it was the voice of Janos and then . . . Unity's own voice. It sounded the same as ever and what a joy to hear it. They both said, when are you coming? She was there in Switzerland and waiting to be fetched.'

What had happened, according to a letter from Rudi von Simolin to Janos Almasy of 5 November 1939, was that immediately after she shot herself she was picked up by the tail that Gauleiter Wagner had put on her and taken by a military car to the surgical clinic. This is indirectly confirmed by a remarkable letter in the *Radio Times* of 11 April 1981 from Mr H. W. Koch of York, who as a child out walking with his mother and elder brother was as near as possible an eye witness to the suicide attempt. He writes:

As we walked along the Königinstrasse where it forms the Western edge of the Englischer Garten, a young fair-haired lady walked towards us, clad in a greyish costume. As she approached us, clutching a handbag to her, with one hand in it, my mother remarked to my brother: 'What a pretty lady, if only she did not have so much powder on her face.' Hardly had she passed when behind us we heard a sharp report; we turned on our heels and my brother caught in his arms the lady that had just passed us. Blood streamed from the side of her face. My mother and brother lifted her from the pavement and put her on the grass verge.

Across the road was some sort of establishment connected with the Luftwaffe; Frau Koch called frantically to the sentry to help, but he would not leave his post. However, shortly afterwards a Luftwaffe car emerged with two lieutenants and an NCO; these picked up the young woman, and her pistol, and drove away. The police later told the Koch family not to talk about the incident, and the Gestapo took statements from them. Mr Koch's brother was also interviewed by his superiors in the Hitler Youth, who told him Unity's name. It is clear from Mr Koch's account that his mother's appeal to the sentry had no effect, and that the emergence of the car must have been the result of a quick and urgent telephone call from someone the Kochs never even noticed.

At first Unity's case was thought to be hopeless. According to Nancy, in a letter to Mrs Ham of 7 January 1940: 'They fetched a nurse to the hospital saying "You can go on your holiday tomorrow, she cannot live the night." ' The bullet had entered her right temple, ploughed its way through her brain and ended up near the back of her head. But she lived.

Rudi went to Munich early next day and contacted Frau Raventos, who said that a girl answering to Unity's description had shot herself in the Englischer Garten and been taken away in a military car. Rudi and Frau Raventos then went together to Unity's flat; the authorities had taken possession of it. Then Rudi went to Gauleiter Wagner, who told her that Unity was still alive. She wrote all this to Janos Almasy next day, 5 September. As people do after an attempted or actual suicide, Rudi accuses herself of not having sought her out earlier and seen to her; Unity had told her of her intention some months before, but at the time Rudi had laughed it off.

Now Rudi proved herself a devoted friend. She saw Unity in hospital, at first still unconscious; she kept Janos in touch at Bernstein by letter and telegram – Bernstein was not on the telephone. Hitler rang the clinic often for news, Rudi said. Unity was X-rayed and the bullet located; the doctors decided not to try to remove it. On 13 September Rudi tells Janos that Unity had a telephone conversation with someone whom the clinic refused to identify; Rudi supposes it was Hitler. Julius Schaub, Hitler's adjutant, confirms this in an article in *Revue* (1950): Schaub himself accompanied him on two visits, the first on 10 September. Unity was staring at the ceiling, only just conscious. Hitler visited her again several times when she was able to talk. Later she told Sydney that he offered her the chance of staying on in Munich, in which case he would give her German nationality immediately, or of being sent back to her family in England. She chose to return.

She had regained consciousness, of a sort. There were early signs of paralysis, but this largely cleared up. She could write a little, though uncertainly enough for her to need some re-education later in using her right hand; she was never able to draw again. There is a letter from her to Janos dated 10 December. It is confused but basically rational; she says, 'Janosh was sad because you didn't answer her telegrams.' 'Janosh' here evidently stands for 'Rudi', and 'sad' for 'worried'.

Hitler arranged for her return. She was taken to Berne with a German nurse in attendance; Janos travelled with her on the train, and rang her parents from the clinic there. Sydney then went to Berne with Debo, intending to return with Unity by train. David would meet them at Folkestone with an ambulance. Unity's voice may have sounded the same as ever to Sydney on the telephone, but this was illusory. She had suffered brain damage that could never be put right, though in certain respects she gradually improved; she even once drove a car on a provisional licence. But she had become an entirely different person; Debo says that this was obvious to her as soon as they met in Berne, and it was certainly obvious to Jonathan when he saw her later. Hitler himself had seen it: 'Out of the active being whom we once knew a quite different one has arisen,' Schaub quotes him as saying.

Sydney and Debo found her in the Berne hospital; she was very thin, her face all eyes, but to Sydney she looked beautiful, and she wrote:

We were all three so happy. She seemed to talk just as usual and asked for news, of everyone. Then suddenly she said something that made me realize what had happened. We were having tea, and she said to me, pushing the sugar basin, 'Will you have some chocolate?' I said, 'I don't see any chocolate.' 'Yes, here it is,' she said, pointing to the sugar basin. Just very occasionally a word would come wrong in this way. But after a time this quite disappeared.

Sydney, Debo and Unity left Berne on the evening of 31 December, with a nurse from the Swiss clinic. They arrived in Calais in the early afternoon of 1 January 1940, too late to catch that day's boat to England, so they went to the Hotel Terminus. It was there, at dinner, that the English press caught up with them, in the shape of George Reid Millar of the *Daily Express*, who sent Sydney a note offering her £3,000 for an interview with Unity about her experiences in Germany. Sydney's reply was a firm refusal, but couched unfortunately in terms calculated to whet a journalistic appetite: 'I am sorry I was not able to see you and my daughter also is too tired after her journey. There is no question of accepting the offer of the *Daily Express*. My daughter has been very ill but is now much better and I am taking her home. She has received the greatest possible care while in Germany.'

So this notorious friend of Hitler's was merely tired, and much better in herself; no mention of brain damage or diminished faculties. If one could only get to her, what a scoop she could give! Millar increased his offer to £5,000, to no avail. Sydney and the hotel staff kept him and other journalists away during the two days they stayed in Calais. This period was a nightmare to Sydney, who began to feel she would never get Unity home. At last, on 3 January, Unity was carried to a boat on a stretcher, while the French police kept journalists away. There was trouble with the customs, who came on board and went through every one of Unity's fourteen pieces of luggage. Sydney says:

A doctor was sent on board and came in with the Customs officers. When they were looking through the contents of her handbag they came upon a little packet of white pills, which they handed to the doctor. 'What are these?' he asked her. She said she could not remember. 'I know what they are,' he almost shouted. 'They are *cocaine*. Anyone can see by looking at her that she's a cocaine addict.' I said, 'She is *not*, and these pills are not cocaine. You will please take them away and analyse them.' Presumably he did so, but he never had the decency to aquaint me with the result.

They had in fact, Unity remembered later, been got for Rebel, her great dane now with some people in Hungary.

The journalists were prevented from meeting the boat: the port was a restricted area, but they evidently felt they should be allowed in. 'Don't waste our soldiers' time or poke bayonets at a Press who still want facts,' complained the *Daily Express*. David was there with the ambulance and they drove away. Then came trouble. About five miles outside Folkestone the ambulance began to make ominous clanking sounds. Sydney looked back and saw the lights of at least twenty cars following them in procession – the press. They stopped, and found that the springs of the ambulance had broken; they could not continue to High Wycombe. They went back to Folkestone, again followed by Fleet Street.

There, the Press was rewarded. Out came the flash light cameras and many photographs were taken as Unity got out of the ambulance and walked unsteadily on her father's arm into the hotel. We came slowly out of the darkness into the brilliantly lighted hall of the hotel to find it full of Press men and women. I stopped and said to them: 'Are you all quite mad? What is it all about?' Of course they didn't care what I said or what I didn't say, but they left us alone to go upstairs, just gazing with all their eyes. There is no doubt in my mind that the Press and Cinema company arranged the breakdown of the ambulance. At the time I was not sorry, it was horrid driving so far in the blackout with very poor lights and she so tired.

But the *Daily Express* got its interview, without paying. One of its reporters at Folkestone had got round David, who had said he could see her for a few minutes. The interview, Sydney says, was not too bad, although Unity did say: 'I'm glad to be in England, even if I'm not on your side.'

Next day they obtained another ambulance and drove to High Wycombe without a hitch. But, as Sydney says, 'not before the cinemas had taken a roll of film which appeared in the newsreels with many scathing and loudly laughing comments'. There were protests about Unity's treatment in *The Times* and in both Houses of Parliament, though questions were also asked in Parliament protesting that the press had been kept from interviewing her as she was carried off the boat. 'The Press were certainly very mad,' comments Sydney. 'They appear to have lost their senses over the arrival of poor Unity back in England. After it had all died down some of them had the grace to admit it.' The fact was that Unity had enraged too many people. It must be remembered in particular that the Jewish community, whom she had publicly insulted, and with whose deadly enemies she was identified, were disproportionately represented in the cinema and press. Happy that Britain was now fighting their enemy, they can be excused their enthusiasm. Unity, in her day, had denied their credentials as Englishmen. Who was now the 'alien'? But the pressure to grant an interview might have been relaxed if Sydney had been franker about the confusion Unity showed following her brain damage. Later Unity was taken to the Acland nursing home in Oxford, where she was under the care of Professor Sir Hugh Cairns. From there in due course she was discharged into her mother's care. After first seeing her, Nancy wrote to Mrs Ham on 7 January 1940:

The whole thing is most poignant. She is like a child in many ways and has very much lost her memory (a mercy I expect), does not know why she was ill but seems to think the doctor made a hole in her head. She is very happy to be back; keeps on saying 'I thought you all hated me but I don't remember why.' She said to me 'You are not one of those who would be cruel to somebody are you?' So I said I was very much against that.

Diana, too, saw Unity; she noticed the change at once, but her account shows that Unity knew more about the immediate past than she had divulged to Nancy. Her German nurses, says Diana, had been nuns, and had as Christians tried to persuade her that her attempted suicide had been a sin. 'She questioned me over and over again: did I think it very wicked to die by one's own hand? She probably knew my answer. To that small extent man must be the master of his fate. He did not ask to be born; if his life becomes too tragic or unbearable he has the right to die.'

The one person who consistently tried to minimize the change in Unity was Sydney. But Sydney was to devote the next eight years to looking after her stricken daughter, and belief in a possible recovery was perhaps necessary to her if she was to face the endless and sometimes heartrending task. Nancy wrote to Mrs Ham on 10 February 1940: 'The Oxford doctor seems to have told Muv she will get quite all right and to have spoken very differently to Farve.' It is doubtful that a doctor would have given such inconsistent opinions to Unity's parents; but any prudent doctor hedges a prognosis, and this could give Sydney the opportunity to draw an optimistic inference. It is also clear from Sydney's account that Unity came to remember much more about the past than seemed to be the case at the time; there are passages in Sydney's memoir about Unity that are dictated by Unity herself, of simple but perfectly lucid recollection. Nevertheless she had regressed to a mental age of perhaps eleven; she had lost all that sense of what might interest others that makes it possible to hold an adult conversation. She trembled, her face would contort, and she became tearful or enraged about little things. Her father's changeable loves and hates emerged in her, in caricature. Generally she liked people the more, the less often she saw them. Her mother of course was always with her; nobody knows, says Debo, what Sydney had to put up with. Unity's relaxed atheism turned into an anxious and erratic religiosity which sent her chasing after different sects in turn, including at one time Christian Science, though she also went regularly to Swinbrook parish church. In a Church of England congregation there usually seems to be one woman whose voice, in tune but indefinably tiresome, rises above the rest. At Swinbrook during the war this voice was Unity's. She had retained some of her sense of humour, in her good moments she could still see a joke. But while having lost rather little of her memory, certainly less than Nancy thought, she no longer had the power of sustained and consecutive reasoning. This was certainly merciful, because it meant that she could not dwell on the implications of her situation in such a way as to renew her despair. She never attempted suicide again, or even talked of doing so. She had blasted away the pains, as well as the faculties, of her adult self, and henceforth her smaller miseries were no more than her diminished abilities could cope with. In a sense, therefore, her suicide attempt had been successful.

She knew that something was wrong with her. 'Am I mad?' she once asked Nancy, whose reply was very characteristic in that it concealed kindness in a tease: 'Of course you are, darling Stonyheart, but then you always were.' She lost her looks completely. After her physical recovery from the wound the tendency to overweight, noted before the war by Dr Sauerbruch, became serious; bad circulation gave her a high colour. She abandoned the make-up that had been disapproved of by Putzi Hanfstaengl and the League of German Girls, and at the very end by Frau Koch. This was fortunate, as she would have been too clumsy to apply it well.

David and Sydney naturally collaborated over Unity's homecoming, but underneath there was a serious rift between them. It started with the outbreak of the war, and finally their differences became such that they found it necessary to live apart for the rest of their lives. They remained in close touch, writing to each other almost every day; they were of course together for Debo's wedding in April 1941, and to comfort each other after Tom was killed in action in May 1945. But from 1940 onwards they could no longer share a house for any length of time.

David always had strong views at any one moment, but was liable to change them suddenly. In the Mitford childhood all accounts agree that the favourite of one moment could become the outcast of the next, and vice versa. David certainly believed himself to be firm as a rock, though a remark to the *Daily Express* on 2 February 1939 may betray some sort of doubt. The newspaper asked him if he stood by a statement he had made two years before, saying that Germany ought to get back its colonies which the Treaty of Versailles had removed. He said he did, adding: 'I never change my views – well, almost never.' He was right to add the afterthought. The invasion of the Czech lands six weeks later began to turn him against Germany, and the attack on Poland in September, together with the British declaration of war, swung him right round. As soon as war was declared he made it clear in the *Daily Mirror* that his views had completely reversed themselves. By 17 March 1940 Nancy could write to Mrs Ham: 'He is more violent now against Germany than anybody I know, and against any form of peace until they are well beaten.' The Hun was filthy again.

Sydney was a very different sort of person. She had never been emotionally captivated by Nazism; her consistent coolness had irritated Unity as much as David's warmth had delighted her. But Sydney was impressed with the new Germany, and felt that Hitler was doing more for the German people than the democratic system was doing for England. By a route of her own, she came round to a view close to that of Mosley, based on her father's vision of England's manifest destiny on the seas. Britain, the great sea power, ought to keep out of the continent on principle. Hitler could be allowed to do more or less as he wished there as long as the British had naval and air supremacy, so that he could never be a danger to the British Isles. That this was a possible development of her father's ideas is shown by the fact that her brother Geoffrey essentially agreed with it; that it was not the only one is shown by her other brother, George, taking the opposite view. For all Thomas's children believed in his gospel, and their differences resembled the quarrels between churches over scriptural inter-pretation.

Sydney was upset when Hitler invaded the Czech lands, but on cooler reflection this merely made her feel more strongly that Britain should keep right out of Eastern European affairs. Hitler, after all, did not meddle in India. In her typescript about Unity, Sydney makes her views clear. When writing about her first visit to Unity in the summer of 1935, she says:

This was the time of the great upsurging of German national feeling. These people were in the grip of a tremendous emotion . . . In England it was contemptuously called hysteria. I suppose when people weep for sorrow or joy it is always hysteria. Of course there should be more self-control. The people wept when Nelson walked through the streets of Portsmouth to embark on the *Victory*, and they tried to touch him as he went. Hysteria.

The bracketing of Hitler in this way with Nelson, Sydney's great hero, is an astonishing accolade. She goes on later: 'In England Hitler was said to be a cruel tyrant. So it was quite strange to find in Germany that the very people who were supposed to be suffering under this tyranny had a semi-adoration for him. I determined to try to find out the truth of the matter, and in the next few years I made up my mind about it.'

She certainly did. In later years a friend, who worked in the BBC, offered to play to her any sound recording in the Corporation's extensive archives. She could have heard anything: most of the music ever written, records of historic events, theatrical performances. She elected to listen to speeches by Hitler. We picture to ourselves this gentle old lady listening in a sound-proofed studio to the high-pitched shouting of the great demagogue, not understanding a word. This was the voice that ruined Unity's life.

Sydney always took longer to make up her mind than David, but when made up no force outside herself would change it. When David 'recanted, like Latimer', as Nancy put it, he and Sydney began quarrelling bitterly. Nancy saw a good deal of this. She writes to Mrs Ham from High Wycombe on 10 February 1940: 'Things here are terrible – Muv and Farve absolutely at loggerheads.' Relations continued to deteriorate; on 17 March Nancy wrote to Mrs Ham that David 'says he can't live with her any more – I really think they hate each other now'. His temper was not improved by the fact that the authorities were forbidding him to go to Inchkenneth, which was in a restricted zone; as far as David was concerned this prohibition was soon lifted, but while it was on David blamed Sydney for it. Sydney and Unity were in fact banned from going to Inchkenneth until 1944.

When in due course Unity came out of hospital, she constituted an additional difficulty between her parents, though not for political reasons. The trouble was that the damage to her brain had made her clumsy and messy. David's phobia about spilling has already been noted; Unity spilt constantly, and she was also incontinent at night. David could not stand her for long in the same house. The imprisonment without trial of Mosley and Diana in the summer of 1940 added to the difficulties between David and Sydney, because to Sydney this action, by a government that kept claiming to be fighting for freedom, was deeply shocking. We do not think that David went so far as to approve of Diana's imprisonment, but he certainly still disapproved of Mosley. Given Sydney's intense sympathy with the Mosleys, this too would certainly have caused trouble.

Eventually David withdrew to Inchkenneth, taking with him as housekeeper Margaret Wright, who had been assistant parlourmaid at Rutland Gate and was also a trained nurse. She was to look after him, first at Inchkenneth and later at Redesdale Cottage, until his death in 1958. She was good-looking in a rather tough way, but most people found her wholly lacking in charm. Her requests were not wrapped up in Mitford fashion, but unvarnished and peremptory; her conversational interventions were as self-confident as they were banal. None of David's daughters enjoyed her company, but opinions among them differ to this day as to whether she was kind to the old man in his last helpless years, or surreptitiously cruel. We are inclined to believe the case for the defence, for two reasons. First, because Iris and Jack Mitford, shrewd observers from his own generation, both thought highly of her; secondly, because Margaret had just the kind of wardress bossiness that was most calculated to irritate David's children and make them tend to think the worst of her. Nor did they like the way she increasingly took their father over. Debo, in particular, used to be deeply offended when Sydney visited David and Margaret continued to behave as mistress of the house, pouring out the tea. Nancy was more relaxed, and used to laugh at the effect Margaret had on David's way of speaking. 'Farve and the Snap!' she wrote to Diana on 19 August 1957. 'I do love it you know he wrote saying my hair-do (on TV) was deplorable.' Probably the sisters sometimes irritated Margaret. What to them were necessary amenities were to her affected airs and graces. Had she known the extent of it, their aversion to her manner might have seemed to her snobbish. But she probably knew of it only dimly. For their father's sake they were always friendly, and this almost certainly sufficed to deceive someone who was not very sensitive. Margaret was rather a trial, but she was fond of David in her way. He certainly had a great regard for her and would never hear a word against her.

At the beginning of the war he had become old rather suddenly. He contracted cataracts in both his eyes, which until then had been perfect, and had the lenses removed. He could see afterwards, with spectacles, but the period of enforced inactivity certainly contributed to his *coup de vieux* at the age of sixty-two. From that time on, Margaret was to be increasingly necessary to him; and the job of looking after an ageing man on a lonely island is not one to appeal to most people. On balance he was lucky to have her.

Sydney from this time devoted her life to looking after Unity.

She went back to Swinbrook village, renting the Old Mill Cottage from the landlord of the inn next door; this was a good choice because everyone in the village, and many people in the little town of Burford nearby, knew them and were used to them. Mrs Stobie, Sydney's faithful cook, looked after them. Sydney reverted to the family's smallholding habits and kept chickens, as well as two or three white goats from whose milk she made cheese and sometimes butter. From time to time they would go to High Wycombe, or to Rutland Gate Mews where Mabel, the parlourmaid, was still there to take care of them. The authorities were deeply suspicious of Sydney, though we doubt if it was ever clear to anyone just what this elderly lady could do to damage the war effort. Servicemen and women in uniform were in general banned from visiting her. As to Unity, it seems never fully to have reached the public consciousness that she was suffering from extensive brain damage. This was certainly Sydney's doing to an extent, for she belonged to a generation which was not frank about illness, and in addition it is fairly sure that she deceived herself on the matter. The authorities knew the score, however; Herbert Morrison, the Home Secretary, refused in April 1941 to imprison Unity using his arbitrary power of arrest.

So during most of the rest of the war, Sydney and Unity lived at the Old Mill Cottage at Swinbrook, occasionally coming to London for various purposes, including visits to Diana in Holloway Prison. Sometimes, too, they would spend short periods at High Wycombe. The Swinbrook cottage looks tiny from the road, but in fact it has at least four bedrooms, as well as outhouses and a large barn which used to contain the mill; operated by the River Windrush. Jonathan and Desmond used to spend part of their school holidays there. Relations with Unity were often difficult. She was unpredictable – occasionally rather frightening, often embarrassingly vulnerable, an adult who was also a cross child. Sydney looked after her with unswerving devotion, putting up with her moods, trying patiently to make her happy. One of Unity's favourite subjects of conversation was her own funeral; she would choose the hymns to be sung at it, from time to time changing the list. It always included 'Holy, Holy, Holy, Lord God Almighty', her favourite hymn. But Sydney's worry was that Unity would outlive her; what would then become of her daughter? The others, especially Diana, always promised that they would share the responsibility, and Diana did indeed sometimes have Unity to stay so as to give her mother a break; but Sydney's mind was never at rest on this point. As to David, he would spend rather more than half the year at Inchkenneth, and the rest in London. In 1944 this was reversed; Sydney and Unity went up to Inchkenneth, and David, with Margaret, went to Redesdale Cottage in Northumberland, where Clementine Redesdale had spent her last years.

It was therefore on Inchkenneth, in May 1948, that Unity suddenly contracted a severe bout of meningitis, from the old bullet wound. Arrangements were made to take her across to hospital in Oban. One morning she looked up and said in a loud voice, 'I'm coming', making Sydney's heart sink, but by the time the journey could be made she seemed to have recovered a little. This enabled her to survive the difficult journey, but once in hospital she took a frightening turn for the worse and died on 28 May. An autopsy was suggested, since her death had been indirectly the result of self-inflicted violence, but the case was sufficiently clear for it to be judged unnecessary. By an odd coincidence, Nancy had chosen 28 May for the death of Linda Radlett, the heroine of *The Pursuit of Love*. David came to Oban to be with Sydney. The funeral was held at Swinbrook, with the hymns which Unity had chosen. Jonathan remembers how sad it was in that church not to hear her voice rising above all the rest. Defiantly, Sydney had this inscription engraved on her tombstone: 'Say Not the Struggle Naught Availeth.'

Not long after this David, now growing old in earnest, became reconciled to Mosley. He wrote to Diana a touching letter apologizing for not speaking to Mosley at Unity's funeral and assuring her that this was inadvertent; three years later he paid a last visit to Paris, and saw both them and Nancy. They took him to see the house they had recently bought, Le Temple de la Gloire. He was most affable; he loved the house, and to Diana's surprise he sent her £500 to buy a pair of curtains. At Nancy's he met the Marquis de Lasteyrie, a friend of both her and Diana who was of a very old family. 'I liked that old relation of Joan of Arc,' David commented.

Old age suits some people better than others. It did not suit David. He never became senile, but he was bored and often lonely. He could no longer shoot, fish or skate; his children were dispersed, his wife partly estranged, and many of his friends dead. He had lost his only son. He no longer had his estate, or his work on the County Council, and he did not care to go any longer to the House of Lords, where he felt increasingly out of the swim. About his last action there was to vote against accepting the United States loan that bridged the gap between the Lease-Lend scheme which had kept Britain going during the war, and Marshall Aid which started a year or two later. Innocent of any knowledge of economics, he felt that the terms of the loan endangered Britain's independence, not realizing that the expense of the war had made Britain in any case dependent on United States bounty and that the loan's terms were in fact extremely easy.

Sydney, from afar, used sometimes to worry about David, up at Redesdale Cottage with only Margaret for company. She wrote to Nancy on 16 May 1949: 'Poor Farve it's very sad and so inexplicable. Why should he choose to go and live like that. And so far as the "comfort" I never think he gets enough to eat.' His surviving letters on the whole seem cheerful enough. He wrote to Nancy in October 1953 asking her to come for Christmas: 'We are asking Iris and Jack so you might get a certain quantum of "copy" too late no doubt for *Pompadour* and in any case quite unsuitable.' Jack was well known in the family for being a card, and his expressions were as much prized as those of David himself. Nancy was just about to bring out her book on Madame de Pompadour.

David died in March 1958. Diana describes some of his last days:

Muv and Debo decided to go to Redesdale for Farve's eightieth birthday, he had not been too well that winter. In the night I woke and suddenly knew that I must go with them. Early next morning I went to Kings Cross and ran along the train until I found them in their carriage. We stayed not at the cottage but at the Redesdale Arms, a comfortable nearby inn. I shall never forget the expression on Farve's face when Muv appeared at his bedside, and his smile of pure delight. All their differences forgotten, they seemed to have gone back twenty years to happy days before the tragedies. She sat with him for hours, Debo and I going in and out. After a couple of days Muv and Debo travelled on to

Scotland and I returned to London. They had hardly arrived when they were wired for to go to Farve; a few days later he died.

There was a certain amount of comment in the press about his will, because he cut Decca out of it. This seemed rather vindictive, but there was a reason. Under Scottish law, Inchkenneth had on Tom's death in 1945 reverted to his sisters in equal shares. As soon as Decca received notification that she owned one-sixth of the island, she announced her intention of presenting her part of Inchkenneth to the British Communist Party. It was, she makes clear in *A Fine Old Conflict*, a marvellous tease, and one that might help on the Revolution. Claud Cockburn, formerly editor of *The Week* and a pillar of the Communist Party, was in San Francisco covering the conference which was to found the United Nations; Decca used him as emissary. He went and saw David; rather to Decca's irritation, David talked him out of accepting on behalf of the party, which had not been very enthusiastic when informed of the proposed gift. Rather naturally, though, David felt that anything he might leave Decca could possibly be treated in the same way. All the same, when the will was made public Nancy felt it was unfair, and presented her own share of the island to Decca to make up. Sydney agreed and approved, writing to her on 1 June 1959: 'It is so much too generous of you to give your share of the island to Decca. I do see your point that she got nothing from Farve, it was unfair and so hurtful to have it all public. She didn't seem to mind very much, but wouldn't say if she did.' Sydney in fact, had been perfectly cool about Decca's *démarche* at the time. But it is her and David's reputation that suffered as a result of this episode. It seems to have stuck in the public mind as an example of narrow-mindedness and vindictive intolerance. The record is seldom fair.

It might have been expected that Sydney's old age would be, if anything, unhappier than David's. Her political views were far more unfashionable than his, and she never changed them. To her the war had been the end of Britain's only hope to avoid decline; Churchill was no saviour of his country, but rather, despite himself, the blind instrument of its destruction. That she saw cousin Winston as a tragic figure rather than a villain is shown by the fact that she did not sever the family connection; she and

David attended the marriage in 1947 of Churchill's daughter Mary to Christopher Soames. She was, and remained, a Mosley supporter, and detested the settlement in Europe after 1945. But she did not repine, and was able to adapt to the post-war world in a way that David never could. Her last years were sunny, surrounded by affection. Her descendants clustered round her, not just from duty but because she was lovable and original. She retained, to the end of her life, Thomas Bowles's freedom from received ideas, his ability to think everything through from first principles. This, in a confusing century like our own, can lead into traps; it led Sydney to Hitlerism, because she relied too much on the evidence of her own senses and believed too little the perfectly valid experience of others. But it enables a person to take things as they come, to see people afresh and as they are; it gives the opportunity for a new start. More important even than this was Sydney's capacity for love. *Amor vincit omnia*, we are told: Love Conquers All. Sydney showed how true this is, most particularly in her dealings with that one of her children with whom she most fundamentally disagreed – Decca. We shall talk about them in due course. She had of course another great advantage over David in facing old age, for she was an avid reader of books and follower of current affairs. She remained interested to the end of her life.

She made of Inchkenneth a small paradise; her descendants remember it as such, as do numerous cousins, nephews, nieces and friends. Nancy used loyally to go, though, as we have seen, she detested the journey. One raw morning she was in Oban, killing the few hours between train and boat in the lounge of a cold hotel. She huddled as close as she could to the single bar of a small electric fire. The door opened and two tough ladies strode in, dressed in tartan tweeds and scarves. 'I like this cold weather, Jeannie,' remarked one to the other. 'Braces y'up.' Nancy was not of this view, though once in Inchkenneth, in the well-warmed house, she would cheer up. In much the same way as, long before, she had teased her sisters, she would now tease their grandchildren. She told Catherine, aged five, that every morning before anyone was up she would swim across the sea to Mull.

'You couldn't,' said Catherine. 'It's too cold.'

'Ah,' said Nancy, 'the angels come and breathe on it and warm it up for me.'

This was too much for Catherine, who looked at her with wide-eyes and finally said: 'You're Octopus Untruth.'

The reference was to a character in *The Kitten Pilgrims*, a Victorian children's book that Sydney had been reading to her. Catherine's sally delighted Nancy, who for a few years afterwards would sometimes sign her letters 'Octopus Untruth', to the bewilderment of Julian Jebb when he was researching, years later, for the television programme about her. But as time went on the island seemed a dangerous place for Sydney, especially when she became really old and contracted Parkinson's disease. Ought she not to abandon it? Her descendants had visions of her slipping on the seaweed of the jetty and breaking a leg. But nothing of the sort ever happened. Her delights were Scrabble and conversation; until Parkinson's disease prevented it, she also liked to play the piano for everyone to sing. Her style at Scrabble was influenced by the songs of her youth; she insisted on the validity of 'jo', a most convenient two-letter word which she insisted meant 'fellow' or 'boyfriend', because of Robert Burns's 'John Anderson, my Jo'. Her daughters would object sharply that Jo was in fact a proper name, short for John, but Sydney would have none of it. Conversation was hampered by her increasing deafness; she would sit in Harrods' bank between two of her daughters, making them bellow out the latest gossip so that other passing customers would turn round in surprise. She acquired a hearing aid, but could never quite master it. Once it slipped down her blouse, emitting a desolate whine.

'Your hearing aid is wailing,' said Jonathan.

Sydney felt for it perfunctorily, then let it be. 'Oh dear, poor thing!' she said, laughing.

However, her deafness was not always a disadvantage. Alexander and Max used to quarrel, and Diana once said to them, 'I hope you boys don't annoy Muv with your fighting.'

'I don't think she minds,' said Alexander. 'You see, she's so lovely and deaf.'

She was protected also by the innocence of a late Victorian upbringing. Diana once asked if her sons were using bad language, a habit to which they were at the time rather addicted.

'No, I don't think so,' said Sydney. 'Only blinking sod.'

In 1963 Sydney's daughters noticed that she really did seem very frail, and tried to persuade her not to spend the summer at the island. She insisted, however; and it was there that she died in May, not long after her eighty-third birthday. Nancy, Pam, Diana and Debo all went to be with her during her last illness, taking turns to sit by her bed and talk to her. She was buried at Swinbrook near David.

Her brother Geoffrey wrote to their sister, Dorothy Bailey: 'Sorry about Sydney. Without pain it is what the Esquimaux call "the long sleep". Acworth said that whenever you go to sleep it makes no difference to you whether it is for a few hours or for ever.'

# 35

# Decca, Marriage and Emigration

Esmond and Decca's wedding may have been unusual, but they received a number of presents. Diana gave Decca an amethyst and pearl necklace and earrings; others gave money, and Esmond also had an advance on *Boadilla* from his publishers. They went to Dieppe, where his mother's house was. While there they also met Roger Roughton, a friend of Esmond's, who had just taken a house in Rotherhithe, in London's dockland. It was agreed that they should share it and in due course, they moved in.

Philip Toynbee, Esmond's old comrade in arms, visited them there and became a constant guest. He liked Decca at once. Esmond told him later that the only thing to do with the English upper class is to marry into it, a more respectable version of a saying of Mosley's in his Labour Party days, 'Vote Labour; sleep Tory'. But Toynbee was probably right in thinking that Decca was about the only member of her class whom Esmond could, in practice, possibly have married.

One of the things Esmond did at Rotherhithe was to give gambling parties. Gambling was a weakness of his, and he was usually unlucky. The Dieppe casino was a snare whenever he visited his mother. But if he took the bank, he now reasoned, the odds would be on his side. He gave up the gambling parties rather soon, however; even as croupier Esmond's luck was indifferent. Friends, relations and connections came, but the 'bank' was not as successful as in theory it ought to have been. Bryan Guinness went once with his new wife, Elisabeth; their purpose was to lose some money to Decca for old times' sake. Settling down to a game of roulette, they unfortunately found that their luck was in. They won and won. By no means a couple for a late night, they grew ever more sleepy and depressed as the chips piled up beside them.

Only when the grey London dawn began filtering through the windows did the law of averages at last enable them to escape with a loss rather smaller than they had intended, and drive back to the West End, more dead than alive.

Esmond and Decca worked for an advertising agency – he as a copywriter on the staff; she, more occasionally, as a market researcher. With a number of other women, she would travel to some target area and canvas housewives on their feelings about some product or other. Political canvassers are familiar with the reactions and retorts received by these researchers; politics and domestic wares can be confused on the doorstep. 'What's your product?' they are occasionally asked.

Decca found her fellow canvassers rather disappointing. Sharing hotel rooms with them, she came to know a number of different sorts of women, for a little extra pin-money is welcome in any quarter. There were married and single, young and middle-aged women; their origins and past histories were various. Decca now had the human contact she had craved as an adolescent and found it, in the event, deeply depressing. These women, whatever their origin or occupation, seemed almost all to share a sad and brutal cynicism. Men obsessed them, and so did sex. Men existed only to be milked and exploited, and sex was the way this could be done. It was the female equivalent of the male bravado, familiar to anyone who has inhabited a barrack-room, in which 'tart' is used as an actual synonym for 'woman', where sex is a valuable commodity which one must try to obtain by force or fraud, exciting some girl's affection being an especially efficient form of fraud. The one moral system is that of the prostitute, the other that of the pimp, and in either it would be considered despicably soft to admit any actual feeling for someone. It is only a convention, for the vast majority of people who talk like this are neither pimps nor prostitutes, nor do they lack feeling; but it does strike the newcomer sometimes with a strange harshness. Decca was generous and idealistic and enjoying a marriage that was in reality as marriages are in story books; she found the talk dismal, and took it, perhaps, too seriously, being too young to guess at the more complex truth underneath the cynicism. It is one of the few instances in her writing where her indignation at the human condition is wholly non-political, where she notices a fault in human nature without attributing it to society.

The Romillys were poorer than they need have been because Esmond lost money most weeks at the greyhounds. Also, Decca had to learn housekeeping from scratch, and was not very good at it. They had a happy time nevertheless, and a raffish social life; they gave bottle parties, trying to end the evening with a profit by consuming less drink than their guests had brought. Philip Toynbee tended to live with them during his vacations from Oxford. Toynbee was at this time chasing girls, keenly and indiscriminately, presenting a comic contrast to the rock-like monogamy of the Romillys. He noticed this himself, regarding his friends as curiously old-fashioned. Their simple joy in each other is indeed reminiscent of David and Sydney when they were first married. Intellectually rejecting their parents' way of life, Decca and Esmond had rediscovered it in practice.

It was Esmond who hardened Decca's feelings against her family. She now began to look at them, as at everything else, through Esmond's eyes – but only to an extent, for she certainly did not stop seeing them. In particular the 'Boud' relationship with Unity was very much alive. Unity would sometimes drive Decca around London as an unpaid taxi; we learn, for instance, from Unity's diary on 2 November 1937: 'All drive to Fortnum and Masons for lunch . . . Then we drive to Selfridges where we buy things for Decca's baby [Julia, born the following month] . . . I drive Decca to dentist, dropping Muv on way . . . Wait for Decca and drive her to Bermondsey . . . Drop her near her home.' 'Near', not 'at': to avoid Esmond? It was a bit like a clandestine love affair. On 23 December that year Unity drove Sydney to Rotherhithe – 'takes an hour to get there', says her diary – with Christmas presents. It was a Thursday, and they arrived at 3 p.m., so evidently the visit had been arranged for a time when Esmond was at work. Unity also saw Decca three times in March 1938; on the twenty-eighth of that month, she notes that she drove sixty miles in London fetching her from Rotherhithe, taking her to Mrs Hammersley's, then shopping for lamps and other things. On two occasions in November 1938, Decca met Unity surreptitiously in Harrods, where Unity bought her a coat. On 6 December, Unity even found her at Rutland Gate Mews with their cousin Ann Farrer, always known as Idden which was the Boudledidge for Ann. They chatted for a while, went to a film together and had tea at a teashop; then Unity drove Decca to Nancy's house at Blomfield Road. There was only one member of the family with whom Esmond actively got on, and that was Tom. He dined with the Romillys now and then, and went to their bottle parties. Despite all the differences between Esmond and Tom, they felt a good deal of mutual respect.

Decca and Esmond conducted a sort of guerrilla war against their own class. With Philip Toynbee, whom they visited in Oxford, they gatecrashed a house party of the socialist peer, Lord Faringdon. First they asked themselves to dinner, where Toynbee and Esmond got drunk; then the Romillys took advantage of Decca's pregnant condition to force themselves on their host for the night. They went to bed late, and kept the servants up all night ringing for sandwiches, tea, rum or cigars. In the morning, according to Toynbee, Decca even proposed to cut down the curtains to take home, but Esmond stopped her. She did, however, fill her bag with Balkan Sobranie cigarettes.

Though pro-Communist, they did not join the Communist Party. Giles Romilly and Philip Toynbee were dedicated party members, Toynbee being one of the most assiduous recruiters for the party among Oxford undergraduates; but Esmond found it too disciplined, too humourless, above all perhaps too full of middle-class intellectuals, to be congenial. He and Decca joined the Bermondsey Labour Party, within which they were, of course, on the left, and particularly interested in activities to do with the Spanish Civil War. Esmond also appears to have joined the Transport and General Workers' Union. We need not doubt that both of them were politically very active, but one incident about which Decca's memory appears to be seriously at fault is her account of a May Day procession to Hyde Park with the Bermondsey Labour Party. She says she took part in this in a pregnant state with Esmond and Philip Toynbee, and that along the way they encountered groups of blackshirts who attacked the procession, only to be repulsed by the Bermondsey men. She spotted Unity and Diana waving swastika flags. The only possible May Day for this to have happened is 1938, for on May Day in 1937 Decca was in Bayonne, about to get married, and in 1939 she was in the United States. She cannot have seen Unity and Diana waving swastika flags. Unity was in Germany at the time, and as for Diana, Mosley never used the swastika symbol and banned Diana from going to marches; apart from which waving flags has never been her style.

The Romillys' baby, Julia, was born on 29 December 1937. They proved devoted parents; Decca surprised Toynbee with her competence. Unity saw the baby, it seems for the first time, on 3 March, having got back from Germany the day before. 'Julia is sweet,' she notes in her diary, though she evidently thought her too thin because she told Diana that her legs were like Marlene Dietrich's. Then came disaster. Decca took Julia to a weekly health clinic to be weighed and given cod liver oil. An epidemic of measles broke out; the baby caught it, probably at the clinic, and gave it to Decca. Esmond engaged nurses. Decca had a bad attack but recovered; little Julia caught pneumonia and died. She was four months old. The family was shattered; Diana cried for two days. The day after Julia was buried, Decca and Esmond left for Corsica, where they stayed for three months.

On their return they resumed the same life. They went down to Eton with Philip Toynbee. As an act of bravado, they took thirty top hats from outside the chapel where the boys were at evensong; the practical joke took a rather unattractive turn when Esmond later sold them to an old clothes dealer. But the political shadows were lengthening. It was the time of Munich, which from the Romillys' point of view was a particularly sinister betrayal because to readers of such left-wing gossip sheets as Claud Cockburn's *The Week*, paranoid about the alleged pro-Nazi tendencies of the government, it looked as if it was the prelude not just to acquiescence in Nazi aims in Europe but to an actual Nazi alliance. It was in fact an illusion to think that any important Conservatives were really thinking in these terms, but the fear of such a conspiracy made Esmond think about going to America. Decca also, providentially, came into some money at this time. On her twenty-first birthday, Sydney suddenly gave her about £100. For all her children, since their births, Sydney had put by a tiny weekly sum in an interest-earning deposit account. It was a complete surprise; none of Decca's elders had told her what to expect. It more than paid their fare. Esmond at first planned that he and Decca, and other friends, should go and lecture all over the United States to women's clubs; the generosity of what has become known as the 'blue rinse brigade' to even rather obscure lecturers was already legendary. But the other friends dropped out, and finally Esmond and Decca went alone.

They left on 18 February 1939. Three people came to the station to see them off: Tom, Blor and Philip Toynbee. Unity, of course, did not come; Esmond would not have welcomed her. But Decca had already said goodbye to her. She had in fact seen plenty of Unity over the previous three days. They had both lunched with Nancy on the fifteenth, walked in the park with Sydney on the sixteenth, and had long chats at Rutland Gate Mews on the seventeenth.

On arrival in New York, the Romillys put up at an hotel found for them by Peter Nevile. From there, they wrote round to various contacts that Nevile and others had given them. They made many friends, mostly media people – advertisers, journalists and publishers. Plenty of them were socialist-minded New Dealers – rather confusingly, these were and are known in the United States as 'liberals' – so that there was no lack of politically congenial company.

The most important contact they made at this time was Katharine Meyer, later Graham, daughter of the owner of the *Washington Post*. She was later to inherit this paper, with dramatic effects on its political line and perhaps on the political history of the United States, for it played a vital part in preparing the American public for the abandonment of Indochina to Communism as well as in exploiting the Watergate burglary to hound President Nixon out of office. Already a committed 'liberal', Katherine Meyer was about their own age. She invited the Romillys to her parents' house in Westchester County, where they met her father, Eugene Meyer. A Jewish millionaire of an older generation, he was very hostile to Fascism but in favour of capitalism. In American politics he was Republican and his daughter Democrat, but common hostility to Fascism meant that in 1939 the political differences between the two were muted, and mainly the subject of friendly banter.

Esmond and Decca found various jobs, some better paid than others. Then Esmond took a short course as a bartender with the idea that he might get employment in that capacity. They bought an old Ford and toured around, wherever possible staying with friends and acquaintances. They found their way to Martha's Vineyard, already a haunt of left-wing intellectuals: Stalinists, Trotskyists and socialists of all varieties. It was August 1939, and war was obviously approaching. The news of the Nazi-Soviet pact struck Martha's Vineyard like a stone thrown into a chicken-run. Esmond defended the Soviet position; Britain and France had always rejected Soviet calls to stop Hitler, so Stalin had done the only thing he could. When Hitler invaded Poland and the democracies declared war, the news came to Esmond as an anti-climax; he expected the British and French to prosecute the war half-heartedly and then change sides and join with Hitler. The lack of any immediate physical move to protect Poland seemed to confirm his view, though this was really determined by geography. The thinking was quite unrealistic in the real world, but one sees how to people in Martha's Vineyard, discussing distant matters while half-dazed by the September sun, such views might seem plausible. Claud Cockburn, ever inventive, was peddling them in *The Week*, of which someone sent Esmond a copy. Intermittently, Decca and Esmond used to believe Cockburn's waffle, though it did not interfere with Esmond's underlying realism. Not for nothing was he Winston Churchill's nephew; the relationship gave him an insight into the point of view of Churchill's anti-appeasement section of the Conservative Party, and a realization at least part of the time that it was this section which in a war situation would come to the top. When Churchill was invited back into the government, Esmond wrote from Martha's Vineyard an article about Churchill, predicting that he would be the next Prime Minister.

They went on to Washington, where Esmond got a job selling silk stockings on commission. At the same time they went to a good many dinners and parties, where they got to know some of the New Dealers. They met Michael Straight, the Communist sympathizer who edited the *New Republic* and caused a stir recently by recounting his equivocal relationship with the Cambridge traitors, especially Anthony Blunt. It was Straight who introduced the Romillys to Clifford and Virginia Durr, who were to be a great mainstay of Decca's life. The Meyers, too, were in Washington, where they owned a large house and invited Decca and Esmond to stay. Eugene Meyer commissioned the Romillys to write a series of articles on their adventures in America. Toynbee turned up his nose at them when they appeared; he found them altogether embarrassing.

Esmond's next venture was a bar in Miami. He and Decca found themselves there by chance, when driving through America. The bar prospered and Esmond threw himself into the work, for several months avoiding too much worry about the war and the world situation.

But in December 1939 this temporary quiet in their lives was interrupted by the press. Unity had returned to England on a stretcher after her suicide attempt, comatose and with a bullet in her brain. The newspapers rang continually, insistently. Decca could tell them nothing, but she was beside herself with worry; it was a burden she had to bear alone, for she remained fonder of Unity than she could ever possibly admit to Esmond. She guessed the truth accurately enough as soon as the calls started, even though the first ones asked her to confirm all sorts of rumours, like those repeated by journalists to Sydney and Nancy. Unity had told Decca, as she had told several others in the family, that if war broke out between Britain and Germany she would shoot herself, and that was clearly what she had done. At least she was still alive; but in what state?

Esmond remained Esmond. They visited Washington in March 1940 and visited Michael Straight and his wife, who took them to a party given by the left-wing American Youth Congress. In *After Long Silence* (published 1983) Straight writes:

The room was filled with liberated Negroes and Jewish students from New York, talking, smoking, sipping drinks and dancing rather self-consciously with one another. Esmond took one look around the room and whispered, 'Five dollars for the first one who says out loud, "Thank God for the British Empire"'. It was no contest. I had barely started up an argument with two leaders of the Congress when I heard an uproar at the bar end of the room. Esmond had shouted out his phrase to the amazement and disgust of those around him. He hurried toward me to collect his five dollars. My companions, two earnest Marxists, looked at me in disbelief.

The Romillys were certainly not going back to Britain, which at this stage they thought might attack the Soviet Union – much of the talk in the papers during this 'phoney war' period was about Stalin's invasion of Finland, and of course the Nazi-Soviet pact was in being. Churchill himself broadcast on 20 January 1940:

All Scandinavia dwells brooding under Nazi and Bolshevik threats. Only Finland, superb, nay sublime, in the jaws of peril, shows what free men can do. The service rendered by Finland to mankind is magnificent . . . Many illusions about Soviet Russia have been dispelled in these weeks of fighting in the Arctic Circle. Everyone can see how Communism rots the soul of a nation – how it makes it abject and hungry in peace, and proves it base and abominable in war . . .

This kind of thing was not at all encouraging. Esmond, we remember, had predicted that Churchill would replace Chamberlain and fight the war with more determination. Yet if even Churchill expressed himself in these hostile terms about Communism, then others in the Conservative Party who were less anti-Fascist might well swing Britain round to neutrality, or worse. Esmond still put some faith in his uncle, but until he or someone of his sort took over, until it was certain that the country would fight seriously against Nazism, Esmond was staying out. Even later, when he had joined the war effort, he did not seem to Toynbee to be a patriot, certainly not in the conventional sense of the word. Ideology, not country, was what determined whether he would fight.

So, quite consistently, when the Germans launched their Blitzkrieg on France and Churchill's coalition replaced the Chamberlain government, Esmond decided that he would take part in the war. We should note that this picking and choosing as to when to volunteer was entirely left-wing. The British Fascists were told by Mosley at the beginning of the war to fight for their country and the vast majority of them did so unconditionally, though the party's policy was against war with Hitler and many of them joined up with a heavy heart. Esmond gave up his bar, and the Romillys headed back to Washington. Decca was pregnant again. The Durrs took them in, and Esmond went to join the Canadian Air Force. This was a way of participating in the war effort without joining the British armed forces. As with so many people on the upper-class left, Esmond could have said with Christopher Isherwood: 'It is *English* authority I dread.' (*Down Here on a Visit*.) The army would be Wellington all over again, everything he had run away from and spent his life avoiding.

Decca stayed with the Durrs, who were congenial and kind. She gave birth to a daughter, Constancia, always known as Dinky; the nickname is a corruption of Donkey, symbol of the Democrats, for she was born in the thick of the 1940 presidential election campaign and the Durrs were, of course, staunch Democrats. Decca had chosen the name after a heroine of the Spanish Republican cause; Spain remained one of her preoccupations. Esmond visited Decca whenever he could get any leave, looking unfamiliar in his Air Force uniform.

In due course Esmond finished his training in Canada, and was posted to Britain as a navigator with the rank of pilot officer. Just before this, in June 1941, the Germans invaded Russia, and he and Decca made up their minds that they would both join the Communist Party, he in England, she in America. He saw a good deal of Philip Toynbee, who was an intelligence officer in the Army. Toynbee writes that Esmond was looking forward to a social revolution; the war only interested him because it might lead to one. His frame of mind was more political than it had been since the Spanish Civil War. It was the Russian campaign which interested him most; he had just read Koestler's *Darkness at Noon*, that grim reconstruction of the interrogation and liquidation of an old Bolshevik by Stalin's secret police, and he firmly supported the interrogators. Esmond seemed to Toynbee like a relic of a simpler age. On his leaves he went to parties, and behaved politely but with a certain reserve, never making a pass at a woman. Decca, even though absent, was the only woman who interested him. In the autumn of 1941 he was posted to a bomber station in Yorkshire. It suffered a steady quota of losses, and from one mission over Hamburg, in November, Esmond failed to return. Churchill, visiting Roosevelt, was staying at the White House, and Decca went to see him to ask if he had heard anything about his nephew. He could tell her nothing, though when he mentioned Diana and her husband she took the opportunity of suggesting to the Prime Minister that they should be put up against the wall and shot.

Esmond never did return. To Decca, he had been the prince who had kissed her awake. No one will ever know how much she suffered. She was from then on scarred, toughened. It was the end of youth.

# 36

# Nancy's War

The declaration of war which drove Unity to shoot herself came to Nancy, on the contrary, as a relief. As she wrote to Mrs Ham on 27 January 1940: 'You see I don't mind the atrocities quite so much now Peter and Christopher [Mrs Ham's son] are in uniform and marching to the rescue. When it tortured me was when your friend Chamberlain was offering that gout-twisted hand to the chief perpetrators.' Life was not easy, though. David did to her exactly what Thomas Bowles had done to Sydney in 1914; he cut her allowance. 'We are utterly broke,' writes Nancy to Mrs Ham on 29 November 1939, 'as Papa has seen fit to retrench on my allowance £50 p.a. and Peter's pay doesn't cover his mess bills.' She herself wrote *Pigeon Pie* in less than three months, and volunteered as a helper in the Air Raid Precautions (ARP) organization. At first, as she put it, this mostly involved waiting about. But quite soon she was on the day shift in the first aid post in Praed Street, Paddington. From there she wrote a comprehensive letter to Mrs Ham on 15 September 1939:

Well my job is writing on the foreheads of dead and dying in indelible pencil. *What* I write I haven't yet discovered. What happens when a coloured man presents *his* forehead I also ignore. I was just about to ask all these little details when the Queen arrived to see over (in fawn) so I have never found out . . .

Meanwhile I sit twiddling my indelible pencil and aching for a forehead to write on. I think I shall write Mrs Hammersley 31 Tite Street and see what happens, it might produce interesting complications in a case of loss of memory . . . Sitting in this hateful cellar (gas and therefore air proof, electric light all day and cold as the grave) my brain has become like the inside of a bad walnut.

She also gives news of the family, expressed in characteristic style.

Muv has gone finally off her head. She seems to regard Adolph as her favourite son in law (the kind of which people say he has been like a *son* to me) and when one says Peter has joined up she replies I expect he will be shot soon which is so encouraging. Poor thing I suppose she is quite wretched so one must make allowances. Bobo [Unity] we hear on fairly good authority is in a concentration camp for Czech women which much as I deplore it has a sort of poetic justice. Peter is going to make the Aostas get her out in a month or two when she has had a sufficient dose to wish to go. This seems a sound plan.

So Peter was still being self-importantly helpful, as over Decca. She continues: 'Farve has publicly recanted like Latimer, in the *Daily Mirror*, and said he was mistaken all along (and how). What THEY have done now any different to before I ask myself.' Decca, Nancy adds, might as well stay in America, since she hears that the forces are not accepting people who fought in the Spanish Civil War. Tom, stationed nearby, is dining with her most nights.

As to Nancy herself, 'I really see nobody, impossible to lunch out and in the evening I am too tired and it is too dark and frightening to go out.' She was never to get used to the blackout; she told Jonathan later of a bag snatcher in the Paddington area where she lived who lurked in the shadows and then felled any passing woman with a rugby tackle, making off with her possessions. She thought this funny, on the surface, but was obviously apprehensive. Her letter to Mrs Ham goes on: 'Darling I am so pleased you are better, that is a ray of good news, better than the Poles holding Wooch [Lodz] or whatever it's called. I find I can only read old dry books like Carlyle's *Life of Sterling* and Macaulay's *Essays*, isn't it funny. Luckily and thank goodness the London library is still with us.' Peter is about to be posted abroad, and she proposes to have Robert Byron as a paying guest to avoid the gloom of living alone.

Nancy's ignorance of ARP skills did not last; she progressed so far as to be invited to broadcast a series of lectures on fire fighting. These, however, were not a success. After a little time she was told they were to be discontinued.

'Do you mind telling me why?' asked Nancy.

'Well, you see, it's your voice. We've had several complaints;

someone even wrote in and said they wanted to put you on the fire.'

*Pigeon Pie* appeared in May 1940, at the time of the fall of France, and did not do well. Nancy says in the preface to the second edition that it was 'an early and unimportant casualty of the real war which was then beginning', her feeling being that the mood of the country was no longer frivolous enough for it. The trouble, really, is that it is the least good of all Nancy's books. It is funny at times, but rather strained, and the plot is excessively silly. Mark Ogilvie-Grant is again the central figure as in *The Old Ladies of Eaton Square*; this time he is the songster of Kew Green in his butter-coloured wig, thought at first to be broadcasting songs for the Germans or to have been murdered, but turning out in the end to have been a hero. *Pigeon Pie* was written extremely fast; more important, it was written when Nancy's mood, far from being frivolous, was sombre. She was worried about the war, about Peter, about money and about her family. Some of her letters of the time catch the 'phoney war' spirit rather well, all the same. In one to Mrs Ham dated 27 January 1940 she says, 'I say what a new horror have you seen – the Nazis are employing pigmy spies so small they can hide in drawers. I just *daren't* open mine now to look for a hanky.' But in this time of anxiety she could not keep this up for the length of a book.

At least Peter turned up safe and cheerful after Dunkirk; Nancy wrote proudly to Mrs Ham that his regiment had done well in the retreat. Chamberlain had meanwhile resigned, and Winston Churchill took over as Prime Minister of an all-party coalition to prosecute the war. Diana and Mosley were arbitrarily imprisoned. There was little real reason for this action, but it was widely welcomed because people were in a fright. Nancy had laughed in the preface to *The Stanleys of Alderley* at the idea of Englishmen shying at the 'distant growling of a dachshund'. When the growling was not so distant, she herself gave way to irrationality. Gladwyn Jebb, in due course to become Lord Gladwyn, was one of the officials detailed to make inquiries about the Mosleys. At this time Mosley had been arrested but Diana had not. On 20 June 1940 Nancy wrote to Mrs Ham: 'I have just been round to see Gladwyn at his request to tell what I know (very little actually) of Diana's visits to Germany. I advised him to examine her passport to see how often she went. I also said I regard her as an extremely dangerous person. Not very sisterly behaviour but in such times I think it one's duty?' Bernard Shaw once said that when an Englishman does something of which he is ashamed, he says he is doing his duty. Not that Nancy was particularly ashamed; on the contrary, she rather took to her role as nark. Five months later she went again to the authorities to make sure Diana stayed inside and to denounce, among several others, Pam. To put two of her sisters in Holloway would have been an achievement of a sort. It is true that Nancy believed, as many people did at the time, that anyone who wanted peace with Hitler must also want him to win the war. In 2003, half a century later, opponents of the Anglo-American operation in Iraq would also be accused of wanting our forces to be defeated. Then again, Nancy may well have harboured a grudge against Diana for taking pompous exception to *Wigs on the Green*.

Nancy settled down to face the war and the blackout at 12 Blomfield Road, Maida Vale, with Gladys, her faithful but rather demanding maid, and her pug Milly. Her little London garden was pressed into service to grow vegetables, and she acquired some hens. 'Words long forgotten like creosote and bran mash are never off my tongue,' she wrote to Sydney (quoted by Harold Acton), 'not to speak of droppings board and nest box.' Then in the autumn came the blitz. She wrote to Sydney on 12 September 1940 (again quoted by Harold Acton): 'We are catching it here all right as they are gunning for Paddington.' Peter had turned up with two small children of one of his soldiers who had been bombed out.

We put them to bed in the kitchen . . . the house next door got an incendiary and caught fire so I in my nightdress put the children into an eiderdown, got a taxi and put them to bed at Zella's [a former governess]. Came back here, having been nearly blown out of the cab when Fitzjohns Avenue went, and shot at by the home guard on the way for not stopping. Then we had a rare pasting here . . . I don't at all advise you to come to London, it is not very agreeable I assure you.

Then on the thirtieth: 'The nights are noisier than ever but I should say fewer bombs – two more of my best friends have lost their houses . . . It is obviously a matter of time before we all do.

Peter spent a night at Blomfield and had an incendiary, if he hadn't been there to put it out that would have gone.' She was staying with Zella for a spell, and had sent Gladys to another friend. But next month they returned to Blomfield Road. The house never was bombed, though others in the neighbourhood were. When Jonathan as a schoolboy first went there to spend a night during the holidays one foggy wartime winter he walked down the street slowly, unable to make out the numbers in the pitch darkness of the blackout, when suddenly he saw a lighted window with ruched blinds, a feature of his mother's decorative schemes and those of his aunts. He felt it must be No. 12, and it was. 'I recognized your house by the blinds,' said Jonathan. 'Of course, that's why I left the blackout off,' said Nancy.

Nancy's attitude to the bombing varied sharply according to mood. Sometimes she was frightened and miserable, as is evident in a letter of 9 September 1940 to Mrs Ham: 'Darling the nights! Nobody who hasn't been in it can have the smallest idea of the horror one is going through. I never don't feel sick, can't eat anything and although dropping with tiredness can't sleep either', and again on 17 November:

Sleep in such a bombardment is impossible . . . Oh I am tired. I sometimes think for hours on end of a very ugly country house bedroom with a large, rather lumpy but soft mahogany bed and a fire in the grate, and going there for a week with meals on a tray and matching china at intervals.

My hair is going quite grey – I don't think you'll know me, my skirts fall off and my clothes hang on me. I feel older than the hills – not a bit young any more isn't it horrid and my own life has honestly ceased to interest me which must be a bad sign.

This depression seems to be of a different sort from that directly caused by the bombing; was she beginning to realize that her marriage was going wrong? At any rate she did not always feel like this. Earlier, on 26 October, she had written to Mrs Ham:

Oh dear I had such a laugh today. Do you remember, by the Albert Memorial a sculptured group called Asia with a lady riding on an elephant? She very coyly lifts a veil, to reveal – that her right breast has been blown off by a bomb. The effect somehow is indescribably

humorous, especially as nothing else in the whole group has even been
chipped. One of Hitty's better jokes . . . People here pay no attention
whatever now to bombs and if somebody does take cover you can be
sure they are just up from the country.

During 1940 Nancy changed her job and began looking after
evacuees; the hours were shorter than at the air raid post but the
job was more demanding. Harold Acton speculates that the
evacuees in Evelyn Waugh's *Put Out More Flags* may have owed
something to Nancy's account of her experiences, but a good
many stories on these lines were circulating at the time. During
the winter of 1940–41 she was caring for a group of Jewish
refugees who were housed at Rutland Gate. There were problems.
'Oh dear a little creature here aged 16 is in the family way. I
advised her in the words of Lady Stanley, a tremendous walk and
a hot bath and a great dose, but will this have any effect on a
tough little Jewess? Or shall I be obliged to wield a knitting
needle and go down to fame as Mrs Rodd the abortionist? I might
join Diana which would be rather nice.' Her parents were being
difficult, too. 'You can't imagine how beastly Muv is being – she
now regards me as a Jewess I believe and is horrid both to and
about me,' she says. Sydney would have been a great deal more
'horrid' had she known that at this time Nancy went again, to Jebb
or a colleague, to urge that Diana be kept in prison. She also advised
that Pam and Derek should be watched. A memorandum dated
14 November 1940 in Diana's MI5 file quotes Nancy as saying that
Diana was 'far the most dangerous character [in the family] and
should on no account be released.' Pam and Derek 'might well be
worth keeping under observation' as being 'fanatically anti-semetic,
anti-democratic and defeatist.' The memorandum adds, though, that
Derek 'for some curious reason . . . entertains an ambition . . . to
become a rear-gunner in the RAF.' Though obviously puzzled, the
authorities had the sense to leave Derek free to fight and earn his
medals.

Nancy's contact with the intelligence services encouraged them
to ask her to do a little spying in the Free French Officers' Club.
An Allied operation against Dakar had been leaked to the Vichy
Government, and it was thought that the leak might have come
from someone in London. Nancy took the job. Whether she

passed on any information we do not know, but she certainly had a love affair with a Free Frenchman known as André Roy. This caused an ectopic pregnancy; the foetus was surgically removed in October 1941 and Nancy was thereafter unable to bear children. It was another and grander Free French officer who was to become the love of Nancy's life.

In the meantime Nancy had taken a job a Heywood Hill's bookshop in Curzon Street. Nothing could have suited her better.

Heywood Hill and his wife were friends of Nancy's; the shop, relaxed though efficient, was a haven of civilization in wartime London, and has retained its essential character to this day. It dealt in all books, new and old, as well as in prints and certain antique toys. After Nancy joined it became a centre for chatting. Lord Berners came there, as did Lady Cunard and the Sitwells and Raymond Mortimer and Cyril Connolly and Cecil Beaton and so on, not to mention any member of Nancy's family who happened to be in London. The telephone was systematically misused. 'A little less "darling" and a little more attention please!' snapped one customer when Nancy was chatting at some length. But Nancy's net effect on the business must have been favourable, for Heywood Hill's developed insensibly into 'a centre for all that was left of fashionable and intellectual London'. Thus Evelyn Waugh; he usually looked in when he was on leave from the Commandos.

It has to be admitted that Nancy, with her colleagues and these regular customers, constituted rather a clique. Harold Acton was himself an habitué, and as he delicately puts it, 'Little did the casual customer suspect that he might be a target of mockery.' He might indeed, especially if American. A formidable lady in United States naval uniform came in once when Jonathan was there, and told Nancy that she wanted something to give her little girl.

'How old?' asked Nancy.

'Waal, she's only th'rrteen,' was the reply, 'but she's v'ry *matoor*.'

Nancy found the lady something, and when she had gone she emitted a high shriek. 'Thirteen and very *matoor*! *Imagine*!' Nancy was a lavish source of amusement to her colleagues in the shop,

Molly Friese-Green and Handasyde Buchanan, who in due course were to marry. Another assistant, quoted by Harold Acton, wrote to Heywood Hill years later remembering those days: 'Mrs Rodd . . . asked what I would do when my age group was called. I said I thought I would be a "clippie" on a bus. Some weeks later a twangy pure cockney voice bawled through the shop "All fares please – pass along there!" ' Altogether one has a sneaking sympathy with the 'new young man' who joined Heywood Hill's in the summer of 1945 and kept murmuring to himself: 'This is a *most* extraordinary establishment.' He wanted to fill the window with a display of the latest work of Mazo de la Roche, a bestselling writer of whom Nancy did not even know the sex. But she only once made a really bad mistake, when she omitted to lock the shop one Friday night and felt too tired to go in on Saturday morning. Heywood Hill himself happened to look in and was not best pleased to find numbers of bewildered people trying to buy books from each other.

What Nancy liked least at the bookshop was when it was her turn to do the accounts. However, when Sydney was in London this problem was solved, for Nancy would turn the task over to her. Sydney rather enjoyed it; she had stated in *All About Everybody* that her occupation if she had unlimited choice would be 'woman at the *caisse*'.

During the second half of the war, then, Nancy was happy in her work. She made light of the V1 bombing, even forgetting how much she had minded the blitz of 1940. To Sydney in July 1944 (quoted by Harold Acton) she wrote: 'Nobody minds the bombs any more (I never did) but they are doing a fearful amount of damage to houses. One going over here knocked panes of glass out of my neighbours' top window simply from the vibration of the engine . . . But how can the Germans be so stupid as to get everybody into a temper now, when as they must see they have lost, it is really too idiotic of them and seriously I think minimizes the chances of a decent peace.'

The liaison with André Roy had been a lighthearted affair, despite its sad result, but it was the first time Nancy had been unfaithful to Peter and showed that the marriage was going wrong. Nancy had taken her marriage vows seriously, though Peter, from the start, had had affairs. When home on leave he would not always see Nancy at all, though sometimes he would turn up at Blomfield Road in the small hours, drunk, and rouse Nancy to pay his taxi. Harold Acton says that 'Her annoyance was noticeable on the rare occasions [Peter] invaded the bookshop.' A note in the back pages of Nancy's diary for 1941 shows the conscious effort Nancy was making to preserve her marriage:

Love is a purely physical affair and therefore should not be confused with any other side of life or form of affection; and while it makes an agreeable foundation from which to begin a marriage the absence of physical love . . . should never be allowed to interfere with the continuity of marriage. Marriage is the most important thing in life and must be kept going at almost any cost, it should only be embarked on where there is . . . a complete conformity of outlook. Women as well as men ought to have a great many love affairs before they marry as the most critical moment in a marriage is the falling off of physical love, which is bound to occur sooner or later and only an experienced woman can know how to cope with this . . .

As far as it goes this is true, but it is also incomplete; for however experienced a woman may be, she needs cooperation from her partner for this transition, and Peter did little to help. We question, too, in what sense Nancy can at this stage be regarded as experienced. She knew the world and she knew literature, so she was aware of what is expected and a good deal of what happens in the domain of love; but how much of it had she personally undergone? She was never to know happy domesticity, and she had not yet enjoyed a passionate love affair. What is more to the point, Nancy's requirement of 'complete conformity of outlook' can be as treacherous a foundation for marriage as sexual attraction; it is not only in bed that a new partner can appear who is more compatible. Yet against all odds she kept the marriage going, after a fashion, for a surprising length of time.

Far more welcome than Peter on his visits to Heywood Hill's was de Gaulle's Directeur du Cabinet, Colonel Gaston Palewski, always known to Nancy and her family as 'The Colonel'. On 13 August 1944 the sharp-eyed James Lees-Milne noticed at a dinner party that Peter was putting Nancy on edge and making her anxious not to displease him. Even Peter's persistent unfaithful-ness, then, was not preventing her from feeling guilty. It was mainly so as to be near the Colonel that Nancy moved to Paris after the war. She and he never lived in the same house, there was never any question of their marrying, and the affair tailed off in due course to remain as a close and deep friendship. The timetable according to which this happened will always remain a mystery, given the extreme discretion of both parties, but we may be certain that the relationship was at nearly all times both happy and rewarding. However, it also suffered from a fundamental lack of symmetry. To the Colonel it was a delightful, extended amatory episode with a kindred spirit, which came to a natural conclusion but was followed by an abiding fondness. It was not his fault that to her he was simply the love of her life.

Still less was it his fault that she was a Mitford. This delightfully funny woman in her late thirties, cultured and with all the appearance of sophistication, was deep down still as unawakened as the Sleeping Beauty. No less than Diana, Unity and Decca, but at a far more advanced age than any of them, she still possessed a hunger for conviction and conversion like a kind of unexploded bomb. This hunger the Colonel was able to satisfy. He was as funny as Nancy herself, he was cultured and his educated taste at least matched her own, but he was also a passionate man with deep convictions and fierce loyalties. Perhaps precisely because he was half Polish, he was a particularly fervent French patriot of the type to whom the defeat of 1940 was quite unacceptable. He was therefore an intense admirer and close colleague of de Gaulle. Under the influence of her love for him, Nancy became from this time onwards as blindly pro-French as Unity had been pro-German, and in an equally partisan way. That is, she was unable to see that there was any other form of French patriotism than Gaullism, just as Unity had been unable to see that anyone opposing Hitler could love Germany. We do not deny that there may have been more to be said objectively for Nancy's view than for Unity's; certainly the course of history has ensured that the Resistance is regarded as the incarnation of French patriotism, while Nazism is regarded as a disgusting aberration. This should not obscure the fact that subjectively, that is to Nancy and Unity themselves, their feelings resembled each other's rather closely. In due course Nancy cooled down to some extent and came to laugh at herself on her adopted patriotism, as is shown in her depiction of Grace de Valhubert in *Don't Tell Alfred*. But her basic feelings remained like this to the end of her life.

The ground had been prepared in her long before she met the Colonel. In fact the Colonel's Frenchness was one of his attractions in the first place, for she had always enjoyed France. So of course had her grandfather Bertie, but he had tended to pick and choose, rejecting for instance the geometrical gardens of Le Nôtre. Nancy employed no such selectivity; one of the things that made the French more heavenly than almost anything else was their habit of bossing nature about and making it run in straight lines. Unimproved nature was a bore anyway. She had written to Mark Ogilvie-Grant on 10 December 1930 expressing relief that she was escaping a prospective trip to Switzerland. 'Like my hairdresser; when I said why do you hate Switzerland, "Ah, *les montagnes*," was all he could say in a sort of groan. I so agree don't you – I think natural scenery is THE END.' But even more attractive than the regimenting of nature was the fact that France had ordered Europe about, both culturally and militarily, during precisely the time – say between the accession of Henri IV and the fall of Napoleon – that Nancy found most congenial. Critics have accused the Mitfords of power worship; there is something in this as long as one emphasizes that the feeling was always essentially subconscious. They directed themselves towards an idea of power not deliberately, as the social climber toadies to a duke or the gold digger makes herself agreeable to a millionaire, but with a plant-like inevitability, as a flower turns towards the sun. We see in it a version of the pre-human urge in the female to secure the best mate; and simply because it is in this way the uncalculated expression of a mental process that existed before reasoning was thought of, it is inappropriate as well as uncharitable to blame them for it. Nancy was too adult and too educated to fall for totalitarianism. Her good taste in politics kept her from the crudities that her sisters, all of course at a much younger age, had accepted. Parades had little appeal to her and agitprop had none, so her version of the power-tropism turned her towards the past, to Napoleon and to Louis XIV. *The Blessing* contains an episode in which one of the Colonel's literary avatars makes his little son learn by heart and recite the inscription on the Arc du Carrousel:

'*À la voix du Vainqueur d'Austerlitz, l'Empire d'Allemagne tombe*', and so on. From the pen of another author this might easily be taken for an attempt to lampoon the French as windy and vainglorious. Nancy means it quite straight.

In later years Nancy's compatriots were sometimes rather put out by her extreme passion for everything French, but it was on the whole regarded as a curiosity rather than, as with Unity's parallel obsession, an outrage. This is essentially because France has on the whole been fashionable among the English talking classes whereas Germany, since 1914, never has been. Influential men of letters of the stamp of Cyril Connolly or Raymond Mortimer even shared Nancy's feelings to a considerable degree. Evelyn Waugh, however, emphatically did not, and he was not the only person to find Nancy a little irritating on the perfections of France. Sydney and Debo used to tease her on the subject; so, once, did Jonathan, getting a genuinely angry rise out of her. On some French people she grated a little, rather as André Maurois used sometimes to grate on the English; for a prophet can be short of honour not only in his own country, but in one which he has too uncritically adopted. Her feeling for de Gaulle, caught from the Colonel, grew to something very like worship. She was quite aware of the family parallel; at an enthusiastic Gaullist meeting after the war she said she had been 'feeling very like my sisters', and Mrs Ham, who was cool about de Gaulle, wrote sharply: 'You Mitfords like dictators; I don't.'

Happiness and fulfilment with the Colonel transformed Nancy's life for the better in the final years of the war; more important, it caused her to grow up as a novelist. After *Pigeon Pie*, so brittle and immature, she suddenly wrote a novel of real quality, *The Pursuit of Love*. Promise ripened into high talent, essentially because she now knew from personal experience what love was. For the first time she produced a book that, despite noticeable blemishes, at least approached the status of a masterpiece; its jokes and bright chatter were underpinned by a solid construction but above all deepened by a new emotional self-knowledge.

Certainly it was an instant bestseller, to such a degree that its sales, and the literary reputation that it secured for Nancy, ensured that she would never again need to worry about money. She also became from then on the best known of the Mitford sisters. Up till then that distinction had undoubtedly belonged to Unity, whose autograph was always the most in demand from those of Jonathan's schoolmates who collected such things. From being an upper-class girl who had written a few books, Nancy became at a stroke an established author.

The work was also the start of what Decca has christened the Mitford Industry: that industry of which this present work is of course a part. This is because the central family in it; the Radlett family, is based on the Mitfords. However it is not a history of the Mitfords, even a fictionalized one. It is a new creation which simply uses certain selected foibles and incidents from Nancy's family as its main building materials; and the selection is made according to a principle, partly no doubt unconscious but partly, we are convinced, deliberate. Lord and Lady Alconleigh, Uncle Matthew and Aunt Sadie, are certainly like Nancy's parents as they were when she was growing up, though Sydney's portrait is really no more than a clever impression. David is drawn in rather more depth; and the more carefully one reads the book the more Nancy's treatment of her father appears actually to be sympathetic. The generalizations about Uncle Matthew, which stand out when one reads the book superficially, are often on the lines of 'this violent, uncontrolled man'. However, many of the individual incidents show David's sensitive and thoughtful side. For instance, having growled his refusal at his daughter Linda when she wanted a dormouse, he takes some trouble to get her one for Christmas. Uncle Matthew does, it is true, thrash his children from time to time, which David did not; but then more of his children are boys than in David's case, and it was always more usual to beat boys than girls. The general keynote is a rough and erratic kindness very similar to David's. David himself did not merely take the portrait in good part; he actually liked it.

There are other portraits from life besides those of Nancy's parents. Lord Merlin, the rich neighbour who at several points acts as a *deus ex machina* to help Linda when in difficulties, is Lord Berners. This has misled some people into imagining that Lord Berners knew the Mitfords from their childhood, which was not the case. In real life it was not until the thirties, and entirely through Diana, that he came to know them at all. Fabrice de Sauveterre, who plays in Linda's life the same role that the

Colonel played in Nancy's very different one, also shares some of the Colonel's traits. Josh the groom, who judges people entirely on their horsemanship and on nothing else, is a vignette of the Mitfords' Hooper, known as Choops. Those who like this sort of thing can search in the book as in a bran tub and find other characters reminiscent of real people, but the more they do this the less they will understand what the book is really about.

For the seven Radlett children, and in particular Linda who is the central character, have actually rather little in common with the seven Mitfords, except certain jokes and tricks of speech. There are outward similarities, but the deeper one delves, the less important these are compared with the differences. For one thing, Tom is omitted. There are indeed three boys, but none of them has anything to do with Tom and all are fairly shadowy. This excludes from the Radletts all concern for music or for general ideas. Secondly, politics is almost omitted, and Fascist politics entirely so. Decca's Running Away Account amuses Nancy too much for her to leave it out, but Jassy, who keeps it, uses it not to elope with a Communist but to go to Hollywood and marry an actor. It is true that Matt, one of the shadowy boys, runs away from Eton to fight for the Spanish Republicans, but this episode is not developed. Linda becomes a Communist, but the conversion is quite clearly shown to be superficial.

Linda talks like the Mitfords, in her youth she sheds their easy tears over animals, she shares with them a basic natural decency and a ladylike self-respect, and also a discretion, all of which give some foundation to her charm. But what she has not, and what Nancy did not mean her to have, is much trace either of their intelligence or of their willpower. More important, she lacks their capacity to change; she is exactly the same in her thirties as in her teens. As to the Mitfords' habit of following a cause and their rather frightening talent for using their charm in its service, here is Linda, already aged about thirty, in her Communist period: ' "Grandi had a dinner-dance last week, and he rang me up himself and asked me to bring Christian, which I thought was awfully nice of him actually – he has always been nice to me – but Christian got into quite a temper and said if I couldn't see any reason against going I'd better go, but nothing would induce him to." ' Count Grandi was Mussolini's ambassador in London. We invite the reader to imagine Decca suggesting to Esmond that they should go to a party of Grandi's.

Linda is, in fact, quite deliberately made out to be a nice little fool; capable of courage, dignity and tact, but a fool all the same. This is because for the particular plot Nancy chose as suitable for her particular talents, a little fool was what was required. Intelligence in her heroine would have introduced complications that would have been beyond her. It is true that she was later to write well of Madame de Pompadour, of Madame de Maintenon, and of Voltaire's brilliant mistress Madame du Châtelet; but this was historical reconstruction, a very different process from invention.

*The Pursuit of Love* in the title is primarily Linda's pursuit of it as narrated by her cousin Fanny Logan. Linda first marries Tony Kroesig, the son of a rich banker. This gives Nancy a chance to develop the theme noted in *Wigs on the Green* and in the introductions to *The Ladies of Alderley* and *The Stanleys of Alderley*: the idea that the essentially feudal social order based on the squirearchy is acceptable, because it entails reciprocal duties; but that wealth based on finance, being wholly irresponsible, is wholly wrong. The Kroesig name is German, and the family is supposed to be soft on Hitler, but the crude stereotype to which its members conform has much in common with that with which anti-semites used to slander millionaire Jews. They are, that is, in the worst sense international, caring for no country or area except where they can be safe and make money. The Kroesigs are smug, cowardly, vulgar, pretentious, humourless and greedy. They live in a 'horrible house' in Surrey, surrounded by garish blossoms that will never turn to fruit. In real life the magnates of finance-capitalism quite commonly develop a social conscience, which at its most typical expresses itself in lavish charitable donations; in the Kroesigs there is no sign of anything of this sort. In real life very rich men have often fought bravely for their country; not so the Kroesigs. During the First World War Tony Kroesig's father wangles a desk job which secures him an OBE and several valuable business contacts. As the Second World War approaches the Kroesigs shift both their money and themselves to America; Uncle Matthew, on the contrary, later organizes his whole family to resist the invader to the death. (We note in this connection that in one country which actually was occupied, Nancy's beloved

France, the landed gentry with some honourable exceptions
tended to accommodate to the realities of defeat and of Marshal
Pétain; it was much more the finance-capitalists with international
connections who were in favour of carrying on the fight from
abroad with General de Gaulle.) In domestic politics, the Kroesigs
profess a conservatism so openly brutal as to be, in the end,
absurd. Tony enters Parliament and becomes 'a perfect mountain
of pomposity'.

' "I hate the lower classes," he said one day . . . "Ravening
beasts, trying to get my money. Let them try, that's all." ' The
trouble here is that Nancy has simply lost her rag. She hates Tony
so much that she is unable to make him credible. For one thing his
remark about the lower classes is not pompous. Pomposity aspires
to dignity; Tony's remark does not. It is selfish and petulant, but
not pompous. It has a simple schoolboy directness about it; the
expression 'ravening beasts' even has a flavour of Uncle Matthew.
There are in truth politicians who think like Tony Kroesig is
supposed to, but this is not the way they speak. A real Tony
would have said: 'I say nothing against the lower classes. Salt of
the earth, splendid people. Badly led, though. Listen to the first
loudmouthed agitator that gets up on a soapbox and couldn't run a
sweetstall.'

Linda has a daughter by Tony, Moira, whom she dislikes from
birth and systematically neglects. Nancy realizes that this is a stain
on her heroine's character, and tries to explain it away. Linda, we
are told, deliberately does not allow herself to get too fond of
Moira because she realizes instinctively that one day she will leave
Tony. This does not really wash, especially in a character whose
charm is supposed to reside in her artless spontaneity; and she in
fact stays with Tony for nine years.

In due course Linda runs away with Christian Talbot, Communist son of a professor. One piece of dialogue about his family
reads oddly to the modern eye:

' "Is his brother a Communist too?"

' "Oh no, he's in the Foreign Office." '

Linda makes herself useful in a Communist bookshop two days
a week. Like Heywood Hill's for Nancy, this shop becomes the
resort of her friends. She is, though, not happy for long with
Christian. He loves humanity, not her. Nancy, we note, accepts

the claims of the Communists to love mankind, even if they spoil this by impersonality and clumsiness. This recalls her remark in *Christmas Pudding* that Communism was a 'high, if boring, ideal'. At all events Christian, like Peter Rodd, goes to Perpignan to deal with the Spanish refugees, and Linda joins him like Nancy, willing but inefficient. Eventually Linda sees that he has fallen for a more competent woman colleague, and leaves in dudgeon for Paris, where she finds herself penniless at the Gare du Nord with a return ticket that is a day out of date. Crying on her suitcase, she is rescued by a short, stocky, very dark Frenchman' who turns out to be the very rich Duke, Fabrice de Sauveterre.

Rescued, and also, not to put too fine a point upon it, picked up; for he is a well-known seducer. There is of course nothing crude about the operation. ' "I invite you to luncheon with me, but first you must have a bath and a rest and a cold compress on your face." ' He does not at first so much as lay a hand on her knee; he merely talks as if it is a matter of course that they have started an affair. ' "With me, it usually lasts five years." ' If the reader sniffs something of the stage Frenchman here, a hint of moustache twirling, it is certainly inadvertent on Nancy's part; she means it to be irresistibly charming. Fabrice knows all about fashion; he tells Linda that her linen suit ' "has ready-made written all over it" ', and is out of date. ' "Jackets are getting longer you will find. I'll get you some clothes – if you were well-dressed you would be quite good-looking . . ." ' He also knows all about politics and international affairs and history and art, and is a superb guide round Paris. ' "Really," she thought with a giggle, "this is a very penny-novelettish seduction, how can I be taken in by it?" But she was filled with a strange, wild, unfamiliar happiness, and knew that this was love.' Exactly in fact like the heroine of a penny novelette.

Fabrice instals Linda in a flat, where she is blissfully happy. Her nights are filled with lovemaking of a type which convinces her that neither Tony nor Christian can have known the facts of life, her days occupied buying clothes with Fabrice's money. She goes back to London when the invasion of France is imminent. Fabrice turns up once, having of course joined General de Gaulle after the fall of France, and tells Linda for the first time that he loves her. They will live together again after the war, he promises. ' "As I love you ten times more than the others that brings it to when I am ninety, and, by then, *j'en aurai tellement l'habitude* . . ."' He goes off, leaving her with child. Linda returns to her parents' house, where the whole family is gathered to sit out the war and resist the Germans if they invade. Fanny's mother is there, known as the Bolter because she has spent her life bolting from husband to husband. Here is a well-observed portrait of a type of woman who did not exist at all in the Mitford family but most certainly existed outside it – a female rake. Ageing now and losing her looks, she has acquired the special street wisdom of her kind, not wholly cynical but resigned to the perishability of love. To the Bolter, Linda's case is clear; she is a woman of her own type. Does not her record show it? To think otherwise is illusion or pretension. Linda is offended; Fanny takes her part, convinced that the love her cousin has at last found is true and permanent. Until the very end of the book it seems that Nancy means the reader to assume this and to write the Bolter's opinion off. But then there is a twist. Linda dies in childbirth, never knowing that Fabrice has been killed in the Resistance. The Bolter discusses Linda with Fanny. ' "Poor Linda," she said, with feeling, "poor little thing. But Fanny, don't you think perhaps it's just as well? The lives of women like Linda and me are not so much fun when one begins to grow older."' Unwilling to wound her mother by denying that Linda was that sort of woman, Fanny simply says that Fabrice was the great love of her life; but the Bolter suddenly comes up with a devastating, indeed an unanswerable reply: ' "One always thinks that. Every, every time."' Since these are the very last words in the book, we are clearly supposed to be left with a doubt. It is far more effective than if the couple had survived and the doubt been resolved one way or the other; and it depends for its effect on the insight that Linda is *not* a Mitford.

As to Nancy herself, the Colonel awakened her at this time as surely as Fabrice awakened Linda, no doubt using some of the same conversational gambits; but since Nancy possessed inner resources that the character she created lacked, the results were less commonplace. The first of them was *The Pursuit of Love* itself, which she dedicated to the Colonel; and never was a dedication more appropriate. Had she been a man and he a woman, there would be no difficulty in defining what he was to her at this stage and during the rest of her life. Although it sounds faintly odd this way round, we shall nevertheless say it: he was her Muse.

In the summer of 1945 Nancy continued to work in Heywood Hill's and corrected the proofs of *The Pursuit of Love*. She received from her father £10,000, of which she used half to buy a partnership in the shop. Her ostensible reason for first going to Paris after the war was to do some business on behalf of the shop; 'trying to sell Cobbett's *Rural Rides* to the French,' said Evelyn Waugh. She wrote to Harold Acton, who was in the Allied headquarters in Paris in July: 'My dream is to be fixed up with some Paris shop and do delicious swops so that I can be the purveyor of highbrow frog books here and vice versa.' Then she switches to London life. 'Tomorrow the Rothermere party for the election. We are asked from 12.30–3.30, fork luncheon. Evelyn says: "I intend to arrive at 12.30 and stay to 3.30 using my fork all the time." ' This was of course the election at which the Labour Party, led by Clement Attlee, unexpectedly ousted the Conservatives by a landslide, despite Churchill's poster bearing the slogan 'Help him finish the job'. Nancy had voted Labour; Peter Rodd had even been to Transport House to seek a constituency to fight, though without success. Having a wife with the maiden name of Mitford had probably not helped. But she was pleased at Attlee's victory and said so. In the following years, when Nancy was in Paris, her friends used often to reproach her for the iniquities of what they called '*your* government', especially as she never stopped teasing them about the marvels of France compared to the austerity of England. They felt she had saddled her country with socialism and then got out herself.

Nancy spent September and October of 1945 in Paris, then returned to Heywood Hill's which she finally left in March 1946. This period was made happy and hopeful by the success of *The Pursuit of Love*. She was now independent and could devote herself to writing. Congratulations, too, came from all sides. Fan letters arrived. She was particularly flattered when an old foreigner who was an occasional customer came in and seized her hand in both of his, saying in a strong Central European accent: 'Miss Mitford, I had to tell you; Uncle Matthew, he *is* my father.' So this creation of hers, apparently so rooted in a particular class and country, had achieved the status of an archetype. Evelyn Waugh agreed: Uncle Matthew, he said, was everyone's father.

As to her time in Paris, Nancy was ecstatic. Harold Acton quotes a long letter from her to her mother in September 1945:

I must come and live here as soon as I can. I feel a totally different person as if I had come out of a coal mine into daylight . . . The angelic *concierge* (how helpful the French are) got into the Métro at rush hour for me, went all the way to Montmartre, and returned with the prettiest *femme de ménage* you ever saw, all like magic. Imagine a London porter, all grumbles and groans and puttings off and certainly no lovely girl at the end of it! . . . I'm doing business in a rather desultory way – writing one or two articles for French papers which pay frightfully well, selling and buying books etc., but really I'm having an absolute rest and the result is I feel so wonderful I don't know it's me. Enough to eat twice a day, always a glass of wine and staying in bed most of the morning have made a new woman of me . . . Oh the food. Every meal is a recurring pleasure. I don't know how I shall be able to drag myself back to starving London . . . And always a *verre de vin*, so good for one.

There is, says Acton, a hint of teasing here; there is indeed, for he quotes another friend, Alvilde Chaplin, afterwards Lees-Milne, as giving a rather different account. According to her, Nancy was 'making do in cold hotels'. She herself was living at the time outside Paris, subsisting mostly on carrots and potatoes; Nancy would 'come and stay, and all the horrors turned into jokes'. But there was no lack of horror to act as raw material; not only food shortages, but above all a lack of heating. Warmth, as we have mentioned elsewhere, was always particularly important to Nancy, and she must have suffered. As in the song, though, Nancy had her love to keep her warm. There she was with the Colonel in the capital, not long liberated, of his beloved country. Her letter to Sydney may have been touched up in the details; her joy was real enough.

# 37

# Pam and Tom: II

By the time the war started, Pam and Derek had been settled at Rignell for some years. He worked in Oxford at his spectroscopy and hunted or raced in his spare time, she enjoyed the quiet Oxfordshire countryside and looked after the long-haired dachshunds they both adored. Nancy wrote from Rignell to Mrs Ham early in the war, on 11 March 1940: '[Pam] lives in a round of boring gaiety of the neighbourly description but all the same I envy a country existence of almost any kind and I feel certain I shall never achieve one.' Derek was not there; if he had been, they would have quarrelled about the war, for Nancy goes on to say:'What are all these diplomatic moves? If peace I shall leave on the next boat and *for good* will you come along? However I learn with relief from today's wireless that a civilian has been killed so perhaps this will be a signal for war.' Derek would not have been able to stand Nancy in this bloodthirsty mood, or she him; he wanted peace, and said so. In December of the same year he and Nancy did have words on the subject. Nancy wrote of it to Mrs Ham on the twenty-sixth: 'Pam and Derek came to London for a few days and talked such Fascism that the whole town is speculating on how they manage to remain OUT [of prison].' As we have seen, it was no thanks to Nancy that they did remain out of prison. We are also rather surprised that Pam, as well as Derek, is said to have spoken in this way. It is out of character.

By now the Mosleys were in prison for their views. In Diana's case this was achieved with some encouragement from Nancy. It was a good thing for the country that she did not have the same success with Derek, for as it was he became a war hero. The irony of Derek's position is highlighted by what Nancy goes on to tell Mrs Ham: 'Cyril [Connolly], Hog Watson [Peter Watson; see p. 592] and many another lefty are avoiding military service by dint of being editors of a magazine [*Horizon*] which is a reserved occupation isn't it brilliant.' The point is that while a number of people who supported the war showed a reluctance to risk themselves, Derek, who as a scientist was in a genuine reserved occupation, volunteered for the Royal Air Force. He experienced some difficulty in doing so. Lindemann did not want to release him from his scientific team at the Clarendon Laboratory, for it was doing important war work; but Pam pulled strings. She knew Group Captain William Elliot, assistant secretary to the war cabinet. He mentioned Derek to Churchill himself. A word from his old friend the Prime Minister, and Lindemann allowed Derek to go. His combination of fearlessness and scientific knowledge made him immensely valuable to the Air Force, and he was repeatedly decorated; yet he never moderated his opposition to the war or toned down his expression of it.

In the meantime he and Pam had come to Diana's rescue by giving a home to her small sons. Shortly after Mosley was arrested, the authorities requisitioned his house at Denham; so Diana, Nanny Higgs, Alexander and Max had to find somewhere to go. They were invited to Rignell. In fact Diana herself was then arrested, so Nanny and the children went without her. Pam and Derek also had Jonathan and Desmond to stay for that half of the holidays when they would normally have been with their mother. These arrangements lasted for about two years. It was particularly kind of Pam in that Nanny Higgs, staunch and faithful as she was, was nevertheless an old-fashioned nanny of the type who once congregated in Hyde Park, each with a polished perambulator and one or two scrubbed children in white boots that had been laboriously cleaned by a nurserymaid. Pam was having to cope with the departure of servants for the war. Without Diana to help, Nanny and the children added to her difficulties. After about two years they left Rignell and became paying guests at Swinbrook House, whose new owners, Duncan and Pamela MacKinnon, had become friends of the family.

Meanwhile Derek joined the Royal Air Force and, after training, went into action in March 1941 as a wireless operator and air gunner in Bomber Command. But he was almost immediately transferred to a night fighter squadron in which, flying as a navigator, he helped shoot down at least five and probably seven enemy aircraft, damaging another two. In June 1941 he won the DFC. He was promoted fairly rapidly, ending the war as a wing commander. In May 1942 he was put in charge of testing 'Window', strips of metal foil dropped by bombers so as to confuse the enemy radar. Later he also worked on ways of jamming the radio transmissions directing German air defences. In the course of this he was awarded the AFC for bravery while testing a captured German aircraft, and his work was of outstanding help to Bomber Command. In due course he was given the OBE for valour, and the United States also decorated him after the war with the Legion of Merit. The brilliance of his service career was perhaps to be expected, for he was utterly fearless and had very quick reactions as well as being dexterous, aggressive and brilliantly intelligent. It is, all the same, rather to the credit of his superiors and colleagues that they put up with him. Most of the time he was charming and funny, but he must at times have irritated them beyond belief. He quickly became convinced that none of the three services was any good except the Royal Air Force.

'Your father's a brown job, isn't he?' Derek asked Jonathan once, a little condescendingly.

Jonathan failed to understand at first, then Derek explained that it was an Air Force nickname for a soldier in the Army. 'Have you got a name for the Navy?' asked Jonathan.

Derek became rather heated. 'The Navy!' he rapped out. 'The Navy isn't worth a nickname; we call the Army the brown jobs, but all we need to call the Navy is *the Navy*!' The tone was one of utter contempt.

But even within the Air Force Derek had no time for those who did not fly: the 'penguins', as they were called, recognizable as such because they had no wings on their uniform. Pam caught this from Derek. 'Do you know what I saw the other day?' she once said to Derek in Jonathan's hearing. 'An *Air Commodore penguin*!' Her eyes were round with amazement as she said this, and her Mitford emphasis could not have been stronger if the man had had two heads. Derek graded the fighting services, in fact, rather as he graded academic subjects: only his own speciality was any good.

He felt of the Army as he felt of chemistry, of the Navy as of biology. As for the penguins, they were no better than history or modern languages.

What made Derek a difficult companion in the mess was not these prejudices, perhaps shared to an extent by some of his companions, but rather his habit of saying things like 'When the darling Germans have won the war I shall have my own *château* on the Loire.' Why he should have such a *château* in the circumstances was never clear; perhaps this made the remark acceptable. But once when an air marshal paid a visit there really was a dreadful scene. The great man was surprised and not best pleased when Derek vehemently contradicted some remark of his.

'Come, come, Jackson,' he said: 'we mustn't get heated.' It was like trying to extinguish a fire with petrol.

Derek exploded, gobbled like a turkey. 'What do you mean, *we*?' he shouted. 'The royal we, the editorial we, or just you and your bloody tapeworm?'

When the war came to an end Derek returned for a time to his work at Oxford. 'I am still dairymaid,' Pam wrote to Sydney on 1 October 1946. 'We now have a cow here belonging to Prof. [Lindemann] and Derek takes the cream into Oxford two or three times a week. We get the skim milk for our calves, so it suits well.' In 1947 Derek was appointed Professor of Spectroscopy at Oxford; despite this, he decided to emigrate to Ireland. The Labour government enraged him. At his high income level the top rate of 97½ per cent tax was payable on much of his fortune; it would have meant retrenchment on horses, and on scientific instruments for the Clarendon Laboratory and the Oxford Observatory to which he liked to be generous. Dr Kuhn, in his memorial paper on Derek, suggests that there was also some residual bitterness from an incident that had taken place during the war. The Home Secretary, Herbert Morrison, made the Mosleys leave Derek's house when he put them up immediately after their release from prison. Since Derek was doing secret work, a security leak was said to be feared. We shall return to this incident in the next chapter. It offended Derek deeply; he felt it to be not only an impertinence but a deadly personal insult. Morrison had been a conscientious objector during the First World War; Derek himself was fighting and winning medals for a cause that was Morrison's far more than it was his own. Yet Morrison was not only telling him whom he should have in his house, but implying that he and his guest might betray secrets to the enemy. Morrison is supposed to have rung Derek up personally and been told: 'When you have won the DFC, the AFC and the OBE for valour, you can speak to me again.' Now, in 1947, Morrison was a prominent member of the government which was proposing to take Derek's money.

After leaving Rignell Derek rented Lismore Castle in County Waterford for a few months during 1947 from Debo's husband Andrew, then Marquess of Hartington. Jonathan and Desmond stayed with them for part of August; Jonathan's clearest memory of this visit is of Professor Lindemann, by now Lord Cherwell. Pale-faced in his city suits, he interested Jonathan as he had interested Diana at the same age twenty years before. He would often argue with Derek about the war, on which subject they were at opposite poles. They were very old friends, though, and loved one another.

Then Derek bought Tullamaine Castle, near Fethard in County Tipperary. The move to Ireland was probably a mistake, despite the money it saved him. At Rignell he had occupied himself with his science and his horses; in Tullamaine he still had his horses, but not his science. He did sometimes go to Columbus, Ohio, as visiting professor, and now and then also to Dunsink Observatory in Dublin, but it was not enough. He became bored and restless; the 'fickleness' to which his identical twin had confessed years before in *All About Everybody* became evident in him once more. He and Pam had no children; two attempts, once before and once after the war, had both ended in miscarriage. In any case Derek's wish for a child was only fitful. 'It might be the wrong colour or the wrong sex,' he said; the wrong sex was female, the wrong colour dark, like himself. He also once told Jonathan that he did not want to bring a child into a world where there might be an atomic war.

Finally he left Pam for Janetta Kee, who had just divorced Robert Kee, the future television producer. They had a daughter called Rose, Derek's only child, but did not remain together long; this indicates that even if Pam had managed to produce a child, it might not have kept Derek with her. Rose was 'the wrong colour

and the wrong sex', but this did not stop him being inordinately
proud and fond of her, even if on the whole from a distance.

Derek married three times after Janetta, thus equalling Henry
VIII, since Pam had been his second wife. He settled in France in
the early fifties, and at the invitation of Profesor P. Jacquinot
became a researcher at Bellevue laboratory near Paris. He worked
there for almost thirty years, till his death in 1982, and continued
to distinguish himself in his recondite field; the French government presented him with the Legion of Honour in 1966. He lived
quite near the Mosleys. When Alexander was at school with the
Oratorian fathers at Pontoise, Derek used to give him arguments
to buttress his atheism. 'Why should there be a higher being than
we are?' he said. 'I believe in a *longer* being – a darling dachshund
ten light-years long.' And he gave the little loving whinny that
went with stroking one of the dogs he had loved so much.

Derek never lost his love of teasing. In the summer of 1976
there was a drought, and the Cardinal Archbishop of Paris prayed
for rain. It did not come; and Derek, at a dinner party where most
of the company consisted of devout Roman Catholics, said that
the Cardinal ought to be flogged in public, like any other failed
witch doctor. Fortunately his last marriage, to Marie-Christine
Reille, was a successful one, ending only with his death. Marie-
Christine made his old age happy, and their marriage lasted about
as long as that with Pam. But Pam had been with him in his erratic
prime, when to keep him for fourteen years was a greater achievement.

Pam herself left Tullamaine not long after Derek. She rented a
small house at Grüningen near Zurich; Nancy was very taken with
it and thought the Swiss landscape something from a picture book.
Pam also bought a house in Gloucestershire, where she still lives.
In Zurich she got to know many a Swiss banker: 'I worship the
gnomes,' she said. They would click their heels, kiss her hand and
invite her out to lunch. She was in constant touch with her family,
and had many friends, including Rudi von Simolin, now the
Baroness St Paul, who had been so helpful after Unity's attempted
suicide. One might nevertheless have thought Pam would sometimes be lonely, but she never seems to have been; of all the sisters
she is the most self-sufficient.

In the autumn of 1969 Pam accompanied Nancy to Dresden

and Potsdam to research for *Frederick the Great*. She was useful as
an interpreter, for her German is good and Nancy's non-existent;
she also had to help look after Nancy, now suffering from the
illness that finally killed her, because as the journey proceeded
Nancy got worse again after a temporary remission from her pain
that summer. As Nancy's condition deteriorated Pam came more
and more to France to help. Diana was really in charge of looking
after Nancy, since she lived near and visited every day; but after
her we think it was Pam who did most. When Nancy was at her
worst, all defences down, all worldly interests forgotten and even
teasing in abeyance, when she was just someone in pain, it was
Pam who knew best, by sheer instinctive kindness, what should be
done. Diana says too that when she herself was ill with a brain
tumour in 1981 it was Pam whose visits gave her the most
comfort. Her mere presence was a reassurance.

Latterly Pam has become well known in the poultry world
since she imported into Britain a picturesque breed of chicken
called the Appenzeller Spitzhaube. The tasteful arrangement of
feathers on its head resembles a pointed cap. The birds had come
as eggs, hatched by Debo (who else?) in an incubator at Chatsworth. Pam also starred in Julian Jebb's television programme
about Nancy, and was heard on the radio. Of all the sisters she is
the best performer, for she lacks all self-consciousness; she also
has the best memory for detail. In preparing this book, both Diana
and Debo have given indispensable help; but, as with most of us,
their memory of the past is selected, packaged, interpreted. Pam
does very little of this; her memories, as she recalls them, retain
the freshness of direct perception. We shall give an example, not
from our own notes which have mostly been woven into this text
already, but from a letter she wrote to Nancy for her birthday on
26 October 1964:

Do you remember 42 years ago on my birthday at Asthall when there
was such a heavy frost that the wire netting on the hen pens was quite
closed with frost sparkles and the sun was shining brightly; Farve gave
us all enough money to take the bus to Oxford and lunch and cinema.
When we arrived we had ages to wait for lunch so as it was icy cold
you insisted on going to the Ashmolean museum, we were against it as
it was costing sixpence each and we would not have so much lunch as

we had hoped. However we agreed to go as it was the only place to keep warm till lunch time. Then, to our joy, we met Uncle George in the museum and he invited us all to a wonderful feast at Fullers!

Here there is no generalization, no seeking after significance, no picking out of the amusing bits; it is a sample of the Mitford childhood as it actually was, a raw piece of the past like the core from a geological test drilling.

It will be recalled that Sydney wrote to Unity, at the time of Munich, complaining that Tom had almost joined the war party and asking Unity to convince him otherwise. This is partial corroboration of what James Lees-Milne was to write of Tom in an 'Appreciation' for *The Times*, after he was killed: 'It was [his] unassailable integrity which impelled him to fight tooth and nail against the Germans whom he had long known so intimately and admired so well. After Munich he was literally overwhelmed with misery and misgiving in fear that England was throwing away its traditional title in the European hegemony. And so he was among the first to join the Territorials . . .' One must read this in the context of the period. Tom had already been in the Territorials for some time – the Queen's Westminsters to be exact. However, though Lees-Milne did not know this, the organization he did join at the time of Munich was Mosley's BUF. His mood at Munich was indeed one of misery and misgiving, but his adherence to Mosley shows that he was blaming the crisis on the British partisans of war at least as much as on Hitler. He did indeed fight tooth and nail against the Germans, though at the end of the war he deliberately chose to fight against the Japanese instead. The 'Appreciation' is angled so as to give the impression that Tom was a full-blooded and conventional supporter of the war; even that he was converted to this belligerence with the best people, at Munich, rather than in March or September 1939. It was loyal and kind of Lees-Milne thus to adapt his friend's views. In the mood of 1945 the full truth about Tom's attitude would only have brought further attacks on his family; even silence on the subject might have been dangerous.

For the newspaper files contained one story which could well have been picked up. Tom went to Mosley's great meeting in favour of peace, at Earl's Court, on 16 July 1939. The *Evening Standard* spotted him. Plenty of other friends and relations were there among the audience of twenty thousand, including Debo, Tom's friend Lord Hinchingbrooke, MP, and Tilly Losch. The trouble was that Tom gave the Fascist salute, and it was reported. Two journalists, who were fellow Territorials, complained to Tom's colonel that they objected to being officered by Fascists; the colonel rejected this complaint, and to do the *Evening Standard* justice it took the same attitude in a leading article on the nineteenth: 'All ranks of the Territorial Army are volunteers. They must not be deprived of their rights as citizens merely because they willingly assume extra responsibilities. It would be otherwise if the officer attempted to obtrude his political views in the course of his official regimental duties. But there is no evidence that Mr Mitford has attempted to do so.'

Earlier in July Tom had been to a ball at Blenheim, where he had a conversation with Winston Churchill. 'Chamberlain says war produces nothing,' said Churchill. 'But look at all this!' He waved his hand to indicate the magnificent house and furniture earned through war by his ancestor, the great Duke of Marlborough.

Tom's attitude to the war when it came was exactly that of Derek, though he was usually as discreet as Derek was flamboyant. It was the attitude Mosley enjoined on his supporters. If one's country is at war, one fights: even if one thinks the war wrong; even if one suspects that it might be nationally suicidal. At this distance in time it might perhaps be admitted that to fight while holding this attitude entails a certain special heroism.

When war broke out Tom left the Territorials and became an officer in the Rifle Brigade; on his leaves he often saw Nancy. Towards the end of 1940 he brought a girlfriend to stay at Biddesden. Bryan wrote to Diana for Christmas 1940: 'Tom came and stayed while we were away for a weekend with a young lady who is he says a "potential fiancée" . . . I wrote and sent him my potential congratulations.' In the abstract, Tom wanted to get married, because he wanted to have children. But when it came to thinking of anyone specific, he could never face it. Nearly four years later James Lees-Milne records a conversation in his diary (*Prophesying Peace*) for 2 August 1944. Tom discusses his girls with such frankness that Lees-Milne is moved to say that none of them would marry him if they knew what he was saying about them. 'Oh, but they don't know,' says Tom, roaring with laughter. What was the trouble with his girls? Did none of them seem to measure up to his sisters?

Tom was sent overseas in early 1942, fighting in North Africa and Italy. He was returned to England in July 1944 for a course at the Staff College, and while there he usually spent his weekends either in London or at Crux Easton with the Mosleys. He and they discussed philosophy, politics and just about everything under the sun.

In London he frequently saw Lees-Milne, whose published diary already mentioned gives some vivid glimpses of him. On 18 July that year he writes: 'On walking past the Ritz I heard Nancy give a cry; and there she was with Tom, back from the Mediterranean after two and a half years absence. He almost embraced me in the street, saying "My dear old friend, my oldest friend," which was most affecting. He looks rather younger than his age, is rather thin, still extremely handsome.' On 27 August they discussed politics. Tom said that if he was a German he would be a Nazi; all the best Germans were; he added '. . . that he was an imperialist. He considered that life without power and without might with which to strike fear into every nation would not be worth living for an Englishman.' This is interesting because British imperialists did not usually think or talk like this; they were rather more apt to think of the money they might make and talk (in the manner either caricatured or exemplified by Nancy in her preface to the Stanley letters) of the good they were doing as world governess among fractious charges. The view Tom expressed belongs not to an island which dominates the seas with little risk, but to a part of a land mass which is always exposed to invading armies. It is continental thinking. Possibly some of his reading in German influenced him, though Kant was his favourite and such ideas are not Kantian. Perhaps it was really the menacing pressure of total war which gave the main impetus. In any case Lees-Milne contradicted him: 'Told him I . . . would prefer to live in a country of tenth rate power, provided there were peace and freedom of action and speech. The sweet side of Tom is that he never minds how much an old friend disagrees with him. But woe betide an acquaintance.' To be fair to Tom, too, he was never an anti-semite. His sympathy with Nazism, such as it was, was in spite of its attitude to the Jews, not because of it. Tom admired Jewish musicianship and scholarship. Had he lived to know of the holocaust he would certainly have been horrified, though perhaps, like Diana, he might think that it would not have happened if Britain and France had not gone to war with Hitler.

Tom asked to be sent to Burma; he did not want to risk being ordered to ill-treat German civilians during the occupation that was clearly about to take place, but preferred to fight the Japanese. In his entry for 22 December 1944 Lees-Milne describes driving Tom down to the Old Mill Cottage, Swinbrook, and lunching with Sydney and Unity. It was one of Unity's good days; Lees-Milne finds that she has become rather plain and fat, but that she is still amusing. She even talks of Hitler, something that at that stage she almost never did, other than in private with Sydney. Four days later Lees-Milne picks Tom up from Swinbrook to take him back to London. 'Bobo made Tom laugh a great deal. He is perfectly sweet and patient with her. Indeed with those of whom he is fond his manner is irresistible. He said good-bye to his mother, who was brave and good about his departure, which he told me might be for three years.'

In the event it was for ever. Tom was killed in Burma in early April 1945. For Lees-Milne it was a double blow. All those years before, in 1919, he had made two friends among the other new boys at Lockers Park; one was Tom, the other was Basil, Marquess of Dufferin and Ava. Both were hit on the same day, 3 April. Dufferin was killed outright, and the news of his death arrived on the 4th: Tom was wounded in the stomach and survived a day.

Diana was still under house arrest, but determined that whatever the authorities said she must go to London to be with her parents. Mosley rang the Home Office, who to give them their due did give permission. He drove Diana to Rutland Gate Mews where she found David, Sydney, Nancy, Unity and Debo. Mosley himself, knowing he might still be *persona non grata* to David, stayed outside in the car. They all tried as best they could to comfort one another.

Nancy was certainly thinking of Tom when she wrote in

*Madame de Pompadour* of the Comte de Gisors that he was 'one of those almost perfect young men who are so often killed in wars'. To us Tom remains mysterious; we think of him with regret, of course, but also with a curiosity that is unlikely to be satisfied, for he was expert at covering his tracks. What would he have done if he had lived? What would finally have emerged from that excellent mind into which so much knowledge was constantly poured? James Lee-Milne's 'Appreciation' raises these questions: '. . . One sensed that Tom Mitford somehow ploughed a solitary furrow, in that his intellectual pursuits were exclusively his own, and his esoteric deductions often eluded those who most thoroughly sympathized with his searching mind. In this age of discursive reading he would reject almost with contumely the latest books in preference for the driest classics which most of us, who are not scholars, merely take for granted. These he, on the contrary, devoured . . . in order to delve the root of those abstract theories that meant so much to him. His favourite recreation was then to expatiate upon what he had just been reading in his own inimitable phraseology, with precise earnestness and . . . engaging but provocative humour . . .' Lees-Milne implies that Tom's theories, however serious their subject, were at bottom a stately kind of game. Perhaps; to see the cosmos as a gigantic tease, and analyse it as such, would be like a Mitford. But to have given such an impression to his friends could have been a way of concealing some profound belief. All his sisters have been reticent; none, perhaps, has ever displayed her deepest feelings. Nor did their grandfathers, nor did Tom. Lees-Milne also notes his fastidiousness, which showed itself in all sorts of ways, such as his failure to choose a bride and his unwillingness to face the occupation of Germany. Someone less fastidious might have thought it his duty, feeling as he did, to go to Germany and take part in the occupation; to try to mitigate the sufferings it caused, even expose the scandals of cruelty and peculation when he found them. But Tom was not that sort of person. The effort to influence events was, finally, antipathetic to him; there remained the grace to submit to them.

# 38

# Diana, Political Prisoner

As Diana had told Hitler he would, Mosley kept up his unrealistic fight for peace right up to the declaration of war and even after it. It seemed to him that, whether or not his country ended on the winning side, a war against Germany could only be followed by Britain losing power, and accordingly influence. His Fascist movement was a scattered minority, strong only in parts of the East End of London; he had repudiated all the 'old parties', and done so in the offensive terms which were one of his political specialities. He still drew large audiences: as mentioned earlier, twenty thousand people came to hear him at Earl's Court in July 1939, but this achievement, though in its way as spectacular, was also finally as ineffective as his resignation speech of 1931. He had gambled on years of peace, after which there would be his expected slump; during the good years he would educate and build up his party as a political force, financed by his commercial radio, and then the slump would make the non-political mass of the people turn to him. In fact what happened was the converse. During the short period of peace that was available, most politically minded people came to dislike him intensely. When what followed was not a slump but a war with Germany, the masses came to follow the leaders of opinion so that it became not just possible, but politically profitable, for the Churchill government to put him and his supporters arbitrarily into prison.

Mosley's biographer, Robert Skidelsky, points out that in the last months before the war he ought to have condemned Hitler for endangering peace. Following Munich, for instance, the Czechoslovak state more or less dissolved itself; but this should have made it seem not more, but less, necessary for Hitler to move troops into Prague and thus calculatedly slap Chamberlain in the face. As Skidelsky says: 'A consistent and reputable public line . . . would have been to warn Hitler that, while there were powerful forces in England working for peace, the only chance they had to succeed was if Hitler moderated his methods . . . Such a warning would have served the cause of peace better than the policy of continued support for German actions.' Diana has said that in private Mosley was taking exactly this line. Why did he not take it in public? We doubt if it would have averted war, but it would have helped Mosley, countering the idea put about by his opponents, and widely believed, that he was a Nazi puppet. It would have weighed with Norman Birkett's Advisory Committee when they examined him after his arrest in 1940, for in their report they say Mosley had a sympathy with the German government 'which forbade criticism, even of the mildest kind, of any of their worst excesses'. (Quoted Skidelsky, *Sunday Telegraph*, 18 December 1983.) We think that the reason why Mosley did not issue a public warning to Hitler was that he was very consciously a revolutionary. He thought of himself, at all events, as being as revolutionary as Lenin. He despaired of the other parties and despised their leaders. His own party would make a complete break with the past. He once told Jonathan that at this time he intended to forbid his people, when elected to Parliament, all social contact with those in other parties. He had the same suspicion of trans-party socializing and what others see as the civilizing role of Parliament as do the zealots of the modern Labour Party. In Barbara Castle's diaries her expression of disgust at inter-party tributes and ceremonial parliamentary backslapping is very Mosleyite. In any case he wanted to abolish Parliament, the 'talking shop', and replace it with a body of experts, representing people in terms not of their residence but of their occupation, who would know what they were talking about and get things done. It would have gone against the grain to advise his fellow revolutionary, Hitler, to respect the susceptibilities of opponents whom he regarded as second-rate and purblind.

So Mosley did nothing to allay the personal dislike, shading into hatred, that was to make otherwise enlightened people want to clap him in prison without a trial. Skidelsky points out that already by the end of 1936 'all the essential measures required to render him ineffective, in so far as that could be achieved by the fiat of a liberal regime, had been taken'; to do this in four years was not bad going, as Skidelsky comments, for a democracy in peacetime. Why was this? Disapproval of his attacks on the Jews was not the decisive factor; the process started before any such attacks took place. It was because he advocated revolution. Certainly this was to be achieved by purely legal means – victory in a General Election followed by enabling legislation. However, many who liked the existing set-up naturally saw it as a threat – those in the left-wing establishment as well as those in the traditional one. Hitler was achieving his revolution within the law and his example was not exactly encouraging to either. His regime persecuted members of the old order as well as the left: Diana writes to Unity on 31 May 1938 from Berlin that she has been to a tea party where 'there were nothing but princes and princesses and the conversation more or less ran on various relations who were in jail'. It is no wonder that many of their English equivalents wondered what might happen under Mosley and felt that it made little difference whether he obtained power legally or not. (The Chilean middle class were to feel much the same during Salvador Allende's abortive revolution, which also started in a legal way.) These fears eventually led the British talking classes to regard Mosley as a pariah. All the same, when war did break out Mosley behaved impeccably. He told his members: 'Our country is involved in war. Therefore I ask you to do nothing to injure our country, or to help any other Power. Our members should do what the law requires of them, and, if they are members of the Forces or Services of the Crown, they should obey their orders . . . But I ask all members who are free to carry on our work to take every opportunity to awaken the people and to demand peace.' More picturesquely, Mosley used sometimes to say that if one's old mother picked an unnecessary quarrel in a pub and got into a brawl, one would defend her as well as trying to extract her from it. The trouble is, of course, that the very fact of being in a war can make people come to see patriotism as equivalent to the will to win that particular war. In the case of the Second World War this effect was very marked indeed. Mosley's message on the outbreak of war is generally ignored, as is his stronger one on 9 May 1940: 'In the event of an invasion every member of British Union would be at the disposal of the nation. Everyone would resist the foreign invasion with all that is in us.'

Until the fall of France, during the months of 'phoney war', Mosley argued that, pending a negotiated peace, Britain and France should fight purely defensively. So they did, of course, because they could do little else. Had Hitler held off from attacking the West, the war might have ended through sheer inactivity. Skidelsky (p. 462, footnote) quotes Mass Observation as saying that during this time 'there was little support for the punishment of Mosley'. But then Hitler invaded and conquered France. As soon as his invasion of France began to succeed, opinion precipitated the replacement of Chamberlain and his Conservative government by Churchill as Prime Minister of an all-party coalition, and it made the mass of the British people for the first time seriously frightened. There is a view that Hitler ordered his generals not to destroy the British Army before Dunkirk; if this is so, it went quite unnoticed by the British. Hitler did then make Churchill a surprisingly favourable peace offer, but Churchill, supported by most of the country, turned this down out of hand; it would, as he pointed out in *The Second World War*, have meant accepting the actions against which Britain had gone to war.

One of the first results of the change of mood was that Mosley was put into prison. Defence Regulation 18b providing for administrative arrest had been in force since just before the outbreak of war, but it was not phrased in such a way as to include members of the British Union of Fascists purely as such. The government hurriedly widened its scope, and arrested Mosley and a number of others on 23 May 1940. Mosley's supporters were not the only people arrested; also imprisoned were an MP, Captain Ramsay, and a retired admiral, Sir Barry Domvile. On the day after Mosley's arrest Mass Observation took a snap poll, whose conclusions were (quoted from Skidelsky): '(1) Very seldom have observers found such a high degree of approval for anything, (2) some people, however, objected to a person being arrested for what he might do rather than what he had done, (3) the commonest comment was that it should have been done a long time ago, and a great many people mentioned this spontaneously.' This reaction was not confined to the populace; in his diary the top civil servant, Sir Alexander Cadogan, greets Mosley's arrest with a laconic 'About time too.' Hitler had finally sunk Mosley.

Mosley and Diana had given up Wootton Lodge in March 1940 and moved into his house, Savehay Farm, at Denham in Buckinghamshire. Diana gave birth to Max, her fourth and youngest son, on 13 April. On the morning of 23 May she drove to London with her husband; they had a small flat in Dolphin Square, and just outside that early high-rise development she saw a group of men waiting who were clearly plain-clothes police. 'Look, coppers,' she said. As soon as Mosley got out of his car one of them produced a warrant for his arrest. It turned out that all the staff of the BUF headquarters had been arrested as well. Diana returned to Denham, and a posse of police arrived to search the rambling house; they did not seem to know what they were supposed to be looking for. Mosley was taken to Brixton Prison, where his cell was full of bedbugs and the shaving arrangements were so insanitary that he grew a beard. Diana visited him next day, and he asked her to get hold of a solicitor. This proved rather difficult: none of those with whom Mosley had previously dealt dared to act for him now. Diana's own solicitor put her on to Oswald Hickson, who was to act for them for the next few years.

There was an extraordinary atmosphere at this time, with Hitler's army racing through France. Lord Berners came once to Denham to spend the day with Diana, and told her that at Oxford, where he was living at the time, various dons had advised him that contact with Diana was dangerous. He had of course disregarded them, but he had other fears; he talked of getting some poison for himself in case he was mutilated in an air raid. He was deeply pessimistic, and thought that the war would destroy all the amenities that made life worth living. Diana tells us that his remarks to her were almost word for word those of the character Lord FitzCricket in his novel *Far From the Madding War*.

It is clear from the recently released Home Office records known as the Mosley Papers that Diana was only kept at liberty, during these weeks, so that she could be watched; Sir John Anderson, the Home Secretary, made arrangements for her telephone to be tapped, her letters opened and her movements monitored. She did make a few administrative arrangements for Mosley, paying the wages of his remaining headquarters staff.

The BUF was not yet banned, so there was nothing unlawful about this. In the meantime pressure built up for her own arrest. The word that keeps recurring is 'dangerous'. Nancy, as we have already mentioned, told Gladwyn Jebb that her sister was dangerous. The Oxford dons told Lord Berners that it was dangerous to visit her. Lord Moyne, Bryan's father, wrote to Lord Swinton to make him aware of 'the extremely dangerous character of my former daughter-in-law, now Lady Mosley'. He enclosed a two-page memorandum based on a conversation he had had with Jean Gillies, Jonathan and Desmond's governess, giving opinions which she claimed to have heard Diana express, together with a partial list of her visits to Germany. Swinton, the recipient of this missive, chaired a committee dealing with these matters called the Security Executive, a Court of Star Chamber so secret that the government even now persists in forbidding disclosure of its files. The reason we know about Moyne's letter is that Swinton thought it important enough to send a copy straight on to Sir Alexander Maxwell of the Home Office. Swinton's accompanying note, dated 26 June 1940, says that Moyne's letter 'confirms information given me very confidentially yesterday, by another member of the family who said that they regarded Lady Mosley as at least as dangerous as her husband . . . that she had been much closer to Hitler than Mosley had ever been'. We need not assume that the unnamed member of the family was Nancy: it might have been one of several who took this view. The button was finally pressed by Brigadier Harker, acting head of MI5 and a member of Swinton's Security Executive, who wrote to Maxwell on the twenty-seventh: 'In view of present circumstances I do feel very strongly that this extremely dangerous and sinister young woman should be detained at the earliest possible moment.' At the same time Harker filed his official recommendation for Diana's detention. Under 'remarks' on this form Harker said that Diana had been 'the principal channel of communication between Mosley and Hitler'. She had been concerned in the wireless project from which 'all the profits were to go to Mosley' and he was to bear none of the risk; this was wrong because the Germans, in fact, were to receive more than half the profits. But the advantage of being in Harker's position is that one's statements remain secret and cannot be queried. His 'remarks' continue: 'Unity Mitford, whose friendship with Hitler, Streicher and such persons and whose enthusiasm for the Nazi cause are notorious, is described by Mosley as "my wife's favourite sister". It must be assumed that Lady Mosley approved of Miss Mitford's disloyal proceedings.' Harker concludes that, since Mosley's arrest, Diana has been acting as a link between Mosley and members of the BUF still at liberty. It was all rather insubstantial, and Maxwell vacillated a little; on the same day he minuted:

In view of the information that Lady Mosley is acting as a liaison between the leaders in prison and the movement outside, it would be justifiable to make an order for her detention . . . As, however, Sir Oswald's case is to be heard by the Advisory Committee on Monday and Tuesday next, I think it would be right to suspend action as regards Lady Mosley till we get the report of the Committee.

But the Home Secretary, to whom he spoke later that day, told him the order should be made at once.

This puts into perspective various speculations which have been made about the arrests under Regulation 18b. Some have thought that the Labour leaders insisted on them as a condition of joining Churchill's coalition. If so they were pushing against an open door. The national panic in our 'finest hour' can be ascribed to the crumbling of certainties since the time of Bertie and Thomas. Nothing of the kind would have occurred in their day, or before. Napoleon had been as menacing as Hitler, but nobody dreamed of putting Charles James Fox in prison or insinuating that his campaign for peace covered an intention to betray his country.

So on 29 June this dangerous and sinister young woman, having breast-fed Max, put him into his pram in the sunny garden at Denham. The policewoman who arrested her advised her to bring enough clothes for the weekend; this seemed to indicate that she was being taken in perhaps for interrogation, and would be released in a day or two. She therefore decided not to take the baby with her but to keep her milk going with a breast pump while she was away. This caused her a good deal of discomfort that turned out to be for nothing, for she was in fact to be kept in prison for nearly three and a half years, a period that, as will be seen later, could easily have been extended to five. Those of her children, and of Mosley's, who were at school and being told that habeas corpus and the right to a trial were features of the British system, received rather a special impression. It was, though, perhaps rather salutary to learn the true relation between words and facts, between pretensions and actions: to learn to count the spoons when pompous men talk of their honour.

Diana was taken to Holloway, where she was evidently not expected; she was left in a broom cupboard known as 'Reception' for four and a half hours. Fortunately she had a book with her, having snatched up a pocket edition of Strachey's *Elizabeth and Essex* as she left Denham. After a couple of hours she was given a mug of tea which looked like soup, and a large sandwich; she did not feel like touching either. Finally she was taken to a woman doctor with dyed hair and long red fingernails. Not liking the look of the doctor, Diana told her she could look after herself despite having been nursing the baby, also that she had already had a bath. Then a wardress took her to F wing, motioning her to go first, for wardresses must always have their prisoners in front of them. Diana continues the story: 'Dozens of women, many of them in dressing gowns, were standing about in groups, most had mugs in their hands. I didn't know it, but it was ten minutes before they were due to be locked in their cells for the night and for this reason they were all on the landings. They crowded round me with kind expressions of sympathy; they knew I had left a little baby and were furious on my behalf.' They were members of the BUF, of all ages and types. Diana knew few of them, since her work on behalf of Mosley had been concerned with his radio project. Nevertheless many of them were to become her great friends, and all were very kind to her for the sake of Mosley, whom they idolized.

In most respects conditions seem to have been worse than Mosley's at Brixton, though at least Diana had no bedbugs. For her first night she was put in a basement cell, its window entirely obscured by sandbags, with a wet floor on which lay a thin and lumpy mattress. She was in pain; she never even took her clothes off, and was unable to sleep. Dawn did not penetrate the sandbags, but finally a wardress came and unlocked the cell, shouting 'Are you all right?' before passing on to the next. This was the only moment of the day, as Diana was to discover, when it was in order to ask to see the governor, or a doctor.

The kind Fascist women came and offered her biscuits and

cocoa; she did not want to eat or drink, but the human contact was a comfort. Fortunately she was moved from the particularly vile cell in which she spent her first night to a rather better one in E wing, where besides British Fascists there were women of German and Italian origin arrested under 18b: they were mostly married to British men and therefore not enemy aliens. She made friends with some of them; one was an unfortunate German Jewess who had done a spell in Dachau, which before the war was not the hell-hole it later became. She complained that Holloway was dirtier. The dirt was what Diana minded most; it came as a surprise to her. It made her glad that she had not brought Max, but worried about herself in case in her condition she caught an infection. The second unpleasantness was the food. This is her description of her first 'dinner':

I was given a pat of margarine, some sugar in a pot and a bit of bread; also a revolting greasy metal container in two parts. The upper part had some small black potatoes with traces of earth upon their wrinkled skins and some yellowish straw-like strings which had probably once been a very old cabbage. When I lifted this tray and looked beneath, the gorge rose; oily greyish water in which swam a few bits of darker grey gristle and meat. The margarine had an exceptionally disgusting taste, as I quickly discovered. I ate the bread and some sugar on it.

The prison food never became any better, except when there was bully beef, which Diana liked. Fortunately Diana and the others were allowed food parcels, and despite wartime shortages something was always available. The parcels took a long time to get through the prison administration, but eventually they did come. Mosley sent her in some Stilton cheese, and for a time she lived mostly on prison bread and his Stilton, becoming quite thin on this diet, which was sometimes supplemented with a little port. She soon became well in herself, even though it became apparent that she was inside for much longer than the weekend mentioned by the policewoman who had arrested her. She was sustained by anger. Solzhenitsyn describes a prisoner in the *Gulag Archipelago* who was such a convinced anti-Communist that he actually throve on the dreadful conditions in his camp; of course, he would say, this is how I've always said Communists would behave. I'm proved right! Diana's attitude to the politicians who had locked her up, the 'old gang' as Mosley called them, was similar. She had always known that they were vile hypocrites – now they had proved her point. She was also, eventually, cheered up by the solicitude of her non-political friends. Four of them wrote to her on the very day she was arrested: Lord Berners, Robert Heber-Percy, Henry Yorke and Lady Mary Dunn, Hamish Erskine's sister. Others wrote later. She did not receive these letters for some months, because at first she was only allowed to send and receive two letters a week, and she gave priority to those giving news of her children. Lord Berners wrote:

Are you burrowing a passage under your cell with a teaspoon? Shall I send you a tiny file hidden in a peach? But you might break your teeth on it, so I'd better not. And I don't suppose this kind of joke will appeal to the prison censor's sense of humour. It would be awful if this laborious typewritten effort of mine was suppressed . . . How do you spend your time when you're not picking oakum? (Prisoners who have been at Oxford call it 'sporting their oakum' I believe.) Are you constructing a philosophy of life? or learning the Bible by heart? or taming a spider?

He was evidently right about the prison censor; this letter arrived riddled with pinholes. Probably it had been to the Home Office and to MI5.

Sydney and Pam used to visit Diana in the early months; she asked them to bring her woollen clothes and hot water bottles, even though it was summer. In due course most of the family visited her, including Nancy, Unity and Debo, and from an early date Jonathan and Desmond. Twenty minutes was the time allowed. Visitors would be first shown to a waiting room near the main gate. The yellow walls and benches resembled those in waiting rooms everywhere, though in a station there would have been graffiti, and in a hospital some dog-eared magazines. There were one or two other people there, women in headscarves and sad, shapeless clothes, sometimes a disconsolate soldier. Nobody talked much. In due course one would be escorted through a yard to a similar, smaller, room where Diana would appear. She looked much as usual, though the absence of make-up made her seem rather washed out and insubstantial. A wardress would sit there; her presence did not seem to matter. In any case Jonathan was later to make friends with several of the wardresses. Everyone chatted quite cheerfully and normally; Jonathan does not remember these first occasions as poignant, though he was sorry when the twenty minutes was up. It was all part of the war: mother in prison, father away in the Army, no sweets, food on the ration, gas mask.

Not long after the arrests under Regulation 18b, the government appointed an Advisory Committee to examine the cases. Mosley appeared before this committee on five occasions in July 1940. The chairman was Norman Birkett, KG, who was later to be one of the British judges at Nuremberg. The Advisory Committee chairmanship may have given this prominent barrister some practice at administering *ad hoc* decrees as if they were law, for Birkett never suggested that Mosley had behaved illegally; his interrogation dealt with how far Mosley had been friendly with Germany and Italy, and also, even less relevantly, with what he intended to do if in power. Birkett tried to get Mosley to admit that his movement had received money from Mussolini; he pressed Mosley on the radio concession, and asked if Diana had been a help. Mosley said her friendship with Hitler had opened doors, since she was one of the three women Hitler most respected in the world, the others being Winifred Wagner and Magda Goebbels. This claim can hardly have been helpful to Diana in the context; Mosley did, however, distinguish her from Unity, who he said had caused embarrassment. Birkett examined Mosley on his dislike of the Jews and on his hope that, if he gained power, opposition would 'fade away'. On both these points Birkett was effective in terms of political debate. However, the matter at issue was not whether Mosley ought to be in power, but whether he ought to be in prison. On this, Mosley said there seemed to be two reasons to keep him in; that he might betray his country, or that his campaign for a negotiated peace was damaging. Birkett said that for him personally the second point was the decisive one, for which Mosley thanked him. This was the line the committee followed in their report to the Home Secretary; they recommended that he be kept inside because his propaganda had harmed the war effort and he might continue it. There was no mention that he might commit treason, but also no thought of releasing him on condition that he did not renew his peace campaign.

The Advisory Committee did not examine Diana till the autumn, because the house where it met was bombed. In the end she was taken to the Berystede Hotel at Ascot. It seemed to her a waste of time, because Mosley had seen the committee in July and no attention had been paid. But she looked forward to it as an outing, and hoped at least for a good lunch.

Birkett's companions were an elderly magistrate called Sir Arthur Hazlerigg, and Sir George Clerk, a diplomat. Clerk had been ambassador to Constantinople when Diana and Bryan had visited Turkey in 1930; they had lunched at his embassy.

The hearing lasted about an hour; much of it concerned her visits to Germany and her friendship with the Nazi leaders. She was a Fascist, she said; Mosley had converted her. Birkett asked her about her visits to Rome in 1933 and 1934, when she stayed with Lord Berners: this was a red herring, and seems to have been accepted as such. The incident in Hyde Park in October 1935 was mentioned, when Diana had voted against trade sanctions against Germany. Why had she given the Fascist salute when the National Anthem was played? 'It was a demonstration against the meeting,' she replied. 'They put this vote to boycott German goods, which seemed to me the most ridiculous idea I ever heard of.' Birkett asked why she had been married in Germany. 'Because we wished to keep the marriage secret.' Why was Hitler present? 'Because he is a friend of mine.' Was he still a friend of hers now that he was bombing London? 'It is frightful. That is why we have always been for peace.' Would she welcome Hitler if he invaded Britain? 'I can never live if England has been conquered.' But she felt she would like to replace the British political system by the German one, 'because we think it has done well for that country'.

Birkett asked how well she knew the other Nazi leaders. She answered that she knew Goering and Hess, had met Himmler once and liked him, but had not asked him about the activities of the Gestapo. Goebbels, whom Diana knew better than most of the others, was oddly enough not mentioned; but Sir George Clerk brought in Streicher. Diana replied: 'He is a very simple little fellow, quite uneducated.' His *Stürmer* was amusing as pornography, but 'nonsense from beginning to end', and Streicher had very little influence.

Birkett asked if Diana agreed with the Nazi policy on Jews, and she replied: 'Up to a point I do. I am not fond of Jews.' Had she heard of atrocities committed against Jews? 'I saw the book called the *Brown Book of the Hitler Terror*, but I did not pay much attention to it.'

Birkett took Diana through the story of the radio concession. 'It is quite plain, is it not, that it was your friendship with Hitler that obtained that?' Diana denied this. She had first gone to Goering and pointed out to him that to give one of Germany's wavelengths for this purpose would be a way of earning foreign exchange. He had liked the idea and gone to the Post Office, who had turned it down. Then she had gone to Hitler who had said yes. 'That was a very great favour,' said Birkett. Diana disagreed. The French had done the same because they thought it was good business; Hitler had followed the same reasoning.

Diana expressed the view that Hitler should have been left alone in Eastern Europe: Austria had been 'longing' for the Anschluss, Hitler was right to take the Sudetenland and had only taken the rest of Czechoslovakia at the Czechs' request, to stop a revolution. Danzig needed to be settled and the Poles were only difficult because Britain and France had guaranteed them. Hitler was friendly to the British, at least until they declared war on him. Sir Arthur Hazlerigg asked how Hitler could admire Britain, considering it was a democratic country? For the qualities, said Diana, which made the British go out and make the Empire.

Diana told Birkett that she had last seen Hitler at Bayreuth, about a month before war broke out. 'Did you tell him then that there was no doubt war was coming?' Birkett asked.

'No. He told me.' She had never hidden from Hitler the fact that there were powerful influences in Britain making for war. But even now she felt Britain could end the war by a negotiated peace, and not lose the Empire.

She had talked to Hitler about Churchill and other anti-appeasement politicians. 'I remember him asking me about Winston . . . I always said he was an extremely clever man and a great patriot according to his own lights . . . in quite a different category from Duff Cooper or Eden.' She had once told Hitler about Churchill and his campaign for rearmament, and Hitler had said he was the German Churchill. Churchill, said Diana, was fascinated by war and his ancestor Marlborough. He envied Hitler.

'The last time I saw [Churchill] he wanted to hear about him. I think he felt to himself, "If only I had a chance like that." '

Sir George Clerk asked: 'You do not think he, as it were, seized this crisis?'

'No,' conceded Diana. 'I do not think he is wicked in that sense. I think he is a patriot. In a way I think he longed for war, but he did not want to bring it about.'

At one point Birkett said that Diana was answering him intelligently. This nettled her: 'You are being sarcastic,' she snapped. Hazlerigg made the chivalrous gesture of sending her half a bottle of claret with his compliments for lunch; she shared it with the wardress who was accompanying her. But the committee's recommendation was unanimous; jointly and severally, Birkett, Clerk and Hazlerigg recommended that she be kept inside.

Diana's next outing was to court; it was a happy occasion because she saw Mosley, for the first time since they were arrested. They were not, of course, in the dock; they were plaintiffs in a libel action.

The popular press, or sections of it, had been behaving towards the Mosleys and other detainees with a viciousness that is at this distance of time hard to credit. There was a piece in the *Daily Mirror* after Diana's arrest, asking why she had at first been allowed at liberty with her baby. 'Does the law act with such delicacy to ordinary women delinquents? It does not. Regardless of their unborn children, women convicted of serious offences get clapped behind bars with abrupt and impolite speed.' The clear implication that Diana was a delinquent, the placing of her in the same category as people convicted of serious offences, was of course a libel.

There were also several stories saying that the Mosleys were living a life of luxury in gaol. The *Sunday Pictorial* on 4 August 1940 said of Mosley in the usual repellent journalese:

Every morning his paid batman delivers three newspapers at the door of his master's cell. Breakfast, dinner, and tea arrive by car . . . Mosley fortifies himself with alternative bottles of red and white wine daily. He calls occasionally for a bottle of champagne . . . He selects a different smartly cut lounge suit every week. His shirts and silk underwear are laundered in Mayfair.

Bearded and undernourished in his oldest corduroys, locked in his bugridden cell for twenty-one hours out of every twenty-four, Mosley found this rather too much. The court took the same view, and found for the Mosleys against the *Sunday Pictorial* and the other newspapers which had written on these lines. The newspapers were made to pay damages: Diana commissioned Sydney to buy with her share a fur coat which she wore all day and put on her bed at night.

Diana adapted to prison life in her own way. She became fond of some of her fellow inmates, who were on the whole, of course, of her political persuasion. With some of the wardresses she had an uncertain start; their view of her was probably conditioned by what they had read. This did not last long. She soon got on well with most of them and particularly liked at least three. Dear, plump Miss Davies was perhaps her favourite, and not far behind came Miss Andrews and Miss Baxter; they were kind people who helped everybody as much as they could, within the limits of the system. Dr Charity Taylor, who looked after Diana once when she was ill, is also remembered kindly by her. With the governor, a rather dour Scotsman called Dr Matheson, her relations were no more than correct. Jonathan came to like him rather more than she did: Dr Matheson was always willing to talk about illness and the workings of the body, and medicine was at this time Jonathan's consuming interest. Diana used to enjoy the prison vocabulary. Reception, for instance, had nothing to do with diplomatic cocktail parties, but meant the introductory broom cupboard. Going to court did not mean Buckingham Palace. Going to Ascot meant not the race meeting, but the Advisory Committee. Garden party meant a group of convicts digging in the prison vegetable garden.

Diana's worst time in the prison came when a bomb, falling nearby, broke the water mains. The lavatories became choked up, their floors awash with urine. Each prisoner was allowed half a pint of water; Diana tried to wash in hers, but it did no good. On the second night there was the sound of repeated vomiting; thirteen women, who had eaten the prison stew, had food poisoning because washing up was impossible. When they were taken to the yard for exercise on the first day there was a rush for the outdoor lavatories; Diana went to one with a red V on the door, which she found fairly clean. What she did not know was the meaning of the V – it was reserved for women with venereal disease. Diana was none the worse; few people really catch these maladies from a lavatory seat.

The mains were repaired after two days, but it happened that on the first of these waterless days Diana saw her lawyer, Oswald Hickson. The report of this visit appears to be missing from the Home Office file, but according to *A Life of Contrasts* Diana asked Hickson to warn the Home Office that unless something was done about the sanitation there would be hundreds of sick women.

Mr Hickson said: 'Don't you know anyone in the government I could appeal to for you?'

'*Know* anyone in the government?' cried Diana. 'I know *all* the Tories beginning with Churchill. The whole lot deserve to be shot!'

News of this remark reached Churchill, through channels, from the listening wardress. He was curiously pained by it; like many prominent politicians he combined egotism with sensitivity. He showed egotism in supposing that someone treated as his government was treating Diana would think of him in any other way, but he showed sensitivity, of a kind, in minding this. Years later that remark led to a kind of reconciliation between Diana and Churchill.

Even at the time it may at least have helped to remind him of her existence, for it was not long afterwards that he began pressing the Home Secretary to alleviate some of the conditions under which political prisoners were held. Mosley had already secured freedom of association for them; the initial practice of locking them in their cells for twenty-one hours a day was against administrative rules, and he had threatened to sue the Brixton governor. But the Home Secretary was now Herbert Morrison, a leading Labour politician who disliked Mosley and did his best to block Churchill's suggestions. Morrison was also pressed in Parliament by a small number of decent and independent-minded members, especially Richard Stokes, Labour member for Ipswich, and Irving Albery, Conservative member for Gravesend. Morrison would in effect tell them that there was a war on, exactly like some shopkeeper delighted that the customer, for the duration, was now wrong.

He was less able to ignore a minute from Churchill on 22 December, quoted by Skidelsky.

Would it be very wrong to allow a bath every day? What facilities are there for regular exercise and games and recreation under Rule 8? If the correspondence is censored, as it must be, I do not see any reason why it should be limited to two letters a week. What literature is allowed? Are newspapers allowed? What are the regulations about paper and ink and for writing books or studying particular questions? Are they allowed to have a wireless set? What arrangements are permitted to husbands and wives to see each other, and what arrangements have been made for Mosley's wife to see her baby, from whom she was taken before it was weaned?

After this Dr Matheson summoned Diana and told her that the government had said she was to have a bath every day. She had to refuse. There were only two bathrooms in the prison wing and enough water in the boiler for four baths; prisoners had baths about once a week. Diana could not hog a bathroom every day and make baths for everyone else even rarer. A little later the rule allowing two letters a week was relaxed, and Diana received her letters from the previous summer. Visits from Mosley also took place, once a fortnight, beginning in the spring of 1941. He would come in a police car with Admiral Sir Barry Domvile, whose wife was also in Holloway. Max also came for the first time since Diana's arrest.

Some of the wardresses' reports of visits by various people to Diana are quite interesting, though they give a strange impression because Diana's own phraseology is quite unpredictably mixed up with that of the wardresses. On one occasion she is supposed to have said she had four 'kiddies', which we do not believe; on the other hand the word 'sweet' often occurs. On 5 December 1941 she was visited by Sydney and Unity.

Lady Redesdale spoke of . . . how upset they all are at [Esmond Romilly] being missing. Lady Mosley said 'I have never seen him of course, he refuses ever to meet Bobo and Kit or I, but of course I am very sorry because poor little [Decca] was so fond of him. Did he come down in the sea?' Miss Mitford said, 'He came down on Berlin so there may be hopes for him.' Miss Mitford laughed for some time after this . . . The conversations at this visit were very difficult to follow as Miss Mitford was very excited and spoke very quickly, and laughed a lot.

Esmond Romilly's name is given as Des Donnelly, and Decca's as Betty. Kit was Diana's nickname for Mosley.

Diana's relationship with Decca has not been symmetrical. Whereas Decca publicly asked for Diana to be put back into prison, refers to her in bitterly hostile terms in correspondence and clearly shows antagonism in her books, Diana's references to Decca are affectionate, if sometimes pained. On 14 August 1943 she wrote to Sydney from Holloway about Decca's second marriage: 'How simply thrilling about Decca, I do hope he is nice enough, she would be a perfect wife . . . Do you think I could write her a line, I never *do* but would love her to know how much I wish her every possible happiness.'

It was Tom who seems to have secured the decisive improvement in the Mosleys' conditions. On leave from the Army, he visited both Mosley and Diana on the same day. He was dining with Churchill that night at Downing Street, and asked both of them if there was anything he could pass on to the Prime Minister.

'Only the same as always,' answered Diana. 'If we have to stay in prison, couldn't we at least be together?'

Mosley had said the same thing, and Tom passed it on. Diana was not very hopeful; she and Mosley had often asked this and always been told it was impossible. Morrison did indeed resist, but Churchill kept at him until he gave in.

Dr Matheson sulked. 'You are under the cabinet now,' he grunted at Diana.

The Preventive Detention Block at Holloway was set aside for the Mosleys and the three other married couples who were still held under 18b; the Domviles, among many others, had by then been released. So, soon, were two of the other couples, leaving Major and Mrs de Laessoe as the only others to share the block. Each couple had what was in effect a small flat consisting of three cells, kitchen and bathroom. In the Mosleys' case the newspapers, still on the lookout for luxury, christened this a suite, so that their readers should think of the Dorchester. This it was not, but nevertheless it was far better than what had gone before. There were other improvements. Instead of being given food cooked in the prison kitchens, they were given the rations from which it was made. These turned out to be unexpectedly wholesome. There was a garden, in which Mosley and Major de Laessoe grew vegetables, including unusual ones like kohlrabi and pea-beans. The authorities even sent two convicts to swab the staircase. 'I'm sending sex offenders,' said Miss Davies; 'they are clean and honest.'

Jonathan and Desmond were now allowed to visit for a whole day, as were Vivien, Nicholas and Michael, Mosley's children by his first marriage. Alexander and Max were allowed to spend the night.

Jonathan remembers these visits clearly. Diana would cook a lunch that seemed worthy of Boulestin. No doubt she put her best foot forward; Mosley would pretend that 'old Sproots', as he called himself in his gardening persona, got his only meal of the month when the young gentlemen came. There would be endless jokes. Mosley would teach the boys what are now known as rugby songs, to Diana's pretended displeasure; he would then quote Robert Walpole as saying he always talked bawdy, then everyone could understand. But he also talked seriously; in his way he was a real educator, and at the age of twelve Jonathan was just beginning to appreciate this. Mosley had learnt German in Brixton, and the German love of the classical world encouraged him to revive the dim memories of Greece and Rome that remained from his Winchester schooldays. He would talk at length about the ancients, especially his hero Julius Caesar, enlivening for his listeners the academic classical education which they were undergoing in their turn. Nicholas, more of an age to appreciate his conversation, remembers talking with his father about Nietzsche and Goethe. Sometimes Dr Matheson would turn up; he was more genial now. On one of Nicholas's visits he caught them all with some brandy which Nicholas had brought in his pocket; he had come to say that Nicholas had outstayed his time, but stayed to accept a glass. To Jonathan he would explain the functions of the thyroid or pancreas. A wardress would escort visitors to and from the block, and stay chatting for a bit. When Miss Davies escorted visitors away in the evening, she would ask Mosley to come too, because the way back led past the condemned cell. She remembered the execution of Mrs Thomson, who in a celebrated case of the twenties had induced her lover to murder her husband; from the time her appeal was rejected to the moment of her death, Mrs Thomson had never stopped screaming. So Miss Davies, the escorter, had to be escorted.

The Mosleys were kept in this place, which following Solzhenitsyn one might describe as the First Circle, for two further years. During the second winter Diana became very ill with dysentery. She refused to go to the prison hospital; Miss Davies, later, said that she had been right. 'It's not so much the hospital,' she said. 'It's the people in it.'

Eventually, in 1943, Mosley contracted phlebitis in the leg which had been injured in the First World War. He had had attacks before, but this was the worst. He became skeletally thin. Diana was seriously worried about him, and various doctors came to examine him. She also sent Sydney to see Clementine Churchill so that the Prime Minister should know what the situation was; rather reluctantly Sydney went. Clementine's attitude was indeed rather irritating. She had been a bridesmaid at Sydney's wedding; now she needled Sydney with a false graciousness.

'Winston has always been so fond of Diana,' she assured her, adding that the Mosleys were better off inside; if they were released people might attack them.

What turned the trick was not this approach but a report by five doctors dated 9 November. It was signed by Mosley's own doctor, Dr Geoffrey Evans, and Lord Dawson of Penn, the King's doctor; three prison doctors noted their concurrence. They said that if Mosley remained in prison he would suffer permanent damage to his health, and he might even die. This was enough to frighten even Morrison; it was one thing to keep Mosley in prison, but if he should die there it would be quite another. He might become a martyr. Even if the worst did not happen, any subsequent ill health, given this report, could be blamed on his imprisonment. The game was obviously up. Most of the political prisoners had in fact already been released. The de Laessoes went at the same time as the Mosleys; no doubt, as Diana says, so that the Preventive Detention Block should be emptied.

Rather oddly, the release was announced to the public before the Mosleys came to hear of it. Miss Baxter heard it on the wireless, and it was she who told Diana, tearful with excitement. They hugged each other, and Diana ran to tell Mosley. In due course the governor turned up and gave them details. It was only a release at all in the sense that they were to leave Holloway. They must not be in London, they must go somewhere approved by the Home Office, they must not have a car or travel about without permission more than seven miles, they must not talk to the press or to their political associates, they must be accompanied by a policeman. The first difficulty concerned where they could go; their flat was in London, and the house at Denham requisitioned by the War Office. They asked Pam and Derek if they could come to Rignell, and they at once agreed.

The press gathered round the main gate in great force and manned the place day and night. The Mosleys were kept in prison two further days, and finally smuggled out of a back gate before dawn and driven straight to Rignell in two police cars.

Most of the newspapers fumed about the release, led of course by the *Daily Worker* who said that Diana at any rate should be put straight back as she was in rude health. Commander Oliver Locker-Lampson was a Conservative Member of Parliament who had never forgiven Mosley for once, years before, making a fool of him in a debate; he suggested in Parliament that Diana should be examined for phlebitis. The Communist Party, and sections of the trade union movement, organized demonstrations against the release; Decca, far away in California, added her voice to the chorus. So did Nancy, but involuntarily. She became caught up in a demonstration outside an underground station; 'Put him back!' people were chanting. She found she had to join in so as to get to the station. Most people disapproved of the release at the time; Skidelsky quotes three Mass Observation opinion polls which averaged 77 per cent against and 9 per cent in favour. Bernard Shaw and Nancy Astor were two public figures who took a different view. Shaw said: 'I think this Mosley panic shameful . . . It was high time to release him with apologies for having let him frighten us into scrapping the Habeas Corpus Act.' Lady Astor, confronted by a trade union delegation, referred back to the Nazi-Soviet pact: 'You're the same lot as stabbed us in the back in 1939.'

At Rignell the Mosleys found affection and comfort. Mosley stayed in bed, and Diana mostly indoors, not too miserable on behalf of the journalists who were lying in wait for them, in the raw December weather, behind every bush. The cold did not inhibit their inventiveness: Rignell became a mansion, and Pam's dachshunds were magnified into baying hounds. Such trivialities were virtually all they could get, for a condition of the Mosleys' release; as just mentioned, was that they should not speak to reporters. But they were not allowed to stay with Pam for long. Someone in the Home Office discovered that Derek was doing secret scientific work; it would never do for Mosley to be in his house.

It looked rather odd, though. Birkett's Advisory Committee had kept Mosley in prison not because he might spy against his country, but to stop him campaigning for peace. Birkett himself had said as much. The implication that he might pass secret information to the enemy was completely new; it was never even formulated as an allegation. It was nevertheless acted on, which shows that when the values of the open society are abandoned one casualty is a certain mental discipline. In any case Derek's research was recondite, and took place in an Oxford laboratory to which Mosley did not have access. If Derek had taken papers home, Mosley could not have understood them. He was also so closely supervised that his only means of communicating with Germany would have been telepathy. Probably the trouble was that Morrison was feeling sore. He hated Mosley; he had let him out because the doctors' report had forced his hand, but we need not suppose he enjoyed it. Nor did he like having to defend the release by using the same libertarian arguments he had blocked when Richard Stokes and others had employed them against the imprisonment. Here was an opportunity to show that he would stand no nonsense.

Diana was rather missed at Holloway. Years later Debo's sister-in-law, Lady Anne Tree, became a prison visitor and came to know Miss Davies, who told her: 'We've never had such laughs since Lady Mosley left.'

Obliged to leave Rignell, the Mosleys first found a rather odd resting place – a half disused pub called the Shaven Crown, at Shipton-under-Wychwood in Oxfordshire. It was a pleasant

Tudor building of weathered Cotswold stone in the main street of the village, and shut up for the duration except for one bar which for some reason was officially placed out of bounds to the Mosleys. They rented the rest and moved in there with Alexander and Max, and faithful Nanny Higgs.

Life was not easy. Diana had to do the cooking and housework. Everyone was obsessed with food; in this regard things were more difficult than when they had been in prison, despite occasional presents of eggs from Sydney, or from the local doctor. When Unity's beloved dachshund was drowned in the River Windrush, Diana came in and said there was terrible news. 'What?' said Desmond. 'No sausages at Hammett's?' To make things worse all four boys, one after the other, got whooping cough. Lord Berners came to stay; he cheered everybody up, but Diana felt she was not making him comfortable.

However, the domestic problem was solved in due course by the continuing hostility of the newspapers. There were gloating pieces about the Mosleys' discomfort, and a picture of Mosley carrying coal for the boiler. The curious result of this was that a very large number of people wrote offering their services. After sifting through the letters, Diana decided to take up two of them. One lady turned out not to be of much use; an overweight, sallow person with dark rims round her melancholy eyes and a trembling, ladylike voice. She did very little except, occasionally, a little sewing; finally she left in high dudgeon after threatening to expose the Mosleys in a novel. 'The thing is,' Diana told Jonathan afterwards, 'her letter was so intelligent.' But the other letter selected was from Mrs Nelson, a former cook of Lord Berners who remembered Diana from when she used to stay in his house in Halkin Street. She came with her husband and stayed several months, seeing the Mosleys into their next house.

This was Crux Easton, between Newbury and Andover, a rambling brick-built house with a magnificent view out over Hampshire. Diana had to have special permission from the Chief Constable of Oxfordshire to go and see it; she went accompanied by two policemen, and lunched on the way at Faringdon with Lord Berners who remarked: 'You are the only person who still has a driver and a footman on the box.' Crux Easton had eight acres and a resident gardener; the Mosleys bought a cow and chickens. They were not allowed a car, but would go bicycling around the undulating roads. '*Herrschaften!*' (gentry), Diana would remark, as they passed some particularly trim house; Mosley claimed to find this embarrassing.

Friends and family came to stay: Sydney, Nancy, Pam, Unity, Debo with her young children, and of course Lord Berners. Tom spent most of his leaves there, when he was at the staff college. Randolph Churchill wanted to go, but the Mosleys would not have him, feeling that at a time when they were not allowed to see their political supporters they preferred not to receive their political opponents. At this time, and for a number of years after the war, the Mosleys kept up a policy of never speaking to any member of the wartime House of Commons other than those they knew to have opposed their imprisonment. Ellen Wilkinson, who had been friendly with Mosley in his Labour Party days but who had certainly not opposed Regulation 18b, got into the Dolphin Square lift with them and impulsively greeted Mosley. 'Don't you remember me? I'm Ellen Wilkinson.' They ignored her. In general they were fairly indifferent to normal party politics. At the time of the 1945 election, when Labour won under Attlee with an unexpected landslide, Diana wrote to Sydney on 29 July: 'I looked in at the shop [Heywood Hill's] and saw Nancy who was jubilant about the election results which were just coming in, and also the Woman who was depressed by them. I felt like a sort of umpire.'

From Crux Easton they moved to Crowood, near Ramsbury in Wiltshire, where there was a large farm of about eleven hundred acres. The Home Office, almost incredibly, had refused permission for them to go and view it, so they had to buy it unseen. This was early 1945; it was the authorities' last opportunity to use Defence Regulations to make themselves pointlessly unpleasant, since the regulations lapsed with the end of the war in Europe. Crowood House is a simple, pleasant eighteenth-century manor house in grey stone; Diana made it classically pretty, with striped fabrics, Aubusson carpets and her furniture from Wootton and Crux Easton. In the dining room were some Mosley family portraits. One included a number of rather plain children dressed in Georgian style, of which the youngest, a baby, looked positively subnormal. 'Did that one make good?' Lord Berners wondered.

# 39

# The French Lady Writer

In 1946 Nancy settled in France, where she remained to the end of her life. Debo and her children were in due course to christen her the French Lady Writer. At first she stayed in hotels, then in borrowed or temporary flats. Jonathan spent three weeks with her at 6 Rue Bonaparte in December and January, 1946–47, being taught French and taken round the Paris museums by a serious but amiable young man who reeked of garlic and seemed carefully to keep his heavy beard at two days' growth. The winter was a hard one, but Nancy was snug in a high-ceilinged sitting room heated to tropical temperature. There was a wood-burning stove which Jonathan called the Cone after the red-hot cone in H. G. Wells's story, on which a factory worker sizzles to death, pushed by a jealous workmate. Nancy shrieked at this, and the stove became the Cone to her too.

The Colonel lived fairly near and used to come round often; he was one of the chief organizers of the Gaullist party that was beginning to form. His own flat was full of beautiful objects, for he was an expert on antique furniture and old masters; it contained one small room known as the rubbish room, where he put everything that was not up to standard. 'Everything I ever give him goes into the rubbish room!' Nancy complained happily, and the Colonel smiled, but did not actually deny it. Some present or other had clearly been given this treatment. Nancy was still occasionally dealing in books for Heywood Hill's, and one evening a French book dealer arrived at her flat. He dealt in expensive books for rich bibliophiles, but was a Communist. 'Are you still seeing Palewski?' he asked Nancy. '*C'est un des conservateurs les plus noirs.*' Nancy fidgeted rather, for the Colonel was expected any minute. When he arrived, he and the bookseller embraced and called each other '*tu*'. They had been at school together.

This shows how, even at the height of their affair, Nancy and the Colonel were never generally regarded in Paris as a couple. But this did not save her from Evelyn Waugh's heavy disapproval: sin was sin. He told her off in a letter, following which she wrote to Mrs Ham on 29 January 1949:

Evelyn's letter *pure wickedness*, not fun at all. I wrote and said you are supposed to be fond of me and you should be glad that I am happy. He replied I am fond of you, very, and that is why I am not glad . . . It all comes from being an amateur not a professional Catholic. You and Madame Costa aren't like that or do you smilingly conceal from one that you see hell fire licking one's toes? (Perhaps smilingly is not the word for *you* my darling.)

Countess Carl Costa de Beauregard, Mrs Ham's close childhood friend, was important in Nancy's life. She had a country house called Fontaines, near Meaux, to which she often invited Nancy. She was devout and saintly; her friends were mostly elderly country gentlefolk and priests. As a rule Nancy was much the youngest of the party. One friend is supposed to have been surprised that Madame Costa spent so long in the confessional; curiosity got the better of discretion, and he asked her parish priest what this blameless old lady could possibly have to confess. 'Very little,' said the priest, 'except that she has been horrid [*odieuse*] to her guests.' Nancy shrieked at this story, because Madame Costa was famous for never being horrid to anyone. To Nancy Fontaines was a haven; she could write there in peace during the day and look forward to undemanding evenings chatting or playing friendly bridge for low stakes. For, alone of the Mitfords, Nancy was a bridge player. She kept rather quiet about this, for she detested arguments and post mortems and only played when she knew there was no danger of them.

Evelyn lectured in vain; Nancy was now happy as never before or since. She had love and she had enough money, both for the first time. She visited England frequently, staying with Sydney, Diana or Debo, and impressing everyone with her elegant French clothes. She was one of the first to appear in England wearing Christian Dior's 'New Look', with its full skirts whose lavish use of fabric, and soft femininity, responded to a post-war reaction against shortages and uniforms. All her life Nancy loved clothes; they were always her greatest extravagance, and of the sisters it was always she who cared most about elegance and had the finest dress sense. She was sharp also about what other women wore. After attending Princess Alexandra's wedding to Angus Ogilvy she wrote to Diana, on 27 April 1963: '*Resolution*. Never again to take any trouble about clothes for an English occasion. I never in my life saw such a jumble sale. The hats were all made by people who had heard of flowers but never seen any except one in front of me, a *green satin top hat* with a real carnation hanging on a ribbon at the back. No skirt had ever seen an iron.'

In December 1947 she found a permanent flat at 7 Rue Monsieur. It was on the ground floor between a courtyard and a garden of stone and ivy. There was good eighteenth-century furniture in it, which she supplemented with things of her own from England, including Bertie's Chinese screens. She stayed there till 1966, and it is the place where we remember her best. She acquired a saintly and devoted maid, Marie, who looked after her perfectly and whom she loved dearly. Perennial French inflation made Nancy put up her wages from time to time; this was always at Nancy's initiative, and whenever it happened Marie would protest that she could not possibly accept such a huge rise – nobody had ever been paid so much. Guests slept in the dining room, known as the Bed-diner. Diana gave her a cat, a ginger and white tom from Crowood. It was soon joined by a white hen, which Marie bought with a view to boiling, but which laid an egg on the kitchen table as she was about to dispatch it. Nancy and Marie agreed that its life had to be spared, and for some years thereafter it had the run of the flat. The cat never bothered it.

One of Nancy's dearest enemies in Paris was Violet Trefusis. She was a rich English writer now best known for her lesbian love affair long before with Victoria Sackville-West. Her relationship with Nancy, half friendship and half feud, was based on real mutual irritation but none the less enjoyable to both. Violet laughed at Nancy's French, Nancy deplored Violet's table manners and punctured her pretence that she was the illegitimate daughter of Edward VII. (Violet's mother, Mrs Keppel, had been one of the King's mistresses.) When Violet thought she might write her memoirs, Nancy suggested the title: 'Here Lies Mrs Trefusis'. She once took Jonathan to tea with Violet and warned him: 'If she rubs the back of her head it means she's telling lies.' Jonathan watched in vain for this interesting sign. He was also distracted by memories of a small clockwork pig – it was the bricklaying pig from the Disney film *Three Little Pigs* – which Lord Berners used to wind up and set going on its hind trotters, observing: 'Violet Trefusis'. It was indeed rather like her.

Soon after moving to Rue Monsieur, Nancy started writing *Love in a Cold Climate*. This was later easy to amalgamate with *The Pursuit of Love* to form a single television serial, because it has the same narrator, covers roughly the same time and contains some of the same characters. This time the Radlett family are not centre-stage, but rustic neighbours of the much grander Mont-dores. Lord Montdore is a former Viceroy of India. His wife is a battleaxe; some of her characteristics are based on Violet Trefusis. Their only daughter, Polly, elopes with a dim and ageing hanger-on, and Lady Montdore is enraged. However, she is finally mollified by a *deus ex machina* – Cedric, Lord Montdore's Can-adian cousin and heir, who turns out to be gay. Polly gets rid of her husband and ends up with a suitable older peer. The homo-sexual is a new element; it was unusual at the time to present one as being happy and pleasant. But Nancy knew many a Cedric, both in London and Paris. Years later, in May 1961, she was to write from Ireland to Mark Ogilvie-Grant (quoted by Harold Acton): 'Went to a shopping centre and purchased a china plaque with in Irish lettering "Everybody's Queer but Thee and Me". Now who can I give it to? Takes a bit of thought.' Nancy also takes a cold-eyed look at life among Oxford academics, for Fanny Logan, the narrator, marries a young don. For this Nancy picked the brains of her friend Billa Harrod, wife of Roy. She wrote to Billa in acknowledgement on 14 February 1948: 'You are a blissful girl and of course ought to write a book yourself. You've said all I wanted to know. Oh your letter did so bring back England and all the sides one forgets, ugly houses and bad food. Here of course professors, that class, all have the very best sort of French food and . . . spend literally every penny on it. Jolly sensible, but you see the English would be shocked at spending money on your stomach.'

Also in this book we notice that Nancy has developed a love of grandeur, to see social life not just as entertainment but as display. This taste is best expressed later in her histories, especially *The Sun King*, but it already appears in *Love in a Cold Climate*. Lady Montdore is a monster, but because she is grand and gives splendid parties the reader is meant on balance to admire her: 'People liked to pretend that it was solely on [Lord Montdore's] account that they ever went to the house at all, but this was great nonsense because the lively quality, the fun of Lady Montdore's parties had nothing whatever to do with him, and, hateful as she may have been in many ways, she excelled as a hostess.' This connects with a strange episode – Nancy's harassment, one might almost say her persecution, of a British ambassador.

Nancy preferred France to her own country in most ways, yet the British embassy was important to her. The first ambassador after the war was her friend Duff Cooper. He had been a prominent opponent of appeasement during the thirties, and Churchill rewarded him for his support with the post of Minister of Information during the war, where he unfortunately instigated the unnecessary vendetta against P. G. Wodehouse. But his book on Talleyrand still reads excellently; he was scholarly and clever. As to his wife, Lady Diana Cooper had star quality; she was famous between the wars for her beauty and presence, and has made another reputation in old age with her scatty, but sometimes inspired, volumes of autobiography. (Lady Diana is in fact as the Mitfords are supposed to have been: a natural writer whose early education was deficient. She writes as Nancy and Decca might have written if their account of their own education had been accurate.) In the Coopers' day, Nancy was always in and out of the embassy. An undated letter to her from Duff Cooper reads: 'Keep an eye, one of your beautiful eyes, on Diana during this week while I in my mad selfishness am deserting my post. I know you will without my asking you, but I know too that your time is full . . . Yet you must eat; and a mouthful with her won't take longer to swallow than alone.' From an ambassador this was a nice letter, if a bit arch.

But the Attlee government evidently thought the Coopers' embassy had more glitter than substance, and they were replaced in 1948 by the career diplomat Sir Oliver Harvey and his wife

Maude. Nancy soon noticed the difference. An American she knew, an habituée of the Coopers, called at the embassy and was not offered so much as a cup of tea. It is rather hard to see why she should have been, but Nancy was annoyed, even though the lady was not a particular friend of hers. Unfortunately, too, the Coopers were still in Paris, for the French government had given them the use of a house at Chantilly. Two parties formed among the sillier Parisians, and Nancy became a Cooper cheerleader.

Princess Elizabeth paid an official visit to Paris while all this was going on, and on 17 May that year Nancy wrote a long account to Diana for sending on to Sydney. She said that Prince Philip had been poisoned by the Harveys' food and was on the lavatory all through the Longchamp races. At a French government function to which the Colonel obtained an invitation for Nancy she was surrounded by the Harveys' friends, who were unbelievable: 'I don't know how they found them. None of us . . . asked to anything at all and the Coopers only asked after dinner one evening Diana having bought an entire evening trousseau for the visit . . . So in my book [*Love in a Cold Climate*] when the utter ghastly drear Boy Dougdale marries the heavenly heroine it is "I Oliver Harvey take thee Leopoldina." Tease?' Furthermore, the Harveys had replaced the dark green curtains in the embassy library by pale beige.

It was odd of Nancy to write like this to Diana and Sydney, of all people. She should have known that neither of them would gnash their teeth on behalf of Duff Cooper, who in their eyes was nothing but a warmonger. We think that Diana quite enjoyed writing to Nancy about an Anglo-French dinner party given by her particular friend Daisy Fellowes at Donnington, near Newbury. Daisy had been pro-Cooper, but changed sides; she announced to the assembled company that Maude Harvey was charming. What was more, she fixed with her beady blue eye the painter Christian Bérard, and forced him to agree. Nancy was put out; she knew better than to tackle Daisy, but reproached Bérard severely.

Some years later Nancy was to use the Cooper–Harvey episode in *Don't Tell Alfred*, her last novel, published in 1960. Time had passed and the Harveys been replaced by Nancy's friends the Jebbs; Nancy was able to think straighter and laugh at both sides.

The incoming ambassadress in the book is Nancy's narrator, Fanny; the leftish don she married in *Love in a Cold Climate* has been unexpectedly made ambassador to France. Lady Leone, the previous ambassadress, remains in the embassy pretending to be ill, and members of the smart set continually call on her and make merry in her room, ignoring Fanny. However, Fanny does get her out, and in the end it is Lady Leone who seems slightly ridiculous. Nancy never lost her critical interest in the British embassy. When Sir Winston Churchill died in February 1965 she wrote to Mark Ogilvie-Grant of a subsequent ambassador, Sir Pierson Dixon: 'The Dixons' last glorious act was keeping the Embassy flag at full mast when the General's [de Gaulle] next door, was at half for Winston. Several thousand people telephoned (so my friends on the exchange tell me) and were informed that the flag is only lowered for Royalty. After this they left, unsung, and no doubt Anglo-Frog relations will look up.'

But this is to anticipate. After *Love in a Cold Climate*, Nancy felt able to devote herself to a labour of love. She translated Madame de La Fayette's *La Princesse de Clèves*, a novel about court life in the sixteenth century that she used to say was her favourite book. Diana commissioned this for her publishing company, Euphorion Books. It reads well, but has had to be corrected for the current Penguin edition, for Nancy was no linguistic scholar. Then came another translation, or rather adaptation: André Roussin's farce *The Little Hut*, about a woman who is stranded on a desert island with her husband and lover. The play had been a success in Paris, but in London the Lord Chamberlain still had power to censor the theatre, and it was thought that he might object to the fact that a black man comes and makes love to the woman. In her version Nancy makes the third man white, so all was well. Nancy toured with the company, starting in Edinburgh. At first she was not happy with them: 'It's dreadful how dull they all are but don't say I said,' she wrote to Harold Acton. 'Also Communists I note.' But later she got to like them, describing Robert Morley as 'blissful'. The success of the tour obviously put them all in a good mood. It was followed by a good London run, and Nancy made money. Bertrand Russell, of all people, loved *The Little Hut*, and saw it many times.

Her next novel, in 1951, was *The Blessing*. It is a funny book with a happy ending, but to those of us who knew Nancy it is rather poignant. How Nancy would have liked to be Grace de Valhubert! Grace is an English upper-class girl married to Count Charles-Edouard de Valhubert, another idealized version of the Colonel – more idealized than Fabrice, because this time he is said to be tall and good-looking. Again he shares the Colonel's knowledge of pictures and old furniture, and his love of jokes. Grace is partly a self-caricature of Nancy, for her love of everything French is made fun of; but we think Nancy also had Diana in mind. Grace is blonde, her face 'beautiful and rather large'. The couple settle in France and have a little son, some of whose habits are based on Alexander and Max Mosley when small. Grace has to grow accustomed to French ways, and one particular thing she has to get used to is Charles-Edouard's practice of making a pass at every woman in sight. This, it is implied, is a civilized French habit at which only the dim and dowdy English would cavil. Finally Grace catches Charles-Edouard actually in bed with a woman, and she divorces him though both are still in love. Their son discovers that it is profitable to play off divorced parents and their respective admirers against each other, and intrigues to keep his parents apart; eventually they see through him and all is well. They reappear in *Don't Tell Alfred*, firmly married.

Frenchmen, then, always chase skirts, and their women are far too poised to mind. In real life it suited Nancy to assume this, for it softened the effect of the Colonel's other affairs. She forbade herself to show jealousy; now and then, perhaps, she even persuaded herself not to feel it. Such are the little igloos of illusion we build for ourselves against the cold facts. For the facts were indeed cold. Nancy was as much in love with the Colonel as ever, but had no sort of right to be jealous. Far from being married or engaged to him, she was still married to Peter. That rolling stone even turned up now and then, and Nancy would be quite pleased to see him; though a day or two would be sufficient for her to become irritated all over again when he stumbled home in the small hours and made unnecessary work for Marie. They did not divorce until 1958, and even then it was on his initiative. Meanwhile she well knew that the most she could hope for with the Colonel, in the long run, was to remain his best friend; she also knew that she would destroy this hope if she showed jealousy. She may have managed this, but in other ways she was not always easy. As a leading Gaullist the Colonel used to address meetings which the Communists would attack and sometimes disrupt. Some were mini-Olympias, and Mosley used to feel sympathy for him since he had faced the same kind of trouble. Now and then Nancy would describe to the Mosleys how she had teased the Colonel after such an incident, when he can only have wanted a little peace and quiet. Afterwards Mosley commented to Diana: 'Poor brute!'

With all her qualities as a companion Nancy lacked one that was crucial: she could never be entirely cosy. It was one reason why she was, as Harold Acton puts it, a natural bachelor. She also preferred living alone; she often said so, and the evidence is that she was sincere. But people are complicated; certainly Nancy was. We think she also envied women whose temperament, unlike her own, allowed them to settle down with the man they loved. She would have liked to be able to hold the Colonel as Diana held Mosley, though he, too, had a roving eye. She could not have told anyone this. Her mother would not have understood, and as to her sisters and her friends, it was with them that she might have laughed at similar predicaments in others. She was in the trap of *Rigoletto*. To be sure, she was successful, respected and sufficiently well off. But at the centre of her life we seem to see, under her bright chat, a dissatisfaction; not with the Colonel, but with her own nature. Long before, when Lily Kersey could not still love her, she teased Pam and the others. Now she took again to teasing; only this time her scope was not the nursery, but the wide world.

She used to go somewhere – Athens, Rome, Moscow, Ireland – and write an article sending it up, often to the rage of the inhabitants. One old Italian countess read out Nancy's Roman article to her friends, then solemnly put it on the fire. An Irishman wrote to her: 'Hell would be a more suitable place for you than Ireland.' Once she even teased the French, at least a number of them, by writing an article saying that Marie Antoinette was rightly executed as a traitor. Prince Pierre of Monaco is supposed to have cut Nancy dead for this.

But the greatest of Nancy's teases was directed at her own countrymen. Unerringly she sought out their sorest spot, the class-consciousness which can be so inhibiting and obsessive.

G. K. Chesterton saw this as a tragedy, his country as divided by 'swords of scorn'. To Nancy it was not tragedy but comedy. She could not, however, have exploited it as she did had she not found a truly brilliant confederate, Professor Alan S. C. Ross of Birmingham University.

To be truthful it was Ross who found her. He was interested in the linguistic usage of the upper class and had just written an article on the subject. She was an obvious source of information because a passage in *The Pursuit of Love* had already made her rather well known in connection with these matters. In that book, Uncle Matthew dislikes girls' boarding schools because they do not teach upper-class usage. 'Education! I was always led to suppose that no educated person ever spoke of notepaper, and yet I hear poor Fanny asking Sadie for notepaper. What is this education? Fanny talks about mirrors and mantelpieces, handbags and perfume . . .' and so on. (Uncle Matthew would of course have preferred looking glasses, chimneypieces, bags and scent.) So Professor Ross wrote to Nancy and they met in due course. They got on famously; she told Diana afterwards, 'He really does get it more or less right.' What was more to the point, the Professor was another tease, as much of a tease as Nancy.

The original version of his article was entitled 'Linguistic Class-Indicators in Present-Day English', and it was published in 1954 in the Helsinki publication *Neuphilologische Mitteilungen*. A condensed and simplified version was first published in *Encounter* in November 1955 under the title 'U and Non-U'. It is written in the scholarly manner; U and non-U are an application of the habit among philologists to designate languages or dialects with initials, as ME for Middle English, or OF for old French. But the article is really one long tease, exactly the kind Nancy most enjoyed; its air of academic authority only heightens it. Ross gives the game away in his second footnote:

In this article I use the terms *upper class* (abbreviated: U), *correct*, *proper*, *legitimate*, *appropriate* (sometimes also *possible*) and similar expressions to designate usages of the upper class; their antonyms (non-U, incorrect, not proper, not legitimate, etc.) to designate usages which are not upper class. These terms are, of course, used factually and not in reprobation (indeed I may at this juncture emphasize a point which is doubtless obvious, namely that this whole article is purely factual).

To which we reply, tell that to the Marines. Words like correct, proper, legitimate and so on contain far too much approval for a single disclaimer to be able to remove it. At times Ross even uses the word 'gentleman' to mean member of the upper class or U-speaker. Ross need have used none of these expressions, and had he really wanted to be purely factual he would have avoided them.

The tease is not only, or even mainly, on the non-U. 'Today', we are told, 'a member of the upper class is, for instance, not necessarily better educated, cleaner or richer than someone not of this class.' Ross is in fact claiming that the upper class is nothing other than a group of people who talk in a particular way. Nancy loved the article; and it happened to reach her just as she was preparing an essay for *Encounter* called 'The English Aristocracy'. She included Ross's material in her essay, published in September 1955, making U and non-U into a cult but leaving the essay a mess. In launching a tease, she sacrificed consistency.

For Ross's material does not fit with the rest of Nancy's article. Her main arguments hark back to Bertie's respect for medieval chivalry and for the samurai; as do her introductions to the Stanley letters, and Eugenia's speech in *Wigs on the Green*. She sees much more to the upper class than a mere dialect. The British peerage, says Nancy, is the only one left in the world with even a little real political power, and it is the core of the upper class. She introduces Ross's thesis with a smooth connecting passage: 'There is in England no aristocratic class that forms a caste . . . Most of the peers share the education, usage and point of view of a vast upper middle class, but the upper middle class does not, in its turn, merge imperceptibly into the middle class. There is a very definite border line, easily recognizable by hundreds of small but significant landmarks.' Most of these, it is implied, concern the use of words, and she then quotes Ross, listing some of his U and non-U equivalents and adding more.

After this she returns to her earlier ideas: 'The purpose of the aristocrat is to lead, therefore his functions are military and political.' But he is averse to working for money. It is not that he is necessarily lazy or unenterprising. He engages in public service, but for its own sake; he does not enrich himself in it. But by bringing in so much of Professor Ross's material she has already half established that none of this is as relevant as whether someone says mirror or looking glass.

She pokes fun at aristocrats for opening their houses to the public, something at which 'the lowest peasant of the Danube' would stick; forgetting that opening a stately home can equally be presented as a modern version of an old aristocratic function, that of display. She concludes that the English lord will probably survive, partly by pretending to be poorer than he is. 'He must, of course, be careful not to overdo the protective colouring. *An aristocracy cannot survive as a secret society.*' (Our italics.) This contradicts Professor Ross, for if an aristocracy is defined as such solely by its use of language, then anyone can become a member simply by using language in the same way. So it depends for its exclusiveness on people not knowing the code; on secrecy. Professor Ross in fact assumes that the aristocracy has become a secret society, while Nancy is telling it not to do so.

But nobody noticed this, and the article caused a fine stir. *Encounter* sold out and had to reprint, a rare event for an intellectual monthly, and it prudently exploited the goldmine for all it was worth. Two months later, in November 1955, it reprinted Professor Ross's learned article in a shortened form. Then Evelyn Waugh wrote an 'Open Letter' to Nancy in the magazine's December issue. He warned her of its contents in a letter dated 19 October: 'Except that I expose you as a hallucinated communist agent there is nothing in it to hurt.' The open letter accuses Nancy of bamboozling 'a great number of needy young persons'. Nancy, a socialist, is inciting the lower orders to class war by revealing that their betters are all the time laughing at the way they speak.

What followed this controversy was not a class war, but simply that some English people became more self-conscious than ever about the way they spoke. Jonathan was once at a party where the host, an unkind humorist, whispered to a girl that she had a bad stain on the back of her dress. She had no such stain, but spent the rest of the party sidling along the walls so as to hide her back. For years, Nancy made some English people embarrassed in a rather similar way.

The business irritated the family. Sydney ticked Nancy off

obliquely, saying in a letter of 9 September 1955 that the *Encounter* article would have been just as good without bringing in Professor Ross. She clearly meant that it would have been better, for in a later letter, dated 26 August 1956, she corrects herself after mentioning writing paper: 'Oh I mean notepaper, being of middle-class origin.' Diana remembers that she, Pam and Debo all 'nearly died of embarrassment' at the time. In Diana's case she suffered more than embarrassment, for her politics caused her to disapprove of adventitious class distinction. Mosley had put his supporters into uniform partly to iron out class differences. Years later, in 1978, Diana had her own say in the collection *U and non-U Revisited*. 'In the long run perhaps [Nancy] wished she had thought of something else to put in *Encounter*, because she preferred to be known as a novelist and a biographer rather than as an expert on etiquette or whatever it was.' Diana adds that the 'rather absurd class feeling' ought to be encouraged to wither away and, since 1955, has to an extent done so. All the same the controversy did contribute to the general gaiety. John Betjeman wrote a poem beginning 'Phone for the fish-knives, Norman'. Perhaps the last word should belong to Osbert Lancaster who drew a cartoon in which his character Maudie, Countess of Littlehampton, pronounces: 'I don't care what Nancy says: if it's me it's U.'

Already before this, in 1954, Nancy had produced her first historical biography – *Madame de Pompadour*. It is a drawing-room history, but it is carefully researched all the same. The reviewers were cold. One of the most eminent of them, Nancy's friend Raymond Mortimer, prepared her for this response when she sent him the book before publication. There would be hard knocks, he said in his letter of 13 August 1953. 'I am enjoying the book, and at the same time I feel that the whole enterprise is questionable . . . Your narrative style is so peculiar, so breathless, so remote from what has ever been used for biography. I feel as if an enchantingly clever woman was pouring out the story to me on the telephone.' In other words, she should stick to the novel. The same point was made much more sharply in the *Manchester Guardian* by the historian A. J. P. Taylor, to whom it seemed that Nancy had simply put the characters from her novels into fancy dress. 'Certainly no historian could write a novel half as good as Miss Mitford's work of history. Of course he might not try.' Nancy's comment to Billa Harrod was: 'In a way it's a compliment when the historians say keep off the grass – which is really what it amounts to, as they can't pretend my facts are wrong.' If Taylor over-reacted, he was nevertheless right to note that *Pompadour* was rather like the novels. 'Once more we have the secret words, the ritual of society, and the blunders of the uninitiated . . .' But this was not untrue to history. Nancy simply chose to write about a period and a *milieu* in which these things existed. Pompadour's time was a time when Nancy would have felt at home, an age of chat, 'cheerful, gossipy, joking chat, running on hour after idle hour, all night sometimes'. There was an eighteenth-century French equivalent of U and non-U; Nancy lists certain pairs of expressions, then says it was 'all quite meaningless', showing what she really thought about the Professor Ross episode which was shortly to take place. Nancy reveals herself in this book as taking a very lukewarm attitude towards the joys of sex; she was, to be sure, fifty when it was published, but the length of time during which she had been satisfied with Hamish Erskine indicates that she was like this even when young. She plays down Pompadour's physical role, both as mistress and later as procuress; she underlines the fact that too much sex made Pompadour ill, and says that what she and Louis XV enjoyed together was 'that particularly delightful relationship of sex mixed up with laughter'. She talks of Pompadour's love of life, and interest in people, being 'perhaps the *base* of what we variously call charm, *sex appeal* or fascination'. (Our italics.) So to Nancy, sex appeal is just charm under another name; its base is not anything so crude as physical desire. This is a little like drawing up the specifications for a car which are accurate except that they leave out the engine. It is the converse of pornography, which assumes that the engine is the whole vehicle. Nancy never came to terms with sensuality. She experienced it, though possibly less than some; but she did not understand it. Also, now that her liaison with the Colonel was on the decline, she had a particular reason to minimize something that tended rather to take him away from her than to bring him closer.

None of these unconscious self-revelations affects the charm of *Madame de Pompadour*, or its accuracy. Dr Alfred Cobban, a specialist in French history which Taylor is not, wrote Nancy a soothing and complimentary letter and later included the book in the bibliography of his *History of Modern France*. Encouragement from him and others helped to make Nancy devote herself to history, and from now on she was to be mainly a historian.

She published *Voltaire in Love* in 1957. This is an account of Voltaire's love affair with the learned Marquise du Châtelet; Evelyn Waugh suggested the title. Harold Acton thinks it is the best of her historical works, and Evelyn Waugh wrote to her on 19 May 1959: 'This is a fan letter. I've just re-read *Voltaire in Love* and must tell you how much I admire it. I enjoyed it hugely at the first reading but I didn't appreciate it. You write so deceptively frivolously that one races on from page to page without noticing the solid structure.' The picture of the young Voltaire is convincing, the account of his endless literary squabbles is lively and clear. It is as good a read as Lytton Strachey's *Voltaire and Frederick the Great*, and much fairer. Bertrand Russell was also complimentary about *Voltaire in Love*, though he found occasion to correct two small points about Leibnitz.

Nancy then wrote one more novel, *Don't Tell Alfred*, published in 1960. She had planned the book years before; already before *The Blessing* appeared she told Mrs Ham that she was going to use the characters in it for another book in which her narrator, Fanny, would become ambassadress to France. Nancy's nephew, Alexander Mosley, provided more raw material. He sometimes worked as courier for a small package tour business, Spanish Travel SA; it organized holidays to Port Bou, which, being the northernmost town of the Costa Brava, was the cheapest place to get to. One day Alexander turned up at Nancy's flat and gave a stark description of what conditions were like for the tourists. She wrote to Diana on 13 September 1957:

Ali ambled in yesterday for a bath and luncheon . . . 'Mm, yes, we call it packing in the meat – we call *them* the Shah.' . . . 'What, like the Shah of Persia?' 'No, like a Shah of rain.' . . . 'Do the same ones ever come twice?' 'The pretty girls do because they go to bed with the waiters and the customs men.' . . . Then he said would I like to come and see him packing in the meat so we had a R.V. Gare Saint Lazare at 6.30. Darling it's too sad. If you could have seen their tired excited faces – all carrying their own luggage – well knowing what I did I nearly cried.

In the book Fanny's younger son Baz also 'packs in the meat' and, owing to a train strike, dumps all his party on the embassy.

Nancy used to say, after *Don't Tell Alfred*, that she would never write another novel because, living in France, she was losing her ear for English dialogue. The book does show signs of this problem. Its young people are particularly unconvincing. She does her best with the boys, bringing in the beginnings of pop fever as well as the Teddy Boy culture; Fanny's elder son is another recognizable type, going in for sandals, sanctimony and Zen Buddhism. But they do not really work. The only girl, Fanny's niece, Northey, belongs entirely to the past, being a rerun of the young Linda. All the same the book is fun, with a lovely silly plot and a portrait of Uncle Matthew in old age which is such an exact and affectionate description of David that we think it is meant as a sort of obituary; he had died in 1958. The reviewers were down on *Don't Tell Alfred*, but it sold all the same. 'Sucks to them,' Nancy commented to Mrs Ham on 2 November 1960. She was also fortified by Evelyn Waugh's opinion; he told Nancy on 27 October that year that it was her best novel, though also, rather mysteriously, that it was her Communist Manifesto. For all that she was wise not to write another for she was indeed losing touch with English life. A letter to Mrs Ham dated 22 August 1960, shortly after publication, shows striking ignorance. Referring to a young people's party, she asks: 'What on earth is Pim –? (what they drank.) I see I'm quite out of it in spite of all the prep I did on young people for my book. Oh bother – what are jeans?' Mrs Ham was able to inform her on the twenty-eighth: 'Pim is a mixed gin and lemonade drink. Jeans are lumberjack trousers which go with locks of hair over the nose.' It is most odd that Nancy did not know about Pimm's No. 1, 'the original gin sling', which certainly existed in her own day and before. If English life was becoming unfamiliar, this was not replaced by a sufficient feel for contemporary France, which she loved without wholly understanding it. She could never have written about the French from inside. Her area was now the interface between French, English, and a few Americans and Italians, in one particular group; neither a broad nor a fertile acre.

Above all, though, Nancy had at last found her true *métier* as a mature writer in the form of historical biography. Raymond

Mortimer and A. J. P. Taylor had both got it wrong. There is an amateurishness in all the novels, including *Don't Tell Alfred*. What is lacking in them is something more important than familiarity with Pimm's; it is the disciplined imagination that can distinguish, among imagined events, between what is believable and what is not. Weaknesses result so that at times the structure seems to collapse. In the histories she submits to the discipline of the facts, about which she is always meticulous. By dealing with things that actually happened, she avoids the improbable, and her writing becomes what in the novels it never quite is: truly accomplished.

In the meantime, to Nancy's joy, de Gaulle had come back to power in France in 1958. The Colonel, whose political views Nancy shared in every particular, was a supporter so close and loyal as to have no doubts. The drama of Algeria virtually passed them by – the fact, that is, that de Gaulle used the supporters of French Algeria to help him get to power and then started negotiations to hand Algeria over to the Moslem majority. Algeria could be French or Arab; de Gaulle was in power, and that was enough. A year before de Gaulle had come to power, the Colonel had been made ambassador in Rome. Nancy, and friends of hers, used to visit him there from time to time; he always made them welcome, though in a letter to Nancy dated 24 March 1960 Evelyn Waugh conveys a hint that he may not have had quite enough to do. 'Colonel Gaston's affection is gratifying and inexplicable. He has grown much prettier but is very restless in his fine house. The footmen literally run behind him as he darts from one salon to another. He eats his food too fast. It is very good and deserves lingering attention . . .' A few years before, Nancy might have missed the Colonel; but by now their relations had settled down to an affectionate friendship. To have a beautiful Roman embassy to visit was compensation for his absence. At this period Nancy spent much of her time in Italy, especially in Venice. Many of her Paris friends used to go there for part of the summer, and from the late fifties onwards she often stayed with Countess Anna Maria Cicogna.

Nancy was now famous, and rather enjoyed it. In connection with *Don't Tell Alfred* she appeared on television, and this was her description of the event to Mrs Ham in a letter of 3 November 1960:

The television – I was very much put out by their dragging in my poor sisters – didn't know they were gossipy like that. Then the questions – why do you live in Paris? One can't very well say because it's 20 times more agreeable than living in London.

The odd thing is, however feeble you are, it sends the sales whizzing. I sold half as many again last week. I think the public feels that you are in some way sanctified if you've *been on telly*. Also, I didn't ask for first class to go back as it wasn't a mealtime, but as soon as I showed my nose at London Airport they transferred me into first class for nothing! I've never been so amazed. But can you tell me why anyone watches? It seemed so deadly dull – a woman with a lot of dogs – a young man cross with the critics and pontificating about his play. Too mysterious.

She never lost a sense of genuine surprise that anyone should bother with her; underneath her social gloss lay considerable humility. Jonathan once took a small group of people to see her, including the eminent actor Paul Scofield. It was rather touching to see them together, because Scofield, too, has this humility. Neither had the least idea that the other might be impressed.

Nancy liked Viscount Montgomery. Her feeling for him was half admiration, half mockery. She played up to him in a way that he liked. To Mrs Ham on 2 July 1957 she wrote: 'Dined with Monty and the Jebbs, just the four of us, you know how he always rather fascinates me. We talked about generals having luck. He said, "I had luck when Gott was shot down." N: "Perhaps it was lucky for us too." M: "Yes it was." ' She loved a particular Christmas card he sent her so much that she left it up for a whole year. It had a photograph with the caption: 'Myself by the grave of Winston Churchill'.

The time eventually came when Nancy left Rue Monsieur. The immediate cause of her departure was that her rent was about to be raised sharply. She had become more and more fascinated with the Palace of Versailles, especially while writing her next history, *The Sun King*. This was originally planned as a rather slight picture book with the palace as its subject rather than the king who built it, but research, and the process of writing, involved Nancy more and more with Louis XIV, so that it ended as a biography. The illustrations remain sumptuous, but do not overshadow the text. This time the reviewers were polite; they had become accustomed to the idea of Nancy as historian. The book sold very well indeed. In the year it was published, 1966, Nancy bought a house at Versailles, and the following January she gave up her flat and moved there. Versailles was a place she had come to love, and besides, the house would be an investment. All the same, looking back on it, the move seems to have been a mistake. Violet Trefusis predicted this, and was probably not wrong. People would not go out to Versailles as readily as they would pop into Rue Monsieur. Nancy used to say she wanted to discourage casual dropping-in; nevertheless we think she came to miss Paris.

Two deaths during 1966 made Nancy very sad – those of Madame Costa de Beauregard in February and Evelyn Waugh in April. Some of her letters at the time have a note of mourning. On All Souls Day she wrote to Christopher Sykes (quoted by Harold Acton): 'I think of Robert [Byron] today – my brother Tom, Victor Cunard, Mrs Hammersley, Evelyn and Roger Hinks. The fact is it's people one has jokes with whom one misses – the loving the good and the upright much less. Robert is still the person I mind about most.'

All the same she enjoyed most of that autumn, when she was preparing the house and planning to put wild flowers in the garden. On 18 December she wrote to Debo: 'I went yesterday and made a huge bonfire in the garden (Oh how enjoyable) and, in spite of being Saturday afternoon the sweet deaf and dumb painter was there and of course joined in. Nobody ever can resist, can they?' Most of her letters at this time are cheerful; though when 12 January, the day of the move, was almost upon her there is a note of foreboding. To both Debo and Mark Ogilvie-Grant she wrote, quite lightly, that she felt moving would be like dying; to Harold Acton she wrote: 'I'm engulfed in my move and greatly enjoying it though I suppose the actual day will be like the death of Damien.' It was not; in fact Nancy's letter describing it to Sir Hugh Jackson (quoted by Harold Acton) makes it sound great fun.

The French movers are extraordinary. They even kept the little heap of pennies under my big clock, to balance it, and put them back in the same place and started it again. The system is, everything is wrapped

up, however small, and every book separately, and all the furniture
from top to toe. Then they load the things at street level on to a
platform which rises to the level of the rooms, and the things float in
through the windows – none of that wrestling on the stairs. It took
three whole days and I haven't got so very much furniture. They even
make your beds and would probably cook your dinner if you asked
them. They were so adorable – we parted in silence and tears and
enormous tips.

She had just two years of contentment at Versailles, during
which she began research on her last book, *Frederick the Great*,
which she dedicated to Diana. Frederick fascinated her in
two quite separate ways. He was a cultured, French-speaking
eighteenth-century monarch, and his love-hate relationship with
Voltaire led her naturally to him. Quite apart from that, he was
one of the greatest generals of history, so he also appealed to
the side of Nancy that liked Viscount Montgomery. She wrote
to Raymond Mortimer in late 1969 (quoted by Harold Acton):
'*Battles*. It is the sorrow of my life never to have been in one. I
suppose a cavalry charge must be the nearest thing to heaven on
this earth. When I was little I was so jealous of my great-uncle for
being killed in one (against the Boers – so wicked when I was a
child and so wicked again now).' It seemed surprising at the time
that she should choose Frederick, all the same, considering her
dislike of Germans. Harold Acton finds her choice perverse.

But before she had begun writing the book, in December 1968,
the pain began. It was like a very bad sciatica, affecting her back
and legs. She wrote to Debo on 24 February 1969: 'The pain is
awful . . . but . . . when I've been in bed a bit it goes away.'
Aspirin was no good; she has 'had it for nearly three months now'.
Nobody ever quite knew what caused it, though all sorts of
theories were put forward. The French doctors at first described
it as a '*colonne vertébrale dégradée*'. In fact it heralded the onset of
the disease that was to kill her, which after many wrong diag-
noses, numerous tests and irradiations and operations, turned out
to be Hodgkin's disease, a form of leukaemia. At least this was
said to be what she had when she died. But was it all she had? We
have known one or two people with Hodgkin's disease, which is
unpleasant enough, in fact usually fatal; but they have not suffered

from this intolerable back pain. Since the back pain was her most
noticeable symptom, the doctors were naturally misled. At first it
seemed that the trouble was simply a recurrence of severe back-
ache which she had had in 1948, forcing her to stay in bed. This
had cleared up by itself, but now, after she had been ill for four
months, Nancy's doctors took tests and found a 'lump' in her
back. Nancy wrote to Geoffrey Gilmour on 29 March 1969
(quoted by Harold Acton):

I did the tests yesterday. The comic relief was so great I hardly minded
them it was like a horror film of the worst variety. One was constantly
left, naked, in the dark while they developed the films, like children
with a Brownie, in a sort of kitchen sink next door. Everybody divine
like they are here at Versailles . . . I wonder if it's my twin brother one
has heard of that; a little old man with a white beard. Little Lord
Redesdale, shrieking away, might be an addition to Rue d'Artois and
Diana's dinner parties.

The lump was removed; it was, apparently, benign. But the
pain came back.

In July there was a real remission; Nancy's cook, a replacement
for Marie who had just retired, turned out to be a trained masseuse
and treated Nancy, who for a time thought herself cured. This
enabled her to get back to *Frederick the Great*, and her letters
become cheerful again. Of a book by Antonia Fraser she wrote to
Raymond Mortimer on the twenty-fifth (quoted by Harold
Acton): 'Peter Quennell says its success is due to prayer – the
whole Pakenham family on its knees for weeks according to him.
It conjures up a vision of Weidenfeld, with Spring and Autumn
lists, at the Wailing Wall and [Hamish Hamilton] at the Kirk.' She
wrote fast: by 10 August she told Sir Hugh Jackson that she had
already done about a quarter of the book and was now only
getting 'sort of growing pains which are nasty but bearable'. She
felt able to go to East Germany in September and October, with
Pam as interpreter. The pains came back gradually, forcing her to
abandon the idea of going to Silesia. In November she wrote to
Alvilde Lees-Milne (quoted by Harold Acton):

I had a lot of pain but no worse than when I'm here and they were so
kind about bringing chairs and bringing the car to forbidden places and

so on. The only thing was no baths, only showers, and I depend greatly on lying in a hot bath so that was rather a blow. Food delicious because they haven't got round to broilers and so on and the taste was what one has forgotten, but of course if you say so they are deeply offended and say by next year all the farms will be factories.

She was greatly taken with Potsdam and worried that the East Germans were about to demolish the pretty old town and replace it with skyscrapers.

For the last years of her life the pain scarcely ever left Nancy. At first she was reluctant to take painkillers for fear of clouding her brain, but her resolution soon evaporated. She consulted French doctors, English doctors, and Italian doctors when she went to Venice for the last time in 1970; she consulted quacks, faith healers and a man who put a sample of her blood into a box. Occasionally some of them seemed to do her good for a time; but it never lasted. Perhaps she never really expected it to. Sydney's scepticism about doctors had sunk in, despite her own habit of blaming Sydney for ignoring medical advice when she was a baby. She had argued with Mrs Ham about this, writing to her on 13 July 1960: 'Do you admit that doctors cannot cure: cancer, heart, exzema [*sic*], madness, paralysis or any of the real human ills?' And in a sombre preview of what was in store for herself, she wrote to Mrs Ham on 8 August the same year of her friend Lady Marriott, daughter of the multi-millionaire Otto Kahn: 'Momo is dying – the cancer has come back. In other words the famed American doctors tortured her, drove her mad and prolonged a terrible death. She has been ill exactly a year. Added to which the expense was so terrific that *even her* trustees demurred. It can't be right.' One of Nancy's last and blackest jokes was made to one of her own doctors. 'If I were as bad at writing books as you are at curing people, I should starve.' English doctors, dressed as for White's as she used to put it, particularly irritated her; when she has a good word for a doctor, he is usually French.

The cook-masseuse in due course left and was replaced by a Moroccan called Hassan. Nancy came to be very fond of him, though he caused a problem because he was away the whole weekend, obliging Nancy to live on porridge because it was all she could cook. At least that was her story. But Nancy kept in touch with old Marie, and was desperately worried when Marie was hit by a car in December 1970. Ill herself, she could not for several weeks get to hospital to visit her. As Nancy became worse, nurses had to be engaged; at the end of her life she was looked after by two Australians, working in shifts.

During 1972 Nancy received honours, both from France and from England: the Legion of Honour and the CBE. It was the Legion of Honour that pleased her the more, but she also liked the recognition from her own country.

By now she was very ill. Throughout her adult life she had been thin; now she was emaciated, and her world often seemed to be reduced to her house and garden, her worries to the problems of saving the blackbirds from the local cats. As we mentioned earlier, her sisters all came to visit and help. It was Diana who really took charge, for she lived nearby. Debo, too, came frequently and she used to worry not only about Nancy herself but about the strain on Diana. Pam also came, and of all of them she was the one with whom Nancy felt easiest when she was really low. With the others she had shared too many unkind jokes. When she had become too weak for jokes it was finally Pam, whom she had teased and who had never teased back, who came into her own.

Decca visited as well, which, considering she lived in Los Angeles, was a great kindness. It meant that she had to see Diana often, but this passed off without any difficulty. We remember their unexpected telephone conversation, years before, when Decca had been staying with Sydney. They now had a really good reason to be friendly, at least for the time. Each knew that Nancy was deeply fond of the other. As to politics, if two people disagree it is probably better if the disagreement is wide. Otherwise the feeling remains that if one got some point across, the other might see sense. Neither Diana nor Decca could have any such illusion and so they could be, and were, perfectly cordial. The legend that Diana and Decca have not spoken since the war nevertheless persists.

The Colonel, too, visited Nancy regularly. He had eventually married in the mid-sixties, but by that time his friendship with Nancy had long settled down to a point where the marriage did not affect it; his wife, too, was a good friend of hers. A sudden impulse made him go to see Nancy on the very day she died; he was the last person to see her alive.

Her final project, which never came off, was to write her memoirs. Harold Acton, for one, used to urge her on with them, but she was too ill. She did, however, write Debo a letter on 29 October 1971 which is interesting, if in parts obscure:

If one writes an autobiography it's not enough, as so many people seem to suppose, to tell how many housemaids one's father employed — one must *unmask* oneself. Roughly speaking I shall say what an unsatisfactory relationship I had with Muv to explain my love for old ladies: Aunt Vi (Peter's), Mrs Ham, Madame Costa, and others. I would like vaguely to try and find out if this relationship, shared with Decca and Honks [Diana] but not with you and Tom, was one's fault or hers. The others loved her in old age. I deeply respected her and liked her company and jokes but never loved her.

Each sister would have a right of veto over the book.

I shan't mind asking questions — shan't leave things out for fear of annoying which might not annoy at all. That was Decca's great mistake in my view. I might make each of you write a review of Decca's book. Incidentally my book will begin in 1945 when I came here with flashbacks at the death of Bowd, Muv and Farve. I won't bore the public again with our childhood to the extent of more than a few pages.

Unmask herself? We agree with Harold Acton; this is something Nancy would never have been able to do. She was too reticent. She compared herself to the water beetle which skims the surface and would sink if it looked down, and she was right. Her memoirs would have had nothing of the confessional in them; the inner Nancy that underlay the kindness, the sharpness, the inconsistency of views and the self-protective jokes would have remained a mystery.

She died in her own bed, peacefully, on 30 June 1973. Ten years before, at Chatsworth, Debo had written her various questions as to what should be done when she died, and she had replied.

*Debo:* Is it true that you have left money in your will for a tomb and that I am to see about it?

*Nancy:* True.

*Debo:* Where do you want to be buried?

*Nancy:* Near to wherever I drop off the perch . . .

*Debo:* Have you got any thoughts on the Tomb?

*Nancy:* Large and showy, with angels and a long inscription saying how lovely I was and greatly missed . . .

*Debo:* Is the Tomb to be where you're buried, I mean to say you die in Timbuctoo, *then* where do you want the Tomb?

*Nancy:* Yes, Timbuctoo. Then it will be something for *visitors* to *visit*.

*Debo:* Lots of clergymen and other fussy people are livid at the idea of angels, but I suppose I'll be able to impose my will.

*Nancy:* Yes, please impose . . .

She must have changed her mind, for these arrangements were not followed. Her remains were flown to England, accompanied by Diana and Mosley, and she was buried in Swinbrook churchyard.

# 40

# The Mosleys Post-war

Mrs Ham saw Diana for the first time after the war in the late spring of 1948. She wrote to Nancy on 4 July that year:

You know, when Bobo died, I wrote to Diana and she came when I spent two nights with Muv at the Mews. So completely unchanged in every way – that was, and is, and shall be. Gay, laughing, enchanted with life and with some wonderful antidote one feels against mortal ills. Can it be 'The Leader?' In her case it is useless to say 'Somehow one had hoped the heart would grow sick.' Tom [Mosley] was there looking quite different. He was very pleasant I thought, and more human – less like a ship's figurehead than I'd remembered.

Mrs Ham was right; Mosley was indeed Diana's 'antidote'. He was the secret, not only of present happiness, but also of the feeling, necessary to someone like her, that her life had purpose and a task. She made Mosley as happy as he made her. Their private life was as near flawless, perhaps, as is possible for two such spirited people. But in politics, which was what really interested them, they were doomed to political failure; not to oblivion, for Mosley remained a notorious political bogeyman, but to impotence. Diana's life after the war was the mirror image of Nancy's. Nancy was to achieve outward success while having a private life that was very largely cheerless; Diana, happy and secure in private, was to devote her considerable abilities to a cause which ensured that they would be disregarded.

At Crowood the Mosleys settled down to live the life of the country gentry. There was quite good shooting, run at first by a black gamekeeper who was more picturesque than competent. Jonathan remembers one occasion when he put up the partridges prematurely and drove them the wrong way. It was not Mosley who reproached him for this but Diana, who suddenly became very much her father's daughter. There was a certain amount of local disapproval, mostly among the village colonels and other minor gentry. It mainly took a negative form; there was none of the effort normally made when new people move into an estate, to 'rope them in' to this or that. They did not mind being ignored in this way; they had their own friends and Mosley was fairly busy, writing and organizing as well as farming. Diana was in fact not best pleased when the local attitude began to change, which happened under the influence of Mr Leigh Williams, a tutor engaged for Alexander and Max. 'I'm afraid Mr Leigh Williams is making friends with Captain X and the rest of them,' she said to Jonathan. 'I hope this doesn't mean neighbour life.' There was nothing that could be called an organized boycott; the shopkeepers were obliging, Alexander and Max made friends with the village children, and Max, who liked horses, sometimes went hunting or showjumping; some of the neighbours would also come over to shoot. But Penelope Betjeman recalls an occasion when Diana wanted to buy a pony for the boys. Penelope knew of a suitable one that belonged to a couple of horsey spinsters who shared a house; but directly she told the ladies who it was that wanted to buy the animal, they made it clear that they would never deal with the Mosleys. Once an Anglican friar turned up on a mission to evangelize Hampshire; on a whim, Diana invited him to lunch. What, she asked, did he think of Ramsbury? – expecting some anodyne reply about its charm. 'It's the wickedest village in Wiltshire,' the friar replied without a smile; he then told the story of the village youth club and its hall. It had been built by the boys of Ramsbury under the well-meaning guidance of a retired army officer. An opening ceremony had been planned, but the night before the same boys who had built the place set fire to it and burned it down. Privately, Diana was rather on the side of the boys as she heard this horror story; if they had built it why shouldn't they burn it? She has an anarchic strain in her character, a hatred of bossiness. Yet bossiness, especially the bossiness of the minor gentry, was one of the raw materials of Fascism; if things had gone her way her system would have depended on a type of person to which she was not drawn. She would no doubt have managed to hide this.

One summer day the doorbell rang; it happened that Diana answered it herself. She found two young aircraftsmen, in a state of obvious embarrassment. They had just won a bet; they had heard stories of armed guards and blockhouses and barbed wire at Crowood, and the general opinion at the men's base was that nobody could penetrate to the Mosleys' front door.

Now and then the Mosleys were visited by a group of young Germans, ex-prisoners of war who had stayed in the countryside as agricultural labourers. One of them asked Diana to explain something: he had been classified as a '*Kaninchen-Nazi*', rabbit-Nazi. What had he to do with rabbits? Suddenly the penny dropped: Diana realized that he had misheard the English phrase '*rabid* Nazi'.

The friends whom they saw were mostly non-political, some from before the war, and several new ones. The Betjemans came over frequently from Wantage where they lived, as did Lord Berners and Robert Heber-Percy from Faringdon. Through Lord Berners the Mosleys came to know Daisy (Marguerite) Fellowes, daughter of a French duke by an American heiress; she was a legendary figure who before the war had been known as the best-dressed woman in the world. Beautiful as well as elegant, she had a wicked sense of humour. Stories about her abounded. She once gave a close woman friend a generous Easter present: a new nose remodelled by a plastic surgeon. 'It's lovely,' said Daisy, 'but she can't breathe through it.'

She was less kind, it is said, to an admirer who was getting on her nerves. Standing by the swimming pool of her house above Monte Carlo, he asked: 'Can one dive in here?'

'If you like,' she said. The depth at that point was about three feet.

Daisy, with her one-legged husband Reginald, genial in his wheel-chair, lived at Donnington Park near Newbury, a mansion in the Strawberry Hill Gothick style furnished with breathtaking elegance. A great friend of Daisy's was the Liberal peer, Lord Sherwood. Other occasional visitors to Crowood were the Yorkes. Prince Stanislas Radziwill used to come; he was later to marry Jacqueline Kennedy's sister. His cousin Dolly was another friend, as was her husband, the Danish painter Mogens Tvede. Diana rather liked shocking Mogens. He and she, with Alexander and

Max, once visited the National Gallery, and near it one of the boys spotted the statue of Nurse Cavell.

'Who's that, Mummy?'

'An old English spy the Germans shot.'

Mogens was shocked. 'Really, Diana, you can't say things like that.'

'Well,' conceded Diana, 'she was a *brave* old spy.'

Now that Mosley's eldest children, Vivien and Nicholas, were grown up, there were also their friends from the younger generation; and separately from them was a small group of Mosley's political admirers among Oxford undergraduates, notably Desmond Stewart. The Mosleys' social life was the more enjoyable because, in their circumstances, no one who was going to be uncongenial would be likely to come at all. Jokes abounded; Nicholas remembers 'fireworks of laughter' with the non-political friends, though he perhaps exaggerates the extent to which Mosley himself would hold forth on politics or philosophy. Sometimes this would happen, but Jonathan's memory is rather of general discussion with Mosley as a kind of chairman, for he could listen as well as talk. Formal argument was rather rare.

Of practising politicians, Jonathan remembers only Robert, later Lord, Boothby, a crony from Mosley's House of Commons days with whom he had exchanged confidences about love affairs and who remained, despite deep political disagreements, an affectionate friend. Boothby's wine-resonant voice introduced an unusual note into nursery tea at Crowood. He was to become one of the first politicians to make his name on television; already he was writing a weekly political article in the *News of the World*.

'It's marvellous,' he rumbled, 'to think that eight million people read what one writes.'

'But Bob,' objected Diana, 'are you sure the *News of the World* readers actually read *you*?'

Boothby was quite firm. '*Every* reader of the *News of the World* reads *every word* of it.'

In the meantime Mosley was starting up again in politics. He wanted to answer the charges that had been made against him, and to publish to a wider audience the political ideas he had developed in prison, where he had done a great deal of reading; and a remnant of his supporters, few but fervent, was waiting for him to give a lead. It was, of course, hopeless. Six years of total war, accompanied by incessant propaganda, had established him in many people's minds as the man who, if Hitler had invaded, would have been his instrument. Mosley's time as a political prisoner was itself taken as discrediting him; it was assumed that those who ran Britain were lovers of freedom, for did they not incessantly say so? Therefore it was further assumed that if they jailed anyone they had a good reason. To the extent that people thought politically, they were hostile to Mosley; he managed to have a pleasant personal life and very rarely encountered trouble, but only because most people, most of the time, do not think politically.

But he was only forty-nine when the war ended, and at the height of his powers. Retirement would have been inconceivable. For one thing he regarded himself as having been proved right, and Diana entirely agreed with him. So, it must be said, did others, not all of them committed Fascists. Osbert Sitwell wrote to Mosley in early 1945: 'To have been deprived, as you have been, of a period of time, is beyond bearing. The only comfort for you must be, that it is impossible to blame *you* for anything that happened in those years.' His opponents had had their war; half Europe had been handed over to Communism, the Empire was clearly doomed, and the world trading system would sooner or later fall victim to over-production and world slump, a worse 1929. Soon Mosley began advocating the union of Europe, in a more extreme form than anyone else. The nationalism of the Fascists was outdated; there must be an 'extension of patriotism'. 'Europe a Nation' was the new slogan. The slump, which Mosley expected about twenty-five years before it occurred, would make people turn to his ideas. In the meantime he must express himself; he must communicate. Diana encouraged him. 'I am glad to say Kit is starting a newspaper,' she wrote to Sydney on 14 October 1946. 'Somebody ought to have a crack at those unspeakable swine: you say you don't listen to the wireless, neither do I, but I often see the newsreel at the cinema and it makes me sick with rage and misery every single time.' This was of course the time of the Nuremberg Trials, over which her old acquaintance Norman Birkett was helping to preside. To her, the trials and the executions seemed a cynical farce. The newspaper referred to was the monthly *Mosley Newsletter*, which in 1947 was replaced by the weekly *Union* (later *Action*). Assisted by Alexander Raven Thomson, Jeffrey Hamm and other pre-war supporters Mosley started a grass roots movement. This would be small and poor at the beginning, but at the right moment it could suddenly mushroom, as Hitler's had done. Money would come with the slump, when people would have a choice between Mosley and Communism. He christened his party the Union Movement; it maintained a presence mostly in the East End of London, and Mosley would address meetings whenever he could get a hall, though they were often refused. In addition, he wrote two books: *My Answer*, dealing with the past, and *The Alternative*, outlining his political philosophy and future intentions. He and Diana also founded a publishing company called Euphorion Books, mainly for non-political works. Many were translations: Goethe's *Faust*, *La Princesse de Clèves* in Nancy's translation, and *Stuka Pilot*, the reminiscences of the German air ace Hans Ulrich Rudel. This last outsold all the Euphorion list put together.

The authorities remained hostile. They were reluctant to allow paper for Mosley's publications: the printers' unions were also difficult. The government even refused to allow the Mosleys to have passports. They began applying for them in 1947, but they were constantly turned down. Their friend Lord Sherwood raised the matter in the House of Lords; it was no use. Diana wrote to the former Conservative minister, Brendan Bracken; he said that if the Conservatives got in they would grant the passports, but there was no immediate prospect of this. Daisy Fellowes went to her house in the South of France at this time and met Churchill, who complained to her that Diana had said he ought to be shot. At first Diana denied this, then remembered her remark in Holloway to her lawyer, Oswald Hickson. Diana was at first unmoved by Churchill's hurt feelings, but Daisy was persuasive, and Diana remembered her admiration for cousin Winston in her youth. In the end she wrote a conciliatory letter to Churchill, and received in reply a telegram and letter which, unlike those to Unity in 1938, were both friendly.

Finally, in 1949, the Mosleys obtained their passports by a manoeuvre that would have made the government, if it had not given in, look uncommonly foolish. In law, a passport is not necessary to leave Britain, but because other countries insist on it in order to let foreigners in, no international carrier will accept a passenger without a passport. So Mosley did two things. He contacted his friends in Franco's Spain and Salazar's Portugal, receiving their assurance that they would accept him without a passport; and he bought a yacht, the 60-ton ketch *Alianora*. A few days before they sailed, the passports were granted. With Alexander and Max they had a leisurely summer cruise, calling at Bordeaux, visiting many places in Spain and Portugal, and then going round to the Côte d'Azur and down the Italian coast to Rome.

During 1950 the Mosleys formed the intention of leaving England. The immediate reason for doing so was a rather complicated tax case which Mosley lost; after it his counsel remarked to him: 'I should have won that case for anyone in the country except you.' This, together with the passport episode, indicated that enough official prejudice against the Mosleys persisted to make it perhaps unwise to make their base in their own country. Lord Berners died in April after a long depressive illness; his death removed one reason why Diana might have wanted to stay in England. It is true that 1950 was a year of meetings and much political activity; nevertheless, it seemed to Mosley that it would be a good idea to emigrate. He used to say: 'You don't clear up a dung heap from underneath it.' In addition, Pam and Derek had moved to Ireland, to Tullamaine Castle, County Tipperary. In 1951 Mosley sold Crowood and bought two houses: Clonfert Palace in East Galway, Ireland, and the Temple de la Gloire at Orsay on the outskirts of Paris. He claimed to be rather embarrassed by the names of his residences: 'One a palace, the other a temple of glory: everyone will say the old boy has finally gone over the top.'

It was not megalomania but chance which determined the names. Clonfert Palace was a solid, pleasant house with very thick walls, mostly perhaps seventeenth-century. It was called a palace because it had been the residence of a bishop; there was a medieval cathedral of the Church of Ireland at the end of the garden, and Jonathan Swift had stayed in the house with the bishop. It was on the edge of the bog, just west of the River Shannon. The Mosleys moved most of their furniture there from Crowood. They decided to put in electric light and central heating, but not a telephone; as it turned out, the combination was disastrous. There was no farm, but there was stabling and paddocks for horses, so the boys' country life could continue as at Crowood.

The Temple de la Gloire is very different: a beautiful house that is also in a way a curiosity. It was built by Vignon for the admiring relatives of General Moreau to celebrate his victory at Hohenlinden. To the front it is a pleasant, ordinary French house of its date, 1800, with a plaster façade and shutters. To the back it really is a temple; above a symmetrical stone staircase reminiscent of Palladio there are Ionic pillars surmounted by a pediment. It has a miniature triangular park mostly occupied by a small, shallow lake; it is partially protected from the surrounding sub-urban *pavillons* by tall old trees. When the Mosleys proposed to buy it, their French financial adviser (*homme d'affaires*) noted the timber potential of the trees, and approved the investment. At the price, he told Diana, '*vous avez là une fortune, rien que dans les arbres*'. This, the third of the beautiful houses in which Diana says she has had the privilege to live, was soon to become the Mosleys' main home. Mosley lived there till his death in 1980. Gradually they made a garden, and in due course installed a small swimming pool; and by general consent Diana surpassed herself in the dec-oration of the house. Most of their own things were at Clonfert, but she combed Paris salerooms, concentrating on the Empire period. Recently the French authorities have paid her the com-pliment of insisting that the colour scheme she chose must now always be adhered to.

In December 1953 a fire broke out at Clonfert; it was probably started by the newly installed central heating, and the lack of a telephone fatally delayed the calling of the fire brigade. Much of the house and contents were destroyed, including the portrait which featured the dim baby and, very sadly for us, all Diana's letters written to Mosley in Brixton Prison. Part of the house was saved, but it was uninhabitable. In due course Mosley bought another Irish house, Ileclash near Fermoy. It possessed a stretch of the Blackwater River for fishing, but he finally used it less and less and after a few years it was sold. Their home was now definitely at Orsay and they lived there from that time on, looked after by a devoted Irish couple, Jerry and Emmy Lehane.

France was the only country in which Mosley refused ever to

be involved in politics. He presented this as the courtesy of a guest; it was also a matter of elementary prudence. However, France was a country where Mosley could find many more friends than in England who were not just politically tolerant but politically sympathetic. Ever since the French Revolution there have been warring definitions of French patriotism. Sir John Harington's remark that if treason prospers none dare call it treason has not applied there, for none of the successive treasons has prospered for quite long enough. This has deprived the French of the unthinking national solidarity which for a long time was Britain's strength and of which a by-product was the reflex disapproval of Mosley. There were right-wing intellectuals, often more or less associated with the Pétain regime, who became friends of theirs: Alfred Fabre-Luce, Jacques Benoist-Méchin, Gaston Bergery. But even someone like Nancy's Colonel, who took a contrary view, would not dream of avoiding anyone because he had a different view about the Second World War. Few of the French minded seeing Mosley. With the French landed gentry, in particular, the Mosleys were probably more at home than was Nancy. Among the equivalents of David and Sydney, the country families without many international contacts, the Resistance was rather a minority taste. Nancy herself notes this in *The Blessing*. Her Gaullist hero has an ancestor who was one of Napoleon's marshals, of whom we are told:

The family, after his death, had once more embraced a cautious Royalism, and a veil was drawn over this unfashionably democratic outburst. Old Madame de Valhubert always pretended that she knew nothing of it, and, if anybody mentioned the Marshal, would say that he must have been some very distant relation of her husband's. All his relics . . . were hidden away . . . in a little outhouse . . . and even Charles-Edouard would not have dared bring them back into the salon during the lifetime of his grandmother.

'It will be the same with me,' he said. 'Sigi's great-granddaughter-in-law will hide away my *Croix de Lorraine*, my *Médaille da la Résistance*, and the badge of my squadron, and say that I was some distant relation of her husband's. They are terrible, French families.'

Relations between Nancy and Mosley illustrate how right Logan Pearsall Smith was when he said: 'If we treat people long enough with that pretence of liking called politeness, we find it hard not to like them in the end.' Both had to be polite to each other because both knew that they would be in trouble with Diana if they were not; Nancy, in particular, had learnt this from the episode of *Wigs on the Green*. They were not at first inclined to get on. To Nancy, Mosley had ruined Diana's life and in the most appalling fashion corrupted her; to Mosley, Nancy was a silly lady novelist catering to his countrymen's worst instincts. 'I've suffered from that type all my life,' he once told Jonathan. But both loved Diana more than they disapproved of each other. The Colonel, too, was a help. From the first, his view of Mosley was on balance friendly. Nancy writes to Mrs Ham on 27 August 1949: 'I've seen a lot of Diana, and the Col. met them (a great secret) and was much taken aback at being talked to as if he were a fellow fascist! He says he thinks Tom Mosley charming but a little bit mad – he adored Diana of course.' A little later Nancy told the same thing to Jonathan – 'Don't tell your mother,' she cautioned. 'It would not be well received.' Jonathan respected this, but asked Mosley what he thought of the Colonel. 'A good lightweight,' was the reply. However, deep down the two men appreciated each other and in old age they became close friends. It is true that in the late sixties Nancy could still write to Decca sharply ridiculing Mosley's denial of anti-semitism. This, like most of Nancy's letters, was no doubt written to please its recipient; it caused some trouble after her death, for it was this letter that Decca insisted should be read out in full during Julian Jebb's television programme about Nancy (see Introduction). But in the letter Nancy also admits that she has become fond of Mosley.

We have mentioned that the Mosleys' political activity was to be ineffective, but their life cannot be understood without noting that this activity was incessant and that both, at all times, believed it would have an effect in the long run. It can be divided into three parts. First there was political philosophy. Second came the promotion of Mosley's party within Britain. Third there were his contacts in other countries, also mostly former Fascists.

Diana helped in all these activities of Mosley's. As regards his political philosophy, if it remained in practice largely unpropagated, it was not for want of trying on her part. For one thing, she used to go through Mosley's books and articles improving his style: being, as he used to complain, a governess. 'Who do we love? Our darling Gov.,' he would say. When she made some correction that he thought pedantic, he would resist; but he usually accepted her view in the end. We ought not, either, to ignore Diana's efficient ordering of the household and the entertainment of guests. The decoration of her houses was always classically beautiful, and Emmy Lehane blossomed with her encouragement into an exceptional cook. Widespread disapproval did not prevent people coming to the Mosleys; Diana ensured that when they did, they almost always enjoyed it. No firm supporter or opponent would be affected by such things, but at the margin they have their effect. Another important contribution was Diana's editing of the intellectual monthly magazine, *The European*, between 1953 and 1959. Its circulation was very small and it never paid; in the end Mosley decided that he could no longer continue it. But while it lasted it brought together a number of writers with real talent. This, unfortunately, did not help their careers. One reviewer told Jonathan that his opposite number on the *New Statesman* had warned him off *The European*, 'as a friend'. This was only a special case of a general feeling among men of letters that anything to do with Mosley ought to be cold-shouldered. Lawrence Durrell reproached Richard Aldington for contributing. No wonder *The European* was slightly uneven; Jonathan used to tell Diana that in every issue there was one very good article, and one really boring one. The number of misprints and mistakes was also high for the time, though thirty years later other publications have caught up in this matter. But Skidelsky is not wrong to describe the periodical as an impressive achievement. It attracted contributions from Ezra Pound, Henry Williamson and Roy Campbell; younger writers to appear once or twice included Robert Aickman, Hugo Charteris, Anna Kavan, Tom Stacey and Mosley's son Nicholas. Some of Mosley's Union Movement supporters naturally contributed – Raven Thomson, Robert Row, Jeffrey Hamm – but its backbone was a group of young writers of whom the best were probably the Arabists Desmond Stewart and Alan Neame, and the drama critic Michael Harald. Neame was a great admirer of Pound, and a number of other Poundians also contributed; Diana, privately, never much liked Pound's work, but she gave his supporters a good deal of space. Some of the regular contributors bear comparison with the very highest standards for style, erudition and originality; Michael Harald was at times truly brilliant. Mosley himself wrote in every issue a column called 'Analysis' which dealt with British and foreign politics. The column is usually shrewd; sometimes, reading it a generation later, it seems visionary. For instance, he clearly foresees in the fifties the coming of the urban guerrilla. At least two non-political articles of Mosley's in *The European* are outstanding: an evaluation of Erich Heller's *The Disinherited Mind*, and a consideration of Shaw and Wagner. But the real discovery of *The European* was Diana herself. She had never written for publication before, but she emerges from *The European* as a natural writer. Here she is in an early number laying into the autobiography of a busybody:

Hardly a day of her long life seems to have passed which did not find her sitting on some committee, interfering more or less with the lives of other people, or presiding as a large frog in some very small puddle . . . Sometimes she is sweeping crippled and defective children into a class at Chesterfield Settlement; sometimes at work in the Anti-Suffrage League; between the wars serving on the hated Unemployment Assistance Board; during the last war running a canteen which (get ready to laugh) she called Topsy because it just growed.

Another of Diana's hatchet jobs was on the autobiography of Elsa Maxwell. That gossip columnist and indefatigable arranger of parties had known everyone, as they say; she once wrote that she liked kings and queens, when they were nice. In her book, she claims that the man she would really like to meet is Dr Albert Schweitzer, the organist and humanitarian world-famous for his hospital in the African bush. Diana comments: 'I have a suggestion for Miss Maxwell. She and a friend, during the Peace Conference in 1919, disguised themselves so successfully as Lloyd George and Clemenceau that "passers-by thought we were the diplomats [*sic*] in the flesh." Why does she not dress up as a local hostess, go to Lambarene, and meet Dr Schweitzer? I believe she might get away with this disguise.' In the later numbers, Diana wrote a regular 'Diary'. Like all such columns it is best when she is being unpredictable. For instance, in December 1957 she makes out that science is a fitter subject for higher education than are the humanities. Her point is that lovers and practitioners of the arts can be self-taught, and are perhaps better if they are; Beethoven and Shakespeare never went to a university. Scientists, however, do need to be taught, and for this purpose must have access to equipment. This idea may well have come from Derek. In the same number there is a gentle tease on Harrods:

Last time I was in London two foreigners stopped me and asked 'Where is Knightsbridge?' I replied that it was the very street we were in. They seemed rather doubtful, and said they had walked twice up and down looking for a shop called Harrods, but couldn't find it. When I told them that, though Harrods may call it Knightsbridge, the street it adorns is Brompton Road, they were puzzled. It is one thing to have your shop in a 'good address', but very strange to muddle customers by giving a good address and then not being there.

*The European* obliged Diana, month after month, to write a great deal. She also had to select and edit what others wrote. It was six years of literary apprenticeship; afterwards she was not just a natural writer, but a practised one.

It might have been better for Mosley to have continued with *The European* and more or less dropped the Union Movement. Desmond Stewart used to plead with him to take this course, and just possibly it might have given him, eventually, some small leverage on the climate of opinion. But the process would have been so slow that no discernible effect would have been felt in Mosley's lifetime. In the meantime Britain's absolute and relative power was declining and it seemed certain that sooner or later there would be a really serious economic crisis. Again, the coloured immigration then beginning, still a cloud no bigger than a man's hand, would cause problems if it continued. He in fact expected quite soon the slump that, in the event, was not to start till the late seventies, and thought it might destabilize the political situation enough to make people turn to his movement. But this never happened. He stood for Parliament in 1959 and 1966, and both times lost his deposit.

Rather more important than Mosley's activity in Britain, though still only on the margin, was his activity in Europe. This took place among the respectable remnants of European Fascism: people who were not planning violence, or accused of war crimes, but aiming at political rehabilitation by constitutional means. One of Mosley's German contacts, Dr Werner Naumann, was arrested by the British occupation authorities in January 1953, partly it seems because he was in touch with Mosley, but he was released without being charged with anything. Mosley was also in touch with the leaders of the nationalistic Deutsche Reichspartei. In South Africa he knew Oswald Pirow. He visited Peron in Argentina, though he missed seeing Evita, who was ill. In Spain his friend was Ramon Serrano Suner, Franco's brother-in-law, who had been Foreign Minister during the war. In Italy Mosley was close to some of the leaders of the MSI, including Giorgio Almirante. There was quite a lot of coming and going over the years, including a libel suit against the Italian Communist paper *Unità*, which Mosley won.

Was this international activity entirely futile? Perhaps not quite. In Germany, Mosley's influence probably reduced the number of committed Nazi sympathizers who took what was called the 'Eastern View': the view that in the ruin of their cause it was the Communism, rather than Western democracy, which would ultimately make a less uncongenial world for them. More generally, it is likely that he had some effect in propagating a European viewpoint among circles on the continent whose instincts were narrowly nationalistic. He got members of the Italian MSI to sign a declaration in favour of European unity: an achievement in its way, since that 'neofascist' party had been exclusively nationalistic.

These activities used intermittently to annoy Nancy. Diana never talked politics with her, but this made her all the more cross whenever she was reminded that the Mosleys were still at it. To Mrs Ham she wrote from Venice on 13 July 1960: 'Sir O. was here for the fascist meeting which never took place but gave rise to a communist riot here – only rather a good riot, damped by rain. He is said to be the chief of a fascist *réseau* [network] in Germany now. The Italians (one's own friends) are enraged about it . . .' And again on 22 August 1960: 'Diana says Sir O. has never been so busy – it makes my flesh creep. No doubt we shall all be in camps very soon. I've ordered a camping suit from Lanvin – the price is so terrible that even I feel guilty and won't dare confess it. But I tell myself old age looms as well as what *you* call the milennium [*sic*], and a new suit is so cheering.' Perhaps what displeased Nancy most was that this should happen in Venice, very much one of her stamping grounds. It caused her embarrassment with her friends there. But Venice was also a place where the Mosleys usually went for pleasure rather than politics. Diana is something like a walking guidebook to it, knowing what pictures are in what churches and finding her way to them without hesitation. It was in Venice, too, that Mosley claimed to have overheard two Jews discussing them.

'Say what you like,' one is supposed to have said, 'old Tom Mosley would never have done us any harm.'

'No,' said his companion, 'but Diana would.'

This was one of those often-repeated teases that are generated by happy marriages; over the years he must have told the story a hundred times, always in her presence because the whole point was to make her playfully slap his hand.

In 1966 he gave up the leadership of the Union Movement. He was seventy, but his age was by the way; he was in good shape still. The idea was not retirement but a change of tack. It is rather impressive that the Union Movement continued to exist, even in a small way. It did so, though from now on it was to be eclipsed by the various organizations which were to unite, temporarily, in the National Front. These groups, often caricaturing in themselves the image of Nazism put about by its enemies, appealed more strongly than Mosley could to those who were seeking stridency and extremism, for in these he fell sadly short. The case Mosley put to his followers for partly abandoning them could only have been accepted by people of a quite different sort; they needed to be sober and realistic as well as exceptionally loyal. The fact he had to make clear to them was that he and they would get nowhere through the old methods of meetings and small-circulation periodicals. He personally had to break through into the orthodox media, for which purpose he needed to be free of formal ties with his movement. He still spoke at their dinners and contributed to their paper; indirectly he also helped financially by maintaining his 'secretariat' of Jeffrey Hamm and Robert Row. Robert Row edited the Union Movement paper, *Action*, and the secretariat also produced Mosley's personal 'broadsheets'. But the fact that most of his committed supporters did not join another group, or lapse into inactivity, shows that many of them loved him. It is not too strong a word.

After Mosley gave up leading the Union Movement, he also stopped his blanket attacks on the system and the existing parties. On the contrary, now and for the rest of his life he stood for a coalition government drawn from elements in all parties. He was consistently in favour of joining the Common Market. He admitted that it had weaknesses, but it was the form the European idea happened to be taking: it would be a first step. We notice a mellowing since 1931, when it had been precisely the insistence on getting everything at once that had driven him towards Fascism and the wilderness.

But how could he get his ideas aired? On private instructions from the government, the BBC had banned him in 1935. It showed no sign of relenting; in fact the Director-General, Sir Hugh Greene, is supposed to have said that Mosley would appear only over his dead body. ITV followed this lead. A number of producers, notably Daniel Farson, had arranged interviews with him over the years. None was allowed to be shown. There was, however, a weakness which Mosley could in the end exploit. Though excluded, he was not forgotten, and every now and then someone would attack him. One such attack perpetrated on the BBC was the repetition of a libel, and he sued for contempt of court. Lord Chief Justice Parker and his colleagues did not find for him, which might have meant jailing the BBC Governors; but Parker did express 'considerable sympathy' with Mosley. 'Someone who has the ear of the whole nation can say things and the unfortunate subject has no means of answering back in the same medium.' This happened in 1966, and not long afterwards he began appearing on both BBC and ITV. In 1968, James Mossman featured him in a *Panorama* programme that was watched by 8½ million people. The programme was balanced, but this in itself means that by the standards of the time it was friendly.

Also in 1968 he published his autobiography, *My Life*, which sold well and in due course went into paperback. The reviews were, in the context, surprisingly favourable; Michael Foot spoke of Mosley's 'political genius', and Norman St John Stevas accepted his denial of anti-semitism. This is what sparked off the controversy in *The Times* correspondence column that we mentioned in an earlier chapter. But essentially Mosley began to be looked on less as a present danger, more as an interesting historical figure. From then on, especially during the early seventies, he appeared on television a number of times. Once he debated the Common Market with Richard Crossman. It is perhaps true to say, with Skidelsky, that debating style had changed in forty years and Mosley, in his seventies, had to learn to cope with this; but he did so. When the American edition of *My Life* came out he even crossed the Atlantic and did a good deal of broadcasting in the United States. Both he and Diana also published articles, especially in *Books and Bookmen*.

The new publicity produced a great many new contacts and acquaintances, many of them in and around the media. Perhaps Mosley thought some of these people took to him more than they really did. To Jonathan he once remarked, 'I love media men'; from the victim of forty years of boycott this was remarkably quick forgiveness. It is a fact, though, that some of them were charmed and impressed by him. His energy was still almost unimpaired; but he now added to it a new, mature geniality. A top advertising man in his forties who met him around 1970 was impressed by his conversation, but even more by the stamina he showed when they lunched together at the Ritz. 'At the beginning he said he lived sparely, like an athlete,' said this man to Jonathan. 'Well, we had champagne before lunch, followed by two kinds of wine and a large brandy. He matched me glass for glass, then went off to take a press conference, alert as ever. As for me, I was knocked out; I went to sleep in my office.' Besides media men, Mosley came to know a number of politicians, writers and intellectuals. Many of them were contacts renewed from before the war; some were quite improbable. Dr Mervyn Stockwood, left-wing bishop of Southwark, came to dinner in a biretta, acquired from his Roman Catholic opposite number with whom he swapped hats. He got to know the Mosleys through becoming a pen-pal of Diana's. She is fond of theological teasing.

This brings us back to her key role in consolidating many of these personal contacts, entertaining both at Orsay and in London. The new people in the Mosleys' lives only added themselves to what was anyway an active and international social life. The end of *The European* was certainly not the end of the Mosleys' contact

with young British intellectuals. In the late fifties they came
to know some of that very disparate group of writers lumped
together under the term Angry Young Men. Colin Wilson, notably, became a friend, though often a critical one; he foresaw the
odium which would follow Mosley's decision to fight North
Kensington in 1959. He has, however, often defended Mosley with
great courage: not a popular operation even when the defence is
entirely reasonable.

Members of the family all probably helped, over the years, in
breaking down personal prejudice against the Mosleys. For one
thing there were all their children. He had three, and she two, by
their first marriages, and they had two together: seven in all. The
total number of people introduced by them to the Mosleys must
exceed a hundred; the most important of these was Professor
Robert Skidelsky, a university friend of Max, who wrote a
masterly biography of Mosley. Six of the seven have their own
children, some grown up; these, too, have carried on the process,
not as a conscious campaign but in the nature of things. Other
relations of Diana's also helped, most notably the Devonshires. In
every way except politics Diana and Debo have been increasingly
close over the years as Debo's late, but formidable, intellectual
development led her to share more and more of Diana's interests.
As regards politics, all Debo will ever say is that she hates the
subject. In her position this is a sane reaction. Andrew is political,
but has always been able to put up with anyone, however extreme,
who does not obtrude his views in private life. This the Mosleys
have never done: on the contrary they were, over the years, a
congenial addition to house parties at Chatsworth or Lismore,
where they met not only practising politicians but artists, sports-
men, businessmen and all kinds of people. Prejudices soften in a
country house weekend, and many who would otherwise not have
known this have become aware that neither Mosley nor Diana was
obsessive or unpleasant.

The high point for Mosley's relative rehabilitation – it can be
likened to the top of a very modest range of submerged hills that
remained far under the sea – was probably the publication in 1975
of Skidelsky's biography. The work is honest, meticulously scholarly, and rather hard to shrug off. Its author clearly likes Mosley,
and though he does not endorse all his actions or agree with him

politically, he gives an objective description of his career and takes his post-war thinking seriously enough to summarize it perceptively.

But two years later, in 1977, Diana published *A Life of Contrasts*; reactions to her book showed a distinct worsening of the atmosphere. Not that it was at all badly reviewed, on balance; Jonathan Raban, in the *Sunday Times*, even noticed that Diana wrote well. Nevertheless there was a wave of real bitterness. She rather expected it; 'I'm afraid it will not be liked,' she wrote to Jonathan not long before publication. *The Times* review was one of the kindlier ones, but said there was ground glass in the *bombe surprise*. This is because Diana presents scenes and people exactly as they seemed to her, making no concessions to generally accepted opinion. Her writing has the direct frankness of Sydney's and some of Thomas's, and in Diana's circumstances that proved a bit too much. Mosley emerges as the man who could have given his country prosperity and peace. Pre-war Germany is a happy country; what was being prepared, what was happening outside Diana's experience, is omitted. Hitler is a marvellous, if rather moody, companion who has abstemious habits and exquisite manners; there is a chapter about him and Churchill, comparing rather than contrasting, which was bound to annoy. Diana's book soon got a label: it was 'unrepentant'. Not only does she quite evidently fail to see what she has to repent of, she is distinctly astringent about at least two Nazis who did repent. One is Putzi; and there is a dig also at Albert Speer, whom she remembers at Hitler's table. 'At that time a young architect, he has grown into an old writer. On the occasions when I saw him he gave a wonderful imitation of being fascinated by his host . . .' She is certainly far too perfunctory in referring to the horrors of the Nazi regime, but some commentators came close to implying that she had committed them. One made out that, far from resenting her imprisonment, she should think herself lucky that worse did not befall her, implying that she ought to have been executed. There was another, distinct, ground of resentment – the fact that Diana had lived most of her life in comfort. This was compounded by Diana's explicit enjoyment of the beauty she had seen and the fun she had had. Too much was 'perfection', from Edward James's house in Italy to the Duchess of Windsor's food. It is true that to read about other people's past enjoyment can pall; but in Diana's case it needed to be described as showing that she had a full life apart from politics, and her political activity could not be attributed to a 'complex'. The trouble is that among modern *literati* a non-political life of Diana's sort is now disparaged. One can imagine the harassed reviewer, typing amid the wails of children and the smell of cooking, resenting Diana's breakfasts in bed. For these, as much as for her politics, he may have felt she deserved a spell in Holloway. After prison, one article commented sourly, it was 'back to the old lush life'. Again, the fact that Diana's is an altogether lighter book than those by and about Mosley meant that it was read less analytically. Ground glass makes people angrier when it suddenly appears in a *bombe surprise*. The book sold, all the same; publishers are said not to read reviews but to measure them, and certainly Diana got the column inches.

Then, in 1980, Diana published another book, *The Duchess of Windsor*. She was encouraged to write it by the Duchess's devoted French lawyer, Maître Suzanne Blum. The Windsors, also living on the outskirts of Paris, had been friendly with the Mosleys for years; the short chapter on them in *A Life of Contrasts* is in its quiet way one of the best things ever written about them. The Duke, in particular, comes to life, with his special mid-Atlantic way of talking, his infallible memory for people, the way his sad expression would suddenly break into smiling animation. Diana's biography of the Duchess was well done, though depending mainly upon published sources; it has perhaps been superseded by Michael Bloch's more recent book about the Windsors, equally friendly and much more complete. But one remark in Diana's book filled her family with foreboding. With a couple like the Windsors, she says, when the first dies it is very hard on the one who is left. It made us think of Mosley's death, for which it showed perhaps that she was now steeling herself.

Ageing, notoriously, is not a smooth process; people stay much the same for years, then with or without reason suffer what the French call *a coup de vieux*. Until his late seventies Mosley was as he had been in middle age; alert in mind and, but for his bad leg, active in body. But from about his eightieth birthday, in 1976, old age caught up fast. Mentally the change was perhaps only noticeable to those who knew him well, but physically he suddenly seemed really old. He moved slowly, he limped more. Parkinson's disease set in and the drug he took for it sometimes made him fall over. He also seemed all at once to accept that he was old, and to tolerate the condition. Diana became tied to him; he did not like her to leave him for long, and she did not care to be away. For this reason she refused to go to the United States to promote *A Life of Contrasts* there.

He died suddenly and peacefully, in his bed, in November 1980; he was just eighty-four. Guests who had been with him the previous weekend said he had been as lively and genial as ever; he had even been intending, a few days afterwards, to fly to London and appear on television.

To Diana, it was as if her own life had ended. Only Jerry and Emmy Lehane, perhaps, can know how she suffered in those first few days. Alexander and his wife Charlotte, who live in Paris, took charge and, did all they could. The funeral took place at the Columbarium at Père Lachaise; music was interspersed with readings. It was an unusually cold December, and the place was unheated. It seemed somehow appropriate that one sat listening in freezing, sepulchral cold. 'Say not the struggle naught availeth': Clough's poem was one of those read out. The words are also on Unity's tombstone. One wondered. Yet he had, on the whole, enjoyed the struggle; he had enjoyed most things.

Nearly a year later it looked as if Diana would die too. She had a series of what seemed like strokes and became half paralysed; she was flown to the London Hospital. Finally Professor Watkins diagnosed a brain tumour and removed it; it turned out to be benign, and she eventually recovered completely, convalescing at Chatsworth, Jonathan found his visits to the hospital poignant – it seemed that his mother was dying, or that even if she recovered she would be incapacitated – but there was usually something to cheer him up. As she improved, a good deal of laughter used to come from her room; one passing doctor who did not know her told the ward sister that Diana sounded hysterical, and ought to be watched. One visitor was Lord Longford; he was not only an old friend but was also connected with the firm that published *The Duchess of Windsor*. 'Frank's so *faithful* the way he comes all the time,' said Diana, and paused, adding: 'Of course, he thinks I'm Myra Hindley.'

# 41

# Decca, the Red Star

After Esmond's death Decca stayed on in Washington with their baby, Dinky. At first they remained with the hospitable Durrs, then lived in a shared flat. Decca went to secretarial school, and was then taken on as a typist by the Office of Price Administration (OPA) which ran price control and rationing. Her gift for office politics soon secured promotion to the rank of investigator. She liked the work. Americans, she found, were much too keen on material comforts, even during the war. They were apt to deal on the black market, and in general thumb noses at the state. In most contexts Decca likes to range herself with the nose thumbers, but not here.

The people she met at work were mostly, like her, dedicated rationers, though there was also what she saw as a fifth column of free market supporters. Many colleagues were left-wingers, some moderate and some extreme, of the type that had taken over Roosevelt's New Deal at the administrative level. One is not surprised to find J. K. Galbraith among them, but many were far to the left of him, natural soulmates in fact for Decca. One of her colleagues was the lawyer Robert Treuhaft, employed as an enforcement attorney. They appealed to each other because both combined extremely left-wing politics with sophistication and a sense of humour. He came from the Bronx and she thought his accent funny, but we may be certain that he was even more astonished at hers. He was also to be permanently amazed by her stories of her family. Their relationship eventually turned into a typically stable and affectionate Mitford marriage, its stability based on politics and jokes. In Washington they had fun at the food counter of the OPA self-service canteen; they had fun catching people wasting petrol by driving to nightclubs. They have had fun ever since.

Bob was the son of Hungarian Jewish immigrants; his mother had by hard work built up a hat shop in New York, and was comfortably off. Very clever, Bob had got into Harvard, then into Harvard Law School; he moved to the political left when apprenticed to a lawyer who did trade union work. Bob and Decca both had Communist sympathies and would have liked to join the party, but at this stage they did not. They were both young and in junior positions; possession of party cards might have damaged their prospects, and in the case of Decca, who was an alien, it could have caused special difficulties. So they contented themselves at this stage with supporting individual Communist causes. In the climate of the wartime alliance with Russia, this attracted no particular attention.

Suddenly Decca shifted herself right across the continent to San Francisco when she was transferred to the OPA office there. Bob saw her and Dinky off on the train. He came out to see them for a holiday, and in due course he and Decca were married; he joined her in San Francisco, getting a job at the War Labour Board. Diana, in prison, heard the news and asked Sydney to transmit her best wishes. 'Is he a deutscher?' she asked, and added that Decca would make a perfect wife. Bob, Decca and Dinky moved in with a friendly landlady in the Haight-Ashbury district, then a modest residential part of the city. Later it was to become world-famous as 'Hashbury', centre of flower power and weed power. Almost as soon as Decca reached San Francisco she had joined the appropriate union, which was the Communist-influenced United Federal Workers' Union. The man who recruited her was Al Bernstein; his son, Carl Bernstein, was to expose the Watergate affair in the newspapers of Decca's friend Katharine Graham. A celebrity by then, Carl Bernstein was also to write a preface to Decca's *The Making of a Muckraker*, making it clear that she had been a guiding light of his.

Decca remained in correspondence with Sydney, but otherwise her complicated family must have seemed very far away. But this was not to last. In November 1943 the Mosleys were released from prison, and the Communists organized their protests. It was a story, even in America, and in no time at all the San Francisco newspapers sniffed Decca out. Her employer at OPA allowed her a day or two off so she sat at home, surrounded by reporters waiting outside. Finally she wrote a letter to Winston Churchill, sending a copy to the *San Francisco Chronicle* as an exclusive. It demanded that they be put back in jail, where they belonged. Their release, she said, was an insult to all anti-Fascists and a betrayal of all those who died fighting Fascism.

This implies that there are people so repellent that it is pedantic to inquire what they may have actually done; jail is *where they belong*. We see in embryo the reasoning behind the Gulag Archipelago, just as in Unity's letter about the Austrian Nazi, who found out he was half-Jewish, we saw the germ of Hitler's death camps. Unity, of course, shot herself before she could have second thoughts; Decca in due course did have some, perhaps, though the half-hearted regret expressed in *A Fine Old Conflict* (1977) applies more to the wording than to the sentiment. She describes her own letter as stuffy, self-righteous and unsisterly. She admits to spitefulness. She claims to have feared that the Mosleys' release might indicate a wish to make a separate peace with Germany, and mentions bitterness about Esmond's death; odd, this, since Mosley had been imprisoned for trying to stop the war in which Esmond was killed. Finally, she hints at a further motive for writing which may really have been the determining one. Opposition to the release was in accordance with the Communist Party line. To come out publicly in this way might help to secure an invitation to become a party member. Among those she consulted before writing her letter had been her superior in the union, and it was this lady who not long afterwards recruited both her and Bob. It must be remembered that the Communist Party is not something one just joins; a party card is regarded as a privilege.

Bob and Decca joined the party when they were all at the state convention of the Congress of Industrial Organizations (CIO), to which Decca's union was affiliated. Outsize pictures of Stalin and Roosevelt dominated this gathering, and Decca, whose union experience up to then had been white collar in character, met up with some genuine working-class militants, people who had experience of picketing. The convention was supporting the election of Roosevelt; this campaign was successful in the next year, but we are reminded how odd was Roosevelt's coalition of supporters, ranging from Communist sympathizers haranguing union meetings beneath pictures of Stalin to southern white supremacists framed by the Confederate flag.

In 1945 Decca lobbied the San Francisco International Conference, which was to be the formative body of the United Nations, and saw several English people there. These included the Conservative MP Robert Boothby, an old crony of Mosley's, as well as Kingsley Martin, the editor of the socialist *New Statesman*. Another Englishman present was the upper-class Communist Claud Cockburn, former editor of *The Week* and future columnist in *Private Eye*. Decca, it will be remembered, had a little errand for Cockburn to do with her share of Inchkenneth. Her main preoccupation in San Francisco was to agitate for the exclusion of Franco's Spain from the United Nations, she told Sydney in a letter.

Apart from this excursion into the international field, the next few years of Decca's life were largely devoted to the United States Communist Party and to the Civil Rights Congress, the Communist-run organization which campaigned for black rights. Her account of this period in *A Fine Old Conflict* manages to hold the reader's interest while not concealing how boring much of it must have been. She liked most of the comrades, admired many of them, yet the reigning atmosphere of prosy self-righteousness comes across fully. She could not always help teasing; this was often, though not always, resented. However, even the grimmest of the comrades evidently recognized Decca's dedicated industriousness and the seriousness which underlay her flippancy. We believe, too, that the flippancy is possibly overplayed in *A Fine Old Conflict*; it suits the image she wants to project of herself to uncommitted readers. She certainly worked hard; when agitating in the Deep South for the blacks she showed physical courage. Bob, meanwhile, pursued his legal career, joining a firm which specialized in trade union cases and in defending blacks. Since many of his clients were poor, the work was often underpaid. Two sons were born to them, Nicholas and Benjamin (Benjy). In 1947 they moved to the industrial town of Oakland, not far from San Francisco.

Decca kept in touch with Sydney all the time, sending photographs of the children and news of her doings. She received Mitford news in reply, or such of it as Sydney felt she would care to read. But we need not doubt that Decca was surprised when in early January 1948 Sydney telegraphed saying that she intended to come out to visit them. It was little Dinky, aged seven, who was responsible. In a letter thanking Sydney for a Christmas present, she had written in her big, childish hand that she wished Sydney would come to see them one day. Sydney was waiting for just such an excuse to visit the daughter she had not seen for so many years, and the son-in-law and grandchildren she had not seen at all. Decca can be forgiven if she wondered how the visit would go. How would Sydney and Bob get on?

In the end everyone enjoyed it. Decca says Sydney's intention was to make friends at all costs. We are sure this is right, but it does not imply any sort of surrender by her mother. Sydney did not take the political views of any of her daughters very seriously, whether or not she agreed with them. She went mainly out of fondness for Decca, but also out of curiosity. At sixty-eight Sydney was still able to accept things exactly as she found them. Her attitude was that of her father when his yacht called at some unfamiliar port: cool, observant and amused. Decca's life seemed perhaps queer in some ways, the American conditions as much as the Communism, but Sydney took it as she found it. Her bedroom, she noted, was furnished only with a bed and a piano. Very well, her suitcase would do instead of a cupboard. She loved the children, and made Bob laugh.

About politics she never argued, but Bob's legal activities met with her approval. 'He helps those poor negroes when they are framed,' she said later to Jonathan; 'so good of him.' But she also told Jonathan there were rather too many blacks in and out of the Treuhaft household; Dinky, she feared, might one day marry one. Bob's mother, Aranka. took the same view, complaining to Debo that Decca had coloured folk in her home. Bob told Sydney that a bill was about to pass Congress that might mean prison for him and Decca; the Cold War had replaced the Russian alliance. Here Sydney took the opportunity for what, in the context of Decca's letter to Churchill, must be construed as the gentlest of digs: she said she supposed they would go to prison, which would be a pity; but of course she was quite used to seeing her children put in jail.

Debo came to see Decca in 1950. Decca invited some Communist friends to meet her; she thought the comrades were rather deferential to the Duchess, though Debo got the impression of being attacked rather insistently on the subject of British imperialism. Perhaps this is an example of the clash of cultures. American conventions allow more aggression in dinner table argument than is normal in Britain, so that what to Decca looked like pulled punches seemed to Debo like hammer blows.

Now and again one is struck by small parallels between Decca and Diana, the Treuhafts and the Mosleys. Both couples, for instance, at times expected the imminent collapse of the capitalist system. Mosley, thinking the British economy particularly precarious, was to sell all his British equities during the fifties, thus probably losing more in capital than he was to gain in income through being outside the United Kingdom. On a much smaller scale the same reasoning trapped Decca and Bob. Their Marxist lecturer proved to their satisfaction that a great depression was impending, so they went short of Sears Roebuck shares, fortunately with a stop-loss order which limited the damage to 300 dollars. Another parallel was a bungled attempt by the United States government to stop the Treuhafts leaving the country for a visit to Europe in 1955, which recalls the denial of a passport to the Mosleys after the war. The Treuhafts' passport application form was returned without acknowledgement. They renewed the application, intending to fight the refusal which seemed certain to follow. But by some administrative oversight a valid passport arrived. It was quickly followed by a telegram telling them it had been issued by mistake, but they used it anyway, setting sail for England with the children and Nebby-Lou Crawford, the seventeen-year-old daughter of a friend.

Debo met them in London and then travelled up with them, and her own children and Nanny, to Inchkenneth. It was Decca's first experience of 'The Worst Journey in the World'. Once on the island she found it hard at first to adjust to the calm routine. But she settled down, and it is certain that the whole family must have enjoyed the visit. Later events prove this. After Inchkenneth the two families went to Edensor, the house near Chatsworth where the Devonshires were living during the years before they moved into Chatsworth itself. Bob was the one who really enjoyed this visit; he saw Decca's family as a splendid spectator sport, which seems always to have been his attitude. Decca was rather on edge;

she was not a good guest, she admits. There is indeed evidence
that this visit did not go smoothly. Nancy picked up a few worries
from Debo, and wrote to Diana about them on 8 September 1955:
'I suppose you've heard all the Decca news from Debo. Oh dear
how I dread their arrival – and I have to keep hypocritically
writing to say I die for them. Ay di me [*sic*]. I bet they're off to
Russia, hence Bob's disguising moustache. The awful thing is it
won't teach them (that'll teach them) because nothing ever does
teach people.'

After a time in London the family went on – not, as Nancy
expected, to Russia, but to Hungary; they were curious to see the
country from which Bob's family had come. It was now a People's
Democracy, under the leadership of Comrade Matyas Rakosi. Just
over a year later, in 1956, there was, as we now know, to be a bit
of bother there. The Treuhafts' first stop was Vienna, to get
a visa. They used an appropriate stratagem to achieve this. After
all, they were genuinely friendly to the regime, true left-wing
militants anxious to be impressed. Rakosi's Hungary seemed, of
course, pretty marvellous on the whole. Signs of socialism triumphant were everywhere. They were entertained on a collective
farm, and told how much the lot of the peasants had improved.
They went to the ballet and the opera and were thrilled that the
audience seemed working-class. They even met a Stakhanovite, a
champion worker who over-fulfilled his norm.

But two incidents occurred which worried Decca. First, a
waiter, evidently not trusting the post, asked the Treuhafts to
take a letter from him to send to his brother in America. She and
Bob thought they had better decline. He might easily be an anti-
Communist. Perhaps his letter contained slander against the
regime. At least Decca did not simply accept his letter and take it
straight to the authorities. The other incident concerned a young
woman teacher who met them in their hotel and asked them to her
house for a drink; her husband wanted help to visit the United
States. She too sounded distressed. They then got a note from her
telling them not to come. A friend on the peace committee, to
whom Decca told these stories, said that naturally there were still
malcontents, especially among non-proletarians like teachers and
waiters. The Treuhafts had better keep away from such people for
the rest of their stay, she added. They did.

On her return to America Decca wrote a lyrical account of the visit to Hungary for a pro-Communist periodical. The original version included these incidents but the editor cut them out, citing reasons of space. Unfortunately editors are like this. By 1977, when *A Fine Old Conflict* was published, time had passed and the Rakosì government was rather disapproved than approved of, even by the left. Fortunately Decca had kept the original version of her article and could accordingly include the stories in her book.

From Budapest the family went straight to Paris to visit Nancy, who had, we remember, been feigning a state of wild excitement about their visit. Nowhere is Nancy's strange two-faced character more evident than in the episode which was now to take place. The Treuhafts arrived unannounced (and dead tired) at Rue Monsieur because Decca had lost Nancy's telephone number. They found Nancy away; she had given them up and gone to stay with Debo. Marie, Nancy's maid, took them in and told them what happened.

Decca immediately telephoned Nancy at Edensor to tell her of their arrival. Nancy's reaction was strange and sharp. She snapped at Decca for ringing from her flat; it was very expensive, she complained, and hung up. To Bob, especially, this seemed just another glorious example of the family dottiness; and in great bon-homie, he and Decca made themselves at home with a comfortable drink. In due course Nancy rang back. This time she sounded relaxed, welcoming and affectionate. The letter to Diana quoted above shows that the sharp reaction to the first call expressed her immediate feelings more accurately than the cooing tones of the second. Years of living alone in her well-ordered flat with the cherished objects she was accumulating were developing in Nancy a spinsterish side. This sudden mass invasion, in her absence, of her calm domain was dreadfully upsetting. She did want to see Decca, far more than she was ever likely to admit to Diana; but in *her flat*, with American children, so notorious for their indiscipline and ill-manners − ! − Perhaps she even remembered the visit to Lord Faringdon: she began to think of the Treuhafts as Visigoths. In a panic, she wrote again on 22 October 1955 to Diana; since she was the one member of the family Decca would certainly avoid, perhaps she could be used to drive the Treuhafts out. Her tone is confused and agitated. 'Oh dereling oi am in great and terrible despair. I'm almost sure, from signs too long to explain, that the Treuhafts have moved into Rue Mr, and I *can't* bear it.' Not so much for her own sake, she says, though she details various fears, but because of the effect on Marie. 'I've written to say she must tell them *you* are both arriving on Monday for a few nights as this seems the only way to dislodge them. (I've sent them £50 for an hotel.)' She beseeches Diana, who is away, as soon as she gets back to ring Marie to find out what is happening. 'No good me ringing up because when I did, and got on to Decca, she merely put on that stonewalling voice and I could get nothing out of her except idiotic giggles.' Diana is to tell Marie that 'once they've gone they're not to be allowed into the flat again – she must shut all up and pretend to be away . . . I know you'll feel for me and do what you can. (And Evelyn says I'm a Communist agitator – the *comble* [limit]).'

The panic was soon over. Nancy wrote again to Diana three days later: 'Oh the relief. In fact they behaved perfectly, and I think Marie must have thought I'd quite lost my head . . . Well, I had, too! I think when Decca telephoned she was a bit drunk – she'd been travelling all day and then settled down to my whisky while waiting for the call . . . Anyway, she's waiting in Paris for my return, which I've put forward one day and will come back on Friday 18th . . . I can't wait to C. for myself.' She duly did, and the rest of the visit went swimmingly. Bob and Nebby-Lou went home soon to job and school respectively, but Decca and Dinky stayed on in an hotel, spending their days at Rue Monsieur. Nancy and Decca had lovely chats together, though their conversation remained superficial. Decca was not going to tell Nancy anything intimate, especially about her political activities; any more than Nancy was going to tell her about her difficulties with Peter Rodd or her feelings about the Colonel. There has always been a paradox about the relations between almost any two Mitfords, which is that, though they both chat fluently and are deeply fond of each other, the affection between them is inarticulate and what they say to each other is independent of it. They rarely unburden themselves; the face they turn to each other is the face they turn to the public. This has never changed through the years. But even when they are hostile, it alters their tone to each other rather little, if at all. Decca's feelings towards Diana did not change as the years advanced. In a letter to Roy Harrod in 1960 she says she has resumed contact with all her sisters, except Diana who she is afraid will make her son Benjy into soap because he is half-Jewish. Yet in fact she and Diana did come into contact – not during this 1955 visit, but, we think, in 1959. Decca was staying with Sydney at Rutland Gate Mews. The telephone rang and Decca picked it up; it was Diana, who had no idea Decca was there. Sydney's heart missed a beat when she realized who was on the other end, but it was soon clear to her that the sisters were chatting away as if nothing had ever come between them. As soon as the telephone was back on its receiver, though, the conversation was as if it had never been.

At this stage, except for the special case of Diana, no difficulty existed between Decca and anyone in the family. She was regarded as rather a curiosity, and Jonathan remembers a vague feeling that she was in some way necessary to the family to balance his mother and Unity. Catherine, with her brother Jasper, went one year for a holiday on Inchkenneth, finding Decca there with her family. Catherine loved them all, and contributed her first seven-year-old articles to an island newspaper that Decca organized. She came back happy and stimulated. Decca and Bob, in fact, took to Inchkenneth so much that they actually bought it; an example of the strange magic the place possesses, because they lived, after all, on the opposite side of the world. Nancy, as we have seen, had given her share of the island to Decca; Decca then proposed to buy out Pam, Diana and Debo, on the understanding that Sydney should continue to occupy and run the island till the end of her life. No one made difficulties, Diana no more than anyone else. A valuer from Oban gave a figure for the island and the deal was done. The Treuhafts owned the island until in due course, some years after Sydney's death, it did seem more trouble than it was worth, and they sold it. The Mitfords did not, like some families, quarrel about money; it was as if their political differences exhausted their quarrelling capacity.

Meanwhile, it was becoming clear in the mid-fifties that the United States Communist Party, with its affiliates, was in a blind alley. All the agitation, all the campaigning, all the fund raising being conducted by the dedicated and often brilliant party comrades was leading nowhere. There was some actual persecution; but Senator McCarthy, the House Committee for Un-American Affairs, the FBI and so on were only the tip of an iceberg whose dim submarine bulk consisted of a rooted dislike of Communism among the generality of the American people. Exposure as a Communist made a person unpopular. One of the distinguishing features of a Communist was his belief that the atrocities of Stalin and other Marxist dictators were invented by the Western media, that what little may have been true was due to residual discontent among feudal or bourgeois remnants. Since this view was quite clearly absurd, the Communists had painted themselves into a corner.

What changed this, and launched Decca on her trajectory, was Khrushchev's speech in March 1956 to a closed session of the Soviet Party Congress. As left-wingers always do, Decca claims much too much for this speech; she says it gave all the crimes of Stalin in all their details. All Khrushchev in fact did was to mention some of Stalin's crimes *against Communists*, concentrating on the purge of 1937–38 which was directed primarily at the party. The huge massacres of peasants, of actual and putative political opponents, were scarcely touched on. But the fact that Communists were the victims was really what made the revelations so sensational within the party; it had not just been Fascists and reactionaries who had suffered, but people like themselves! Also, of course, a pronouncement by the leader of the Soviet Union had to be true; it was not enemy disinformation. Communists all over the world were taken by the scruff of the neck and forced to think. Since many Communists were, in different ways, extremely bright, a result was the release of a good deal of brainpower that was in due course to have a profound influence on American society. It was to help complete the emancipation of the blacks, and in due course to further the abandonment of non-Communist Vietnam. It directed the student unrest of the 1960s, and the campaigns against nuclear armaments. The end purpose pursued by most of these bright Marxists is worldwide Communism, and on balance they have probably moved us all in this grim direction. But some of the campaigns with this ultimate end have had good results, notably Decca's. As so often we are reminded of the devil in Goethe's *Faust*, willing destruction but unable to help doing good.

What happened in Decca's special case when the atmosphere changed in this way? She had left her family and country and she detested her class, but it was easier to take herself out of the upper class than the upper class out of her. Hilaire Belloc had noticed that aristocrats 'talk of their affairs in loud and strident voices'; Decca was always to retain something of this attitude. In the meantime, she was well-educated and had a natural feeling for words. In addition she possessed a sharp sense of the ridiculous. She liked and respected her party colleagues; but she could not help noticing that whatever they might one day do to the class enemy, they were most certainly torturing the English language. Nancy had not long published *Noblesse Oblige*; Stephen Potter, a year or two earlier, had produced little books on *Gamesmanship* and *Lifemanship* and pointed out some of the linguistic ploys by which people get the better of each other without actually cheating. She began looking through their eyes at the turgid jargon of the comrades. Marxists are rarely stylists, and American Marxists most rarely of all. The result was a duplicated pamphlet called *Lifeitselfmanship, or How to Become a Precisely-Because Man*. Communist rhetoric often talked about ideas being tested in *life itself*, and claimed that something was the case *precisely because* something else was. The solemn circumlocutions, the clichés that fell like leaden lumps, were indeed a dialect that Decca could describe as L, for left-wing, and contrast with non-L.

Collaborating with some like-minded comrades, she wrote a clever and funny pamphlet. It met with party approval; it was a blow against left-sectarianism, that is, the tendency within Communism to look inwards, and this was exactly the tendency which the party leadership was at that time frowning on. There were of course people who objected, linguistic Stalinists as it were; it was, in fact, fair enough from a Marxist viewpoint to complain that some of the expressions she mocked were necessary scientific terms, and to abolish them was to deny that Marxism was an exact science. But the pamphlet did well; the Communist and fellow-travelling press gave it good reviews, and Philip Toynbee printed extracts in the *Observer*. At this time Communists, in endless meetings up and down the United States, were telling each other that they must find their way back into the mainstream of American life. *Lifeitselfmanship* helped this by stimulating thought among the faithful, by making their language clearer, and by making outsiders see that they could laugh at themselves.

At this stage Bob and Decca left the party. The resignation was not due to any change of heart, as emerges clearly enough from the scorn Decca heaps on all who resigned because they ceased to believe in Communism. They remained proud to have been in the party but felt they could work better outside it for the causes they had at heart. Bob and Decca now worked as non-Communists in pro-black movements, agitating against the Vietnam War and so on. From now on they classed themselves as Liberals which in the American sense they are.

She now wrote *Hons and Rebels*. Her early life and family gave her, of course, a rich vein to exploit; Nancy's novels had made the public familiar with the Asthall and Swinbrook world. Then there was Unity's involvement with Nazism, Diana's marriage to a notorious Fascist leader and her own romantic elopement; Debo's status as a duchess, too, was no bad thing. We must not suppose that Decca sat down cold-bloodedly to make of the Mitford story a sort of Brechtian tract. Primarily, the book was written to make people laugh, which indeed it does. However, her deeply rooted beliefs put her against her family and all its ways; these were people to laugh at, not with. *Hons and Rebels* is what Marxists call a work of 'critical realism'.

It grew bit by bit, starting as no more than an introduction to what was intended as a book about Esmond. Decca seems at first to have been reluctant to contemplate her own past systematically. But she had always enjoyed telling stories about particular happenings; her family loved hearing about these, and Bob, in particular, never ceased to find her anecdotes amazing. Friends, too, used to enjoy them, told in her only very slightly Americanized Mitford voice. She showed her writing to Bob, to Dinky, to some of the friends who had helped with *Life-itselfmanship*. They made her put in things that had slipped her memory. The essay grew into a book.

Was it the work of these helpers that Evelyn Waugh spotted? He told Nancy in a letter of 18 May 1960 that *Hons and Rebels* 'seems by two hands, half fresh and funny if false and half trite and stodgy'. He wondered if the second author was Bob. It would seem not; Bob's role was mainly to remind Decca of jokes she had told him in conversation. There is a sense in which the book is written by two people, but in fact both are Decca: the funny child Decca of the Swinbrook nursery, and the stern adult Decca of the Communist *apparat*. In Freudian terms, Communism has got hold of her superego, and the charm remains in her id. Superego lets id out of her cage like a child actress, painted and bedizened, for her antics to attract the public. With practice, Decca came to knit these two elements seamlessly together, and develop a very effective writing style. It was rather a conservative style, asking no concession to the fashion for the 'touchy-feely'. Her reticence as regards anything truly personal remained in the tradition of Bertie, and of Thomas.

Only parts of *Hons and Rebels* attain her best level; the elements are there, but they do not always harmonize. In the same letter to Nancy Evelyn Waugh said: 'All that stealing and lying combined with sermons on socialism seems very odd.' The parts about Decca's family and early life in *A Fine Old Conflict* are more polished.

To outsiders *Hons and Rebels* is on balance truly funny; but what concerned family or friends was whether it was accurate or fair. Decca admits 'that inaccuracies and distortions there are bound to be, as always when relying entirely on recollection'. But Decca did not rely entirely on recollection. Ideology also made a contribution, and facts, for Decca, were by no means sacred.

Nancy's novels are an important source for *Hons and Rebels*, at least as important as Decca's real life memories. The reduction of David and Sydney into caricatures had already been done; in effect all Decca needed to do was refer to it. The uncles and aunts went the same way, reduced to humoristic types. Uncle Tommy is badly treated. His claim to have tasted human flesh is blown up into a story that he enjoyed a stew of black babies. Nancy's picture of a deficient formal education suits Decca very well, and the governesses are lampooned. There is the one who is supposed to have fainted at the sight of Unity's grass snake, twined around the lavatory chain. Another did in fact take the children shoplifting, though only for tiny items. We thought this story was one of Decca's tall ones, until Debo confirmed that it had happened.

Diana, after her marriage, is depicted as a vain and empty-headed doll. Politics may not be the only factor here; we sense also a grievance about the playmate who has left the schoolroom where one is still stuck. Who was Diana to think she could treat Decca as a stuffed toy she had outgrown, like Christopher Robin abandoning Pooh when he went away to school? Diana denies that she ever did anything like this, but this evidently is how it seemed to Decca herself. On Pam Decca makes one good joke as well as the rather silly one of describing Derek as a jockey. Pam is said to have been so keen on horses that she went to a firm of solicitors called Withers. This firm was an eminent one, and knew it. At least one City merchant banker known to Jonathan fell off his chair laughing at this. Tom comes over sympathetically as an indulgent big brother, and the nursery games are described with charm.

On balance, though, it was understandable that the family disliked *Hons and Rebels*. Decca's personal legend has it that her family rejected her when she eloped. This is wrong; there was a panic, a momentary row, but afterwards everyone was on as good terms with her as Esmond, and she herself, would allow. David cut her out of his will, but only because he thought that anything he left her would go to the Communist Party, to which she had offered her share of Inchkenneth. Otherwise it was she who did the rejecting. *Hons and Rebels* did, for the first time, cause some real resentment.

Sydney was old and wise, and her reaction was moderate. She wrote to Nancy on 19 March 1960:

I was really rather pleasantly surprised that it was not *more* furious against everyone. I am truly sorry about the Aunts and Tommy, most uncalled for, and hurtful. Why did she have such an unhappy childhood. I think it may partly have been that we were so taken up with anxieties for the elders of the family that the young ones got forgotten. Also her wide reading in Communism at such a young age probably did have its effect.

She adds that the book is very funny, and asks in what way it is not honest; this must have been a point made by Nancy. Mrs Ham, too, gave Nancy her views on 30 March that year. Characteristically, and uniquely, her main worry seems to be that she herself does not appear.

One would conclude from the book, I think . . . that Muv was a good-natured queer fool, Farve, of course, a madman. But I think it is a sad book, and leaves a reader wondering why this country home and large family of children and much of the 'good things of life' should have been so utterly intolerable.

As a matter of fact I don't think Muv minds half as much as Diana, or even Debo. I think I'm rather offended at not being brought in, who really played as great a part as any of the uncles and aunts, and a special part in being liked by the parents and the children.

Nancy replied next day, 1 April: 'I think it just as well you're not IN, I don't think anyone who is has much cause for pleasure.' But Nancy was, as so often, playing a double game. In her capacity as writer, Nancy saw very well that the book would succeed; she wrote to Decca congratulating her and telling her so. Later Nancy came further under the influence of her other sisters. Not long after the book came out she was with Pam, Diana and Debo in Ireland, and all four signed a letter to Uncle Tommy regretting that Decca had written of him in the way she had, and dissociating themselves from it; they felt it might have hurt the old man. They received a cheerful reply saying he had not read the book, did not intend to, and would pay no attention to what Decca said anyway.

The reviews were on the whole favourable, but they did sometimes twist the story further, highlighting what was wrong in the book and ignoring what was right. Mostly, though, they at least struck a light note. Not so *The Times Literary Supplement*, which said in a heavy-handed article that Decca describes 'an early environment of almost incredible aridity – tasteless, stupid, wasteful and idiosyncratic only in its scorn of all intellectual and aesthetic values'. The reviewer goes to town on the unfortunate Redesdales, saying that they emerge as 'monsters of arrogance and dullness, whose neglect, in all but a material sense, of their children might well have resulted not in that rebellious pattern of behaviour so prized by the author but in alcoholism or the analyst's couch'. The reviewer rubs salt in the wound by wondering if Decca realizes 'how supremely unpleasant her father and mother appear . . . If she does, she is too wise and loyal to stress these points.' This provoked two letters of rebuttal. One was from Mrs Ham, who says that the Mitford home was charming: 'on the face of it, all that heart could desire'. She admits that the parents were '*sui generis*, not to say eccentric': in Sydney's case she traces this back to Thomas. She points out that David could not have been a real tyrant if he allowed the pranks Decca describes. She draws the parallel between the Mitfords and the Stanleys. The other letter was from Diana, who points out that Swinbrook contained an excellent library: 'Scorn of intellectual values was a matter of choice for the individual child, not of necessity.' She adds that Tom filled the house with music. She also mentions that Pam's 'jockey' is a Fellow of the Royal Society and former Professor of Spectroscopy, and ends: 'The portraits of my parents are equally grotesque. My sister's book was probably meant to amuse, rather than to be "wise", "loyal", or truthful.' This is all understandable, though it is really this particular reviewer who makes the Redesdales seem grotesque, not Decca's book itself.

*Hons and Rebels* was a great success on both sides of the Atlantic. At a stroke Decca was an established author, in demand to write articles and invited on to television chat shows. She took full, and intelligent, advantage of this, especially in an article about the anti-segregation campaign in the south and another about an early student rebellion in the University of California. But soon she began working on *The American Way of Death*. Published in 1963, it is by far her best and most effective book.

Evelyn Waugh's grim little novel *The Loved One* had already dealt with the grotesque burial rites practised by at least some Americans. His 'Whispering Glades' cemetery was modelled closely on Forest Lawn; even to its description of its inventor as The Dreamer. But the matter was by no means confined to one pretentious Californian cemetery. Most Americans, even working people to the extent that they could afford it, had taken to having their dead embalmed, laid out in grand caskets where they were exposed, faces massaged into a jolly smile, then buried in stately mausoleums. The underlying theme of Waugh's book is that this was the result of a materialist denial of death and rejection of its religious implications. That this is perhaps a part of the truth is indicated by the growth since Waugh's time of a much more expensive and gruesome habit than embalming – deep freezing for ultimate resuscitation. In any case the spread of the over-elaborate funeral was only possible because in the United States a uniquely large proportion of simple and ordinary people have a great deal of money. Many of these people were pretty naive, willing to listen to the most dubious salesman. This is in fact why dubious salesmen like Sinclair Lewis's Babbitt abound in the United States; general prosperity creates for them what naturalists call an ecological niche. The undertaking profession was a particularly nasty example, because a person who has just been bereaved is more than usually vulnerable and suggestible. Habits of wastefulness and profiteering took root, supplemented by moral blackmail and even direct falsehood: for example, people were often given to understand that it was legally compulsory for corpses to be embalmed, which was not the case. People were blackmailed into buying elaborate caskets, then further milked by the cemeteries. The average burial had come to cost $1,450, or more than ten times the British average.

There were 'funeral societies' here and there which arranged cheaper burial for their members, and it was Bob's involvement in one of them which drew Decca's attention to the subject. She began by drawing on Bob's files about the funeral industry to help a journalist write an article in the *Saturday Evening Post*. The response to this article made her seriously interested.

*The American Way of Death* is very hard-hitting, though as far as one can see never unfairly so, and above all very funny. Decca's Marxist commitment actually improves it. It is this that inspires her to emphasize in her foreword that she is not just dealing with a few undertakers who do not conform to business ethics, but with the whole profession, with the system of ethics itself. For Marxists are taught to regard systems of ethics as weapons fashioned by dominant groups so as to suit themselves. As a general understanding of human society this view results in a kind of tunnel vision, and as a prescription for the behaviour of Marxist governments it has proved disastrous because it tells them it is right to fashion a moral order in which their own convenience is the highest good. But in particular cases this discipline of cynicism can be helpful. The American funeral business was an industry whose whole system of ethics had become malign. It was Marxism that taught Decca to ignore particular malpractices, which her research uncovered in large numbers, and to concentrate on the scandal of the whole.

Already, before publication, the book worried the undertakers, and their trade press expressed this worry. It was not their first piece of bad publicity, and the more intelligent of them knew that there was enough wrong for a hostile exposure to be dangerous. But they little knew what was in store for them. Decca's book became a bestseller; its sales dropped off, for some reason, after Kennedy's assassination. The funeral men only discovered Decca's Communist background after the book was published. When they did find out, they got a California congressman to detail her political career in the House of Representatives. It did them little good. By 1963 domestic anti-Communism was beginning to be unfashionable in the United States; 'McCarthyism' had become a vogue insult. William Buckley became rather confused: his *National Review*, having first praised the book, turned against it when Decca was shown to be a former Communist. This did not matter. She never tried to deny her past; for one thing this would have been futile, while for another she probably sensed that, far from her politics discrediting her book, it was more likely that this successful and justified campaign by someone known to have been a Communist would help make the left respectable. Nobody seems to have made the political point that in our view needed making, which is that the American funeral business in all its unpleasantness was just one side effect of general prosperity. Communism never produces the affluence on which alone such orgies of tastelessness can be based. Accept Decca's case against such side effects by all means, but do not follow her into advocating changes which will eradicate the underlying prosperity. The signs are that non-political Americans did follow some such reasoning, for funeral spending did moderate, but capitalism continued.

Decca, however, never let up in her campaign against American society. She became an established 'muckraker'. She continued to make left-wing propaganda, sometimes cleverly, sometimes less so; but she also uncovered some real scandals. As a political propagandist she was most effective, perhaps, when she was surreptitious. An article about individuality in women that appeared in American *Vogue* on 15 April 1966 was consciously angled to equate individuality with political radicalism, while it also included stories about aristocratic English eccentrics so as to make it attractive to those who like such things. In *The Making of a Muckraker* Decca explains the technique in just these terms, casting some light on *Hons and Rebels*. On the other hand, the book *The Trial of Dr Spock* falls flat. This is an account of the arraignment of the famous child care expert and four others for conspiring to encourage young men to evade military service in Vietnam. All but one were sentenced, but none spent any time in prison. The whole thing was a non-event, and we doubt if the book had much appeal to anyone not already committed to the cause. As regards scandals, though, one of her articles certainly repeated on a smaller scale the triumph of *The American Way of Death*. This was her exposure of the Famous Writers School, which ran a correspondence course on writing. The course was overpriced and oversold. Very few of its customers succeeded as writers. It made much of its money from the fact that most pupils dropped out, yet had either paid in advance or could be bluffed into keeping up instalments by the empty threat of legal action. Decca arranged to be present when a salesman was making his pitch; his claims were outrageously inflated. But the real giveaway occurred when she interviewed some of the school's Guiding Faculty, a group of fifteen more or less well-known writers who figured in the advertising. They were supposed to be intimately involved, to look at the aptitude tests sent in by candidates, in general to supervise the operation. They did nothing of the sort; what is more, they made it clear that they were entirely aware of how their names were being used. They were also well paid. One of them felt insulted when Decca hazarded a guess at what she was receiving; it was appreciably more, she implied. One who was a publisher as well as a writer said he never published the work of the school's pupils, and went on to tell Decca that mail order selling appeals to the gullible. He tried to retract this, but really made it worse because his grounds for not wanting to be quoted were not that the remark showed unscrupulousness, but that it might annoy the mail order industry. As a result of this article and the publicity surrounding it, the school had to close. It was a successful operation, thoroughly, ruthlessly and beautifully done.

Then in 1973 came Decca's longest book, *Kind and Usual Punishment*, a study of the prison system in the United States. This is a half-success. It has the incisiveness of her best work, and the skill at getting people to reveal themselves, and it certainly shows that the prisons are as a rule degrading and frightening places. The chapter on the use of prisoners for medical research stays especially in the mind; they are bribed with better conditions or more remission to undergo risks that no one on the outside is ever asked to face. The trouble is that Decca is relentlessly one-sided. The inmates are presented entirely as victims; that some of them are dangerous, and indeed systematically cruel to others within the system, is glossed over. There is nothing about the vicious bullying that forced Gordon Liddy (see his book *Will*) to learn the art of dirty fighting, or about the homosexual gang rapes. Worse, Decca's political opinions work in this instance against the book rather than in its favour. In *The American Way of Death* Marxism honed her sword; here it blunts it. The intervening sixties have seen her views become fashionable. This has made her self-indulgent; instead of keeping her head down and accordingly sticking to the point, she now feels able to chase political hares. She talks of the misdeeds of the influential; breaches of health and safety regulations by landlords and employers, misleading packaging, corruption organized by criminal syndicates. The passage is, frankly, woolly; it lumps together too many disparate malpractices, confusing law breaking with law manipulation and with bad law. It is irrelevant to the guilt of individual convicts, or the danger they may pose to society. She is here attacking the social order itself rather than the practice in its prisons, and when we consider the prison system developed in countries whose social order she appears to prefer to the American one, uneasy thoughts are produced. The point to which she should have stuck is that prison, which can never be pleasant, ought at least to be decent. She amply demonstrates that in the United States it is unnecessarily beastly and in places actually horrifying, but pours scorn on those who try to improve matters piecemeal. Her demonstration is done in a manner likely to turn many people off it; had she been as successful with prisons as she was with funerals and famous writers, she would have subtracted far more from the sum of human misery.

In 1977 Decca published the second volume of her autobiography, *A Fine Old Conflict*, to which we have frequently referred. It gives a full account of her Communist activities in the fifties. As regards her family it is more balanced than *Hons and*

*Rebels*, showing in particular far more sympathy with Sydney. It is a reticent book; Decca omits all reference to one dreadful personal tragedy: the death of Nicholas in a traffic accident at the age of eleven. More oddly, she also fails to mention the purchase of Inchkenneth.

*The Making of a Muckraker* is a collection of Decca's articles on various subjects; funerals of course and prisons, the misdeeds of an unscrupulous restaurant, the Deep South, the Famous Writers, even a very funny account of a spell in a health farm. We have noted Decca's touch of upper-class arrogance; this appears here, coupled with an open cynicism that is less attractive, perhaps, than Decca seems to think. An introduction gives very shrewd hints on how to rake muck, or be an investigative journalist. She makes a great deal of her documentary research and of the art of picking experts' brains. She is always accurate, she insists – a claim that has caused sour smiles in the family, remembering *Hons and Rebels*, but one that is probably justified in her journalism. Her most memorable comments are on interviewing, which is where, as she puts it, the fun really begins. Questions should be prepared beforehand, graded from 'kind' to 'cruel', and the victim should be asked them in that order. Lulled by the kind ones and charmed, no doubt, by Decca's manner, he may when confronted by a cruel question give himself away. Though admitting that ethics is not one of her strong points, she does think that, in general, an understanding to keep a conversation off the record should be respected. If possible the interviewee should be bounced out of asking for this by fast talking. Altogether Decca's technique seems so formidable that we were dreading interviewing her for this book; she would subject us to cold-eyed expertise, tell us our kind and cruel questions were all mixed up and perhaps end by exposing *us*. It was strange that when it came to the point it was she who would not see us. Of course if *everyone* had talked to us it would have been a breach of family tradition.

# 42

# Debo

Happy is he, says Pushkin in *Eugene Onegin*, who is young in his youth and whose character develops in line with his age, who can learn to cope with life by degrees, over the years. Debo has had the luck to be like this. Just as Pushkin recommends, her abilities have always appeared when required, neither too soon nor too late. It is a great gift.

Like the others, she loved country life and country things when she was young. But with her this was not just a phase, as in the cases of Nancy, Diana and Decca; she did not, like them, sink into cosmic boredom in her teens, because as new interests arose she still kept her old ones. Certainly she could be moody, and the others would sometimes irritate her unbearably, 'Shut up, all of you!' was her greeting to the family one morning as she sat down to breakfast at Rutland Gate: a pre-emptive strike. Annoyed once with Tom, she told him: 'This family consists of three giants, three dwarfs, and one brute.' (The giants: Nancy, Diana, Unity. The dwarfs: Pam, Decca and herself.)

Debo grew up during the thirties, that decade of such unease for the world, such drama for her family. She was a child of eight when Diana married Bryan, a young woman of nineteen when Unity put the bullet in her brain. How did she cope? How did she avoid Communism, Fascism or neurosis? To answer this we recall characters in two famous children's books. She was, first, like Sarah in Belloc's *Cautionary Tales* who is 'Confirmed in her instinctive guess/That literature breeds distress.' She was, that is, careful not to worry her adolescent mind with Aldous Huxley, like Diana, or with Beverley Nichols, like Decca. Then we remember L. Leslie Brooke's *Johnny Crow*. Bored by philosophy, '. . . the Hippopotami/Say "ask no further what am I?"' Debo shared the viewpoint of these prudent beasts. She never dissipated her curiosity in speculation about general principles. She did her lessons, of course; and she absorbed from them the skills to make herself, in middle age, as cultivated as anyone in the family. For the moment it was enough to try to be sufficiently quick-witted and resilient to withstand the teasing of the others. Being the youngest in this particular family was no sinecure.

The main ones to tease her were Unity and Decca, who were nearest her age; but it would also have gone against nature for Nancy to allow the age difference of sixteen years to come between her and the sport. 'Everybody cried when you were born,' she used to assure Debo, referring to the disappointment that she was yet another girl. She made her weep with the rhyme about the house-less match. Another Debo tease, by Unity and Decca, was based on a newspaper story which had carried the headlines:

SLOWLY CRUSHED TO DEATH IN A LIFT
Man's Long Agony in a Lift Shaft

At first this was recited as versicle and response. When banned in this form, the headlines were converted to a series of taps:

—.—.—.—
——..—.—

Debo was soon brought to a state in which not many of these taps were needed to set her off.

Evidently her technique for dealing with teases was to cry easily, and yet learn not to mind too much underneath. That is, when one of her sisters started some rigmarole designed to upset her, she would begin weeping *soon*, so that the perpetrator would desist and perhaps, if there was a grown-up in earshot, be scolded. Debo was most of the time David's favourite; being the youngest she appealed to his protective side, and in addition her tastes were close to his. They became closer still when in middle life she took up shooting; in her youth her main passion was the horse. Aged fifteen, in *All About Everybody*, she put her favourite pastime as hunting; her occupation if she had unlimited choice was also hunting, bracketed with racing.

Except when she was sent with Decca for one term to Oakdene near High Wycombe, Debo never went to school. She hated

Oakdene as much as Decca liked it. Again unlike Decca, she enjoyed life at home, especially in the country at Swinbrook. She did not like leaving it for High Wycombe or Rutland Gate. She enjoyed the foreign trips more than Decca did, though we suspect she was pleased to get back to her animals. This puts into perspective Sydney's sad letter to Nancy after *Hons and Rebels* appeared, already quoted, in which she wonders whether Decca's childhood was unhappy because her parents concentrated too much on the troubles of the older ones. The point is that Debo had fun, even if Decca did not.

In interview, Debo summarized what life was like in those few years at Swinbrook. She remembers her father for his charm and courtesy: 'He made people feel marvellous.' He did have rages, sometimes about small things; Gladys, Duchess of Marlborough, was never asked to the house again because she left a paper handkerchief on a hedge. Sydney's manner was unusually vague, 'but she could come down like a ton of bricks and it was then awful'. Debo also remembers that neither of her parents bothered very much about what others thought. We think this self-confidence made all their children feel more secure, even though some of them could find it annoying.

The Redesdales asked few people of their own age to Swinbrook, other than from the family. Mrs Ham came regularly; otherwise their guests were their own brothers, sisters and cousins with their spouses and children. Visitors from outside the family were mostly of their children's generation. Some of these were more welcome than others, but by this stage most were tolerated. There was the odd embarrassment. Peter Watson, future proprietor of Cyril Connolly's *Horizon*, rang up once and David picked up the receiver. 'It's that hog Watson,' he said, not bothering to cover the mouthpiece. To the family Peter Watson was of course Hog Watson from then on. David also turned one young man out of the house because a comb fell out of his pocket. To have been unkempt might equally have earned expulsion, but this was a problem David expected a gentleman to solve, by magic if necessary. Tom, for instance, was always tidy, yet never carried a comb. He was a hero figure to Debo; she looked forward to his visits, accompanied as often as not by a glamorous and scented lady. Not that his affairs always ran smoothly: once, after being crossed in love, he was in a depression for three months, during which time he hardly spoke.

Debo's 'Honnish' relationship with Decca is important for understanding both of them. Hon, as we have seen, meant hen; they used to do things like imitate the expression on a hen's face when it is laying an egg. But the Honnish way of speaking was loosely based on the Oxfordshire accent, and there was in the whole cult an implicit desire to identify with ordinary people. In Decca's case this was one of the origins of her later political stand. With Debo it was just as important and its influence equally permanent, but it has shown itself in a different way. This is because Decca, early in life, felt the need to turn her feelings into explicit general principles; she also read books. Class became an *evil* to her, its beneficiaries including her own family became enemies. What started as a desire for closer human relationships turned into a dehumanization of her dealings with her parents and most of the real people she actually knew. (This was *tragedy* in the most literal sense.) But Debo, innocent of slogans and generalizations, regarded class more as a misfortune, since to her it showed itself in her day-to-day experience simply as an obstacle to getting to know particular people. She found that the best remedy for it was to ignore it. This is what she learned to do; she has always behaved in exactly the same way to everyone. Some might say that for a duchess this is easy. Is it? People have reticences, chips on the shoulder. Debo's sure touch in dealing with them is not just technical deftness; subliminally the message comes across that, deep down, she is on their side.

At first the activities of Debo's sisters, much as they worried her parents, reached her mostly as 'noises off'. She stayed with Diana and Bryan when they were married; after their divorce she was not allowed to go to Eaton Square, though Diana sometimes came to Rutland Gate or Swinbrook. We remember that Nancy wrote to Debo in confidence to tell of her probable engagement to Peter Rodd, before she even told Sydney. This was quite a compliment to the discretion of a thirteen-year-old.

Swinbrook was sold in 1936 when Debo was sixteen. She was bitterly unhappy about this, and her sadness was increased by the knowledge that none of the others shared it. She knew and loved every leaf of the countryside, and was deeply attached to the house. To her, the others seemed callous and supercilious about Swinbrook. A few months after the sale came the first of the family dramas to affect Debo directly and deeply: Decca's elopement, in February 1937. Debo was not quite seventeen. Decca was not just her closest sister in age, but her particular crony and confidante: her Hon. At first, we must remember, Decca just vanished. She could have been killed; she might be, in sober truth, one of the white slaves in Buenos Aires she liked to joke about. It was only a day or two before Peter Nevile came to Rutland Gate with Decca's letter, but the time seemed endless. After what had happened became known, it sank in that Decca's departure had been planned in detail, without Debo knowing anything about it. Debo felt let down. She saw quite well that Decca had needed to keep quiet; but when we find that a friend has for some time had a preoccupation we did not know about, it does make him or her seem less close. A solidarity Debo had thought unconditional had turned out to have had its limits. Perhaps most people have gone through some such experience; it is a sad fact of growing up, and for Debo an important part of her youth was now gone beyond recall. The £1,000 she won from the *Daily Express* in libel damages cheered her up, of course; she bought a fur coat with it. For her this was more than adequate compensation for a pursuit of her family by the press which seemed to her parents like a persecution; though it was nothing to what was to occur over Unity.

Next year, in 1938, Debo came out. David gave a ball for her at Rutland Gate on 22 March: Unity arrived home in time to attend, just after seeing the celebrations as Hitler entered Vienna. Unlike Decca, Debo enjoyed her debutante 'season'; unlike Unity, she enjoyed it in the conventional way. She and three other debutantes gave another party at Rutland Gate in June; Debo put on the invitation cards 'Beer and sausages', though in fact there was champagne. Her nickname that year was Swyne. Unity wrote to Sydney from Bayreuth on 3 August: 'Swyne seems to be having a wonderful time. I bet she is enjoying it. But *who* will the romance be with? I'm all on tenterhooks to know, the stars generally foretell right.' They did. Debo was at Goodwood races on 25 July, and at Cranborne on 29 July. At both these places she saw Lord Andrew Cavendish, younger son of the Duke of Devonshire. He, too, was eighteen. They became great friends, though not at that stage officially engaged. In August, as mentioned earlier, they surreptitiously visited Diana and Mosley at Wootton with another friend, and were surprised to find the place peaceful and unguarded. But a great deal was to happen before they were married, three years later.

In September of the next year, war broke out and Unity shot herself. For Debo and her parents it was another crisis like that of Decca's elopement, but longer, more harrowing and with no happy ending. At first, Sydney was surprisingly unworried. 'I did not feel terribly anxious for her as I knew she would be looked after, but we did realize what an awful shock [the outbreak of war] must be to her.' (Sydney, *Unity*.) This was odd, as eleven months before, after the Munich crisis, Unity had written on 8 October 1938: 'I must say that during those awful two weeks I was certain I would never see any of you again, as of course it would have been impossible for me to go on living if there had been a war.' She could not have put it more plainly, and had at various times said the same thing to others; yet Sydney managed to put it out of her mind. Then the rumours started; Unity was in a concentration camp, had been murdered and so on. Teddy Almasy's letter and telegrams during October reassured the family that she was alive, but the likelihood of a suicide attempt still does not seem to have occurred to Sydney. Then, gradually, the essentials of the story became clear. On Christmas Eve Janos and Unity rang from Berne; and as we have seen, Debo went with Sydney to fetch her.

'We were all three so happy,' says Sydney of the reunion in the Berne clinic. This was so only up to a point, for Debo at once realized that Unity was now in effect a different person. Sydney was always protected, in the matter of Unity, by a degree of self-deception; Debo was not. Then came the nightmare of their reception in England by the Fleet Street pack, the broken-down ambulance, the offensive stories and newsreels. Debo went through it all with her parents.

The year 1940 was a bad one for Debo. She had to witness the miserable quarrels between her parents, and when Unity was released from hospital into her mother's care she experienced the heartbreak of helping to cope with her frequent incontinence and her difficult moods. She wrote to Diana in Holloway on 4 October:

Birdie [Unity] . . . *so* hates me that life here has become almost impossible. The sitting room is so small and two enormous tables in it belong exclusively to her and if one so much as puts some knitting down on one for a moment chaos reigns because she . . . shrieks bloody fool very loud. I think in some ways she's better though but she seems to have completely lost her sense of humour and never roars at the funniest thing . . . Farve has gone to Scotland and taken Margaret-the-maid-who-had-a-young-man-who-took-her-to-Ascot-in-a-Rolls-Royce. I expect he will have a gay time.

But she had not lost touch with Andrew, who was now serving in the Coldstream Guards, Early in the following year they got engaged, and Debo wrote to Diana on 4 March 1941:

It *is* so exciting because Andrew and I are going to be married . . . His parents have been so wonderful about it, I didn't know people could be so nice, they really seem pleased . . . I expect we shall be terrificly [*sic*] poor but think how nice it will be to have as many dear dogs and things as one likes without anyone to say they must get off the furniture. I *do* so wish you weren't in prison, it will be vile not having you to go shopping with only we're so poor I shan't have much of a trousseau.

Andrew was, of course, a younger son, and probably did not have much more than his Army pay at the time. Debo was also worried that the newspapers had got hold of the story before it was officially announced and before Andrew could tell his colonel: 'I hope lividry hasn't set in.'

They were married on 19 April, at Saint Bartholomew the Great, Smithfield; a reception was held at Rutland Gate. Two days before, all the windows had been smashed by a bomb. Unity was spotted at the wedding: there are press photographs of her looking rather overweight in a flowered hat. A Labour MP called Evelyn Walkden noticed this, and spitefully asked the Home Secretary to imprison her since she had evidently recovered from her illness, 'on account of her past close association with Nazi leaders and her declared pro-Nazi views'. Morrison refused; he knew her condition well enough.

Debo then followed Andrew around the country as he was posted from place to place. In 1941 she gave birth to a son, but he died. Then in March 1943 Emma was born, her first surviving child; later that year Andrew was posted overseas, to Italy. Debo was roped into war work, writing to Diana on 12 January 1944: 'I do disgusting work now, do feel sorry for me. It's in the YMCA canteen and it's very embarrassing because they all copy my voice.' In due course, to Debo's delight, Andrew won the Military Cross, and she gave birth to a son, Peregrine or 'Stoker', in April 1944. In May Andrew's brother William, Marquess of Hartington, married Kathleen Kennedy, elder sister of the future President of the United States. But in the Russian roulette of war he was unlucky; he was killed fighting in Belgium in September. Andrew was now heir to his father.

After the war Debo and Andrew had a good life, not too worried by the prevailing austerity. Debo once appealed to her friend, Mr Tom Egerton: 'Oh Mr Tom, who is the most pathetic person in the world?'

'He, he!' he replied: 'not *you*.'

He was right of course, though her life was not all roses. She had three children after Peregrine, of whom only Sophia, born on 18 March 1957, survived. So of her six children, three died at birth; and nobody will ever know how much this cost in depression and misery.

In November 1950 Andrew's father died unexpectedly; he was only fifty-five and in reasonable health. This left Andrew with the appalling problem of 80 per cent death duties; they were not finally settled for seventeen years. Enormous amounts of land all over the country, and large numbers of works of art, had to be sold, but finally Andrew, with Debo at his right hand, successfully carried out an orderly retreat and consolidation on Chatsworth and his Irish house, Lismore Castle. It was from Lismore that Nancy wrote to Diana on 6 July 1957: 'Debo has become the sort of English duchess who doesn't feel the cold, it is the only drawback to complete pleasure.' But Nancy always felt the cold badly; her correspondence is full of references to not being warm enough.

Until 1959, Debo and Andrew lived in Edensor House near Chatsworth; then they moved into Chatsworth itself. Curiously enough, this was a measure of economy. If Chatsworth was to be fit for the public to see, indeed if it was not to fall down, the enormous place had to be cleaned and looked after. It was sensible to take advantage of this for their own living quarters. Necessary repairs, alterations and decorations took eighteen months, Debo tells us in her book *The House*; this seems quite fast, considering all that needed to be done. Debo chose all the decorations herself. She says: 'When I was young I watched my mother doing up whatever house we were living in and making it far prettier on far less money than those of our friends who employed professionals to do the job, and I felt that I could probably do as she did.' Nancy and Diana had always done the same – better, in fact, than Sydney; it was a talent with which some, though not all, of the family were endowed. So, it now turned out, was Debo: and in Chatsworth she had a task really worthy of her abilities. She also had access to the armies of skilled men and women attached to the Chatsworth estate. We think she rose fully to the challenge. Yet she adds: 'I am thankful that I was thirty-eight when I found myself making these decisions. The house had had time to impress its powerful character on me and prevented the wholesale use of pink paint, which was my only idea of decoration when I first grew up.' There is perhaps something in this, though false modesty is something that needs to be looked out for in all Debo's statements. Quietly, all this time and in many fields, Debo was learning. The Devonshire possessions made her gradually into an expert on art, on fine furniture. Edensor House we remember as charming but unremarkable; perhaps there was some pink paint used. Chatsworth, on the other hand, is a decorative masterpiece, bold and imaginative as well as harmoniously conceived. We shall not describe it; it must be seen.

Another clue to the surreptitious development of Debo's intelligence that was going on at this time, despite her continuing claims to be unlettered, can be identified. As soon as Chatsworth was ready, she began to invite intellectuals to stay. On 20 November 1959 Nancy wrote an ominous warning of what they might do to her fixtures and fittings: 'Tell about these intis. They are terrible wreckers, worse than puppies and will give a mellow old look to the house in no time at all. I expect that's why you have them.' They have come since in increasing numbers. Patrick

Leigh-Fermor, for one, has provided neat titles for the false books on the door to the gallery in the library.

Debo also encouraged Andrew in his purchase and commissioning of contemporary works of art. Lucian Freud painted the whole family, and there are works by Epstein, Derek Hill, Angela Conner and others. Debo's portrait by Lucian Freud was painted when she was thirty-four. An old lady was overheard saying of it: 'That's the Dowager Duchess. It was taken the year before she died.'

With all this Debo has retained the country interests of her childhood. Her friend Elizabeth Winn wrote to Diana on 4 March 1968: 'It's amazing the way that Deborah Feodorovna has managed to turn the whole place into a smallholding. Beneath every ledge or statue is a batch of chickens, some with houses designed by famous architects, and then, those *ponies*. It's a real rodeo viewing them. One has to arm oneself with sticks and stones, as they bite viciously.'

Debo has also become a businesswoman, with an actively managed share portfolio. (She loves the word 'portfolio' used in this sense.) Latterly she has become a non-executive director of Tarmac, the road surfacing company. She runs shops at Chatsworth for food, mementoes, books and garden furniture. She has written the steadily selling successful book about Chatsworth, *The House*, in which she still dares to describe herself as a 'non-reader'. By the time she is ninety she will probably have done everything under the sun.

With one exception. It is a safe bet that she will never take up politics.

# 43

# Twenty Years On

Twenty years ago, when this book was first published, the Mitford story was complete in its essentials; yet neither the family nor the world have stood still. Pam died on 12 April 1994. She was 86, but was active and retained all her senses until the end. She had an accident on a visit to London; she fell down some steps and broke her leg. She was taken to hospital where it was pinned, and within twenty-four hours she was sitting up in bed and cheerfully talking to visitors. But a clot from the operation reached her heart, and suddenly she was no more. Her funeral was at Swinbrook, where she is buried near Sydney, Nancy and Unity; a country funeral, simple and evocative, attended by family and masses of friends. She had aged well. Teased all her life by her more quickwitted sisters, yet expert at surfing these breakers without loss of face, Pam developed in old age a sunny humour that earned the deep love of her sisters and all their descendants. Pam's last years evoked the prelude to the last act of *Falstaff*, that masterpiece of Verdi's genial old age.

Decca died of lung cancer just over two years later, on 22 July 1996. Alone of the sisters, she was a chain smoker and heavy drinker. Drink she had managed to give up by sheer willpower, frightened by falling over when tipsy and breaking her ankle. Giving up smoking was more difficult. She was supposed to have given up some years before and even lectured on giving up smoking. She remained true to her earlier admission that ethics was not one of her strong points by interrupting these very lectures from time to time when she slipped into the ladies' for a surreptitious drag. However when Dinky, by then a trained and dedicated nurse, caught her at it and told Bob, she really did give up, though she never lost the craving. The cancer was diagnosed in June 1996 almost by chance – she was getting trouble from her broken ankle and consulted a doctor, also telling him that she was coughing blood. Blood tests and X-rays showed up the cancer. At first she tried to shrug it off, not cancelling plans for a holiday in August in Cape Cod. On 11 July she was given three months to live, which she only half believed. She was dead in eleven days.

Her send-off was very different from Pam's quiet funeral at Swinbrook. The funeral itself followed the guidelines of *The American Way of Death* to the extent of keeping the cost down to $475. But Decca was a celebrity and admired by celebrities. She was a darling of the media, a best-selling author, a renowned lecturer, a star of the leftwing Establishment on both sides of the Atlantic. She was good company; her political commitment may, as we suggested, have harnessed her funniness and charm, but it never suppressed it. So the Spartan funeral was followed by two enormous and star-studded memorial services, the first in San Francisco attended by more than five hundred people, the second, a few months later, in a London theatre. This was compered by the television announcer Jon Snow and featured a performance by the singer Maya Angelou. Born into the old upper class, Decca had made a smooth transfer into the new media élite.

Nobody reproached Decca for her long years of promoting Leninist Communism, a doctrine which on one estimate was responsible for 94.35 million deaths worldwide (Source: *Le Livre Noir du Communisme*, Stephane Courtois and others, Laffont, 1997) and which she never convincingly renounced. There was always a queer contrast between her treatment in the media and that of Diana, who in her lifetime had Hitler's holocaust thrown into her face by every interviewer and whose death unleashed a media frenzy, much of it disapproving.

She died in her Paris flat on 12 August 2003, aged 93, following a mild stroke probably caused by the unusual heatwave. Like Pam she was active to the end and continued reading, writing and entertaining; but unlike Pam she became profoundly deaf, as Bertie had been in old age. Even a modern hearing aid helped little, and the telephone was useless to her though she often used the fax. She complained to Jonathan that she missed her telephone conversations with her friend Lord Lambton. 'You could fax him,' said Jonathan, but she replied: 'One can't gossip on a fax.' By her wish she was cremated and her ashes buried in the churchyard at Swinbrook with the family.

It was the *Daily Telegraph* which led the press pack; probably the editor felt that this figure from the past might interest its rather mature readership. The edition of 13 August had an enormous colour photograph of Diana on the front page, both the second and third pages were dominated by articles about her and pictures of her and the Mitford family, she occupied most of the obituary page, and on the page opposite the editorial there was yet another long article. Even the day's cartoon was dedicated to her: two figures in S.A. uniform were goose stepping under a giant wreath. It was odd that a serious broadsheet newspaper should pay this sort of attention to a 93-year-old woman who had done nothing to change the course of history.

The most hostile article was a creepy effort by Andrew Roberts in which the writer shudderingly admits to have enjoyed being 'subjected to the full force of her Mitfordesque charm'. Expecting horrors, he is disappointed that Diana fails to deny Hitler's responsibility for the Holocaust. However she lives up to expectations when she says that she found Hitler attractive. As so often, Diana spoke only of that which came within her experience, like her personal impression of Hitler, and left alone that which did not, like the Holocaust. Rather oddly for a visiting journalist, Roberts seems to have nursed the unlikely hope that Diana would blurt out an admission that her husband had 'wasted his undeniable talents upon a foul lie'. He is too horrified even to answer a debating point. When she says that the recent secession of Slovakia shows that Czechoslovakia could not last in its 1938 form, implying that there might have been a case for Hitler's actions in 1938, he simply regards this as further evidence of her infamy rather than giving a reasoned answer, which would have been quite easy. He perhaps sensed that Diana made the point to irritate, rather than to convince; and knowing Diana we do have the feeling that she may have enjoyed winding Roberts up.

If so, the gambit succeeded; Roberts 'lost it'. He says: 'Lest anyone still believe that [Diana's] imprisonment was somehow undeserved . . . it is recorded that, during a Hyde Park rally in October 1935, she silently gave the Heil Hitler salute when the rest of the crowd was singing God Save the King.' To make a gesture which Roberts dislikes, then, is to deserve imprisonment. Anne Chisholm says in her review of Anne de Courcy's book about Diana (*Sunday Telegraph*, 9 November 2003): 'No one reading [Diana's replies to the Advisory Commission in 1940] can doubt that she deserved to stay where she was.' If Roberts and Chisholm would calm down they would see that once opinions, as such, become punishable, people will conceal them. The investigators will require the methods of Torquemada, Witch-Finder Hopkins or Senator McCarthy. As to Regulation 18b in particular, it put out of action many who otherwise would have fought for their country, as Mosley told them to. It could have caught Tom Mitford, who belonged to the British Union of Fascists before being killed fighting in Burma, and Derek Jackson, who though openly opposing the war against Hitler won two medals for gallantry and conducted scientific research important for the war effort. Nancy, we remember, had a tail put on Derek. The reasoning behind Regulation 18b is not in opposition to tyranny; it is an early stage in the process that can lead to it. The prisoners now kept indefinitely and without trial, in Belmarsh Prison and Guantanamo Bay, are silent witnesses to this.

Not all criticism of Diana is wrong. When she said to her Advisory Committee during the war: 'I am not fond of Jews,' this is rightly condemned. One should never condemn a whole group in this way. Yet we have never seen anyone taken to task for saying they were not fond of, for example, Germans. Again, Diana is accused of being callous about the Holocaust. She did often deplore this horror, but is given no credit for this. On the programme *Desert Island Discs* she ventured to doubt the figure of six million killed. This was foolish; she had not studied the subject. It is true that some of those who have suggested a rather lower figure are accepted as respectable, but from her this idle speculation was inevitably seen as 'Holocaust denial'. Of course the Holocaust was not the only mass atrocity in living memory. The most massive ethnic cleansing of the twentieth century occurred in the parts of Germany that the Allies allotted to Poland at Yalta, and in the formerly German-speaking parts of Czechoslovakia. These areas were systematically and by State action emptied of German men, women and children to the accompaniment of beatings, rape and mass murder. Something like

16 million are said to have been expelled of which perhaps two million lost their lives. This is almost forgotten; when it is referred to it is generally in passing and never with any sympathy for the victims. Margaret Macmillan, in her magisterial study of the Treaty of Versailles, *Peacemakers*, says this about events during and after the Second World War: 'Poland was emptied of its Jews by the Nazis and of its Germans by the Soviets and moved 200 miles to the West.' This is pretty brisk, about Jews as well as about Germans. But turning to Czechoslovakia she refers to the brutalized Germans with something unattractively like a sneer: 'The Germans had fled, with considerable encouragement from the Czechs.'

Returning to Decca, we have already mentioned that she refused to see us when we tried to interview her for this book; she also forbade us to quote her or her writings and threatened to sue us if we did so. When this book appeared she did more. To quote Mary S. Lovell's *The Mitford Girls*:

She sent sheets of quotable material to her circle of literary friends in England for them to use in their own reviews of the book . . . Several reviewers used extracts from these 'crib sheets' of Decca's, and at least one major review was copied almost word-for-word from Decca's comments.

That reviewers should lazily pass off Decca's material as their own indicates that the 'chorus of indolent reviewers' has not much changed since Tennyson's tease. But their behaviour was also, surely, a touch disreputable. Unnecessary, as well; the particular hostile reviewer we most enjoyed reading thought up his own strictures. Decca herself, in an interview quoted by Mary S. Lovell in *The Mitford Girls*, had already referred to the world of English reviewing, disapprovingly, as 'a small pond where people scratch each other's backs – or bite each other's backs – and they all know each other. At least in California if your book is reviewed well you know it's because they like it.' She was not above using this when it suited her.

Decca's concern was that the crypto–Marxist version of the family story presented by *Hons and Rebels* should continue to be the accepted one. But she also had against the two of us a more personal grudge. In 1977, Catherine was in New York working for Andy Warhol's *Interview*. It was some years before we thought of writing this book. She suggested that she might interview her great-aunt Decca, and the magazine agreed. The interview itself is quite bland, until the moment when Catherine makes it clear that she is very fond of Diana, who was her grandmother. Decca: 'Oh. You love her.' The shock appears clearly in the two full-stops. To which Catherine, rubbing it in, replies: 'Oh, I love her so much!'

In few other families would Decca have been shocked that Catherine was fond of her grandmother. But from Decca's standpoint, Catherine, as a member of the younger generation, ought to have deplored her Fascist forebear. The job of the young was to be on their way towards the sunlit uplands of the Left. Instead of which, 'I love her so much!' What were the young coming to?

There was worse to come. When the interview was published, Catherine prefixed it with a letter from Jonathan which called Decca 'a hardened and intelligent Marxist agitator who knows very subtly how to play on her upper-class background so as to enlist residual snobbery (on both sides of the Atlantic) in establishing Marxism.'

Decca had never before met anything like this. Certainly there had been many protests from the family about *Hons and Rebels*. Her aunt Dorothy Bailey, Sydney's sister, had given her a proper dressing down when she met her in London: 'I for one will never forget the savage cruelty with which you treated your mother and father.' Decca was taken aback; it is rare in normal life to be attacked directly like this, even by an aunt. But the complaint was entirely private, relating to Decca's treatment of individuals. Jonathan's letter to Catherine was a hostile political assessment. Decca saw the two of us as having stitched her up, and stitching people up, we remember from *The Making of a Muckraker*, is a skill of which Decca was proud. Those who most enjoy biting are most resentful at being bit, which is why Decca took the trouble to disparage us to reviewers.

In real life, as we have said, Decca did far more good than harm. She and her friends failed utterly to persuade the United States to surrender to Communism, or to adopt it. Diana and Mosley were not shot, and Decca did not prolong their stay in prison by even a day. On the other hand her achievements were notable. It was right that the American funeral industry should be made to clean up its act, and the people she exposed in her career as a muckraker on the whole deserved what they got. Her son, Benjamin Treuhaft, is continuing her beneficent radicalism. He is a restorer and tuner of pianos. One of the sillier aspects of the United States embargo on trade with Cuba concerns these instruments; if the Americans had their way, no pianos would reach Cuba and those already on the island would be getting more and more decrepit and out of tune. Perhaps some bureaucrat in the United States treasury department can explain how a cacophony of superannuated pianos can help the Cuban people free themselves from Communism, but it seems a mystery. Anyway, in 1993 Benjamin restored a grand piano and sent it to Havana's Museo National de la Musica, and persuaded other tuners to send numbers of pianos there. The US Treasury Department tried to fine him $10,000 dollars for this activity but failed to press the matter, perhaps fearing ridicule. Benjamin now runs a charitable outfit called 'Send a Piana to Havana' which has delivered more than two hundred used pianos. Good for him.

Debo is the survivor. We have mentioned her book on Chatsworth, *The House*. Besides describing the house itself, with its garden and amazing collection of art and furniture, it gives a history of the Cavendish family from the sixteenth century and accounts of many of the people who have worked at Chatsworth. Imaginatively illustrated, it deserves its continuing steady sales. In recent years Debo has also become more and more in demand as a writer of articles, some of the best of which are collected in her book *Counting My Chickens* (Long Barn Books, 2001). This is similar to the writings of Nancy, Diana and Decca. Like theirs, it is full of jokes. 'Could some clever reader tell me what a quantum leap is and where I can see one performed?', she asks, and pokes fun at the computer which addresses her as 'Mr/Ms Hess Of.' Packaging, she points out, 'has gone too far, and the simplest things have become impossible to open'. Then when you buy a pair of scissors for the purpose 'they are similarly encapsulated in a thick shiny film, which human hands and nails are not designed to penetrate.' The only solution, she concludes, is a scalpel. She was delighted when, a few days later, a scalpel arrived in the post.

It would be wrong, though, to be lulled by the jokes into thinking Debo has no agenda. With great skill, she promotes what

Tony Blair calls the 'forces of conservatism'. 'The past,' wrote L. P. Hartley, 'is another country; they do things differently there.' Debo, in her eighties, is an emissary from that country and speaks up for it. She keeps out of politics in the strict sense, though a giant portrait of her and Andrew presided over the Countryside March in September 2002. She is a sharp critic of what she sees around her today, always supporting the country and praising the old skills. Quite often one laughs aloud, but the humour is like Mary Poppins's spoonful of sugar which helps the medicine go down; and the medicine is a defence of the countryside and its habits, including field sports and, notably, foxhunting. Decca, too, used the Poppins technique, though in her case the idea was to abolish the past rather than to preserve or revive it. Consciously or unconsciously, Debo has picked up some hints from her sister, but she has refined the technique. Sometimes she reminds one of the ancient Chinese executioner whose victim remarked that the passes he made with his sword seemed to have had no effect, but who said with a smile: 'Just nod your head.'

Her writing derives from the job into which she married, helping her husband to run the Devonshire family estates. Faced in 1950 on his father's death with estate duty of 80 per cent on the enormous family assets in land, houses and works of art, it was Andrew whose skill in selecting what to sell and when to sell it ensured that after 17 years the liability could be met while keeping the essential part of the Chatsworth Estate and all the really important art works. However it is Debo who redecorated the huge house and still sees that the visitors so essential to pay for its upkeep are looked after, Debo who oversees the successful businesses that are its spinoffs: the souvenir shop which she has made a thing of beauty in itself, the popular farm shop. It is Debo, too, who writes in its defence.

It needs defending, because the Chatsworth estate is more than a thriving business; it is also a survival. Andrew passed no exams, he was on no shortlist, he was selected by no committee of the great and the good. The same applies to Debo as his wife. Let us not mince words; they owe their position to privilege. As much as the old House of Lords, and indeed the Monarchy, they constitute a standing offence against the principle of equality of opportunity.

The alternative to privilege is of course bureaucracy, and Debo is very sharp about that, in all its forms. Otherwise she simply describes in detail how her own set-up works. She demonstrates that Chatsworth is a happy community as well as a productive business, that the employees are valued and looked after. She never makes the mistake of claiming that the whole of Britain could be run on the same lines; Chatsworth after all is part of the countryside, pre-industrial. William Cobbett, almost two centuries ago, would have liked Britain to return to this condition, but even in his day it was too late. She talks only of Chatsworth, but in describing in detail how the organization works, she shows that the Devonshires run it better than any official committee could do. Any change would be for the worse.

Debo brings in general principle only once, and that obliquely, in her favourable review of the Duke of Bedford's *How to Run a Stately Home*, written in collaboration with George Mikes. She quotes the owner of Woburn Abbey as mentioning Robert Ardrey's Territorial Imperative: 'It all started with the monkeys who each insisted on having his own private place up in the tree . . . I happen to be the owner . . . of a magnificent stately home; I am also the monkey on the tree.'

In *Counting my Chickens* Debo refers back to old jokes and affectations, for instance her pretence that she does not read books. Asked to suggest ten books for a journey on the trans-Siberian railway she only produces six, one of which consists of blank paper and another is one she admits to not having read. She decides not to take Thomas Hardy's *The Woodlanders* because it would make her homesick – but how does she know this? She describes the novels of Henry Green, real name Henry Yorke and not one of her favourite men, as dreary. Clearly she has at least dipped into them. Her favourite writer seems to be Beatrix Potter. *Ginger and Pickles*, about a cat and a dog who run a shop but go broke through giving credit, is according to Debo the best book on retailing ever written, and she treasures *Peter Rabbit* as a manual of garden design.

Using the Chatsworth farm, open to the public and in particular to children who may be interested in what farmers do, Debo does her best to teach town-dwellers the facts of life. Some find them shocking, like the boy who, when seeing a cow milked, thinks the process so disgusting that he will never drink milk again. More surrealist is the criticism by a group of children that the trout in their tanks are bored and that 'the cluster of people round the rabbit pen put the animals in a predator–prey situation.' The sillier sort of environmentalist gets mocked: Debo quotes a lady who angrily accused a gardener of poisoning her dahlias when they had merely faded in the autumn, and attacks those who want to stop quarrying in the Peak District National Park, quoting a television comedian – unnamed – as saying that 'allowing more quarrying in the Peak Park is like grinding up York Minster for motorway hardcore.' Debo's comment: 'I wonder what material he thinks York Minster is built of and where it came from. No quarry, no Minster.' A favourite periodical of hers, often to be seen lying about at Chatsworth, is *The Waller and Dyker*, official magazine of the Dry Stone Walling Association of Great Britain.

There is no consensus about the Mitfords, either as individuals or collectively. On their extreme politics, perhaps most of us now agree with what Nancy wrote in a letter in 1940: 'There isn't a pin to put between Nazis and Bolshies.' (Quoted by Mary S. Lovell, *The Mitford Girls*.) In the thirties, Nazis and Communists were thought of as opposites. Since both had countries in their grip, they could hide many of their own atrocities, so that others could choose what to believe and what to disregard. There were people whose loathing for Nazism gave them a soft spot for Communism, and others of whom the exact converse was true. It is now known that each variety of totalitarianism committed horrors which exceeded the worst that its opponents could uncover. Nancy's instinct, in fact, was spot-on.

As time passes it becomes easier to see how alike the sisters were. Decca and Diana, the two political extremists, were in some ways the closest in character. Both fell blindly for totalitarianism, through men to whom they remained permanently loyal: both were adored by their own friends and family; both were funny, brave, charismatic and persuasive. But all the sisters inherited the confident style of their grandfathers. This style goes down rather badly with those who are affected with contemporary *angst*; the Mitfords in general, and those in particular of whom the commentator disapproves, are regularly attacked as overprivileged, overpromoted, strident, opinionated brats. *Hons and Rebels* has contributed to the spread of this point of view; it is certainly the most widely read of all the 'factual' books about the family, having sold continuously during the forty years since it first appeared. Fashionable public opinion was in any case tending in this direction; only recently has a young person mounted a reasoned defence of Mitford values as compared with some of the absurdities of the modern talking classes. This was Laura Thompson in her recent biography of Nancy, *Life in a Cold Climate*. Yet whatever the prevailing tendency, some people have always felt the Mitfords to be not only interesting in their engagement with the stormy history of their time, but also rather fun. Some, also, are impressed by the sisters' romantic side, their real-life 'pursuit of love', of a love that could truly last for life.

There is, though, a genuine case against them. Oddly enough it was young Randolph Churchill who as a schoolboy put his finger on it. His motives were characteristically impure; he was boyishly in love with Diana, and cross because she had got engaged to Bryan. But he made a shrewd point. He accused Diana of having 'no fundamental moral sense. In other words, though you rarely do wrong, you do not actually see anything *wrong* in sin.' (Quoted by Anne de Courcy in *Diana Mosley*.) Randolph's accusation here was in effect that Diana based her good behaviour on what the Earl of Chesterfield wrote to his son: 'Do as you would be done by is the surest method that I know of pleasing,' rather than on Immanuel Kant's categorical imperative which elevates 'do as you would be done by' into the general principle that one should do nothing that cannot be made into a universal law. To a Kantian or a serious Christian, Chesterfield's maxim seems desperately inadequate even if in practice it can lead to decent behaviour; and for this purpose Randolph was ranging himself with Kant.

What he said can be applied to all seven Mitfords. Decca's sense of sin was every bit as deficient as Diana's. Unity had nothing of the sort until she was brain damaged; there was not much sign of it in Nancy either. Pam and Debo were too concerned with practicalities to bother with it; Tom, who was an admirer of Kant but not particularly religious, would have known all about sin but seen it rather as a philosophical problem than as cause for a dark night of the soul. Earlier, we referred to the Mitfords' viewpoint as Pelagian, and traced it back to Thomas Bowles; here we are making more or less the same point. Does it matter? Lewis Carroll's poem 'The Walrus and the Carpenter' may be relevant. The Walrus, who weeps as he devours the oysters, is a spoilt Kantian; he is upset because he is doing to the unfortunate bivalves something he would not want done to him. The Carpenter is unmoved; Chesterfield's point would be the one to appeal to him, if any, but he regards the oysters as not worth pleasing. Neither Walrus nor Carpenter do credit to their respective standpoints, but what of the rest of us? Is Kant the better influence on people's actual behaviour, or is Chesterfield? Would a sense of sin have made the Mitfords behave better? Who knows?

One final thing must be mentioned, which we were very pleased to discover in our most recent researches. When Mosley died, Decca wrote a brief note to Debo asking her to convey sympathy to Diana. In the end, then, Decca was not as implacable as she sometimes made herself appear for public consumption.

# Family Trees

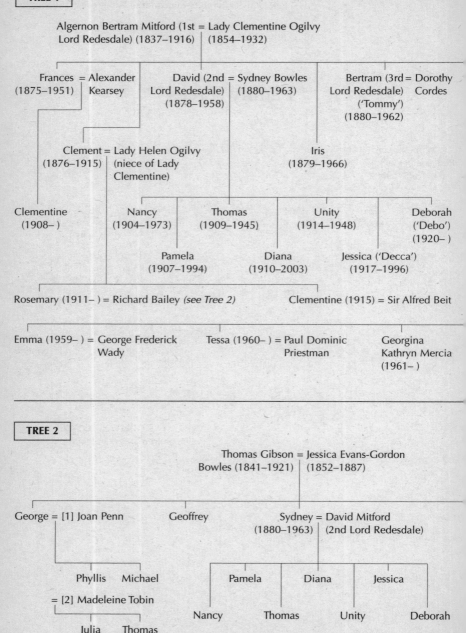

**TREE 1**

Algernon Bertram Mitford (1st = Lady Clementine Ogilvy
Lord Redesdale) (1837–1916)   (1854–1932)

Frances = Alexander
(1875–1951)   Kearsey

David (2nd = Sydney Bowles
Lord Redesdale)   (1880–1963)
(1878–1958)

Bertram (3rd = Dorothy
Lord Redesdale)   Cordes
('Tommy')
(1880–1962)

Clement = Lady Helen Ogilvy
(1876–1915)   (niece of Lady
Clementine)

Iris
(1879–1966)

Clementine
(1908– )

Nancy
(1904–1973)

Thomas
(1909–1945)

Unity
(1914–1948)

Deborah
('Debo')
(1920– )

Pamela
(1907–1994)

Diana
(1910–2003)

Jessica ('Decca')
(1917–1996)

Rosemary (1911– ) = Richard Bailey (*see Tree 2*)

Clementine (1915) = Sir Alfred Beit

Emma (1959– ) = George Frederick
Wady

Tessa (1960– ) = Paul Dominic
Priestman

Georgina
Kathryn Mercia
(1961– )

**TREE 2**

Thomas Gibson = Jessica Evans-Gordon
Bowles (1841–1921)   (1852–1887)

George = [1] Joan Penn

Geoffrey

Sydney = David Mitford
(1880–1963)   (2nd Lord Redesdale)

Phyllis   Michael

Pamela   Diana   Jessica

= [2] Madeleine Tobin

Nancy   Thomas   Unity   Deborah

Julia   Thomas

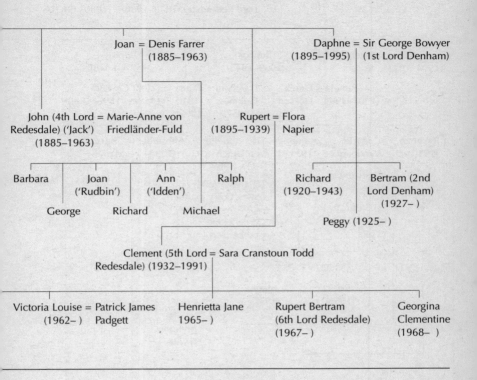

## ALGERNON BERTRAM (1st Lord Redesdale)
### his children, grandchildren and great-grandchildren

Joan = Denis Farrer
(1885–1963)

Daphne = Sir George Bowyer
(1895–1995) | (1st Lord Denham)

John (4th Lord = Marie-Anne von
Redesdale) ('Jack')   Friedländer-Fuld
(1885–1963)

Rupert = Flora
(1895–1939) | Napier

Barbara

Joan
('Rudbin')

Ann
('Idden')

Ralph

Richard
(1920–1943)

Bertram (2nd
Lord Denham)
(1927– )

George

Richard

Michael

Peggy (1925– )

Clement (5th Lord = Sara Cranstoun Todd
Redesdale) (1932–1991)

Victoria Louise = Patrick James
(1962– )   Padgett

Henrietta Jane
1965– )

Rupert Bertram
(6th Lord Redesdale)
(1967– )

Georgina
Clementine
(1968– )

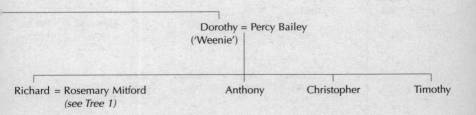

## THOMAS GIBSON BOWLES
### his children and grandchildren

Dorothy = Percy Bailey
('Weenie')

Richard = Rosemary Mitford
*(see Tree 1)*

Anthony

Christopher

Timothy

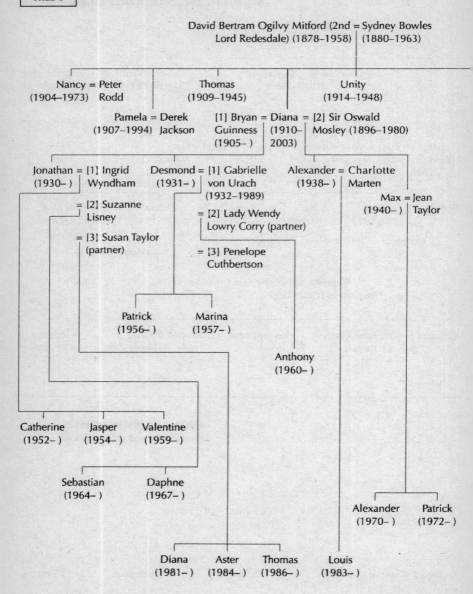

David Bertram Ogilvy Mitford (2nd = Sydney Bowles
Lord Redesdale) (1878–1958) | (1880–1963)

Nancy = Peter
(1904–1973) Rodd

Thomas
(1909–1945)

Unity
(1914–1948)

Pamela = Derek
(1907–1994) Jackson

[1] Bryan = Diana = [2] Sir Oswald
Guinness (1910– Mosley (1896–1980)
(1905– ) 2003)

Jonathan = [1] Ingrid
(1930– ) Wyndham

= [2] Suzanne
Lisney

= [3] Susan Taylor
(partner)

Desmond = [1] Gabrielle
(1931– ) von Urach
(1932–1989)

= [2] Lady Wendy
Lowry Corry (partner)

= [3] Penelope
Cuthbertson

Alexander = Charlotte
(1938– ) Marten

Max = Jean
(1940– ) Taylor

Patrick
(1956– )

Marina
(1957– )

Anthony
(1960– )

Catherine
(1952– )

Jasper
(1954– )

Valentine
(1959– )

Sebastian
(1964– )

Daphne
(1967– )

Alexander
(1970– )

Patrick
(1972– )

Diana
(1981– )

Aster
(1984– )

Thomas
(1986– )

Louis
(1983– )

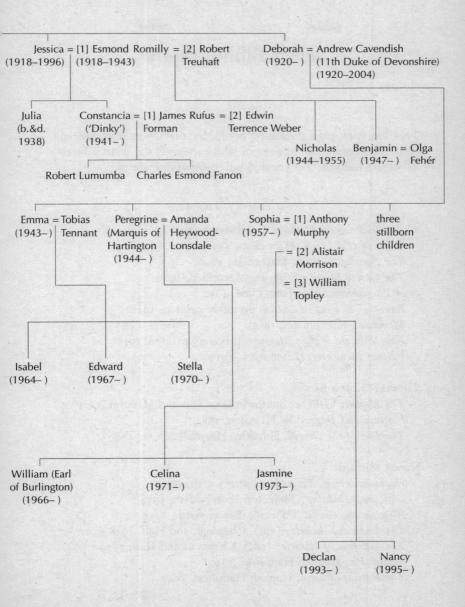

**DAVID BERTRAM OGILVY (2nd Lord Redesdale)**
his children, grandchildren and great-grandchildren

Jessica = [1] Esmond Romilly = [2] Robert
(1918–1996) (1918–1943) Treuhaft

Deborah = Andrew Cavendish
(1920– ) (11th Duke of Devonshire)
(1920–2004)

Julia
(b.&d.
1938)

Constancia = [1] James Rufus = [2] Edwin
('Dinky') Forman Terrence Weber
(1941– )

Nicholas
(1944–1955)

Benjamin = Olga
(1947– ) Fehér

Robert Lumumba Charles Esmond Fanon

Emma = Tobias
(1943– ) Tennant

Peregrine = Amanda
(Marquis of Heywood-
Hartington Lonsdale
(1944– )

Sophia = [1] Anthony
(1957– ) Murphy

= [2] Alistair
Morrison

= [3] William
Topley

three
stillborn
children

Isabel
(1964– )

Edward
(1967– )

Stella
(1970– )

William (Earl
of Burlington)
(1966– )

Celina
(1971– )

Jasmine
(1973– )

Declan
(1993– )

Nancy
(1995– )

# Select Bibliography

This list comprises published books by the seven Mitfords and their grandfathers, and books of which they are the main subjects. All books published in London unless otherwise stated.

## BOOKS BY THEM:

Algernon Bertram Mitford, Lord Redesdale
*Tales of Old Japan*, Macmillan, 1871
*The Bamboo Garden*, Macmillan, 1896
*The Garter Mission to Japan*, Macmillan, 1906
*A Tragedy in Stone*, John Lane, 1912
*Bayreuth in 1912, a Sketch*, privately printed, 1912
*Memories*, Hutchinson, 1915
*King Edward VII, a Memory*, privately printed, 1915
*Further Memories*, Hutchinson, 1917

Thomas Gibson Bowles
*The Defence of Paris*, Sampson Low Son and Marston, 1871
*Flotsam and Jetsam*, W.H. Allen, 1882
*The Log of the Nereid*, Simpkin, Marshall & Co., 1889

Nancy Mitford
*Highland Fling*, Thornton Butterworth, 1931
*Christmas Pudding*, Thornton Butterworth, 1932
*Wigs on the Green*, Thornton Butterworth, 1935
*The Ladies of Alderley* (ed.), Chapman and Hall, 1938
*The Stanleys of Alderley* (ed.), Chapman and Hall, 1939
*Pigeon Pie*, Hamish Hamilton, 1940
*The Pursuit of Love*, Hamish Hamilton, 1947

*Love in a Cold Climate*, Hamish Hamilton, 1949
*The Blessing*, Hamish Hamilton, 1951
*Madame de Pompadour*, Hamish Hamilton, 1954
*Noblesse Oblige* (contr.), Hamish Hamilton, 1956
*Voltaire in Love*, Hamish Hamilton, 1957
*Don't Tell Alfred*, Hamish Hamilton, 1960
*The Water Beetle*, Hamish Hamilton, 1962
*The Sun King*, Hamish Hamilton, 1966
*Frederick the Great*, Hamish Hamilton, 1970
*A Talent to Annoy* (ed. Charlotte Mosley), Hamish Hamilton, 1986

Nancy Mitford
Translations:
   *La Princesse de Cleves*, Madame de la Fayette, Euphorion Books, 1950

Diana Mosley
   *A Life of Contrasts*, Hamish Hamilton, 1977
   *The Duchess of Windsor*, Sidgwick and Jackson, 1980
   *Loved Ones*, Sidgwick and Jackson, 1985

Jessica Mitford
   *Hons and Rebels*, Victor Gollancz, 1960
   *The American Way of Death*, Simon & Schuster, 1963
   *The Trial of Dr Spock*, Knopf, New York, 1969
   *Kind and Usual Punishment*, Random House, 1974
   *A Fine Old Conflict*, Michael Joseph, 1977
   *The Making of a Muckraker*, Michael Joseph, 1979
   *Faces of Philip*, Heinemann, 1984

Deborah Devonshire
   *The House*, Macmillan, 1982
   *The Estate*, Macmillan, 1990
   *Counting my Chickens*, Long Barn Books, Ebrington, 2001

## BOOKS ABOUT THEM INDIVIDUALLY:

Algernon Bertram Mitford     .
  *Mitford's Japan*, Hugh Cortazzi, Athlone Press, 1985

Thomas Gibson Bowles
  *The Irrepressible Victorian*, Leonard E. Naylor, Macdonald, 1965
  *Never Forget*, Julia Budworth, privately printed, 2001
    (Biography of Thomas Bowles's son George incorporating much about his father.)

Nancy Mitford
  *Nancy Mitford: a Memoir*, Harold Acton, Hamish Hamilton, 1975
  *Nancy Mitford*, Selina Hastings, Hamish Hamilton, 1985
  *Life in a Cold Climate: Nancy Mitford*, Laura Thompson, Review, 2003

Diana Mosley
  *Diana Mosley*, Jan Dalley, Faber and Faber, 2000
  *Diana Mosley*, Anne de Courcy, Chatto and Windus, 2003

Unity Mitford
  *Unity Mitford: A Quest*, David Pryce-Jones, Weidenfeld & Nicolson, 1976


## BOOKS ABOUT THEM COLLECTIVELY:

*The Mitford Family Album*, Sophia Murphy, Sidgwick & Jackson, 1985
*The Mitford Girls*, Mary S. Lovell, Little, Brown, 2001
*Les Extravagantes Soeurs Mitford*, Emile Guikovaty, Bernard Grasset, Paris 1983
*Ces Extravagantes Soeurs Mitford*, Annick le Floch'moan, Fayard, Paris 2000
*De Osannolika Systrarna Mitford*, Albert Bonniers Forlag, Stockholm, 2002

## BOOKS ABOUT THEIR HUSBANDS:

Sir Oswald Mosley
  *My Life*, Oswald Mosley, Thomas Nelson and Sons Ltd., 1968
  *Oswald Mosley*, Robert Skidelsky, Macmillan, 1975
  *The Rules of the Game*, Nicholas Mosley, Secker & Warburg, 1982
  *Beyond the Pale*, Nicholas Mosley, Secker & Warburg, 1983

Esmond Romilly
  *Friends Apart*, Philip Toynbee, MacGibbon and Kee, 1954
  *Rebel, the Short Life of Esmond Romilly*, Kevin Ingram, Weidenfeld & Nicolson, 1985

# Acknowledgements

The authors owe this book in the first instance to the close and generous co-operation of three of the subjects: The Hon. Mrs Pamela Jackson, Diana Lady Mosley, and Deborah Duchess of Devonshire. All gave us numerous, comprehensive interviews and access to all material in their possession, and they examined the parts of the typescript relevant to them. Mrs Jackson was particularly helpful in establishing contact for us with other members of the family; Lady Mosley read the proofs of the whole work; and the Duchess of Devonshire opened for us the archive at Chatsworth, which contains a great deal of important material. All three have been most patient in answering questions as they have occurred to us.

We are also grateful to Lord Moyne for talking to us and making useful corrections to part of our typescript. James Lord Neidpath also read the proofs and pointed out several errors and solecisms.

We are deeply indebted to the following for interviews, which gave us vital information: The Hon. Mrs Bailey; Lady Beit; Lady Betjeman; Mr Thomas Bowles; Mr Ian Curteis; Daphne Lady Denham; Lord Dulverton; Miss Georgina Evans Gordon; Lady Harrod; Mrs Jean Howard; Mr James Lees-Milne; Lord Redesdale; and Miss Madeau Stewart. Mrs Bailey and Lady Denham also lent us photographs and sent us written notes which we have found most useful. Mr Bowles lent us a quantity of valuable material, as did Mr Max Mosley. Lady Harrod showed us her correspondence with some of our subjects. Lord Redesdale kindly allowed us to reproduce the family portraits in his possession.

For permission to quote printed material we thank Sir Harold

Acton, Mr James Lees-Milne, the Duchess of Devonshire, Sir Osbert Lancaster and Macdonald & Company, publishers of Leonard Naylor's *The Irrepressible Victorian*.

Finally, we would like to thank Ms Hellen Marchant, the Devonshires' secretary, who was most helpful; also Mrs Constancia Weber, Benjamin Treuhaft, Marina Guinness and Patrick Guinness.

# Index